THE AGE OF
REAGAN

THE AGE OF

REAGAN

★ ★ ★ ★ ★

A History, 1974–2008

SEAN WILENTZ

HARPER

An Imprint of HarperCollins*Publishers*

www.harpercollins.com

HarperCollins books may be purchased for educational, business, or sales promotional use. For information, please write: Special Markets Department, HarperCollins Publishers, 10 East 53rd Street, New York, NY 10022.

Grateful acknowledgment for permission to reproduce illustrations is made to the following: Text: *Bettmann/Corbis*: pages 12–13. *Stewart Mike/Corbis Sygma*: pages 430–431. Insert: *Bettmann/Corbis*: page 1, top; page 3, top, bottom right; page 7, middle left; page 8, bottom left. *The Granger Collection*: page 1, bottom left. White House Photograph courtesy *Gerald R. Ford Library*: page 2, all. White House Photograph courtesy *Jimmy Carter Presidential Library*: page 4, all; page 5, all. White House Photograph courtesy *Ronald Reagan Library*: page 6, all; page 7, top, bottom right; page 8, top, bottom right; page 9, top, bottom right; page 10, all. White House Photograph courtesy *George Bush Presidential Library*: page 11, all. White House Photograph courtesy *William J. Clinton Presidential Library*: page 12, top, bottom left; page 13, all. *Patrick Robert/ Sygma/Corbis*: page 12, middle right. *Jeffrey Markowitz/Sygma/Corbis*: page 14, top. *Wally McNamee/Corbis*: page 9, middle left; page 14, bottom. *Reuters/ Corbis*: page 15, all. *Matthew Cavanaugh/epa/Corbis*: page 16.

"Idiot Wind":
Copyright © 1974 Ram's Horn Music. All rights reserved. International copyright secured. Reprinted by permission.

"High Water (for Charley Patton)":
Copyright © 2001 Special Ride Music. All rights reserved. International copyright secured. Reprinted by permission.

FIRST EDITION

Designed by Nicola Ferguson

Library of Congress Cataloging-in-Publication Data

Wilentz, Sean.
    The age of Reagan : a history, 1974–2008 / Sean Wilentz. —1st ed.
        p. cm.
    Includes bibliographical references and index.
    ISBN: 978-0-06-074480-9
    1. United States —Politics and government —1945–1989. 2. United States —Politics and government —1989. 3. Political culture —United States — History —20th century. 4. Political culture —United States — History —21st century. 5. Conservatism —United States —History — 20th century. 6. Conservatism —United States —History —21st century. 7. Reagan, Ronald —Influence. I. Title.
        E839.5.W535 2008
        973.927—dc22   2007047333

08 09 10 11 12 ID/RRD 10 9 8 7 6 5 4 3 2 1

TO THE MEMORY OF

ALFRED KAZIN

AND

ARTHUR M. SCHLESINGER JR.

CONTENTS

Introduction   1

Prologue: July 4, 1976   14

1   Memories of the Ford Administration   26

2   Détente and Its Discontents   48

3   Jimmy Carter and the Agonies of
Anti-Politics   73

4   Human Rights and Democratic Collapse   99

5   New Morning   127

6   Confronting the Evil Empire   151

7   "Call It Mysticism If You Will"   176

8   "We Have an Undercover Thing":
The Iran-Contra Affair   209

9   "Another Time, Another Era"   245

10   Reaganism and Realism   288

11   The Politics of Clintonism   323

12   Clinton's Comeback   355

13   Animosities and Interest: The Impeachment
of Clinton   382

14   Irreparable Harm: The Election of 2000   408

Epilogue: October 13, 2001   432

Acknowledgments 459

Notes 461

Selected Sources and Readings 515

Index 545

THE AGE OF
REAGAN

INTRODUCTION

J UST AS THE PERIOD of American history from 1933 to the late
1960s—between the rise of the New Deal and the fall of Lyndon B.
Johnson's Great Society—was chiefly one of liberal reform, so the past
thirty-five years have been an era of conservatism. Although briefly interrupted in the late 1970s and temporarily reversed in the 1990s, a powerful
surge of conservative politics has dominated American politics and government. This book relates the basic story of the political trends and events of
the era, and interprets conservatism's ascendancy. I have not been motivated
by a wish to discover the deep cultural, economic, social, or psychological
factors that might explain recent political history, although all these factors
do come into play. Nor do I wish to add to the copious literature of either
hagiography or vilification about our recent and current political leaders. I
want instead to provide a fresh, succinct, and accessible chronicle of American history, focused on political history, after 1974. I especially hope to
account for how a conservative movement once deemed marginal managed
to seize power and hold it, and what the consequences have been.

The title points to the straightforward proposition that Ronald Reagan
has been the single most important political figure of the age. Without
Reagan, the conservative movement would never have been as successful
as it was. In his political persona, as well as his policies, Reagan embodied
a new fusion of deeply conservative politics with some of the rhetoric and
even a bit of the spirit of Franklin D. Roosevelt's New Deal and of John F.
Kennedy's New Frontier. This is not to say that Reagan alone caused the
long wave of conservative domination—far from it. But in American politi-

cal history there have been a few leading figures, most of them presidents, who for better or worse have put their political stamp indelibly on their time. They include Thomas Jefferson, Andrew Jackson, Abraham Lincoln, Theodore Roosevelt, Franklin D. Roosevelt—and Ronald Reagan.

It says something about the literature of American history, and the relative paucity of historical scholarship thus far about Reagan and his era, that he is the outstanding conservative figure on the list. Almost immediately after Franklin Roosevelt died in office in 1945, historians began chronicling and debating the history of the New Deal. By contrast, although some biographies of varying quality appeared—the best of them by the journalist Lou Cannon—nothing like this kind of outpouring by historians followed Reagan's departure from office in 1989. Only recently, approaching twenty years later, have historians begun to produce a substantial body of work on Reagan's presidency and its effects.* It is no secret that much of the American intelligentsia disliked Reagan, whereas intellectuals—and, for that matter, Ronald Reagan—admired Franklin Roosevelt. But that difference does not fully explain the lack of historical scholarship on the age of Reagan—because admiring conservatives, like dismayed liberals, have until recently written fairly little about Reagan except memoirs or panegyrics. In part, historians have been badly hampered by tightened restrictions on the release of presidential and related papers, especially the rules imposed by the George W. Bush administration in 2001, which, although ostensibly intended to aid the "further implementation" of the Presidential Records Act of 1978, effectively overturned the act by executive order. As a result of these restrictions, a great deal of interesting material from the Reagan administration onward is now under lock and key. If this unfortunate secrecy was intended to protect certain reputations, it has had the additional effect of rendering its chief beneficiaries less imposing historically than they might otherwise be, because their full stories, quite simply, cannot be told.

But there are deeper explanations as well. Historians have long been

---

*A brief but incisive historical interpretation of Franklin D. Roosevelt and the New Deal appeared only three years after Roosevelt's death in the final chapter of Richard Hofstadter's *The American Political Tradition and the Men Who Made It* (1948). Soon after came important works by Eric F. Goldman, Frank Freidel, and James MacGregor Burns, as well as Hofstadter's *The Age of Reform: Bryan to F.D.R.* (1955), and the first volume of three that appeared in Arthur M. Schlesinger Jr.'s uncompleted *The Age of Roosevelt* (1957). Important historical works on Reagan and his era that have begun to appear in the last several years are discussed in Selected Sources and Readings (page 515).

drawn to leaders whom they identify with progressive efforts to humanize the workings of American democracy and other conditions of American life. There are more books about Theodore Roosevelt than there are about all of the six "gilded age" presidents who preceded him *combined*. Reagan doesn't fit the preferred mold. A conservative hero in a conservative age, he is either so admired by the minority of conservatives in the academy or so disliked by the others that it has seemed as if he and his administration have been difficult to evaluate fairly. I sometimes have the impression that the preponderance of American historians would prefer simply to skip over the Reagan era as a bad dream and write instead of times and figures they find more attractive.

Edmund Morris, a distinguished biographer of Theodore Roosevelt, was selected as Reagan's authorized biographer and granted unprecedented access during and after his presidency. Morris discovered that Reagan was not the two-dimensional icon he had imagined. Yet he was so confounded by what he described as Reagan's strange combination of passivity, neglect of important issues of the day (especially the AIDS crisis), and murky motives that he retreated into partial fictionalization, inventing characters to interact with a Reagan he confessed he could not truly understand. Morris's book contains a great deal of useful information—but his limited comprehension and odd literary decisions also render it an enormous opportunity lost.

Although I am sharply critical of Reagan's leadership, my views have ripened over time, and, in any case, I believe Reagan and his presidency were so important that they deserve more scholarly attention than they have received. I hope that this book, building on some fine, very recent works, can help remedy the situation and spur further historical assessments of the era in which Reagan was the preeminent political figure. The book draws on numerous primary documents that have either been previously neglected or only recently released to the public, and that offer interesting revelations. But I do not pretend to be presenting a treasury of archival riches, let alone to be rendering a final judgment. I instead hope to provide a new and longer view of the subject, offer definitions of some important matters, and open up lines of inquiry and debate.

Taking the longer view requires expanding the chronological frame of reference. The age of Reagan was not limited to Reagan's eight years in the White House, any more than the ages of Jefferson, Jackson, and Franklin Roosevelt were limited to their respective presidential terms. Like all major periods in our political history, the Reagan era had a long prelude, in which an existing political order crumbled and the Republican right rose to power, as well as a long postlude, in which Reagan's presidency continued to set the tone for American politics. Taking the story back through the end of the Nixon administration is essential in order to understand both the political dynamics that contributed to Reagan's success and many of the individuals who played important political roles through the 1980s and after. (These include such figures such as George H. W. Bush, Donald Rumsfeld, and Dick Cheney—veterans of the Nixon administration who served as important officials under Nixon's successor, Gerald Ford.) Extending the story into the presidency of George W. Bush shows how, for good or ill, Reagan's legacy has played out in foreign as well as domestic affairs. It also shows how, under Reagan's Republican successors, as well as under Bill Clinton, his legacy gradually began to unravel. Limitations of sources and historical (as opposed to political) writing persuaded me to restrict the discussion of George W. Bush's presidency to an epilogue. I do not at all intend this as a commentary on the relative importance of the period after 2000. Rather, I want to convey due respect for the endeavors of future historians who will examine the period in far greater detail than I can now—and, I hope, test the broad interpretations I offer of Bush's White House and its war on terror as part of the age of Reagan.

Reagan's rise was hardly inevitable; it resulted from a complex confluence of factors. Eight years before Reagan's election, President Richard M. Nixon, beginning his second term, contemplated what he called "an epic battle" aimed at greatly augmenting the power of the executive. Had it not been for the Watergate scandal—which came close to being suppressed—Nixon could well have succeeded in creating his own imperial presidency. Without Watergate, the large political opening that gave Reagan his first strong shot at the presidency probably would not have existed—and Reagan, the shining hope of the conservative movement, might never have been nominated, let alone elected. (Neither, in all likelihood, would the Democrats have fallen into the false sense of assurance that misled them so badly following Nixon's downfall.) In terms of voter alignment, the conservative turning point came in 1968, not 1980. It was by no means certain, though, that the turn would bring about the Reagan era, or conservatism as it then developed. But for the highly contingent turns of fortune, this book might have been titled "The Age of Nixon."

The Watergate affair did not, to be sure, cause an utter break with the past. Reagan benefited enormously from the so-called southern political strategy that Nixon pioneered, and by building on it he won two smashing electoral victories. Several of Nixon's policy positions, notably in the areas of school desegregation and judicial appointments, foreshadowed Reagan's. As would become clear during Gerald Ford's presidency, some of Nixon's men, including Rumsfeld and Cheney, drew closer to Reagan in their thinking, especially on foreign policy. And after he entered the White House, Reagan, who admired Nixon's knowledge of foreign affairs and world leaders, quietly consulted with the ex-president, especially during his second term.

In addition, some of Nixon's top aides, as well as some of his younger political strategists and operatives, remained very much a part of both the conservative movement and the Republican Party after Nixon's departure. They included two of Nixon's speechwriters: Patrick J. Buchanan (who became ubiquitous on the radio and, in the early 1980s, on cable television) and William Safire (who left the White House in 1973 to become an influential political columnist for the *New York Times*, where he would remain for the next three decades). They also included two men who got their start as national leaders of the College Republicans under Nixon: Lee Atwater and Karl Rove. In all these respects, the age of Reagan carried forward political proclivities and personalities of Richard Nixon's aborted presidency.

Still, the political as well as temperamental differences between Nixon and Reagan were fundamental. Reagan, a committed ideological conservative, attempted to push American government and politics in a more decisive conservative direction than Nixon did—and far more so than his chief Republican rival in 1980, George H. W. Bush, would in later years. In foreign affairs, Nixon's policy of détente was anathema to the Reagan forces, who followed a very different set of assumptions and priorities regarding the Soviet Union. How successfully Reagan accomplished what he set out to do is one of this book's basic themes. Another theme concerns how much these successes and failures actually had to do with conservative ideology about supply-side economics and confronting the Soviet Union and its proxies around the globe (the heart of what became known as the Reagan Doctrine).

The conclusions I have reached differ greatly from those advanced with increasing fervor in recent years by Reagan's admirers. They differ from those of his most vociferous critics. And they differ in several ways from the conclusions I would have expected myself to draw about Reagan's presidency and about much else when I began work on this book several years ago.

The Reagan era unfolded amid major social and political transitions in the United States. An urban society that had emerged during the decades before the Second World War became a society dominated, at least numerically, by suburban dwellers. While older industrial centers in the North and Midwest declined, sunbelt areas boomed. The civil rights revolution of the 1960s and later feminist agitation broke down old barriers of prejudice but also fostered potentially inflammatory resentments. The economy fell prey by 1973 to an alarming new syndrome, stagflation, which led many expert economists to believe that America's world economic supremacy was ending. A system of national party politics governed by old big-city and statewide machines and entrenched political professionals gave way to another party system, superficially more open, in which party loyalties among the voters became attenuated and individual candidates' success depended increasingly on their ability to raise large sums of money to cover heavy media costs. The trauma of President Kennedy's assassination in 1963, followed by the foreshortened presidencies of Lyndon Johnson and Richard Nixon, generated widespread public alienation from electoral politics and mainstream politicians. The disastrous war in Vietnam cracked open the bipartisan consensus over containment that had held during the cold war and badly divided Democrats against Democrats and Republicans against Republicans, as well as against the opposing party.

The capture and command of the political initiative by the "Reagan right" resulted from all these changes. Above all, Reagan and his supporters, unlike the battered Democrats and the disgraced Republican establishment, gave the voters a compelling way to comprehend the disorienting and often dispiriting trends of the 1970s—and to see those trends not as a product of their own defects (as Reagan's Democratic predecessor, Jimmy Carter, came to imply) but as a consequence of bad leadership. With Reagan as its likable, ever-optimistic standard-bearer and ultimate symbol, the Republican right delivered what sounded like straightforward, commonsense solutions to the nation's ills: cut taxes, shrink government domestic spending, encourage private investment, and keep the military strong while aiding those abroad who were fighting communist tyranny.

"They say we offer simple answers to complex problems," Reagan proclaimed in the speech that first brought him attention as a politician. "Well, perhaps there is a simple answer—not an easy answer—but simple: if you and I have the courage to tell our elected officials that we want our national policy based on what we know in our heart is morally right." Compared with the various Democratic appeals—the updated, moderate southern progressivism of Jimmy Carter; the retooled New Deal liberalism personified by Walter Mondale; the cool rationalism of Michael Dukakis—this seemed a forward-looking message with conviction as well as confidence. With some brilliant turns, Reagan and his supporters managed to appropriate the bold, unapologetic nationalism once celebrated by Franklin D. Roosevelt and John F. Kennedy and attach it to political causes that Roosevelt and Kennedy would have found anathema. Into the early 1990s, that mixture helped cement what looked for a time like a formidable national electoral coalition. And after the bitterly contested, strange presidential election of 2000, conservative Republicanism received a new lease on life in a highly radicalized form, made possible through a majority decision by five activist justices on the Supreme Court.

Political pundits have been forecasting the imminent collapse of the Reagan era for many years, since the middle of Reagan's own first term. Harsh public reaction to economic catastrophe, and large electoral gains by the Democrats in 1982, prompted David Broder, the dean of political journalism in Washington, to observe that Reaganism was merely "a one-year phenomenon," and that Reagan's presidency had quickly reached its "phaseout" point. In 1986, the Republicans lost control of the Senate, and only weeks later the outbreak of the Iran-contra scandal sent Reagan's public opinion ratings crashing. Bill Clinton's victory in 1992, followed by public disgust at the Republicans' shutdown of the government in 1995 and at their impeachment of Clinton three years later, seemed to presage the conservatives' demise. Yet the Republican Party, by now thoroughly Reaganized, rebounded.

In 2006, midway through George W. Bush's calamitous second term, the Democrats won majorities in the House and Senate for the first time in a dozen years. With Democrats taking charge of congressional committees to oversee and, if necessary, investigate the White House, an important power shift took place in Washington. Nevertheless, even after the debacle in Iraq, the loss of a major American city to hurricane Katrina, the Bush administration's failed assault on Social Security, and numerous scandals, the Democratic majorities were small, especially in the Senate, where the Democrats clung to a one-vote majority. During the early phases of the fight for the presidency in 2008, there were signs that the age of Reagan had run its course, but the political outcome remained far from predictable.

The true measure of the success of any political movement, though, does not rest simply on which party controls the Congress and the White House at any given moment. There are other government institutions to consider. Looking to the long term, Reagan and his Republican successors managed, through highly politicized appointments, to push the ideological makeup of the federal judiciary far to the right. The federal courts, once pilloried by conservatives, have become something of a bulwark of conservatism and will remain so for decades to come, impervious to the ups and downs of electoral politics.

The impact of the age of Reagan is indicated even more strongly by the guiding assumptions and possibilities of American politics and government, and the hold they have on public opinion. Thirty years ago, the proposition that reducing taxes on the rich was the best solution for all economic problems inspired only a few on the right-wing fringe. Today, it drives the national domestic agenda and is so commonplace that it sometimes appears to have become the conventional wisdom. It is only one of many such notions—including proposals that public schools teach the pseudoscience of "intelligent design" as well as Darwin's theory of evolution, the idea that wealthy business buccaneers should have a large say in formulating federal policy, and the so-called unitary executive theory of presidential power—that have moved from the political margins to the center of power. Buttressed by mythical accounts of the past thirty-five years, as well as by changed standards of truth and objectivity in the news media, conservatives in the age of Reagan learned how to seize and keep control of the terms of public debate—skills that liberal Democrats had once mastered but lost amid their political complacency in the 1970s and disarray in the 1980s.

Finally, the Reagan era witnessed fundamental challenges to the nation's constitutional order, and how Americans understand it. The era began with a severe constitutional crisis, caused by Nixon's usurpation of executive powers that produced the Watergate scandal. Three more spectacular constitutional confrontations (which might easily have turned into crises) ensued during the next quarter century—over the Iran-contra scandal, the impeachment of President Clinton, and the Supreme Court's decision to determine the presidential election of 2000.

The first two revived issues that had hovered over Nixon's self-destruction —in Iran-contra, the proper powers of the president in foreign and military affairs; and in the impeachment of Clinton, the standards by which a president should be impeached and removed from office. All three struggles raised profound questions and provoked passionate debate about the legitimate structure of authority in modern American democracy. Since 2000, President George W. Bush has provoked renewed and even deeper concerns by repeatedly asserting his virtually absolute authority as president to run what he has called his war on terror—a war that Congress has never formally declared—however he sees fit. Although conservatives have not always triumphed in these constitutional confrontations, the fact that the confrontations recurred after Nixon reveals once more how powerful the right became after 1980—and how the right has attempted to change, fundamentally, the nation's political order.

Readers may be skeptical about my decision to extend this book to cover the very recent past. How can a historian write authoritatively and with detachment about events he or she has lived through, right up to the near present? Some readers might also ask why, given my own writings about politics as well as history over the years, this book ought to be considered objective and above partisanship. How, in particular, can I write as a historian about events in which I played a public, albeit minor, role, including testifying as an expert witness before the House Judiciary Committee during Clinton's impeachment and supporting Al Gore's candidacy in the election of 2000?

Most of the book involves events that occurred a decade ago and more— far longer than it took the historical literature on other eras, including the age of Franklin D. Roosevelt, to begin the task of interpretation. Sufficient time has now passed to produce a sound (if, in some respects, incomplete) body of scholarship about these events—as well as for passions to have receded sufficiently to permit analysis with convincing documentation and reasoned argument. It is true that, more than for earlier eras, accounts of this one will long be hampered by the disturbing new rules governing release of official materials. Historical judgments may be subject to greater revision than such judgments usually are, when and if these materials see the light of day. But to succumb to these artificial limitations, ignore the abundant documentation that does exist, and refrain from writing the nation's history during the last quarter of the twentieth century would be an abdication of responsibility for a historian.

The analysis of more current events in the Epilogue flows from my contention that Ronald Reagan's presidency has had an enduring impact. With regard to assessing the present and recent past as a historian, the late Theodore Draper, writing in defense of what he called "present history," expressed my own view:

> I have written for the reader who was no longer interested in the daily or even weekly ration of news; this reader wanted to understand it in some organized form and in some historical perspective. No doubt the organization and perspective would change as time went on and more information or insight became available. Life cannot wait, however, for historians

to gather enough evidence to satisfy them or to make up their minds once they get it. Even a preliminary organization and perspective represent an advance, however provisional. We must make do with what we have while it is still possible to do something about the matter.

Like Draper's, my purpose in this final portion of the book is "to analyze present-day events historically." That kind of analysis seems to have sadly diminished in our public deliberations. This book is not an exercise in projecting the concerns of the present into the past—what is sometimes called presentism. My aim is exactly the opposite, to see what light the recent and not so recent past throws on the present.

Also like Draper, I did not conduct a single interview in connection with this book. In part, this decision was a matter of practicality: arranging for, conducting, and sorting through the scores (possibly hundreds) of interviews demanded by a study of this scope would have delayed the book's completion for many years—and might even have prevented me from ever finishing. More important, I am suspicious of interviews as a reliable source for historians, especially political historians. Journalists, in their normal role of reporting on deadline, must depend on interviews to establish basic facts quickly. But historians who rely heavily on interviews run the risk of being manipulated by their informants, in ways they cannot be by primary documents and secondary sources. Trying to write an unbiased account of recent times is difficult enough using the kinds of materials that historians traditionally have interpreted. Written sources have abundant lures and snares of their own. I am certain, though, that opening my evidence and analysis to the dance of subjectivities that interviewing involves would have made it all the more difficult to attain detachment. (My past experiences interviewing political leaders of various stripes for magazines and journals of opinion reinforced that judgment.) If I have thereby sacrificed the conceit of insider, "fly on the wall" immediacy, or forfeited juicy quotations and anecdotes, for the sake of pursuing dispassionate history, I think that the book is the better for it.

Concerning issues of objectivity and partisanship, I firmly believe that it is possible for a historian to lay aside personal views, commitments, and earlier judgments when writing about the recent past—including events in which he or she has had a small hand. Judging the past scrupulously requires a willing suspension of one's own beliefs. No historian is perfect at it; it is an elusive, even impossible goal but also an essential one if history itself is to be more than propaganda, more than a reaffirmation of one's own prejudices. Indeed, one of the most satisfying if humbling aspects of writing history is to find one's prejudices and expectations challenged by the historical record and sometimes undone, as has happened to me repeatedly in writing every chapter of this book.

I reject, however, the now fashionable claim that objectivity involves reporting all views or interpretations as equally valid. Objectivity instead involves judging validity for oneself, fairly, and then inviting others to consider and argue over the evidence, logic, and fairness on which that judgment is based. More perfect truths about the last thirty-five years of American history will arise from those considerations and disputes. But, for now, let us enter the age of Reagan.

JULY 4, 1976

F LAGS FLEW, BELLS RANG, and mammoth fireworks bombarded the night. The nation's bicentennial came as a cause for immense celebration—and also as a relief and an escape. After an embittering political decade, culminating in the Watergate crisis, the country seemed to be pulling through. Americans desperately wanted to think so. Their outpouring proclaimed a yearning for simple unity and a national sense of purpose. At least for a day, disappointment and disorientation gave way to exuberance and Old Glory.

Years later, Gerald R. Ford, who had succeeded the disgraced President Richard M. Nixon on August 9, 1974, recalled the bicentennial events as a national triumph, a "super Fourth of July" of hugs and joyous shouts:

> I can still see those seas of smiling faces with thousands of flags waving friendly greetings. . . . I can still hear the Liberty Bell toll, echoed by church bells across this beautiful land. It was a long day, and just before my head hit the pillow that night, I said to myself, "Well, Jerry, I guess we've healed America."

Ford returned to this idea often: if he was remembered at all, he said on a later occasion, it would be "for healing the land"—and the bicentennial was the symbol of his success.

The president spent part of the day attending its grandest spectacle, a massing in New York Harbor of sixteen large sailing vessels from around the world, dubbed the "tall ships," surrounded by an armada of small recreational craft. Hundreds of thousands of ordinary celebrators crowded the shoreline of Manhattan island to witness the extravaganza, finding choice seats at the southern end near the Battery. Above them, and dwarfing the old-fashioned wooden barks and brigantines in the harbor, soared twin monuments to the immense wealth and power of the city's political and business elite—two 110-story office towers, officially opened barely three years earlier as the tallest buildings on earth, the World Trade Center.

The throngs in New York, like the scores of millions who rejoiced throughout the country, suppressed any signs of trouble, as if a single discouraging word would wreck the day. President Ford received a patriotic reception from New York's city fathers, and replied with a wide fraternal smile. But the benevolent mood was just as wishful in Manhattan as it was elsewhere. Eight months earlier, the president had refused to lend federal aid to lift New York out of a grave fiscal crisis, inspiring a classic tabloid headline, run by the New York *Daily News*: FORD TO CITY: DROP DEAD. Ford soon reversed course and approved a federal loan, but enmities still ran deep; and ordinary New Yorkers, like the residents of many older American cities, sank into gloomy shabbiness and worse. By the time of the bicentennial, the reporter John Russell of the *New York Times* wrote that New Yorkers were searching for "a climate of reasoned confidence," feeling so disheartened by urban blight, racial fear, and political inertia that "even the will to learn has new obstacles to overcome."

Out in the harbor, a topsail schooner bore silent witness to how the country had awakened to past injustices: *La Amistad*, outfitted in Philadelphia, had been named after the vessel of the same name seized by captive Africans in 1839, an important moment in the rise of the American antislavery movement. But there still was trouble on the waters this Fourth of July, churned by international politics. One of the tall ships, the Chilean four-masted barkentine *Esmeralda*, had stirred protests by human rights advocates upon reaching America. According to critics, the ship, when not in ceremonial disguise, was being used as a floating torture chamber for political prisoners held by the American-backed right-wing dictatorship of General Augusto Pinochet. Two invited sailing ships from the Soviet Union, meanwhile, complained of harassment, threats, and generally rude treatment, which New York police spokesmen adamantly denied. The Soviet government ordered the vessels home immediately after the ceremonies of July 4, canceling scheduled port calls in Boston and Baltimore.

Then the other ships departed, the show was over, and the country at large looked for reasoned confidence and leaders who might offer it. For

nearly two generations, since the onset of the Great Depression, the country and its politics had moved, unevenly, in a liberal direction, inspired by
the idea that alleviating the burdens of the unprivileged and poor was a
national good, and that prudent but muscular vigilance, founded in international alliances, would protect the nation's security. All this was quickly
changing. Americans, in a phrase John Russell used about New Yorkers,
had found their old ideals "eaten away by realities no one cared to face."
The liberal tradition of the New Deal, the Fair Deal, the New Frontier,
and the Great Society could not go on forever—"and," as Russell wrote
presciently, "a lot of people would like to see it stop now." Far more conservative presumptions about recovering and expanding the nation's greatness
were gathering force, forged by a political movement that stood well to the
right of Richard Nixon and Gerald Ford.

The foremost proponent and hero of this reborn conservatism was a
man who was nowhere near New York on July 4, 1976, the former governor of California, Ronald Reagan. The next day, buried amid its bicentennial coverage, the *New York Times* carried an article by its veteran political
reporter, R. W. "Johnny" Apple, about how the governor's strategists were
thinking up ways to snatch the Republican nomination from President
Ford at the party's national convention later in the month. Those efforts fell
short, but four years later, Reagan would seem to take the nation by storm.
To some shocked Democrats and liberals, who had deluded themselves that
they still owned the future, the triumph of the Republican right came out
of nowhere. Yet for decades, Republican conservatives had been carefully
planning their own updated American Revolution.

Richard Nixon's resignation abruptly ended the nation's gravest constitutional and political crisis since the Civil War and Reconstruction. The misdeeds collectively known as Watergate had no precedent in their scope and
severity. The actual break-in at Democratic Party headquarters at the Watergate complex in 1972, the associated violations of campaign ethics, and
the effort to cover them up, were the least of it—although Nixon's own
former speechwriter, the conservative columnist William Safire, would
describe, many years later, those "evil" offenses alone as "a serious assault
on the foundations of democracy" which "rightly resulted in the resignation of the President." Systematically, and with full knowledge, Nixon had
also used the machinery of government to spy on, or prepare to spy on, domestic radicals, mainstream critics, and dozens of other citizens who he

imagined had conspired against him. (The White House's "enemies list" included well-known journalists; congressional leaders from both parties; the presidents of Yale, Harvard, and the Massachusetts Institute of Technology; the actor Steve McQueen; and the author Judith Martin, better known as "Miss Manners.") Nixon had underlings fabricate official documents, while he secretly conducted foreign policy, including the coup in Chile and the bombing of Cambodia, and prepared for a more dramatic expansion of executive power, to be completed after his reelection. By reorganizing the federal bureaucracy from the cabinet level down, replacing career professionals with political loyalists, and reducing their independent power, Nixon would thoroughly politicize the executive branch and federal agencies. (Secretary of State Henry Kissinger, one of the few cabinet members spared in the abrupt second-term shakeup after Nixon's landslide victory, was horrified by "the frenzied, almost maniacal sense of urgency about this political butchery.") Nixon later boasted: "I have thrown down a gauntlet to Congress, the bureaucracy, the media, and the Washington establishment and challenged them to engage in an epic battle."*

In attempting to cover up the details of the Watergate break-in, Nixon wanted to keep hidden the far longer list of what his complicit attorney general, John N. Mitchell, called the "White House horrors." Yet even Mitchell's stark phrase failed to capture the magnitude of the president's transgressions. Had Nixon succeeded in evading detection or frustrating his accusers, he would have fundamentally changed the character of the federal government, vaunting the White House over Congress and the courts, and permitting presidents to violate citizens' privacy at will. In flagrant contradiction of the framers' conception of divided power and of checks and balances as the surest guarantees against tyranny, Nixon sought to establish an imperial presidency, operating in the shadows, without accountability, pushing his power beyond its constitutional limits.

The bills of impeachment hammered out by the House Judiciary committee over the summer of 1974 cited a few of Nixon's more obvious violations of his oath of office and other constitutional obligations, and hinted at their larger implications. The committee specifically charged that Nixon had abused his power by conducting illegal surveillance of citizens and un-

---

* Nixon had already challenged constitutional fundamentals during his first term when he repeatedly impounded funds appropriated by Congress for domestic programs he did not like. Federal courts ruled against the president, but the issue was not settled until 1974, when a weakened Nixon signed the Budget Impoundment and Control Act.

lawfully using both the Internal Revenue Service (IRS) and the Central Intelligence Agency (CIA) in covert operations that, among other things, violated the Bill of Rights, which guarantees to all Americans a fair trial. These accusations, if proved, amounted to high crimes and misdemeanors against the Constitution, and warranted Nixon's removal. Evidence of additional illegalities would surface after Nixon left office, particularly an elaborate scheme called the Huston Plan, partially implemented, which would empower the White House to spy on and even lock up, without legal authorization, Americans it deemed dangerous or undesirable.

In late June 1974, the Supreme Court spurned Nixon's claims to executive privilege and forced him to release incriminating secret tape recordings of his conversations inside the Oval Office. On August 5, the White House made an announcement that clinched Nixon's doom: one taped conversation revealed Nixon, only days after the break-in, ordering the CIA to block the inquiry by the Federal Bureau of Investigation (FBI) into Watergate. Bitter-end Nixon loyalists, including Vice President Gerald Ford, finally gave up. "No longer was there the slightest doubt in my mind as to the outcome of the struggle," Ford recalled. "Nixon was finished." (Nixon's chief of staff, Alexander Haig, had already apprised Ford a few days earlier of the contents of the so-called smoking gun tape, and Ford had begun preparing to become president.) Four days later, Nixon departed and Ford took the oath of office. According to conventional wisdom, Nixon's resignation proved that the system worked. (These encouraging assessments generally ignored how lucky the system had been. Had Nixon been more selective in recording his Oval Office conversations or had the White House simply destroyed the incriminating tapes, the Watergate investigation would have fizzled.) But Nixon's downfall had other far-reaching implications for the future of American government and politics.

Richard Nixon had built his political career by shrewdly navigating the shoals of Republican Party politics. A leading conservative anticommunist crusader after his election to Congress in 1946, Nixon fervently accused the Truman administration of cowardice and appeasement, while he also befriended the Republican mainstream center-right. As President Eisenhower's vice president, Nixon contributed little of substance on policy, broadly endorsing the acceptance of New Deal Keynesian essentials that distinguished Eisenhower and the moderate, so-called modern Republicans, from the party's mossback anti–New Dealers, whom Eisenhower described as "stupid." Nixon did, though, shrewdly tack with the political winds, finally disowning the choleric red-baiter Joseph R. McCarthy, building up his own foreign policy credentials with high-profile visits to Latin America and the Soviet Union, and otherwise preparing himself to succeed Eisenhower in the election of 1960.

Nixon's narrow defeat at the hands of John F. Kennedy put him, and the Republican Party, in an awkward position. As the cost of gaining liberals' support for his nomination, Nixon had struck a truce—the so-called treaty of Fifth Avenue—with the party's leading liberal, Governor Nelson A. Rockefeller of New York, which gave Rockefeller effective control over drafting the party's platform. The party's conservative wing—which had passed from the dour, midwestern, anti–New Deal isolationism of Robert A. Taft to a far feistier right-wing anticommunism proclaimed by younger westerners such as Barry Goldwater—called Nixon's compromise a sellout, "the Munich of the Republican Party," Goldwater protested. Nixon's failure in 1960 (and his ill-starred run for the governorship of California two years later) then created a vacuum in party leadership. After President Kennedy consolidated his popularity in the middle of his term, none of the Republican liberals wished to take him on in 1964, and the center-right party establishment had no attractive candidate. That left the Goldwater right, which, from the moment Nixon lost the presidency, pulled itself together to take over the party. Kennedy and Goldwater, despite their sharp political differences, were personally friendly, and even spoke of opposing each other in a series of debates like those between Lincoln and Douglas, arguing out their clashing philosophies around the country.

Kennedy's assassination in November 1963 changed the Republicans' political calculus only slightly, as Rockefeller and another party liberal, Governor William Scranton of Pennsylvania, made feeble efforts to slow the Goldwater juggernaut. They failed miserably at the party's convention in San Francisco, a roaring conclave of hard-edged conservatives who practically booed a doggedly ebullient Rockefeller off the podium during his allotted speech. In nominating Goldwater, the Republicans backed a candidate who equated Social Security with socialism, opposed the landmark Civil Rights Act of 1964 as a violation of states' rights, and denounced as pusillanimous the bipartisan anticommunist foreign policy of containment. As one of his supporters, Phyllis Schlafly (who was then still obscure), put it in the title of a best-selling campaign tract, Goldwater offered the country "a choice, not an echo." Yet the hard-right Republican crusade seemed to fall apart in November, when Kennedy's successor, Lyndon Johnson, who had pledged to continue the policies of the New Frontier, crushed Goldwater in the greatest popular landslide to that time in presidential politics.

In 1968, Nixon, having moved to New York after his defeat in California, was well positioned to take back his party's mantle. President Johnson's travails in Vietnam, rioting in urban black ghettos, the Republicans' strong comeback in the congressional elections of 1966, and the widening cracks among the Democrats, made it all the more likely that this would be Nixon's year. But the party he hoped to lead was different from the one he had grown up in. Hostility to racial desegregation, dating back to the Dixiecrat schism among the Democrats in 1948, as well as disillusionment about Democratic welfare-state policies, had led large numbers of white southerners to bolt to the Republicans, especially in 1964, when Goldwater, an enemy of the Civil Rights Act, headed the Republican ticket. As forecast by the Republican strategist Kevin Phillips, the Democratic "solid south" was transforming itself into a Republican solid south. (Some northern urban ethnic voters had also already switched parties; they were labeled, together with the southern bolters, by the distinguished political commentator Walter Lippmann as "Goldwater Democrats.") By adding upwardly mobile, conservative white southerners and southwesterners to the party's traditional base, along with northern Catholics and working-class voters offended by both Johnson's civil rights programs and the resurgence of a radical left, Nixon could forge a new, long-lasting Republican majority that would replace the New Deal coalition and its updated successor that ushered in the Great Society.

Claiming he had a secret plan to end the war raging in Vietnam, Nixon won the election in 1968 over Vice President Hubert H. Humphrey, but just barely; and his success was not nearly enough to secure Republican majorities in Congress. Still, the country's politics augured a strong conservative shift. (Attorney General Mitchell, who knew whereof he spoke, proclaimed two years after the election, "This country is going so far to the right, you are not even going to recognize it.") The third-party campaign of the arch segregationist George Wallace of Alabama swept the Deep South in 1968, winning five states and finishing second in three. If Wallace cost the Republicans votes in the short run, his candidacy drew voters away from Humphrey and eventually proved a way station for southern whites and some northern working-class voters who had not yet completed their migration from the Democrats to the Republicans.

Once in office, Nixon actually widened the war in Southeast Asia, as an agonizing face-saving prelude to an American withdrawal that would begin in his second term. His administration's attacks on critics of the war, sometimes including liberal Republicans, as effeminate bums and defeatists—"nattering nabobs of negativism," in a line coined in 1970 by William

Safire for Vice President Agnew—revived the conflation of liberalism and quasi-treasonous defeatism that Nixon had helped perfect during his early days in Washington. Nixon also tried to keep faith with his southern supporters, as well as with the party's Goldwater wing, through choices for the federal bench. Above all, by naming to the Supreme Court an attorney from the Justice Department who was a confirmed Goldwater conservative—William H. Rehnquist of Arizona—Nixon stood up for those ultraconservatives who despised the court, under Chief Justice Earl Warren, as a bulwark of liberal subversion.*

On other fronts, to be sure—his secretive realpolitik approach to foreign policy, including his overtures to the Soviet Union and the People's Republic of China; his misbegotten adoption of wage and price controls to combat rising inflation; his support for a minimum guaranteed income plan and for the first phases of what became known as affirmative action—Nixon riled hard-line conservatives, including their new darling, Ronald Reagan. (Reagan, after serving as governor of California for less than two years, had mounted a last-minute challenge to Nixon at the 1968 convention. Nixon thwarted it by gaining all-out support from the former Dixiecrat turned Republican Strom Thurmond.) The disquiet deepened early in Nixon's second term when his secretary of state, Henry A. Kissinger, negotiated a treaty with the North Vietnamese that virtually ended American military involvement in the war—more an abandonment than an honorable peace in the view of many on the Republican right. But inside the Oval Office, Nixon enjoyed complete command of his party. The growing disarray of the Democrats reinforced his ascendancy.

Lyndon Johnson's policies regarding Vietnam had bitterly divided the Democratic Party. The divisions had begun under Kennedy as intramural arguments in the White House between one set of anticommunist liberals who favored aggressive action in Vietnam, Cuba, and elsewhere; and another set who favored more restrained anticommunist policies based on international treaties, foreign aid, and nuclear deterrence. After Kennedy's murder, Johnson, although torn about what he would call his "bitch mis-

---

* Nixon failed to win approval for his nomination to the Supreme Court of Clement F. Haynesworth Jr. and G. Harrold Carswell, both staunch southern conservatives of marginal talents. Judge Harry Blackmun of the U.S. Court of Appeals, a close friend of Chief Justice Warren Burger, eventually won confirmation for the contested vacancy, without opposition in the Senate. A Minnesota Republican, Blackmun would go on, in 1973, to write the majority opinion in *Roe v. Wade*, to the horror and chagrin of many Republican conservatives.

tress" of a war in Vietnam, heeded the more aggressive voices, fearing a domestic resurgence of the right wing if he did not. Ironically, by fighting the war as he did, authorizing intense bombing, restricting targets, and barring nuclear weapons, Johnson invited accusations from the right that he was halfhearted in his defense of freedom. "It's silly talking about how many years we will have to spend in the jungles of Vietnam when we could pave the whole country and put parking stripes on it and still be home by Christmas," Ronald Reagan pronounced in October 1965.

The escalation of American involvement not only divided anticommunist cold war liberals but led to a resurgence of the political left unseen since the demise of Henry Wallace's Progressive Party in 1948, and the rise of the anticommunist witch hunts of the McCarthy period. Students and other alienated baby boomers became one face of the antiwar movement, led by a small but noisy self-described "new left" on the nation's college campuses. But many of their prominent, more moderate elders, ranging from the civil rights hero Martin Luther King Jr. to liberal but decidedly mainstream Democrats such as Eugene McCarthy and Robert F. Kennedy, who had been elected to the Senate from New York in 1964, also broke with Johnson over the war.

Challenges by McCarthy and Robert Kennedy, along with collapsing public approval ratings, persuaded Johnson early in 1968 not to seek renomination. Subsequent events—King's assassination in April and Kennedy's in June; left-wing uprisings at Columbia University and on other campuses; the party's disastrous, blood-spattered convention in August capped by the nomination of an erstwhile liberal hero, Johnson's loyal vice president Hubert Humphrey—sent the party into a tailspin. Late in the campaign, Humphrey backed off slightly from his support of the war and recovered nearly enough to beat Nixon; and the Democrats retained control of Congress. But a struggle had begun over the national party's soul. Gone were many of the old party brokers who had helped select Democratic candidates such as Franklin D. Roosevelt, Harry Truman, and John F. Kennedy. Into their places moved more earnest liberal and left-wing reformers, for whom the Vietnam War and the slowed pace of civil rights reform had bankrupted what they called the "old politics."

The political crisis within the party was also an intellectual and social crisis. Since the late 1940s, Democrats had gravitated to the pro–New Deal, anticommunist liberal ideas expressed in works such as Arthur M. Schlesinger Jr.'s *The Vital Center*, published in 1949. With a pragmatic sense of irony about the limits of public endeavor, anticommunist liberals still thought of themselves as the inheritors of what Schlesinger called a "fighting faith," dedicated to the unending struggle to expand human freedom, material opportunity, and social decency, at home and around the globe. In domestic affairs, they relied on the neo-Keynesian idea that, through adjustments of tax and monetary policy and judicious regulation, the federal government could help steer an expansive American capitalism toward mass prosperity with acceptable levels of inflation. Although some were cautious, most of them also embraced the civil rights movement. In foreign affairs, they were dedicated to what John Kennedy had called a "long twilight struggle" against the tyranny of the Soviet Union, to be won through a policy of containment that would reward democratic Western allies in the third world, check Soviet expansionism, and in time cause communism to collapse under its own weight of oppression and inefficiency.

Established Democratic liberalism had suffered through numerous shocks, but now it was philosophically at loose ends. The debacle in Vietnam confounded the expectations and allegiances that characterized liberals during the cold war. Many of the initiatives of Lyndon Johnson's Great Society, when not starved for funds because of the war's expense, became bogged down in poor management, waste, and political feuding at the local level, and showed that many social problems were more complicated and intractable than initially imagined. Radicals on the campuses and rioters in northern black ghettos seemed to repudiate the very system the liberals prized, leaving vital center Democrats dazed and confused.

To compound the liberals' difficulties, developments in the 1960s discredited their core idea that the federal government could successfully manage the economy. Increased spending, first on Great Society programs, then on the Vietnam War, sustained the economic boom, but also spiked inflation. Thereafter, rising oil prices combined with poor economic management brought worsening inflation, even as the boom slowed and unemployment rose. As inflation ate away at the hard-earned gains of professional and middle-class Americans and stoked anxiety about the future, economists began to challenge Keynesian orthodoxy, especially about government regulation, which, it was discovered, created hidden costs that abetted inflation without preventing corporate collusion and price-fixing. New Deal liberalism, with no ready solution, seemed to have run out of steam; it was more apt to look back to the glory days of yore than to propose coherent policies for the present and future.

Finally, the nation's changing social landscape bewildered the old liberals. Their cultural as well as political instincts, shaped by the Great Depression and World War II, were attuned to the great cities, with effective political machines, masses of pro-Democratic workers, and teeming immigrant neighborhoods. In the 1960s, though, the American people, having moved eighty years earlier from the country to the city, moved from the city to the suburbs; and they also moved to the South and West. That dramatic demographic shift—made possible, ironically, by many of the policies formulated by the New Deal liberals—created a new and enormous body of voters who tended to hold liberal views on social and personal issues but despised the old political machines, lost interest in the problems of cities they had successfully escaped, and were generally skeptical about (if not hostile toward) ambitious social programs or government-led solutions to economic problems.

Many of the younger Democratic liberals had grown up in the new postwar suburbs; others came from backgrounds where traditional party hierarchies were suspect. Although they stood to the left of many in their cohort, they also disdained machine politics—indeed, in some respects, disdained partisanship itself—which they held responsible for what they saw as the corruption and intellectual blindness that had led to Vietnam and undone the Great Society. The new Democratic liberals shifted the party to the left and consolidated their power by promulgating, among other things, revised rules governing national nominations, which curtailed the influence of old-line party leaders. In 1972, after the mainstream liberal candidacy of Humphrey's former running mate, Edmund Muskie, faltered (thanks in part, it was later revealed, to dirty tricks played by the Nixon forces), the new rules helped ensure that the presidential nomination went to a leading party reformer, George McGovern of South Dakota. A man of enormous drive and humanitarian inclinations (under President Kennedy, he had headed the international Food For Peace program), McGovern was also a capable mainstream politician, having helped build a Democratic Party almost from scratch in a conservative Republican rural state, and then having won a Senate seat in 1962. But this year his political gifts totally failed him. His antiwar campaign, with the motto "Come home, America," alienated traditional Democrats (many of whose leaders sat on their hands, much as many antiwar liberals had during the national elections in 1968). It also sounded anemic compared with Nixon's robust flag-waving and renewed promises to secure an honorable peace in Vietnam. McGovern wound up winning a slightly smaller percentage of the popular vote than Goldwater had won in 1964, and earned only seventeen electoral votes, less than one-third of Goldwater's total.

* * *

Nixon's defeat of McGovern was so lopsided that historians and pundits have puzzled over why his campaign would have even bothered to break into Democratic National Committee headquarters in 1972. The ironies were numerous. The Watergate caper may have been one of the few "horrors" about which Nixon knew nothing in advance. Except for a series of unpredictable and chancy factors, from the haphazard discovery of the burglars by a night watchman at Watergate to Nixon's decision not to destroy the White House tapes to the doggedness of reporters Carl Bernstein and Bob Woodward of the *Washington Post*, Nixon's unconstitutional activities might never have come to light.

Now that they had, though, leaving Nixon in ignominy, the entire political scene changed. The "long national nightmare" of Watergate, as the new president called it, was over. But the end of the affair raised an array of difficult questions. Who, if anyone, would inherit the revamped center-right coalition and the southern strategy Nixon had so carefully constructed? Would Gerald Ford, with strong political ties to Nixon dating back to the 1940s, continue his predecessor's policies at home and abroad? Or might the president, as some of his early moves suggested, shift closer to the political center? If he did move toward the center, could Ford contain his party's restless right wing? Would the Democrats, who still controlled both houses of Congress by substantial majorities, undo the damage Nixon had inflicted, while also learning some hard political lessons from McGovern's loss in 1972? Or would the divisions between party traditionalists and new liberals worsen after McGovern's resounding defeat?

There were also questions about the country's political temper after two consecutive failed presidencies. Would Americans still thrill, as they did during John F. Kennedy's inauguration in 1961, to calls for self-sacrifice on the nation's behalf? Or would they grow cynical about politics and government? If cynicism won out, could any national leaders curb it—or, perhaps, harness and transform it to advance their own political ends?

Above all, it remained unclear, in the aftermath of Watergate, what kinds of American leaders would prevail and where they would lead the nation.

1

MEMORIES OF THE FORD
ADMINISTRATION

JOHN UPDIKE'S SATIRICAL NOVEL *Memories of the Ford Administra-tion*, which was published in 1992, concerns a stumblebum, would-be promiscuous historian named Alfred Clayton. While struggling to finish a sympathetic biography of James Buchanan—one of the few presidents in all of American history more vilified than Nixon—Clayton agrees to write, as a distraction, a chronicle of his impressions and memories of Gerald Ford's presidency. Clayton's recollections revolve around the Boston Red Sox and sex—delightful sex, desperate sex, and default sex. "What had been unthinkable under Eisenhower and racy under Kennedy had become, under Ford, almost compulsory," he writes. But what about Gerald Ford? The politics of the mid-1970s had barely seemed to intrude on Clayton's consciousness. "For that matter, was there ever a Ford Administration?" he asks. "Evidence for its existence seems to be scanty."

Post-Watergate America lingers in Americans' memories as a jumble of bad clothing fads, shag haircuts, an embarrassingly puerile popular culture, and political stasis. The economy was in deep trouble. Much of what remained of the idealistic social movements of the 1960s descended into the mad violence of grouplets such as the Weather Underground and the Symbionese Liberation Army, before burning out altogether. The frenzied pursuit of consumerist pleasures—through electronic gadgets, mail-order rendezvous, and other life-enhancers—gave rise to what the journalist Tom Wolfe called "the Me Decade" and the historian Christopher Lasch judged more severely as a culture of narcissism. The poetic songwriter Bob Dylan, who had survived the 1960s and somehow kept his head, no longer heard freedom blowing in the wind; he heard something mindless and sinister:

> Idiot wind, blowing like a circle around my skull,
> From the Grand Coulee Dam to the Capitol.
> Idiot wind, blowing every time you move your teeth,
> You're an idiot, babe.
> It's a wonder that you still know how to breathe.

Dylan could have been berating a lover, the entire country, or both.

Yet there were also fresh breezes, or what seemed to be. In 1975, a drop-out from Harvard named Bill Gates joined up with a friend, Paul Allen, to found a company they originally called "Micro-soft," with the utopian motto, "A computer on every desk and in every home." The feminist movement, the strongest outgrowth of the activism of the 1960s, was on the march following the Supreme Court's decision in 1973, in the case of *Roe v. Wade*, to strike down state laws that criminalized abortion. (A year earlier, Congress had sent an Equal Rights Amendment, which would ban civil inequality based on sex, to the states; and by 1977, thirty-five states had approved the amendment, leaving only three more to make it the law of the land.) Out of the morass of popular culture emerged, in 1976–1977, a televised series called *Roots*, on the ordeals and triumphs of one supposedly representative black family, beginning with the enslavement of an African, Kunta Kinte, in the eighteenth century. Based on a wildly successful book by the black writer Alex Haley, *Roots* attracted 130 million viewers to its final episode and appeared to be a milestone, marking how Americans had begun laying aside the racial stereotypes and hatreds that had disfigured their history. (Only later did charges surface that Haley had fabricated portions of the book that were purportedly true.)

New departures were also stirring elsewhere on the fragmented cultural and political scene. The feminists' success alarmed cadres of conservatives, including Goldwater's campaigner Phyllis Schlafly, who seized the opportunity to drum up a movement that would help revive the right and rally it around cultural issues. In 1973, another conservative activist, Paul Weyrich, established a new think tank, the Heritage Foundation. With Heritage at its disposal, Weyrich hoped that the political right would at last win the battle over ideas and policy planning long ceded to the liberals.

Even more prominent, although little understood at the time, were the struggles in Washington over how to govern after Richard Nixon's down-fall. The press corps paid the most attention to liberal congressional Demo-crats who, emboldened by sweeping victories in the elections of 1974, moved to retrieve the power they said Nixon had usurped, especially over foreign policy. The White House did its best to fend off these efforts, while it battled Congress over pressing economic issues. But the Ford administration, which very much existed, was also riven from within—and haunted by Nixon's political ghost. Ford himself was determined to govern from the ideological center: he knew this would dismay conservatives and, in some instances, leave them "sputtering." Inside the White House, though, a faction consisting of former Nixon hands faced off against more moderate elements, pushed the administration to the right, and tried to create a mainstream conservative alternative to the Goldwater hard-liners, now led by Ronald Reagan. While they counseled a fight to the finish with Congress over economic issues, con-servatives in the White House undermined the stature and power of the most celebrated holdover from the Nixon era, Secretary of State Kissinger, whose so-called realist approaches to domestic and world affairs they con-sidered tired, timid, and unprincipled. Disgruntled traditional "cold war Democrats," who would soon be known as neoconservatives, also attacked Kissinger's policies. Reagan and the Republican right, meanwhile, regarded Ford's White House with dismay and, finally, with disgust.

Overshadowed by Watergate while facing new and bewildering prob-lems at home and abroad, the Ford administration was torn by competing ideologies and political agendas. Its tribulations would leave a lasting mark on the next thirty years of American history.

A modest and easily underestimated man, Gerald Ford had gained the presidency not because of any executive expertise but because of his skills as a congressional insider in the backslapping, hard-driving style that once dominated Washington politics. His calm demeanor and reputation for in-tegrity initially won him great credit from the Washington press corps as exactly the kind of leader the country needed after Watergate. Before long, though, commentators of differing persuasions began questioning whether he was up to the job.

Born as Leslie Lynch King Jr. in 1913, Ford emerged from a broken home (he later took the name of his stepfather, Gerald Ford Sr., a paint salesman); earned an athletic scholarship to the University of Michigan, where he starred in football; and then took a law degree at Yale. After combat duty as a naval officer during the World War II, he returned to Grand Rapids, Michigan (where his mother had raised him), and in 1948 successfully ran for Congress. A center-right Republican—he would later describe himself as moderate on domestic issues, conservative on economic and fiscal issues, and an internationalist in foreign affairs—Ford was popular with his colleagues, who thought of him as an open, regular guy, trustworthy to a fault, even if his deliberate midwestern manner led some to misjudge him as slow-witted.

In 1965, after Goldwater's debacle, Ford's friends in Congress elevated him to the post of minority leader, a job he retained until 1973, when Nixon's embattled Vice President Spiro Agnew was charged with corruption and forced to resign under a cloud. Nixon would have preferred to replace Agnew with the formidable conservative ex-Democrat John Connally of Texas, who had already served as his secretary of the treasury. But Connally was as controversial as Ford was popular; and with the Watergate scandal simmering, Ford was the better choice to shore up Nixon's political base inside Congress. When that base disintegrated months later, good old Jerry Ford was suddenly the chief executive of the land.

The instant transition of power proved, not surprisingly, the most troubled the country had ever seen. Determined to bind up the wounds of the Vietnam War, Ford ventured a bold early stroke, in a speech delivered to a convention of the Veterans of Foreign Wars (VFW) in Chicago only two weeks after he assumed the presidency. Although he knew his audience would be unsympathetic, Ford declared that he would grant limited clemency to young men who had evaded the military draft for Vietnam by fleeing to Canada and Sweden. To Ford's press secretary, Jerald terHorst, it was a difficult decision "and a noble thing to do," and would help wipe away the stain of Nixon's disgrace. To the news media, which had been celebrating Ford since the day he took office, the president now looked like one of the wisest statesmen ever to occupy the White House. But the praise was not universal. Superpatriots (including many of the VFW delegates in the hall) considered Ford's gesture rank capitulation. Suspicious liberals wondered whether Ford's show of mercy was really a calculated preemptive trick to clear the way for the unthinkable—the official pardoning of Richard Nixon to spare him criminal prosecution for his alleged crimes.*

---

* Ford's program withheld honorable discharges and veterans' benefits from military deserters, and required twenty-four months of alternative national service. Of the 350,000 persons eligible, only 27,000 even applied for clemency, and slightly fewer than 22,000 of them received it. The program was generally considered a failure, even by those who administered it.

The question of pardoning Nixon had bedeviled Ford from the moment he was sworn in. During the congressional hearings over his own nomination as vice president earlier in the year, Ford testified that the public would never stomach the pardoning of a suspect president. Prospects for a pardon dimmed even more in March 1974, when a federal grand jury named Nixon as an unindicted coconspirator in the Watergate affair. Yet as soon as Ford entered office, he sounded equivocal. As he had predicted, public opinion polls, by wide margins, favored inflicting on Nixon the full measure of justice. But from many quarters, above all from Nixon's loyalists still inside the White House (especially Haig and Kissinger), Ford felt pressure to acknowledge that Nixon had suffered enough and that a pardon was in the best national interest. Neither the Watergate special prosecutor Leon Jaworski nor the federal judge who had overseen the final phases of President Nixon's agony, John J. Sirica, showed any zeal to press charges against him as a private citizen.

Ford faced a terrible political and personal dilemma. Although a pardon would implicitly concede Nixon's guilt, it might also look like the result of a prearranged corrupt bargain—absolution in exchange for a resignation. Inconveniently, barely a week before Nixon stepped down, the White House chief of staff, General Alexander Haig, obviously speaking on Nixon's behalf, had reminded Ford that, as president, he would have the power to issue a pardon—an incident that, on its face, would look like the latest smoking gun in the Watergate saga were it ever disclosed. Yet allowing the wheels of justice to grind on would incur the risk of eclipsing and even crippling Ford's efforts to mend the country. The long national nightmare that Ford spoke of at his swearing in would continue, and might easily produce damaging new revelations about Nixon that would further sour the country's bad mood.

After struggling with the matter for exactly one month, Ford announced on September 8, out of the blue, that he would issue a full pardon of Nixon for all federal crimes he had committed "or may have committed" while in office. (Ford had actually reached his decision at the end of August, but he delayed going public until he quietly built a consensus among his staff members and his emissaries had worked out an agreement with Nixon in San Clemente over the disposition of Nixon's tapes and papers.) All hell immediately broke loose. Aghast, the reporter Carl Bernstein telephoned his partner in the Watergate investigation, Bob Woodward, with the news: "The son of a bitch pardoned the son of a bitch!" The Democratic elder statesman Senator Mike Mansfield, choosing his words carefully, spoke for most of his party when he complained that, in America, the rule of law ought to apply to everyone, "presidents as well as plumbers." Republicans also fiercely objected: the party's right wing suspected that a diabolical pact had been struck to save Nixon's skin; and more moderate conservatives feared that the voters' reaction would worsen what already promised to be heavy losses in the congressional elections the following November. The White House press secretary, terHorst, who had been kept in the dark, resigned on the spot, infuriated at what he considered his boss's abdication of conscience, and convinced that Ford had squandered the goodwill he had earned with his offer of clemency to draft resisters.

More than thirty years later, the accumulated evidence points to a more benign interpretation of Ford's motives and actions. By the time Haig and Ford held their suspicious meeting, Nixon's political fate was virtually sealed, so he had little leverage for extracting a pardon. The conversation seems to have involved little more than Nixon, through Haig, reminding Ford obliquely of his only viable option if he wished to govern without disabling distractions. Although the televised speech announcing the pardon betrayed no emotion, Ford was sincerely moved by the anguish of the Nixon family, who, he said, had been caught up in "an American tragedy in which we have all played a part." (Ford was also genuinely concerned for Nixon's physical and mental health, having received reports that the ex-president was falling to pieces in seclusion at his estate in California.) The new president knew that many honorable Americans would condemn him, and acknowledged that "if I am wrong, ten angels swearing I was right would make no difference." Between two evils, he chose what he decided was the lesser. Either the tragedy "could go on and on and on," he told the country, "or somebody must write the end of it." He acted out of a decent compassion for Nixon and patriotic concern for his country.

Granting Ford his noble motives, however, does not at all vindicate his handling of the pardon. Over the days and weeks before his announcement, the president held his cards closely, even when meeting with his chief advisers. Although he was well aware of where the public stood, he made no effort to prepare the country for what was coming. Had he chosen, once he had made his decision in late August, to begin explaining his reasoning before revealing his conclusion, he could have forestalled at least a portion of the outrage. Instead, he looked as if he was defying the people's will over a momentous issue in order to shield his political benefactor. He even quietly implied that all America had somehow played a role in the national nightmare.

Most important, Ford pardoned Nixon after failing to extract in return a formal confession of wrongdoing beyond a mushy admission by Nixon that he had been "wrong in not acting more decisively and more forthrightly in dealing with Watergate." A desire to prevent the negotiations between the White House and San Clemente from turning nasty, as well as concern for Nixon's mental and physical health, held Ford back. But by failing to follow up more forcefully, Ford left a skeptical country with a corrosive sense that the course of justice has been artificially interrupted, and that a powerful man (but not his hirelings, some of whom faced, and ultimately served, serious jail time) had outrageously been held above the law. Instead of alleviating public cynicism, as intended, the pardon actually deepened it. Ford's failure would also permit Nixon, for the rest of his life, to proclaim his innocence of any criminal wrongdoing. And it would permit pro-Nixon propagandists in the future—including, until very recently, the former directors of the Nixon presidential library and museum—to whitewash the entire episode. Absolution might have implied, at the moment, Nixon's culpability, but over time it acquired overtones of exoneration, which fed the fantasy that Watergate was nothing more than a power-grab by Nixon's adversaries in Congress and the press.

The tense situation in the White House, which had contributed to the controversy over the pardon, deepened the sense of disorder. Surrounded by old Nixon hands as well as his own staff, Ford, with little preparation, had had to make important personnel choices and impose order. The Nixonians most tainted by Watergate, including Attorney General John Mitchell and the staff members John Ehrlichman, H. R. "Bob" Haldeman, and Charles Colson, were gone, either serving time or awaiting trial on federal charges. But Ford, believing that continuity was essential during the sudden transition, had retained as many of Nixon's officials as he could, including six major appointees untouched by the scandals: Secretary of State and National Security Adviser Henry Kissinger, Secretary of Defense James Schlesinger, Secretary of the Treasury William Simon (who had been appointed shortly before Nixon's resignation), Director of the Office of Management and Budget Roy Ash, Assistant for Domestic Affairs Kenneth Cole, and General Haig, given his old duties as Nixon's chief of staff but with the more modest title of staff coordinator. (Ford would soon persuade his old congressional friend and colleague, a veteran of the Nixon administration, Donald Rumsfeld, to leave his job as ambassador to NATO and take Haig's place.) The remainder of the cabinet consisted of holdovers from Nixon's time. Ford's men served as important staffers, led by the head of the White House Editorial Office, Robert Hartmann, each of whom received an appointment as a presidential counselor with cabinet rank.

Nixon's and Ford's teams never blended, and this problem was exacerbated by the loose managerial style Ford brought over from Capitol Hill. Hartmann and Haig (and later Hartmann and Rumsfeld) were particularly allergic to each other, typifying what Hartmann, a longtime stalwart and aide-de-camp of Ford's, later described as a more general problem: there was never, he wrote, "for all thirty months he was President, a truly Ford Cabinet or Ford Staff. There was an incompatible, uncontrolled, contentious collection of Praetorians, many bitterly resentful of the few Ford loyalists who hung on to the end." The inside jockeying over Nixon's pardon was the first clear sign to Ford's old friends that the White House was filled with men who had priorities other than serving the president's best interests. In a setting rife with intrigue, it was only a matter of time before Ford's factionalized White House divided against itself.

Ford's lack of a vice president compounded his organizational problems, and the issue hung in the air for five weeks into his presidency. One strong candidate was the former governor of New York, Nelson Rockefeller. Although many Republicans distrusted Rockefeller as an incurable liberal and a womanizer, his aura of recognized national leadership would add credibility to Ford's accidental presidency. Rockefeller also desired the job, despite his professions that he had never wanted to be the vice president of anything. Ford, not trusting his own instincts, conducted a private poll of leading Republicans, and Rockefeller came in second behind George H. W. Bush, a patrician Connecticut Yankee and party scion who had made his name in the oil capitals of Texas and had served Nixon loyally as ambassador to the United Nations and chairman of the Republican National Committee. (Ford's friend Rumsfeld also campaigned vigorously for the job, but was crowded out by the better-known aspirants.) Suddenly and mysteriously, reports surfaced in the press charging that Bush's failed campaign for the U.S. Senate in 1970 had received approximately $100,000 from a slush fund at Nixon's White House. Ford turned to Rockefeller, who quickly accepted.

The announcement, made in mid-September, caused Ford additional trouble. Right-wing Republicans gagged at the thought of their old adversary Rockefeller now standing so close to the presidency. They wondered whether Ford was taking them seriously as a political force. Others in Washington, across the entire political spectrum, worried about Rockefeller's immense wealth; his net worth turned out to be, on official investigation, $182.5 million, a staggering amount at the time. News stories told of how Rockefeller had spread his largesse among his political allies and protégés (preeminently Henry Kissinger), and how he owed roughly $1 million in unpaid back federal taxes. The congressional hearings over Rockefeller's nomination dragged on for more than two months; Rockefeller won approval in early December only after he agreed to pay his delinquent taxes and place his remaining assets in a blind trust. Two weeks later, he was finally sworn in.

The pardon, as well as the rancor over Rockefeller, cost Ford and the Republican Party dearly. Even White House insiders, braced for criticism, were shaken by the intensity of the response to the pardon. Ford's honeymoon with the press corps abruptly ended and cordial relations would never resume. The president's personal favorability in the opinion polls crashed, falling from a high of 70 percent when he replaced Nixon to figures in the low forties at the end of the year. Infuriated liberal and left-wing House Democrats, led by the fiery New Yorker Bella Abzug, launched an investigation into whether the new president had acted improperly or illegally. The acrimonious hearings drew no blood but put Ford in the humiliating position of having to testify on Capitol Hill in his own defense—the first president so compelled in more than a century. Right-wing Republicans were nearly as angry as the Democrats. Immediately following Nixon's resignation, only Barry Goldwater's outspoken support of the new president had kept the hard-liners reconciled to Ford, whom they considered a run-of-the-mill Washington hack, in over his head as president. After the pardoning of Nixon, though, followed quickly by Ford's choice of Rockefeller, all bets were off.

In the November elections, the Republicans lost forty-eight seats in the House and four in the Senate, returning to the Democrats the commanding congressional majorities they had enjoyed in their heyday of the middle to late 1960s. The great political realignment begun under Nixon seemed to have broken down. There was even loose talk among Republican strategists that the party ought to change its sullied name. The Democratic Congress was now in a position to assert itself forcefully against a weakened White House, restoring checks and balances over foreign as well as domestic policy while paving the way for what Democrats hoped would be a runaway victory in the presidential election of 1976. Some buoyant liberals even conjectured that the fallout from Watergate had revived American liberalism in a new form, imbued with the reformist spirit of the new politics. Liberal Democrats, however, were not the only ones aroused. At the other end of the political spectrum, the frustrated Republican right wing, led by Ronald Reagan, started putting aside any doubts about the propriety and political wisdom of challenging an incumbent Republican president.

Political lines sharpened early in 1975, as the augmented Democratic majority in Congress girded for all-out war with the White House. Yet if liberals, or for that matter moderates or conservatives, were to govern effectively, they would have to tackle severe and baffling economic and fiscal problems that had beset the country for years and had grown acute since 1973. The Watergate crisis had crowded the difficulties out of the headlines, but they affected the everyday lives of all Americans as the political controversies inside Washington did not. They were long-term structural problems that seemed independent of the usual ebb and flow of the business cycle. They sharply challenged what had become the prevailing wisdom about how the American economy operated.

The word coined to describe the new phenomenon strangling the economy was "stagflation," which meant a rising inflation rate coupled with slow economic growth and rising unemployment. The combination made no sense by standard measures: inflation normally followed a drop in unemployment, whereas declining employment and average real wages were supposed to cause consumer prices to fall. To suffer from both miseries at the same time mystified professional economists and laypersons alike, yet that had been the case since 1969. The Nixon administration, heeding Keynesian economic principles, had imposed government controls on wages and prices and devalued the dollar in order to boost American exports, to some noticeable effect. But in 1973, following America's support for Israel in the Yom Kippur War, Arab oil ministries formed the Organization of Petroleum Exporting Countries (OPEC) and imposed an embargo. By early 1974, the price of crude oil had jumped to ten dollars a barrel, more than a fivefold increase since the previous October. The effect on prices at the gasoline pump (when gasoline was available at all) was severe, but the larger ripple effect on the cost of goods throughout the economy was devastating, pushing the annual inflation rate in 1974 to 12.4 percent, double what it had been five years earlier. On the same day Ford became president, the government announced that the Wholesale Price Index (WPI) had risen by an alarming 3.7 percent in July alone, the second-largest monthly increase in nearly thirty years.

The oil crisis compounded other economic problems, causing a vicious spiral. The nation's automobile industry was ailing badly, outperformed by foreign manufacturers, especially in Japan, which produced attractive and affordable vehicles that were far more fuel-efficient than their American competitors. Steel production and other heavy industries were also declining precipitously, underpriced by foreign firms and hit hard by union unrest. Traditional urban economic powerhouses such as Detroit and Cleveland were hemorrhaging jobs; this situation helped raise the national unemployment rate to 7.5 percent in 1975. With lucrative manufacturing jobs disappearing, replaced (when they were replaced at all) by lower-paid service employment, average hourly wages dipped in 1973 and 1974, after a quarter century of steady growth. The annual gross national product per capita, which had expanded at an average rate exceeding 3 percent during the 1960s, actually fell by more than 2 percent during Nixon's final year in office.

The crisis led economic doomsayers to predict the imminent decline and fall of the American century and the irresistible future dominance of the Japanese. These assessments proved overly gloomy. For all its afflictions, the nation's economy remained basically strong. Although the old manufacturing centers in the so-called rust belt were in terrible shape, the sunbelt cities, including Houston and San Diego, were booming, thanks partly to government aid and partly to lower regional labor costs. The foundations of what had long been promoted as the American way of life—decent and affordable housing, low food costs, sound and improving services—were still available to a far greater extent than in any other country. Still, the sharp reverses of the early 1970s raised doubts about how long the American way would last, and for how many Americans. Economic anxieties tested the nation's nerves in ways that affected many realms of life, ranging from race relations, crime, and the divorce rate to faith in government itself. Political arguments over how best to conquer stagflation and the rest of the country's economic woes would have far-reaching effects.

Gerald Ford, who had served on the House Appropriations Committee, took a greater interest in economics and fiscal policy than Nixon ever did, and he held more orthodox Republican views about government's limited role in economic life. His created a new cabinet-level superagency, the Economic Policy Board (EPB), and installed as its head an even more doctrinaire upholder of free-market economics, Treasury Secretary William Simon. The chairman of the president's Council of Economic Advisers (newly appointed by Ford), Alan Greenspan, a longtime associate of the exuberantly pro-capitalist writer Ayn Rand, favored similar assumptions, but was more alert to political realities than his rival Simon, and showed greater willingness to deal with Congress. Ford took inspiration from Simon's steely assurance, though his pragmatic side generally led him to favor Greenspan's more measured conservatism. Yet Ford was in a difficult position, trying to chart his own course on economic issues (and related matters of energy policy) while caught between Simon and Greenspan, and while also battling both congressional liberals and the right wing of his own party. Buffeted about by political as well as economic challenges, Ford wound up looking inconsistent.

Ford decided to place economic issues at the center of his first presidential address to Congress—but what would he propose? A tax hike and severe cuts in the government budget might curb inflation but also further retard the economy. A tax cut could spark economic growth but feed the inflation. Simon and Greenspan, who regarded inflation as the greater immediate threat, believed that lowered prices would eventually create new jobs, and they counseled Ford to put first things first. Ford duly told Congress that inflation was "public enemy number one." He announced that he would meet the crisis in the time-honored Republican way by slashing government spending, but would also raise federal income taxes for the first time since 1968, with a 5 percent surcharge on high-income individuals and corporations. To reinforce his call for sacrifice and fiscal severity, Ford created the EPB, by executive order, to oversee the American economy; it was the first cabinet-level body of its kind. And to stimulate a spirit of popular engagement, he announced a national volunteer organization called Whip Inflation Now, or WIN. By wearing red WIN buttons (dimly reminiscent of the Blue Eagle buttons issued by Franklin Roosevelt's National Recovery Administration during the early years of the New Deal), citizens could show that they had enlisted in the struggle to keep prices down.

Ford's proposed tax hikes and service cuts contributed to the Republicans' dismal showing in the 1974 midterm elections. (The plan to increase taxes also further alienated many right-wing Republicans; Ronald Reagan fired off a stiff telegram of complaint to the White House.) The unfortunate WIN campaign, basically a propaganda ploy, turned into a rare example of instant political kitsch, mocked by newspaper editorialists and late-night television wits. ("[A] lot of people in the Ford White House thought it was idiotic before they did it," the respected Washington reporter Lou Cannon later remarked of the WIN folly.) The White House retreated, at the urging of the more moderate members of the EPB as well as the conservative Greenspan (although not, emphatically, the more ideologically driven Simon). After finally admitting that the economy was in recession, Ford jettisoned his proposed tax increase in favor of a onetime $16 billion cut in individual and corporate taxes, while vowing to hold the line against federal spending. He also called for abandoning the price controls on domestic oil that Nixon had imposed before the OPEC boycott, on the assumption that supply and demand would now regularize prices for heating oil and gasoline at lowered levels. To assuage a public that believed the oil companies were gouging consumers, Ford further proposed to increase taxes on the companies' profits.

In what became a familiar pattern, Ford's efforts to unite the country around what he considered reasonable proposals succeeded chiefly in enraging and emboldening his political adversaries. Anti-inflation hawks, including Simon, said that Ford's flip-flop on taxes looked like a betrayal of sound economic doctrine. Congressional Democrats, who favored a tax cut for the middle class, called the president's reversal halfhearted, and they proposed a far deeper, permanent tax cut, weighted more heavily for middle- and lower-income families. The Democrats also called, in standard Keynesian fashion, for sharp increases in federal spending to offset recessionary pressures. Ford retaliated by repeatedly vetoing spending bills, as he would continue to do for the rest of his presidency; and in the great majority of cases he beat congressional efforts to override him.

Congress counterattacked in March 1975 by approving a bill that permanently cut taxes by $22.8 billion, over 40 percent more than the president's proposed temporary reduction, and was more progressive in its targeted beneficiaries. Furious, Ford listened sympathetically to Simon's advice that he veto the bill, both for economic reasons and because anything less than a veto would allow the Republicans' right wing to accuse him of caving in to Congress. However, Ford's other economic advisers, including Greenspan, countered that a veto would make him look foolish—he had, after all, already changed his mind once and proposed his own tax cut—and that in any case, Congress could easily go ahead and pass an even larger tax cut as a prelude to the presidential race in 1976. Ford ended up signing the bill but promised to kill any proposals that would add even a single dollar to the federal deficit (which actually had been declining substantially, as a percentage of the gross domestic product, or GDP, since 1972). "We will swallow something on the tax side," he later told Republican congressional leaders, "but fight against increases on the spending side."

Similar unsteady dynamics developed in Ford's complicated struggle with Congressional Democrats over energy policy. In addition to a plan that combined deregulation of oil prices with a tax on windfall profits, the White House announced that it intended to impose a tariff on oil imports. Democrats in the Senate immediately responded that the tariff measure exceeded the president's constitutional authority, and Congress passed a joint resolution blocking it. Once again, the president initially sided with conservatives' entreaties to hold firm, and this time he seemed to stick by his guns by vetoing the anti-tariff bill in early March, a month after Congress had passed it. But Ford accompanied the veto with major concessions: first, he would delay the full phasing in of his tariff plans; second, he would postpone indefinitely all plans to end the oil price controls. Two months later, he ordered the Federal Energy Administration (which Congress had established the previous year) to proceed with oil deregulation, but on a very gradual schedule. Democrats offered their own energy bill, which restored oil quotas and heavily taxed both gasoline and automobiles that did not conform to minimal fuel-efficiency standards—but then, in the face of complaints about new taxes, they stripped the bill and finally killed it.

The Democrats' defeat did not, however, presage a victory for the White House on energy policy. After Congress repeatedly rebuffed new deregulation proposals (and after Ford vetoed a congressional bill extending the controls), the administration took a strategic decision to give way over energy (though not without a fight) while fighting fiercely over taxes. After strenuous negotiations, Congress approved, in November, an Omnibus Energy Bill, which fixed domestic oil prices at $7.66 per barrel but authorized the president to decontrol that price gradually over a period stretching for more than three years. The president reluctantly signed it, in the hope of taking the energy issue off the table in the coming presidential election.

Simultaneously, Ford tried to flummox Congress with a new proposal for a permanent tax cut totaling $28 billion, coupled with spending cuts of at least the same amount. Preparing for the election, Ford would present himself as a responsive but responsible fiscal and economic manager. Democrats, not surprisingly, passed the proposed tax cuts without the spending cuts, and insisted that only additional federal expenditures, including deficit spending, could offset the recession. The ensuing back-and-forth was predictable. First, Ford vetoed the Democrats' bill. Then the Democrats, after failing to override the veto, pledged themselves to cut spending in the next fiscal year and passed a much smaller permanent tax cut of $9 billion. Once again, Simon advised stiff-necked resistance to the proposal; Greenspan and the moderates called it the best available compromise; and Ford signed the bill.

While Ford and the Congress wrangled, New York City's fiscal crisis intruded on national affairs, with immediate political as well as economic implications. New York had been the nation's foremost financial and cultural capital for more than a century. Since the mayoralty of Fiorello H. La Guardia in the 1930s and 1940s, it had also been a beacon of liberal urban policy in the New Deal tradition. By the early 1970s, though, everything seemed to be falling apart. Rising municipal outlays were badly outstripping the city's income from a shrinking tax base (diminished by a decline of manufacturing in New York and by a middle-class flight to the suburbs). During the decade after 1965, the city's expenditures rose, on average, 12 percent annually, more than twice as fast as its revenues. The accompanying deterioration of its services and quality of life made New York a prime example, to some observers, of how bankrupt—literally—New Deal liberalism had become. Politics aside, widespread resentment around the rest of the country of New York's prestige, polyglot population, and perceived arrogance produced reactions that ranged from indifference to schadenfreude.

From the spring through the early fall of 1975, officials in New York struggled to meet the city's financial obligations, and enormous tensions developed between Vice President Rockefeller and the dominant conservatives within the Ford administration. After Simon, Greenspan, and, finally, Ford flatly rejected a request by the mayor of New York, Abraham Beame, for a $90 billion federal loan, Beame sought relief from state officials, who established new agencies to shift the city's debt into long-term bonds and otherwise oversee the city's finances. When these measures proved insufficient, Rockefeller, previously cool to the city's requests, changed his mind and became New York's advocate. Should the city default, the vice president told one cabinet meeting, the impact, politically as well as economically, would be "far more serious than anyone thinks." In part, Rockefeller was standing up for his own beloved city; in part, he had become persuaded that his political adversaries inside the administration, especially William Simon and Donald Rumsfeld, were trying to undercut him by stiffing New York. In mid-October, after Ford spurned his private pleas to provide financial aid, Rockefeller publicly broke with the administration and demanded federal assistance. Soon after, Ford held a meeting of his chief advisers and asked them about changing course on New York; Rumsfeld summed up the prevailing mood with a loud, "Hell no!" Ford announced his latest decision to rebuff the city, and the *Daily News* ran its famous "drop dead" headline.

Ford would never completely heal the political breach with Rockefeller, but he did relent over aiding New York, and fairly quickly. In November, the New York state legislature enacted a series of emergency measures providing $4 billion in assistance in exchange for guarantees of higher city taxes, layoffs of municipal workers, and a hike in the city's subway fare. The White House then announced it would pitch in by requesting from Congress an additional $2.5 billion in loan guarantees over a three-year period. Ford later said that the acts of good faith by both the city and the state persuaded him to act. Historians have wondered whether he was more interested in gaining the political backing of New York's junior senator, James Buckley, an unorthodox member of the Conservative Party (and brother of William F. Buckley Jr.). Buckley's endorsement in the following year's Republican New York primary would be invaluable (and Ford duly received it); accordingly, the president's motives may have been more narrowly political than they were generous.

Either way, Ford could claim once more that he had gained what he basically had wanted—but at the cost of exposing himself to charges that he was a feeble executive, indecisive on economics and fiscal policy. Ford's fate was, in some ways, unkind. Over time, it became obvious that the countercyclical effects of the tax cut in 1975 and the restraints imposed by the Omnibus Energy Bill had helped curb the insidious stagflation. By the end of 1976, the consumer price index (CPI) fell to about half of its high point two years earlier; and the civilian unemployment rate, which peaked at 9 percent in mid-1975, dropped to 7.5 percent at the start of 1977, and would continue to drop for the rest of the decade.

The lion's share of the credit, to be sure, belonged to Congress, which had repeatedly forced the hand of the White House, especially over the tax cut. Inside the White House, the canny and persuasive Alan Greenspan played a crucial role as a conservative counseling compromise. Yet Ford did, finally, sign the bills in question. In a less fractious political time, he might have capitalized on that more fully—and historians today might even look back on his presidency as a notable success, at least in the economic realm. Instead, each time Ford changed course, he looked less like a shrewd pragmatist or a man with the courage to change his mind than a confused flipflopper. The Democrats, who battled Ford all down the line, hoping to regain the White House in 1976, would never warm to him. Right-wing Republicans, who had not trusted Ford to begin with, increasingly thought him treacherous.

* * *

Different dynamics existed on other, even more inflammatory domestic matters concerning race relations and civil rights. Here, Ford stood much firmer. Yet the man who prided himself on healing America after Watergate also ended up widening the racial breach, despite his best intentions.

In the early 1970s, battles against racial segregation focused, as they had for nearly twenty years, on public schools. Civil rights organizations contended that the nation had been too sluggish in promulgating the Supreme Court's order, contained in its decision of 1954 in *Brown v. Board of Education*, to pursue school desegregation "with all deliberate speed." The Nixon administration complicated the issue by distinguishing between formal de jure racial discrimination, a problem restricted almost entirely to the South; and de facto segregation, prevalent throughout the country, where segregated housing patterns and local zoning restrictions, though not explicitly dictated school segregation, had kept black and white children in separate schools. By opposing de jure segregation, Nixon had made a strong impact on the rules governing once strictly segregated southern public schools (although not on segregated schooling, as he could not prevent white parents from simply withdrawing their children from the system and sending them to all-white private academies). By refusing to attack de facto segregation, however, Nixon (partly as an extension of his southern strategy) willfully sided with those northern parents, nearly all of them white, who opposed achieving racial balance by busing white children to black schools and black children to white schools. As thousands of school districts across the country confronted court-ordered busing plans, Ford's White House sustained Nixon's policy—and immediately found itself embroiled in passionate controversy.

No northern city faced deeper problems over race and compulsory school busing than Boston. Alongside its heritage of abolitionist liberalism, Boston also had a long history of racial animosity, especially between the growing number of black migrants to the city and neighborhoods long settled by Irish and Italian immigrants and their children. The worst conflicts pitted the black ghetto of Roxbury against nearby South Boston, populated almost exclusively by white Catholics, most of them of Irish extraction. Tension worsened in July 1974, when Judge Arthur Garrity Jr. of the U.S. District Court ordered the city of Boston to implement a school busing desegregation plan in preparation for the coming fall term. The white local school board vowed to resist the order. Resistance turned violent when the schools reopened on September 12, and a mob of South Bostoners screamed racist insults, attacked black students, and otherwise attempted to prevent the desegregation of their beloved South Boston High. Local leaders, including a popular and confrontational former congresswoman and school board head, Louise Day Hicks, quickly endorsed a white boycott of city schools led by Hicks's group, Restore Our Alienated Rights (ROAR).

The White House strongly opposed the court-directed desegregation effort. President Ford, to be sure, unlike the conservative wing of his party, had a pro–civil rights record. He had supported *Brown v. Board of Education*. In 1964, he voted in Congress to approve the landmark Civil Rights Bill, as he did a year later in favor of the Voting Rights Bill. But like Nixon, he had also opposed compulsory legal remedies for de facto segregation; and he was wary of federal involvement in local school systems. As president, Ford proudly reminded reporters, "I was one of the original members of the House or Senate that said that court-ordered forced busing to achieve racial balance was not the way to accomplish quality education." After Judge Garrity announced his decision, Ford used the occasion of his first formal press conference to denounce it.

Richard Parsons, a member of the administration's Domestic Counsel, would eventually advise Ford through aides that his stance—opposed to both segregation and busing—was inadequate. "Since busing is the law of the land, like it or not," he wrote, "[the president] ought to be actively encouraging people to comply with the law and not fueling frustrations with the law by criticizing it." Parsons urged that Ford consider some alternative strategy for achieving desegregation, including formation of a presidential commission or conference, instead of simply fanning the flames of discontent. Ford decided against any such commission and rejected any other federal option as improper. Sticking to his often repeated line that he favored desegregation so long as it did not interfere with quality schooling, he fitfully searched for a voluntary local solution to school segregation. In his failure, he ended up giving aid and comfort to hard-core foes of desegregation.

In Boston, the freshly revamped Justice Department decided not to get involved on either side. With a strong push from his chief of staff, Donald Rumsfeld, Ford had replaced his interim attorney general, William Saxbe, with Edward Levi, the president of the University of Chicago and former dean of its law school. A distinguished university administrator with centrist leanings, Levi was a fine choice to lead the Justice Department out of the squalor left behind by Nixon's attorney general, John Mitchell. Among other reforms, Levi would introduce new guidelines restricting the ability of the FBI to use wiretap surveillance. On the issue of the Boston schools,

Levi decided that "because the Governor [of Massachusetts] has not yet used all of the means at his disposal," the Justice Department would not intervene. Black leaders in and outside Boston, including Ford's own secretary of transportation, William Coleman, objected strongly to the department's refusal to implement the rulings of a federal court, claiming, as Coleman told the cabinet, that history would show the federal judges had "acted with great restraint, judgment, and wisdom in assisting the court-ordered busing"—but they objected in vain.

Ford did have some heavy intellectual artillery to support his basic position, in the person of Daniel Patrick Moynihan, a former domestic policy official under Johnson and Nixon, now U.S. ambassador to the United Nations. Moynihan, an Irish Catholic liberal who had been a sociologist at Harvard, had won a reputation as a brilliant maverick willing to flout the liberal establishment (and especially the civil rights establishment). Unlike more dogmatic liberals, whom he disdained as leftist Puritan ideologues, Moynihan would work in government with conservatives while presenting himself as the consummate social scientist who stood above party, ideological politesse, and academic convention. In a long memorandum written to Ford in October 1975, Moynihan expressed a strong premonition that conservative politicians and demagogues might use the issue of busing to turn Americans completely against racial integration. But he also explained that the best social scientific evidence showed that school integration did little or nothing to improve the learning and life chances of blacks and other minorities. Once pro-busing forces came to understand this, he conjectured, their ardor over the issue would fade. Armed with Moynihan's prestigious reflections—"Talk with me. Excellent," the president wrote to Donald Rumsfeld in a note covering Moynihan's memo—Ford felt justified in viewing his opposition to busing as the essence of enlightenment.

The administration did try to draw a clear line against violence, and as the situation in South Boston degenerated, Ford put on alert status units of the Eighty-second Airborne Division—much as President Eisenhower had decided to mobilize troops to enforce school desegregation in Little Rock, Arkansas, eighteen years earlier. Push came to shove on December 11, when the stabbing of a white student at South Boston High impelled a mob of white parents to surround the school, trap the black students inside, and then threaten to storm the place. Although further violence was luckily averted, black leaders, including Representative Charles Rangel of New York, head of the Congressional Black Caucus (CBC), demanded federal action. But Ford, having been told that the situation was less dangerous than had been feared, and that local law enforcement officials had contained it, refused to send in troops.

Judge Garrity eventually prevailed in Boston. After he held the members of the school board committee in contempt for refusing to comply with his plan, the committee submitted a desegregation plan of its own in January 1975. Although insufficient to persuade many white parents to abandon their boycott, a relatively successful busing program began in the autumn, causing minimal violence. Undeterred, Ford instructed Levi to take up cases in which the government could claim before the Supreme Court that mandatory busing had gotten out of hand. In July 1974, the Court, after a bitter fight, had ruled five to four, in the case of *Milliken v. Bradley*, that mostly white metropolitan school districts had no constitutional obligation to achieve racial balance by merging with mostly black cities. But the White House's strategy of finding further support for *Milliken* got nowhere; and in the case of *Runyon v. McCrary*, one of the few cases on race in the schools before it in 1976, the Court ruled that the Constitution forbade private schools from discriminating on the basis of race. Ford had better luck in Congress, where moderate Democrats were having second thoughts about busing as a solution to the nation's racial ills. In 1975, Ford signed a law forbidding the Department of Health, Education, and Welfare to require school systems to transport children beyond their neighborhood schools.

The White House stance in the Boston struggle, and in a related school desegregation conflict in Louisville, did nothing to persuade advocates of civil rights that Ford's party now wished to reclaim its heritage as the party of Lincoln. Neither did the administration's ultimate proposal, announced in late June 1976, for a School Desegregation Standards and Assistance Act. Ford proclaimed that the proposed legislation would respect individual rights and help to guarantee the best possible public education, while also affirming "our common belief in civil rights for all Americans." But the plan—which would have effectively nullified busing by confining the courts to correcting racial imbalance caused by illegal acts and limit court-ordered busing plans to no more than five years—offended even moderate black leaders. "There is no level at which this bill can be condoned," Coleman told Ford in a memo detailing the proposal's objectionable features. The bill died in committee.

At the beginning of his unexpected presidency, Ford had hoped to halt the Republican reaction against civil rights reform. In retrospect, he wrote of how the Nixon administration had closed the door to minorities, especially blacks, and of how, as vice president, he had wanted to open it. He pointed proudly to a meeting he held, in his early days as president, with the Congressional Black Caucus (CBC)—which Representative Rangel had described, according to Ford, as "absolutely, fantastically good." And when the busing issue began to boil over in 1975, Ford arranged discussions at the White House with civil rights leaders and educators as well as elected officials and members of his own administration. But racial politics in America had moved into areas where good intentions and personal relations at the top carried little weight.

On the one hand, ordinary black parents as well as civil right leaders were demanding the full measure of their civil rights, with the backing of the federal courts and by compulsory programs if necessary, so that their children would not be trapped in inferior, even dangerous, schools. On the other hand, working-class and middle-class whites across the country— by no means all of them given to the ugly racism and violence that flared up in Boston—insisted that *their* rights as citizens and parents were under attack by federal judges and liberal politicians who cared nothing about the value of traditional neighborhood schools, and who would debase education in the name of redressing ancient wrongs. (That certain prominent pro-busing judges and elected officials, including Senator Edward M. Kennedy of Massachusetts, sent their own children to private schools inflamed class passions as well, reinforcing the idea that in this period, unlike the New Deal era, all liberals were uncaring, hypocritical "limousine liberals." Kennedy, in fact, was physically attacked and forced to flee a mob of irate white parents at a demonstration outside Boston's federal building in September.) In this clash of race and rights, no amount of goodwill could mollify either side.

On the distinct issue of court-ordered busing, Ford, the pro–civil rights Republican, had steadfastly supported one of the sides, whose deepening social and economic anxieties and repeated judicial setbacks were stoking resistance to civil rights legislation as a whole—including the early programs, endorsed by Nixon, for affirmative action in government hiring and contracting. By feeding the hurt and outrage of conservative northern whites, Ford deepened their alienation not simply from liberal Democrats but from what had long been the Republican mainstream on civil rights. Ford's actions were perfectly consistent with traditionalist midwestern Republican conservative views about the evils of federal power; but they were also consistent with the Nixonian southern strategy. And by further agitating instead of calming racial tensions, Ford's policies would, ironically, end up helping to push many ex-Democrats as well as longtime conventional Republicans into the political camp of the pro-Reagan right.

Early in 1976, the Republican opinion poll expert Robert Teeter asked his sample population a simple question: "What has Ford done that particularly impresses you?" Sixty-one percent of those polled replied, "Nothing." The results were particularly striking on domestic issues, above all on the economy, in which the poll showed considerably higher public confidence in the ability of Congress and the Democratic Party to handle inflation and unemployment. Ten months before the presidential election, there was deep concern in the White House—and renewed hope among liberals—that the voters were flocking back to liberalism.

Circumstances were more complex in foreign policy and diplomatic matters. But abroad as at home, Nixon's ghost haunted the Ford administration.

2

DÉTENTE AND ITS
DISCONTENTS

EALING WITH THE AFTERMATH of Nixon's presidency required
coming to terms with the Vietnam War as well as with Watergate. So long as America had been heavily involved in the war,
public debate took the form of searing arguments about the legitimacy of
American military involvement overseas. In the calmer political climate
after 1974, debate shifted to questions about how the country's failures
in Vietnam had altered its military and political position, and whether
the United States should temper its cold war military commitments—
or expand them. The arguments focused in particular on the policies of
détente designed by Nixon's all-powerful voice on foreign affairs, Henry
A. Kissinger, whom Ford retained as both secretary of state and national
security adviser.

To liberal and left-wing Democrats, the war had been a moral and political catastrophe, an utter disgrace that had been brought about by what they
considered a corrupting anticommunist truculence common among traditional cold war Democrats and conservative Republicans alike. Two disastrous presidents, one from each political party, had, they believed, escalated
and then prolonged a cruel and unwinnable conflict by severely stretching
their constitutional mandates. Accordingly, even before Nixon's resignation, Democrats on Capitol Hill began trying to curb the executive's power

to wage war independent of Congress. In November 1973, after eight previous failures, the House and Senate finally overrode Nixon's veto of what had become known as the War Powers Resolution.

Henceforth, presidents would have to consult with Congress before commencing any hostilities abroad, and continue such consultation regularly until hostilities ceased. If Congress did not formally declare war or enact "a specific authorization for such use of United States Armed Forces," within sixty days, the president would have to end military engagement. Supporters of the resolution claimed that it did no more than restore to Congress, in part, the sole authority to declare war, as explicitly stipulated in the Constitution. Critics, however, called the resolution an unconstitutional infringement on the president's explicitly delegated powers as commander in chief. In his veto message, Nixon denounced what he called Congress's "clearly unconstitutional" effort "to take away, by a mere legislative act, authorities which the President has properly exercised under the Constitution for almost 200 years." But Nixon was now in serious political trouble—widely distrusted for his intense secrecy in conducting foreign affairs, as in much else—and Congress was ready, willing, and able to assert itself.

After the elections of 1974, the resurgent Democrats turned to exposing the dirty secrets of recent American foreign policy. The covert activity of the CIA became their primary target. Late in 1974, the investigative reporter Seymour Hersh of the *New York Times* revealed some of the details (the "family jewels") about numerous unsavory and sometimes flatly illegal secret CIA operations, ranging from clandestine actions leading up to the coup in Chile in 1973 to the surreptitious surveillance of domestic antiwar protests and protesters. Caught off guard, President Ford, early in 1975, had the director of the CIA, William Colby (whom Nixon had appointed in 1973), quickly provide a report on the allegations, and then appointed a commission headed by Vice President Rockefeller to investigate the CIA. Although established to get at the truth, the Rockefeller Commission was also designed to limit investigation to the specific abuses Colby detailed, thereby allowing the White House to get out in front of Congress on the issue, and forestalling what Deputy Staff Coordinator Richard B. Cheney called "a serious legislative encroachment on executive power."

The commission's report, released six months later, chronicled various sordid ventures, including a large domestic surveillance project called Operation CHAOS, and concluded that "the CIA has engaged in some activities that should be criticized and not permitted to happen again." But the commission also sidestepped (some observers said whitewashed) several disturbing allegations about plans by the CIA, dating back to the Eisenhower administration, to assassinate foreign leaders, including Rafael Trujillo of the Dominican Republic and Fidel Castro of Cuba. By failing to exonerate the CIA, the report alienated the agency's conservative supporters; but by failing to criticize the CIA more harshly, the report angered many members of Congress.

Dissatisfied Democrats, led by Senator Frank Church of Idaho, picked up where the Rockefeller Commission left off. With the active cooperation of the CIA's director, Colby, Church's special select committee on intelligence activities assembled information on matters previously slighted, including the assassination plots. In December 1975, the committee released a detailed six-volume report, which called the CIA a "rogue elephant" and recommended far more intense congressional oversight of it. Soon, both houses of Congress established permanent intelligence committees to do just that. Pressure on both the CIA and the White House grew when Senator Dick Clark of Iowa guided through Congress legislation that shut down a shadowy CIA project, approved by the Ford administration, to fight forces in Angola that had been backed by the Soviet Union.

Meanwhile, in the White House, it was decided that the disloyal Colby, a holdover from the Nixon administration, had to be removed. In July, after consulting various top White House officials, Staff Coordinator Donald Rumsfeld sent Ford a list of possible replacements headed, somewhat oddly, by the name of U.S. Solicitor General Robert Bork. (Although Bork lacked even the slightest experience in intelligence work, he was considered, according to the capsule description that accompanied Rumsfeld's memo, a "strong team player"—reflecting his controversial actions on Nixon's behalf as a participant in the so-called Saturday-night massacre, which had removed Special Prosecutor Archibald Cox at the height of the Watergate scandal late in 1973.)

Finally, Ford himself undertook a major reform of intelligence gathering, including the establishment of a three-member Intelligence Oversight Board of private citizens to whom all federal intelligence entities were required to report regularly. But Ford's actions came too late to let him grab the mantle of reform away from Congress, or prevent the further shift to Capitol Hill of powers formerly exercised exclusively by the White House.

In due course, the CIA would find itself accountable to nine different congressional bodies.*

A larger struggle loomed over the entire direction of American foreign affairs, as shaped by the policy of détente with the Soviet Union and the People's Republic of China, fashioned by Henry Kissinger. Kissinger, a former professor at Harvard, had established himself as the indispensable man of American foreign policy—a tough-minded, supremely well-connected intellectual and bureaucratic infighter who, thanks to an admiring press and his reputation as a ladies' man, had also become a celebrity. But Kissinger faced growing criticism from across party lines. Leftists and liberal Democrats held him equally responsible with Nixon for secretly widening the conflict in Southeast Asia and for an assortment of smaller but equally nefarious covert actions, above all the coup in Chile. Kissinger, the former academic, for his part thought the liberals were his most formidable political foes; indeed, his policy of détente can be interpreted, at one level, as an effort to delegitimize the left by reducing cold war tensions. In a costly miscalculation, he and Ford paid far less heed to traditional cold war Democrats and conservative Republicans who charged that Kissinger's realist philosophy debased American power, prestige, and principles by placing stability above other considerations. With its Metternich-like obsession about the global balance of power, and its post-Vietnam pessimism about America's military standing, Kissingerian realism, these critics claimed, actually encouraged aggression by the Soviet Union and China.

The leading Democratic hawk, Senator Henry "Scoop" Jackson of Washington, had strongly supported Johnson's and Nixon's policies regarding Vietnam, and was appalled by the antiwar ascendancy within his own party. Long a critic of arms control negotiations with the Soviet Union—in 1963, he had opposed President Kennedy's Test Ban Treaty, holding out for tougher inspection requirements—Jackson attracted other alienated, hard-line cold war Democrats. Their ranks included leaders of organized labor who were staunchly anticommunist and now sharply opposed Nixon's and Kissinger's proposals for free trade with the Soviet Union. They also in-

---

* The congressional efforts to rein in the CIA accompanied other legislation designed to make government and political operations more transparent. The Privacy Act, passed in 1974, enlarged the scope of the Freedom of Information Act of 1966 by granting individual citizens access to files about them compiled by the federal government. A year later, Congress created the Federal Election Commission to disclose information about campaign finances and oversee the public funding of presidential elections.

cluded the coterie of intellectuals and policy specialists who were becoming known as neoconservatives. (Among the latter, on Jackson's own staff, was a tough young arms control expert, Richard Perle, whom liberal opponents on Capitol Hill quickly nicknamed the "Prince of Darkness.")

With an eye on a presidential run in 1976, Jackson seized on the plight of observant Jews in the Soviet Union who were being persecuted and prevented from emigrating to Israel. In order to prod the Russians, Jackson added provisions to impending trade bills that would require the Kremlin to loosen its emigration quotas for Jewish citizens. Late in 1974, the Soviet Union quietly agreed to step up its issuing of exit visas, in accord with Jackson's stipulations—but Jackson quickly turned around and helped win unanimous approval in the House of legislation that demanded even larger concessions on Jewish emigration. The Soviets, who had already protested to Kissinger that Jackson's activities were meddlesome, felt manipulated and betrayed. Ford, infuriated, blamed Jackson's double cross on his presidential ambitions. But Jackson's goals were principled as well as political, and his main target was Henry Kissinger.

Other antirealists came chiefly, although not exclusively, from the Republican right. The aggressively anticommunist Goldwater-Reagan wing of the party had always regarded Nixon's and Kissinger's realpolitik as a craven sellout, in a direct line with what they believed had been Franklin D. Roosevelt's capitulation to Stalin at the Yalta Conference in 1945. (That Kissinger had risen to power largely thanks to his friend and patron Nelson Rockefeller redoubled the Republican right's contempt.) Yet even more moderate Republicans, including a close friend of Ford's, the former secretary of defense Melvin Laird, complained that détente had created the illusion that the Russians had abandoned their quest for global domination. And at the center of power, Ford's own secretary of defense, James Schlesinger—who had served as the director of the CIA before Nixon added him to the cabinet in 1973—clashed repeatedly with Kissinger. The disputes stemmed in part from Schlesinger's and Kissinger's conflicting, outsize egos. But Schlesinger had long opposed any expansion of détente with the Soviets, and with a domineering manner all his own, he voiced that opposition inside Ford's cabinet.

Ford had to walk a delicate line among the contending forces. Late in 1974, he held a summit meeting with the Soviet leader Leonid Brezhnev in the Siberian port of Vladivostok, chiefly to renegotiate Kissinger's Strategic Arms Limitation Treaty (SALT). The agreement had been approved in 1972 and was due to expire in two years. Ford quickly had to decide whether to sustain the realist spirit of the original treaty, which permitted the Soviet Union to have superiority in land-based missiles and the United States to have superiority in multiple-warhead missiles, or to heed calls from Schlesinger and the Joint Chiefs of Staff to press for strict equality in all areas. (Kissinger, who thought multiple warheads of superior strategic importance, feared that the Pentagon's hard line on Soviet land-based missiles could destroy any hopes of renewed arms limitation—but he had learned in advance from Brezhnev that the Soviet Union was prepared to negotiate on the basis of equality, if the Americans so desired.)

Despite Kissinger's commanding presence in Vladivostok, the president sided with the antirealists—and, exceeding Schlesinger's best hopes, Ford stuck to his guns. A SALT II agreement would place equal ceilings on both countries regarding their numbers of intercontinental ballistic missiles, in which the Soviet's arsenal outstripped the Americans'—the antirealists' main area of concern. But even that victory was insufficient for Senator Jackson, who charged that the bargain granted the Soviet Union too much in the way of airpower and required the Americans to scuttle an important weapon, the Tomahawk cruise missile. (Ford was persuaded that both the medium-range bombers permitted to the Russians and the American Tomahawks were obsolete and of no importance except as bargaining chips.) With quiet assistance from Schlesinger, Jackson blocked any vote in the Senate on SALT II. Ford, looking to his own reelection campaign, dropped the issue, and the treaty was effectively put aside. Round one had gone to Kissinger's adversaries.

Kissinger's efforts on other diplomatic fronts were equally fruitless, and this outcome further emboldened his critics. In the Middle East, Kissinger continued the "shuttle diplomacy" that he had undertaken after the Yom Kippur War in 1973, trying to arrange separate agreements between Israel and each of its Arab neighbors, and pave the way for a general peace in the region. A particularly promising series of negotiations between Israel and Jordan advanced through the summer of 1974. But the bargaining broke down in October, when Prime Minister Yitzhak Rabin of Israel dragged his feet, and Yasir Arafat's Palestine Liberation Organization, supported by the other major Arab nations, forced King Hussein of Jordan to abandon the effort. A possible Egyptian-Israeli accord also collapsed, chiefly, Kissinger concluded, because of political pettiness and disarray within Rabin's government.

Dramatic events in Southeast Asia further damaged the realist camp. The Treaty of Paris that ended America's active military involvement in

Vietnam in 1973 had earned Kissinger the Nobel Peace Prize. (His North Vietnamese counterpart in the negotiations, Le Duc Tho, declined the honor.) But by the middle of 1974, it was perfectly clear that the flimsy South Vietnamese government, for which nearly 60,000 Americans had lost their lives, was doomed. Virtually every policy maker had foreseen as much even before the ink had dried on the Treaty of Paris—except, perhaps, Kissinger, who would claim he thought the long war had worn out the North Vietnamese. Adequate American financial aid could, he contended, prevent a communist victory, although, he admitted, it could take two or three years before the South Vietnamese "will be able to handle themselves adequately." The Ford White House, under pressure from the State Department, duly reassured the South Vietnamese that help was on the way. Congress, though, was thoroughly sick of the war and rejected any proposed expenditures that might prolong the United States' involvement. In any event, the peace treaty that Kissinger himself had negotiated, in recognizing the proclamation of Vietnam's sovereignty by the Geneva Convention of 1954, removed the original cornerstone of American involvement—the idea that North Vietnam had invaded Vietnam South. The treaty looked more like a sop to American pride than a serious recommitment to the region.

The situation in Cambodia, the region's other war-torn country, was even grimmer than in Vietnam. Although Kissinger and Ford felt a persisting commitment to the South Vietnamese, they had more or less given up on the Cambodians, whom Kissinger had always regarded as useful but minor allies in the struggle in Vietnam. Congress, for antiwar reasons, also abandoned Cambodia to its fate. Even minimal requests from the administration for Cambodian aid were dead on arrival on Capitol Hill.

On April 17, 1975, Khmer Rouge troops marched into Cambodia's capital, Phnom Penh, force-marched its population of 3 million into the countryside, and renamed the country Democratic Kampuchea. A four-year reign of murder and terror began under the dictator Pol Pot, which would result in the deaths of approximately 2 million Cambodians—between one-quarter and one-third of the nation's entire population. On April 21, South Vietnam's president, Nguyen Van Thieu, his army in retreat and facing certain defeat by a massive North Vietnamese military offensive, resigned. Two days later, President Ford, in a speech at Tulane University not vetted by Kissinger, announced that, "as far as America is concerned," the war in Vietnam was finished.

The North Vietnamese and the Vietcong—encouraged, Kissinger suspected, by Ford's words—pushed into Saigon more quickly than expected, necessitating a sudden evacuation of 1,400 Americans and 5,600 of their Vietnamese allies. The next day, April 30, South Vietnam formally surrendered. The chaotic departure scenes, especially the last American helicopter lifting off the roof of the embassy in Saigon, were disturbing as well as embarrassing, and would be seared into the memory of a generation. But Americans in and outside the administration were also palpably relieved that a national nightmare far longer than Watergate had ended at last. Any criticism directed at Ford, his political backers thought, could be deflected toward the recalcitrant antiwar Democratic Congress. In any event, leading Republicans as well as Democrats made it clear to the administration that, across party lines, as the House minority whip Representative Bob Michel of Illinois put it, "the sentiment in Congress is no military aid." Conservatives had expressed a vestigial desire to back a last-ditch effort but were doubtful that the South Vietnamese could regroup and mount a credible offensive. Antiwar liberals simply took heart at the war's conclusion. Among the war's chief architects, only Kissinger, who had begun coming to terms with its certain outcome in the days and weeks before the surrender of Saigon, expressed open anguish and bitterness at the final defeat.

Less than a month after Phnom Penh fell, the new Cambodian regime gave the administration an opportunity to flex America's muscle—and to ease, at least temporarily, the tensions between the realists and their adversaries. Just after five o'clock in the morning on May 12, the Pentagon received an alert that the Khmer Rouge had fired on, boarded, and seized the crew of the American merchant vessel *Mayaguez*, which had been sailing in the Gulf of Siam. The Kampucheans charged that the ship had strayed into their own waters, a highly disputable claim. Determined to prevent any display of American weakness so soon after Cambodia's and South Vietnam's surrender, the White House quickly devised and put into motion plans to rescue the captives and punish the Khmer Rouge. Amid the emergency, differences inside the White House over détente disappeared.

After a tense day of military maneuvering, the White House confirmed that the Kampucheans had taken the *Mayaguez* and its crew to the island of Koh Tang, just off the Cambodian mainland. The next evening, about 100 U.S. Marines invaded Koh Tang, and two hours later American air strikes hit entrenched Kampuchean positions on both the island and the mainland. The early fighting was costly to the Americans, leaving eight helicopters destroyed; eighteen U.S. servicemen, including fourteen Marines, killed; and forty-one more servicemen, including thirty-five Marines, wounded. (Total casualties in operations connected with the affair would come to eighty-two, of whom half were killed and half were wounded—more than twice the number of captive crew members.) But less than two hours after the bombing began, a Navy reconnaissance pilot spotted the released crew of the *Mayaguez* in a small fishing vessel, waving white flags. Minutes later, the men boarded an American destroyer that had been sent to the scene. The incident was over—although on Ford's orders, American planes briefly continued to bombard the Cambodian mainland, in what some commentators later contended was purely an act of reprisal.

For the moment, Ford's decisiveness under fire appeared to have recouped his presidency. The cover of *Time* magazine featured a no-nonsense portrait of the president, glaring, tight-lipped, beside a triumphant declaration: FORD DRAWS THE LINE. Ford's languishing public approval ratings instantly rose by eleven points. By refusing to consult with congressional leaders before making his decisions, the president had pushed back hard against the War Powers Act. Above all, after years of drifting and despair, there was some bracing news. Ford later recalled the remark of a freshman House Democrat from Kentucky: "It's good to win one for a change."

There was less to this triumph, though, than initially met the public eye. Ford himself was upset by the inordinately high number of American casualties. A report released soon after the crisis by the General Accounting Office (GAO) concluded that pressure on the Khmer Rouge government from the People's Republic of China had played a major role in obtaining freedom for the crew of the *Mayaguez*. Subsequently declassified documents reveal that Ford approved bombing missions that, for all he knew at the time, might easily have killed the men he was trying to rescue. That Ford was able to look like a composed, tough president without also losing the *Mayaguez* crew—the best possible outcome, from the White House's perspective—was as much a matter of good luck as military prowess.

In any event, the artificial solidarity in Washington over foreign policy did not last long. Kissinger finally secured an Egyptian-Israeli accord in early September 1975, but only after Ford's coolness to Israel following the earlier failure provoked a fierce counterreaction from American pro-Israel groups (led by the American Israeli Political Action Committee, AIPAC)—and only after Ford and Kissinger agreed to provide Israel with direct mil-

itary aid above and beyond a previously promised arms shipment worth
$1.5 billion. While he fended off foul personal attacks from AIPAC and
conservative Israelis, Kissinger helped to contain what became known as
the Solzhenitsyn affair—an episode that left behind abiding anger among
both right-wing anticommunists and neoconservatives. In the late spring,
the AFL-CIO labor federation arranged for a banquet to be held in Washington at the end of June to honor the Soviet novelist, Nobel laureate, and
recently exiled dissident Aleksandr Solzhenitsyn. Conservative Republicans
including Senators Jesse Helms and Strom Thurmond, asked the president
to make the time to meet with Solzhenitsyn on the day of the banquet,
and perhaps even attend the festivities. Helms and Thurmond—neither of
whom was friendly to organized labor or famous for his literary interests—
knew that such a powerful symbolic act would sour relations between the
United States and the Soviet Union at a delicate moment.

Some White House staffers, including Staff Coordinator Rumsfeld's
normally circumspect, conservative young deputy, Dick Cheney, strongly
urged the president to go ahead. Refusing to do so, Cheney argued in a
memo to Rumsfeld, was based on "a misreading of detente" as a policy
which declared that "all of a sudden our relationship with the Soviets is all
sweetness and light." An emblematic gesture, Cheney reasoned, would aug-
ment "the President's capability to deal with the right wing in America,"
and thereby improve the chances of ratifying a SALT II pact. In any event,
Cheney charged that the Soviets "have been perfectly free to criticize us for
our actions and policies in Southeast Asia over the years, to call us impe-
rialists, war-mongers, and various and sundry other endearing terms, and
I can't believe they don't understand why the President might want to see
Solzhenitsyn."

Kissinger, sorely provoked, intervened and suggested a brief private
meeting with Solzhenitsyn at the White House. Ford, fed up, and deep
in preparations for an impending second summit with Brezhnev, spurned
both arrangements. (Although he privately called the sometimes imperi-
ous and prickly Solzhenitsyn "a goddamned horse's ass," the president did
offer the writer an open invitation to visit the White House after the meetings with Brezhnev concluded.) Robbed of their chance to obstruct détente on the eve of the summit, Helms, Thurmond, and the others said
nothing more; and Solzhenitsyn never took up Ford's invitation to the
White House. But Ronald Reagan harped on the incident, blasting what
he called Ford's snub of the courageous Russian. The political damage to

Ford and to Kissinger was done, and the affair would rankle for many years to come.

The second summit, held in Helsinki in late July, caused Ford even greater political headaches. His private meetings with Brezhnev were contentious, and made no progress toward achieving a revised SALT II pact. More portentously, the Helsinki meetings were held in conjunction with a climactic series of meetings of a multinational group founded in 1973, the Conference on Security and Cooperation in Europe, which had drafted a wide-ranging agreement on economic and scientific cooperation, freer movement of peoples, and the settling of disputes between East and West. Kissinger, who saw the accords as nonbinding but a positive step toward relieving cold war tensions, insisted that Ford attend the meetings and place his personal stamp of approval on the accords.

Along with its provisions renouncing the use of force and advocating human rights, the agreement included a passage that recognized the borders of communist-controlled Central and Eastern Europe as permanent, although they could be altered by peaceful negotiations. To Kissinger, the language amounted to little more than a recognition of existing realities that were not likely to change anytime soon, and in any event had no deleterious effect on American power. Compared with what the Russians had hoped to gain from the accords—and compared with the far more aggressive line about the Soviet Union's control of Central and Eastern Europe contained in the so-called Brezhnev Doctrine—the Helsinki document actually represented a step backward for Soviet hard-liners. Above all, Kissinger told Ford in an emphatic briefing paper, "[T]he philosophy which permeates most of the CSCE's declarations is that of the West's open societies." Ford agreed, and delivered a speech that, while praising efforts to resolve world tensions, insisted on the primacy of Americans' devotion "to human rights and fundamental freedoms and thus to the pledges that this conference has made."

Among the American foes of détente, "Helsinki" immediately became a byword for "sellout." Even before Ford left the United States, Scoop Jackson denounced the accords as a formal capitulation to Soviet tyranny, and told the president not to go. The entire anti-détente coalition, from Eastern European immigrant and ethnic organizations upholding the rights of "captive nations" to the editors of the Wall Street Journal, ripped into Ford and Kissinger for ratifying the "new Yalta." "I am against it," Ronald Reagan announced, "and I think all Americans should be against it." Three decades later, the attacks look ridiculous, even hysterical, in light of how the accords' human rights provisions contributed to the rise of dissident movements inside the Soviet Union and its satellite states.* Kissinger, known as an amoral, pessimistic realist, grasped the agreement's pervasive anticommunist philosophy, and its political importance, better than his more stridently anticommunist critics did. "All the new things in the document are in our favor—peaceful change, human contacts, maneuver notification," he told the cabinet shortly after he and Ford returned to Washington. "[I]t was the President who dominated the Conference and it was the West which was on the offensive. . . . Anyone observing from another planet would not have thought Communism was the wave of the future." But in the White House, concern grew that Kissinger's latest exploit had handed the Republican right a new and powerful political weapon. And this fear was no longer hypothetical. On July 15, less than two weeks before Ford departed for Europe, the conservative senator Paul Laxalt of Nevada announced the formation of a Citizens for Reagan committee that would explore the option of battling the president for the Republican nomination.

By mid-autumn, several currents of agitation converged within the administration to force a major shakeup. Schlesinger, the secretary of defense, had long since worn out his welcome with Ford, who thought him arrogant, condescending, and disloyal. (Some people suspected that the conservative Schlesinger was actually working behind the scenes with the Reagan camp.) Vice President Rockefeller, still the living emblem of Republican liberalism, was dragging down Ford's chances for the party's nomination; and in mid-October, Rockefeller's break with the White House over the debt crisis in New York City would put him at odds with the president as well as the president's men. William Colby, the director of the CIA, had survived through the summer but remained in a precarious position because he had provided assistance to congressional investigators (although Ford would later say he supported Colby's candor). As ever, there were the problems surrounding Henry Kissinger, made all the graver because he still

---

* In 1976, the dissident Soviet physicist Yuri Orlov and ten associates formed the Public Group to Promote Fulfillment of the Helsinki Accords, which later was linked with the American-initiated private group Helsinki Watch; thereafter, similar groups arose around the Soviet bloc and fostered the internal resistance to Soviet domination that would culminate in the revolutions of 1989–1991. Norman Podhoretz, who as editor of the neoconservative *Commentary* indignantly criticized the accords, has since acknowledged that the agreement "put a very powerful weapon in the hands of dissidents . . . in their struggle against the Communist regime. Ultimately, Helsinki, instead of ensuring the permanence of the Soviet empire, contributed to its eventual demise." Podhoretz, "Bush, Sharon, My Daughter, and Me," *Commentary*, April 2005, p. 38.

held his dual position as secretary of state and, in the West Wing, as head of the National Security Council.

Two other men were also at the center of action in the White House that autumn: Staff Coordinator Donald Rumsfeld and his deputy and longtime protégé, Dick Cheney. Outwardly, they were an unlikely pair. Rumsfeld—voluble, brash, openly ambitious—had attended Princeton (where he was a varsity wrestler), flown as a naval aviator, and worked two years in Chicago as an investment broker at the venerable firm of A. G. Becker before he entered public service in 1962, winning the first of four elections to Congress from a district in suburban Chicago. In the House, Rumsfeld befriended Gerald Ford, whom he helped elevate to minority leader in 1965. Considered a moderate, dovish on Vietnam, Rumsfeld went on to make his mark as Nixon's director of the Office of Economic Opportunity (OEO). One of Lyndon Johnson's antipoverty initiatives in his Great Society program, OEO was a bureaucratic cog slated for oblivion, but Rumsfeld improved its management and effectiveness.

It was while he was at OEO that Rumsfeld hired as his personal assistant Cheney, a taciturn man who was raised in Wyoming, had dropped out of Yale, and had been a graduate student at the University of Wisconsin. Cheney flunked a job interview with Rumsfeld in 1968 but was more impressive a year later, and he thrived as the details man for a mentor who was better at issuing edicts than actually seeing them through. The laconic westerner's political views were, at least initially, markedly more conservative than those of his boss. (Robert Hartmann, who disliked both Rumsfeld and Cheney, said of the latter that, during the Ford years, "whenever his private ideology was exposed, he appeared somewhat to the right of Ford, Rumsfeld, or, for that matter, Genghis Khan.") But amid the Watergate affair, as congressional liberals attacked executive authority, Rumsfeld began moving to the right, notably on arms control and other issues related to détente, as well on resisting Congress; and he and Cheney became an almost inseparable team within the White House bureaucracy. Cheney did stay in Washington, solidifying his finances as vice president of an investment consulting firm there, while Rumsfeld was in Brussels serving as the U.S. envoy to NATO in 1973 and 1974. But as soon as Ford tapped Rumsfeld to become his staff coordinator, Rumsfeld brought Cheney along as his assistant.

Between the summer of 1974 and the summer of 1975, Rumsfeld and Cheney took charge of White House operations and tried their best to shape domestic and, in time, foreign policy. Although their politics had closer affinities in many ways to the Republican right than to the moderates in the administration, they resisted the temptation represented by Reagan and saw in Ford a surer instrument for their own designs—provided that the liberal Republicans and moderates were cast aside. Ford's old friend Hartmann found himself turfed out of his office (and deprived of his easy access to the president) after Rumsfeld helped arrange to have the room turned into a private presidential study. Rockefeller, to whom Ford had promised broad powers over domestic policy making, complained bitterly about Rumsfeld's repeated efforts to undermine him. (These included helping to force the vice president, in Rockefeller's own words, to "relinquish my responsibilities for overseeing the work of the Domestic Council," the major in-house body advising the president on domestic affairs.) Kissinger saw in Rumsfeld a formidable, sharp-elbowed political infighter opposed to détente who, he wrote years later, "understood far better than I did that Watergate and Vietnam were likely to evoke a conservative backlash, and that what looked like a liberal tide after the election of the McGovernite Congress [in 1974] in fact marked the radical apogee."

Cheney, quieter but ideologically edgier than Rumsfeld, expanded his purview beyond gofer duties such as inspecting the White House bathrooms and ordering new salt shakers for the private residence in the East Wing. He had never had any truck with Nixon's accusers in the Watergate scandal, which he regarded, according to one of his close business associates at the time, as "just a political ploy by the president's enemies." The only unconstitutional aspects of the affair, Cheney thought, involved Congress's unflagging efforts to establish its supremacy over the executive, as foreshadowed by measures such as the original War Powers Resolution in 1973. Cheney carried that Nixonian spirit with him into his new job, urging in his draft memo on the CIA that the administration try to head off any congressional investigation lest it cause "a serious legislative encroachment on executive power." In a top-level meeting in May 1975, he considered as one option investigating the reporter Seymour Hersh of the *New York Times*, and the *Times* itself, when the newspaper published a story of Hersh's about a secret submarine reconnaissance mission inside Soviet waters. (The participants at the meeting also weighed the possibility, according to Cheney's notes, of obtaining a search warrant "to go after Hersh papers in his apt [that is, his apartment]." The White House ultimately did nothing.) Cheney later admitted helping Rumsfeld's efforts to undermine Rockefeller by putting "sand in the gears" to kill the vice president's projects.

Cheney combined his preference for a strong executive with his conservative distaste for détente—the latter ran closer to Reagan's views than to either Nixon's or Ford's—and he started weighing in. In his memo to Rumsfeld over the Solzhenitsyn affair, he warned that the administration had contributed to "the illusion that all of a sudden we're bosom buddies with the Russians." Cheney, along with Rumsfeld, also encouraged inviting leading neoconservative thinkers such as Irving Kristol to the White House for seminars with the president, as well as for the circulation of their articles, coordinated through a protégé of Rumsfeld's, Robert Goldwin, who worked in the operations office as the White House's liaison to an emerging right-wing intelligentsia. "Why don't you come see me on Irving Kristol," Cheney wrote to Goldwin early in 1975. "We need to come up with a specific proposal as to how he might be utilized full time."

Since there is no paper trail, how much influence Rumsfeld and Cheney had in orchestrating the "Halloween massacre" late in 1975—the largest reshuffling of any cabinet to that point in modern American history—remains a subject of speculation. But without question Rumsfeld and Cheney were the major beneficiaries. On Sunday, November 2, Ford, now hard-pressed by the right, took care of his administration's family business, *Godfather*-style, in a single day. He fired Schlesinger and (finally) Colby. He relieved Kissinger of his position as national security adviser; thus Kissinger would no longer work out of the White House and would no longer have ready access to the president. While he was at it, Ford arranged for a successor to his ailing secretary of commerce, Rogers Morton. Morton's job went to Nixon's former attorney general, Elliot Richardson (whom Nixon had fired when he would not cooperate over Watergate, and who was therefore well-liked by party moderates and independent voters). Kissinger managed to see his friend and fellow realist, General Brent Scowcroft, handed the job as security adviser. As for Colby's job directing the CIA, Bork's name did not survive vetting at the highest levels. After the Washingtonian lawyer and power broker Edward Bennett Williams turned down the job, the president settled on George H. W. Bush, who was serving as his envoy to China and had privately expressed a desire to come home. (Bush, as chairman of the Republican National Committee, had stayed loyal to Nixon during Watergate until the bitter end, much as Bork had—but Bush had experience with foreign policy, knew Ford from Congress, and was far better liked than Bork on Capitol Hill.) The biggest plum, the position of secretary of defense, went to Donald Rumsfeld. His major qualification for that particular job, the White House claimed with a straight face, was that he had been a Navy flier; now Rumsfeld would have as much formal power (and access to his old friend President Ford) as Henry Kissinger. The new White House chief of staff (with the former sonorous title now restored) would be Dick Cheney.

And that was not all. The very next day, Vice President Rockefeller, acting at Ford's request (or so Rockefeller stated much later), announced publicly he had withdrawn his name from consideration for the Republican ticket.

So many conflicts, personal and political, got settled in the shuffle, with so many winners and losers from different sides of the policy wars, that it was difficult to interpret what had happened.* Ford himself insisted simply, to his staff as well as to the press, that the time had come for him to name his "own team" in foreign policy, consisting of "the very best men w[ith] whom he can work comfortably." But many political pundits initially thought that Kissinger had pulled off a coup by toppling his adversary Schlesinger while bringing his friend Scowcroft into the White House. Conservative Republicans, furious at the firing of Schlesinger, certainly thought that Kissinger was the man pulling the strings. But that is not at all how Kissinger understood the changes: for several nights running, he consulted with friends about whether he should resign completely, and nearly did so. Schlesinger, with his insolent treatment of the president, had been a marked man for some time; Ford later confirmed that, except for his concern about stability and continuity after Nixon's resignation, he would have fired Schlesinger right away. But, to repeat, conservative Republicans were livid at Schlesinger's dismissal, and Ford's hopes that reducing Kissinger's duties would mollify the right wing proved illusory.

The biggest losers in the shuffle, in fact, were Kissinger (now demoted from his office inside the White House) and his old benefactor, Rockefeller (now a lame duck). Bush's sudden ascendance at CIA has since been widely interpreted as a move to make Bush unavailable as a vice presidential candidate in 1976 (such a candidacy, after Bush's near miss in 1974, was a real possibility). The biggest winners were Rumsfeld and Cheney, who would

---

* Ford had originally hoped to announce Rockefeller's withdrawal first, thereby leading off with news that would please the Republican right. But when *Newsweek* magazine received leaked information that Schlesinger would be fired, the president hastily rearranged his plans. As a consequence, the right absorbed the first heavy blow, and the disorderliness conveyed an impression that Ford, who had hoped to appear forceful, was actually losing control of his own administration.

have more power than ever to set the administration's course. (One of the shrewdest and best-informed reporters in Washington, Lou Cannon of the *Washington Post*, claimed immediately that Rumsfeld was in fact, as the *Post*'s headline put it, the "silent architect" of the shake-up.) Despite Schlesinger's departure, the Ford administration took a large step to the right, especially in the conduct of foreign policy.

During the year to come, Secretary of Defense Rumsfeld buried Henry Kissinger with regard to a variety of issues large and small, including the revival of the SALT II talks. Simultaneously, Chief of Staff Cheney, whom Washington reporters nicknamed "the Grand Teuton," imposed a more efficient, centralized, secretive regime in the White House, and also took charge of the president's election campaign as the White House liaison to the Ford for President committee. By March 1976, Ford would tell a campaign audience in Peoria, Illinois, "We are going to forget the use of the word détente"—a shift Rumsfeld and Cheney had been working toward for several months.

None of this, though, soothed hard-line conservative Republicans. "I am not appeased," Ronald Reagan said, when asked about the demotion of Henry Kissinger. Less than three weeks later, Reagan telephoned the White House and got right to the point. "I am going to make an announcement," he told Ford, "and I want to tell you about it ahead of time. I am going to run for President."

As 1976 began, Gerald Ford could not be blamed if he wished he'd never left Congress. The previous September, amid the continuing controversy over Helsinki and with the cabinet shake-up impending, two women, on separate occasions within three weeks of each other, tried to shoot him while he was on political trips in California. (The first of the two, Lynette "Squeaky" Fromme, had been a member of the notorious Charles Manson murder gang that, gruesomely, marked the descent into criminal insanity of one current in the 1960s counterculture.) Ford's vivacious and candid wife, Betty, once a modern dancer with the Martha Graham troupe, had won enormous public respect and affection by forthrightly facing and recovering from breast cancer surgery in 1974. A year later, though, in a widely watched television interview, she matter-of-factly condoned abortion, extramarital sex, and smoking marijuana. It was a refreshingly honest and unscripted performance for a first lady; but her husband, who adored her, had to worry about the political repercussions among right-wing moralists—and he had to hear his wife mocked in those quarters as an unlady-like loudmouth and worse. (Ford needn't have worried: his wife's public approval ratings were already higher than his, and they would improve over the coming months. Her comments, although offensive to religious conservatives, probably did the Ford campaign more good than harm overall.)

The turbulence subsided a bit in December when Ford held a successful summit with Mao Zedong and the Chinese Communist leadership in Beijing, and elicited, for once, only muffled growls on the right. At home, the economic news had been gradually brightening for several months. Still, in the first week of January Ford's public approval rating stood at a dismal 39 percent, and his disapproval rating was 46 percent. No modern president with such poor polling numbers in January had ever gone on to win in November.

There was never a doubt, though, that Ford would run, and his gradual awakening to the genuine threat posed by Ronald Reagan reinforced his determination to do so. By March, the Ford campaign had become tight-knit and disciplined, headed by Cheney, the political consultant (and former adviser to Reagan) Stuart Spencer, and the pollster Robert Teeter. Knowing that Reagan would present himself as an outsider and as a conservative, Ford's men decided to eschew presenting their candidate as "nice guy Jerry," and to stress his seriousness and solid presidential mien—the President Ford who had persevered in the *Mayaguez* crisis without losing his cool. And Reagan, who led Ford decisively in the early polling, had already handed the Ford campaign a political gift that kept on giving. Back in September, in a speech to the Executive Club of Chicago, Reagan proposed to cut federal spending by $90 billion, balance the budget, and cut personal income taxes to an average of 23 percent—all by transferring authority from the federal government to the states. It was a wild idea that, if ever put into effect, would cause massive unemployment for public workers and force states to raise their taxes, including income taxes. The Ford campaign fully exploited the speech as evidence that Reagan was a pie-eyed extremist who literally didn't know what he was talking about. All the better for the Ford campaign, the first Republican presidential primary would be in New Hampshire, where there was no state income or sales tax at all.

Reagan should have won New Hampshire. It was the most conservative of the New England states, and its elections often turned on intensely personal, small-town campaigning; the charismatic Reagan, although known mainly as a master of television, was also an excellent stump speaker. But the continuing reverberations from his "$90 billion" speech did him in, along with a higher than expected voter turnout (which normally favors incumbents) and his handlers' poor tactical decision to have him campaign elsewhere for two days before the vote. Although Ford barely prevailed, with 51 percent of the total, his victory had the feel of a tremendous upset.

Ford's campaign picked up steam and Reagan's now seemed plagued by slipups. Florida, the site of the next major primary, had large numbers of elderly voters and Hispanics (including many Cubans), two groups normally stirred by attacks on the Washington establishment and Kissinger's détente policies. But Reagan decided to throw into the mix an old idea of Goldwater's about investing Social Security funds in the stock market. The idea was anathema to retired senior citizens who relied on their monthly checks, and who could recall conservatives' hostility to Social Security dating back to inception of the program during the New Deal. Ford condemned Reagan's plan as foolish and risky—and wound up with 53 percent of the vote in the Florida primary.

The Reagan forces, badly in need of a victory, regrouped in North Carolina, where Senator Jesse Helms placed all his political resources at Reagan's disposal. These resources included Helms's own campaign genius, an ultraconservative lawyer from Raleigh, Thomas Ellis. A veteran of southern-style hardball politics, Ellis was well schooled in stimulating the political id of the state's white voters. (At the time, although it received little publicity, he was also a director of the Pioneer Fund, a eugenicist group that funded efforts to prove the genetic superiority of whites over blacks.) Ellis failed to bring all his campaign tricks into play. (Early on, he tried to publicize a local newspaper's speculation that Ford would pick Senator Edward Brooke, a moderate black from Massachusetts, as his running mate, but Reagan nixed the plan.) Yet Ellis demanded and received complete control of the statewide Reagan organization. And presumably he could see how, in North Carolina, special dividends would accrue from focusing fire on Kissinger—the secretive Svengali who had supposedly destroyed U.S. military superiority and who just happened to be (it went without saying) a foreign-born Jew from Harvard who spoke with a funny accent.

Ellis and Helms also selected the ideal foreign policy issue for the Reagan camp to use against Kissinger and the administration, an issue that Reagan had already begun raising in Florida: the United States' rights to the Panama Canal. Since the late 1960s, the United States had sought unsuccessfully to renegotiate the terms of the original canal treaty, signed in 1903. Kissinger, fearing that Panama could become another Vietnam, reopened negotiations in 1974. Immediately hard-line conservatives in the

Senate turned the halting of any new treaty into a hot-button cause, made hotter because Panama's strongman ruler, General Omar Torrijos, had been linked to Fidel Castro. Ford was seeking a compromise that would permit a continued limited American presence in the Canal Zone. Reagan seized on the issue, declaring in one stump speech after another: "[W]e built it, we paid for it, it's ours and . . . we are going to keep it." Some Republicans of differing persuasions criticized the hard-liners in Washington as well as Reagan for their inflammatory and divisive rhetoric on Panama: Vice President Rockefeller accused Reagan of being "totally deceptive" and "telling the American people things that are not true," and Senator Barry Goldwater firmly supported Ford with regard to the canal and said he thought Reagan might, too, "if he knew more about it." Not only did Reagan's public statements contain "gross factual errors," Goldwater charged; they reflected either "a lack of understanding of the facts" or "a surprisingly dangerous state of mind which is that he will not seek alternatives to a military solution when dealing with complex foreign policy issues." But even Goldwater, the pro-military conservative hard-liner, could not persuade everyone; indeed, some voters in the primaries thought the narrow militarism Goldwater criticized in Reagan was exactly what the country needed. Thanks to his friends in North Carolina and the imbroglio over the canal, Reagan wound up winning 52 percent of the vote—the first time a competitor had ever defeated a sitting president in a Republican primary.

The result in North Carolina shifted the momentum in favor of the challenger. Reagan hit his stride, taking to national television and repeating his litany of the administration's sellouts to the Russian communist slave masters. His rhetoric was a throwback to the early 1950s, when Republicans attacked the Truman administration by caricaturing its "striped pants" diplomats as effete, un-American, and soft on communism, and accusing these diplomats of having stabbed the country in the back. Now, however, a right-wing Republican was turning the tables on a Republican administration. Stunned, Ford replied feebly that Reagan's attacks were "irresponsible." (Kissinger wanted Ford to counterattack fiercely, by saying that Reagan's rhetoric was endangering America's international standing; but the president heeded Cheney's advice to tread softly lest he permanently antagonize Reagan's supporters.) An attempt by the Ford camp to lighten things up by allowing the president's press secretary, Ron Nessen, to appear on an acidly satirical network television show, *Saturday Night Live*, long one of the president's main tormentors, fell flat. In May, Reagan scored impressive victories in Texas, Alabama, Georgia, Indiana, and Nebraska, followed, in June, by another win in California—his home state, to be sure, but also a huge trove of delegates.

With many moderate Republicans saying that they would refuse to support Reagan if he won the nomination, and many pro-Reagan conservatives saying they would bolt the party if he did not win it, some insiders feared that the party was on the verge of collapse. "There's just no comparison with 1964," one veteran Republican in California fretted, alluding to Goldwater's debacle in the election of that year. "Our party was viable then. The devastation in 1976 is likely to be far deeper than just a party losing in a Presidential campaign." Yet Ford found his second wind, and held the support of just enough influential conservatives (including Goldwater) to create a semblance of party unity. Long political friendships helped him gather support from so-called superdelegates, party insiders named as delegates above and beyond those selected in the primaries. The president campaigned hard across the country, fully exercising his powers of patronage. Ford generally ran better in the northern and border states than in the South, winning primaries in Michigan, Maryland, West Virginia, Ohio, and New Jersey.

On the eve of the Republicans' national convention in Kansas City in August, the president held only a narrow lead in delegates but had come within a whisker of winning the nomination. Reagan, at the last minute, called a Hail Mary play and named a moderate Republican, Senator Richard Schweiker of Pennsylvania, as his prospective running mate. The maneuver mainly earned derision as a stunt. Ford finally prevailed, on the first roll call of the delegates, but with a margin of only 117 votes out of a total of 2,257 cast—an embarrassing result for a sitting president. Although the center held for Ford, the outcome also indicated how close the Republican right had come since 1964 to recapturing the party.

Other developments at the convention humiliated the president. In the platform committee, the Reagan forces advanced a plank called "Morality in Foreign Policy" that summarized their candidate's talking points on foreign policy and defense from the primary campaign. Kissinger (once again) and Rockefeller objected furiously, but Cheney and other campaign insiders countered (once again) that the right had to be placated and that, in any case, a platform was not a binding statement. Ford reluctantly allowed the plank into the platform, along with another calling for a constitutional amendment to prohibit abortion. On the choice of his running mate, Ford was leaning strongly toward naming a moderate, until Reagan's southern delegates informed Ford's camp that they would place Reagan's name in nomination unless his preferred candidate—the blunt conservative senator Robert J. Dole of Kansas—got the nod. Ford crumpled.

Having staved off one "outsider" candidate, Ford now prepared to face another, very different, outsider: the Democratic nominee, Governor Jimmy Carter of Georgia. Unlike Reagan, Carter seemed to have come out of nowhere in 1976. Nearly a dozen other Democrats contested him during the primaries, a measure of how highly the party thought of its chances in the aftermath of Watergate and Ford's pardoning of Nixon. The candidates included Scoop Jackson, a diminished but determined George C. Wallace (who had survived an assassination attempt in 1972), and Senator Birch Bayh of Indiana (backed strongly by organized labor), as well as liberals such as Congressman Morris "Mo" Udall of Arizona and the former senator Fred Harris of Oklahoma. Carter had three enormous advantages over the others: he was identified with neither the new liberal faction nor the traditionalists in the party; as a governor, he could run untainted by any association with the Washington establishment; and, perhaps most important, as a southerner, he would attract states that had fallen into Republican hands since 1960. He quickly gained another unanticipated plus by capturing the imagination of influential sectors of the national press, including the *New York Times*, whose friendly coverage helped catapult him out of obscurity.

After winning the precinct caucuses in Iowa and the first primary in New Hampshire, Carter turned aside Wallace's heavily favored forces in the South, narrowly beat Udall in several races, then staved off a late challenge from the young liberal governor of California, Reagan's antithetical successor, Edmund "Jerry" Brown. At the nominating convention—which the Democrats held, pointedly, in New York City—Carter came across as a moderately liberal Democrat. In his acceptance speech he lauded his party's "progressive" heritage of reform, called for a national health care program, and even quoted one of Bob Dylan's lyrics from the 1960s. Carter chose as his running mate Walter Mondale of Minnesota, a figure congenial to party traditionalists and liberals alike. On certain issues, though, in both the primaries and the general election, Carter positioned himself close to Scoop Jackson (and to the right of the administration), criticizing the Helsinki accords as an authorization of "the Russian takeover of Eastern Europe," and blasting Ford over the Solzhenitsyn affair. It was as if he was trying to reweave the different strands of Democratic thinking that had unraveled during the convulsion over Vietnam.

Yet Carter's main appeal was less political or ideological than personal and moral. A proud, upright Southern Baptist and Annapolis-trained Navy engineer who still ran his family's peanut farm in a small town in Georgia, he presented himself to the voters as a God-fearing, hardworking meritocrat, ready to sweep away the corrupt barons of Nixonian Washington (who, by dint of Nixon's pardon, included by implication Gerald Ford). Carter pledged never to lie to the voters and claimed that, by reflecting "the high moral character of the American people," he would lead the nation out of the morass of Vietnam and Watergate to higher ground. His campaign slogan—"Why not the best?"—promised an alternative to the insiders' mediocrity. The public responded favorably: in mid-August, as Ford limped to victory at the convention in Kansas City, Carter led by a wide margin in the opinion surveys, as high as 29 percentage points in the Harris Poll.

The Ford campaign devised a multitrack response to Carter's high-minded appeal. In order to project gravitas, the president himself would adopt the familiar "Rose Garden strategy," sticking close to the White House and receiving free publicity from television and the newspapers simply by doing his job. Bob Dole, like Spiro Agnew before him, would be the campaign's attack dog, ridiculing Carter as a slick neophyte who should not be trusted with the presidency. The campaign's paid televised advertising would amplify Ford's down-to-earth, regular-guy persona, making special mention of his popular wife and personable family. Finally, beleaguered by the dismal polls, the Ford camp challenged Carter to a series of televised debates. Carter, who still needed to connect with a public that hardly knew him, accepted, and three appearances were scheduled. No presidential candidates had debated each other since the famous contests between Kennedy and Nixon in 1960.* Carter and Ford's debates have not left the same historical mark, but they proved crucial to the campaign.

The first debate, in late September, gave Ford an enormous lift. Like an overprepared student in an oral examination, Carter looked stiff and sounded tentative. (He would later say he was overawed by the occasion.) Ford, who had worked hard on his delivery in a mock television studio, appeared, by

---

* In August 1964, the Senate, with the acquiescence of President Lyndon Johnson, killed a bill that would have suspended the equal-time provisions then governing broadcast media, thereby ending any possibility that Johnson would debate Barry Goldwater. In 1968, Hubert Humphrey challenged Richard Nixon to one-on-one debates, but Nixon refused, on the grounds that it would be unfair to exclude the third-party American Independent candidate, George Wallace. In 1972, Nixon saw no reason even to consider debating George McGovern.

contrast, calm, authoritative, and even expansive. As previously agreed to by the candidates, the questioning focused on domestic affairs and the economy, and Ford reeled off impressive figures about rebounding growth and receding inflation. Carter, however, was forced to explain himself over proposals he had made or appeared to have made about raising taxes and generating a huge federal surplus. In a clever maneuver, Ford also attacked the Democratic Congress as the real source of the current mess in Washington. The charge was unjust, especially given Congress's contribution to the economic recovery for which Ford now took credit. But Ford's attack was effective in offsetting Carter's image as an outsider and in deflecting memories of Watergate and the pardoning of Richard Nixon. Instantly, Carter's once forbidding lead in the polls dropped to eight percentage points.

In the second debate, held ten days later, the specter of Helsinki reversed the campaign's momentum. The general topic was foreign affairs, and Ford was asked a predictable question about the Helsinki agreements and the Soviet Union's control of Eastern Europe. The president had a reasonable answer already prepared, to the effect that the American government's official policy was to recognize the sovereignty and independence of each of the Eastern European countries. But Ford botched his lines, declaring, "There is no Soviet domination of Eastern Europe, and there never will be under a Ford administration." What was supposed to be a careful distinction between the accords and the actual governing principles of American diplomacy turned into a bizarre statement that sounded as if Ford had lost touch with reality. Worse, when pressed, Ford repeated the mangled line, then failed to clarify it for several days, stalling his campaign and reviving all the old questions about his basic competence. Carter, handed an unexpected favor, made the most of it, both during the debate and after: "And I would like to see Mr. Ford convince the Polish-Americans and the Czech-Americans and the Hungarian-Americans in this country that those countries don't live under the domination and supervision of the Soviet Union behind the Iron Curtain," he declared, minutes after Ford's gaffe.

Ford never fully recovered, although he came close. In the last days of the campaign, he cut loose from the White House, barnstormed the country around the clock, and changed the subject to the economy, which continued to show signs of improvement. The third debate, on general subjects and with an awkward format, did not make much of an impact. On Election Day, a large number of eligible voters took a pass on both candidates, so that the turnout was the lowest since 1948, a mere 54 percent—normally a boost for the challenger. Carter made his most impressive showings in the South: he broke the hammerlock of the Republicans' southern strategy and even managed to carry Mississippi, which had not voted for a Democratic presidential candidate since 1956. But nationwide, Carter, who had once looked invincible, won only 50.8 percent of the popular vote, to Ford's 48.2 percent. Carter's margin in the electoral college was the slimmest since Woodrow Wilson's in 1916. The Democrats did hold on to their commanding congressional majorities, but picked up only one seat each in the Senate and the House.

The morning after Election Day brought the victors more a sense of relief than elation. With virtually nothing to claim in the way of a mandate, Jimmy Carter would still have to prove he was the leader the country was looking for after the shocks of the early 1970s. If he failed, there were many others who would be ready to lead very differently—including the man who had only barely lost to Gerald Ford.

3

JIMMY CARTER AND
THE AGONIES OF
ANTI-POLITICS

J IMMY CARTER HAD REASON to be pleased when he gave an extended interview to *Playboy* magazine during a break in his campaign in the summer of 1976. Many American voters still did not recognize his name, and *Playboy* reached more than 5 million readers every month. Its previous interviewees included the Reverend Martin Luther King Jr., William F. Buckley Jr., Jawaharlal Nehru, and Dr. Albert Schweitzer. The interviewer, Robert Scheer, formerly of the left-wing magazine *Ramparts*, had difficulty understanding Carter's religious views, which some people suspected were prudish and holier-than-thou. But Carter did his best, explaining himself patiently while trying to sound like an up-to-date regular guy. "Christ set some almost impossible standards for us," he said at the conclusion of the interview. Quoting from the Book of Matthew, he admitted that like any other human he had sinned and "committed adultery in my heart many times," but that his redeemer forgave him. In any event, he would not judge another man lest he commit the sin of pride: "Christ says don't consider yourself better than someone else because one guy screws a whole bunch of women while the other guy is loyal to his wife."

Carter's remarks were wholly in line with his Baptist faith. Yet they were also open to malicious interpretation—and as soon as the interview appeared in late September, doubts arose about his political acumen. Political professionals and press commentators thought he had erred badly by even appearing in *Playboy*, sacrificing his seriousness to gain some name recognition. Sophisticated liberals read Carter's equation of fantasy and actual adultery as the jabbering of a hayseed religious weirdo. Conservative evangelical Christians interpreted Carter's mixture of scripture, semi-profanity, and unashamed sex talk in a girlie magazine as the latest revelation that America was doomed to hell.

The interview in *Playboy* hurt Carter but did not cost him appreciable liberal support or prevent him from winning the votes of most born-again Christians in 1976. (That Carter's opponent was a veteran Washington insider whose wife publicly condoned premarital sex and supported abortion rights may have helped prevent evangelicals from defecting—or so Carter himself surmised.) Four years later, however, public perceptions had curdled. A fledgling army of politicized right-wing Christians now fervently believed that Jimmy Carter and the entire Democratic Party were Satan's lieutenants. Democratic liberals had decided that beneath Carter's outward weirdness lay a sanctimonious southern conservative who had betrayed their party's traditions, especially the legacies of John and Robert Kennedy. The pols and pundits who once found Carter refreshing rejected him as rigid, small-minded, and self-righteous, incapable of understanding the workings of Washington politics.

Carter's best day as president may have been his first. After his swearing in, he left his armored limousine and walked hatless down Pennsylvania Avenue to the White House with his wife and family—a populist touch that recalled the inaugurations of Thomas Jefferson and Andrew Jackson.* Like Jefferson and Jackson, the new president—Jimmy, not James—would renounce pomp and circumstance, and return the nation's government to the people. A vigorous fifty-two-year-old with a beaming smile, Carter conveyed all-American virtues, having risen out of the small town of Plains, Georgia; left a promising career in the Navy to take over the family's peanut business when his father fell ill; and only later turned to politics, eventually winning the governorship on his second try in 1970. Succeeding the notorious segregationist Lester Maddox as governor, Carter seemed to embody the spirit of a new South where, he declared at his inaugural in Atlanta, "the time for racial discrimination is over." Now, as president, he would bring his spirit of decency to a national government that still seemed adrift—with the

---

* The idea actually originated in a letter from Senator William Proxmire of Wisconsin, an advocate of physical fitness who thought the president's walk would be a good example to the rest of the country.

support, he expected, of a Congress firmly controlled by his own party. The throngs along Pennsylvania Avenue roared with approval.

No less than Gerald Ford, though, Carter faced large problems that defied conventional wisdom—and he had even worse luck than his predecessor. A new energy crisis, compounded once again by treacherous turns in foreign affairs, brought stagflation back with a vengeance. Carter's handling of the economy exacerbated divisions among Democrats without reconciling Republicans to him. In foreign policy, his attempts to rebuild American power and prestige on the principles of human rights appeared to neoconservative Democrats and Reagan Republicans like a warmed-over version of McGovernism. When new cold war crises led him to turn those same principles against the Soviet Union, liberal Democrats thought he had swerved to the right.

Carter's lack of experience in Washington, his faith in technical expertise, and his disdain for the capital's ordinary politics—all assets in winning the presidency—would be routinely cited as the main sources of his enormous difficulties after he entered the Oval Office. Many of Carter's most severe political wounds certainly were self-inflicted. But the challenges and misfortunes of the late 1970s also left a president of Carter's centrist political sensibilities with little room to maneuver. And while the Carter administration floundered, the resurgent Reagan Republicans enlarged their operations and honed their message, determined to win their revolution at last.

Carter's homespun appeal cloaked the fact that he had deliberately expanded his horizons before he ran for president. In 1974, he persuaded Robert Strauss, the head of the Democratic National Committee, to have him chair the party's congressional campaign committee for the fall elections. The position gave Carter valuable national political experience and contacts. Official trips to Latin America in 1972 and to Europe and Israel in 1973 had enhanced his knowledge of foreign affairs. Carter also happily accepted an invitation to join the newly formed Trilateral Commission in 1973. This group, a private organization of scholars, corporate heads, philanthropists, and political leaders, was founded by David Rockefeller to promote greater cooperation among North America, Europe, and Pacific Asia, and to help bridge the gap with undeveloped countries. Carter had never mingled in such powerful company before, and he forged some important friendships at the commission, not least with its chairman and cofounder, the foreign policy expert from Columbia University, Zbigniew Brzezinski.

Carter's administration, sometimes derisively called the "Georgia Mafia," was actually an uneasy mixture of the president's political loyalists and a retinue of nationally known figures. The Georgians included the whiz kids Hamilton Jordan (who served as an all-around adviser until being appointed chief of staff in 1979); the press secretary Jody Powell; and the advertising expert Gerald Rafshoon. Stuart Eizenstat, a lawyer from Atlanta, former junior aide to Hubert Humphrey, and policy director of the Carter campaign, became the president's chief domestic policy director. An older Georgian lawyer, Judge Griffin Bell of the federal district court, took over the Justice Department. Carter's closest friend in politics, the businessman Bert Lance, served as director of the Office of Management and Budget (OMB) until charges of earlier financial improprieties, of which he was eventually cleared, forced him to resign in September 1977. But the rest of Carter's team included notables: Brzezinski (named head of the National Security Council); Secretary of State Cyrus Vance (who had been deputy secretary of defense under Lyndon Johnson); Johnson's top domestic adviser Joseph Califano Jr., whom Carter named secretary of health, education, and welfare; Johnson's former budget director Charles Schultze, now head of the Council of Economic Advisers; and, from the Nixon-Ford years, James Schlesinger, Carter's chief adviser on energy issues.

There never was any doubt that Carter was in charge—at times overly so. The president centralized lines of communication so that his cabinet agencies would report directly to him, with little collaboration on their own. Carter was early to arrive at the Oval Office and late to leave, and he quickly earned the reputation of a technocratic micromanager—the man who made every decision, right down to the hourly playing schedule on the White House tennis courts. Although all this was not without precedent—historically minded observers compared his passionless expert's style to that of another engineer, Herbert Hoover—Carter could display an irksome, self-confident aloofness that some ascribed to deep-seated insecurity and others called arrogance.

In two ways, Carter's White House departed significantly from previous presidencies. As a man of the new South, Carter was determined to increase the number of minorities and women in senior government positions and as his personal counselors. Vernon Jordan, president of the National Urban League and the civil rights activist and lawyer Marian Wright Edelman were members of a select group that vetted Carter's cabinet appointments. Congressman Andrew Young, formerly an aide to Martin Luther King

Jr., was named U.S. ambassador to the United Nations. Two black women headed cabinet agencies: Juanita Kreps as secretary of commerce and Patricia Roberts Harris as secretary of housing and urban development. No previous administration had come close to this inclusiveness, which boosted Carter's standing among blacks and white liberals.

The more informal but conspicuous presence of Carter's pollster, Patrick Caddell, affirmed a different kind of change in American politics. Every modern president has had political gurus who stay constantly in touch with the quirky trends of public opinion. But Caddell represented a new breed of adviser. The advent of television as the primary vehicle for campaigning and the decline of traditional party machines in the 1960s and early 1970s created a need for political media consultants. These specialists understood both the ever-changing new technology and the nuances of creating a campaign message—and their political identity changed from valued campaign statisticians to frontline strategists. In 1976, Pat Caddell, although only twenty-six, was the most celebrated pollster and consultant in the country, and electing Jimmy Carter president became his new crusade. After the election, Carter could not afford to lose Caddell's expertise, lest he lose touch with the people and the people lose touch with him.

Four years earlier, when he was just out of Harvard College, Caddell had worked for the McGovern campaign. Now, he said, as the offspring of Irish Catholic parents from Massachusetts who had raised him in the South, he had a special affinity for the southern outsider Carter. He also had his own special philosophy about national politics, based on a belief that the electorate had become deeply disaffected with traditional party politicians. Seeing voters as frustrated investors who were receiving an inadequate return for their votes, Caddell contended that this growing alienation, which he sometimes called "malaise," was causing Americans to yearn not just for new leaders but for an entirely new kind of leaders. These leaders would be straight-shooting anti-politicians who eschewed the old-fashioned party trappings, valued expertise over ideology, spoke candidly, and won voters over by earning their trust. By these lights, someone like Carter was an ideal figure, practically destined to become president. The wunderkind Caddell would help shape both the candidate and his candidacy—and then the president and his presidency—to fulfill that destiny. "Jimmy Carter," Caddell would later remark, "is a natural extension of the change in American politics. It'd be crazy not to be."

During Carter's early months as president, his popularity with the general public seemed to vindicate Caddell's theories. On his first full day in office, Carter issued an executive order fulfilling a campaign pledge to scrap Ford's measured clemency program; in its place, he offered unconditional amnesty to all who had evaded the draft during the Vietnam War.* Conservatives immediately protested, and a wave of negative phone calls hit the White House, but Carter weathered the storm and enhanced his reputation for decisiveness and independence. Thereafter, he proposed to Congress an enormously ambitious legislative agenda on matters ranging from national energy policy to streamlining the federal government. He demanded and received emergency authorization to deregulate natural gas prices and end sudden acute shortages. He revived Franklin Roosevelt's homey "fireside chats" with the American people (though on television, not radio) and held "town meetings" in local communities. Reinforcing his image as an anti-politician, he also reduced some of the ostentatious splendor of the White House by ordering that the presidential yacht be sold and that his public appearances not begin with a band playing "Hail to the Chief."

Lawmakers in Washington, unimpressed by Carter's large agenda, formed negative early impressions of the new president, who seemed to hold the capital's peculiar cultural and political folkways in contempt. But by the end of April, Carter's public approval rating had soared to 75 percent. For the moment, it looked as if the country had found the leader it had been searching for since Richard Nixon's downfall.

Carter's steady decline after his propitious start was caused chiefly by the country's renewed economic woes. The rate of inflation, which stood at 6 percent the month he took office, rose on average every year for the rest of his presidency, reaching the low double digits in 1979 and 1980. Efforts by the Federal Reserve to curb rising prices by raising interest rates succeeded mainly, in the short run, in slowing down the economy. Civilian unemployment, although appreciably lower than it had been during the recession of the mid-1970s, seemed stuck at an uncomfortable level of about 6 percent until it rose in 1980 to the same figure as when the administration began, 7.5 percent. (The figures were far worse in some heavily industrial states.) The federal deficit, which by the time Carter took over was the highest in American history, $68 billion, would stand at $73 billion in 1980, despite

---

* Like Ford's clemency program, though, Carter's pardon withheld unconditional amnesty from military resisters, and sustained many of the burdens imposed by Ford. Very few Vietnam-era military deserters and AWOLs would ever receive any form of legal relief.

the president's campaign pledge that the government would show a surplus by the end of his first term.

The political wrangling over Carter's policies started during the period of his honeymoon with the public. In order to stimulate the economy and reduce unemployment, Carter agreed with congressional leaders in the first days of the administration to sponsor a quick fifty-dollar rebate to each taxpayer, as part of a major package that included a cut of $900 million in corporate taxes and a modest jobs program. The bill speedily passed the House, but stalled in the Senate—and when, in April, Carter learned that he had inherited a much larger deficit than he expected, he withdrew his support of the rebate and declared that, henceforth, he would focus on fighting both the deficit and inflation. Liberal congressional Democrats, some of whom had had quiet doubts all along about the fairness of the rebate but supported it anyway, now felt as if Carter had double-crossed them. And both the U.S. Conference of Mayors and the AFL-CIO denounced the entire stimulus plan as insufficiently attentive to reducing unemployment.

The fallout aggravated bad feelings already created in February, when Carter, in an austerity move, eliminated from his budget $5 billion in proposed pet dam construction projects earlier approved by Ford. Congress reacted fiercely to the cuts—"The road can be smooth or the road can be rough," the Senate majority leader, Robert Byrd, warned the president— and Carter quickly agreed to a compromise. But a pattern of discord had been established. Some congressional Democrats would never trust Carter again, especially on fiscal issues; and Carter would forever regret not holding the line on the dam expenditures as an early, politically damaging sign of weakness.

Individual parts of Carter's stimulus package, including a $20.1 billion jobs program and a bill to aid state and local governments during economic downswings, did pass Congress. And the president had some early victories in energy policy, which was now of central importance to any national economic strategy. Taking the matter more seriously than Ford, Carter successfully proposed the establishment of a new cabinet-level department of energy, where he would eventually install James Schlesinger as secretary. In his role as anti-politician, he set a public example of energy conservation by ordering thermostats at the White House lowered. He also put Schlesinger in charge of secretly preparing a complex major energy bill. Schlesinger's proposal called for a tax on all domestic oil production, a special "gas guzzler" surcharge on automobiles that failed to satisfy federal fuel-efficiency standards, mandates for public utilities and certain heavy industries to switch from oil and gas consumption to coal, and a variety of tax incentives to encourage conservation. Calling it the "moral equivalent of war," Carter unveiled the proposed bill in mid-April, and received favorable responses from the press and the public. Four months later, thanks to strenuous efforts by the House speaker, Thomas "Tip" O'Neill, the bill passed the House by a substantial margin.

These triumphs turned out to be fleeting exceptions. Carter had wanted to act quickly to reform the nation's welfare system, but fell into heated arguments with the secretary of health, education, and welfare (HEW), Joseph Califano, over such fundamentals as whether "reform" meant increasing federal spending, as Califano believed, or holding expenditures steady, as Carter had always assumed. The bill finally proposed in August reflected Carter's espousal of the work ethic by providing jobs for those on welfare who could work—but it displeased conservatives, who saw it as a vast expansion of federal welfare, as well as organized labor, which feared that new federally sponsored jobs paid at the minimum wage would undercut union wages. By summer's end, differences within the White House over tax reform, another of Carter's high priorities, had caused bitter squabbling between Eizenstat and Secretary of the Treasury Michael Blumenthal, prompting Carter to delay proposing a bill to Congress. The energy bill that had easily passed the House faced much tougher going in the Senate. Nine months into his presidency, Carter's legislative agenda seemed to be going nowhere.

Neither political nor economic developments broke in Carter's favor. In early September, the White House hunkered down when accusations started flying concerning allegedly suspicious bank dealings in Georgia by the director of OMB, Bert Lance. William Safire, now a columnist for the *New York Times*, made what would prove to be baseless charges against Lance concerning influence peddling; and the *Washington Post* amplified Safire's claims. Lance, called to account, defended himself well before the Senate Government Affairs Committee, and in succeeding years he would be fully cleared—but the political damage had been done, and Lance resigned soon after he testified to the Senate. Suddenly, Carter, who had stubbornly defended Lance, lost his most trusted economic adviser and closest friend in the executive branch—and his public image as the antidote to Richard Nixon was sullied.

The economic growth rate, which had been robust for the first half of the year, slowed during the third quarter, and Charles Schultze feared that the administration had predicated its policies on overly optimistic forecasts. The average annual rate of inflation seemed to be running at about 6 percent, and unemployment at 7 percent, roughly the same as in Ford's last year—not an emergency, but a continuing cause for concern. Carter's economic programs faced even more dismal prospects during his second year in office. Carter had shocked Tip O'Neill by saying that he intended to preside over the country much as he had done in Georgia, and that if he encountered resistance from Congress, he would simply take his case to the people. O'Neill resented having the House and Senate of the United States likened to the Georgia state legislature, and he knew that Carter's misunderstanding of reality in Washington could paralyze the legislative process, with politically fatal consequences.

O'Neill did his best to shield the White House and Congress from what he considered Carter's folly. When, for example, Carter's proposal for a new federal office of consumer affairs seemed headed for certain defeat in the House despite heavy lobbying by the White House, O'Neill simply removed the item from the House calendar at the last minute, sparing Carter and the Democrats embarrassment. But O'Neill could not fully contain the rebellious impulses within the House Democratic caucus, and he had no day-to-day influence at all over the Senate.

After receiving Carter's energy bill from the House, the Senate balked. The main sticking points were Carter's proposals for federal regulation of intrastate natural gas prices and for a "wellhead" tax on domestic crude oil that would raise the price to consumers to match levels in the rest of the world. Led by a Democratic senator, Russell Long of Louisiana, representatives of oil- and gas-producing states, previously not consulted, stalled the plan. After protracted negotiations over the bill between the House and Senate collapsed in May 1978, O'Neill threatened to break the proposal down into five separate bills—a move that would almost certainly have doomed the wellhead tax, which Carter considered the most important piece of the package. On another front, Califano, soon after taking office as secretary of HEW, had declared the Social Security Administration in a financial crisis due to the continued inflation. The administration's call to rectify matters with a modest hike in payroll taxes met with denunciations from senators about a raid on the treasury, and provoked the House into passing an even greater increase in tax rates and a provision lifting the wage ceiling on which Social Security taxes were paid. Carter went along with the House proposal, hoping to compensate for it by providing tax relief in other areas. But by breaking his campaign promise not to raise taxes, Carter further damaged his image of trustworthiness and created special anxieties among business leaders.

In order to offset the payroll tax increase, Carter's annual budget called for income tax cuts amounting to $25 billion, accompanied by reductions in spending on numerous social programs, especially those involving development of blighted urban areas. Carter was not being callous: in October 1977 he had visited a despairing, rubble-strewn neighborhood in the South Bronx, which one newsman had pronounced "the worst slum in America," and ordered an action plan for which the Bronx would serve as a test case. But much as with welfare reform, Carter was more interested in finding new ways to help the cities by encouraging private investment and make existing programs more efficient than he was in spending massive federal funds. Left-liberal Democrats, as well as the Conference of Mayors, bridled, and their reaction compounded Carter's political difficulties with other major interests groups, including organized labor. His remarks in his second State of the Union message—that federal resources were limited, and that "[g]overnment cannot eliminate poverty or provide a bountiful economy or reduce inflation or save our cities or cure illiteracy or provide energy"—sounded to enraged liberals like surrender to Republican laissez-faire doctrine dating back to Herbert Hoover. Only on environmental policy did liberals give Carter high marks for signing new clean air and water bills, establishing a federal superfund to finance the cleanup of toxic waste sites, and strengthening the Environmental Protection Agency (EPA).

The deepening cleavage between Carter and liberal interest groups illustrated anew how badly the two sides misunderstood each other. Carter was not the conservative that liberal and left-wing Democrats believed he was, but neither was he the New Deal Democrat (let alone the left-wing populist) they had once fantasized he was. Carter's politics, which meshed well with Caddell's prescribed anti-politician style, were more of an updating of the tradition of southern progressivism that had evolved during the era of Woodrow Wilson. Originally, southern progressives combined a dedication to clean, efficient government with unwavering support for racial segregation. Although Carter had quietly pandered to racist voters in his gubernatorial campaign in 1970, he thereafter firmly, at times movingly renounced that part of the southern political heritage. Otherwise, though, he remained very much a progressive, who thought vested interests were parasites on good government, and who wanted to reform government to make it more rational, efficient, and responsive to the larger public interest.

Massive federal programs of social reform, like those of the New Deal and the Great Society, were, to Carter, deeply suspicious, as likely to corrupt government and impede social progress as they were to uplift the unfortunate. Carter firmly believed in fiscal prudence and reducing federal expenditures, but he also believed that less could well mean more, especially for the truly needy, so long as expertise and efficiency overcame fraud and waste. The more he described himself and his outlook as truly progressive to his party's left wing, the more he might as well have been speaking in a foreign language.

In Washington, where Congress had been reasserting its institutional power against the executive since Nixon's departure, truculence arose among offended congressmen who would not allow a Democratic president they deemed retrograde push them around, any more than they would a bona fide Republican. Complacent in their power and in their own preconceptions about liberal government, Democrats could imagine no alternative to themselves. But instead of addressing and overcoming this destructive mood, the Carter White House worsened it, goaded by a moralistic tendency to regard adversaries as selfishly corrupt, as well as by the imperatives of Carter's new style of anti-politician leadership. In a preinaugural memorandum, Caddell had warned Carter that he would face stern opposition from "traditional" Democrats such as Edward Kennedy and Morris Udall, "as antiquated and anachronistic a group as are conservative Republicans." Determined, as Caddell put it, to "Carterize" the party and to scrap forever the liberal dogma and bromides of the New Deal, Carter had an opportunity to carve out a bold new rhetoric and philosophy, offering the country a revised liberalism and liberal leadership befitting the confusing rigors of the 1970s. Instead, he revived an older progressive spirit and then fell back on familiar formulations about fiscal responsibility and the gospel of frugality—while treating the Democratic majority on Capitol Hill as benighted obstructionists.

From the spring through the fall of 1978, the tensions between the White House and the Democratic left became dangerously personal. In mid-October, Congress finally sent the president his energy bill, but in a diluted version that stressed deregulation and tax credits rather than new taxes to encourage conservation—and that completely eliminated Carter's cherished wellhead tax. Congress also passed a new tax bill that reduced taxes by $18.7 billion but contained none of Carter's original tax reform agenda.

More irksome politically for the White House was its escalating conflict with Senator Edward Kennedy over national health insurance. Democratic presidents and candidates since Harry S. Truman had pledged to enact some sort of comprehensive national health insurance plan, just as Carter had in 1976. But the president's concept of a feasible plan, mandating private health insurance with federal coverage of catastrophic illnesses, clashed with Kennedy's preference for a universal federal program financed by payroll and income taxes. Carter also wanted to move more slowly than Kennedy did, insisting that no major social welfare proposal get in the way of more pressing economic and fiscal legislation. The president did consult closely with Kennedy during the early phases of his presidency, but the more they disagreed about the correct timing for introducing a health insurance bill, and about the proper scope of federal responsibility, the frostier their relations became. Finally, in July 1978, Kennedy accused Carter of a "failure of leadership," and the break was complete. National health insurance became a dead letter, at least for the moment, and the likelihood of a liberal revolt in 1980 to replace Carter with Kennedy as the Democratic nominee became almost certain.

The congressional elections in November would, however, give little comfort to any segment of the Democratic Party. The warning signs were everywhere. Despite the administration's efforts to curb inflation by tightening bank credit and through voluntary wage and price controls (and, beginning in October 1978, more formal restrictions and incentives), the overall annual inflation rate was climbing, and would reach 9 percent by the end of the year. Around the country, mounting anger in the middle class at high property taxes and government costs, as well as rising prices, had bred a full-fledged revolt. It was most successful in California, where, in July, Howard Jarvis, a hard-right businessman and longtime supporter of Ronald Reagan, spearheaded the passage of a referendum, Proposition 13, which slashed state property taxes and placed at risk some basic public services, including schooling.

Democratic liberals might consider the president an atavistic fiscal conservative, but the electorate, especially in rural areas and in the South and West, seemed to be warming to economic policies more drastically regressive than anything Carter had in mind. The election returns affirmed the shift in public mood. Although the Democrats retained their majorities in both houses of Congress, five leading liberal Democrats in the Senate and one moderate Republican lost their reelection bids, whereas a new crop of conservative Republicans, including Gordon Humphrey of New Hampshire and Thad Cochran of Mississippi, would now be in the Senate to reinforce older heads such as Strom Thurmond and Jesse Helms. The new House Republican caucus would include Dick Cheney, elected from his home district in Wyoming, and a brash young Georgian from suburban Atlanta, Newt Gingrich. In the congressional tallies, Democratic support dropped in rural, small-town districts where Carter had done well in 1976. Most portentously, the traditionalist white evangelical vote that had opted for the Southern Baptist Democrat Carter shifted in large numbers to the Republicans. That shift involved concerns above and beyond the rate of inflation.

While economic policy and federal assistance programs dominated debates about domestic issues in Washington, what eventually became known as "social" or "culture war" issues began roiling the country. Originating partly in the attacks by the Nixon administration on its critics, partly in broader reactions to the civil rights reforms of the 1960s and 1970s, and partly in much older currents in conservative politics, a loosely knit conservative counterestablishment—and even a conservative counterculture—fully emerged after 1976. Combining grassroots organizing, think-tank policy mongering, and sophisticated marketing techniques, these conservatives activists—called by one of their leaders, Richard A. Viguerie, the new right, in contrast to the new left and the "new politics" Democrats—were determined to bring what they viewed as the eastern liberal establishment to its knees.

Having wandered in the political wilderness for decades, the activists of the new right refined yet another populist image, deeply conservative and attractive to the southern and western political base that Carter had partly filched in 1976. The new left populism of the 1960s, more interested in protest than politics, had disintegrated, leaving behind a reflexive suspicion among left-wing Democrats about the uses of American military power abroad. The populism of the new right, however, was intensely political, focused on winning power by packaging new ideas for policy and feeding off the resentment of what Richard Nixon had called the "silent majority." The Democratic southern outsider Jimmy Carter once again found himself stuck in a dwindling political center between his party's increasingly embittered left and the energized pro-Republican right.

On racial issues, the political spotlight shifted from school busing (which Carter, like Ford, opposed) to affirmative action—and conservatives sustained the shift from support of repressive Jim Crow practices to the rhetoric of equal rights. Since the late 1960s, numerous federal and state programs had been established to compensate for previous injustices in hiring, education, and government benefits by giving preference to qualified minority and women candidates for government jobs and for admission to public colleges and universities. A backlash set in amid the economic troubles of the mid-1970, as whites claimed they had been victimized by what they called reverse discrimination. A discontented former Marine, Allan Bakke, twice denied admission to the medical school at the University of California at Davis, filed suit in 1973, claiming that the university had discriminated against him by accepting black students with grades and aptitude-test scores lower than his own. After the supreme court of California ruled in Bakke's favor, the university appealed to the U.S. Supreme Court. Its impending ruling in *The Regents of the University of California v. Bakke* in 1978 sparked a constitutional debate over affirmative action that inflamed anew the basic conflict raised by the earlier disputes over busing: in a clash of asserted civil rights, which side's claim would be respected?

President Carter had a divided mind over the *Bakke* case, and, for once, he tried to stay above the fray within the administration. Others inside the White House, however, became passionately engaged, and on both sides of the issue. Attorney General Griffin Bell was already an object of suspicion to liberals in the administration, having run into difficulty during his confirmation hearing when his past membership in an all-white social club came to light. Handed the *Bakke* case in 1977, Bell wrote a brief that favored Bakke and claimed that the admissions plan utilized by the university was an artificial quota system violating both the letter and the spirit of affirmative action. Stuart Eizenstat as policy director and Carter's legal counsel, Robert Lipshutz, both Georgians who were considered more liberal than Bell, ripped into the brief and urged a more ringing endorsement of affirmative action. They suggested asking the Supreme Court to remand the case to lower courts in order to adjudicate the constitutionality of the university's plan. Carter rejected the latter proposal, but he sent the brief back to the Justice Department and demanded a new draft with a less equivocal statement supporting affirmative action. He thereby touched off a bitter intramural fight whose details found their way, via leaks, into the press.

On one side, White House liberals, including Califano and the chair of the Equal Opportunity Employment Commission, Eleanor Holmes Norton, as well as the Congressional Black Caucus, prepared arguments in opposition to *Bakke*. "The entry of the United States for the *first* time in such a suit on the side of an individual claiming reverse discrimination," Holmes warned the president, would accelerate what she saw as a "deterioration" of affirmative action programs in higher education. Vice President Mondale beseeched Bell to uphold vigorously the administration's support for affirmative action. On the other side, Bell complained of interference by liberals; and in the middle, Eisenstadt and Lipshutz tried to formulate a consensus position. Carter ended up supporting a brief by the Justice Department which argued that "only one question" should be decided by the court: whether a state university could take race into account as a factor in admitting students. The Supreme Court went further, ruling, in a hotly contested five-to-four decision reached in June 1978, that race could be a factor in university admissions, but that the program at Davis was unconstitutional because it applied a strict percent quota for minorities. In the narrowest sense, the University of California had lost and Allan Bakke had won—but in a watered-down version, affirmative action had survived.*

The Carter administration hailed what it called the court's vindication of affirmative action. (A few weeks after the ruling, Carter sent a memorandum to the heads of all executive departments and agencies, stating that he was "strongly committed to a policy of affirmative action" and that "the recent decision by the Supreme Court in Bakke enables us to continue those efforts without interruption.") But the White House was more of a loser than a winner, less because of the court's ruling than because of its own internal squabbling and its apparent irresolution. The bickering, as reported in the press, made the White House look both divided and petty. The president, in trying to parse the difference between quotas and affirmative action, sounded to the public as if he was trying to please everyone and succeeding in pleasing no one. Civil rights leaders, who viewed the decision as a blow to affirmative action, became especially irked at Carter—and not for the last time.

Less than three months after the *Bakke* decision, leaders of the Black

---

* Although the Supreme Court divided five to four, only one justice supported the entire ruling—Associate Justice Lewis Powell, who wrote the majority opinion. Four of the justices wanted to support affirmative action in general and quotas in particular, in line with the Constitution's stipulations about equal protection under the law. Four of the justices wanted to kill affirmative action as inherently a quota system and thus an unconstitutional violation of equal protection. Powell split the difference, fashioning a compromise that backed affirmative action but rejected quotas. The result was a decision that displeased both sides of the debate over affirmative action. The *Bakke* decision showed, above all, how widespread the confusion was over affirmative action—extending even to the Supreme Court.

Congressional Caucus came to the White House to complain about the administration's slackness in funding federal aid for jobs and housing, and in passing fair housing legislation, as well as its seeming indifference about the Humphrey-Hawkins full employment bill, then stalled in Congress. Carter had originally supported the bill, which guaranteed federally funded jobs as a "last resort" to provide full national employment (variously defined as an unemployment rate of between 3 and 6 percent)—but later he insisted on important revisions of the bill that would take rising inflation into account. The meeting at the White House degenerated into a shouting match. Carter tried to mend fences at a later meeting and promised to work harder on behalf of Humphrey-Hawkins. But when the bill finally passed, it came with an unlikely provision, added by the Senate, which required that the inflation rate be lowered to 3 percent by 1983 and to zero by 1988. Although the black legislators were glad to have won anything, what had begun as an attack on unemployment had become a government anti-inflation manifesto.

Carter was running into similar difficulties with advocates of women's rights. On gender issues, as on race, Carter reasonably considered himself a liberal. As president, he came through reliably on appointments, not just by including women in his cabinet but by selecting more women for the federal bench than any of his predecessors had. And he firmly endorsed most feminist political demands, including an Equal Rights Amendment (ERA) to the Constitution. Passed by Congress in 1972, the ERA had gained the approval of all but three of the number of state legislatures required for its ratification. But the state approvals had languished after an initial rush (only two states passed the amendment from 1974 through 1977), and there were rising doubts that the amendment would succeed before the seven-year limit included in the original legislation ran out. A National Women's Conference gathered in Texas in 1977, in part to rally the ERA movement. Carter not only supported the delegates' call for an extension of the time limit for ERA (and arranged for a large media splash when he signed an extension bill in 1978), he also supported the original legislation that financed the conference with federal money. In June 1978, Carter formed a President's Advisory Committee for Women, and appointed as one of its cochairs the confrontational left-wing Democrat (and now a former Representative) Bella Abzug.

Still, Carter ran afoul of the feminists. Some leaders of the movement accused him of merely paying lip service to the ERA, leaving it to his increasingly active and influential wife, Rosalynn, to do the hard work of telephoning and stump speaking on behalf of the amendment. Even more troublesome to feminists was Carter's position on abortion. Since *Roe v. Wade* in 1973, women's rights organizations had pushed hard to ensure that abortion be kept affordable for all women who chose it. Although Carter backed *Roe*, he drew the line at supporting federal funding of abortion, except in cases of rape or incest, or when the woman's life was endangered. He had made his position clear during the election campaign; nevertheless, feminist leaders (including, eventually, Abzug) assailed him, linking his views on abortion funding with his economic policies, which, they charged, victimized poor women, including single mothers, in order to fight inflation.

Just when Carter became embattled over civil rights and cultural issues with blacks and feminists on his left, a resounding attack on both him and the left arose from hard-line conservatives over the same issues and related ones. The leaders of the charge, including the Reverend Jerry Falwell of the Moral Majority and Phyllis Schlafly of STOP ERA, were unfamiliar to most Americans and seemed to come out of nowhere. But the political origins of this emerging cultural right lay in more conventional right-wing organizations that had been growing rapidly in numbers and influence since the early 1970s—including some that had existed for decades.

Before Goldwater's campaign, and for many years after it, conservatives had been at a considerable disadvantage in presenting their anti–New Deal, anti–civil rights, and aggressively anti-Soviet ideas to policy makers and the general public. William F. Buckley Jr.'s weekly magazine, *National Review*, founded in 1955, was an important conservative counterweight to *The New Republic* and *The Nation*, and Buckley's nationally syndicated television show, *Firing Line*, gave conservatism an enlarged public presence. The American Enterprise Institute (AEI), established in 1943, served as a forum for pro-business anti–New Dealers and, through the AEI's subsidiary Center for Strategic and International Studies, for foreign policy conservatives. The Intercollegiate Studies Institute (begun in 1953 with Buckley as its first president) was engaged in what its founder, Frank Chodorov, called a "fifty-year project" to sway colleges and universities toward conservative ideas; the Hoover Institution at Stanford University, dating back to 1919, became an academic beachhead for conservative writers and scholars; the best-selling anti-collectivist novels of Ayn Rand made a national cult of Rand's professed philosophy of "objectivism." But none of these scattered enterprises enjoyed the prestige and influence in policy-making and media circles of more liberal organizations such as the Brookings Institution, the Twentieth Century Fund, and the Council on Foreign Relations. Despairing because of their intellectual marginality, some conservatives had long berated themselves (in a line adapted from John Stuart Mill, on the nineteenth-century British Tories) as "the stupid party."

In the 1970s, conservatives got smart. In 1973, a staffer on Capitol Hill, Paul Weyrich—a young, right-wing, activist, anti–Vatican II Catholic from Wisconsin (and an admirer of his home state's late senator, Joseph R. McCarthy)—joined with another Republican staffer, Edwin Feulner, to found a new conservative think tank, the Heritage Foundation, with financial backing from Joseph Coors, the conservative heir of a beer company in Colorado, as well as from a wealthy right-wing native of Pittsburgh, and heir to the Mellon fortune, Richard Mellon Scaife. Under Feulner and Weyrich's guidance, Heritage would not simply formulate new ideas and approaches, as Brookings and similar institutions did, but would package and forcefully advocate conservative policy proposals among sympathetic lawmakers. The appearance of the Heritage Foundation goaded the AEI to broaden its efforts and also become a policy-making adjunct to the rising new-right movement. And Coors's involvement (along with the formation in 1972 of the Business Roundtable, a conservative consortium of corporation chief executive officers) inspired other conservatives of immense wealth to fund right-wing institutes, publications, and foundations, often through private foundations of their own.

By the end of the decade, almost every shade of conservative opinion had some sort of vehicle (and usually more than one) to enlarge its public voice and give conservatism new legitimacy and greatly enlarged influence. Alongside AEI and Heritage, there were now the Manhattan Institute, the Shavano Institute, the Center for Public Choice, the Center for Judicial Studies, the Richard Mellon Scaife Foundation, the John M. Olin Foundation (headed by the former secretary of the treasury William Simon), the Ethics and Public Policy Center, and the National Institute for Public Policy. Weyrich left Heritage to form several new-right political action committees and advocacy think tanks, including the Committee for the Survival of a Free Congress.

Under Robert Bartley's direction, and with able writers such as Jude Wanniski, the editorial pages of the *Wall Street Journal* became an assertive national voice for conservative ideas and politics, chiefly but not solely on economic issues. The neoconservative intelligentsia had Norman Podhoretz's magazine *Commentary* and *The Public Interest* (cofounded by the veteran controversialist and expert fund-raiser, Irving Kristol) as well as the Committee on the Present Danger, a group headed by Podhoretz's wife, Midge Decter, which argued fervently that the Soviet Union had achieved an imminently dangerous military superiority over the United States. From the more traditional precincts of the right came countless policy papers, pamphlets, and new periodicals, including a sarcastic magazine, *The American Spectator*, as reminiscent of the latter-day right-wing version of H. L. Mencken's *American Mercury* as of *National Review*, edited by a young polemicist named R. Emmett Tyrell.

In its variety and forcefulness as well as its ubiquity, the new right's counterestablishment caught moderate as well as liberal intellectuals and policy makers by surprise. The CEO of Citibank, Walter Wriston, active at AEI, would later remark that it took "about twenty years for a research paper at Harvard to become a law," whereas the conservatives had figured out how to put their proposals directly into the marketplace of political ideas and sell them much more swiftly. The constellation of richly endowed centers and publications picked up on and publicized each other's proposals about everything from cutting taxes on corporations and wealthy individuals to rejecting the evils of détente, creating a sound-chamber effect that made the proposals appear not simply plausible but inevitable. By facilitating personal as well as political contacts among the different segments of the right, and by reaching out for younger people who would become tomorrow's columnists and political staffers, the conservative institutions began, collectively, to resemble an independent political machine.

The new right also brilliantly turned the tables rhetorically and intellectually on liberals and Democrats. In his charter for *National Review*, written in 1955, William F. Buckley had defined conservatism, in its defense of property and religion, as the willingness to "stand athwart history, yelling Stop, at a time when no one is inclined to do so, or to have much patience with those who so urge it." (Among the historical developments the magazine wished to halt was the southern civil rights movement, which, the editors wrote in 1957, was trying to deny the "sobering" reality that for the time being "the White community . . . is the advanced race.") By the early 1970s, the new right would seize the initiative, re-formed as a force for progress as well as history—casting the New Dealers as the old fogies of collectivism while dropping their own overt racism, elitism, and haughty tone and presenting themselves as the harbingers of change, risk, and experiment. No matter how much their ideas on economics, race, and social equity repackaged "old right" principles, the new right unfailingly claimed to be the party of hope and newness, and not memory—leaving the liberals as the exhausted, clueless, corrupt defenders of an outmoded era.

The political implications of these developments were enormous. As late as 1976, William Rusher—the publisher of *National Review*—and the direct-mail expert Richard Viguerie were so discouraged that they proposed conservatives think hard about forming a new party to run a ticket consisting of Ronald Reagan and George Wallace. But the brilliantly orchestrated rise of a new-right intellectual and institutional infrastructure made such desperate moves unnecessary. The decline of old party mechanisms had fragmented the Democrats into dozens of disconnected interest groups, but hard-line conservatives were organizing to supply much of the expertise, publicizing skill, and élan required of any political party. With center-right Republicans on the defensive after Gerald Ford's defeat, the new right would not have to slog through the party trenches to win national power; instead, it could engineer a corporate-funded takeover that, in time, would turn the Republican Party into a wholly owned subsidiary of the conservative movement. The major requirement for advancing the takeover was for the new right to unite in 1980 behind a national candidate—a relatively simple matter, given the ascendancy of Ronald Reagan.

The swelling clamor from the right over cultural issues resulted from a convergence of this new counterestablishment with two other existing currents: conservative evangelical activists (many concerned chiefly with protecting the racially segregated, fundamentalist so-called Christian academies against government efforts to remove their tax-exempt status), and veteran Goldwater Republicans who had seized on the backlash against affirmative action and feminism. In 1978, Weyrich, Viguerie, John "Terry" Dolan of the National Conservative Political Action Committee, and Howard Phillips of the Conservative Caucus, allied with the hard-line conservative evangelical Reverend Robert Grant to form a group called Christian Voice. By building on successful local evangelical campaigns (notably a successful effort a year earlier, led by the pop singer Anita Bryant, to defeat a homosexual rights referendum in Dade County, Florida), Christian Voice aimed to mobilize conservative Christians in politics, combining opposition to abortion, women's rights, homosexuality, and pornography with a defense of "traditional" pro-business economics. Grant, however, quickly felt crowded by his new partisan allies, denounced the religious right as a sham run by an unholy combination of three Catholics and a Jew, and went his own way—to give especially vital support to right-wing Republican

congressional candidates in the 1980 campaign.* Weyrich, Dolan, Viguerie, and Phillips found another, more politically reliable evangelical leader,
Reverend Jerry Falwell of Lynchburg, Virginia. In 1979, they organized a
new group, Moral Majority.

Falwell was a superb choice. The pastor of Lynchburg's fundamentalist Thomas Road Baptist Church, with a membership of 17,000, he had
built his congregation from a tiny assembly into an enormous enterprise, including its own independent, fully accredited Liberty Baptist College (later
Liberty University), which Falwell founded in 1971. A pioneer in using
television to spread his preaching about biblical inerrancy and the nation's
moral chaos—his syndicated *Old Time Gospel Hour* ran on 300 stations and
could reach 1.5 million viewers—Falwell was, in his own way, as expert a
media personality as Ronald Reagan. Shrewd in politics as well as in fund-
raising, he was perfectly comfortable merging his roles as pastor and conservative partisan, abjuring the traditional evangelical position (which he
himself once upheld) that ministers ought not become political spokesmen.
(In the mid-1960s, Falwell, then an explicitly staunch segregationist, had
denounced Martin Luther King's fight for desegregation as communist-
inspired and insisted that ministers stay out of politics—but in 1977, he
had joined with the Baptist minister Tim La Haye to fight against the
homosexual-rights ordinance in Dade County.) Falwell's political beliefs
—on taxes, foreign policy, and civil rights for racial minorities, as well as
on abortion and homosexuality—aligned neatly with those of the more
secular new right. "If you would like to know where I am politically," he
remarked, "I am to the right of wherever you are. I thought Goldwater
was too liberal." Indeed, Falwell's chief original goal in joining Weyrich
was to preserve the tax-exempt status of his private academy in Lynchburg,
founded in 1966 as an alternative to integrated public schools.

The antifeminist leader Phyllis Schlafly came from a different corner
of right-wing politics. A veteran conservative campaigner (and a Roman
Catholic), she had first gained national notice among conservatives during
the campaign of 1964, when her self-published pro-Goldwater manifesto, *A
Choice Not an Echo*, sold 3.5 million copies by Election Day, largely through
the efforts of local activists. Considered, even by some of her fellow conservatives, a strident hard-liner, Schlafly had refused to distance herself from

---

* Weyrich, Dolan, and Viguerie were the Catholics; Phillips was the Jew. Grant continues to be
the guiding spirit behind Christian Voice, which has outlasted Moral Majority as an important
liaison between right-wing evangelicals and Republican Party officials.

the militantly right-wing John Birch Society. Her pro-Goldwater writings, with their attacks on the sinister eastern establishment "kingmakers" who supposedly ruled the Republican Party and much of the world, epitomized the kind of conspirational thinking that the liberal historian Richard Hofstadter described as the "paranoid style." After Goldwater's defeat, Schlafly turned to writing alarmist best sellers (with her coauthor, the retired rear admiral Chester Ward) on the growing military threat from the Soviet Union. Not until 1972, when Congress passed the ERA, did Schlafly show much interest in women's issues—but then she quickly turned her enormous energy, organizational experience, and slashing style to opposing the women's movement, in order to help ignite what her biographer calls "a conflagration on the Right."

Schlafly initially relied on longtime contacts among Republican activists to build her new STOP ERA group; and by early 1973, the organization had established chapters in twenty-six states, concentrated in states considered critically important to the ratification of ERA. Many of the themes of STOP ERA—that the ERA would, for example, destroy the traditional family and women's valued legal protections, including protection from combat military service—had been standard antifeminist fare for decades. Yet by stressing what she claimed women would actually lose from the ERA—from single-sex bathrooms to exemption from the military draft—Schlafly advanced the broader conservative shift from nay-saying to what sounded like a commonsense, conservative permutation of feminism. She was also innovative in reaching out to religious conservatives, including Mormons and Southern Baptists, by denouncing feminist leaders as out-of-touch elitists. Above all, she linked the antifeminist reaction and the militant conservatism she had long championed on other issues. In 1975, Schlafly founded the Eagle Forum, a new group dedicated to upholding "family values" and opposing the United States' membership in the United Nations. That same year, she and Admiral Ward published an 800-page attack on the Ford administration's "suicidal" foreign policies, *Kissinger on the Couch*; simultaneously, STOP ERA's lobbying in the states bore fruit, most impressively in the Illinois legislature, where infighting and Democratic defections twice sent ERA down to defeat.

Although STOP ERA would never gain anything close to the membership of its main antagonist, the National Organization for Women (NOW), it gained clout far beyond its numbers. Schlafly—who somehow found the energy to enter and complete law school in addition to working against ERA—was adept at both insider lobbying and outsider pressure politics. When the International Women's Year (IWY) Conference (for which Carter had supported giving a federal grant) met in Houston in 1977, Schlafly called for a counterdemonstration, and succeeded in attracting 20,000 "pro-family," antiabortion, anti-ERA women to the city, about twice as many as the number of delegates and supporters who came to the IWY gathering. Early in 1978, the ERA either lost or failed to receive a scheduled vote in four states. Although Congress would eventually extend the time limit on state approvals to June 30, 1982, the ERA was obviously on the ropes, mainly because of Phyllis Schlafly and her supporters. A year later, Beverly La Haye, wife of the conservative evangelical Tim La Haye, would establish yet another traditionalist, anti-ERA group, Concerned Women of America—and would eventually enlist 500,000 members, far more than the liberal NOW.

For Jimmy Carter, it was the latest sign that politically, the time was out of joint. While civil rights leaders and feminists to his left challenged him for being too tepid, the right was massing its forces to wipe away even his measured, updated southern progressivism. His every step toward placating his liberal critics, over *Bakke*, over federal jobs programs, and over women's issues, emboldened the conservative counterestablishment and its proliferating support groups about the political outlook for 1980. After the midterm elections in 1978, he would have to deal with a Congress that was even more polarized, and decidedly more conservative, than its predecessor. To make matters worse, new developments overseas suggested that the already unsettled economy was headed for far deeper trouble.

On January 16, 1979, the shah of Iran, Mohammad Reza Pahlavi, left Tehran for Egypt, on what he called a brief vacation, thereby touching off a chain of events that led to his overthrow and to the installation, in April, of an Islamic republic under the control of the Shiite supreme spiritual leader, Ayatollah Ruholla Mussaui Khomeini. The Carter administration could not have predicted how thoroughly the Iranian revolution would disrupt its own political fortunes over the next two years. But as early as the spring of 1979, it became clear that the short-term economic effects would be severe and politically costly.

To the continued consternation of liberal Democrats, civil rights leaders, and organized labor, Carter remained committed to fighting inflation as the chief cause of the nation's economic woes. Primary responsibility for holding the line fell on the president's Council on Wage and Price Stability

(COWPS), now headed by the economist Alfred Kahn. By the end of 1978 COWPS was beginning to implement official standards for wage and price hikes. But despite rosy expectations, the administration was losing its war on inflation. The annual inflation rate had hit 9 percent, with food prices rising especially quickly. Although economists generally expected the rate of inflation to fall, they also expected that this was more likely to happen because of higher prime interest rates and a further slowing down of the economy than because of efforts by COWPS.

The consequences of the Iranian revolution ended even guarded optimism. For nearly a year, petroleum prices had been stable because of a worldwide glut in crude oil. After the overthrow of the shah, however, Iranian oil production virtually stopped, and OPEC seized the moment to raise prices by 17 percent. The cost of food and other consumer necessities continued to rise, but it was the price of oil that threatened to raise the overall inflation rate well into double digits. As oil shortages loomed, Carter decided, in April, to announce a gradual lifting of existing caps on domestic oil prices, telling Americans that they would have to become reconciled to using less oil and paying more for what they did use. He would couple this measure with a tax on excessive profits by oil companies, with the proceeds going to research and development of alternative energy sources and to helping poor families pay for their rising fuel costs. Only a week earlier, OPEC had announced a second sharp price rise of 9 percent.

The wheels seemed to be falling off Carter's domestic agenda. Liberal Democrats, led by Kennedy, wanted to know how the president could declare inflation the primary economic enemy and decry the windfall profits accruing to American oil companies, yet still call for the decontrol of oil prices. The new chairman of the Federal Reserve Board, Paul Volcker, whom Carter named to replace William Miller in 1979, responded to inflation by raising the board's interest rates, thus leading the nation's banks to raised their prime rate to 14.5 percent—a level some economists feared would start a recession. Lines of irritated motorists at gas pumps nationwide grew ever longer; in June, angry truck drivers in Levittown, Pennsylvania, barricaded expressways, causing two nights of rioting that led to more than 100 injuries and nearly 200 arrests. A week later, OPEC announced its largest price increase yet.

The main question on Americans' minds seemed no longer to be tied to any specific issue, but rather to be whether Jimmy Carter was competent to address any issue at all. One poll found his personal favorability rating nearly as low as his already miserable rating for job performance, which in some surveys was lower than Nixon's had been in his final weeks in office. These numbers made Pat Caddell blanch. Returning hurriedly from an economic summit in Tokyo, Carter, on his aides' advice, arranged with the television networks for airtime on July 5, when he would deliver a major presidential address on the energy crisis—but suddenly, late on July 3, the White House canceled the arrangement, without stating any reason. After strong urging from Caddell, Carter had decided to withdraw and reflect on the state of the nation, and then to compose a speech that would move far beyond the energy problem to consider a broader calamity of the American spirit.

For eleven days, Carter stayed at Camp David behind a thick veil of secrecy. Speculation raged. Was Carter finally getting his act together? Was he planning a major shakeup in the White House? Had the president gone mad? In fact, he was listening to a steady stream of specially invited visitors criticize, exhort, and pontificate, as he tried to come to grips with the nation's mood. The visitors included detractors such as civil rights activist Jesse Jackson; wise old Washington hands such as Clark Clifford; labor leaders, including Lane Kirkland of the United Auto Workers; and some clergymen and academics, including the historian Christopher Lasch, whose recent study of American maladjustment, *The Culture of Narcissism*, was the rage among the intelligentsia that summer. Finally, though, Carter would compose an address that owed its crispness to his media adviser Gerald Rafshoon and his speechwriters Hendrik Hertzberg and Christopher Matthews, and owed much of its philosophy and tone to Patrick Caddell.

The speech, delivered on July 15, contained new proposals on the energy crisis, including new limits on oil imports and the creation of an Energy Security Corporation to finance the development of alternative fuels. But Carter started with the unsettling proposition that "the true problems of our Nation are far deeper," and that they amounted to a "crisis of confidence" concerning "the meaning of our own lives" that was striking "at the very heart and soul and spirit of our national will." In framing his remarks around fundamental moral and spiritual issues—the country's soulless materialism; a growing disrespect for government, churches, and schools; the triumph of private self-interest over community—Carter was speaking from his own heart. But at times his bleak account of a nation adrift read almost exactly like Caddell's memos and speeches about the disorienting conditions that had sent Americans in search of new anti-politician leaders, supposedly epitomized by Carter.* And by sermonizing about those conditions, Carter appeared to be abdicating his role as leader and blaming the people themselves for their own afflictions. It was a form of anti-politics unlike any Americans had ever seen—the chief magistrate, who was supposed to inspire the nation and lift it out of its slough of despond, was instead complaining about unrelieved anguish and emptiness.

Early response to Carter's speech actually was favorable, as commentators expressed a slightly astonished admiration for his candor as well as his eloquence. Anything, in the short run, was better than nothing; and Carter's ratings in the polls immediately rose. But once the full purport of Carter's sermon sank in, it boomeranged on the White House. Editorialists and pundits began claiming that there was nothing wrong with the country that new, responsible leadership couldn't fix. Whatever political goodwill Carter gained disappeared completely when, two days after the speech, he announced that he had asked all his cabinet secretaries for letters of resignation and that he had accepted five of them, including those of Bell, Blumenthal, Califano, Schlesinger, and transportation secretary Brock Adams.. The president had not lost his mind, but he looked panicked. His positive job performance rating soon dropped, in one survey, to 23 percent—lower than when he had slipped away to Camp David.

In the summer of 1979, the administration seemed to have finally crashed and burned. Yet there was even worse to come for Carter and the country, also stemming from the Iranian revolution. There were cruel ironies in this. By stoking patriotic fervor, the debacle in Iran would help Carter stave off political challenges from his left, even as his inability to solve the mess whipped up the Republican right. And there was a deeper irony: during his first years in office, Carter's essentially moral outlook had paid off most in some of his foreign policy ventures, particularly in the Middle East.

---

* The speech quickly became known as Carter's "malaise" speech, even though that word did not appear in the text. It did appear, however, in one of Caddell's memorandums, as Caddell later informed reporters.

4

HUMAN RIGHTS AND DEMOCRATIC COLLAPSE

PRESIDENT CARTER CARRIED HIS southern progressive views into his conduct of foreign policy. During the campaign of 1976, this high-minded outlook helped him outflank Ford on the left and the right simultaneously, blaming the realists' secretive diplomacy for prolonging the disaster in Vietnam while complaining, much as conservatives complained, about Ford's and Kissinger's amorality in pursuit of détente. Once in power, Carter melded his positions into an updated Wilsonian internationalism, pledged to open diplomacy and a marriage of ethics and power. Some specific elements of Carter's foreign policies, notably his eagerness to help underdeveloped countries, stemmed from his experience with the Trilateral Commission. Others, especially in the area of arms control, presumed a continuation of détente in modified form. All converged in Carter's ideas about the primacy of human rights in world affairs.

Unfortunately, geopolitical realities did not always make the world a consistent place, let alone a safe one, for policies based on humane principles. Carter understood this well enough, even before he became president. He had studied the influential writings of the theologian Reinhold Niebuhr, and recognized that good resided with evil in all of humanity. The burden for world leaders, he thought, was to fight for justice in the face of that humbling knowledge. But the challenges to Carter's chastened idealism could be sharp and sometimes overwhelming once Richard Nixon's and Henry Kissinger's system of global alliances began to crumble.

On New Year's Eve, 1977, Shah Mohammad Reza Pahlavi honored the Carters, who had decided to visit Tehran for the holiday, with a luxurious state dinner. The shah's regime had become, during the Nixon years, a singularly valuable ally of the United States, the linchpin of American policy in the Persian Gulf—a reliable (if, after 1973, price-gouging) supplier of large oil shipments, a moderating political force in the Middle East, and a bulwark against the Soviet Union's designs there. In exchange, Nixon and Kissinger had increased the numbers of American military advisers in Iran and had permitted the shah to go on a spending spree, purchasing the latest U.S. military technology and hardware.

The shah's program of rapidly modernizing Iran, however, offended the country's Shiite Muslims and their autocratic fundamentalist clerics, whose dissident activities the shah squelched with a brutal secret police force, SAVAK. The repression, as well as the regime's ostentatious splendor, made bitter enemies of Iran's secular leftist and liberal intelligentsia, both inside the country and in exile. At once pro-Western, antitheocratic, and cruelly repressive, Iran presented difficult conundrums and choices for Carter's foreign policy. But Carter left no doubt about his priorities during that New Year's Eve in Tehran. Lifting his glass, he praised the shah's devotion to "the cause of human rights," and the stability that had earned him "the respect and the admiration and love" of the Iranian people—and the shah toasted the "special relationship" between Iran and the United States.

Two years later, the repercussions of Carter's toast would batter his presidency and help seal its doom. But Iran was only one example, albeit the most dramatic, of Carter's travails in world affairs. On a few critical matters—bringing the controversy over the Panama Canal to a successful, negotiated conclusion; signing a SALT II treaty; and coming as close as any president before or since to achieving an accord in the Middle East—Carter could rightly claim substantial, even spectacular success. Yet each of those efforts, along with Carter's failures in foreign policy, roused political reactions that further eroded his narrow centrist ground. And the tumult in Iran, coupled with mounting domestic troubles, led to one of the most miserable years in modern American history.

There was never much doubt, least of all in his own mind, that Carter would be the master of his administration's foreign policy. Lacking personal experience, he relied on the veteran Cyrus Vance, his secretary of state, to fill the role of chief diplomat. As head of the National Security Council,

Carter's friend Zbigniew Brzezinski of Columbia University and the Trilateral Commission offered incisive thinking about the shifting geopolitical situation. By appointing Andrew Young as ambassador to the United Nations, Carter broke new ground, symbolically and substantively, by naming the first black to the post and thereby announcing his intention to shift American policy vis-à-vis the third world. But Carter intended to stamp American foreign relations with his own sense of rectitude, even if it meant having to overcome stiff political opposition at home. He would enjoy his earliest success by dealing deftly with the outstanding issue of American sovereignty over the Panama Canal. His exertions elsewhere in Central America and in Africa were less fortunate.

Carter picked up the controversy regarding the canal where Gerald Ford and Ronald Reagan had left it during the primaries in 1976. Military experts agreed with political moderates, liberals, and some conservatives (among them Barry Goldwater) that the existing pact for the Canal Zone dating back to 1903, needed to be scrapped. The American military presence in Panama deeply offended not just the Panamanians but Central Americans generally, as an enduring emblem of Yankee imperialism. The canal—about fifty-five miles long and lined by thick jungle—was highly vulnerable to sabotage. Continued American control was an open invitation to terrorist mischief that could easily escalate into a major and potentially disastrous American military intervention. Although the canal remained a significant thoroughfare, its military as well as commercial significance had dwindled sharply since World War II. Not only would a new treaty be a Wilsonian bow to national self-determination, it would also rid the U.S. military of an albatross. When Carter decided to pursue the matter, he had the backing not just of Ford, Kissinger, and various Republican moderates in Congress but also of the Joint Chiefs of Staff.

On September 7, 1977, Carter and Panama's leftist strongman leader Omar Torrijos signed two treaties: the first guaranteeing the canal's permanent neutrality and availability to ships of all nations; the second securing a reduced American military presence until 2000, when sovereignty over the canal would pass to the Panamanians. Immediately, the Republican right, led by Strom Thurmond and Jesse Helms, united to block ratification by the Senate. Carter, they cried, was trying to surrender a vital American asset to a Marxist dictator. Under the proposed neutrality agreement, there would be no way to stop the Soviet Union's ships from using the canal, even in time of war. (The critics did not seem to notice that, in the direst circumstances, American naval forces could easily prevent any hostile ships from entering or leaving the canal.) In any case, the Canal Zone was as much a part of the United States as Puerto Rico or Guam—or, for that matter, Thurmond fancifully declared, Florida or Texas. To abandon one inch of American territory—let alone an essential territory such as the Panama Canal—would be further proof, the critics charged, that America was beating a full-scale retreat from the communist menace.

The new right mobilized—Thurmond headed the American Conservative Union's Task Force to Defeat Ratification—but the administration at last prevailed narrowly in April 1978. For Carter, the triumph was sweet. By pushing hard publicly as well as behind the scenes, he managed to move public opinion for the first time ever (albeit by a small margin) in favor of granting control of the canal to Panama. Whereas previous presidents going back to Lyndon B. Johnson had failed with regard to the Panama Canal, he had not.

Yet there was less to the victory than Carter and his supporters wanted to admit. Many senators who fully understood the rationale of the new treaties were frightened of a backlash from their constituents, and in the final tally, both treaties scraped through the Senate by a single vote. (The wary senators' fears would in time prove justified: twenty of those who voted in favor were defeated for reelection either in 1978 or in 1980.) Above all, Carter had won, barely, but at great cost—and only with the outspoken support of Republican moderates and Kissingerian realists against the Republican right. That support was not forthcoming on other foreign policy issues.

In Nicaragua near the Canal Zone, a long-standing anticommunist autocracy—allied to the United States—was in deep trouble. Since 1937, the Somoza family had ruled the country. The current leader, Anastasio Somoza Debayle, had been elected president shortly after his brother Luis died in 1967. Then, just as his term was due to end in 1972, Anastasio maneuvered to retain effective control as head of the national guard. A devastating earthquake struck Managua in 1972, killing 10,000 people and destroying the city. The catastrophe allowed Somoza to retain all power, and in 1974 he was reelected president. But popular opposition to the regime also mounted in the aftermath of the earthquake. The country's Roman Catholic clergy began openly criticizing the regime; human rights groups complained of systematic abuses by Somoza's national guard; and support grew for the leftist Sandinista Front (named for a rebel leader of the 1920s and 1930s, Augusto César Sandino), which had been fighting a nasty guerrilla war against the Somozas since 1963.

In early 1979, his regime tottering, Somoza refused to hold new elections supervised by the Organization of American States (OAS), and Carter imposed U.S. sanctions on Nicaragua. This strong show of American displeasure greatly encouraged the anti-Somoza forces, including the Sandinistas, who undertook what they called their final military offensive—and this put the White House in difficult straits. Somoza's bloody rule had cost him considerable support in Washington, but the dictator still had his backers, including Kissinger and a solid phalanx in Congress. And although Carter would have no truck with Somoza, he and his aides were troubled by reports about the Sandinistas' not very covert political and military ties to Cuba.

Searching for a middle path, Carter sent Vance to the OAS with a proposal that it should send a peacekeeping force to supervise the formation of a new government, thereby staving off an outright victory by the Sandinistas. The Sandinistas' rejection of the plan surprised few outside the White House; and in July, the rebels forced Somoza to flee the country and then installed their own junta. Lacking any control over the situation, Carter tried to cooperate with the new government by sending emergency food and medical supplies and asking Congress for $75 million in economic aid. But the Sandinista radicals soon pushed the revolution farther leftward by receiving military aid from Cuba and voicing solidarity with other leftist guerrillas in the region—thereby deepening concern in the White House. Left-wing liberals on Capitol Hill, still resentful of America's past support for Somoza, deplored Carter's initial efforts to forestall the Sandinistas' victory as arrogant tampering, and they remained suspicious of the administration's intentions. Somoza's many American supporters, meanwhile, were furious at the administration's abandonment of an old ally. The idealist Jimmy Carter was left stranded, a hapless man in the middle.

Carter reoriented American policy more forcefully and dramatically in Africa than in Central America, chiefly to support black self-determination. In 1978, he took a historic journey to Nigeria and Liberia, the first state visit by an American president to sub-Saharan Africa. With substantive as well as emblematic measures, he also made clear his belief that racism and the political subordination of blacks—rather than communism—were the chief threats to American interests in Africa. One especially critical hot spot was Rhodesia. In 1977, Carter persuaded Congress to reimpose a ban on buying Rhodesian chrome, which the lawmakers had lifted in 1971 even though white supremacists under Prime Minister Ian Smith remained in charge of the government. The following year, Secretary of State Vance met unsuccessfully with the leaders of the black oppositional Patriotic Front

(PF). The rebels, with military assistance from Cuba, had been fighting a guerrilla war since 1972, and Vance hoped to broker a compromise that would lead to a peaceful transition to black majority rule. Smith then announced an "internal settlement," in which black moderates would join the government while he remained prime minister. The PF ignored the arrangement and continued its armed attacks.

Vance thought Smith's reforms were merely a gambit to preserve white minority rule. Carter, however, agreed with Brzezinski that the new arrangement offered a decent chance for blacks less radical and violent than the PF's leaders, Robert Mugabe and Joshua Nkomo, eventually to take the reins and extinguish white supremacy. Although he resisted conservatives' demands to remove the U.S. economic sanctions, Carter ordered Ambassador Andrew Young to abstain on a UN resolution condemning Smith's "internal settlement"—thereby, once again, angering congressional liberals and black leaders without mollifying conservatives, led in this instance by Jesse Helms. In April 1979, the White House moved closer to the liberals by refusing to honor an allegedly rigged election that had selected the moderate Bishop Abel L. Muzorewa as the country's first black prime minister. Finally, in September, the British government ironed out an agreement between Muzorewa and the PF, authorizing a cease-fire and a new constitution, and scheduling new general elections. Three months later, Carter lifted the sanctions. He had reached his original goal, but mainly through the ministrations of others—and at the cost of further straining his relations on both sides of the aisle in Congress.

Elsewhere, superpower politics overwhelmed Carter's policies in Africa. The apartheid government in South Africa, long considered an essential ally of the United States in the cold war, was one of the administration's original targets. In 1977, Vice President Mondale confronted Prime Minister B. J. Vorster and demanded cooperation in the still roiling mess in Rhodesia, along with action by South Africa to hasten majority rule both in neighboring Namibia and in South Africa itself. Yet the administration, faced with a regime far more formidable than Ian Smith's in Rhodesia, pushed for only moderate reforms, despite its strong rhetoric. Careless, controversial statements by Andrew Young about, among other things, South Africa's racist supporters in America, forced Carter to replace him in 1979—another setback. Continued military involvement by the Soviet Union and Cuba in the newly liberated former Portuguese colony of Angola prevented formal American recognition of the Angolan government, and prompted Carter to seek congressional support for the Angolan rebel army, UNITA, which was headed by Jonas Savimbi and backed by South Africa.

Despite Carter's good intentions, and despite his close victory in the fight over the Panama Canal, continuing cold war tensions and rivalries played havoc with his human rights policies in the underdeveloped world. And Carter's direct dealings with the Soviet Union did little to ease those tensions and rivalries. Carter had fleeting success with the Russians over arms control, reviving the main lines of détente, even as his appeals for human rights helped set principles that would in time undermine the Soviet empire. But American-Soviet relations soured badly in the late 1970s. By 1980, it appeared as if the United States, more than ever, was on the defensive.

In 1977, Leonid Brezhnev, just past his seventieth birthday, ruled over a stagnating, hollowed-out, repressive superpower. A member of the first generation of Soviet leaders who had no adult memories of prerevolutionary Russia, Brezhnev had risen through the Communist Party hierarchy under Stalin. Even though he backed his mentor Nikita Khrushchev's "de-Stalinization" program after 1956, his Stalinist predispositions quickly showed through after he helped overthrow Khrushchev in 1964.* The trials of the dissident writers Yuri Daniel and Andrei Sinyavsky in 1966 marked a return to cultural repression. Although Brezhnev would not repeat the purges of the 1930s, he did restore to the state police, the KGB, much of the power it had wielded in Stalin's time. In his orchestration of the invasion of Czechoslovakia in 1968 by the Warsaw Pact Nations, Brezhnev brutally enforced the Kremlin's absolute rule over its satellites and also gave the policy a name—the Brezhnev Doctrine. Yet by expending so much of the national treasure on the military and on related, high-profile programs such as space exploration, he left the Soviet Union's hamstrung command economy to deteriorate. His command brought with it chronic food shortages (and dependence on foreign grain), drastic declines in health services and public housing, and the rise of an official, corrupt "informal" economy trading scarce consumer goods and services on the black market.

The aging, vain Soviet leader—in time, he would award himself more than 100 medals for his heroic patriotism—seemed to exemplify his country's

---

* The coup installed Aleksey Kosygin as prime minister beside Brezhnev as first party secretary, but Brezhnev had the upper hand. In April 1966, he changed his designation to general secretary, the same title Stalin had held.

sclerosis. He was nearly deaf; his heart was kept beating by a pacemaker; and his stiff movements and rheumy eyes led to persistent rumors that he was heavily medicated. (He was also rumored to be less than brilliant: one of the milder jokes making the rounds in Moscow claimed that the reason the general secretary gave speeches lasting six hours was that he read both the original text and the carbon copy.) Yet Brezhnev had the advantage that the Americans had been disgraced by Watergate and defeated in Vietnam; and by pushing proxy wars in Africa and continuing his military buildup, he gave some analysts the impression that the Soviet Union was actually on the verge of winning the cold war.

Jimmy Carter's appeals for human rights would have rung hollow, especially in the United States, had he failed to criticize the Soviet Union. The extent to which Carter actually intended this criticism merely to placate American conservatives—and gain what Jody Powell called, in one memo, sufficient "domestic flexibility . . . to make progress in other areas"—remains unclear. But if that, and not moral consistency, was the White House's main intention, the results were disappointing. Barely a week after Carter took office, the State Department issued official statements condemning Czechoslovakia for cracking down on dissenters in violation of the Helsinki accords, and warning the Kremlin against making any attempt to intimidate the dissident Soviet physicist Andrey Sakharov, described in the statement as "an outspoken champion of human rights." Any "flexibility" Carter gained at home from these moves was invisible to the naked eye, but they infuriated Brezhnev, who had his ambassador to the United States lodge an official protest about interference in the internal affairs of the Soviet Union. Brezhnev then ordered the arrest of more dissidents, including Yuri Orlov of the Moscow group monitoring the Kremlin's compliance with the Helsinki agreements.

It would take many years before the bracing effects of supportive appeals like Carter's became evident among dissidents in the Soviet bloc, and by then Carter would receive little of the credit he deserved for undermining communism. At the time, the president seemed to be sending the Soviet Union a mixed message: on the one hand, the new administration had rejected Kissinger's realpolitik and would hold the Soviet Union responsible for human rights; on the other, it would pursue Kissinger's détente and press for an agreement on SALT II. The confusion grew when Cyrus Vance made his first trip to Moscow and publicly proposed actual reductions in the nuclear arsenals on both sides, as opposed to the ceilings agreed to at the meetings in Vladivostok. Brezhnev erupted, in part because he thought the cutbacks proposed were one-sided, and in part because of Vance's (and Carter's) preference for open diplomacy. Brezhnev concluded that the arms proposals, combined with Carter's remarks about the dissidents, were really a brazen attempt to embarrass the Soviet Union and its general secretary before the entire world.

The Soviets were still interested in following up on the Vladivostok agreements and securing a SALT II pact, just as the Americans wanted to relax the tension caused by Vance's initial proposals (and soothe the alarm of their West European allies). In May, the two sides reconvened in Geneva, and worked out the broad outlines for SALT II, including an agreement by the Americans to limit development of their cruise missiles in exchange for a similar concession by the Soviet Union regarding its so-called backfire bombers (which the Americans claimed could be modified to attack the United States). Carter, for his part, also ordered a halt to developing the expensive B-1 bomber, which was supposed to be the successor to the nation's aging B-52s but which many strategists, including Carter's secretary of defense, Harold Brown, thought had been rendered obsolete by advanced missile technology. Still, numerous important differences remained to be ironed out before any new SALT pact could be signed. And although Carter softened his tone, and spoke publicly about the imperative of calm cooperation between the superpowers, he did not completely cease remarking on the Soviet Union's restrictions of free speech and free emigration.

Over the next eighteen months, Vance and his Soviet counterpart, Andrey Gromyko, made fitful progress in the SALT negotiations. At one point, in late December 1977, there was speculation about an impending summit meeting between Carter and Brezhnev. But on other fronts, the gaps in Soviet-American relations were widening. In 1977, Brezhnev began deploying, behind the iron curtain, advanced SS-20 ballistic missiles, capable of hitting any target inside Western Europe. Cuban troops, acting as proxies for the Russians, stepped up their involvement in Angola, as well as their support of Ethiopia in its continuing war with its neighbor, Eritrea.

Carter became increasingly enamored of the view of his national security adviser, Brzezinski, that world politics was based on the conflict between American democracy and Soviet communism. Brzezinski, gaining greater influence than Vance with the president, pushed Carter to take an even firmer line by linking any SALT II agreement to cessation by the Soviet Union of its military adventures in Africa. Carter balked at this but was open to the idea of making a diplomatic approach to China, then on the brink of war with the Soviet Union over a border dispute, in order to exert pressure on the latter.

In May 1978, Brzezinski flew to Beijing and met with Chinese officials. Yet instead of relenting, the Soviets became even more outraged, especially when they received the news that Brzezinski had made insulting remarks about the "international marauders" who were fighting in Africa on behalf of "the polar bear to the north." The State Department recoiled in horror at Brzezinski's tactlessness; yet Carter stood by his new commitment to normalize diplomatic relations with the People's Republic of China before the year was out. The president also toughened his rhetoric with the Soviet Union, still supporting détente and arms limitation but also accusing the Kremlin of aggression and declaring that the United States was fully prepared for the worst should Brezhnev choose confrontation over cooperation.

The United States' overtures to China plunged Soviet-American relations into a deep freeze—and made Carter look more uncertain than ever. In January 1979, Deng Xiaoping, having outmaneuvered Maoist hardliners inside his own government, emerged as Mao's de facto successor and paid an official visit in the United States. He was ostensibly celebrating America's formal recognition of the People's Republic, but he also was permitted to attack Moscow, further endangering the SALT negotiations. Americans, since Nixon, had talked of playing China off against the Soviets—but now it looked as if the Chinese were using the Americans to gain the advantage in the widening Sino-Soviet conflict. Yet the SALT negotiators persevered, and in months of secret talks, Vance and the Soviet Union's ambassador to the United States, Anatoly Dobrynin, worked out the final details concerning verification and the size of missiles to be capped under the agreement. On June 19, 1979, Brezhnev and Carter at last held their summit, in Vienna, and signed a second SALT treaty limiting the manufacture and deployment of strategic missiles.

American voters supported the SALT agreement by a margin of two to one, and a substantial majority approved of recognizing the People's Republic of China—and so Carter appeared to have regained some of the ground he had lost in superpower politics. But arms limitation, though at the core of Carter's foreign policy from the start, was just one element in the complex, continuing cold war. During the same month that he signed the new SALT treaty, Carter, feeling obliged to toughen the American posture, approved full development of an MX missile system, which would permit the shuffling of American intercontinental ballistic weapons around the country on an underground rail system. Six months later, the White House was on an even more militant footing in response to startling events in Iran, and the Americans joined with NATO in declaring that unless the Soviet Union removed its nuclear weapons from Eastern Europe, the West would deploy powerful new Pershing II missiles as well as cruise missiles, aimed at strategic Soviet sites. Soon after, Soviet-American relations virtually collapsed when the Soviet Union announced a military invasion of Afghanistan to prop up an unpopular pro-Soviet government in Kabul.

The motivations and intrigues behind the Soviet Union's entry into Afghanistan were always unclear, and in recent years they have become even murkier. Some American analysts offered the straightforward judgment that the Kremlin was coming to the aid of a political ally, under the terms of the Brezhnev Doctrine. Others feared that the Soviet Union had larger ambitions on gaining control of the Persian Gulf. Secretly, though, the Carter administration had issued directives in June, long before the invasion, for the CIA to engage in clandestine propaganda operations against the Marxist regime in Kabul. Nearly two decades later, Brzezinski would claim that those efforts were part of a trap intended to lure the Soviets into a costly, perhaps disastrous military quagmire—"the opportunity," he wrote to Carter when the invasion began, "of giving to the USSR its Vietnam War." This boast, if true, would make the Carter administration the brilliant covert instigator of a war that would indeed help dig the Soviet Union's grave.

At the time, however, the overwhelming impression in Washington was that the invasion was a major and alarming escalation of Soviet militarism—a sign of the Kremlin's growing strength and ambition. After the cold war ended, it would become clear that these views ignored how the deterioration of social and economic conditions under Brezhnev was leading to a crisis that would hasten collapse of the Soviet Union. Debates would rage over whether American intelligence had reported this decline accurately or had sustained the myth of Russian might. But in 1979, the conventional political wisdom was that the invasion of Afghanistan, far from a sign of desperation, heightened the Soviet Union's direct threat to American national security.

Carter seemed caught completely by surprise by the invasion and acted more hawkish than ever—and his popularity ratings soared. Yet his responses to the invasion also seemed reactive and only marginally effective. He withdrew the SALT treaty from consideration for ratification by the Senate, thereby undercutting one of his administration's few hard-won achievements in foreign policy. He imposed a boycott of American grain to the Soviet Union, which would most directly harm ordinary Russians and American grain producers and suppliers. He announced the Carter Doctrine, whereby the United States would use armed force in order to protect the Persian Gulf from outside interference; he called for a resumption of registration for the draft for men eighteen and older; and he canceled U.S. participation in the upcoming Olympic Games, scheduled to be held in Moscow in 1980. But all of this amounted mainly to saber-rattling or mere symbolism. At home, Carter's newfound bellicosity further alienated liberal Democrats, some of whom thought the SALT II treaty too timid in its arms reductions, and who were already lining up behind Edward Kennedy to challenge the president for the nomination. Among conservatives and neoconservatives, Carter's foreign policy, no matter how hawkish, would always pale beside the robust cold war militancy proclaimed by Ronald Reagan and the Republican right.

The only solid achievements Carter could point to in international affairs, apart from the Panama Canal treaties, stemmed from his handling of the violently fractious Middle East. Yet even here, Carter's persistence would have not paid off but for the imagination and courage of other world leaders, especially Anwar Sadat of Egypt. And after the autumn of 1979, his successes in the Middle East would be overshadowed by events in Iran.

Although the president's advisers warned him not to invest too much of his time in the thickets of Middle Eastern politics and diplomacy, Carter, the relentless overachiever, ignored them. Convinced that Kissinger's shuttle diplomacy could never produce a comprehensive regional settlement, Carter dispatched Vance to the Middle East in February 1977 to start laying the groundwork for a reconvening of the Geneva conference that, though largely failed, had produced the Sinai Agreement of 1975 binding Egypt and Israel to settle their differences peacefully. But the obstacles to any new conference were formidable. Would moderate Arab leaders resist the pressure of Muslim radicals to forgo the peace process and prepare for another war against Israel? More important, would the Israelis permit any representation of the Palestine Liberation Organization (PLO), Yasir Arafat's armed group inside Israeli-occupied Palestine, which denied Israel's right to exist?

For more than a year, Carter's efforts failed. The Israeli prime minister, Yitzhak Rabin, who at first had suggested a possible compromise over setting Israel's borders, informed Washington that under no circumstances would his government parlay in Geneva with the PLO; or withdraw completely from the Golan Heights or the West Bank; or permit the creation, on the West Bank, of an independent Palestinian state. Carter, whose disappointment with the Israelis prompted some miffed public statements, continued to meet in Washington with Arab leaders, including the anti-Israel hard-liner Hafez al-Assad of Syria, which further enraged both the Israelis and American Jewish leaders. On May 23, in part out of concern that Carter was proving unsupportive, Israeli voters handed power to the uncompromising Likud Party and its head, the new prime minister, Menachem Begin. Begin traveled to Washington in July to meet Carter—and made it emphatically clear that he would neither budge over the PLO and Palestinian independence nor halt the construction of new Israeli settlements in the occupied territories. Indeed, as soon as he returned to Jerusalem, Begin unveiled plans for numerous new settlements on the West Bank.

Only two glimmers of hope appeared in all of Carter's and Vance's negotiating over the Middle East. When meeting with the Egyptian president, Anwar al-Sadat, Carter achieved nothing substantial, but found Sadat friendly and approachable. And although Begin was tough, he was not the belligerent hard-liner Carter had expected. In his own way, Begin could be charming. In his sessions with Carter, he expressed a desire to find some way to reassemble the Geneva conference, and said that he was willing to negotiate the withdrawal of Israeli troops from occupied lands in exchange for the Arabs' recognition of Israel. Sensing some slight flexibility, Carter denounced Begin's decision to build new settlements, but pressed forward in seeking a new meeting in Geneva. His hopes rose in September, when the Israeli foreign minister, Moshe Dayan, informed him and Vance that Israel would delay commencing construction of the settlements for a year, that it was eager to get on with the Geneva plan, and that it might even accept the Palestinians' participation as part of a pan-Arab delegation.

A clumsy effort at fashioning a joint U.S.-Soviet appeal to resume negotiations over the Middle East scuttled the Geneva conference, but at least there had been movement. Carter asked his new friend Sadat for assistance; Sadat replied with a proposal for a different conference, in East Jerusalem, involving the permanent members of the United Nations as well as the interested parties in the Middle East. Carter thought the idea was hopeless, but Sadat proceeded anyway, let Begin know that he wanted a meeting, and then accepted Begin's invitation to Jerusalem. Sadat's three-day state visit, highlighted by his eloquent, emotional address to the Israeli Knesset, was a triumph, suggesting to the world that the impossible might yet be attainable in the Middle East.

As Carter and Vance had feared, the other Arab states, including moderate governments in Morocco and the Sudan, furiously turned their backs on Sadat, but he replied that he would go it alone if necessary. Unfortunately for him, the outstanding differences between Egypt and Israel remained enormous, especially regarding Palestine and the permanent withdrawal from the occupied territories. Efforts by the United States to keep the peace initiative going led to mutual recrimination between Washington and Jerusalem. The situation deteriorated badly in March 1978, when a terrorist raid by the PLO near Haifa killed thirty-five civilians and wounded seventy-one. This raid prompted Israel to invade the PLO's strongholds in southern Lebanon; the invasion resulted in more than 1,000 deaths and left 100,000 people homeless. Official negotiations were at a standstill. A secret meeting in Vienna—approved by Begin and involving Sadat; the Israeli defense minister, Ezer Weizman; and Shimon Peres, head of the opposition Israeli Labor Party—backfired when the Israeli cabinet censured Weizman and Peres for exceeding their authority. Sadat retaliated by expelling a small Israeli military mission established in Cairo months earlier.

Carter finally decided that the United States, rather than serve as a mere go-between, had to take a more active role in brokering any kind of agreement, and he invited Begin and Sadat to a summit meeting at Camp David, to last as long as it took for them to work out a settlement. It was an extraordinary proposal for two heads of state to bargain without any prearranged agreements worked out at lower levels. It was especially risky for Sadat, who had become a pariah among the so-called rejectionist Arab states and could not afford to leave Camp David empty-handed. The many months of squabbling had also sapped the spirit of amity that had prevailed during Sadat's trip to Israel. After ten days of meeting separately, each man one-on-one with Carter, the two principals had made no progress. Sadat announced that he was packing his bags, and he relented only after Carter beseeched him to continue the negotiations.

After surviving this near collapse, the meetings progressed with astonishing quickness. On September 18, Carter was able to announce that a consensus had been reached on the basic terms of a new treaty. Israel agreed to withdraw its troops from the Sinai Peninsula and return the area to Egypt, as well as to limit its forces on the Egyptian border; Egypt agreed to restrict its own forces in the Sinai and to establish normal diplomatic relations with Israel. Guarantees were also exchanged for free passage along the Suez Canal and nearby waterways, and between Egypt and Jordan. On the West Bank and the Gaza Strip, the parties could agree to no more than a proposed framework for later negotiations. A final statement offered "associated principles" that should henceforth govern relations between Israel and all the Arab states.

It was a fragile set of accords, which evaded the crucial issues of the Palestinians' autonomy and the Israelis' withdrawal from the remaining occupied territories. Continued wrangling between Israel and Egypt, as well as within these countries, nearly doomed the agreements in December, especially with regard to differing interpretations of the ambiguous framework for negotiations over Palestine. Carter himself had to intervene by visiting Begin and Sadat in March 1979, when he resolved the last outstanding issues. The future of the treaty remained shaky, especially since the reactions to it from Sadat's Arab neighbors ranged from angry hostility to sullen silence. But with the SALT II talks proceeding well, Carter could take pride as well as relief in what he had accomplished, both at Camp David and in his follow-up negotiations. When his plane from Cairo landed at Andrews Air Force Base, a crowd of thousands of invited spectators, who had stood waiting late into the night, cheered him as a gallant peacemaker. On March 26, Carter, Begin, and Sadat smiled and embraced at the treaty-signing ceremony on the White House lawn—the happiest scene in Carter's presidency since his stroll down Pennsylvania Avenue on Inauguration Day two years earlier.

For Carter, the joy was short-lived. Two days later, a serious accident occurred at the Three Mile Island nuclear reactor in Pennsylvania, raising grave questions about promoting atomic energy as an alternative to imported oil. In May, the Gallup poll reported that Democrats preferred Edward Kennedy, the prospective challenger for their party's nomination, over Carter by a margin of 54 percent to 31 percent. In July, Camp David became the site of the prolonged retreat that led to Carter's unfortunate "crisis of confidence" speech. Less than two months after that, on September 8, antigovernment protesters, some chanting "Death to the shah," filled Tehran's Jaleh Square in defiance of a new government ban on public demonstrations. The shah's troops opened fire, killing more than 700, and the Iranian revolution had begun.

The United States' debacle in Iran originated in the collapse of an important piece in Nixon's and Kissinger's global realpolitik. In order to fortify the shah as a check on the Soviet Union in the Middle East, Nixon and Kissinger had turned a blind eye to his repression and tolerated Iran's role as prime instigator of the early price hikes by OPEC in 1973. Dangerous dynamics developed: to pay for the costs of sustaining his authoritarian rule and purchasing an arsenal of American military supplies, the shah needed additional oil revenues, which he and the other heads of oil-producing states extorted from American consumers. As popular opposition inside Iran grew, these dynamics produced furies that could not be contained after Nixon and Kissinger were gone. Carter, concerned chiefly with forging peace between Israel and Egypt, and receiving conflicting advice on Iran, did not fully grasp, until much too late, the depth of popular support for Ayatollah Khomeini.

The shah's departure in January, and Khomeini's triumphant return a few days later from exile in Paris, forced Carter and his advisers to contemplate seriously what would become of the Iranian government. Some officials and commentators in Washington took the shah's view that Khomeini was a reactionary fundamentalist who would settle for nothing less than the establishment of a Shiite theocracy. Others were not so sure. At the very least, the new government would be adamantly anticommunist. And Khomeini had gathered around him secular democrats, including Mehdi Bazargan, who was the leader of the moderate Iranian Liberation Movement, and Abolhassan Bani Sadr, who had accompanied the ayatollah from Paris. There was good reason, the optimists argued, to think that Khomeini and the other religious leaders, having finally overthrown the shah, would step back from the political front lines. Khomeini had signaled as much when, soon after his return, he announced that Bazargan would be the new prime minister, and that all government posts would be placed in secular hands. Were Washington to work in good faith with the Iranian moderates, some analysts believed, the new regime might even evolve into that ever-elusive third force in cold war politics: a government neither pro-Western and repressive nor pro-communist.

Carter took the hopeful view and sustained more or less normal relations with the new government, not realizing that he was playing directly into Khomeini's hands. The ayatollah indeed intended to establish a Shiite theocracy, but he had needed to ally himself with the secular moderates in order to overthrow the shah and then launch a new government. In time, the moderates would prove expendable, and Khomeini would rid himself of them. Carter, by maintaining official contacts with the new government, handed the ayatollah a pretext for doing so by attacking the moderates as collaborationists of the "great Satan," America.

A perfect opportunity presented itself to Khomeini in November, and he seized it. Since leaving his throne, the shah had taken up residence, successively, in Egypt, Morocco, the Bahamas, and Mexico. After initially inviting him to stay in the United States, Carter now refused to admit him, fearing anti-American repercussions in Iran. In early autumn, however, the shah's health began to deteriorate, because of what was eventually diagnosed as malignant lymphoma. Henry Kissinger and David Rockefeller, with Brzezinski's support, pleaded with the White House to admit the shah temporarily, so that he could receive the best possible emergency treatment in New York. Over Vance's objections, Carter relented. After informing Iranian officials of his decision, the White House received reassuring word that Tehran had reacted with "moderation." Even when the shah's stay had to be prolonged by several weeks to allow him to recover from surgery, Bazargan's government seemed to have the situation in hand. "There were objections in Iran," Carter later recalled, "but no reason for alarm about the safety of Americans there."

Suddenly, on November 4, about 3,000 militants, claiming to be students acting in Khomeini's name, overran the American embassy in Tehran, took fifty-four Americans hostage, and issued three demands: that Washington immediately hand over the shah to face charges before a revolutionary tribunal, that the Americans give back the immense stashes of wealth that the shah had supposedly hidden in the United States, and that the Carter administration issue a formal apology. The affair seemed amateurish, led by red-hot fundamentalists who had no clear plan but seemed to be improvising as they went along. Khomeini—who appeared to have known nothing about the attack in advance—thoroughly exploited the situation and turned it into a shattering international crisis.

Prime Minister Bazargan, aghast at the takeover, immediately ordered the militants to release the hostages and depart from the embassy. Khomeini, however, refused to support Bazargan's order, praised the militants, and instructed them to stand their ground. Outmaneuvered and disgusted, Bazargan resigned, removing one of the leading moderates from the revolutionary leadership. The hostage takers, emboldened by the rapturous commendations from Khomeini and, in time, from other Muslim extremists, began digging in for the long haul. On November 6, forty-eight hours after the takeover, a shaken Carter, as if living in a nightmare, presided over the first meetings to plan a rescue operation, making clear from the start that he would never accede to the militants' demands. He also ordered a freeze on all Iranian assets inside the United States, halted all imports of Iranian oil, and expelled all Iranian students who lacked proper U.S. visas.

Three days after the attack on the embassy, Senator Edward Kennedy, with monumental if unintended mistiming, went through with the scheduled formal announcement, in Boston, of his presidential candidacy. Rumors that Kennedy would challenge Carter had been circulating for a long time, going back at least as far as the breach over national health insurance in 1978. In September 1978, Hubert Harris of the Office of Management and Budget reported back to the chief of staff, Hamilton Jordan, about suspicious meetings of Kennedy and his supporters in Boston, offering few specifics but concluding: "They are clearly *planning*." Kennedy actually decided to run during the summer of 1979 (and informed Carter of his decision in late September), but delayed launching his campaign officially until he could gather his ramshackle network of supporters into the semblance of a national organization. Now, at last, Kennedy's candidacy would become a vehicle for Democratic liberals infuriated for years by what they considered Carter's apostasy—but it would do so under the shadow of the hostage crisis in Iran.

Kennedy's effort carried heavy symbolic and emotional freight. His name had first circulated as a possible Democratic nominee in 1968, after the assassination of his brother Robert, when, still grieving, he declined to cooperate with an ad hoc "draft Kennedy" movement at the convention in Chicago. The notorious car accident and consequent drowning of Mary Jo Kopechne at Chappaquiddick a year later—when Kennedy's behavior was, at best, irresponsible—squelched any talk of his running in 1972. But Kennedy's steady service in the Senate in the 1970s (despite continued reports of drunkenness and womanizing) had regained him considerable respect and standing. Announcing his candidacy at Faneuil Hall, surrounded by his family (including his sister-in-law Jacqueline Kennedy Onassis), the survivor was picking up the torch at last. Most of the campaign's advisers were veterans of John Kennedy's administration or of Robert Kennedy's campaign for the presidency in 1968, or of both; others were family friends and loyalists. Kennedy's election would not simply vindicate liberalism but restore a star-crossed political clan.

Through the summer of 1979, the polls had showed Kennedy as the odds-on favorite. (Carter, in a strained, testy moment, remarked contemptuously to a small group of congressmen that if Kennedy ran, "I'll whip his ass!" The comment only made the president sound petty.) The polls still looked promising for Kennedy in November, but there were reasons for qualms. Despite all his skills as a liberal on Capitol Hill and despite his enormous personal magnetism compared with Carter's, Kennedy lacked the articulate deftness of his brothers. Nor did it seem clear that, a dozen years after 1968, Kennedy and his staff had any clear idea how to solve the nation's problems, or that Kennedy even had any compelling reason to run apart from his disdain for Carter. Without due preparation, Kennedy could appear unfocused and tentative: blindsided by CBS's reporter Roger Mudd in an interview broadcast nationwide two days before the official announcement, Kennedy stammered when asked about his troubled marriage, then hemmed and hawed about why he was seeking the presidency and never delivered a convincing answer. And although the voters of Massachusetts appeared to have forgiven him for Chappaquiddick, it remained uncertain if a national campaign could withstand the inevitable resurrection of the story.

The taking of the hostages in Tehran, at precisely the moment he had planned to start his campaign, badly damaged Kennedy's chances. Kennedy did not help his own situation when, in response to reporters' questions, he denounced the shah and criticized Carter for admitting him to the country—remarks that, with Americans being held hostage in Tehran, sounded nearly unpatriotic. But from the very beginning of the crisis Carter and his aides understood the dire political implications for Kennedy (now referred to disdainfully inside the White House as "our friend from Massachusetts"). By stoking patriotic feeling, the televised scenes from Tehran had immediately led the public to rally around their beleaguered president. Simply by acting presidential in a time of great urgency, Carter could fend off any challenge from within his own party. Carter's increasingly hawkish, all-American stance following the Soviet Union's invasion of Afghanistan in December made Kennedy's run even more problematic, reinforcing the challenger's liberal base but raising fresh questions with the rest of the voters about his wisdom and even his loyalty.

Two months after the invasion of the embassy in Tehran, Carter's popularity rating had jumped faster than that of any other president in the history of the Gallup poll, exceeding even Franklin D. Roosevelt's just after Pearl Harbor. In the earliest of the important caucuses and primaries of 1980, held in Iowa, New Hampshire, Florida, and Illinois, Carter defeated Kennedy handily. That might have been enough to persuade most challengers to quit. Even Kennedy's vaunted money machine became clogged after his early defeats in the primaries. But Kennedy and his supporters believed that the fate of the Democratic Party was at stake, and that it was imperative to fight to the finish. Oddly, the more his challenge seemed likely to fail, the stronger Kennedy became on the stump, berating Carter as a failed president who had abandoned liberal ideals. Events at home as well as in Iran soon rewarded the Kennedy forces' tenacity.

After taking his first retaliatory steps against Iran, Carter had set Vance to work on laying out possible options for opening serious negotiations with the militants inside the embassy, while he conferred with Brzezinski about plans for a rescue mission. But as the crisis dragged on, the press seemed to focus on it almost exclusively, and as a mounting disgrace. (The ABC television network began following its regular evening news reports with nightly supplements, bearing the dispiriting title "America Held Hostage.") The news that did get reported apart from the crisis was just as bad. By early spring, the Federal Reserve Board had raised its prime interest rate to 18.5 percent; the rate of inflation, increased by the cutoff of Iranian oil and further OPEC price hikes, had reached around 20 percent; leading economic indicators, including new housing starts, were sinking; and the stock market, after a rally following Carter's announcement of new defense spending after the invasion of Afghanistan, suffered a steep decline.

Carter now seemed to be floundering once more. His announcement, on March 14, of a new anti-inflation plan that would slash $13 billion in federal spending, much of it on programs for the needy, privately infuriated even Vice President Mondale, and gave Kennedy's candidacy a shot in the arm. An electoral wild card appeared when a moderate Republican congressman from Illinois, John Anderson, reacting to the rightward march of his party, began mentioning the possibility of a third-party candidacy in the fall that would crowd Carter in the political center. Then, in a diplomatic blunder, the United States voted in favor of a UN resolution calling on Israel to dismantle all its settlements in the occupied territories, including Jerusalem. Carter, who thought, incorrectly, that Jerusalem had been excluded from the resolution, managed, through a technicality, to get a swift revote, on which the United States abstained, but it was too little, too late. Three weeks later, in the New York Democratic primary (where the Jewish liberal vote was critical), Kennedy trounced Carter; and Kennedy won the Connecticut primary to boot.

The denouement of the effort to rescue the hostages in late April made Carter look worse than helpless. The mission, Operation Eagle Claw, involved sending a rescue team aboard eight helicopters deep into central

Iran, where C-130 cargo planes would refuel the helicopters for a flight to a secret site 100 miles outside Tehran. There, the rescuers would board unmarked trucks, rush into the city, overpower the captors, and take the hostages to a nearby abandoned airstrip, where transport planes would be waiting to fly them to safety in Saudi Arabia. But the mission had to be aborted at the very first staging ground, where a dust storm and hydraulic problems disabled three of the helicopters. Before the tragedy of errors was over, another helicopter crashed into one of the cargo planes, causing a huge explosion that killed eight American soldiers and maimed four others. The White House was plunged into gloom. Cyrus Vance, who had opposed the mission as too risky, resigned as secretary of state even before he learned the dolorous outcome.

All, however, was not lost. Carter addressed the nation the next day to take full and unflinching responsibility for the disaster. And even though Vance's resignation deepened the president's embarrassment, the failure of the mission may, ironically, have snuffed out any chance that Kennedy would win the nomination. With his "Rose Garden strategy" now in tatters, Carter's political advisers, above all Vice President Mondale, implored him to fight for his job on the campaign trail. Kennedy had been scoring points, not with any fresh proposals but with criticisms of Carter's economic policies as unfair to blacks, Hispanics, and the poor, and with familiar, even tired calls for wage and price controls, fuel rationing, and an expansion of social programs. When Kennedy won narrow victories in Pennsylvania and Michigan in April, it became all the more important for the president to show the voters that he had not himself become a hostage inside the White House. The next round of primaries, mostly in border states, were more promising for the moderate Carter; and after campaigning hard in May, he defeated Kennedy in Indiana, Tennessee, and North Carolina. On June 3, Kennedy won in California and New Jersey, but Carter's victory in Ohio gave him sufficient delegate votes to win the nomination on the first ballot.

It remained uncertain how much the nomination would actually be worth. An exhausted but relieved president reached out to Kennedy—but Kennedy, who had come to detest Carter, spurned him and proposed a televised debate to argue out their differences. In July, while the Republican National Convention met in Detroit, news coverage of the White House suddenly focused on Carter's unfortunate younger brother, Billy. A genial former beer-guzzler who still lived in Plains, Billy Carter had played the role of clown for the media since Carter's election, to his brother's growing discomfort—but now he stood accused of influence peddling in connection with a deal he had made to represent the Libyan government of strongman Muammar Qaddafi in oil sales. Having entered treatment for alcoholism, Billy made a perfectly reasonable, even sympathetic impression when he testified before a Senate investigating committee; and the charges against him turned out to be groundless (much like those made earlier against Bert Lance by the columnist William Safire, who had also led the way in hyping the "Billygate" nonscandal). Yet even though his brother persevered, there seemed to be no end to adverse events and press coverage for President Carter.

Carter faced having to deal with a Democratic National Convention that, though it would renominate him, could easily turn nasty and divisive, especially as Kennedy still refused to pledge his support. There was little in the offing to suggest a quick end to the hostage stalemate, or a dramatic improvement in the economy. And on July 16, the Republicans nominated Ronald Reagan for president, fulfilling a long-held dream of the party's right wing. Ordinarily, Carter might have relished a campaign against a candidate whom even some Republicans viewed as an extremist. But apart from the little-noticed absence of the moderate John Anderson, who had decided to pursue his third-party candidacy, the Republicans seemed remarkably united in Detroit. At the end of the convention, the polls showed Reagan with a lead of 28 percentage points over the president.

Ronald Reagan, with the full backing of the new right's machine as well as the nomination of the Republican Party, seemed poised to become the first presidential candidate to defeat an elected incumbent since Franklin Roosevelt's victory over Herbert Hoover in 1932. Yet Reagan's early advantage quickly melted, and from the middle of the fall campaign until Election Day, it seemed highly possible that Carter would win.

There is a myth in modern American politics that, whereas the Democrats are perpetually disorganized and fractured, the Republicans are a disciplined party that always puts forward its most electable candidate for the White House. And according to the myth, Ronald Reagan lost the nomination in 1976 when he wasn't quite ready, but seasoned himself and was prepared to run as a mainstream Republican in 1980. Yet that is not what happened. Although many observers (including Carter) believed as early as 1979 that Reagan would be the nominee, the Republican establishment initially preferred George H. W. Bush, whom President Ford had appointed to direct the CIA in the "Halloween massacre."

In the opening weeks of the primaries, Reagan stressed the wonders of a fiscal theory called supply-side economics, in whose mysteries he had been tutored by its chief publicists, Arthur Laffer and Jude Wanniski, and their young acolyte, the former professional football quarterback and conservative congressman from upstate New York, Jack Kemp. Supply-siders held, as a matter of irrefutable science, that large cuts in taxes for corporations and the wealthy would greatly expand the economy. (Some of them also suggested that the expansion would create higher government revenues and, in time, a balanced federal budget, although those claims were more tentative and of secondary importance.) Bush, whose roots lay in the modern Republicanism that had made its peace with the New Deal, attacked Reagan's new dogma as "voodoo economics"—and promptly edged Reagan out in their first contest, the Iowa caucuses. Stunned, the Reagan campaign headed for New Hampshire and, as it had in North Carolina four years earlier, tacked hard to the right, hammering away on issues such as the giveaway of the Panama Canal and the alleged conspiratorial perfidy of Carter's associates at the Trilateral Commission. Further stirring the conservative base with an artful putdown at a "raucous" candidates' debate in Nashua, Reagan carried 51 percent of the vote. This result made Republican moderates worry about where the party was heading but also forced most of Reagan's rivals other than Bush out of the race. In May, despite his important victories in Michigan and Pennsylvania, Bush finally gave up as well. Only then did the disciplined Republican leaders, except John Anderson, unite behind their nominee. After failing to lure ex-president Ford, Reagan sealed the party's unity in Detroit by naming Bush as his running mate.

The Democrats, convening in New York, conformed more to political stereotypes. After fighting Carter all the way to the convention, Kennedy gave a rousing concession speech—his best speech of the campaign—claiming that he and his supporters had kept faith with the spirit of the New Deal and the New Frontier, and concluding, partly in elegy, partly in defiance, that "the work goes on, the cause endures, the hope still lives, and the dream shall never die." But Kennedy then offered Carter at best a lukewarm endorsement and barely acknowledged the president's presence during the ritual show of unity at the finale of the convention. In 1968, many liberal Democrats had spurned Hubert Humphrey; now, Carter would have to try to win over the liberal base by convincing voters that Reagan would be a dangerously extremist president. As it happened, Reagan nearly did that job for him.

Reagan's strategy involved mobilizing the growing constituencies of the new right, above all northern blue-collar whites and evangelical Christians, as well as the Republicans' "southern strategy" base, while lambasting the Carter administration nationwide for its failures in the economy and (amid the continuing hostage crisis) in foreign affairs. By giving his first major postconvention speech in Philadelphia, Mississippi (site of the notorious murders of three civil rights workers in 1964), with a declaration of his devotion to "states' rights," Reagan indicated to white southerners where his heart lay regarding civil rights reform. By attacking abortion and having Robert Billings, the executive director of Moral Majority, named as his campaign's "religious adviser," he hoped to energize right-wing evangelicals. Everywhere, he said the Carter presidency was a rank failure. "There is only one phrase to describe the last three years and eight months," he told a crowd in Chicago early in the campaign. "It has been an American tragedy."

Through the first weeks of the campaign, Reagan excited important elements of his new would-be coalition. In August, he addressed the Religious Roundtable's annual national affairs briefing in Dallas and cleverly embraced the Christian evangelical right, declaring, "You may not endorse me, but I endorse you." At the formal launch of his campaign on September 1, in Jersey City, New Jersey, he addressed a large crowd of white ethnic workers, many of whom were nervous about the difficult economic times, and he gave a direct and winsome speech. Standing without a jacket or tie, framed by the Statue of Liberty, and with Stanislaw Walensa (father of the dissident Polish trade union leader, Lech Walensa) by his side, Reagan blamed Carter for bringing on a true depression. ("A recession is when your neighbor loses his job," the candidate explained. "A depression is when you lose yours. And recovery is when Jimmy Carter loses his.")

Yet if Reagan was often eloquent, he also seemed prone to weird stump oratory—some of it old-time far-right claptrap, some of it just strange— that called into question his fitness to serve. After Carter opened his campaign in Alabama and actually confronted a group of Ku Klux Klansmen who had turned out at his rally, Reagan said in so many words that his opponent was pandering to racists. Reagan expressed personal doubts about Darwin's theory of evolution. He said the New Deal had patterned itself on Italian fascism. He revived his ill-fated proposal from the primaries of 1976 to make the Social Security system voluntary. He repeated an absurd claim he had picked up somewhere that a recent volcanic eruption in Washington state had polluted the atmosphere with more sulfur dioxide than the last ten years of automobile driving. "If Reagan keeps putting his foot in his mouth for another week or so, we can close down campaign headquarters," Pat Caddell exulted. Carter settled on a strategy of portraying Reagan as an inexperienced, dangerous reactionary and warmonger.

The news also started shifting in Carter's favor. Official figures on the economy showed stronger signs of improvement than expected. The "Billygate" affair ended with a Senate report that dismissed the charges of influence peddling. In the Middle East, Iran informed the United States, in early September, that it was prepared to discuss a resolution of the hostage issue, and exploratory talks began in Germany on September 13. (Soon thereafter, the Iraqi dictator Saddam Hussein invaded Iran, starting a war that eclipsed the crisis at the embassy and compelled the Iranians to negotiate all the more in earnest.) Watching Carter's sanctions begin to take effect, Reagan's camp became obsessed with the suspicion that the president was planning an "October surprise" to release the hostages and win the election. Their fears redoubled when, on October 13, Iran's new prime minister came to the United Nations to argue the case against Iraq, and told reporters that with regard to the hostage crisis, both sides were ready to cooperate. The Reagan campaign's own polls showed that Carter had come all the way back from his deficit in July and now held a narrow overall lead, while Reagan's lead was melting quickly in states such as Illinois and Texas whose electoral votes were crucial.

Reagan's strategists responded by reversing their position concerning televised debates. Until now, Reagan had insisted that any debate between the candidates ought to include the third-party candidate, John Anderson. Carter refused, afraid that such an arrangement would pit two Republicans against him, and Reagan and Anderson actually held one debate on their own. But with the election now slipping away, the Reagan camp changed its mind. Carter's counselors were divided on whether to go ahead. Pat Caddell feared Reagan's ease and verbal skills, but the majority, including Hamilton Jordan, thought that ducking the debate would do the president great harm and that, in any case, Carter's superior grasp of the issues would defeat Reagan's slick salesmanship. For once, Carter did not listen to Caddell—and his decision may have cost him the election.

The debate, held in Cleveland on October 28, a week before Election Day, was a rout. Carter handled himself well, took the offensive, and cogently outlined his substantial policy differences with Reagan. But he also made the error of mentioning a conversation he'd had that day with his daughter, Amy, in which he'd asked her what she thought the top issue of the day was, and she had answered, "Nuclear weaponry and the control of nuclear arms." In trying to come across as a warm family man, Carter sounded odd, as if he would trivialize his job by talking to a precocious teenager about weighty affairs of state. Carter's media adviser, Gerald Rafshoon, winced, but there was worse to come. Reagan, looking confident, parried Carter's criticisms with little shakes of his head, followed by amusing remarks such as "There you go again." Reagan did not look at all like the fiery extremist Carter had denounced around the country; here, instead, was a calm, friendly, attractive man who seemed to know exactly what he was talking about. Then, in his final statement, Reagan looked straight into the camera and let loose his barrage: "Are you better off than you were four years ago? Is it easier for you to go and buy things in the stores than it was four years ago? . . . Is America respected around the world as it was?"

If Carter had bested the challenger on fine debating points, Reagan completely took over the event—and, now, with less than a week to go, he took over the election. His performance had turned Carter's worst vulnerabilities into the campaign's keynote, and Carter was boxed in. Even when the president announced, on the Sunday before the election, a significant advance in the negotiations with Iran, he appeared to be trying to grab back the public's attention at the last minute by playing politics with the hostage issue. In that final week of the campaign, more than one out of four voters settled on their candidate, an unusually high proportion—and among those who settled on one of the two main contenders, Reagan topped Carter by 8 percentage points. The final tally gave Reagan 51 percent, Carter 41 percent, and Anderson 7 percent of the popular vote. And Reagan crushed Carter in the electoral college, winning 489 electoral votes to Carter's 49—the third largest electoral margin to that point in American history, surpassed only by Franklin Roosevelt's in 1936 and Richard Nixon's in 1972.

It was far from clear that Reagan and the Republican right had swept the nation with their ideas and proposals, since they had won only a bare majority of the popular vote. The 2 percent decline in voter turnout compared with that of four years earlier made this the lowest turnout since 1948, so the picture was even fuzzier. But the results certainly reflected a collapse of the Democrats, especially of the liberal Democrats. Having endured the divisive Democratic primaries, traditional core Democratic constituencies—Catholics, Jews, blacks, union members, and urban residents—voted in significantly lower numbers than in 1976. (By contrast, the white evangelical vote, an important constituency for Carter in 1976, split about evenly between Carter and Reagan while voting heavily for conservative congressional candidates.) Not only did the voters repudiate Carter, they rejected Democrats everywhere. To the amazement of seasoned political observers, the party lost a net total of twelve Senate seats, handing the Republicans a majority in the Senate for the first time since January 1955. Seven of the defeated Democratic senators were leading liberals, including George McGovern and Frank Church. The Republicans also had a net gain of thirty-three seats in the House, cutting into the Democrats' majority by nearly 60 percent. In the states, there would be four more Republican governors in 1980 than there had been in 1979.

The election—Tip O'Neill called it an unforeseen tidal wave—mocked the Democrats' false confidence that public revulsion at Watergate had brought liberalism back to its natural place as the dominant force in American politics. The returns also showed that, although Americans might well be anxious after years of disillusionment and disorientation, Jimmy Carter's brand of anti-politics was not, finally, what they were looking for in their leaders. Whereas Carter spoke philosophically of ambiguities and limits, Reagan spoke with splendid simplicity about an unbounded American future. Whereas Carter projected honesty, Reagan projected adventure. Whereas Carter's presidency had become mired in failure at home and abroad, Reagan promised a bright new future. After hesitating over Reagan's unsettling ideas about natural selection and Social Security, the voters greatly preferred a new sort of Hollywood politician, a hard-line conservative who refashioned the bold New Deal faith, in a line Reagan had long before lifted directly from Franklin Roosevelt, that the American people had a "rendezvous with destiny."

The election also pushed the Republican Party farther to the right, a major advance in the absorption of the party by the new right. The White House would now become firmly attached to the conveyor belts of proposals and personnel built by the conservative counterestablishment. And the Republicans on Capitol Hill would tilt more strongly rightward than ever. Not only did Democrats lose their majority in the Senate, but they lost to hard-right Republicans such as Jeremiah Denton of Alabama, Frank Murkowski of Alaska, Steven D. Symms of Idaho, and J. Danforth ("Dan") Quayle of Indiana. One of the pillars of liberal modern Republicanism, Jacob Javits, defeated in the New York Republican primary, would see his seat occupied by a very different kind of Republican, Alfonse D'Amato.

Whether this new political phalanx would succeed in destroying the New Deal order, as the new right had pledged, remained to be seen. As in

all revolutions, seizing power and consolidating it were two different matters. But the seizure of executive power was complete. The country's politics
would begin to look unlike any it had ever known.

The symbolic transition occurred not at Ronald Reagan's inauguration
on January 20, 1981, but in the hours that preceded it. After ten weeks
of additional strenuous negotiations with the Iranians, Jimmy Carter, now
sleepless for two nights and worn to the marrow, received word just after
six-thirty a.m. that a final agreement had been arranged for the release of
the hostages in Tehran. At seven o'clock, he placed a call to the official presidential guest residence, Blair House, to tell his successor the joyous news,
but the call was taken by an aide of Reagan's who said that the governor
had had a long night, was sleeping, and could not be disturbed.

"You're kidding," Carter said.

"No, sir, I'm not," the aide replied.

As dawn began to break, the ashen-faced president jotted down what
had happened in his meticulous, minute-by-minute log. Outside the White
House, all over Washington, limousine chauffeurs, gown fitters, sous-chefs,
and gofers awoke to begin making final preparations for the most sumptu-
ous presidential inauguration in American history.

5

NEW MORNING

Politics is just like show business," Ronald Reagan told his campaign consultant Stuart Spencer in 1966, the year he was elected governor of California. "You have a hell of an opening, coast for awhile, and then have a hell of a close." Reagan could not have better foreseen the course of his presidency.

Reagan's Inauguration Day extravaganza exploded Carter's down-home simplicity. In a mixture of stateliness and expense account chic, the events observed a victory of party but also a celebration of freedom as propounded by the conservative political movement, now triumphant after decades in the wilderness. Some participants, even on the right, thought the festivities offensive: "When you've got to pay $2000 for a limousine for four days, $7 to park, and $2.50 to check your coat, at a time when most people in this country just can't hack it, that's ostentatious," Barry Goldwater growled. The torrents of wealth and privilege—"a bacchanalia of the haves," one critic called it—was the farthest thing from a ceremony of and by the people. But it was very much for the people, broadcast to the nation and the world in television images as the start of a new dispensation, one that despised government but reveled in power. To emphasize the stylistic as well as the symbolic dimensions of the change, Reagan's men switched the swearing-in ceremony from the East to the West Front of the Capitol, a more telegenic site that also happened to look out toward Reagan's real America.

Reagan's inaugural address at once repudiated and evoked Franklin Delano Roosevelt's address of 1933. Reagan outlined the coming of a new order that would break completely with the New Deal and the "modern

Republicanism" that accepted the New Deal's premises. Whereas Roosevelt
had blamed economic disaster on a "generation of self-seekers" and "the
rulers of the exchange of mankind's goods," Reagan assailed a "federal establishment" that had overtaxed the people, stifled business innovation, and
worsened inflation. Roosevelt had promised bold, swift government action
to attack the Great Depression; Reagan charged that "in the present crisis,
government is not the solution to our problem," and promised to get government to "work with us, not over us; to stand by our side, not ride on our
back."

Yet although Reagan preached pro-business conservatism, he spoke in
a heroic idiom that purposefully echoed Roosevelt; and he exaggerated the
direness of the difficulties he faced, so as to make 1981 look like 1933 and
justify major actions. Like Roosevelt, Reagan said that the country was
gripped by "terror," which he aimed to banish with American optimism
and hard work—though in Reagan's case, the terror involved "runaway
living costs," not mass unemployment, catastrophic business failures, or a
collapse of the banking system. Like Roosevelt and the New Deal generation of Democrats (of which he had been one), Reagan identified chiefly
with common Americans: shopkeepers, miners, and factory workers. (His
speech did not once include the word "business" or "corporations.") To overcome the genuine emergency of stagflation, he proposed drastic anti–New
Deal means while promising to achieve the New Deal ends of economic
recovery and mass prosperity. But all of Reagan's Rooseveltian exhortations
were misleading. The "present crisis" of which he spoke was an impetus
but also a pretext for eliminating the New Deal—which had been the chief
goal of the Republican right, new and old, for nearly half a century.

About foreign policy (a subject that, except for one sentence, Roosevelt
omitted from his first inaugural address), Reagan spoke only briefly, sounding more statesmanlike than belligerent. He issued no clarion call to roll
back the influence of the Soviet Union, let alone to win the cold war; he only
vowed never to sacrifice national security. When John F. Kennedy pledged
in 1961, at the height of the cold war, to "pay any price, bear any burden"
in the cause of liberty, he spoke of "our foe," the communists; Reagan, in a
more chastened tone, referred to "our potential adversaries"; "the enemies of
freedom." Reagan did speak, if only indirectly and in passing, about buga-
boos of the right wing such as the Panama Canal ("our own sovereignty is
not for sale"), and he upbraided undemocratic terrorists who "prey upon
their neighbors." More conspicuously, Reagan mentioned neither arms control, the centerpiece of détente; nor human rights, the foundation of Jimmy

Carter's foreign policy. The spirit of another Roosevelt dominated these passages on foreign policy: Reagan promised to speak softly and carry a big stick. (In time, he would give his ultraconservative supporters the impression that he was Theodore Roosevelt in reverse, speaking loudly but carrying, as Richard Viguerie put it, "a small twig.") If he intended to reassure the nation and the world that he was no trigger-happy extremist, Reagan also signaled that a new, more combative day had arrived in the conduct of American foreign affairs.

It was an impressive opening for a movement-inspired administration that eschewed traditional partisanship, yet which, unlike Carter's, could not have been less enamored of anti-politics. Over the next eight years, the Reagan administration would have early political successes despite failures and near-tragedy, but then coast and drift, at several points nearly being wrecked, before Reagan recovered and ended with a hell of a close. The politics of the Reagan administration were deeply conservative, even when some of its policies were not; and its triumphs in devastating the fiscal, judicial, and ideological foundations of liberal reform have left an enduring mark on American politics and government. Yet the Reagan years also defy easy definition as "conservative"; "hawkish," or "pro-business," let alone "Republican." Reaganism was its own distinctive blend of dogma, pragmatism, and, above all, mythology. Although it had tens of millions of followers, its theory resided not in a party, a faction, or a movement, but in the mind and the persona of one man: Ronald Wilson Reagan.

Reagan spent much of his life becoming someone else, turning himself from a midwestern small-town college boy into a leading man in Hollywood "B" films; from a leftist liberal Democratic union leader into an informant for the FBI and a Goldwater conservative Republican; from a television host into a right-wing celebrity and governor of California; and, finally, into the president of the United States. His abilities as an actor and his aptness for changing roles have fooled some critics into thinking he was merely a pitchman for his wealthy conservative backers—or even, as his absorbing if eccentric authorized biography put it, "an apparent airhead." But Reagan's experiences as a self-made and remade man formed the core of an American-style myth that became part of the substance as well as the style of his politics. He celebrated new departures, knowing that this was how Americans liked to think about their own lives, and about their nation, and he offered voters what they wanted—a new morning in a land where tomorrow is always sunny and lies just around the corner. For Reagan, this was not just rhetoric; it was part of a worldview that deeply informed his presidency.

Reagan's humble upbringing contained as much shadow as sunshine. He was born in Tampico, Illinois, in 1911, the son of an alcoholic, unsuccessful traveling salesman and ardent Democrat, Jack Reagan; and his supportive, pious wife, Nelle (who brought her children into the Disciples of Christ church). Reagan then moved with his family to a succession of towns until they settled in Dixon, when he was nine. Reagan's father would never own his own home or business; his mother explained away the father's drinking as "a sickness"; the son dressed in hand-me-downs from his older brother, Neil. When the Great Depression hit Dixon in the early 1930s, Jack Reagan, his dreams of independence shattered, won a New Deal patronage job as the town's highest official for the Works Progress Administration. Squabbles with local relief officials ensued, throwing him into what his son recalled as "almost permanent anger and frustration." Ronald Reagan would later mold the story into a parable not of New Deal hopes but of big government's clumsy destructiveness.

By his own account, Reagan, as a boy, escaped from reality by becoming a "voracious reader," and his favorite books included uplifting tales of morally sound heroes and do-gooders who pull themselves out of poverty. The small-town rural, rhythms of life in Dixon—100 miles due west of Chicago, and much closer to the Mississippi River than the big city—left Reagan remembering his childhood as "a rare Huck Finn idyll." Twain's actual character, though, did not have an idyllic life; and much like Huck's friend Tom Sawyer, Reagan survived on his almost hyperactive imagination. Many children of alcoholics are said to have trouble separating illusion from reality. Whether or not this was true of Reagan, he did have a proven propensity in adulthood to conflate the two—thereby stoking his own desires while turning politics into a realm of dreams. "He had an inability to distinguish between fact and fantasy," one of his early girlfriends recalled.

After graduating as a scholarship student at the Disciples of Christ's nearby Eureka College (where, he later said, he majored in extracurricular activities, including drama and athletics), "Dutch" Reagan landed a job as an announcer at a local radio station in Davenport, Iowa, just down the Mississippi. There he re-created entire baseball games played by the Chicago Cubs in what is now called real time, relying only on sparse ticker tape reports. While traveling in California with the Cubs during spring training

in 1937, he took a screen test at the Warner Brothers studio, chasing his ambition to become a Hollywood leading man. He would never become a star
like Clark Gable or Jimmy Stewart, but Reagan successfully freed himself
from the obscurity of Davenport, and gave his imagination an enormous
new range to roam.

During his quarter-century career as a film actor, Reagan played a wide
assortment of character roles, including the dying football star George Gipp
in *Knute Rockne: All-American*; the slightly moronic Professor Peter Boyd,
who tries to teach human morals to a chimpanzee, in *Bedtime for Bonzo*;
and, in 1942, the hero Drake McHugh, a carefree small-town trust fund
heir who, with pluck and optimism, recovers from unspeakable horror in
the dark melodrama *Kings Row*. During World War II, Reagan stayed
in Hollywood and made films for the Army. Thereafter, he returned to
acting, although his employer, Warner Brothers, decided not to make him
a leading man, despite his success in *Kings Row*. Reagan also threw himself into politics by joining the Hollywood Democratic Committee, a pro–
Soviet Union, pro–New Deal group, in 1943; by serving as president of the
Screen Actors Guild (SAG) from 1947 to 1952; and by making speeches on
behalf of President Harry S. Truman and the senatorial candidate Hubert
H. Humphrey in 1948. It was a natural extension for Reagan, a passionate
leftist New Dealer.

Reagan's transition from what he called a "hemophiliac liberal" to a
hard-line conservative occurred incrementally. His battles with communist
organizers and sympathizers of the Hollywood left within SAG made his
earlier leftist sympathies seem naive—and persuaded him that liberals in
general were well-intentioned dupes. (If, as his later backer Irving Kristol
is suppose to have remarked, a neoconservative is "a liberal who has been
mugged by reality," Reagan—who in the 1940s was close enough to members of the Communist Party to be considered a fellow traveler—was one
of the original neoconservatives.) A crushing divorce from his wife, the celebrated actress Jane Wyman, pushed old friends to the background; his
remarriage in 1952 to a bit-part actress, Nancy Davis (a former Chicagoan
debutante and the stepdaughter of a wealthy conservative neurosurgeon,
Loyal Davis), reinforced his move to the right. Reagan also complained that
his personal income taxes were so high that he could actually put more
money in the bank by cutting down on his acting work—a Hollywood
lesson in how the welfare state penalized honest labor and encouraged sloth.
When his film career faltered, he found television work as host of *G.E. Theater* and *Death Valley Days*, and as a publicist for General Electric, preach-

ing its antiregulatory gospel at the company's plants around the country in a stump speech that gradually became more pointedly political.*

Until he reached his mid-fifties, Reagan was more successful at shedding old roles than excelling in new ones. By 1964, he was a fading but still familiar Hollywood celebrity, who also happened to be the brightest star backing Barry Goldwater's run for the presidency against Lyndon Johnson. Late in the campaign, Goldwater's camp, in desperation (and over the strong objections of one insider, William Baroody of the American Enterprise Institute, but with the candidate's full approval), bought national television time for Reagan to deliver his standard anti–New Deal speech, now tweaked to become a plug for Goldwater. Appearing before a studio audience on October 27, Reagan pushed his various long-standing right-wing themes, including the charge, first made by an embittered Al Smith and familiar on the political fringe, that the New Dealers had taken the Democratic Party in the direction of Marx, Lenin, and Stalin. Here and there, the speech was callous and dismissive in a country-club jokester kind of way. ("We were told four years ago that 17 million people went to bed hungry every night. Well, that was probably true. They were all on a diet." The line brought resounding laughter from Reagan's conservative audience.) Yet in contrast to the bespectacled, unsmiling, at times prickly Goldwater, Reagan mostly said these very conservative things in a way that was startlingly attractive as well as authoritative. And instead of borrowing from conservative ideological gurus, Reagan took his rhetoric straight from Jefferson, Lincoln, and, especially, Franklin Delano Roosevelt. "You and I," he concluded, "have a rendezvous with destiny. We will preserve for our children this, the last best hope of man on earth, or we will sentence them to take the last step into a thousand years of darkness."

Conservative lore relates that Reagan's address electrified the nation, but it did not: one week later, Goldwater was trounced, and right-wing Republicanism seemed to have stepped into the darkness. But Reagan's appearance did bring in a windfall of campaign contributions; and it aroused conservatives, among some of Reagan's closest friends, a group of self-made sunbelt tycoons including the nursing home magnate Charles Z. Wick, the

---

* In 1959, alarmed executives at General Electric made Reagan remove from the speech an assault on the Tennessee Valley Authority, with which their company did business. Three years later, still frustrated by his ideological appeals, the corporation cut its ties with Reagan and canceled *G.E. Theater*. Reagan viewed the company's demands as outright censorship by establishment liberals.

drugstore multimillionaire Justin Dart, and the oilman Henry Salvatori. "We recognized that he had a certain magic quality—he didn't lose the audience," Wick recalled. California had a long tradition, dating back to the Progressive era, of citizen politicians coming to the fore irrespective of party ties—a large advantage for a would-be Republican political candidate who was a former Democrat. In 1966, a year of an intense backlash by voters against President Johnson and his Great Society programs, Reagan, financed by his millionaires' club, ran for governor and defeated the two-term incumbent, Edmund G. "Pat" Brown, by nearly 1 million votes.

Reagan was badly underprepared for his new position. (When asked, after the election, what he would do, he replied with a quip that was both amusing and revelatory: "I don't know. I've never played a governor.") Yet during his two terms in Sacramento, the character actor gradually learned his part—and he displayed an unexpected pragmatic side that belied his simplistic antigovernment rhetoric. Publicly, he took a very hard line against dissenters on campus who had made Berkeley and then other branches of the University of California hotbeds of antiwar protest. He stood firmly, in speech after speech, for reducing the size and power of state government. But once the novice found his footing, and understood that governing was far more complicated than he had imagined, Reagan displayed his greatest skills as a behind-the-scenes, bipartisan negotiator—listening as well as preaching, compromising when necessary with Democratic legislators, and then taking the lion's share of credit for whatever was achieved. Never deeply engaged either in the day-to-day duties of his job or by its substantive details, Governor Reagan eventually learned how to set a basic ideological direction for his hardworking staff and then jump into the fray when needed, with a stirring speech or some backroom charm and persuasion. It was a style he would carry with him into the White House, along with his openness to bargaining and compromising when the chips were down.

The overall results in California were mixed. Although he sharply curbed the growth of the state bureaucracy and delivered $4 billion in relief from property taxes, Reagan sponsored and signed state tax increases higher than Californians had ever known, to offset the hidden deficits he had inherited from the Brown administration. (To ease the pain of the tax hike, he also approved an overhaul of the state's regressive revenue by increasing the tax burden on corporations, banks, and high-income individuals.) In 1966, Reagan pledged to attack the state's soaring crime rate, and in office he signed scores of bills stiffening the criminal justice system; but by the time he stepped down in 1974, the state's homicide rate had doubled, and the figures for armed robbery were even worse. The signal reform of his second term, cleaning up what Reagan called the state's "welfare mess," significantly reduced the welfare rolls by tightening eligibility requirements and substantially increased payments to those who remained on relief—but Reagan exaggerated his own role in what was actually a bipartisan effort to address what liberals as well as conservatives recognized as a serious state problem. One feature of welfare reform in which the governor took special pride, a community back-to-work program, proved a dismal failure and was discontinued six months after he left office.

Still, if his accomplishments were uneven, Reagan had successfully exchanged the role of "citizen-politician" for that of a competent "citizen-governor." His tax increases (as well as his reluctant decision, in 1967, to sign a liberal abortion law) caused some hard-line conservatives to denounce him as a heretic, but Reagan shrugged the attacks off, knowing that they would soften his own image as a dogmatic extremist. His negotiations with the Democratic kingpins in California, including the state assembly speakers Jesse Unruh and, later, Bob Moretti, schooled him in the arts of legislative cajoling, wheeling, and dealing. Although his last-minute try for the Republican nomination in 1968 was amateurish, he handled his defeat with grace. Two years later, amid heavy Republican losses nationwide, he won reelection by routing Unruh. He left Sacramento in January 1975 a popular Republican governor, even as his party was gasping for breath after Watergate. Over the next five years, he expanded his political connections and refined the mythos of Reaganism, which eventually lifted him into what his finest biographer has called "the role of a lifetime."

In 1972, George McGovern ran on the slogan, "Come home, America," and was clobbered by Richard Nixon. To Republicans and, finally, the majority of voters, McGovern's appeal signaled a retreat from the liberal cold war interventionism of the Truman Doctrine into a defeatist isolationism, as well as an embrace of the permissive counterculture of the 1960s. In 1980, and then throughout his presidency, Ronald Reagan, in his own way, also bade America to come home, while he conjured up visions of a brave new national destiny. The odd mixture of restoring traditional assets while creating new opportunities, prospects, and benefits formed the mythic core of Reaganism. Its slogan might have been borrowed from the title of one of the hit films of the day: *Back to the Future*.

Home, in Reaganite mythology, was a re-created bygone place of close-knit families and neighbors. It might be a small town like Bedford Falls in Frank Capra's film *It's a Wonderful Life* (1942); or a heartwarming big-city immigrant and ethnic enclave like those evoked in the 1950s by the hit television series *I Remember Mama* and *The Goldbergs*; or the nineteenth-century pioneer family settlement shown in the 1970s in the perennial television series *Little House on the Prairie*, which stayed on the air two years into Reagan's first term. Home, in this half-remembered, half-invented rendering, was a simpler America, where folks never bothered to lock their doors and friends helped friends—where friends, in fact, formed one big happy family. ("The success story of America," Reagan would remark as president, "is neighbor helping neighbor.") It was a land before a time of ghetto riots, flag-burners, and national leaders who broke the law or who spoke of the country's malaise. Trouble—as personified by Lionel Barrymore's evil Mr. Potter in *It's a Wonderful Life*—sometimes reared its head in the Reaganite homeland, but decent Americans always rallied 'round and, by the grace of God, defeated the villains' plots. At home, in Reaganite mythology, there were only happy endings.

Reaganism's mystique of home stood in paradoxical relation with a decidedly unparadisaical element of Reaganite myth, the legend of the rugged, competitive individual, willing to brave fortune in chancy ventures, his eye fixed on the horizon. The classic film figure in this connection is the lone cowboy, stoic but adventuresome; translated into Reagan's America, it was the unfettered, hardworking entrepreneur who takes risks and, living by the inexorable market laws of supply and demand, either fails the test or makes a fortune. The accumulation of great wealth, exemplified by Reagan's own self-made backers in the sunbelt, was not incidental to this side of Reaganism. ("What I want to see above all," Reagan remarked as president, "is that this country remains a country where someone can always get rich.") But there were broader moral and collective virtues in the individualist legend, which made it seem compatible with the communitarian romance. According to Reaganism, anything less than perfect freedom to pursue one's individual dreams was the surest sign of tyranny and privilege. Without its fearless pioneers, America could never have achieved the material progress that makes possible the continued security and happiness of home. But without the support, pleasures, and moral constraints of home, individualism has no direction. Together, they defined what Reagan celebrated as "the extraordinary strength and character of this breed of people we call Americans," people of all backgrounds and conditions "bound together in that community of shared values of family, work, neighborhood, peace, and freedom."

It followed, in Reaganite myth, that the great destroyer of homes and individuals was intrusive big government. Big government tried to supplant the bonds of neighborhood and community; it blocked individual initiative and risk; it weakened the people's moral fiber (and even denied the existence of God's grace); it sought to make freedom-loving Americans into its servile dependents. Socialism and communism (interchangeable terms in the Reaganite vocabulary) were the perfect examples of big government, but New Deal liberalism was a dangerous variation which, unless destroyed root and branch, would lead America down the totalitarian path of the Soviet Union. Some liberals (as Reagan had learned during his union days) worked consciously and secretly toward sovietizing America; others were well-intentioned do-gooders seduced by a satanic force that disguised itself as humanitarian. While stealing from hardworking people what was rightfully theirs (through taxes), big government also promised things to others (prosperity, security in old age, income supplements) that they could truly earn only on their own. Big-government liberalism was as un-American as the British monarchy was in 1776. "Did we forget," Reagan asked, "that the function of government is not to confer happiness on us, but to give us the opportunity to work out happiness for ourselves?"

Reaganism was nostalgic in the literal and original sense of the term, a longing to return to the homeland, which the afflicted one desperately fears he will never see again. Such nostalgia was, as it remains, a recurring theme in American literature, appearing in works as different as *The Great Gatsby, Gone With the Wind*, and the stories of Zane Grey. And it was hardly unprecedented in American politics, especially in the aftermath of social or political trauma. In the late 1940s, one cumulative effect of the Great Depression and World War II was a rage for upbeat, entertaining Americana, "in the spirit," the historian Richard Hofstadter wrote, "of sentimental appreciation rather than critical analysis." Nor was Reaganism the only nostalgic response to the social, economic, and political shocks of the 1960s and 1970s: Jimmy Carter's appeal to moral purity and Edward Kennedy's rhapsodies to the good old liberal cause and "the dream [that] shall never die" cast their own nostalgic glow. But Reaganism alone, with its attack on big government, capitalized fully on the antigovernment mood created by Vietnam, Watergate, the hostage crisis in Iran, and the losing battle against stagflation. Whereas Nixon had promised law and order and governed lawlessly, and Carter had promised Americans a government as good as its people and then failed to govern effectively, Reaganism promised to get government out of the way almost entirely, recover the first principles of the American Revolution, and (in a conservative twist on a radical slogan of the 1960s) return power to the people. Restoring the energetic spirit of the past, according to Reaganite myth, was the only way to ensure a prosperous, innovative, secure, communal American future, where a free citizenry could dream big dreams, begin all over again, and make its dreams come true—just as Ronald Reagan did.

The myths of Reaganism defied American history. From the era of Alexander Hamilton to the era of the Internet, major economic innovation has proceeded in this country with substantial government aid and involvement. Even at its most entrepreneurial, American corporate capitalism had long since outgrown the simplified, market-driven individualism that Reaganism posited as the essence of freedom. For the vast majority of Americans, activist government, working on their own behalf or their forebears', had overcome economic and social conditions that blocked access to the full promise of American life. The three major policy changes Reagan promised in 1980—deep cuts in taxes, sharp increases in military spending, and an end to federal deficits—flatly contradicted each other in the light of all experience. Past conservatives who had advanced the stripped-down principles of Reaganism on the national level had been repudiated.

But Reagan had the excellent fortune to emerge as a presidential contender just as Democratic liberalism fell into intellectual confusion and political decay. The electorate, despite misgivings, was prepared to give antigovernment conservatism a chance. More important, Reagan had the optimistic temperament and rhetorical skills to turn right-wing Republicanism into Reaganism—no longer a crabby rejection of modern life or a dour Calvin Coolidge–like promotion of big business (much as Reagan admired Coolidge),* but an outgoing, energizing, even sensuous ideal of a bountiful, limitless American future open to everyone who was determined to succeed. His conservatism had nothing to do with veneration of tradition or a fixed hierarchy: "[T]here never was a politician less interested in the past," one biographer has written. Nor was the relaxed, divorced former actor from California in the least priggish or moralistic, no matter how much his politics appealed to those who were. In aiming to undo the actual New Deal, Reaganism represented a New Deal in American conservatism,

---

* On taking office, Reagan replaced Harry Truman's portrait in the Cabinet Room with Coolidge's. And the important elements of the supply-side economics Reagan embraced recapitulated ideas first propounded by Coolidge's secretary of the treasury, Andrew Mellon.

aligning, as never before in the nation's history, pro-business economics and regression on civil rights with democratic, even populist, forward-looking political appeals.

There was a final utopian element in Reaganism, in the area of foreign policy, which surfaced only toward the close of Reagan's presidency and which more than anything else distinguished his outlook from ordinary right-wing Republicanism—the myth of everlasting world peace coupled with Reagan's abiding abhorrence at the thought of all-out nuclear warfare. With his unyielding anticommunism, Reagan, to be sure, was second to none in championing military preparedness. After taking office, he began the nation's largest military buildup since World War II. Describing the intervention in Vietnam as a "noble" war long after conventional wisdom deemed it a needless disaster, Reagan resolutely insisted that the United States had to overcome the postwar defeatist syndrome he associated with liberal Democrats and conservative realists alike. He distrusted negotiations with the Soviet Union over arms control, approved secret military actions in Central America that flouted the Constitution, and expressed fascination with scriptural forecasts of Armageddon.

Yet deep down, Reagan was neither a doomsday man nor especially militaristic. In what his aides considered some of his loopier moments, he would muse aloud about how the nations of the world might drop all their differences if the planet earth were to come under serious threat of attack by aliens from outer space. The scenario (like many of Reagan's scenarios) seemed to come straight out of Hollywood—in particular, from a science-fiction thriller of 1951, *The Day the Earth Stood Still*, in which an alien threatens to destroy the world if the earthlings do not eliminate their nuclear weapons. (Reagan spoke openly and fairly frequently about this film and about its lasting impact on him.) But Reagan's scenario also contained elements of his old liberal self, only inverted: beyond the cold war, according to Reaganism, beckoned a world that neither liberals who favored "peaceful coexistence" nor more orthodox conservatives and neoconservatives could yet imagine in the 1980s—a postcommunist world of peace and harmony where, as Reagan said, "we would find out once and for all that we really are all human beings here on earth together." At bottom, Reaganism had its own global humanitarian vision. This vision of decency, in combination with utterly unforeseen events at home and abroad, would help the Reagan presidency, after severe testing and failure, achieve its own happy ending.

* * *

Reagan opened his first term by displaying a political shrewdness that had usually seemed to elude Jimmy Carter. With the Republicans suddenly in command of the Senate, and with conservative Democrats in the House, especially those from the South, feeling political heat, Reagan was in a position to turn his bare popular majority into an electoral mandate. But he left little to chance. Well before his inauguration, Reagan traveled to Washington to charm and establish working relations with leaders on Capitol Hill, including his main future adversary, Speaker of the House Tip O'Neill. The inauguration itself was partly a signal to the city's high society that, unlike its austere, vaguely scolding predecessor, the Reagan administration would exude glamour and excitement. Tongues wagged with enthusiasm, a relieved Hugh Sidey of *Time* magazine reported, that at last "fun and class would return to social events."

Reagan brought with him from California longtime advisers and aides, including his firmly conservative former chief of staff Edwin Meese III (who had led the crackdown against the rebels at Berkeley) and his close friend and chief media consultant Michael Deaver. His cabinet also included former associates in California—among them his personal attorney, William French Smith, whom he appointed attorney general—as well as some Washington holdovers (above all, as secretary of state, Nixon's favorite, Alexander Haig). As secretary of the treasury, he chose the Wall Street maverick and champion of free markets Donald Regan, who had been chairman of Merrill Lynch. But Reagan installed as his chief of staff a redoubtable former adversary with experience in Washington, George Bush's campaign manager in 1980, the canny Republican (and ex-Democrat), James Baker III.

Given the new president's inverately passive management style, Baker promised to bring efficiency and drive as well as inside-the-Beltway political intelligence to the Oval Office. And under Baker, the new administration would not make Jimmy Carter's mistake of trying to accomplish too many different things right away; nor would it fail to cultivate harmonious and productive relations on Capitol Hill. Initially (and at the urging of, among others, the exiled Richard Nixon, whose advice Reagan quietly sought and took very seriously), the administration would focus on its domestic priorities—passing enormous budget reductions to go along with the largest tax cut in American history, as well as restricting the federal regulatory oversight of corporate America.

The push for deregulation had actually begun in earnest under Jimmy Carter, who worked with a coalition of congressional conservatives and liberals (including Edward Kennedy) to help consumers obtain lower prices and to aid ailing industries, including the airlines and trucking, by lifting federal restrictions and demanding sharper competition. But under Reagan, the cause became an all-out pro-business crusade that drew no distinctions between regulations restraining business competition and those designed to enforce laws protecting the public's health and safety.

When Reagan was sworn in on January 20, he immediately signed an order imposing a hiring freeze on all federal agencies, including regulatory agencies. Nine days later, a second order from the White House forbade the agencies from issuing any new rules. Reagan also appointed strong advocates of deregulation as the heads of the Securities and Exchange Commission, the Federal Communications Commission, the Commerce Department, and the Department of the Interior. (The new secretary of the interior, James Watt, vowed to follow what he called the scriptural injunction "to occupy the land until He returns," by which he meant more mining, more cutting of timber, and more drilling for oil.) Secretary of Commerce Malcolm Baldrige, the former CEO of Scoville, a manufacturing corporation, released a hit list of the most offensive, antibusiness regulations; the list included restrictions on hazardous waste, air pollution, and the spread of potential carcinogens.

While Reagan quietly made his appointments and began waging revolution by bureaucratic decree, public attention was fixed on economic and fiscal policy. Opinion inside the White House was not unanimous in support of the supply-side fiscal ideas that Reagan favored. Baker was deeply skeptical. Richard Wirthlin (the president's chief pollster, who had a PhD in economics), Reagan's campaign research director Martin Anderson, and Anderson's friend and ally Alan Greenspan, all argued that although huge tax cuts would certainly worsen the federal deficit (which Reagan had pledged to erase by the end of his first term), they were unlikely to generate business expansion on the scale that the supply-siders predicted. Reagan, however, staunchly believed that federal taxes were confiscatory, that they stifled growth, and that government spending on social programs was the primary cause of inflation. Although his grasp of supply-side theory remained uncertain, he found irresistible the supply-siders' exuberant forecasts of a painless fiscal revolution.

One strong influence on the president during the campaign of 1980, Congressman Jack Kemp, had already cosponsored legislation, the Kemp-Roth Bill, which would slash federal tax rates by about 27 percent over three years—the basis for what would become Reagan's own proposal, the innocuously named Economic Recovery Tax Bill of 1981. At the new Treasury Department, Donald Regan installed several supply-side crusaders, including, as assistant secretary for economic policy, Paul Craig Roberts, who had helped draft the Kemp-Roth Bill. The point man for the president's effort, however, would be the young former congressman from Michigan David Stockman, whom Reagan appointed as head of the Office of Management and Budget (OMB). As an undergraduate Stockman had espoused the fervent antigovernment ideology of the left (he had been a member of the radical Students for a Democratic Society), but he now had an equally fervent, antigovernment devotion to the magical properties of Arthur Laffer's supply-side curve. At the OMB, Stockman feverishly prepared the administration's new budget proposals, running through the computer one set of data after another about projected economic growth, in order to affirm that sharply reduced tax rates would, indeed, produce both prosperity and higher government revenues.

On February 18, Reagan announced his budget cuts, amounting to $47 billion in new reductions from Carter's final budget, with the heaviest burden falling on programs designed to aid the poor. Combined with the tax cuts, the spending reductions would, the administration predicted (on the basis of Stockman's numbers), reverse the $55 billion deficit projected for 1981 and, by 1984, produce government surpluses. The next day, Donald Regan announced projections that business investments, as a portion of gross domestic product, would rise to unprecedented levels over the next two years.

The public, looking for any bold move that promised to remedy the economy, immediately registered its approval in opinion surveys, and leading bankers expressed their joy. Economic forecasters, though, were dubious about the administration's rosy predictions; and the Dow Jones average immediately dipped by more than thirteen points. Reagan had gathered support for his program in Congress from leading so-called boll weevil southern conservative Democrats (including the cosponsor of the budget cuts, Representative Philip Gramm of Texas, who would soon switch parties); but it remained unclear whether Reagan's program could overcome Tip O'Neill's opposition, survive the committee vetting process, and siphon off enough Democratic support to gain approval in the House for the cuts. By March, the president had begun an all-out public relations offensive, both on television and on Capitol Hill.

Fate intervened on March 30. John Hinckley Jr., the twenty-five-year-old, delusional son of an affluent Republican family in Texas, had, after repeated viewings of the film *Taxi Driver*, developed a fixation on the young actress Jodie Foster. Picking up on the film's subplot of an assassination, and hoping to impress Foster, Hinckley obtained a .22-caliber Rohm RG-14 revolver and, as Reagan was leaving a meeting with AFL-CIO delegates at the Washington Hilton, emptied it in the president's direction. Hinckley missed his target (though he severely wounded and permanently disabled Reagan's press secretary, James Brady), but a bullet ricocheted off the presidential limousine, slammed into Reagan's chest, and lodged near his heart. News bulletins, repeatedly showing film of the attack, reported that the president had weathered it well, rattling off one-liners to the doctors and to his stricken wife ("Honey, I forgot to duck"), unflinching in the face of the assault. In fact, he collapsed when he reached the hospital, and the bullet very nearly killed him.

Reagan's brush with death had an enormous impact. Right away, at the White House, Secretary of State Haig's sincere attempt to reassure the world that the government was secure—"As of now, I am in control *here*, in the White House, pending the return of the vice president" he said—sounded arrogant to reporters, who initiated Haig's fall from grace. More important, the fact that Reagan, now seventy, had survived a shooting after two decades of shocking assassinations seemed to many people a providential reversal in the nation's fortunes. Chief of Staff Baker certainly sensed as much. Once it became clear Reagan would live, Baker began planning a political strategy to capitalize on the new wave of public affection for the president, whose positive public approval ratings instantly soared to 70 percent. In mid-April, while Reagan was still convalescing in the White House residence, Baker and Michael Deaver asked him if he would make a special appeal for his economic program in a televised joint session of Congress. Reagan needed little persuading. Although several months of wheeling, dealing, and coaxing lay ahead—in which Reagan would play an active role—he more or less ensured the passage of his program when, exactly four weeks after he had been shot, he delivered his speech to Congress. ("The aura of heroism which has attended him since his wounding, deserved in large part by his demeanor under the extreme duress . . ." the House majority leader Jim Wright of Texas wrote in his diary, "assured a tumultuous welcome. It was a very deceptive, extremely partisan and probably very effective presentation.") On August 13, Reagan signed into law both the tax bill and the

budget bill, only slightly modified from the White House's original proposals.* The total cost in revenues over the next three years would be $280 bil-
lion—to be more than covered, the administration insisted, by the wave of
new receipts generated by new investment and aggressive new growth.

During the brief interim between the passage of these bills and presidential enactment, Reagan had another opportunity to display his unbend-
ing resolve. In 1980, although he was generally disliked by organized labor,
he had received the endorsement of the Professional Air Traffic Controllers
Organization (PATCO), a union of federal employees. But in early August
1981, when PATCO voted to strike over demands for increases in wages
and benefits, Reagan ordered the controllers back to work within two days,
after which, he declared, they would be fired. Some observers thought the
president was bluffing; others that he was unnecessarily putting the entire
airline industry at risk. But Reagan, convinced that the walkout was illegal and that it endangered public safety—and taking courage from the example of Calvin Coolidge who, as governor of Massachusetts, had broken a
strike by policemen in Boston in 1919—did not back down.

Within two weeks, 11,000 controllers, more than half the membership
of PATCO, had been dismissed; with support from military air personnel
who had been reassigned as strikebreakers, the compliant remainder had
returned 80 percent of all flights to their normal schedules; and PATCO
was destroyed. Not in living memory had the federal government crushed a
strike so effectively. "It struck me as singular," Donald Rumsfeld, now chief
executive officer of the multinational pharmaceutical corporation G.D.
Searle and Company, observed. "You had a president who was new to the
office and not taken seriously by a lot of people. It showed a decisiveness and
an ease with his instincts."

For liberals, in and outside the labor movement, the downfall of PATCO
capped a seven-month political disaster even worse than the electoral tidal
wave of 1980 had portended. A Republican president who had earned
barely half of the popular vote—the lowest percentage of any victorious Republican since Benjamin Harrison in 1888—had, through merciful fortune
and political skill, become a popular hero. Thanks to the boll weevil Dem-

---

* In its final form, one act cut income taxes by 5 percent on October 1 and by 10 percent in each
of the next two years; taxes on capital gains fell 40 percent and taxes on investment income fell
28 percent. The budget-cutting Omnibus Budget Reconciliation Act wound up reducing federal spending by $35 billion over the next fiscal year.

ocrats, the Reagan administration had a working majority in the House to go along with its majority in the Senate.

Important social programs for the needy and unprivileged—public assistance, food stamps, school lunch and job training programs, Social Security disability payments—had been slashed. With a 9 percent tax cut scheduled for each of the next three years, and with top marginal income tax rates reduced by nearly one-third, wealth would be redistributed toward the wealthy, while the government would be starved of funds to meet nonmilitary needs—a reduction, by the administration's own estimates, of $750 billion over the next five years. The labor movement, its numbers and influence tumbling into a drastic decline, was on the defensive as it had not been since the passage of the Taft-Hartley Act in 1947. The Reagan revolution was under way in earnest, with still more than three years to go, at the very least. Not since President James K. Polk came to office in 1845 had any president succeeded in completing so much of his announced agenda so quickly.

Demoralized liberals and leftists had no clear idea about how Reagan's assault might be stopped, let alone any strategy for stopping it. In the Senate, Edward Kennedy, having put his presidential ambitions aside at least temporarily, did lead some successful rearguard actions from his post as ranking member of the Committee on Labor and Human Resources. Kennedy, emerging as a skilled parliamentary tactician, struck tactical alliances with Republican moderates and blocked some of the most drastic proposed cuts in social services, including legal aid to the poor, assistance to low-income families for fuel purchases, and subsidies for school lunches. For the remainder of Reagan's presidency, Kennedy would fight relentlessly to salvage what he could of the liberal legacy. Still, when asked by a constituent in May 1981 to assess the political situation, Washington's highest-ranking Democrat, Tip O'Neill, was blunt: "I'm getting the shit whaled out of me." And all was elation at the other end of Pennsylvania Avenue, continuing the giddy mood that had begun with the inauguration and had intensified after John Hinckley's failed, mad assault on Reagan in March.

One day Michael Deaver said to the president, "Sometimes I have to pinch myself to see if this is real." Reagan just smiled and replied, "So do I."

By the end of 1982, the mood in Washington and across the nation had changed drastically—except, perhaps, inside the circles closest to the ever-upbeat Ronald Reagan.

The long-term economic and political effects of Reagan's early triumphs remain hotly debated to this day. Critics point out that the tax cut failed to stimulate business investment as promised, vastly increased the costly federal deficit, did nothing to improve real average hourly wages (which in 1986 would be lower than they had been for most of the 1970s), and severely aggravated economic inequality. Some detractors, most starkly the late senator Daniel Patrick Moynihan, have charged that "Reaganomics" was actually a cynical scheme to bankrupt the federal government and permanently forestall any resurgence of liberal reform. Reagan's admirers, especially supply-siders, have countered that the dramatic legislation of 1981 led to a recovery from the economic doldrums of the Carter years—a rebound in which the real disposable income per capita of the American population eventually rose. Clearly, though, events during the weeks and months after August 1981 raised serious doubts about the revolutionaries' economic stewardship.

Although he was always more interested in starving government to death through tax cuts than in anything else, David Stockman would never, at least publicly, renounce the supply-side dogma he proclaimed so loudly in the early months of Reagan's presidency. The title of his memoir, *The Triumph of Politics*, summarized his main charge: that Reagan (and virtually everyone else in Washington) betrayed the ideal by failing to legislate the requisite budget austerity and then return to the gold standard. Yet all through 1981, when he was at the height of his power and his celebrity in the media, Stockman was talking to his friend William Greider of the *Washington Post*—and he said things that did more to discredit supply-side theory than anything Reagan did or failed to do. Greider had promised Stockman that he would publish nothing of their conversations until after the Reagan program became law. The reporter was true to his word—and so his article, "The Education of David Stockman," was all the more explosive when it appeared in the *Atlantic* in November.

Stockman's insider view of how the Reaganites actually operated was devastating. He confessed that he had jiggered the figures he fed into the OMB computers in order to produce optimistic projections. He acknowledged that supply-side was less an economic theory than a faith, based on certain a priori assumptions about, in the supply-sider Jude Wanniski's phrase, "the way the world works." Worst of all, Stockman admitted that the original Kemp-Roth Bill, and supply-side theory in general, was just a euphemistic cover (he called it "a Trojan horse") for the so-called trickle-down idea dating back well into the nineteenth century and discredited since the onset of the Great Depression—the idea that further enriching the already rich would eventually produce great economic benefits for lowlier Americans. "It's kind of hard to sell 'trickle-down,' so the supply-side formula was the only way to get a tax policy that really was 'trickle down," Stockman said; then he added, for emphasis, "Supply-side is 'trickle-down' theory."

Stockman's revelations were deeply embarrassing to supply-siders such as the *Wall Street Journal*, and an unexpected boon to congressional Democrats. (On receiving an advance copy of Greider's article, Senator Gary Hart of Colorado, a possible aspirant for the presidency in 1984, cheerfully read it into the *Congressional Record*.) In the White House, Meese, Deaver, and the always protective Nancy Reagan wanted Stockman fired for insubordination. Only the intervention of Jim Baker saved Stockman's scalp. (Baker was apoplectic because Stockman had allowed Greider to quote him directly, but he also prized Stockman's knowledge and was wary of the even more extreme supply-siders at the Treasury Department and on Capitol Hill.) After a much publicized "woodshedding" meeting with Reagan—in actuality, a mild scolding over a lunch of soup and tuna salad—Stockman kept his job.[*]

Unfortunately for the White House, though, its predictions about a fiscal turnaround and a brightening economy had begun to seem illusory even before the *Atlantic* article hit the newsstands. Stockman's budget calculations turned out to be woefully mistaken. In all his number crunching, Stockman had simply assumed strong economic growth and moderate inflation; he also budgeted in much deeper cuts in spending than were actually enacted. His projected new revenues never appeared; desperately, he tried, without success, to squeeze additional reductions out of various cabinet secretaries. The picture looked exceedingly grim: running revised figures through his computers, Stockman now projected that the deficit would rise from $74 billion in 1980 to $300 billion per year in the mid-1980s.

The deficit, generally viewed as inflationary, was blamed in part for pushing up interest rates and hampering the expected economic growth. The tax cuts and budget cuts, meanwhile, met with a disastrous reaction

---

[*] That same afternoon, Stockman held a press conference. Although he affirmed that all of Greider's quotations were accurate, he also denied that they really meant what they plainly did mean—a remarkable performance. Stockman also asserted that the president had never intended to mislead the public. See Douglas Brinkley, ed., *The Reagan Diaries* (New York, 2007), entry for November 12, 1981, 48–49, quotation on 49; "Transcript of Stockman's Statement and His News Conference," *New York Times*, November 13, 1981, p. D16.

on Wall Street, not at all what the administration had expected. Fearing the huge deficits, worsening inflation, and higher interest rates, investors stampeded to sell off their holdings. Stock prices began falling as soon as Reagan signed the new legislation in August. By the time the Dow Jones industrial average hit bottom in September, at 824 points, the overall value of blue-chip stocks had declined by 20 percent since April. As interest rates rose, bond prices fell. Other economic indicators were similarly dismal: purchases of new cars hit a twenty-year low; housing starts declined precipitously; businesses (chiefly small businesses) were going bankrupt at a rate 42 percent higher than in 1980. Reagan, unswayed, vetoed a congressional budget resolution and shut down some government offices for a day, thereby forcing lawmakers to trim an additional $4 billion in proposed spending. But it was a drop in the bucket; and after Stockman's revelations were released, anger fixed on the administration, and especially on Reagan's supposed supply-side wizard. "Stockman was the original interior decorator of this economic house of ill repute," said Lane Kirkland, president of the AFL-CIO. "Now he has his story ready. He only played the piano in the parlor. He never knew what was going on upstairs."

In January 1982, the president publicly acknowledged what economists already knew, that the economy was in a recession. Stubbornly, Reagan vowed to seek no tax increases in 1982, as he blamed the downturn on the economic mismanagement of the Carter administration and the preceding thirty years of "binge" tax-and-spend government. If only Americans gave his reforms the chance to take hold, all would be well. But as winter turned to spring, and spring to summer, the turnabout did not arrive. Unemployment averaged out at 9.7 percent in 1982, the highest rate since the Great Depression. By November, 9 million Americans were out of work; also, 17,000 businesses had failed—the second highest figure since 1933. Reagan's personal popularity remained high, but his job performance rating plummeted below 50 percent. As the midterm congressional elections approached, the impression grew that Reagan's policies had brought not recovery but catastrophe on a scale unseen since the presidency of Herbert Hoover.

In fact, the recession could be described reasonably as both a legacy of Carter's presidency and a product of Reagan's policies, but not in a sense most voters understood. Since Carter had appointed him chairman of the Federal Reserve System in 1979, Paul Volcker had continued to clamp down on the money supply, determined to rid the American economy of the inflation that he believed remained the chief obstacle to prosperity. The policy worked—between 1980 and 1982, the rate of inflation dropped by more than half, from 13.5 to 6.2 percent—and this was enough for Reagan to ignore entreaties from Republicans on Capitol Hill that Volcker be removed. But after a slight, unexpected economic uptick in 1981 pushed Volcker to be more vigilant than ever, the Fed's tight money policy created, in effect, an intentional recession of surpassing severity.

During the 1980 campaign, Reagan had publicly opposed using recession as a cure for inflation. How much he quietly understood what the effects of Volcker's policies would be is unclear. Yet if he did understand and approve of Volcker's harsh measures, he paid politically for the economy's continued deterioration. Under pressure from James Baker and a chastened and alarmed David Stockman as well as congressional leaders (including traditional Republican conservatives headed by the Senate majority leader, Robert Dole), Reagan had to scale back his tax cuts in 1982 by negotiating and then signing the Tax Equity and Fiscal Responsibility Act (TEFRA)—a measure which, combined with added federal taxes on gasoline in an accompanying highway bill, produced what Baker's assistant Richard Darman called the greatest single tax hike in American history. These measures brought lamentations from supply-siders that perfidious forces within the White House had stabbed them in the back. Many, including Assistant Secretary of the Treasury Paul Craig Roberts, quit the administration in disgust; stories began circulating among true believers (and appearing on the editorial page of the *Wall Street Journal*) that Baker and Stockman were purposefully undermining the president's supply-side intentions.

They were utterly mistaken. Reagan was fully involved in these crucial decisions, and as fully in charge as he had always been on matters he cared about deeply. Far from being a dupe, he was governing as he had done since his days in California, holding out as long as possible, compromising when necessary, protecting his important gains while preparing to fight another day. With the tax bill of 1981, Reagan had cut the top marginal rate from 70 percent to 50 percent and slowed the growth of revenue—so much so that, even if some existing social programs proved too popular to be eliminated or to be severely modified, others would be cut drastically. And the chance that any new, expensive nondefense government program would win approval (or even be proposed) was vastly reduced for many years to come. Greider's article had affirmed Stockman's belief that the act of 1981 was intended to place a "tightening noose around the size of government." With that law in place, Reagan was willing to take the one step backward that became necessary to safeguard, even fortify, his earlier two large steps forward.*

The enactment of TEFRA, moreover, was not the administration's first retreat on its economic proposals. Social Security payments had climbed by over 500 percent in the 1970s. To help salvage the system, Secretary of Human Services Richard Schweiker, in May 1981, proposed immediately reducing benefits for those who retired before the age of sixty-five—a more sudden and drastic version of a proposal already forwarded by a House subcommittee on Social Security. The plan, in its revised form, was a political gift to the Democrats, who did not waste it. Tip O'Neill said the proposal was a "breach of faith with those who have worked their whole lives" and vowed to do everything in his power to stop the president. The impact was devastating, even among Republicans. The Senate rejected the proposal, ninety-six to none; the House resoundingly turned down a move by the administration, proposed earlier, to eliminate a statutory provision setting minimum Social Security provisions; and the White House, facing political reality, chartered a bipartisan, public-private commission, chosen in part by O'Neill, to look into Social Security's difficulties.

Reagan himself had long criticized Social Security as a coercive government program, and the administration did succeed in cutting the system's disability payments. But overall the political blundering of the administration succeeded mainly in establishing Social Security even more as the untouchable "third rail" of national politics. Combined with the effects of the recession in 1982 and some of the earlier, highly publicized spending cuts that seemed hard-hearted, the fracas over Social Security put the White House (and Republicans generally) on the defensive about what became framed as the "fairness" issue.** Congressman Peter Rodino of New Jersey, a

---

* Reagan, by his own account, justified TEFRA to supply-siders as a necessary pragmatic and tactical move. "Met with Jack Kemp (alone) and later in leadership meeting," he wrote in his diary in early August. "He is adamant that we were wrong on the tax increase. He is in fact unreasonable. The tax increase is the price we have to pay to get the budget cuts." Douglas Brinkley, ed., *The Reagan Diaries* (New York, 2007), 96, entry for August 4, 1982.

** The most notorious of the cuts involved sharp reductions in the federal government's school nutrition program and caused the Department of Agriculture to allow participating schools to lower nutritional standards—for example, to classify tomato ketchup, inanely, as a vegetable. After Democrats ridiculed the changes, Reagan quickly backed down and blamed unnamed agency officials, whom he accused of trying to "sabotage" his budget policies. Steven R. Weisman, "Reagan Abandons Proposal to Pare School Nutrition," *New York Times*, September 26,

major figure during the Watergate investigations, called on Republicans to save themselves and the country from "the wolves in wolves' clothing" who had taken over their party. Entering the midterm campaign season, the Democrats devised a new slogan: "It's not fair: It's Republican."

In the elections in November, the Democrats picked up twenty-seven House seats, solidifying their majority. Two months later, Reagan's job approval rating sank to 35 percent, and less than 20 percent of those polled believed that the economy was improving. That Reagan could win reelection in 1984, let alone climb back onto his heroic pedestal, seemed, suddenly, a highly doubtful proposition.

Reagan the optimist appeared unfazed. During the congressional election campaign, he beseeched the voters to stick with his policies and "stay the course"—a course about which the country's confidence had been shaken but not destroyed. (Polling data showed that although Republicans were taking the blame for the economic woes, nearly half the country still had a cautious wait-and-see attitude toward Reagan's larger policies.) Into the new year, Reagan's rhetoric did not change. In February 1983, he claimed that "all signs we're now seeing point toward an economic recovery." On economic policy, Reagan's chief initial concern, his presidency's hell of an opening was now over. He betrayed no doubt whatsoever that the show had several more reels to run.

6

CONFRONTING THE
EVIL EMPIRE

EFORE RONALD REAGAN BECAME president, he had a long conversation about foreign relations with Richard Allen, who would later become his first national security adviser. "My idea of American policy toward the Soviet Union is simple, and some would say simplistic," Reagan said. "It is this: We win and they lose. What do you think of that?"

The words now sound prophetic, and they form the basis of claims about Reagan's historical achievement. Yet Soviet communism had begun to rot long before Reagan took office, and resistance within the Soviet bloc was rising steadily in the late 1970s. Three decades earlier, when Reagan was still a left-wing Democrat, Harry Truman initiated policies that, as carried on by administrations of both political parties, contributed mightily to the eventual collapse of the Soviet empire. Reagan's own foreign policy was not a coherent plan for the downfall of communism but a patchwork of policies in different parts of the globe, sometimes successful, sometimes vacillating, and often disastrous. In retrospect, the chief efforts of the so-called Reagan Doctrine either were irrelevant to winning the cold war or helped set in motion forces that would challenge the United States after Soviet communism collapsed. A novice in foreign affairs when he came to the White House, Reagan headed a divided administration whose foreign policy was long on style and symbolism (and at times on mendacity and deception) but chronically incapable of winning substantial diplomatic victories, especially during his first term.

Part of Reagan's strength—which, however, also contributed to his worst failures—was his simple and absolute certainty that the West would triumph in the cold war. More important, Reagan eventually adjusted to new political realities and recognized when the cold war was ending, even though foreign policy experts within his administration, and conservative critics outside, refused to believe it. In this, Reagan differed from his fiercely anti-Soviet friends and conservative allies (who for a time denounced him as a turncoat) nearly as much as he differed from the advocates of détente and liberal defenders of permanent peaceful coexistence. Beneath Reagan's harsh rhetoric lay his peculiar imaginings of a world after communism, derived from his uncomplicated, humane conviction that the Soviet Union was a lie, that no lie could live forever, and that Russians and Americans would one day live in peace and friendship. Those imaginings drove the greatest achievements of his presidency.

Yet it took years of covert folly and lawlessness, bogus dogma masquerading as diplomacy, and barbaric bloodletting in the third world—all leading, in Reagan's second term, to a constitutional confrontation that sent his popularity plummeting and might have destroyed his presidency—before Reagan salvaged success from failure. And although Reagan was not the passive cipher some people made him out to be—for ill and for good—that success required fundamental shifts in his own thinking, a drastic rearrangement of his administration in its final year, and the outsize good fortune that came with the advent of the Soviet leader Mikhail Gorbachev.

Reagan's inaugural address made it obvious that domestic matters, especially taxes and the economy, would initially take precedence over foreign policy. The primacy of domestic concerns became even clearer in March, when, over objections from the State Department, the White House heeded agribusiness interests and lifted the embargo on grain sales to the Soviet Union that Jimmy Carter had imposed in retaliation for the invasion of Afghanistan. In stark contrast to the grain deal, however, Reagan's early speeches, as well as his cabinet appointments, announced a new toughness toward the Soviet Union. Détente, Reagan said nine days after taking office, had been "a one-way street the Soviet Union has used to pursue its own aims." Carter and the Democratic Congress had allowed the nation's military defenses to fall into shameful neglect, exposing America to what Reagan called a "window of vulnerability." When, on close examination, the idea of a window of vulnerability turned out to be a sham, administration officials dropped the phrase—but not the broader claim that the United States had permitted its military preparedness to deteriorate in the 1970s. Reagan's chief advisers on foreign policy—Secretary of State Alexander Haig, Secretary of Defense Caspar Weinberger, and William Casey, director of the CIA—were hard-line hawks who shared his desire to establish unquestionable U.S. military superiority, no matter what it cost.

The (now) former Democratic neoconservatives grouped around the Committee on the Present Danger (CPD) greatly reinforced that desire. Reagan himself had joined the CPD's executive board in 1979; and after he won in 1980, as many as fifty CPD members took posts in his administration. Convinced that the CIA had badly underestimated the Soviet menace, the neoconservatives had gained considerable influence as early as 1976, while the CPD was still being formed, when President Ford—at the urging of George H. W. Bush, who was then the director of the CIA—mandated the creation of a secret Team B intelligence group to provide alternative reports on national security outside the CIA's established channels. Not surprisingly, the neoconservatives who dominated Team B—including Richard Pipes, a professor at Harvard who would later become a member of CPD—drew a much darker picture of the Soviet Union's superiority over the United States in armaments than the career professionals at the CIA did. Described by one former deputy director of the CIA as "a kangaroo court of outside critics, all picked from one point of view," Team B disbanded in 1977, but some of its findings continued to carry weight in the Carter administration, especially in debates over arms control. After Carter's defeat, the neoconservatives carried their exaggerated worst-case projections back with them into the Reagan White House.

The neoconservatives also pushed for a reversal of what they called the "Vietnam syndrome," which they believed had crippled America's will to use military force against the Soviet Union's proxies in Africa, Asia, and Latin America. Ending the syndrome, they insisted, required abandoning the squeamishness over human rights that had characterized the Carter administration, and acknowledging frankly that support for authoritarian anticommunist regimes abroad was a necessary check on expansive totalitarianism. A former supporter of "Scoop" Jackson and a prominent member of the CPD, Jeane J. Kirkpatrick, gave this blunt formulation a theoretical gloss, borrowing from conservative ideas that dated back to Edmund Burke. Writing in *Commentary* in 1979, Kirkpatrick argued that "traditional autocracies" (that is, anticommunist regimes), no matter how corrupt, hierarchical, and repressive, were susceptible to democratic reform and therefore tolerable, whereas "revolutionary autocracies" were utterly closed societies, impervious to change, devoted to controlling every nook and cranny of civic and private life. Impressed by Kirkpatrick's article, Reagan appointed her U.S. ambassador to the United Nations—placing in the UN a figure who held it in contempt for its toleration of "anti-American" resolutions and votes by the General Assembly, and who would apologize for murderous regimes from Argentina to Iraq in pursuit of her neoconservative abstractions.

The accuracy of the conservative and neoconservative reassessments of the Soviet Union's strength and the United States' weakness remains a subject of intense criticism and controversy, but there can be little doubt that they included selective readings of the evidence. The United States had hardly been neglectful of defense in the late 1970s. After bottoming out at mid-decade under Gerald Ford, military spending increased substantially under Jimmy Carter, rising by nearly 12 percent overall between 1977 and 1981. Much of the increased spending went toward improving the nation's nuclear capabilities; it included large outlays for new warheads, new cruise missiles, and development of the nuclear-powered Trident submarine. And contrary to the Reagan administration's claims, military expenditures by the Soviet Union had remained fairly steady since 1975.

Still, the Reagan White House was determined from the start to exempt U.S. defense spending from budgetary constraints, and to remove any doubts about America's global military supremacy. During Reagan's first term, defense outlays climbed from $171 billion to $229 billion, roughly a 34 percent increase when the figures were measured in real 1982 dollars. Reagan resumed development of the B-1 bomber, funded further work on the B-2 Stealth bomber, and spent billions on cruise missiles, the MX missile, and a major expansion of the Navy. The rationale was twofold: enlarging American defense would deter enemies abroad from military adventures such as the Soviet Union's invasion of Afghanistan, and would also force the Kremlin to undertake its own arms buildup, which it could not afford. "They cannot vastly increase their military productivity because they've already got their people on a starvation diet," Reagan observed in October 1981. "But now they're going to be faced with [the fact] that we could go forward with an arms race and they can't keep up." The Democrats' fecklessness, supposedly, had permitted the Soviet Union, an economic basket case, to threaten becoming the world's dominant military superpower. Reagan's arms buildup would supposedly ensure that the United States was dominant. The Soviet Union would then have to curtail or cease its cold war adventures.

Having substituted military pressure for diplomacy, the administration coupled the arms expenditures with a new, one-sided approach to arms control negotiations, heavily influenced by a leading neoconservative strategist, Assistant Secretary of Defense Richard Perle. Although uneasy with the SALT II treaty negotiated under Jimmy Carter, Reagan announced late in 1981 that the United States would abide by it—but he then proposed a fresh round of negotiations called the Strategic Arms Reduction Talks (START). These new talks would begin with a proposal described as the "zero-zero" option, whereby the United States would withhold scheduled missile deployments in Western Europe if the Soviet Union removed its intermediate-range missiles aimed at Europe.

The proposal seemed symmetrical, and the emphasis on arms *reduction* instead of arms limitation sounded more dramatic. But the plan actually weighed heavily against the Soviet Union, which was being asked to remove the heart of its nuclear defense—land-based missiles that were already in place—in exchange for promises by the United States to abstain from future deployments, and to do so without reference either to sea- and air-based systems (where the U.S. held the great advantage) or to the nuclear capabilities of the British and the French. Rather than a fresh departure, START looked to many Western observers, as well as many of the Soviet leaders, like a disguised attempt to foreclose substantive arms control.

Relations between the United States and the Soviet Union, initially brightened by the lifting of the American grain embargo, worsened in 1981–1982 after the Polish government cracked down on Solidarity, the democratic anticommunist trade union movement. Claiming angrily and correctly that Moscow had ordered the repression, Reagan imposed economic sanctions on the Soviet Union, including a ban on its commercial air traffic to and from the United States, and he approved covert support by the CIA to the Polish rebels. The administration then affirmed, in March 1982, a secret document calling for new preparations to prevail over the Soviet Union in either a prolonged conventional war or a nuclear exchange. Formalized in May as National Security Defense Directive 32, the new policy committed the United States to exert what pressure it could to weaken the Soviet Union's economy and to ally itself with dissident forces inside the Soviet bloc. A month later, the administration followed through by blocking the sale of American technology to aid the Soviets in completing a Siberian gas pipeline. During his first major presidential trip abroad, speaking before the British Parliament, Reagan declared that the final conflict had finally come, "a great revolutionary crisis" that would "leave Marxism-

Leninism on the ash-heap of history." Earlier, Reagan had quoted Franklin Roosevelt against the New Deal; now Reagan, the former leftist, paraphrased Leon Trotsky to foretell the doom of communism.

The administration also stepped up its efforts to halt what it perceived as expansionism by the Soviet Union in the third world, especially in Central America, which had supposedly turned the cold war into a clandestine hot war. The most hawkish members of the administration, including Secretary of State Haig, were especially alarmed at the continuing left-wing insurgency in El Salvador, and urged committing American forces to support the ruling junta, which was heavily influenced by a right-wing military officer corps. A splendid little war in El Salvador, Haig argued, would end the Soviets' adventurism and reverse the Vietnam syndrome.

Reagan's advisers were unstinting in their political and their financial support of the Salvadoran junta. When, on the eve of Reagan's inauguration, four American Maryknoll nuns involved in humanitarian relief among the peasants were found slaughtered, the UN ambassador-designate Kirkpatrick denied that the Salvadoran dictators were responsible and said that the nuns had been "political activists." (Independent investigators eventually proved that Salvadoran National Guardsmen had been ordered to target and murder the Maryknoll sisters.) Late in 1981, Elliott Abrams, the assistant secretary of state for human rights, who was Kirkpatrick's closest neoconservative comrade in the administration, testified falsely before a Senate committee that reports of involvement by government death squads in the killing of 900 peasants in the town of El Mozote were "not credible." Yet Haig's idea of a full-scale American military intervention to crush the Salvadoran insurgents gained scant support from Reagan's advisers, who feared another tropical quagmire.

With Reagan's approval, the administration adopted a different strategy that was aggressive but more circumspect. The revolutionary Sandinista government in Nicaragua was one of the chief suppliers of arms to the Salvadoran insurgents. Shortly after taking office, Reagan approved of a covert plan by the CIA to disrupt the flow of weapons from Managua. And in November, the administration took the additional step, again in secret, of setting aside $19 million to arm and train antigovernment guerrillas in Nicaragua, known familiarly as the contras. When informing congressional leaders of the new action, the White House, wary of the Democrats, referred only to its preexisting efforts to stop shipments of weapons to the Salvadoran leftists, and said nothing about helping to hasten the overthrow of the Sandinistas.

The interventions in Central America were part of a larger rearrangement of foreign policy that became known, informally, as the Reagan Doctrine—a shift away from the cold war policy of containment. Under the new doctrine, the United States would try to "roll back" communism outside Europe by supporting, by any means necessary, anti-Soviet autocracies and diverse military insurgencies in pro-Soviet nations around the world.* The basic idea had been present at the beginning of the administration and had been prefigured by the Carter administration's support for the anti-Soviet Muslim mujahideen in Afghanistan; but it was now advocated, in greatly expanded form, by activists in the new right. The Heritage Foundation was especially vociferous in proclaiming the Reagan Doctrine: its reports on foreign affairs identified eight countries, in addition to Afghanistan, where the United States could most easily beat back communism and the Soviet Union's influence: Angola, Cambodia, Ethiopia, Iran, Laos, Libya, Nicaragua, and Vietnam. (Aid to anticommunist rebels would later go to Jonas Savimbi's UNITA forces in Angola.) The idea quickly won support from important officials in the administration, including Weinberger and Kirkpatrick. Among the "traditional autocracies" backed by the United States was the military government of Argentina—until the spring of 1982, when the Argentine generals' embarrassing invasion of the Falkland Islands, which were controlled by Great Britain, brought American policy into collision with the British Tory government of Prime Minister Margaret Thatcher. (Thatcher's victory in her own little war to recapture the Falklands quickly led to the generals' downfall, but caused no basic reassessment of thinking about foreign affairs in the Reagan administration.)

By the end of 1982, the main elements of Reagan's militant foreign policy were advancing at a rapid clip. Détente had been abandoned. So had Jimmy Carter's idea that human rights ought to be the cornerstone of foreign affairs. Yet like Carter before him, Reagan would soon be stymied by events in the Middle East. And, although barely noticeable at first, countervailing forces within the administration, as well as alarming disturbances in U.S.-Soviet relations, began nudging Reagan, though not his neoconservative officials and their hard-line allies, in very different directions.

---

* The term "Reagan Doctrine" was coined by the conservative Washington, D.C., columnist Charles Krauthammer in "The Reagan Doctrine," *Time,* April 1, 1985, p. 54. Although never embraced by the White House, it accurately conveyed the thrust of the administration's policy.

* * *

The limitations of the Reagan Doctrine emerged earliest and most sharply in the Middle East. Concerned chiefly with forestalling any advance into the region by the Soviet Union, the administration initially stressed reaching what it called "strategic 'consensus'" among Israel and the Arab states. This entailed the expansion of the U.S. military presence in the region and increased sales of arms and other military equipment. But political realities continually undermined the Americans' hopes. Although happy to receive American men and matériel, the Arab governments remained far more concerned about actual deeds by the Israelis and the revolutionary Iranian regime of Ayatollah Khomeini than about countering a conjectured Soviet menace. Iran's success in staving off defeat in its war with Iraq made Tehran appear the chief threat to stability in the Gulf. The shocking assassination of Anwar Sadat by Egyptian jihadists in October 1981 deepened concerns about fundamentalist threats from within; given Sadat's unpopularity (resulting from the Camp David accords and his subsequent suppression of internal dissent), his murder also refocused attention on Israeli-Arab relations, especially with regard to the Palestinian question. And in Israel, the United States' efforts to achieve strategic consensus, capped by the sale of AWACS surveillance aircraft to the Saudi Arabian monarchy in the aftermath of Sadat's assassination, badly strained the alliance with Washington.

During his first year as president, Reagan put on a show of toughness against the Libyan leader Muammar Qaddafi. Qaddafi, an eccentric autocrat who had taken power after a coup d'état in 1969, preached a peculiar blend of pan-Arabism, socialism, and Islam, and had long been a strong supporter of the Palestine Liberation Organization (PLO) and other international terrorist groups. At the end of the 1970s, he established a measured alliance with the Soviet Union, which placed him higher on the Reagan administration's hit list. After claiming the Gulf of Sidra as Libyan territory, Qaddafi threatened to attack American naval forces if they performed their usual maneuvers there. Reagan duly ordered the Sixth Fleet into the Gulf; two Libyan fighter jets fired on American F-14s accompanying the fleet; the American fliers summarily destroyed the Libyans. "Let friend and foe alike know that America has the muscle to back up its words," Reagan declared. Yet apart from this passing encounter, during his first term Reagan would undertake no major offensive against Qaddafi.

To contain the Iranians, the Reagan administration implemented the neoconservative policy of supporting the lesser of two evils, who in this instance was the vicious Iraqi dictator, Saddam Hussein (even though Iraq had long been the strongest ally of the Soviet Union in the Persian Gulf region). Iraq had some initial successes after it invaded Iran in 1980; but the invasion faltered in 1981, and Khomeini's theocracy seemed about to overrun Iraq and seize control of its considerable supplies of oil. To buttress the secularist Iraqis, the U.S. State Department, early in 1982, while formally adhering to a strict neutrality, removed Iraq from its list of outlaw terrorist nations, thereby permitting the Iraqis to trade with American businesses. A year later, with the U.S. government now committed to regarding "any major reversal of Iraq's fortunes as a strategic defeat for the West," Reagan plucked Donald Rumsfeld from the private sector and named him special presidential envoy to the Middle East. Rumsfeld met with Saddam in Tehran, raised the possibility of normalized diplomatic relations, and offered assistance with military intelligence and enormous business credits to Iraq.

Iraq's usefulness as a check on Iran overrode concerns about human rights, including the growing evidence that Saddam, in violation of international law, had used chemical weapons against both the Iranians and his own domestic opponents. When, in 1983, Iran complained to the United Nations about Saddam's deployment of what would later become known as weapons of mass destruction, the Americans called for what Ambassador Kirkpatrick called "restraint" and lobbied successfully to defeat any specific condemnation of Saddam. "Our long-term hope," a former ambassador to Baghdad later explained, "was that Hussein's government would become less repressive and more responsible."

As the United States drew closer to Iraq, American policy in the Middle East began falling apart with regard to Lebanon. Since the mid-1970s, Yasir Arafat's PLO, with support from Syria, had used Lebanon as a base for waging war against fractious Lebanese Christian forces and for staging raids against Israel. In early June 1982, Israeli troops under General Ariel Sharon invaded Lebanon, with the ostensible aim of clearing out the PLO's border camps but with the additional hope of inciting Lebanese Christians to establish a pro-Israel government in Beirut. The Israeli offensive continued into August, capped by an eleven-hour aerial bombardment of West Beirut. Having taken no action for more than two months, and thereby giving the invasion tacit approval, Reagan finally told Prime Minister Menachem Begin to stop the bombing. A cease-fire was soon declared and, following intricate negotiations, the PLO's militants agreed to leave Lebanon for several other Arab countries, under the protection of a multinational armed force. But in September, Muslim extremists murdered the Lebanese president-elect, the pro-Israeli Christian leader Bashir Gemayel. Gemayel's supporters in the Christian militia took revenge by invading two camps of Palestinian refugees in Beirut. Then, with the tacit approval of the Israelis, they slaughtered more than 1,000 men, women, and children. Reagan, who had sent 800 Marines as part of the force to oversee the PLO's withdrawal, responded to the atrocities by committing 1,800 Marines to join a new multinational peacekeeping force in a vague, open-ended mission to restore order.

Badly exposed, with no clearly defined political or military objectives, the Americans in Beirut, civilian and military, became targets for Islamic militants. On April 18, 1983, suicide terrorists drove a van of explosives into the American embassy, killing sixty-three people, among them seventeen Americans including the CIA's leading expert on the Mideast. The U.S. forces replied by shelling Muslim militia positions. This reaction deepened the impression among ordinary Arabs that the U.S. forces were acting not as impartial peacekeepers but as allies of the Israelis and Lebanese Christians. American military experts, believing that no vital national interest was at stake, urged withdrawal of the Marines, but Reagan, who saw the Islamic radicals as surrogates for the Soviet Union, refused. Six months later, on October 23, a suicide bomber drove a Mercedes-Benz delivery truck packed with explosives into the U.S. Marines' main barracks at the Beirut airport, destroying the barracks, killing 241 Marines, and injuring sixty others. It was, as it remains, the deadliest single overseas attack on American military forces since the Second World War—and it would lead to one of the most humiliating acts of Reagan's presidency.

The White House's reaction to the bombing was swift and, it seemed, unswerving. Reagan denounced the attack as "despicable" and, backed up by Weinberger, vowed that the American mission in Beirut would continue. Vice President Bush toured the destroyed compound and declared that the administration was "not going to let a bunch of insidious terrorist cowards shape the foreign policy of the United States." Yet apart from some desultory shelling of Muslim militia positions, the United States undertook no military retaliation. Instead, the Marines were moved offshore, out of harm's way. In early February, Reagan ordered the force to begin a withdrawal, and in April the last of the troops departed. By bowing before political and military realities, which had been apparent for months to experts at the Pentagon, the administration had made a mockery of its tough talk about terrorism. What had begun as a policy of strategic consensus had become a strategic nightmare.

Except for the fortuitous unfolding of unrelated events during the weeks surrounding the bombing of the barracks, Reagan might have paid a serious political price for the debacle in Lebanon. But on September 1, military personnel in the Asian part of the Soviet Union mistook a Korean Air Lines passenger jet that had strayed into Soviet airspace for an American reconnaissance plane. When the jet failed to respond to warnings, the Soviets shot it down, killing all 269 persons aboard, including sixty-one Americans. American intelligence reports, later confirmed by a large mass of evidence, showed that the Soviets, their defense systems on a hair trigger, had handled the matter worse than incompetently, but had genuinely mistaken the jet for a spy plane. Reagan, however, denounced the episode as "the Korean Air Lines massacre," a "crime against humanity" that was "born of a society which wantonly disregards individual rights and the value of human life and seeks constantly to expand and dominate other nations." His retaliatory actions—reaffirming the ban on Aeroflot flights and suspending negotiations on various bilateral agreements—was relatively mild, even wispy, and led some observers on the right to question his will. But the American public, already outraged by the incident, became inflamed when the Kremlin, after putting out false stories that the plane had crashed on its own, accused Reagan of having fallen into a "military psychosis." Americans' anger intensified when Marshal Nikolai Ogarkov of the Soviet army insisted that the Korean flight had actually been a "deliberate, thoroughly planned intelligence operation."

Several weeks later, and just one day before the bombing in Beirut, the cold war reached a crisis on another front. The tiny Caribbean island of Grenada, a former British colony 1,000 miles off the American mainland, had been ruled since 1979 by a Marxist People's Revolutionary Government (PRG), headed by the charismatic chief of the New Jewel movement, Maurice Bishop. To the alarm of Grenada's neighbors, the PRG developed close ties with Cuba, and Fidel Castro sent hundreds of Cuban engineers and construction workers to the island to build a long, modern airstrip suitable for commercial and, potentially, military use. In mid-October 1983, rival elements within the PRG ousted Bishop and his allies, brutally executed them, and installed their own communist government. Six Caribbean heads of government from the Organization of Eastern Caribbean States (of which the United States was not a member) requested American intervention, and on October 22, Reagan secretly authorized an invasion, despite opposition from the United Nations, the Organization of American States, and the British government. ("In the middle of a meeting Margaret Thatcher called," Reagan wrote two days later. "She's upset & doesn't think we should do it. I couldn't tell her it had started.") Mishaps plagued the operation, but there was never any doubt about the final outcome. Within a week, American forces overwhelmed the tiny Grenadan military, removed armed Cuban forces dug in at the airstrip, and evacuated several hundred American medical students who had been training in Grenada at St. George's University—the last of which the administration had cited as a major humanitarian reason for the operation.

Reagan immediately sought to entwine the bombing in Beirut and the victory in Grenada and depict them as large and fateful turns in the cold war. After claiming, falsely, that the invasion force in Grenada had turned up huge caches of weapons for supplying communist insurgents, the president described a nightmare vision of the island as a potential major Soviet outpost for exporting terror and tyranny. The American invasion, like the cavalry's arrival at the end of a western movie, had, supposedly, saved the day: "We got there just in time," Reagan told the nation. The president then linked Grenada and Lebanon as places where the Soviet Union had supported violence through its proxy governments and insurgent movements. The claims were unreal; yet the events in Grenada had the double effect of distracting public attention from the catastrophe in Beirut and allowing the president's supporters to claim that the United States had finally won a combat victory against the Soviets and dispelled the ghosts of Vietnam.

Although the invasion of Grenada gave Reagan a clear-cut, albeit easy, military victory, American foreign policy, especially toward the Soviet Union became increasingly inconsistent and difficult to read after 1982. A shift had been presaged in June 1982, when Reagan replaced his stormy secretary of state, Alexander Haig, with George Shultz. Haig's arrogant penchant for bureaucratic infighting had long alienated him from other administration officials, including the president. After Haig had served uneasily for six months under the newly appointed national security adviser William P. Clark (a longtime conservative ally of Reagan's), Reagan summoned Haig and handed him a note that regretfully accepted his letter of resignation— a letter that Haig had threatened to tender during earlier contretemps but had never actually written. "The precipitous way in which you're conducting yourself, Mr. President," Haig told Reagan, "means I just can't get up and leave, I will have to make it clear publicly . . . that I no longer support your policies and that is the case." By the time Haig finished with the formalities, Reagan had already announced Shultz's appointment.

Shultz was a former academic economist who had served the Nixon administration in several posts (including secretary of the treasury from 1972 to 1974) before leaving public service to become president and director of the Bechtel Group, a multinational engineering conglomerate based in San Francisco. Known as an unflappable, poker-faced, highly intelligent man, Shultz appealed to Reagan as calm and solid, in marked contrast to the volatile Haig. William Clark, as national security adviser, was impressed by Shultz's evenhanded views about the Middle East and his respect for the Arabs' grievances. But in time, Shultz would also show far more flexibility and pragmatism in dealing with the Soviet Union than Haig did—or than his new colleagues Clark, Weinberger, Kirkpatrick, and Casey would.

In February 1983, Shultz arranged for a secret private meeting in the White House residence between Reagan and the longtime ambassador from the Soviet Union to the United States, Anatoly Dobrynin. This was the president's first face-to-face encounter ever with a high-ranking Soviet official. The timing was propitious. Leonid Brezhnev had died the previous November, and his successor as general secretary, the former head of the state police, Yuri Andropov, was eager to recommence serious negotiations for an agreement on arms control. Reagan and Dobrynin talked for two hours about relations between their countries, violations of human rights in the Soviet Union, and the future possibilities for arms reduction. Reagan was, as ever, less stridently ideological in person than he could be in his public speeches; he repeatedly emphasized his desire to be constructive, and he told the ambassador that he wanted Shultz "to be a channel for direct contact with Andropov—no bureaucracy involved." It was a small but important first step away from confrontation. As they left the White House, Dobrynin told Shultz that "this could be an historic moment."

Reagan's thinking about the Soviet Union remained divided—in part deeply skeptical about the communists' motives and devoted to putting the Soviet empire on the road to extinction; in part optimistic about his ability to bargain and persuade, and thus spare the world a nuclear conflagration. Soon after his meeting with Dobrynin, Reagan put his harsher side on display to the entire world. On March 8, in an address in Orlando, Florida, to the annual convention of the National Association of Evangelicals, he blasted the Soviet Union as "the focus of evil in the modern world" and "an evil empire." Two weeks later, he followed up with an extraordinary proposal that the United States abandon its traditional policy of nuclear deterrence through mutually assured destruction in favor of building a system of space lasers and rockets as a shield against any attack by the Soviet Union. Formally called the president's Strategic Defense Initiative (SDI), the plan soon won the derisive nickname "Star Wars," after a popular science-fiction film series depicting a mythic battle between good and evil.

The announcement of SDI came as a complete surprise to Shultz and Weinberger, as well as to the Joint Chiefs of Staff (who had been consulted about the idea, but not about when Reagan would publicize it). The plan blended various aspects of Reagan's thinking.

An often-told tale dates the origins of SDI to 1979, when Reagan, while touring the facilities of the North American Air Defense Command (NORAD), was shocked to learn that the United States lacked any defense against even one incoming Soviet missile. Long before then, however, conservative defense experts, enraged by the restrictions imposed on defense systems by the Anti-Ballistic Missile Treaty signed in 1972 and convinced that the Soviet Union had already devised some sort of missile defense system of its own, had been thinking about designing and deploying a defensive shield in space. The Republican Party platform in 1980 pointedly rejected the principle of deterrence and called for rapid research and development of an American antiballistic missile system "such as is already at hand in the Soviet Union." A group of lobbyists from the new right, called High Frontier, pressed the idea on the new administration. The story about Reagan's eye-opening tour of NORAD—a story that reflects extremely poorly on the would-be president's readiness for the job—may have been true, but his proposal four years later reflected well-established conservative opinion.

The SDI also reflected aspects of Reagan's outlook above and beyond implementing conservative ideas. The president appears to have been greatly aroused by a meeting in November 1982 with the renowned nuclear physicist (and father of the hydrogen bomb) Edward Teller. Teller sketched out a space station combining X-ray lasers mounted on platforms and nuclear weapons that could be used solely for the interception and benign destruction of enemy missiles. The outline appealed to Reagan's dreamy fascination with technological gimmickry, his cinematic science-fiction imaginings of immobilizing the enemy and ushering in world peace, and his frustration at what he saw as one-sided efforts to restrain American military superiority. It also appealed to a side of Reagan at odds with those conservatives, including influential elements within his own administration, who believed that American strategy ought to be directed solely toward winning a nuclear war. Reagan's basic hatred of nuclear weaponry had not changed since his days as a liberal; he believed that no winner could emerge from the radioactive ashes of a nuclear war. The SDI would mobilize American ingenuity and technical prowess to ensure that the ultimate human catastrophe would never occur.

Most of Reagan's aides involved with foreign policy shrugged off his fantastic proposition, believing that it would never have much utility except as a bargaining chip in negotiations with the Soviet Union. The technology required to develop SDI, let alone to implement it, was utterly conjectural—far more remote in 1983 than the technology that had been available to develop the atomic bomb during World War II (a crash effort that Reagan likened to his new proposal). Secretary of State Shultz, however, was extremely troubled when he received an eyes-only copy of the speech on SDI two days in advance. To Shultz, the proposal seemed muddled and incomplete. (How, for example, could an antiballistic missile shield in space protect Americans from nuclear-equipped bombers or low-flying cruise missiles?) More important, the speech strongly implied that the United States was radically altering its basic strategic doctrines—a destabilizing shift that was bound to confuse, alarm, and enrage the Soviet leaders only weeks after Reagan had privately and emphatically pledged to Ambassador Dobrynin his constructive cooperation.

The reaction of the Soviet Union was swift and unequivocal. General Secretary Andropov, although contending with severe kidney disease, took only three days to denounce SDI and accuse the Americans of "attempting to disarm the Soviet Union in the face of the U.S. nuclear threat." If SDI ever became operational, the Soviet Union would lose the core of its nuclear arsenal. The plan did not completely eliminate the possibility that the United States would threaten the Soviets with a nuclear attack, or perhaps even launch an attack, secure against massive retaliation. Even if the space shield was a fantasy, at best many years away from realization, Reagan's proposal was a clear invitation to a redoubled arms race, which the Soviets (who had already begun cutting the rate of spending increases for military procurements) were ill-equipped to undertake.

Reagan, unfazed, continued to pressure the Soviet Union and to combat Soviet-backed movements around the world. In Western Europe, despite enormous popular protests (reinforced by an American "No Nukes" movement that favored a freeze on nuclear deployments), Reagan moved ahead with plans to send Pershing II and Tomahawk cruise missiles—the so-called Euromissiles—to NATO, in order to offset the Soviet Union's deployment of intermediate-range SS-20 missiles during the 1970s. In Central America, the administration maintained its support for repressive regimes in Guatemala as well as El Salvador, ignoring marauding, right-wing anti-insurgent death squads that had murdered tens of thousands of civilians. The CIA's covert support for the Nicaraguan contras expanded to include gaining the assistance of Panama's new president, Manuel Noriega, in supplying arms and training grounds, despite Noriega's connections to outlaw Colombian cartels that were flooding the United States with illegal drugs. Skeptical critics in Congress pushed back hard. The Senate had already passed, late in 1982 (and compelled Reagan to sign), a resolution, originally sponsored by the respected chairman of the House Intelligence Committee, Edward Boland, that outlawed American financial aid for efforts to overthrow the Sandinistas. Yet Reagan repeatedly backed the insurgents. At one point he praised the Nicaraguan contras as "freedom fighters," a term that quickly became the White House's description of choice for every variety of anti-Soviet force. On September 16, the president signed a new secret directive ordering the CIA to aid the contras in ending Nicaraguan support for leftist guerrillas "and to bring the Sandinistas into meaningful negotiations . . . with their neighbors on peace in the region."

Simultaneously, though, Reagan was working on a very different track. With encouragement from Shultz, as well as from Nancy Reagan and her close friend Michael Deaver, the president continued to give private assurances to the Kremlin that he intended no attack on the Soviet Union and wished to pursue peace. "If each of us determined we would not resort to war as a solution to any problem," the president said in a handwritten, secret letter to Andropov on August 4, "arms reduction would be simply and easily achieved." A turning point in Reagan's thinking came in November 1983, when apprehension in the Soviet Union about a massive war simulation exercise by the United States and NATO (the exercise was called Able Archer) turned into panic among some Soviet military leaders who believed that the Americans were about to launch a first-strike nuclear attack. The Kremlin, leaving nothing to chance, placed some of its nuclear fighters on combat alert. The exercise ended without incident, but Reagan, severely rattled, backed away from his more militant rhetoric. "A nuclear war can never be won and must never be fought," he declared; and he expressed a fervent desire that he would live "to see the day when nuclear weapons will be banished from the face of the earth." In his memoirs, Reagan recalled both his shock at discovering that Soviet leaders genuinely feared a first-strike attack by the United States and his new resolve to "get a top Soviet leader in a room alone and try to convince him we had no designs on the Soviet Union and the Russians had nothing to fear from us."

It would take a long time before Reagan's policies caught up with his private words and resolutions. The START talks in Geneva, which had commenced in mid-1982, broke down completely in November when, after diplomatic feints on both sides, NATO began to deploy the Euromissiles. In March 1983, the world discovered the extent of the United States' clandestine support for the Nicaraguan contras after a Soviet tanker struck a mine off the Nicaraguan coast—and the *Wall Street Journal* revealed that the CIA, contrary to repeated public assurances from its director, Casey, had with Reagan's approval secretly mined Nicaraguan harbors. Outrage was no longer confined to left-wing Sandinista support groups or foreign policy liberals and leftists in Congress, who had opposed Reagan from the start. "I am pissed off," Barry Goldwater wrote to Casey, in a warning that was all the more powerful considering the source. "This is an act violating international law. It is an act of war." In the Republican-dominated Senate, Edward Kennedy led the way to the approval, by an overwhelming margin, of a resolution calling for a ban on U.S. funds to mine Nicaraguan harbors—"a first step," Kennedy said, "to halt President Reagan's secret war in Nicaragua." Congress then stiffened its earlier Boland Resolution and cut off any aid whatsoever to the contras.

The controversy over Nicaragua eventually contributed to the near collapse of Reagan's presidency. At the time, however, it was overtaken by a mass patriotic fervor that had been building since the invasion of Grenada. In June, at ceremonies on Omaha Beach marking the fortieth anniversary of D-day, Reagan delivered a widely acclaimed sentimental speech that symbolically linked the victory over the Nazis with the continuing struggle against Soviet communism. Nearly two months later, the Summer Olympics opened in Los Angeles, boycotted by the Soviet Union and most of its Eastern European satellites in retaliation for Jimmy Carter's boycott of the games at Moscow in 1980. American contestants, as might have been expected, won more than their usual share of Olympic medals, to the raucous delight of flag-waving American fans, who chanted "USA! USA!" Broadcast by satellite to televisions around the globe, an athletic competition became, in effect, an electronic political rally.

Also drowned out by the wave of American jingoism, however, was an important nationally televised speech that Reagan had delivered on January 16, 1984, in the aftermath of Able Archer. Adopting his friendliest tone yet toward the Soviet leadership, Reagan returned to his vision of a world free of nuclear weapons, and urged "a better working relationship" between the superpowers, "marked by better cooperation and understanding." He concluded with a typically Reaganesque sentimental anecdote, in which two imaginary Russian children meet up with two American children and discover that their similarities and hopes vastly outweigh their differences and fears. "Together," Reagan declared in a direct appeal to the Kremlin (now paraphrasing John F. Kennedy's inaugural address), "we can strengthen peace, reduce the level of arms, and know in doing so we have helped fulfill the hopes and dreams of those we represent and, indeed, of peoples everywhere. Let us begin now."

The wary Soviet leaders denounced the speech publicly as one of Reagan's "hackneyed ploys" intended to win him public support in preparation for his reelection campaign later that year. Such assessments were normal in the two countries' exchanges of propaganda. In this instance, the Soviet leaders thoroughly misconstrued Reagan's popularity, which in 1984 would derive far more from resurgent patriotism than from appeals to international cooperation. Yet behind the scenes, there was another subtle but important shift in Soviet-American relations. Immediately after Reagan's speech, Secretary of State Shultz met for five hours with the Soviet Union's foreign minister, Andrey Gromyko. Although they achieved nothing of substance, the two diplomats spoke calmly, raised issues concerning arms control and human rights, and agreed that negotiations over reducing conventional East-West forces in Europe, now suspended, would resume. "[T]he ice was cracked," Shultz later told his aides.

Nine days later, on January 25, Reagan announced that he would run for reelection.

At the nadir of the recession in 1982, when Reagan's job approval rating plunged to 35 percent and the Republicans fared poorly in the midterm elections, Democratic leaders lulled themselves into thinking that the New Deal's old-time religion had been vindicated. The hard times, supposedly, had exposed Reaganomics as a return to the disastrous trickle-down Republican policies that the Great Depression had discredited. The election of 1984 loomed as a chance for the Democrats to reassert their old verities and rebuild in new form Franklin D. Roosevelt's electoral coalition. Happy days would be here again once the electorate realized that Reagan was really, as Tip O'Neill described him, "Herbert Hoover with a smile."

Reagan's domestic program ran into additional difficulties in 1983. For decades, hard-line conservatives had been calling for the privatization or outright abolition of Social Security. Yet the bipartisan presidential commission on Social Security, headed by Alan Greenspan, recommended that the system be preserved but strengthened with a number of reforms, including an increase in payroll taxes. Congress duly passed the regressive tax increase, and Reagan approved it, claiming that the adjustments had been planned all along and that they represented no new tax burden at variance with his economic philosophy.

The effects of Reagan's deregulation policies proved even more costly. Vice President Bush's Task Force on Regulatory Relief handed down its recommendations in August 1983, foreseeing $150 billion in savings by eliminating what it called unnecessary government interference and red tape—but at the price of either removing or severely modifying hundreds of regulations that protected safe conditions for wage earners and clamped down on threats to public health. Public interest groups and organized labor challenged the administration and won some important victories in the federal courts—including one ruling that the Occupational Safety and Health Administration, a favorite target of Reagan's, was legally bound to protect employees from exposure to toxic substances.

Inside the regulatory agencies, meanwhile, indifference among conservative jobholders to their appointed tasks led to neglectful enforcement and, in some cases, blatant corruption. At the Department of Housing and Urban Development (HUD), Assistant Secretary Emmanuel S. Savas had emerged as a theorist on reducing big government, with particular expertise in cutting federal aids to the cities. In 1983, however, came revelations that a firm for which Savas had consulted before taking office had received a $500,000 HUD contract under his aegis, even though two other companies had submitted lower bids. It also came to light that Savas had bilked HUD for thousands of dollars in travel costs—while using its workers, at public expense, to help prepare his new manuscript on (of all subjects) privatizing the public sector. Savas resigned in July before he could be removed for abuse of office. His case would prove to be a fairly minor indiscretion in a series of scandals to come at HUD.

Officials charged with protecting the environment also became mired in controversy and scandal. Secretary of the Interior James Watt had been a lightning rod for criticism since the day he took office. He finally stepped over the line in September 1983, when he defiantly replied to critics that one commission he had created included "every kind of mixture you can have. I have a black, I have a woman, two Jews and a cripple. And we have talent." Labeled a social troglodyte by the press, Watt resigned. But a more serious affair had broken the previous February, when the budget-cutting chief administrator of the Environmental Protection Agency (EPA), Anne Gorsuch Burford, fired an administrator, Rita Lavelle, a political protégée of Edwin Meese's, over alleged abuses of the $1.6 billion Superfund set aside by Congress for emergency cleanups of chemical spills and hazardous waste dumps. (Superfund monies were allegedly being steered to Republican officeholders to boost their chances for reelection.) Weeks later, Gorsuch Burford herself, along with twenty of her high-level employees, resigned when Congress cited her for contempt after she refused to hand over Superfund records. ("This whole business has been a lynching by headline hunting Congressmen," Reagan bitterly remarked.)* Lavelle was eventually convicted of lying to Congress, served three months in prison, and paid a $10,000 fine.

Compared with these misdeeds, the various alleged scandals of the Carter administration, notably the trumped-up Bert Lance affair, amounted to nothing. Yet the early exposés involving Reagan's administration proved negligible when weighed against a spectacular economic recovery that commenced in 1983—beginning the longest continual period of peacetime economic expansion ever recorded to that point in American history. The inflation rate, which had climbed above 11 percent in January 1981, fell to 2 percent; the average unemployment rate declined from 9.6 percent in 1983 to 7.5 percent in 1984; the annual rate of economic growth jumped from 4.5 to 7.2 percent. Reagan's slogan "Stay the course," which had once sounded like whistling in the dark, now reverberated like an irresistible political battle cry.

Reagan and his supporters were, of course, quick to credit the tax cuts of 1981 for the turnaround, and for curing the maladies of the Carter years, but they greatly overstated their case. Several factors fed the boom. In part (as David Stockman would later concede), the recovery was a normal phenomenon of the business cycle: the economy was bouncing back from Reagan's own recession of 1981–1982. Oil prices coincidentally fell by roughly one-third between 1981 and 1983, reducing the inflation rate. The vast increase

---

* Reagan often referred to press and congressional investigations as lynchings. After James Watt resigned, for example, the president allowed that Watt "has an unfortunate way of putting his foot in his mouth," but insisted that "he's really the victim of a 2 ½ year lynching." Douglas Brinkley, ed., *The Reagan Diaries* (New York, 2007), 185, entry for October 8–10, 1983.

in federal spending on armaments—what some critics called military Keynesianism—increased aggregate national demand. Above all, in mid-1982, as soon as inflation had begun to recede, Paul Volcker and the Federal Reserve Board slashed interest rates, thereby greatly boosting business activity. Still, it was difficult for the Democrats to argue with the evidence that the economy, overall, had improved markedly under Reagan—as it had not done under Carter and the Democrats.

Reagan's political fortunes further benefited from the Democrats' worsening disarray. A crowded field of veteran liberals, including Carter's vice president Walter Mondale and the diehard George McGovern challenged the president in 1984. Senator John Glenn of Ohio, the astronaut, ran as both a moderate and a national celebrity who could match Reagan's Hollywood appeal. Senator Ernest "Fritz" Hollings of South Carolina and Ruben Askew, a former governor of Florida, sought to repeat Carter's success in salvaging the South for the Democrats.

Two other candidates for the presidency—Jesse Jackson and Gary Hart—dramatized the party's evolution since the heyday of Lyndon Johnson's Great Society. Jesse Louis Jackson was the standard-bearer for what had become of the black civil rights movement since the death of Martin Luther King Jr. in 1968. Born to an unwed mother in South Carolina in 1941, Jackson had risen somewhat testily through the civil rights movement to become one of King's young lieutenants in the Southern Christian Leadership Conference. After King was killed in Memphis, Jackson rushed to the forefront as part of an apostolic succession. Based in Chicago, Jackson headed up a variety of organizations, most notably People United to Save Humanity (PUSH), as vehicles of black economic power and self-improvement. As he raised his national and international profile, though, Jackson also sought to unify the entire spectrum of black opinion, initially by incorporating some of the trappings of black nationalism in his rhetoric, and then (most controversially) by allying himself with Louis Farrakhan of the Nation of Islam. Farrakhan's presence in Jackson's entourage in 1983 and 1984, as well as Jackson's own statements about third-world politics, the Middle East, and relations between blacks and Jews, raised clear signals of anti-Semitism inside the Jackson campaign. To Jackson, they marked his abiding hatred of colonial oppression and his determination to become the political tribune for all of black America.

Gary Hart was five years younger than Jackson and came from a very different background—and he represented a very different, more moderate future for the Democrats. He was born in Ottawa, Kansas, and was originally named Gary Hartpence (he changed his surname in 1961). His up-by-the-bootstraps experiences had carried him from the home of a poor railwayman's family to Bethany Nazarene College in Oklahoma and then to Yale, where he earned degrees in both divinity and law before he relocated to Denver as a private attorney. After comanaging George McGovern's failed presidential campaign in 1972, Hart won two elections to the Senate, where he earned a reputation as one of the most promising leaders in the Watergate generation of Democrats—deeply knowledgable, articulate, and attractive, if sometimes aloof and self-absorbed. In 1984, though little known to the general public, Hart stepped forward as the latest version of the antipolitician—a neoliberal, promising an exciting campaign of new Democratic ideas different from the tired nostrums of New Deal and Great Society liberalism, open to reforming the welfare state and, in international affairs, to questioning the Vietnam-era divisions between hawks and doves.

The nomination was a battle among Democratic splinter groups, the fragments of what had once looked like an impregnable national majority. The favorite of the party establishment was Mondale. After leaving the vice presidency in 1981, Mondale had shown signs of being restless with the traditional liberal orthodoxies on which he had built his political career in Minnesota and in Washington. He publicly sympathized with some of Reagan's cuts in taxes and in spending on failed social programs; he talked about the importance of maximizing economic growth while battling inflation. Yet as the favored candidate, Mondale decided to run a cautious campaign, reaching out to all of the major party constituencies while counting chiefly on the support of his old friends in organized labor. On the campaign trail, he stuck mainly to attacking Reagan, promising new social and jobs programs, and speaking in platitudes about America as "a future each generation must enlarge; a door each generation must open; a promise each generation must keep."

Mondale won by a wide margin in the Iowa caucuses, but Hart stunned the other candidates by finishing second and by then defeating Mondale in the New Hampshire primary by 10 percentage points. (Hart's campaign had been working hard in New Hampshire for five months.) Thereafter, the field was reduced to these two front-runners plus Jesse Jackson, who was intent on establishing an African-American presence (as well as his personal power) in Democratic presidential politics. Jackson would eventually win three southern state primaries and carry half of Mississippi's delegates. But his unguarded, outrageous overheard references to Jews as "Hymies" and to New York City as "Hymietown" all but destroyed his political viability, then and in the future, no matter how much he tried to apologize.

Hart, meanwhile, won in Ohio, California, and several western states. Yet although he was effective at taunting Mondale as "a candidate of the establishment past," Hart could never develop his own promise of "new ideas" into a compelling program. When Mondale (borrowing a slogan from a fast-food chain) asked Hart, "Where's the beef?" during a televised debate in Atlanta, Hart's campaign shriveled.

Mondale's nomination at the Democrats' national convention in San Francisco marked the triumph of stolid, old-style liberalism, its roots in the 1930s, over the "new politics" and the antipolitics of the 1970s as well as the embryonic neoliberalism of the 1980s. Yet Mondale's party was not the same as that of his mentor Hubert Humphrey. In a bow to the changed realities, Mondale made history when, after eliminating three possibilities (two of them male), he named Geraldine Ferraro as his running mate—the first woman ever selected for the national ticket of a major party. Ferraro, a third-term representative from Queens, New York, had a great deal going for her quite apart from the breakthrough her nomination represented: she contributed a tough, white, working-class ethnicity that Mondale hoped would rally the New Deal coalition once more. Unfortunately for the Democrats, Ferarro's husband, John Zaccaro, would not permit public disclosure of his income tax returns, as she had promised he would. His refusal raised doubts about her own truthfulness and competence as well as about her family's possibly shady business connections.

Six weeks later, in Dallas, the Republicans renominated the Reagan-Bush ticket in a cascade of patriotic imagery and speeches. Orators on the podium regaled the delegates with denunciations of the opposition as effete elitists—the "blame America first" party of "San Francisco Democrats," in Jeane Kirkpatrick's undisguised attack on the Democrats' virility. A Republican campaign memo explained, more calmly, how the party should approach the general campaign: "Paint Reagan as the personification of all that is right with or heroized by America. Leave Mondale in a position where an attack on Reagan is tantamount to an attack on America's idealized image of itself." Two television advertisements, written and narrated by Hal Riney, conveyed the mixture of hope and underlying fear that drove the Reagan-Bush campaign. The more famous of the two, called "Prouder, Stronger, Better," showed gauzy images of small-town America awakening to a fresh, dewy dawn, accompanied by a voice-over script in Riney's dulcet tones:

It's morning again in America. Today, more men and women will go to work than ever before in our country's history. With interest rates and inflation down, more people are buying new homes, and our new families can have confidence in the future. America today is prouder and stronger and better. Why would we want to return to where we were less than four short years ago?

The other ad depicted a fearsome brown bear wandering through the woods, as the narrator darkly implied that America would be far less secure against annihilation by the Soviet Union without Ronald Reagan in the White House.

Mondale proposed a combination of increases in taxes and cuts in defense spending to reduce the deficit, while shifting $30 billion in spending out of defense and agriculture to fund new social initiatives on education and the environment. He also lambasted Reagan as a frightening reactionary who had nearly ruined the country. But the strategy was wrongheaded, because voters as yet cared little about the deficit and cared a great deal about new taxes. With his attacks on the sunny optimist Reagan, Mondale came across as a gloomy naysayer instead of the crusader for liberal justice he imagined himself to be. Mondale's only chance of overtaking Reagan came in mid-October. In Louisville, during the first of two scheduled debates, the president, crammed by aides with facts and figures, had appeared distracted, faltering, and confused about his domestic policies. The veteran actor knew it—"I have to say I lost. . . . I guess I just flattened out," he wrote—and his sizable lead in the polls began to shrink. Tellingly, though, the news media's analyses of Reagan's poor performance focused not on the merits of his actual policies but on whether he was too old for the job. Better rested and primed for the second debate on foreign policy two weeks later, Reagan buried the age issue by joking that he would not exploit the youth and inexperience of his opponent. Mondale smiled gamely; and with that, the election was virtually over.

In the final tally, Reagan won 59 percent of the popular vote and carried every state except Mondale's home state, Minnesota (where the Democrats' margin of victory was fewer than 4,000 votes), as well as the District of Columbia. Reagan was now in a position to be the first president since Dwight D. Eisenhower to serve a second full term. Even more impressive, only one presidential candidate since James Monroe—Franklin D. Roosevelt in 1936—had won a larger proportion of the electoral vote. Having held their

Senate majority and picked up sixteen seats in the House, some Republicans talked enthusiastically of an impending, permanent partisan realignment. What had begun as the Republicans' southern strategy to overturn the New Deal–Great Society coalition now looked like an impregnable national majority.

The Democrats, in shock, tried to blame the avalanche on the Republicans' ability to lull the voters and rob politics of any serious debate by substituting slick, feel-good advertisements. Ironically, in a party that supposedly championed the interests of ordinary Americans, these analyses showed a certain contempt for the intelligence of the average American voter. Without question, Reagan's campaign handled the media skillfully, both in the press and in its own campaign advertising. But Reagan now also had a record as president, which the voters could judge. As the opinion polls showed, he had built a new coalition of educated white middle-class voters (especially younger voters) and blue-collar families who claimed that he had restored national pride. Between Mondale's traditional Democratic ideas and the now tested Reaganism, there was really no contest as far as the great majority of voters were concerned—especially at a time of renewed prosperity and patriotic fervor.

Few Democrats, meanwhile, appeared willing to face some hard facts about their own party. One who did, the liberal lion Edward Kennedy, observed after the election, "There is a difference between being a party that cares about labor and being a labor party . . . a party that cares about women and being the women's party. And we can and we must be a party that cares about minorities without becoming a minority party. We are citizens first—and constituencies second." Yet even the most astute of the leading liberal Democrats had no concrete program or clear vision for reforming and updating Democratic liberalism to create a unifying party core.

The Republican claims that the landslide heralded a full-scale political realignment were, at the same time, highly debatable. Despite Reagan's lopsided margin, the Democrats would still hold a strong if diminished majority in the new House, and would command a majority of the nation's statehouses. It was not at all clear that the voters had shifted as far to the right ideologically as the presidential election might seem to indicate. Without question, though, Ronald Reagan had earned an enormous personal vindication. And he had won an electoral mandate to pursue, in his pragmatic way, policies that before 1980 had struck conventional pundits as far outside the political mainstream. Despite the administration's numerous setbacks, scandals, and internal contradictions, the age of Reagan had reached a new political peak.

7

"CALL IT MYSTICISM
IF YOU WILL"

A COLD WAVE HIT WASHINGTON in mid-January, forcing the ceremonies for Reagan's second inauguration to move inside the Capitol and curbing the televised splendor of 1981. The president's second inaugural address was also very different from his first. After claiming credit for the economic recovery, Reagan offered only a sparse domestic agenda focused on a reform of the tax code (which he would achieve) and a balanced budget (which he would not achieve). Reagan was more expansive on foreign policy—and more militant than he had been four years earlier. The Soviet Union, he declared, had completed "the greatest military buildup in the history of man." The threat demanded an all-out American response, including full funding of the Strategic Defense Initiative. In his State of the Union message several days later, the president asked Congress not to "break faith with those who are risking their lives—on every continent, from Afghanistan to Nicaragua—to defy Soviet-supported aggression." Paying no heed to the Boland Amendments, he described the Nicaraguan contras as "freedom fighters," and in March he praised the contras as "the moral equivalent of our Founding Fathers and the brave men and women of the French Resistance." It appeared that the conciliatory track with the Soviet Union had hit a dead end, that the Reagan Doctrine was coming into its own, and that the struggle to roll back communism would dominate Reagan's second term.

As it happened, Reagan still had ambitions regarding domestic policy—

and rolling back the liberal welfare state. Yet on some fronts, his administration, having already fallen far short of the new right's goals, advanced no further. On others, early success gave way to internal dissension and some signal defeats. These failures, as well as numerous compromises, demonstrated the limits of the new right's popular appeal and political muscle. It also showed how the forces of pragmatism often restrained the more zealous elements inside the Reagan administration. To be sure, Reagan continued to build an enduring conservative legacy, above all in his judicial appointments and in a fresh round of fiscal reform. Even when the administration gave ground, its symbolic and rhetorical gestures on civil rights and other issues helped sustain the electoral base that had elected Reagan twice. Still, coming after the president's stunning victory in 1984, the Reagan revolution often seemed divided and oddly adrift during his second term.

Almost forgotten today, meanwhile, are the numerous costs of the Reaganites' attack on "big government" that began accruing after 1984. The rush to deregulate business and finance led to some disasters, most dramatically the collapse of a large segment of the nation's savings and loan system. Huge federal deficits, a direct result of the administration's fiscal policies, effectively forestalled any new major social programs. This met with the approval of supposedly fiscally austere conservatives—but the deficits also drained away valuable economic resources. Although the Reagan years are now frequently recalled as a time of moral rearmament and patriotic pride, the administration overlooked and sometimes indulged negligence and permissiveness on a grand scale. The toll of that neglect, in venality and arrant lawlessness, piled up during the second term, leaving Reagan's presidency with a record of official corruption unsurpassed, except by Nixon's administration, since the end of World War II. Lawlessness also became a feature of Reagan's foreign policy—and created a scandal that nearly brought the administration to its knees.

The start of a second presidential term is commonly a time for reshuffling White House personnel, but Reagan began making important changes even before his reelection. Early in 1984, Attorney General William French Smith decided to return to his lucrative practice in Los Angeles, and Reagan immediately named the presidential special counsel Edwin Meese as his successor. Reports quickly surfaced alleging that Meese had received financial rewards from several individuals whom he had helped obtain federal jobs, and the uproar compelled Smith to delay his departure and appoint an independent counsel. The counsel's report, issued in September, concluded merely that there was insufficient evidence to indict Meese, a less than ringing vindication. The Office of Government Ethics, meanwhile, charged that Meese had indeed committed fundamental violations of ethics. The revelations were damaging enough to keep the issue roiling until the Republican-dominated Senate finally confirmed the nomination in February 1985. Reagan had won, but at a considerable political cost. Meese took office with his reputation badly clouded.

Reagan also followed through, after the election, on a curious proposal by his secretary of the treasury, Donald Regan. Regan had been feuding with the chief of staff, James Baker; and after one blowup in late November, Regan suggested (during a conciliatory private chat) that they swap jobs. Regan said that Baker looked tired, and Baker conceded that he was: the strain of running the White House day to day had taken its toll. With tax reform on the agenda for the second term, the job of treasury secretary looked inviting to Baker; and as chief of staff, Regan, who had come to government service only recently after a long and successful career at the brokerage house Merrill Lynch, would be at the very center of executive power. The more the switch was discussed, the more sensible it seemed, and the president signed off on the plan. Nancy Reagan was reluctant to lose Baker's effectiveness inside the Oval Office, but her friend Michael Deaver reassured her about Regan and she grudgingly assented.

Regan's arrival abruptly changed the tone inside the White House. Unlike the patrician Baker, Regan was a self-made man, a son of Irish Catholic South Boston who had succeeded in graduating with highest honors from Harvard and then worked and maneuvered his way up the corporate ladder. Prone to bluntness and, at times, irascibility, he lacked both the experience and the politician's diplomatic impulses that Baker had in abundance; indeed, Regan regarded politics and politicians with contempt, a severe handicap in dealing with Congress. The president liked Regan's persona as an up-from-under individualist, and the two men, closer in age than Baker and Reagan, shared a generational affinity. But whereas Baker was prudent, collegial, and protective of the president, Regan was self-promoting, argumentative, touchy about his prerogatives, and perfectly willing to let Reagan follow his own instincts, no matter how politically damaging they might be. Familiar with the corporate hierarchy, Regan combined the functions previously performed by Baker, Deaver, and Meese; established himself as the maximum boss; and presented no dissenting views to the president. The structure as well as the style of the new operation was very different from Baker's, and the difference would prove costly during the two years that Regan was chief of staff—until a Washington insider more like Jim Baker, the moderate former Republican leader in the Senate, Howard Baker, took over the job in 1987.

The transition from Jim Baker to Don Regan had additional consequences. When James Baker moved to the Treasury Department, he took with him a talented group of aides, including Richard Darman, who had helped check the more dogmatic new-right currents inside the administration. In May, Michael Deaver, the last remaining member of Reagan's original trio, left the White House to run his own public relations firm; David Stockman and the political director, Ed Rollins, also left in due course. Regan brought in new faces. One group of Regan's aides, called, derisively, "the Mice," were known for reserving their loyalty mainly for their boss, the chief of staff, instead of the president. Another new face—not mousy in the least—was the veteran right-wing polemicist and former speechwriter for the Nixon administration, Patrick J. Buchanan, whom Regan hired in February to replace the middle-of-the-road establishment Republican David Gergen as White House director of communications and to oversee the speechwriting department. Although politically astute and often shrewd, Buchanan was also an ideologue with a well-known weakness for rhetorical bomb-throwing. In his own way, he too injected a style very different from that of the departed, judicious Baker-Darman group.

The personnel changes had the additional, unintended effect of elevating the importance of the first lady. During her husband's first year as president, Nancy Reagan had become notorious as a frivolous, big-spending Hollywood socialite, with little sense of public responsibility beyond her adoration of Ronald Reagan. The subsequent revelation that, after the assassination attempt in 1981, she regularly consulted an astrologer, Joan Quigley, regarding her husband's schedule, made her seem flaky as well as selfish. But these impressions were misleading. Beginning in 1982, Mrs. Reagan heeded her critics, relied on advice from Deaver, and focused on various public issues—most conspicuously discouraging drug use in schools, leading to her famous "Just Say No" campaign. More important, the first lady had proved to be a source of sound, insider political intelligence on matters ranging from personnel appointments to debate strategy, always placing her husband's well-being above all other considerations. She was allergic to the more dogmatic conservatives (for whom the cause always took precedence over the president) and suspicious of hard-chargers, who she thought lacked class and tact; and she developed a particularly intense dislike of Donald Regan—a man, she privately quipped, who liked the sound of "chief" but not of "staff." After her closest ally within the White House, Michael Deaver, left in 1985, Nancy Reagan discovered that, more than ever, she would have to take it upon herself and what allies she could find to help protect and guide her husband. During Reagan's second term, this would be a continual and demanding task.

The hard-fought installation of Ed Meese as attorney general reaffirmed that the White House would continue to push the staunchly conservative social and cultural agenda of Reagan's first term. This included civil rights—an issue much less urgent to Reagan than taxes and fiscal policy, but highly sensitive and important for political as well as ideological reasons. Meese had made his reputation in California as Reagan's hard-edged, conservative chief of staff, best known for his instrumental role in cracking down on campus protesters. And during his climb to the White House, Reagan deployed his version of the Republicans' law-and-order southern strategy originated by Richard Nixon, appealing to conservative whites in the South as well as to alienated blue-collar whites and suburban conservative Catholics in the North. On the campaign trail in the 1970s and 1980, Reagan showed that he was not above pandering to white bigots: he repeatedly alluded to an unnamed "welfare queen" and (in at least one speech in the South) a "strapping young buck" who allegedly defrauded the welfare system. In 1980, Reagan's "states' rights" speech opening his general election campaign at the annual Neshoba County, Mississippi, fair, near the site where James Chaney, Andrew Goodman, and Michael Schwerner had been murdered in 1964, sent a clear message: although, perforce, he would sometimes speak in praise of tolerance and racial harmony, his administration would side with those who wished to curtail the civil rights reforms of the 1960s and 1970s, including the Voting Rights Act of 1965 (which Reagan derided as "humiliating to the South").

Meese had made clear his hostility to enforcement of civil rights laws during Reagan's first term, but other controversial figures were much more involved in the administration's day-to-day gutting of civil rights mandates. They included two men with utterly different backgrounds: William Bradford Reynolds and Clarence Thomas. Reynolds would later be described as Meese's alter ego. He was a descendant of an eminent Puritan divine, Governor William Bradford of Massachusetts, and of the Du Pont family of modern industrialists; had graduated from Vanderbilt Law School; had worked briefly in the Justice Department during Nixon's administration; and had spent more than a decade as a corporate lawyer in Washington before entering the Reagan administration in 1981 as assistant attorney general for civil rights, the nation's highest-ranking enforcer of civil rights laws. His ideological ally, Thomas, a descendant of southern slaves, had risen from a broken home in Pin Point, Georgia, and had graduated from Holy Cross and Yale Law School. With the aid of his mentor John Danforth of Missouri (elected to the U.S. Senate in 1976), Thomas made his way in the public and private sectors. In 1981, after two years of working for Danforth as a legislative assistant, he was named assistant secretary of education for the Office of Civil Rights, and the following year he took over as chairman of the Equal Employment Opportunity Commission, or EEOC. (Reagan would later describe Thomas as "my man on the Equal Opp. board," and praise him for doing "a h—l of a good job.")

For all their dissimilarities, Reynolds and Thomas were both relatively young (Reynolds turned thirty-nine in 1981; Thomas was six years his junior). Both would help spearhead the attacks by the Reagan administration on what the Department of Justice called the "reverse discrimination" of affirmative action laws, school busing plans, and other liberal endeavors to accelerate racial integration and civil equality.

Reynolds quickly won attention for his outspoken attacks on existing civil rights legislation, including the Voting Rights Act of 1965. When the act came up for renewal in 1982, he pushed hard for the president to kill it. The federal government, Reynolds argued, ought to limit itself to barring voting rules that intentionally discriminated against minorities, rather than those, targeted by the renewal bill, which merely had a demonstrably discriminatory effect. (Reagan strongly sympathized with Reynolds, but when more mainstream traditional Republicans in both the House and the Senate, led by the Senate majority leader, Robert Dole, worked out a compromise, Reagan signed the extension legislation.) Reynolds also helped assemble and galvanize a cohort of well-schooled, activist ideologues, including religious conservatives and adherents of the pro-free-market, so-called law and economics movement.

Reynolds's collaborators turned the Justice Department, as one of the most thoughtful of their number later boasted, into "one of the most conservative agencies" of the Reagan era. Under Reynolds's direction, the civil rights division of the Justice Department ignored alleged violations of the Voting Rights Act and intervened to overturn affirmative action plans in numerous cities, counties, and states—plans that previous administrations had helped to formulate. At the EEOC, meanwhile, Clarence Thomas quietly dropped the use of class action suits to enforce the hiring of minorities and allowed thousands of job bias complaints, including more than 10,000 allegations of age discrimination, to languish unattended, compelling Congress to pass the Age Discrimination Claims Assistance Act in 1988.

The more that administration officials either disregarded or turned against existing civil rights laws, the more critics charged that the White House was not simply conservative but actively siding with die-hard segregationists. In the most glaring episode, President Reagan, early in 1982, backed the racially discriminatory Bob Jones University of South Carolina, and the Christian Schools of Goldsboro, North Carolina, in a lawsuit against the Internal Revenue Service (IRS), which had denied them tax exemptions under civil rights guidelines authorized by President Nixon in 1970. Supported by Meese, Reynolds, and Attorney General Smith, the case for opposing the IRS arrived on Reagan's desk as a simple matter of checking harassment by "big government." The public reaction was instant and overwhelming. "It is nothing short of criminal," declared Benjamin Hooks, executive director of the National Association for the Advancement of Colored People (NAACP). Some of the small number of comparatively conservative blacks who held responsible positions in the administration bridled, wondering, as one of them said, "whether it is the intention of this Administration to appear antiblack." James Baker and Michael Deaver, disturbed by the political fallout (and fearful especially of losing support among socially tolerant white independents), prevailed on Reagan to pull back and ask Congress for legislation to enable the IRS to act as it had already done. The point soon became academic: for differing reasons, both religious-right groups and advocates of civil rights rejected the president's new proposal, and in May 1983, the Supreme Court decided, eight to one, that the original decision by the IRS had been perfectly lawful.

Repeatedly, the White House undermined its own protestations of good faith in pursuing evenhanded, "color-blind" justice. The president had an especially difficult time over honoring the memory of Martin Luther King Jr. Reagan publicly praised King for freeing Americans from "the burden of racism," and claimed that by rejecting affirmative action programs, he was trying to retrieve the original antidiscriminatory spirit of the civil rights movement—but he also opposed efforts by civil rights organizations and congressional liberals to make King's birthday a federal holiday. Only when congressional support for the holiday became overwhelming did Reagan change his stance. Yet a few weeks before he signed the legislation establishing the holiday, when asked by a reporter about the holdout Senator Jesse Helms's accusations that King had been a communist sympathizer, Reagan replied, flippantly, "We'll know in about thirty-five years, won't we?" and then defended Helms for demanding that King's sealed FBI files be opened. "I almost lost my dinner over that," said David Gergen, still the communications director.

Pent-up ire among civil rights groups and liberal Democrats deepened the animosity on Capitol Hill to Meese's appointment as attorney general. The ire exploded soon afterward, early in the second term, when Reagan nominated William Bradford Reynolds to become associate attorney general, the third-highest post at the Justice Department. More than fifty witnesses testified before the Senate Judiciary Committee in opposition to Reynolds; Democratic committee members harshly criticized Reynolds's record at the Justice Department, aghast that such an outwardly intelligent and decent man could, in Senator Howard Metzenbaum's words, "come down in some of these cases on the side of the bigots."

The judiciary committee's rejection of Reynolds's nomination—an outcome that few had foreseen—stung the White House. Essentially, the situation did not change: Reynolds kept his post at the Justice Department, and the administration remained generally hostile to wielding federal authority in order to combat discrimination (including discrimination against women, disabled persons, and the elderly as well as racial minorities). But Reagan took some symbolic steps during his second term, to make amends. At one White House ceremony in 1987, marking the second national observation of King's birthday, he gave an affecting speech to high school students, in which he praised King as a martyr to America's "promise of liberty and justice for all." And efforts by hard-liners in the administration to advance their agenda ran into increasing difficulties, chiefly because of mounting political cross pressures inside the administration and on Capitol Hill.

In May 1985, Reynolds, with support from Meese, William Bennett, and other cabinet members, stepped up a major intramural campaign he had begun a year earlier to overturn an executive order, originally signed by Lyndon Johnson two decades before, which required government contractors to adopt affirmative action guidelines. Reynolds's efforts, though, met stiff opposition from Secretary of Labor William Brock. Not only did Brock want to protect his department's authority over compliance by government contractors, but many business leaders and organizations (including the National Association of Manufacturers), although strongly favoring deregulation in other areas, preferred sticking with predicable, long-established procedures on hiring goals to entering uncharted legal waters and facing new "reverse discrimination" lawsuits. Brock rallied several other cabinet members to his side, including Secretary of the Treasury Baker and Secretary of State George Shultz (who, as Richard Nixon's secretary of labor, had supported mandatory affirmative action by government contractors). Reynolds fought back with a report documenting allegations of improper demands by the Labor Department for fixed racial quotas, but he succeeded only in redoubling the resistance of Brock and Brock's allies. By mid-1986, Reynolds's campaign was over.

Protracted wrangling over a Supreme Court decision in 1984 in the case of *Grove City v. Bell* became the major civil rights imbroglio in Reagan's second term—and ended in another setback for the administration. The court's decision sharply narrowed the effects of existing legislation by declaring that federal agencies could not withhold public funds from colleges and other institutions found guilty of discrimination; the agencies could withhold funds only from the specific departments within those institutions that had violated the law. Civil rights groups organized to have the decision overturned, and several bills appeared on Capitol Hill with the intent of remedying the ruling. The White House, however, remained silent, aside from issuing a brief statement in 1985 favoring the weakest of the proposed remedy bills.

Early in 1988, Congress finally passed the Civil Rights Restoration Bill, designed to undo *Grove City* and extend antibias laws, in line with what its sponsors called the clear intent of the Civil Rights Act of 1964. Reagan promptly vetoed the bill, claiming that it would "vastly and unjustifiably expand the power of the federal government." Instead, he proposed his own Civil Rights Protection Bill, which would overturn the *Grove City* ruling but specifically exempt educational institutions "closely identified with religious organizations" from the provisions about discrimination by sex. The administration's bill was dead on arrival on Capitol Hill and Congress overrode Reagan's veto, with dozens of Republicans crossing the aisle.

Overall, Reagan's civil rights policies resulted more in political rewards than in long-term legal changes. While earning the enmity of civil rights advocates and black voters, the administration signaled to the new southern Republicans and the "Reagan Democrats" its militant opposition to civil rights laws that they felt threatened their social and economic status. In foreign affairs, Reagan's policy of "constructive engagement" with the apartheid-based government of South Africa, and his veto (subsequently overturned) of economic sanctions against the South African regime in

1986, had a similar effect, while also suggesting that, more than ever, the search for anticommunist military allies and lucrative private trade contracts took precedence over simple racial justice. At home, the seeming indifference of officials in the administration to urban problems of crime and poverty, including a fearsome scourge of crack cocaine in the late 1980s, had perceived racial overtones. Women's rights' groups, already angry at the administration's friendliness to antiabortion activists, complained bitterly about nonenforcement of Title IX of the Education Amendment legislation of 1972, which had outlawed sex discrimination in schools and colleges.

The president's failure, until late 1985, to address seriously the spreading contagion of acquired immunodeficiency syndrome, or AIDS, reflected both a deep-seated public antagonism toward homosexuality and a political determination by the White House not to rile its supporters in the religious right. "The poor homosexuals," Pat Buchanan sneered, before he joined the White House staff. "They have declared war on nature and now nature is exacting an awful retribution." Other conservatives called AIDS a "gay plague," unleashed by the Almighty to punish sexual perversion. Reagan thought homosexuality "a sad thing," but he harbored no particular dislike of gays and lesbians; Reagan's aide Martin Anderson has recalled him saying "that in Hollywood he knew a lot of gays, and he never had any problem with them." (His gay friends included the actor Rock Hudson, whose death from AIDS in 1985 shook the Reagans badly.) Early in 1986, the president asked his surgeon general, C. Everett Koop—an evangelical Christian originally appointed because of his opposition to abortion—to issue a full report on AIDS. But Koop's scientific findings, his recommendation of sex education in schools, and his encouragement of condoms earned him condemnation from many prominent conservatives, including Reagan's secretary of education, William Bennett.

Gay activists responded with both outraged street-theater protests and calmer efforts to build public support for increased funding of AIDS research and public awareness programs. Having previously defended levels of federal funding that medical experts thought woefully insufficient, Reagan finally declared, in 1987, that AIDS was "public enemy number one." But the president, cautious of appearing too untraditional or even slightly progay, held off talking with Koop about the report on AIDS. He refused, despite his wife's entreaties, to endorse condoms (a bugbear of hard-line Catholic conservatives). And he left it entirely up to Congress to appropriate substantial monies for AIDS research—thereby disappointing members of his own family. "He can be as stubborn on a couple of issues & won't listen to anyone's argument," the president wrote after his son, Ron, criticized the administration's inaction on AIDS in an article for the popular weekly magazine *People*. At the start of Reagan's second term—by which time researchers had identified the viral source of the infection—AIDS had claimed the lives of 5,600 Americans, most of them young male homosexuals. Four years later, the death toll had climbed to nearly 50,000. By comparison, in Britain, where the Conservative government undertook broad public health initiatives, the incidence of infection by the AIDS virus was one-tenth as high as the figure in the United States.

The controversy over AIDS illustrated how, by the mid-1980s, issues of civil rights had begun to blend with broader convulsions over gender, sexuality, and race, in what would soon be called, offhandedly, the "culture wars." Nothing signified so clearly the displacement of 1960s-style liberalism than the ferocity of these struggles, over issues that included prayer in schools, federal funding of controversial art exhibitions, and the future of legalized abortion. On the right, conservative evangelicals, increasingly a major force at the grassroots of the Republican Party, proclaimed America a Christian nation that had been degraded by the secular humanist cultural vandals of the 1960s, and they vowed a complete moral and cultural restoration. Neoconservatives joined in the attacks on feminism and gay rights as products of a subversive counterculture. On the hard left, discouraged, pessimistic minority-rights activists, joined by some influential writers in the universities, increasingly spurned the old universalist, integrationist credo in favor of a group-centered ideal—later known, loosely, as multiculturalism—that emphasized the cultivation and celebration of distinct ethnic, gender, and sexual identities in order to offset what they perceived as the Anglocentrism and conventional white male domination of American life.

The Reagan administration and the regnant conservatives in the Republican Party repeatedly paid obeisance to the right-wing culture warriors, especially their leading allies in the religious right, such as Jerry Falwell. (Falwell, whom Reagan described in 1983 as "a good friend & highly supportive," delivered the benediction prayer at the Republican National Convention a year later.) Yet while the White House strongly encouraged the growth of the religious right, it was also very careful, as ever, not to get out too far in front of mainstream public opinion over specific issues such as legalized abortion (on which a small but steady majority of Americans was pro-choice) or affirmative action (on which public attitudes, as well as business opinion, regarding programs that did not involve rigid racial quotas tended toward moderation and, in some cases, general approval). After lending presidential prestige, during his first term, to proposed constitutional amendments that would overturn *Roe v. Wade* and restrict federal authority over controversial matters such as school prayer, Reagan backed off after 1984, realizing that such measures were doomed on Capitol Hill. Confident that the religious right and other cultural conservatives would never defect to the Democrats, the administration tried to control its base with token gestures and rhetorical solidarity, refraining from risking too much by initiating more dramatic, substantive efforts.

In the late 1980s, some implacable antiabortion conservatives, frustrated by the administration's failure to nullify *Roe v. Wade*, undertook forcible civil disobedience campaigns to block access to abortion clinics. Violent fringe elements (sometimes with the implied sympathy of more mainstream conservatives) would later bomb abortion offices and shoot several abortion practitioners. In their embitterment, however, the right-wing militants failed to appreciate that the Reagan administration, and in particular the Justice Department, was quietly waging its own pragmatic version of the culture wars with a long-term strategy that was as comprehensive as it was deliberate. The key to this strategy was to reverse the philosophy of judicial decision making bequeathed by the New Deal and the Great Society. The main fights were in the area of judicial appointments. These fights led to rough confrontations in the Senate over Supreme Court confirmations in 1986 and 1987. They also brought a pronounced rightward shift in the federal judiciary, which would be one of Ronald Reagan's chief political legacies.

During the campaign of 1980, Reagan pledged that he would appoint to the federal bench only qualified candidates who would oppose "judicial activism," adhere to strict construction of the Constitution, and promote "family values"—familiar conservative bywords for checking liberal jurisprudence on federal economic regulation, civil rights, and abortion rights. As president, Reagan actually showed little interest in any direct involvement in selecting nominees—yet his administration wound up having more influence over the composition of the judiciary than any since Franklin Delano Roosevelt's. Whereas Reagan's two predecessors named, between them, only one associate justice to the Supreme Court, Reagan had the chance to appoint three new associate justices and to elevate one sitting justice, Nixon's appointee William H. Rehnquist, to the position of Chief Justice. During his two terms, Reagan also appointed 368 district and appeals court justices—more than any other president in history. These appointments accounted for nearly half the judgeships in the lower federal courts. Not surprisingly, the vast majority of those appointed were white conservatives of the sort Reagan had promised in 1980, including numerous conservatives in the new-right movement, who were especially favored at the Justice Department.

Necessity combined with opportunity to increase the importance of judicial nominations. It would be far easier to gain the required Senate approval for ideologically friendly judicial nominees than to win legislative fights with Congress. (Quite apart from the implicit assumption that, except in extreme cases, any president was entitled to have his judicial nominees approved, the Republicans held on to their solid majority in the Senate through the first half of Reagan's second term, and Strom Thurmond was the powerful chairman of the crucial Senate Judiciary Committee.) Lifetime appointments to the bench were also impervious to the cycles of American politics. The new judges, as Meese said, could "institutionalize the Reagan revolution so it can't be set aside no matter what happens in future presidential elections."

A continuing expansion of the size of the federal judiciary to deal with mounting caseloads made that prospect all the more tantalizing. Presented with upwards of fifty judicial vacancies annually, above and beyond normal attrition, the administration had an extraordinary opportunity to overhaul prevailing judicial outlooks for a long time to come. To maximize that opportunity, Reagan's officials abandoned the customary method of treating judicial appointments as patronage rewards, political bargaining chips, or bipartisan bows to individual competence. In its place, said Stephen Markman, the assistant attorney general for legal policy during Reagan's second term, these officials built on the tough, politicized, conservative approach of Richard Nixon's Justice Department and devised a process that emphasized the "philosophical grounding" of potential judicial appointees—and they vetted candidates on ideological criteria much more carefully than even the Nixon administration had.

Under Reagan, a new centralized screening process drastically diminished the influence normally exerted by the American Bar Association in rating nominees. (The White House simply eliminated consultations, begun under Jimmy Carter, with the National Bar Association, the leading black lawyers' organization.) Instead, officials and staff members at the Office of Legal Policy at the Justice Department scrutinized the records of possible judges and conducted daylong personal interviews, asking candidates directly about their opinions on abortion, affirmative action, and criminal procedure. (Interviews of any sort were unprecedented, and previous officials at the Justice Department, including President Eisenhower's attorney general Herbert Brownell, denounced what they deemed a shocking ideological politicization of the process.) Once approved, candidates' names advanced to a new White House Judicial Selection Committee, consisting of presidential advisers and the chief of staff as well as the attorney general and other Justice Department officials. This committee convened weekly to decide exactly which names the president would nominate. Reagan's officials defended the procedures and claimed that there was no single litmus test for selection, but the White House had plainly expanded its direct authority over judicial selections and made ideological considerations paramount.

Reagan's rearrangements proved enormously effective in placing new hard-line conservatives in the federal appellate and district courts. The process did not, to be sure, always advance smoothly. Senators, including moderate Republicans, came to resent the administration's treading on their patronage turf as well as the narrow ideological sluice through which successful candidates now had to pass. A few of the White House's nominees seemed irredeemably inferior and blatantly political. One, Jefferson B. Sessions (later to be elected to the U.S. Senate), was denied a seat on a district court in Alabama in a narrow vote by the Senate Judiciary Committee—only the second such rejection in fifty years. A few other nominees aroused such stiff opposition that the White House withdrew their names before the Senate began deliberations. But these defeats were negligible when weighed against the administration's hundreds of victories.

The administration was only superficially more flexible in making nominations to the Supreme Court. In October 1980, when his election campaign seemed to be faltering, Reagan had tried to increase his political momentum by promising to name a woman to the Court. When the first vacancy appeared four months after his inauguration, Reagan reminded his advisers of his pledge and fixed on nominating a suitable woman right away. With strong support from Associate Justice Rehnquist, the conservative senators Barry Goldwater and Paul Laxalt, and Attorney General Smith, the name of Sandra Day O'Connor, a federal district court judge in Arizona, quickly rose to the top of the list.

O'Connor faced fierce opposition from Jerry Falwell as well as from Richard Viguerie and the National Right to Life Committee. Her past support for the Equal Rights Amendment was one reason; also, in 1973, as a state senator in Arizona, she had cosponsored a bill that would have permitted state agencies to make "all medically acceptable family planning methods and information" widely available. But Reagan found O'Connor charming when they met at the White House, believed her conservative views on the Constitution and jurisprudence wholly sound, and took as sincere her statements that she personally found abortion abhorrent. The president was also happy to shake up his liberal critics by making history with the first appointment of a woman to the Court. The nomination cleared the Senate by a vote of ninety-nine to none.

Reagan's later maneuver concerning the Supreme Court encountered more difficulties. Shortly after O'Connor's confirmation, Attorney General Meese directed William Bradford Reynolds to identify potential nominees in case another opening should occur on the Court. Reynolds's team made a list of twenty choices, headed by two adamant conservatives with excellent academic and judicial pedigrees: the recently appointed D.C. district court judges Robert Bork (a former professor at Yale Law School) and Antonin Scalia (a former professor at the law schools of the University of Virginia and the University of Chicago).

A vacancy did arise, in 1986, in a wholly unanticipated way when Chief Justice Warren Burger resigned in order to lead full-time a commission established to commemorate the bicentennial of the Constitution in 1987. With Meese's backing, Reagan named the most conservative of the court's associate justices, William H. Rehnquist, as Burger's successor. The White House then decided that Scalia's ethnic and religious background (no Italian-American and very few Catholics had ever served on the Court) and his relative youth (at fifty, he was eight years younger than Bork) were in his favor as the nominee for Rehnquist's seat as associate justice.

Unlike his friend and fellow Arizonan Sandra O'Connor, Rehnquist raised the hackles of Democratic liberals. In his long judicial and political career, he had emerged as the most prominent advocate of what one writer has called "conservative statism," a concern for upholding the status quo, as opposed to the claims of outsiders or the protection of individual rights, with regard to power. During his fifteen years as an associate justice, Rehnquist had been an uncompromising critic of what he viewed as his colleagues' continuation of the unconstitutional liberal jurisprudence of the Warren Court. He had led the charge against the court majority in such prominent cases as *Roe v. Wade*, and he had also written more than four dozen solo dissents.

Senator Edward Kennedy, who had opposed Rehnquist's original nomination for the Court in 1971, now led the opposition to his promotion, declaring that he was "too extreme on race, too extreme on women's rights, too extreme on freedom of speech, too extreme on separation of church and state, too extreme to be Chief Justice." During his televised appearance before the judiciary committee, Rehnquist adopted an uncharacteristic tone of evasive blandness; he refused to discuss his past judicial opinions, and he parried allegations that he had supported school segregation in the 1950s and harassed minority voters at the polls in the 1960s. The Republicans charged that Kennedy and the Democrats were out of bounds and that they were threatening to turn the hearings into what Senator Orrin Hatch called a "Rehnquisition." The thirty-three votes against Rehnquist in the full Senate were the most cast against any successful nominee to the Court to this point in the twentieth century. But Rehnquist's confirmation was never seriously in doubt. And having exerted so much energy over Rehnquist, liberals in the Senate had neither the strength nor the desire to work up much opposition to Scalia, who in any case possessed sterling credentials and unquestionable intellectual force and agility. The judiciary committee gave Scalia its unanimous approval and, after barely five minutes of debate, the full Senate voted ninety-eight to none to confirm him.

A year later, Justice Lewis Powell announced his resignation, and the White House duly nominated Robert Bork to the Court—but the political atmosphere had changed dramatically. Heavy Republican losses in the midterm elections of 1986 had given the Senate majority back to the Democrats, and with it control of the confirmation process. Bork would have to face a Senate Judiciary Committee chaired not by Strom Thurmond but by the centrist-liberal Democrat Joseph R. Biden, who was an aspirant for the presidency. And even though Bork's views were almost identical to Scalia's, he was a much more problematic candidate. Liberal Democrats still remembered that, as solicitor general during the Watergate affair, he had agreed to carry out Richard Nixon's notorious "Saturday night massacre," firing the overly inquisitive special prosecutor Archibald Cox, after Bork's superiors, Attorney General Elliot Richardson and Deputy Attorney General William Ruckelshaus, had refused to comply and left their jobs.

A self-assured, at times prickly personality, Bork had conducted something of a personal crusade in lambasting the Court's decision in *Griswold v. Connecticut* (1965), which had laid down standards of individual privacy that became a basis for many other decisions, including the majority ruling in *Roe v. Wade*. Justice Powell, in his last two terms on the Court, had cast the crucial vote in rejecting positions of the Reagan administration in cases involving abortion, affirmative action, and other issues. It seemed certain that Bork, if confirmed as a justice, would tip the balance the other way.

With the stakes so high regarding Bork's nomination, both the administration and its opponents organized furiously. Discounting the objections of Attorney General Meese and other go-for-broke militants in the Justice Department, the White House portrayed Bork as far more moderate than his reputation suggested (or his record disclosed), in order to make his liberal critics seem shrill and irresponsible. ("We'll get Bork confirmed to Supreme Ct. but it will be a battle with left wing ideologs," Reagan wrote in his diary.) Liberals in the Senate and advocacy groups such as People for the American Way provided evidence to back up Edward Kennedy's polemical charge that Bork envisaged an America "in which women would be forced into back alley abortions, blacks would sit at segregated lunch counters, . . . school children could not be taught about evolution, writers and artists could be censored at the whim of government." Biden and other more moderate Democrats based their opposition on broader principles regarding the Constitution's protections of individual rights and privacy, instead of specific divisive issues such as abortion and affirmative action. Organizations of the new right, unhappy with the administration's approach, countered the liberal groups with their own expensive lobbying campaigns in favor of confirmation, portraying Bork in the brightest conservative hues. ("Some of Judge Bork's right wing supporters," the White House counsel Arthur B. Culvahouse Jr. noted, thought that trying to cast him as a mainstream figure "is an extremely poor strategy destined to ensure Judge Bork's defeat.")

Bork himself, certain of his intellectual mastery and confident of his eventual confirmation, followed a course very different from Rehnquist's a year earlier—sometimes speaking his mind bluntly, sometimes adopting the White House's strategy of tactical moderation, but always engaging the issues laid before him. In five days of testimony before the judiciary committee, he gave an unsettling performance, elucidating his implacable positions on issues such as abortion, and offering unusual assurances about how he would vote on specific issues before the Court, while also trying to reposition himself as an equable, even "centrist" jurist. Some of Bork's disquisitions varied so blatantly from his case opinions and other writings that the Democratic senator Patrick Leahy asked if he had undergone a suspicious "confirmation conversion." Other replies by Bork sounded so flip and so mechanistically abstract and legalistic that they reinforced his image as an out-of-touch ideologue. The president understood all this differently—

"They never laid a hand on him," he wrote when Bork finished testifying—but by the time the hearing ended, the nomination was in trouble. After the judiciary committee voted nine to five against his appointment, the full Senate rejected him, fifty-eight to forty-two.

Republican conservatives, who had originally expected an easy confirmation and were alarmed at this latest sign of the political times, tried to salvage the situation by hurling ferocious allegations at the Democrats. Scurrilous, unpatriotic, and partisan liberals, they said, in and outside Congress, had supposedly defiled the confirmation process by indulging in an unprecedented public campaign. This claim ignored a long history of contentious, sometimes ugly confirmation proceedings for the Supreme Court going back to George Washington's presidency. The claim also ignored the fact that new-right groups had mounted their own strident public campaign on Bork's behalf (even though the administration, for tactical reasons, tried to tone it down). The anti-Bork publicity, without question, damaged his candidacy, but complaints that it was politicized, inaccurate, and even mendacious were mostly far-fetched. (They were also somewhat brazen, given the administration's single-minded politicization of the judicial nomination process.) And if the liberal critics injured his image, Bork's strange testimony damaged his candidacy far more decisively, leaving the impression that he either was exactly the kind of extremist his critics claimed he was or else lacked integrity.

The main reason for Bork's downfall, though, was neither the liberals' harshness nor even his own odd "confirmation conversion," but his own previously and clearly stated views. Uncharacteristically—and far more than in Scalia's case—senators had become well acquainted with Bork's writings. For months before his actual nomination, his name had been bandied about as a probable nominee to the Court, and this gave liberal lawmakers and their staffs ample time to study his record. His reputation as a great scholar of the law, exaggerated though it was, goaded liberals in the Senate to do their homework with special vigilance. And what they found—in Bork's highly charged defense of an "original intent" approach to the Constitution; in his outspoken writings about privacy law, abortion, and other matters; and in his close association with the hard political right—made him unacceptable. A feeling of chagrin on Capitol Hill for having given Scalia a free pass may also have contributed to the intense opposition. Unease at Bork's ideas explains why six moderate Republican senators voted against his confirmation, along with numerous southern conservative Democrats who would have happily supported a more conventional conservative nominee.

Stunned and angered, Meese and Bork thought the White House staff had been lax. (Howard Baker, by now White House chief of staff, was known to be lukewarm about Bork's nomination.) To avenge their loss, they persuaded Reagan to nominate a young admirer of Bork's and close friend of William Bradford Reynolds's: a proponent of law and economics named Douglas Ginsburg, who had been appointed to the D.C. circuit appeals court in 1986. Ironically, Ginsburg would draw fire from some on the right, including William Bennett, who considered him insufficiently reliable to adhere to the jurisprudence of "original intent." In their haste, meanwhile, the White House and the Justice Department failed to complete full background checks on the nominee, and ten days later, public disclosures about his private life (including his past use of marijuana) forced Ginsburg to withdraw. A few days after that, the White House turned to a more traditional conservative, Anthony Kennedy, who had been passed over in favor of Ginsburg. After Kennedy distanced himself from some of Bork's more controversial statements about privacy law and original intent, his nomination breezed through the Senate.

From one angle, the Bork affair was an unmitigated disaster for the administration, and especially for the true believers of the new right centered in the Justice Department. It certainly indicated that the administration had fallen out of step with mainstream thinking about numerous critical legal issues. But from another angle, it was the exception that proved just how successful Reagan's White House had been in remaking the federal judiciary. Bork's failed nomination would be the only major setback in judicial appointments that Reagan suffered during his eight years as president. By successfully centralizing procedures for selecting nominees, making ideology a critical factor in selection, and turning federal judgeships into an emblem and instrument of executive power, the administration had profoundly politicized the process of appointing federal judges. In the short term, this augured further partisan polarization, and rougher campaigns, in confirmation proceedings across the board. But it also reinvigorated conservatism on the federal bench.

One area in which Reagan's reformers held out high hopes for long-term judicial revision was deregulation, and in continuing the assault on what they considered ludicrous, government-imposed shackles on free enterprise and economic growth. Even more than with civil rights, the administration undertook its deregulatory efforts chiefly with decrees from various cabinet agencies, hoping that the reformed conservative courts would eventually ratify and expand on the changes. But Reagan's sweeping approach to deregulation had produced calamities during his first term, and it produced even more in his second. "If you thought about deregulation in 1979, it seemed a brave new world," a senior analyst at the nonpartisan Urban Institute remarked shortly after Reagan left office. "Now the very idea seems disreputable. People at the outset of the Reagan administration thought we were drowning in government red tape. Now they think we're not being protected."

There were a few successes in deregulation, following up earlier successes with the airlines and trucking industries—though like the others, these were rooted in changes introduced before 1980, and sometimes contained an antitrust element out of keeping with the policies of the Reagan administration. After the government, in 1969, had permitted the MCI corporation to begin competing with the American Telephone and Telegraph (AT&T) monopoly for long-distance service, more competitors arose, prompting the Justice Department to file suit against AT&T in 1974. In 1981, AT&T settled with the government, agreeing to divest itself of its local operations (which were taken over by seven new regional companies, known as Baby Bells). Although local rates to customers rose, the intense unregulated competition among hundreds of companies offering long-distance services brought those rates down precipitously. That competition, along with AT&T's fight for the market in equipment sales, hastened the drive for technical innovation just at the moment when fiber-optic technology became available. In retrospect, the breakup of AT&T and the loosening of some regulatory functions by the government helped pave the way for a telecommunications revolution in the 1990s, a revolution that would include the immense growth of the Internet. Although many longtime employees of AT&T were either demoted or dismissed because of the change, the long-term benefits to the mass of American consumers were obvious.

A more deleterious result—although it was not deleterious in the eyes of many conservatives—came from the abandonment of old regulatory rules by the Federal Communications Commission (FCC), in particular the so-called fairness doctrine. The doctrine, which dated from before the FCC's creation in 1934, stipulated that all broadcast licensees not only present important controversial public issues, but do so in an honest, fair, and balanced way. Upheld as constitutional by the Supreme Court in 1969, the fairness doctrine nevertheless came under attack by hard-line conservatives such as Reed Irvine, a longtime activist of the new right, who argued that it enshrined a hidden liberal conspiracy in the broadcast media. In 1987, the FCC summarily dropped the rule, and later the new Rehnquist Court upheld the change. (In the late 1990s, the D.C. circuit appeals court would order the elimination of a few remaining vestiges of the doctrine that gave private citizens as well as political candidates the right to respond to broadcast attacks on them.) Conservatives celebrated the deregulation as a blow for true balance and fairness that permitted the rise of blatantly right-wing political programming on radio and eventually, in 1996, the appearance of the television Fox News Network—expensive operations that liberals lacked either the funds or the imagination to match. Yet as critics accurately charged, abandoning the rule, regardless of the allegations about building conservative bias in the media, blurred the distinctions among news reports, political advocacy, and political campaigning, and opened the way for a new era of cacophonous talking heads and degraded political debate and discourse.

The most spectacular failure of the Reagan administration regarding deregulation came with the near collapse of the nation's savings and loan industry in the late 1980s—the costliest recorded case of government malfeasance in history. Savings and loan institutions (also known as S&Ls or thrifts) dated back to the nineteenth century and had become increasingly popular during the hard times of the 1930s. Borrowers could obtain home mortgages from the S&Ls for periods of up to thirty years at low, fixed interest rates; and depositors were free to withdraw their money at any time to earn higher interest with other investments. So long as interest rates remained stable, the heavily regulated S&Ls could run profitably as unglamorous institutions appealing to Americans of modest means. But the system faced a crisis during the inflation of the 1970s, when depositors withdrew their funds in favor of banks and brokerage houses, whose newly established money market accounts paid higher rates than the strictly regulated thrifts were permitted to offer.

In 1980, Congress came to the rescue by removing the limits on interest rates paid by S&Ls, lowering the capital reserves required of each institution, and raising the amount of federal depositor insurance guaranteed to each S&L customer from $40,000 to $100,000. Two years later, fresh legislation permitted the S&Ls to expand their lending beyond home mortgages to include a large range of investments, including so-called junk bonds and other high-risk securities. Ostensibly, the changes would salvage an ailing industry that had once helped humble citizens attain the American dream. But lifting the old restrictions was also an open invitation to mismanagement and even fraud by the directors of marginal institutions. If, as a result, an institution failed, the federal government would cover the depositors' losses.

The situation called for new forms of federal regulation, sternly enforced. Instead, the agency with oversight authority, the Federal Home Loan Bank Board (FHLBB), deregulated even more. With the backing of Donald Regan who was then secretary of the treasury, the FHLBB devised a series of bookkeeping changes that made it easier for failing thrifts to hide their situation and abolished the requirement that a thrift must have at least 400 stockholders. As a result, an individual entrepreneur could buy or even create an S&L and invest its monies in all sorts of dubious ventures, with little or no oversight. And unscrupulous sharpsters could also move in, strip away an S&L's assets, and make sweetheart investment deals with friends (including buying real estate at grossly inflated prices with S&L funds). Either way, since the federal government had insured the depositors, the real losers would be the taxpayers—as would become painfully clear at the end of the decade.

Greater vigilance in Washington could have minimized the damage. Financial experts have estimated that if the administration had stepped in by 1983 (by which time nearly 3 percent of the nation's S&Ls had collapsed over the previous three years), the cost to the taxpayers would have been $25 billion; had it acted by 1986, the losses still would have amounted to less than $100 billion. But when Edwin Gray, a longtime associate of Meese's who was chairman of the FHLBB after 1983, became alarmed, asked for additional bank examiners, and proposed new restrictions to halt the mounting disaster, administration officials (including Regan and David Stockman's deputies at the OMB) turned him down flat and accused him of being a "reregulator." Thereafter, as the wave of failures continued, the problem grew so immense that no responsible appointee (not even James Baker, after he took over as secretary of the treasury) would be candid about it publicly, lest the ballooning payouts to ruined depositors discredit the White House's low budget estimates and projections about federal deficits. Gray's efforts to reimpose some of the discarded regulations met with some success before he left office in 1987, but always in the face of strenuous resistance from the S&L's lobbyists and their friends at both ends of Pennsylvania Avenue. Three months before Gray's departure, the nonpartisan Government Accounting Office declared that, under the strain of S&L failures, the Federal Savings and Loan Insurance Corporation (FSLIC) fund was insolvent by at least $3.8 billion. Failures of S&Ls, which had already been especially intense in Ohio and Maryland, would soon rip through Texas; in 1987, Texas accounted for more than half of the total losses nationwide.

Congress's complicity with the White House in shielding the industry from scrutiny—and thereby providing cover for criminality as well as for mere ineptness or misfortune—became clear from the events that led to Gray's dismissal. In April 1987, Gray was summoned to the office of Senator Dennis DeConcini, Republican of Arizona, who, with four other senators from across party lines—Alan Cranston, John Glenn, John McCain, and Donald Riegle—questioned Gray hard about the appropriateness of a continuing investigation by the FHLBB into the Lincoln Savings and Loan of Irvine, California, run by the entrepreneur Charles Keating. After telling his employees to solicit "the weak, meek, and ignorant" to invest in Lincoln Savings, Keating had hired family members at exorbitant salaries while keeping politicians happy by providing them with campaign contributions and low-interest loans. When auditors for the FHLBB alerted him to Lincoln's questionable practices, Gray ordered Keating to invest more of his own money in the enterprise.

Keating accused Gray of conducting a vendetta against him, and called on his friends in the Senate to put pressure on Gray to exempt Lincoln Savings and Loan from federal regulatory rules. When Gray refused to back off, President Reagan fired him and appointed a new FHLBB director, who rejected pleas from bank examiners to shut down Lincoln. Two years later, Keating's enterprise collapsed. The denouement took several years, but under the terms of a plea agreement, Keating finally admitted to a relatively minor charge—extracting $1 million from Lincoln Savings and Loan even when he knew it would fail. All told, the estimated cost to the taxpayers of the ruination of Lincoln would exceed $2 billion. The senators, each of whom had received large campaign contributions from Keating and other S&L operators, were called to account for influence peddling, although two—McCain and Riegle—were exonerated of serious infractions.

The "Keating five" scandal and the collapse of Lincoln Savings and Loan were the most notorious episode in the wider catastrophe. Lincoln was not typical of the devastation among the S&Ls: the great majority of failures involved honorable directors who had invested poorly. Yet no matter what the causes were, the failures, unprecedented in the history of the thrifts, could have been checked had the administration been less blindly devoted to deregulation. The growing problem was evident as early as 1984, when the federal government had to bail out the Continental Illinois Bank to save it from folding. And numerous early cases of criminal conduct and neglect should have alerted Regan, Stockman, and other responsible officials to that side of the catastrophe. In March 1984, federal officials shut down the Empire Savings and Loan of Mesquite, Texas, near Dallas—the first closing explicitly attributed to fraud in the history of the thrifts. In time, more than 100 people would be convicted of crimes connected with Empire's fraudulent land schemes; in 1987 Empire's chairman, Spencer H. Blain Jr., would settle a racketeering suit brought by the FSLIC for $100 million. Yet the laissez-faire cycle of fraud and collapse continued. In 1987 and 1988, a combined total of 249 thrifts failed, with a combined total cost that exceeded $50 billion. Only after Reagan left office did Congress approve a federal bailout of the S&Ls, followed by a complete overhaul of the regulatory procedures in which oversight was handed to a new Office of Thrift Supervision with tougher regulatory powers, and another new entity was created to handle the affairs of insolvent trusts: the Resolution Trust Corporation. In 1996, the General Accounting Office estimated that the total cost of the S&L deregulation spree, including interest, would be almost $370 billion, including $341 from the taxpayers.

There were numerous bad actors in the savings and loan scandal, at all levels of government and in both political parties. But even if Reagan himself knew little about the details, the effects of bad legislation were compounded many times over because his administration applied his favorite cure for any economic problem—deregulation and restoration of the "free" market. In part, the president and his aides could not distinguish between industries in which private investors take all the risks and those in which the taxpayers foot the bill. "The administration was so ideologically blinded," the chastened Edward Gray related, "that it couldn't understand the difference between thrift deregulation and airline deregulation." Nor did the administration understand the simple rule that deregulation also requires supervision and close inspection, especially in the case of financial institutions, to protect innocent investors and the general public. The Reagan officials' overtly pro-business agenda in deregulation—sometimes pursued more ardently by the ideologues inside the administration than by the businessmen themselves—made a mockery of its appeals to grand abstractions such as "freedom"; "competition," and "the market." "Overall," writes Reagan's most knowledgable biographer, "Reagan left a ruinous regulatory legacy."

The S&L crisis, in its various manifestations, also signified the rise of a buccaneer mentality, abetted by flaccid management and oversight that the free-market enthusiasm of Reagan's boom years encouraged. Some of this freebooting affected the administration itself: contempt for big government fostered an attitude that laws existed to be evaded, not executed. Inside the Department of Housing and Urban Development (HUD), the early scandal involving Emmanuel Savas paled beside revelations of subsequent high-level corruption involving, according to an investigation by the House, "influence peddling, favoritism, abuse, greed, fraud, embezzlement and theft." With abandon, HUD officials approved payouts to well-connected Republicans, who used agency funds earmarked for low-income housing in order to build luxury apartment buildings, swimming pools, and golf courses. Called to testify about the looting, the secretary of HUD, Samuel Pierce, took the Fifth Amendment, the first cabinet official to invoke this constitutional protection since the Teapot Dome scandal of the 1920s. It would take an independent counsel nine years to sort out the mess at HUD, in a criminal investigation that led to seventeen convictions and more than $2 million in fines.

The notorious procurement scandal at the Pentagon—actually, dozens of little scandals involving bid rigging and other infractions, the costs folded out of sight, for a time, by the size of the military buildup—had been predicted by a blue-ribbon presidential commission in 1986, but Reagan did nothing. (As early as mid-1985, forty-five of the nation's largest defense contractors were under investigation in 135 separate inquiries.) The extent of the damage would never be fully assayed, although it ran at least into the tens of billions of dollars, and the scandal, when uncovered in 1988, indicated (as the Republican senator John Warner said in an unguarded moment) "rampant bribery in Government." More than fifty officials at the Defense Department and private contractors would be convicted for rigging bids and falsifying results of quality-control tests.

Although Reagan himself was never implicated in personal wrongdoing, neither did he regard government ethics, according to James Baker, as "something in the big picture"—and accusations about various frauds and scandals did reach the upper echelons of the executive branch and even reached the Oval Office. After he left the White House, Michael Deaver was indicted for committing perjury before Congress in connection with his testimony about a lobbying scandal involving his new communications firm. Convicted, he would be sentenced to three years in prison; the sentence was later commuted to three months of community service and a $3,000 fine. Reagan's longtime crony and political counselor Lyn Nofziger was convicted of illegal lobbying on behalf of the Wedtech Corporation, a defense contractor in New York City, although the conviction was later overturned on a technicality. Assistant Attorney General Theodore B. Olson, one of the leading lights at the activist Justice Department, faced an independent counsel's investigation over alleged false testimony to Congress; after failing to get the case quashed on constitutional grounds by the D.C. federal district court, Olson won his case in 1988 in the D.C. federal appeals court and, finally, the Supreme Court. Secretary of Labor Raymond Donovan confronted continual scrutiny over allegations of illegal payments and underworld connections before his appointment, and was compelled to resign in March 1985. He was acquitted after being indicted in New York for alleged corruption, but then faced a delayed investigation by an independent counsel into charges that he gave false testimony to a grand jury in 1982, a process that ended in 1987 when the counsel gave up, owing to insufficient evidence.

Attorney General Meese left himself the most exposed. Even after receiving his dubious exoneration from the independent counsel in 1985, Meese attracted attention for possible wrongdoing. In 1987, the independent counsel looking into the Wedtech scandal expanded his probe to include Meese. Wedtech, originally founded decades earlier in the Bronx by a Puerto Rican immigrant, had passed largely into the hands of one Fred Neuberger—yet with forged papers, the company hid that fact in order to qualify for a special program of granting no-bid contracts to minority-owned companies. Working through Nofziger and Meese, Wedtech managed to arrange with the White House public liaison officer Elizabeth Dole (the wife of the Senate Republican leader Robert Dole) a $32 million no-bid contract to produce small engines for the U.S. Army. More than $200 million in additional no-bid contracts with Wedtech followed. Once exposed, the scandal eventually cost two congressmen from the Bronx their jobs and led to the conviction of more than a dozen state, local, and federal officials. Meese was spared prosecution when the report of an investigation by an independent counsel found insufficient evidence on which to indict him. But the report stated nevertheless that he was certainly guilty of complicity in the scandal, and had indulged in "conduct which should not be tolerated of any government employee, especially not the attorney-general." Under heavy attack in the press and elsewhere—the United States attorney in New York, Rudolph Giuliani, reportedly authorized having one of his assistants call the attorney general a "sleaze"—Meese resigned as soon as the counsel's report was released.

According to figures gathered by the veteran Washington journalist

Haynes Johnson (who was no fan of Ronald Reagan's), by the time Reagan left office 138 officials from his administration had been convicted of, indicted for, or subjected to official investigations for official misconduct, criminal violations, or both. Even allowing for the acquittals and for the investigations that did not lead to official charges—about three-quarters of the total—this was an exceptionally high number, especially relative to statistics for the two administrations that preceded Reagan's. One irony, even perversity, of the in-house scandals of the Reagan administration is how often they involved abusing and exploiting some of the very programs that pro-Reagan ideologues denounced as wasteful or discriminatory—environmental protection, federal housing assistance, no-bid set-asides for minority contractors. Yet the scandals also flowed from the same do-nothing inertia that lay behind the dogmatic deregulation that created the S&L catastrophe—a general disregard for oversight safeguards as among the evils of "big government." "All in all, I think we hit the jackpot," the president quipped in his usual upbeat way when he signed the legislation that deregulated the S&Ls in 1982. He would never stop believing that the key to mass prosperity was to get meddlesome government bureaucrats out of the way. He would scarcely acknowledge the S&L crisis and the other scandals, and how they reflected on his views about government regulation. Yet estimates of the overall costs of Reagan's antigovernment dogma, in scandals and corruption, run into the trillions of dollars.

Outside government, Reagan's philosophy also contributed to a cultural paradox. The vaunting of individual effort and local community over government encouraged a spurt in voluntarism in the 1980s, as increasing numbers of Americans worked, unpaid, for their favorite religious, charitable, civic, and educational causes. Yet this generous side of Reagan-style individualism accompanied a coarsening of the culture, in which the accumulation of wealth and material goods became, more than ever, the chief marker of personal achievement—and even, for some, a sign of spiritual transcendence. The administration's relaxed enforcement of most antitrust laws permitted investors to raise money with high-interest junk bonds, which fueled the corporate merger mania of the 1980s. Applauded by conservatives who advocated survival of the fittest in business, the mania created massive new enterprises that carried a dangerously high debt load and that in some cases, contradicting Reagan's own dogma, tended to contribute to reduced competition and higher prices to consumers.

While the underfunded and understaffed Securities and Exchange Commission failed to keep up with the sheer volume of new business, fraud at the nation's brokerage houses worsened. Yet corporate raiders and junk bond dealers became culture heroes; celebration of the hard-nosed art of the business deal crowded out other kinds of aesthetics (except regarding financial investments in blockbuster paintings by old masters and approved hot new artists); corporation CEOs, whose average annual compensation rose fourfold between 1980 and 1988 to more than $12 million, spent lavishly on luxury goods and private parties, setting a new standard of fantasy and aspiration even as average real hourly income for the nation's wage earners stagnated or fell.

One trouble with this spurt of unrestrained free enterprise was that it twisted the bracing, acquisitive, get-ahead elements in the American psyche—and the genuine economic improvements of the Reagan era—into crasser, sometimes callous, and reckless impulses. The bull market on Wall Street and the rise of numerous new financial services and institutions drew middle-class Americans into profitable investing (if only indirectly) as never before. Overall, middle-class material standards rose, as prosperous but hardly affluent Americans filled newly bought homes (their mortgage rates reduced) with all sorts of new appliances and minor luxury goods, such as microwave ovens and VCRs, whose prices had become reasonable. Yet many of these purchases were made with credit cards or other forms of easy credit, and consumers put off financial reckoning to enjoy the good life right now while burying their families under a mountain of debt. And at the top of the financial ladder, a considerable portion of the new wealth was built on insubstantial paper transactions, overleveraged credit, and sharp dealing that from time to time crossed over into illegality.

The fabulously successful Wall Street financier Ivan Boesky drew considerable attention, most of it flattering, when he declared to a cheering audience at a university in May 1986: "I think greed is healthy." Boesky seemed to have expressed, as none before him had dared, one credo of the Reagan era. But only a year and a half later, Boesky, having been convicted of criminal insider trading, was sentenced to three years in prison, fined $100 million, and permanently barred from dealing in securities. And at precisely that moment, the broader weaknesses of the Reagan boom, and of the economic and social policies associated with it, were starting to become apparent.

According to Ronald Reagan, the tax reforms of his second term completed the main work of his revolution. "With the tax cuts of 1981 and the Tax

Reform Act of 1986, I'd accomplished a lot of what I'd come to Washington to do," he claimed in his memoirs. Tax reform certainly stands as the administration's outstanding accomplishment on economic issues after 1984. How far-reaching the reforms actually were, though, is subject to debate, as are their long-term effects on Americans' thinking about taxes. Equally debatable are claims that the celebrated economic recovery under Reagan greatly strengthened long-term opportunity and growth for the American public at large.

On matters other than taxes, the more dramatic efforts to extirpate the New Deal and the welfare state stalled during Reagan's second term. The report by the Greenspan commission on Social Security reform had stimulated Congress, in 1983, to raise the age at which benefits payments would commence, but at a much more gradual pace (not taking full effect until the year 2027) than the politically disastrous Schweiker proposal had asked for in 1981. Two years later, Republican leaders in the Senate barely won approval for a one-year freeze in cost-of-living adjustments, but Republicans in the House opposed it, and Reagan dropped the idea in exchange for a promise from Tip O'Neill to maintain the Senate's outlays for defense spending. Even then, the Republicans' efforts to reduce Social Security were widely interpreted as a major factor in the party's heavy losses in the Senate in the midterm elections in 1986. "[I]t was seared into the consciousness of the Republican Party: Social Security is the one area of spending that you must not touch, no matter what," a Republican staff member in the Senate later wrote. Nor, it seemed, was Congress willing to cut other so-called entitlement and social welfare programs. Quite the opposite: as the Democrats' strength grew, first in the House and then in the Senate, Congress defied Reagan, changed the course of the early 1980s, and increased spending on food stamps, Aid to Families with Dependent Children (AFDC), and, above all, Medicare. By 1989, federal spending on welfare was higher than it had been in 1980.

At the very end of his presidency in 1988, Reagan did sign into law the Family Support Bill, which was described at the time as the most important reform of federal welfare programs since the 1930s. The act tightened various aspects of welfare payments, transferred federal responsibilities to the states, and required many recipients, including mothers of preschool children, to participate in job-training programs and in some cases to work. Yet the act won support from prominent liberals, including Senator Daniel Patrick Moynihan of New York (credited with many of its important provisions), who, now questioning old liberal orthodoxy, hoped to end the cycle of welfare dependency and hopelessness that the existing system encouraged. The act also would cost the federal government a projected $3.3 billion over five years, contrary to the White House's earlier insistence that welfare reform be "budget-neutral." In some areas, such as the law's guarantee of AFDC payments to families with two unemployed parents, the reforms were mandatory; in others, including job training, states were expected to meet standards established by the federal government. And although Reagan signed the bill, many of his own experts on welfare found its chief provisions so tainted by liberal ideas that they were, as one aide remarked, "abominable."

The Tax Reform Act of 1986 was more popular on the right, although it too was something of a compromise. In 1983, largely to fend off further proposals for increased taxes, the president, urged by Regan as secretary of the treasury, began championing the idea of comprehensive tax reform in order to remove loopholes and, above all, to continue the work of 1981 by again slashing income tax rates for individual taxpayers in the upper brackets. In his State of the Union message of 1984, Reagan announced that he was asking the Treasury Department to devise a plan "so all taxpayers, big and small, are treated more fairly." But by the time work on a legislative proposal got under way in earnest, Regan had swapped jobs with the chief of staff, James Baker. As a result, Regan was in a position to press Reagan all the harder for tax reform, and Baker and his aides were able to fashion a proposal that would win bipartisan support on Capitol Hill.

The final bill was actually sponsored by two liberal Democrats—Senator Bill Bradley of New Jersey and Representative Richard Gephardt of Missouri—and made the most dramatic changes in the federal tax system since World War II. It was strictly a balancing act. On the one hand, the bill increased personal exemptions and standard deductions so that 6 million poor Americans would pay no federal income taxes at all; it increased capital gains taxes for high-income individuals; and it removed numerous tax shelters, especially in real estate. On the other hand, it cut the marginal rate for the highest incomes from 50 percent to 28 percent (while raising the rate for the lowest incomes from 11 percent to 15 percent) and reduced the top corporate tax rate from 48 percent to 34 percent. By broadening the tax base and completing the reduction of the top marginal rate to half of what it had been in 1980, the bill satisfied conservatives, who proclaimed it Reagan's second great tax cut. But by also reducing special exclusions and reductions and eliminating breaks that favored one form of capital over another, it advanced reforms favored by liberals. It also may have strengthened popular political support for the income tax itself—an ironic result, given the initial hostility of Reagan's revolutionaries to the very system of federal taxation.

Dramatic as they were, meanwhile, the tax reforms did not alter a greater irony of Reagan's economic stewardship: exploding federal deficits. Contrary to Reagan's original supply-side hopes, and in spite of the tax increases that Reagan supported in 1983, 1984, and 1986, the federal debt tripled between 1980 and 1989, from $994 billion to $2.8 trillion. Although the administration and its supporters were quick to blame a spendthrift Congress, the administration itself (which never submitted a balanced budget) was chiefly responsible. Also, although federal tax receipts increased in the 1980s—thanks partly to the tax increases in 1982 and after—they came nowhere near the levels required to cover the immense new outlays on the military. By forcing the treasury to borrow huge amounts to service the debt, and to pay high interest rates to its creditors, the deficits stripped the government of funds that might have been invested in the nation's economic infrastructure. The requisite borrowing from abroad to cover the government's obligations also turned the United States from a major international creditor into the world's largest debtor in world markets. But if he wanted to reduce the deficits, Reagan would have been forced either to forgo the military buildup and the tax cuts that were the pillars of his presidency, or to ask the American people to make sacrifices in their material standard of living. Neither choice, for Reagan, was an option.

The mounting deficits caused some economists to warn that the continuing boom was dangerously built on government borrowing—and there were other signs of trouble. Although economic growth continued, and although the wealthiest Americans enjoyed unprecedented prosperity, the real wages of full-time male production workers stagnated. Southern and western regions of the country were living in sunny times, but the bad climate worsened in the so-called rust belt. Much of the boom was powered by a consumer spending spree that was, in turn, fueled by credit card debt and other forms of individual and household borrowing. Overall, the nation's private wealth, adjusted for inflation, grew only 8 percent between 1983 and 1988 (compared with 31 percent during the apparently troubled period from 1975 to 1980). During the same period, outstanding household debt as a percentage of gross domestic product jumped by more than 20 percent. And through the first two years Reagan's second term, the faint rumblings of the S&L crisis began to grow louder.

The people at large, however, thought they were enjoying prosperity too much either to notice or to care about the federal deficit or the rising government and consumer debt. The stagflation of the early 1970s and the malaise of the Carter years were over, as were the hard times of 1981–1982. The new, buoyant Reagan economy offered shimmering promises of material abundance. New jobs were appearing at an average of 200,000 a month (even though a great many of them were for low-wage service work). The Dow Jones industrial average, one of the more popular indications of the nation's economic health, rose from just over 950 on the day Reagan took office to a peak of over 2,700 in August 1987. And as the good times kept rolling, so, it seemed, did the public's enthusiasm for Ronald Reagan.

A high point, for Reagan, came when he arrived in New York Harbor for a gala Fourth of July weekend in 1986. It had been exactly ten years since Gerald Ford had visited the same spot during the grand bicentennial festivities that supposedly completed the exorcism of Watergate. The events of 1986 were to commemorate the centenary of the Statue of Liberty, which had been refurbished for the occasion at a cost of $250 million (provided not by the federal government but by a private foundation of corporation heads). The ceremonies, orchestrated by the renowned television producer David Wolper, provided a perfect television and photo-op setting for Reagan and his entourage—the statue standing nobly in the middle distance, the twin towers of the World Trade Center soaring in the background. Just as in 1976, there was a long procession of tall ships, as well as stunning fireworks. There were also new spectacles: a mass administering of the oath of allegiance to 13,000 new citizens by Chief Justice Burger; a presentation by the president of Medals of Freedom to a dozen celebrities who were naturalized Americans, including Henry Kissinger and Irving Berlin; a grand finale featuring speeches and performances by, among others, Charlton Heston, Willie Nelson, the Pointer Sisters, 300 jazzercise dancers, and 200 Elvis Presley impersonators. America—at its benign silliest and pulse-quickening finest—displayed itself proudly to the world.

The president started his remarks by saluting the nation's immigrant heritage, but then he veered into the larger patriotic themes and images that had stood him so well for so long. The statue's centennial, he said, reminded him once more of the Puritans, of the good ship *Arbella*, and of John Winthrop's God-inspired vision of building "a shining city on a hill":

> Call it mysticism if you will, I have always believed there was some divine providence that placed this great land here between the two great oceans, to be found by a special kind of people from every corner of the world, who

had a special love for freedom and a special courage that enabled them to leave their own land, leave their friends and their countrymen, and come to this new and strange land to build a New World of peace and freedom and hope.

As the jubilation of 1976 had supposedly wiped away the stain of Nixon's presidency, so the patriotic affirmation of 1986 marked the nation's triumph over the malaise and defensiveness of the Carter years. America was back, and the American dreamer, Ronald Reagan, had brought it back. As the glorious weekend ended, the president's public approval rating stood at nearly 68 percent.

Fifteen months later, the nation's mood was very different, as was the president's standing. On October 19, 1987, "black Monday," panic suddenly struck the Wall Street markets. The Dow Jones industrial average fell more than 500 points, representing 23.6 percent of its total value, or $500 billion. Although the Federal Reserve System stepped in immediately to ease the crisis—an example of "big government" doing its job—prices fell dramatically again later in the month, and once again in late November. To this day, economists debate why the crash occurred, but at the time, many observers blamed the collapse on anxiety created by the federal deficit. "[W]e are finally paying the piper for seven years of profligacy by this administration," an executive at the Chrysler corporation told the *Wall Street Journal*.

Four days after the crash, Reagan's popularity rating had fallen below 50 percent, a huge decline from the heady days of mid-1986. But unlike the Dow Jones average, Reagan's ratings had collapsed much earlier, in December 1986. A month before that, a shocking scandal in foreign policy had surfaced, and it quickly led to a grave and prolonged constitutional battle. For most of the next two years, the White House would struggle to recover. The stock market crash did not help, but the state of the economy turned out not to be the sole determinant of President Reagan's popularity.

8

"WE HAVE AN
UNDERCOVER THING":
THE IRAN-CONTRA AFFAIR

As soon as President Reagan indicated the toughened line of his second term, the White House's foreign policy faltered. The first major setback was symbolic but sensational—and it revealed a disturbing shallowness in Reagan's understanding of history. In April 1985, the White House press spokesman Larry Speakes announced that the president had accepted an invitation from the German government to commemorate the fortieth anniversary of V-E day by visiting a cemetery of slain German soldiers in Bitburg. (Reagan's media wizard Michael Deaver had made an advance scouting trip of the cemetery two months earlier, when the grave markers were covered with snow.) Reagan was grateful to Chancellor Helmut Kohl for his help in deploying the Euromissiles in 1983, and after the highly successful D-day theatrics in 1984 he felt obliged to honor the postwar German-American reconciliation.

Neither Reagan nor Kohl appreciated how such a ceremony would mock the actual significance of May 8, 1945. Worse, both governments overlooked the fact that the Bitburg cemetery contained the graves of nearly fifty members of the Nazi Waffen SS, or Armed Storm Troopers. (At the Nuremberg trials, the Waffen SS had been specifically condemned for war crimes.) Worse still, the White House had rejected an invitation from a West German officeholder to include on the itinerary a visit to the site of the Dachau death camp. And so the symbolism was truly horrendous: Reagan would be honoring not Kohl's country but Hitler's henchmen, while ignoring the Holocaust. The president then added to the disgrace with his defense that most of those buried at Bitburg had been young German draftees who "were victims, just as surely as the victims in the concentration camps."

A serious public relations blunder turned into a political crisis—"my 'Dreyfus' case," Reagan called it privately, in a thoroughly abysmal historical analogy. Chancellor Kohl received strong backing for the visit in West German opinion polls; told Reagan that his remarks about the dead soldiers as victims of the Nazis, analogous to the Jews, were being well-received; and selfishly insisted that Reagan go through with the commemoration at Bitburg. Some people inside the White House, including Patrick Buchanan, Reagan's communications director, agreed. ("Buchanan argued for a harder line, a bigger gesture, a clearer defense of the new Germany and virtually an amnesty for the Third Reich," Michael Deaver recalled, whatever his own early errors in the affair.) Reagan stubbornly assented, insisting that he was indebted to Kohl and that in any case there was nothing the least untoward about the ceremony at Bitburg. "What is wrong with saying 'let us never be enemies again'?" he asked in his diary.

A firestorm of criticism followed—from, among others, the prominent Jewish writer and Holocaust survivor Elie Wiesel, numerous veterans of World War II, Jewish conservatives, liberals generally, fifty-three U.S. senators, and the popular punk-rock band the Ramones (who recorded *Bonzo Goes to Bitburg*). Most important, perhaps, was that Nancy Reagan, aghast at the implications for her husband's reputation, pushed for changes in the president's schedule in Germany. The White House avoided utter disaster by keeping the visit to Bitburg as brief as possible, and, at Kohl's invitation, adding a trip to the Bergen-Belsen death camp (where Reagan, looking genuinely shattered by what he saw, gave one of his patented moving and highly effective speeches). But Reagan still could not comprehend the original criticism over Bitburg, and he remained not just unrepentant but proud of his decision. "I always felt it was the morally right thing to do," he later wrote in his diary.

The affair left permanent political scars. "Reagan would never again fully recapture the moral high ground he had sacrificed at Bitburg," his biographer Lou Cannon later wrote. And the incident portended far worse disasters that were already taking shape. These crises also involved logistical bungling, and an ill-conceived reading of history and the national interest, but on a far greater and more grievous scale. They stemmed directly from the administration's pursuit of the so-called Reagan Doctrine in Central America and the Middle East, and thus went to the heart of what the president had proclaimed as the central mission of his second term—to challenge the Soviet Union's military expansion on all fronts. Reagan's determination to sustain that mission led him and his administration to proceed covertly and in flagrant violation of the expressed will of Congress. Exceeding the secret operations of earlier administrations, a cabal of well-placed officials inside the White House, with the help of the president, perverted the constitutional rule of law. Their exploits were harebrained and counterproductive as well as illegal. Once exposed, they led to a serious constitutional confrontation.

On the morning of May 28, 1986, a team of American government officials traveling undercover with fake Irish passports sneaked away from a former Hilton hotel in Tehran and headed for Mehrabad airport. The group was headed by Reagan's former national security adviser, Robert McFarlane, and a member of the staff of the National Security Council (NSC), Marine officer Lieutenant Colonel Oliver North. After three days of fruitless secret meetings with high-level Iranian officials, at which the Americans offered gifts for Ayatollah Ruholla Khomeini—a chocolate cake in the shape of a key from a kosher bakery in Tel Aviv and a Bible that Reagan had inscribed with a passage from the New Testament—the American visitors departed angry and disappointed. When they learned that news of their presence had been leaked, they were also alarmed. Already nervous that their unexplained absence was raising questions at home, they did not want to be spotted inside Iran, even for a moment. (North later spoke of carrying a concealed suicide pill in case of capture.) Instead of taking the main superhighway to the airport, their driver meandered through the city's back streets, while their jet taxied to one of the airport's secluded runways. Once the group had safely returned to Washington, though, their undercover operation continued.

Five months later, radical university students in Tehran circulated thousands of leaflets exposing the earlier meetings in May, complete with a photograph of McFarlane. On November 3, an obscure Lebanese weekly magazine, *Al-Shiraa*, provided a fuller account, which, although inaccurate in some details, succeeded in telling the world that the United States had been dealing secretly with Iran. Immediately, the head of Iran's parliament, Akbar Hashemi Rafsanjani, confirmed the report, and two days later, the revelations swamped the American news media. The first of many shocking stories about the Iran-contra scandal had broken.

The affair had originated more than two years earlier. In October 1984, President Reagan signed the second of the Boland Amendments as part of an omnibus budget appropriations resolution. In sweeping language, the amendment barred any intelligence agency of the government from offering assistance of any kind to the Nicaraguan contras, and specifically prohibited gaining indirect help from "any nation, group, organization, movement, or individual." In anticipation of the amendment, Secretary of State Shultz had warned the president that approving any further assistance to the Nicaraguan resistance would constitute an impeachable offense. Chief of Staff James Baker had expressed concern that what he called "crazies" in the administration would try to circumvent Congress by secretly soliciting funds from other countries for the contras—now a legally as well as politically dangerous step.[*]

The most important of these "crazies" turned out to be the president himself. Months before the second Boland Amendment passed, Reagan began secretly pushing his aides to seek alternative means of financing the contras' operations. Thereafter, he endorsed the jerry-built argument of his hard-boiled director of the Central Intelligence Agency (CIA), William Casey, that because the NSC was not, narrowly speaking, an intelligence agency, it could lawfully operate to aid the contras without disclosure to Congress. (Casey's rationale ignored, among other things, that the stated statuary functions of the NSC were in the areas of policy review and coordination, not implementation or operations.) Reagan's instructions to his national security adviser, McFarlane, were unequivocal, "I want you to do whatever you have to do to help these people keep body and soul together."

In placing the full weight of his office behind the contras, Reagan at once defied Congress and spurned continuing diplomatic talks with the Nicaraguan government that had been undertaken by the State Department. (The U.S. government dismissed out of hand as pro-Sandinista a peace and cooperation agreement reached in September 1984 by the so-called Conta-

---

[*] In addition to the second Boland Amendment, the so-called Casey accords were supposed to constrain the administration. The first of these, signed by William J. Casey, director of the CIA, after the deception over the mining of the Nicaraguan harbors, stipulated that the administration would give to the Senate Intelligence Committee the text of any presidential findings on covert actions. The second, signed two years later, pledged notification to the committee when significant military equipment was used in a covert operation. The White House violated the first agreement in 1985 and both agreements in 1986. See *Report of the Congressional Committees Investigating the Iran/Contra Affair, with Supplementary, Minority, and Additional Views* (Washington, DC, 1987), p. 118.

dora group of Latin American governments, although Secretary of State Shultz stated that the American government "fully supports the objectives" of the Contadora process.) Reagan also doubted that the Sandinistas could be ousted by peaceful democratic means—an outcome that had actually become increasingly plausible.

Under pressure because of rising popular discontent within Nicaragua, the Sandinista government held national elections in early November 1984. Encouraged by the State Department, a former Sandinista ambassador to the United States, Arturo Cruz, still living in Washington, strongly considered running for the presidency against the junta chief, Daniel Ortega. But Cruz backed out when Reagan and the hard-liners, certain that no leftist regime would yield power voluntarily, withheld their support. Cruz soon regretted his decision, as one-third of the voters cast their ballots against the government despite the lack of any credible opposition campaign. The White House, though, interpreted the result as affirmation that only military force could remove the Sandinistas.

With Reagan acting as the driving and presiding force, three very different personalities assumed the primary everyday roles in providing the contras with arms and money. Casey, at age seventy-one, had had a long and varied career—as an overseer of clandestine operations for the Office of Special Services (OSS) during World War II, as a tax lawyer in New York, and at several high posts in the Nixon and Ford administrations, including the chairmanship of the Securities and Exchange Commission. A deeply conservative Republican—in 1955, he had a hand in the establishment of the pioneering journal of the right, *National Review*—Casey was tough and impatient, with a reputation for arrogance intensified by his habit of mumbling his words.

The national security adviser, Robert "Bud" McFarlane, almost a quarter century younger than Casey, was a former Marine officer who, after two tours of combat duty in Vietnam, had entered government service as Henry Kissinger's military assistant during the closing years of the Nixon administration. An assistant to Secretary of State Alexander Haig, McFarlane joined the NSC as William Clark's deputy in 1982, and succeeded Clark as national security adviser a year later. As mild and self-effacing as Casey was brusque ("the perfect No. 2 man—or maybe No. 2 and one-half," one insider at the White House remarked), McFarlane was also ambitious and emotionally complex, exhibiting both a sharp wit and a chronic lack of self-confidence.

Lieutenant Colonel Oliver North came out of an entirely different mold.

He was in his early forties and, like McFarlane, had graduated from the Naval Academy and was decorated for combat service in Vietnam—but there the similarities ended. After returning from the war in 1974, North suffered a mental breakdown, formally diagnosed as "emotional stress," that required hospitalization for twenty-two days. (The details remain mysterious, as North's psychiatric records at Bethesda Naval Hospital were inexplicably expunged.) North then returned to active duty, underwent a profound conversion to Christian fundamentalism, and in 1981 was posted to the NSC. Willful, even fanatical, in pursuit of his goals, he impressed some associates as an ingratiating derring-do patriot, and others as a sordid fraud and congenital liar. With his unswerving dedication to the contras' cause, North fit in well with his admirer Casey (who would provide political guidance as well as cover at the top) and with the able but uncharismatic McFarlane.

The mission to supply the contras originated in February 1984, when McFarlane, in consultation with Casey, came up with ideas on how to contract the effort out entirely to another country. After unsuccessfully approaching the Israelis, McFarlane revised his plans in favor of asking governments friendly to the United States simply to fund the contras in secret. In June, the last of the aid that Congress had appropriated earlier for the contras was gone. With no new funds expected, McFarlane reached an agreement with the Saudi ambassador, Prince Bandar ibn Sultan, for monthly "contributions" of $1 million for the rest of the year. Saudi Arabia would become the largest donor. (Early in 1985, when the contras' funds were again running out, King Fahd ibn Abd al-Aziz directly promised Reagan an additional $24 million.) But McFarlane and North raised pledges of additional millions from South Africa, Israel, Taiwan, and (with assistance from the assistant secretary of state for Inter-American Affairs, Elliott Abrams) Brunei, as well as other cooperative nations, and deposited the funds in Swiss bank accounts.[*]

North also traveled across the United States, working with a group of fund-raisers attached to nonprofit, tax-exempt organization, the National Endowment for the Preservation of Liberty (NEPL). Supposedly, the

---

[*] Abrams's solicitation of $10 million from the sultan of Brunei, with Shultz's knowledge and approval, went awry. Oliver North's secretary, Fawn Hall, transposed two digits in typing out the number of the Swiss bank account where North had arranged for the money to be sent. The money's nonappearance in the proper account allowed Abrams to say later that, as far as he knew, the contras' effort had not received any money from foreign governments.

NEPL was dedicated to educational ends; in fact, its purpose was to obtain cash from wealthy conservatives for distinctly noneducational and noncharitable (and, thus, unlawful) purposes, including the purchase of armaments for the contras. In letters to the NEPL's donors, North left no doubt that the administration not only condoned the group's activities but also considered them a "crucial contribution in helping our President in this vital endeavor." Reagan played his part by attending at least half a dozen "photo opportunities" arranged as rewards to the donors by North and the NEPL's founder, Carl "Spitz" Channell, a conservative direct-mail consultant. More than half of the $6.3 million raised wound up paying for Channell's and the other fund-raisers' own commissions, overhead costs, and salaries.

To complete the delivery of military hardware, North recruited, on Casey's recommendation, an arms dealer who had been a major general in the U.S. Air Force, Richard V. Secord. Calling themselves "the Enterprise," North, Secord, and Secord's partner—an Iranian-born businessman, Albert Hakim—established a virtual private army of ships and planes, equipped with the latest communications equipment, manned by various arms merchants, mercenary adventurers, and veterans of the Bay of Pigs, and funded through Swiss bank accounts and dummy corporations. Some of the money, men, and matériel involved in aiding the contras also had connections to smuggling cocaine and other drugs into the United States—with North's full knowledge, as his notebooks and memos from the time revealed. To Casey, North later testified, it was just the start of what he envisaged as an ambitious, permanent secret military operation, which would allow the White House to pursue every variety of covert operation completely free of congressional scrutiny or any constitutional constraint.

James Baker had foreseen that soliciting foreign governments for aid to the contras might illegally contravene the will of Congress. But President Reagan dismissed such objections and instead backed Vice President George H. W. Bush's contention (also supported by Casey, Attorney General Smith, and the NSC legal counsel) that the donations were lawful so long as the United States demanded no quid pro quo. This argument was at best disingenuous: in such international dealings (as McFarlane later admitted) there would always be at least a tacit quid pro quo: later generosity from, and the political favor of, the United States. (Reagan later acknowledged, under oath, that in separate negotiations with the Honduran government, he made it absolutely clear that, in return for assurances of aid and security, the United States would expect cooperation in offering covert assistance to the contras. Other documents revealed similar direct agreements and exchanges with other governments, in Central America and elsewhere.) The president wanted desperately to keep all the solicitations secret, seemingly because he recognized that they were politically and possibly constitutionally dubious. "If such a story gets out," he told one high-level meeting, "we'll all be hanging by our thumbs in front of the White House until we found out who did it." He specifically ordered that Congress be kept in the dark about every aspect of the undertaking. To avoid accountability, the White House had moved beyond the routine covert operations of the cold war toward the creation of a covert foreign policy beyond the law.

The administration faced no such political obstacles in its other main venture under the Reagan Doctrine, aiding the Afghan rebels (or mujahideen) in their continuing fight against the Soviet Union and its local clients. To be sure, the war in Afghanistan exacted terrible costs from the American people, as many of the rebels were supplementing the aid they received from the United States by trafficking heavily in drugs. (A report on the international drug trade released in February 1985 identified Afghanistan as the world's leading source of heroin for the United States and Europe.) But the Reagan administration turned a blind eye, determined to defeat the Soviet aggressors. In March, Reagan approved a directive formally establishing as a matter of national policy the defeat of the Soviet Union's forces in Afghanistan, "by all means available." Working through the Pakistani government, the administration approved $300 million in fresh covert aid, with most of the money and arms going to anti-Soviet Islamic radicals. Equipped with the latest in military hardware, the rebels more than held their own, turning the struggle in Afghanistan into what some observers described as the Kremlin's Vietnam. Unlike the Nicaraguan struggle, the Afghan war met with general approval in Washington and with the American public. Apart from encouraging the drug trade, the blowback effects would not fully hit the United States for many years to come.

Politics, intrigue, and terrorism in the Middle East, meanwhile, continually tested the will of the administration. In early March 1984, less than six months after the Americans' ignominious military withdrawal from Lebanon, the CIA's new station chief in Beirut, William Buckley, was taken hostage by Islamic extremists linked to the pro-Iran Shiite terrorist group Hezbollah. Buckley was the fourth American kidnapped in Lebanon since 1982, and over the coming year, several more Americans would be seized, leaving a total of seven still in captivity at the end of 1985. But Buckley was also a close friend of William Casey, who had personally recruited him for the posting in Beirut. His abduction—and the reasonable suspicion that his captors would torture him—stirred the upper echelons of the administration. In early April, President Reagan signed a new national security directive aimed at redoubling secret antiterrorism efforts while also calling for broad new legislation to prohibit firms and individuals from "supporting or cooperating" with "groups or states engaging in terrorism." Oliver North drafted the directive.

The terrorist situation worsened. A few weeks after the fiasco at Bitburg, Arab terrorists hijacked a TWA jet during a flight from Athens to Rome; 135 Americans were aboard. The hijackers forced the pilot to fly to Beirut, then Algiers, and finally back to Beirut, where they beat and shot to death an American Navy diver and dumped his body on the airport tarmac. Reagan, keenly aware that terrorists had ruined his predecessor, put on a tough public face, declaring that the United States "gives terrorists no rewards and no guarantees." He won enormous public support when the hijackers finally freed the rest of the hostages unharmed. Nobody seemed to notice that the White House had pressured the Israeli government into capitulating to the terrorists' principal demand by freeing 700 Shiite political prisoners. Contrary to Reagan's stern talk, terrorism in this case had paid off handsomely.

Reagan acknowledged no contradiction and instead heated up his rhetoric, linking Iran and Nicaragua (along with Libya, North Korea, and Cuba), as "outlaw states run by the strangest collection of misfits, Looney Tunes, and squalid criminals since the advent of the Third Reich." But despite his bold talk, he was increasingly on the defensive. Terrorists around the world struck again, with impunity, later in the month, killing four Marines in a bombing in El Salvador, wounding forty-two people and killing three when a bomb exploded at the airport in Frankfurt, and killing all 329 passengers on an Air India jet downed by Sikh terrorists during a flight over the Atlantic Ocean. The uncertain fate of Buckley and the other American hostages in Lebanon, meanwhile, was corroding the president's peace of mind.

The day after the burial of the slain Navy diver at Arlington Cemetery, the national security adviser, McFarlane, met in the White House with the director general of the Israeli foreign ministry, David Kimche, who informed him that the government of Israel had forged a connection with a group of "moderates" in the Iranian leadership. According to Kimche, these reasonable Iranians looked forward to an orderly takeover of power on the death of the aged Ayatollah Khomeini, when they would lead Iran away from theocratic extremism. Kimche thought that these moderates could be persuaded to help arrange for the release of Buckley and the other hostages as the first step toward a dialogue with the West. The United States would show its good faith by approving a small shipment of antitank armaments to Iran—weapons that the Iranian military sorely needed in the continuing war with Iraq. The arrangements could be worked out through an exiled Iranian businessman and arms dealer, Manucher Ghorbanifar, who enjoyed the financial backing of the legendary, fabulously wealthy Saudi-born arms dealer Adnan Khashoggi.

McFarlane had ample reasons to turn Kimche down flat. Any arrangement that looked even slightly like a trade of arms for hostages would outrageously violate the United States' long-stated position on terrorism. Kimche's proposal also directly contradicted Operation Staunch, a continuing effort led by Secretary of State Shultz to cut off the flow of all armaments, worldwide, to Iran. (The effectiveness of Operation Staunch was a major reason the Iranians so desperately needed weapons.) By law, the White House was required to report to Congress all sales of arms to foreign countries, but such a report would be politically unthinkable as regarded Iran. Although the Israelis were leaning toward helping the beleaguered Iranians (formerly their friends) in the war with the Iraqis (their constant enemy), the Reagan administration had made strong overtures to Baghdad while adopting an official public stance of neutrality. Finally, had McFarlane investigated the matter, he would have discovered that the CIA had had its own dealings with the appointed contact, Ghorbanifar, and considered him thoroughly untrustworthy.

Yet McFarlane had long been enamored of opening some sort of diplomatic initiative to Iran. Knowing that Khomeini's days on earth were numbered, he convinced himself that a well-executed transformation of the Iranians into American allies would be a stunning achievement, greatly improving the strategic global position of the United States while ruining any and all Soviet designs on oil-rich Iran. McFarlane was also well aware of the president's growing fixation on freeing the hostages. The more he thought about Kimche's proposed overture to Iran, the more attractive it looked. He was even seduced into believing—or talked himself into believing—that a covert approach to Iran could be as momentous as Nixon and Kissinger's opening to China in the early 1970s, overlooking the fact that Kissinger had negotiated with the Chinese premier, Chou En-lai, not with shadowy arms dealers like Manucher Ghorbanifar, and that the Chinese and the Americans faced a common adversary in the Soviet Union. McFarlane's interest deepened several days later, when another Israeli emissary briefed and left a favorable impression on McFarlane's trusted adviser, a neoconservative adventurer named Michael Ledeen.

A former vagabond university teacher, banned from Italy because of his shadowy links to right-wing extremists there, Ledeen had turned up as an antiterrorism adviser to Secretary of State Alexander Haig in 1981. He had contacts with certain Israeli intelligence agents, and McFarlane had brought him into the NSC as a part-time consultant in 1983. A few months before Kimche's visit, Ledeen was tipped off by an intelligence source that the political situation in Tehran had become surprisingly fluid, and that the Israelis knew more than anyone else about how the United States might capitalize on this. His receptiveness to Kimche's overture more than matched McFarlane's. So did the interest expressed by William Casey as director of the CIA—who, if he was aware of his own agency's contempt for the "moderate" middleman Ghorbanifar, chose to ignore it. McFarlane was ready to move when, on July 10, Ghorbanifar, working through an Israeli intermediary, proposed to Ledeen that Israel sell several hundred U.S.-made antitank TOW missiles to Iran as a first step toward cooperation.*

Three days later, President Reagan underwent surgery for a precancerous growth in his large intestine. Four days after that, recuperating in Bethesda Naval Hospital, he wrote in his diary: "Some strange soundings are coming from the Iranians. Bud M. will be here tomorrow to talk about it. It could be a breakthrough on getting our 7 kidnap victims back." Reagan did not mention political initiatives or aiding Iranian moderates: from the start (although he would later deny it), his overriding objective in pursuing the "strange soundings" was to free the American hostages in Lebanon. On August 6, still recovering from his surgery, Reagan, dressed in pajamas and bathrobe, convened a meeting in the White House private quarters of his principal advisers on foreign affairs. The Israelis were pressing for a decision about their proposal, and Weinberger and Shultz firmly opposed the entire idea. (Shultz later recalled saying that "we were just falling into the arms-for-hostages business and we shouldn't do it.") McFarlane and Regan, the chief of staff, favored going ahead. The president's position was ambiguous—so much so that Weinberger came away thinking the plan was basi-

---

* TOW was an acronym for "tube-launched optically tracked wire-guided." The Iranians' other preferred weapon was a medium-range surface-to-air missile, the HAWK (or Homing All the Way Killer).

cally dead, whereas McFarlane believed he had heard Reagan express approval, provided that the arms sent to Iran actually went to anti-Khomeini forces. The meeting reached no decision.

What happened next is still disputed. According to McFarlane, whose account is probably the most accurate, the president phoned him several days after the meeting at the White House and gave what investigators later called "oral authorization" to an agreement whereby the Israelis would sell missiles to Iran with the understanding that the United States would replenish Israeli's arsenal. The chief of staff, Regan, later claimed that the president gave no such prior authorization. Reagan himself initially recalled that he had approved the arrangement, later said that he had not, and finally claimed that he could not remember. Two things are certain: McFarlane notified the Israelis that the deal was set; and on August 20, Israel shipped ninety-six TOW missiles to Iran.

No hostages, however, were freed; instead, ominously, the Iranians asked for hundreds more missiles. (Ghorbanifar claimed that the first shipment had mistakenly fallen into the hands of Khomeini's Revolutionary Guard.) While the Americans pondered how to respond, Ghorbanifar informed the Israelis that only one hostage would be released in exchange for the latest missiles requested. At this point, McFarlane could have backed out of the deal—but when Kimche said McFarlane could choose whichever hostage he wanted, McFarlane seized the chance and named William Buckley. Ghorbanifar replied that Buckley was too ill to travel. (In fact, Buckley had died in early June, a victim of torture.) But the bargain moved forward anyway, this time with Reagan's clear approval. On September 15, Israel delivered an additional 408 TOWs to Iran. That same day, the kidnappers released the Reverend Benjamin Weir, an American Presbyterian missionary who had been held captive for more than a year. The dealing would continue.

In November, the Israelis, concerned about the pace of replenishment by the Americans, and also hoping to cover their own tracks, tried to arrange delivery of a modest new cargo of arms without flying directly from Israel to Iran, but ran into severe logistical problems. Into the breach stepped Oliver North and Richard Secord, who devised a plan to transship eighty HAWK missiles from Israel to Iran via Portugal. The delivery—eventually completed by an airplane belonging to a company that was a front for the CIA—was plagued by bungling, sudden changes of plan, and numerous other mishaps. Eventually, the Iranians received only eighteen missiles instead of the expected eighty, and then quickly rejected the reduced shipment after test-firing one of the missiles and finding that it did not meet their requirements. For a time it looked as if the entire project was turning, North said, into "a bit of a horror story." Yet Reagan, ever the optimist, stood squarely behind the initiative. ("We have an undercover thing going by way of an Iranian," he wrote in his diary on November 22, "which could get [the hostages] sprung momentarily.")

On December 5, in response to complaints from the CIA's lawyers that North had violated an intelligence oversight law of 1980, Reagan signed an official presidential finding that fully (albeit retroactively) authorized the three earlier arms shipments to Iran. The finding, with an attached background summary titled "Hostage Rescue—Middle East," justified the shipments solely as means to "obtain the release of Americans being held hostage in the Middle East." It declared unambiguously what had effectively been the case all along: the Iranian initiative was a straightforward deal of arms for hostages. It also explicitly ordered Casey not to inform Congress without direct orders from the president, even though the White House was legally required to notify Congress of all such findings "in a timely fashion." Reagan himself knew exactly what was going on, in what he described explicitly (although privately) after signing the finding as "our undercover effort to free our 5 hostages held by terrorists in Lebanon." He knew that "only a few of us" were "in on it." And he knew enough about the arrangement's possible implications to cover his tracks. "I won't even write in the diary what we're up to," he wrote—in the diary.

Two days later, Reagan convened in the family quarters of the White House a special meeting of his highest-ranking advisers to discuss the future of the arms sales. Shultz and Weinberger forcefully reiterated their opposition to any dealings in arms with a nation the United States had declared a sponsor of international terrorism. But Reagan's motive was fixed and his mind was made up, regardless of either the administration's publicly stated policy or the law. "President sd. he could answer charges of illegality but he couldn't answer charge that 'big strong President Reagan passed up chance to free hostages,'" Weinberger wrote in his diary. Michael Ledeen, who was not present at the meeting but was close to the arms sales, later recounted a more dramatic version: "Reagan was not moved, and, with a twinkle in his eye, told them: 'I don't care if I have to go to Leavenworth; I want the hostages out.' He joked that Thursday was visiting day, and brought the meeting to an end."

In early December, just before Reagan signed the "Hostage Rescue" finding, McFarlane, weary of bureaucratic infighting, resigned as chairman of the NSC and was succeeded by his deputy, retired rear admiral John M. Poindexter, a reclusive, tight-lipped bureaucrat but also a firm backer of Casey and North. Over the next six weeks, the scheme, as pushed along by Casey, Poindexter, and North, turned into a secret arrangement for the direct sale of arms by the United States to Iran, with the CIA and then Oliver North's Enterprise acting as intermediaries. Shultz and Weinberger restated their vehement objections; and one analyst at the CIA broke with Casey and warned that all arms delivered to the so-called moderates would end up in the hands of the Khomeini regime. But Reagan, unyielding on the imperative of freeing the hostages, ignored the doubters.

On January 7, Reagan assembled his advisers, and Weinberger later described in his diary what happened: "Met with President, Shultz, Poindexter, Bill Casey, Ed Meese, in Oval Office—President decided to go with Israeli-Iranian offer to release our 5 hostages in return for sale of 4000 TOWs to Iran by Israel—George Shultz + I opposed—Bill Casey, Ed Meese + VP favored—as did Poindexter." Also in January, Reagan signed two additional findings approving the covert activities and authorizing the direct sale of U.S. arms to Iran—without informing either Shultz or Weinberger. ("I gave a go ahead," the president wrote after signing the second finding.) After considering resigning, but deciding that his resignation would make no difference, a disappointed Weinberger—who, along with Shultz, would henceforth be shut out entirely from the Iran initiative—directed his military aide, Major General Colin Powell (who had also opposed the arms sales), to arrange for the release of more than 3,500 TOW missiles to the CIA.

Over the ensuing ten months, 1,500 of the missiles, along with planeloads of spare parts for HAWK missiles, arrived in Iran, as did 500 more TOWs from Israel (which, as before, the United States replaced). Through the end of October 1986, only one more American hostage was freed; meanwhile, the kidnappers murdered one of the original hostages and seized three more Americans. The secret operation had been going on for more than a year, and tens of millions of dollars worth of American-built armaments had been sold to Iran, but the number of those released and those taken captive remained the same. Yet North was unfazed—for in conjunction with his partner, Secord, and the NSC's chairman, Poindexter, he had altered the operation so that it would pay great dividends regardless of the hostage situation.

During the eighteen months after the House passed the second Boland Amendment, the Enterprise had sent tens of millions of dollars in guns and money to its original beneficiaries, the contras—but the scheme for Nicaragua, and the broader effort on behalf on the contras, had also encountered difficulties. Efforts to overturn the Boland restrictions, undertaken by congressional conservatives (notably the former White House chief of staff Dick Cheney, who had won a seat in the House from Wyoming), failed. Reports by humanitarian groups on atrocities committed by the contras inflamed opinion in Washington and around the country. The contras themselves—reorganized in 1985 as the United Nicaraguan Opposition with a leadership that included some former Sandinistas, notably Arturo Cruz, as well as some of Somoza's former officials—were riven by factionalism. Despite growing popular dissatisfaction with the Sandinista regime, the contras seemed incapable of toppling it, even with the millions in aid they received via the Enterprise.

By August 1985, the White House, under pressure from newspaper reports, acknowledged that Oliver North was involved in some sort of operation to support the contras, and members of Congress began asking disquieting questions. Members of the administration, led by President Reagan, insisted that nothing illegal was afoot. McFarlane flatly told the chairman of one House committee that there were no "parallel efforts to provide, directly or indirectly, support for military or paramilitary operations in Nicaragua." What an official investigation would later describe as the White House's "deliberate attempt to deceive Congress and the public" largely succeeded. But late in the year, North, now drawn into the scheme for Iran while struggling to sustain the contras, complicated matters by pursuing what he would later call "a neat idea."

After the "horror story" transaction in 1985, the Enterprise still had substantial unexpended funds left over from $1 million given to it by the Israelis to cover overhead costs. With the Israelis' HAWK shipments now in abeyance, North received permission from Israel to use the $800,000 however he pleased—and he duly told Secord to spend the money on the contras. Now, he realized, if he could take over the entire operation by shipping U.S. arms directly and then sharply raise the prices charged to the Iranians, he could pay the unshakable Ghorbanifar a hefty commission, amply reward Secord and Hakim for their trouble, and divert what was left of the windfall to the anti-Sandinistas. The initiative in Iran was quickly degenerating into an arms-for-profits scam, formally connected to the illegal funding of the contras.

Through the spring of 1986, President Reagan, still preoccupied with the hostages, also faced a new round of terrorist attacks, including, in early

April, the bombing of a discotheque in West Berlin that killed three persons (two of them American servicemen) and wounded 200 others. Despite his combative rhetoric, Reagan had failed to mount any direct military response amid the recent waves of terrorist violence—but this time, after learning of intelligence reports that Libya was involved, he retaliated swiftly. An intense burst of coordinated American bombing raids destroyed several important Libyan government and military sites and only narrowly missed killing Muammar Qaddafi (thought to be a main target). But the raids also killed at least fifteen civilians, including Qaddafi's two-year-old adopted daughter, and inflamed anti-American opinion.

As Arab states united to condemn the attacks, North and Second pressed to keep the Iranian channels open, still hopeful that at least some hostages might be freed and that more money could be raised for the contras. Now the former national security adviser, McFarlane, thoroughly disgusted with Ghorbanifar, persuaded Reagan to send him and North to Tehran for direct talks with the Iranians in late May—talks that would prove fateful in ways the Americans never imagined. Along with the cake and inscribed Bible for Khomeini, the visitors and their entourage brought with them a shipment of spare parts for HAWK missiles. The negotiations over further releases of hostages broke down, and the thwarted Americans made their frenzied departure from the former Hilton hotel through Tehran's back streets to Mehrabad airport. "This was a heartbreaking disappointment for all of us," Reagan wrote in his diary. But North took solace. He told McFarlane during a layover on the long journey home not to be "too disappointed," and finally let him in on the secret: the one bright spot, McFarlane later recalled North saying, was that "some of the proceeds or dollars from the sale of weapons to the Iranians was going to be available in Central America."

Reagan's popularity ratings, already high, climbed even higher after the attack on Libya, with nearly 70 percent of those polled approving of his overall job performance. On the eve of July 4 and the Liberty Weekend celebrations in New York—and following a determined publicity blitz begun in March, in advance of the midterm election season—the White House managed to win narrow approval in the House of a $100 million aid package for the contras, thereby repealing the Boland Amendment. A euphoric Oliver North now set his sights on freeing hostages and boosting Reagan's popularity ever higher. He tried unsuccessfully to arrange a release of prisoners to coincide with the extravaganza at the Statue of Liberty; then he sought to get a prisoner freed at the height of the midterm election campaign. In August, North and Secord's partner, Albert Hakim, opened up a so-called second channel, establishing contact with a new intermediary, identified as an officer in the Iranian Revolutionary Guard, who met with Secord and Hakim in Brussels. Ghorbanifar, meanwhile, also kept scrambling for deals with the Iranians, in order to pay off his heavy back debts to Adnan Khashoggi.

North's priorities suddenly shifted on October 5, when the Sandinistas' ground fire downed a droning Fairchild C-123K cargo plane carrying five tons of ammunition, uniforms, and medical supplies to the contras. North and the CIA had leased the plane as part of their effort (paid for with some of the funds diverted from the arms sales to Iran) to sustain the contras until the new appropriations voted by Congress actually reached the field. One of the mercenaries—a former Marine, Eugene Hasenfus—had, against orders, packed a parachute and, after bailing out of the doomed cargo plane, was captured by a Sandinista patrol. Hasenfus's confession that he believed he was working for the CIA to supply the contras, as well as incriminating documents found in the wreckage, threatened to expose the entire covert American supply effort only a month before the midterm elections. North turned his energy to damage control; his efforts included intervening to curb probes by the FBI and U.S. Customs Service into the cargo flight. President Reagan (who may not have known the exact details) and Assistant Secretary of State Abrams (who was in a position at least to suspect, but later said he did not) denied categorically that Hasenfus and the others had any connection to the government, saying they were simply private American citizens acting on their own.* Abrams also categorically denied before Congress having knowledge of any foreign government providing aid to the contras—even though he had personally arranged for an agreement from Brunei for a $10 million contribution. If the White House hung tough, a timely release of one or more of the hostages in Lebanon might deflect the public's attention.

Just after midnight on the morning of Sunday, November 2, two days

---

* Two weeks later, Abrams learned that the CIA's station chief in Costa Rica had actually played a part in Hasenfus's flight; Abrams would later testify to Congress that he had unwittingly spoken inaccurately in denying any involvement by the U.S. government. North, however, testified to Congress that even if Abrams did not know the details, he was in a position to know generally what had happened, without having to ask.

before the elections, a phone call from John Poindexter awakened Reagan at his ranch in California with joyous news: another hostage, the hospital director at Beirut's American University, David Jacobsen, had been set free. Yet even that delight was tempered by the Americans' failure to free a second hostage, and by Jacobsen's confirmation that his fellow hostage, William Buckley, had died four months earlier. And neither the last-minute news about Jacobsen nor Reagan's personal popularity proved sufficient to stave off heavy losses by the Republicans in the elections—losses that cost the party control of the Senate. It was the worst political setback the administration had yet suffered. Worse still, the day after the elections, November 5, the U.S. press began reporting the shocking story out of Lebanon that exposed the arms sales to Iran.

The early responses by the White House regarding Iran were disturbingly Nixonian. On November 6, Reagan issued a false statement that the article in *Al-Shiraa* had "no foundation." (He also recorded in his diary that the press corps was "off on a wild story" that "we bought hostage Jacobsen's freedom with weapons to Iran.") When Congress refused to be mollified, and when news reports presented fresh evidence that the administration had indeed sold arms to Iran, the White House clumsily made matters worse. In a televised speech to the nation on November 13, Reagan admitted the transactions but claimed, defensively, that they were intended to aid Iranian moderates, put an end to the Iran-Iraq war, eliminate state-sponsored terrorism, and last (almost incidentally) "effect the safe return of all hostages." He emphasized, though, "We did not—repeat did not—trade weapons or anything else for hostages; nor will we." He also said that he had authorized the transfer of only "small amounts of defensive weapons" which, "taken together, could easily fit into a small cargo plane."

Casey, Poindexter, and North, having long foreseen possible exposure, hastily pulled together joint cover stories, with falsified chronologies of the events. They placed full responsibility for the early shipments on the Israelis, who, they claimed, had proceeded on their own and over objections by the United States. As for the later HAWK shipments coordinated by the Enterprise, they claimed that the cargo was oil drilling equipment. On November 21, Poindexter and Casey presented false accounts, under oath, to the House and Senate intelligence committees—but the neither Congress nor, for once, the public believed the administration's reassurances. Attorney General Meese, frightened that an impeachment inquiry might be opened, met with the president and obtained authority to gather all the facts from the NSC over the weekend, so that White House officials would be "speaking with one voice." Meese, habitually disorganized under the best of circumstances, took his time getting the investigation under way. But he made sure that neither the Criminal Division of the Justice Department nor the FBI—that is, the agencies with the most experience in criminal investigations—would be involved in the fact-finding. He alone would be the point man, with three reliable loyalists—assistant attorneys general William Bradford Reynolds and Charles Cooper, and the chief of staff at the Justice Department, John Richardson—acting as his detectives and advisers.

At about three p.m., the attorney general telephoned Poindexter (who had attended Meese's meeting with the president) and requested that he make available all materials connected to the initiative in Iran. Poindexter duly destroyed the most sensitive documents, including the only copy, so far as he knew, of the damning presidential finding of December 5 on arms and hostages. (The text of the finding survived, however, in draft form at the CIA's headquarters, and soon afterward it came to light.) Poindexter also tipped off North, who, after conferring with McFarlane, retreated to his office. There, with the help of his secretary and an aide, North held what McFarlane later remembered him calling a "shredding party." North had been destroying files since October, following the Hasenfus incident. Before the weekend was over—even with Meese's men searching through his files on Saturday, and with Meese, on Sunday, questioning him about what they found—North and his helpers had managed to gather and surreptitiously alter or destroy 5,000 pages of documents relating to the contras and Iran. Across the Potomac in McLean, Virginia, General Secord, helped by a secretary and two aides, destroyed incriminating records of the Enterprise in his office files.

With their deliberate destruction of evidence, Poindexter, North, and Secord pushed Reagan's White House beyond even Richard Nixon's obstruction of justice. But North's wholesale shredding apparently missed a memo that revealed the diversion of funds to the contras, and one of Meese's investigators quickly discovered it.* When informed by Meese on Monday

---

* The swiftness with which William Bradford Reynolds found the damning memo raises the suspicion that North left it in the open on purpose, possibly with Reynolds's foreknowledge, thereby implicating himself and the NSC in the diversion, but not the president. This deduction raises the possibility that the cover-up was more complex than subsequent investigators were able to discover, that Reagan himself was aware of the diversion, and that North was agreeably playing the fall guy in order to protect the president. But barring some future revelation, this, like much else about Iran-contra, remains purely speculative.

of the Iran-contra link, Reagan reportedly blanched; and in his diary, he recorded that neither "our Col. North" nor, "worst of all," Poindexter had told him of the arrangement. ("This may call for resignations," he concluded.) Yet even if the president was truly surprised, he expressed no anger about the diversion per se, which he immediately knew to be "a violation of the law against giving the Contras money without an authorization by Congress." His chief concern was that the revelation, which he described as "a smoking gun," would expose the secret U.S. arms sales to the Iranians—an arrangement he continued to defend privately against the complaints of Secretary of State Shultz, whom he described as "still stubborn that we shouldn't have sold the arms to Iran."

The next day, November 25, Reagan, in the worst performance of his presidency if not his entire career, read to the White House press corps a prepared statement about his discovery that "in one aspect," merely, the "implementation" of his policy regarding Iran had been "seriously flawed." As a result of that discovery, he said, Poindexter had resigned and North had been removed from the NSC staff—and a special White House review board would investigate what went wrong. (Behind the scenes, Reagan told Poindexter that he would reluctantly accept his resignation because he knew "the press would crucify him if he stayed & he didn't deserve that.") Then, strangely, the president disappeared and left Meese on the podium alone to tell the press about the diversion to the contras and take questions. A feeding frenzy began in the press. Leaders from both houses of Congress announced that they would start their own investigations.

By December 2, Reagan's approval rating in the Gallup poll had, within a month, dropped by twenty-one points to 46 percent—the sharpest one-month decline Gallup had ever recorded. Before the end of the year, the Justice Department appointed Judge Lawrence Walsh, a respected senior Republican lawyer, judge, and former deputy attorney general in the Eisenhower administration, as a special prosecutor to begin an independent investigation. Despite his credentials and although he had no partisan motive, Republicans in Congress demonized Walsh, falsely accusing him of numerous malfeasances, even of being a tax evader, while conservative allies of North and the other coconspirators assassinated his character. Walsh expressed shock at these tactics.

For months, in private as well as in public, Reagan continued to assert that he had not approved of any trade of arms for hostages. Even when he apologetically changed his story at the end of February—after the special White House review board, headed by Senator John Tower, Republican of

Texas, released its report contradicting him—the president insisted that he had never *intended* to trade arms for hostages. But these claims were patently false. Abundant evidence, including his own private diary entries, those of Caspar Weinberger, and the presidential finding of December 5 "Hostage Rescue—Middle East," indicated that Reagan had authorized arms sales precisely because he hoped that they would, as he wrote, get the hostages "sprung momentarily." Early in the affair, the president seized on the rationalization that because the United States was not sending arms directly to the kidnappers, this was not an arms-for-hostages arrangement. Given Reagan's propensity to appear disengaged and self-deluding rather than dishonest, he may have persuaded himself that this semantic dodge was truthful. But nobody else seriously claimed it was.

By sticking to his story for so long, however, and then claiming he had been confused and misled, Reagan bought valuable time and contained the political damage. Other factors and developments—some fortuitous, others planned—also helped shield the president from the truth. Six weeks after the news of the arms sales broke, the director of the CIA, Casey, suffered a debilitating stroke, and in May he died of brain cancer. Without Casey's further sworn testimony (and without the documents that Casey's protégé North and North's accomplices Poindexter and Secord had destroyed), further investigations into what the press now called the Iran-contra affair were severely hampered. Hours before he was to testify before Tower's review board, the unnerved Robert McFarlane attempted to commit suicide by swallowing twenty to thirty Valium pills—a near tragedy that elicited, in Washington, more empathy than suspicion. Meanwhile, in early January, Reagan had undergone prostate surgery that left him, for a time, physically weakened. Although the president's withdrawal worsened the chaotic mood within the White House, it touched another vein of public sympathy.

Precedents, timing, and the political calendar all worked in Reagan's favor. The Watergate scandal had turned serious at the very beginning of Nixon's second term; Reagan's presidency, in contrast, had less than two years to go. With the Democrats back in command of the Senate, realists reasoned that a lame-duck Reagan, damaged by scandal, could not accomplish too much in any case. If, moreover, Reagan were to face impeachment proceedings, they would come at the very close of his administration, and overwhelm the presidential elections of 1988—a disastrous prospect for Republicans, but also unsettling to Democrats, many of whom had already rejected impeachment on the grounds that elevating George H. W. Bush to the presidency would strengthen Bush's hopes for 1988. The Democrats also did not want to be seen as the party that regularly impeached Republican presidents. An inflamed partisanship, they feared, might lead some future Republican Congress, out for revenge, to look for excuses to impeach a Democratic president.

The example of Watergate had also primed Congress, the press, and the public to look for a so-called smoking gun that would decide the president's fate. Speculation now focused, not surprisingly, on the most shocking (and thus, it seemed, the most damaging) of the recent revelations. Americans rephrased a famous question originally asked by Senator Howard Baker in 1973: "What did the president know about the diversion of funds to the contras, and when did he know it?" But this formulation helped the president enormously. The diversion was hardly the gravest episode in the Iran-contra affair, yet making it seem so swept everything else to the background. It also placed undue importance on the single sequence of events about which the president may well have known nothing and where no smoking gun would be found—the events that he himself had singled out, in his disastrous press conference of November 25, as the "one aspect" in which the "implementation" of his policy had been "seriously flawed." The near obsession with the diversion to the contras was itself a diversion from more significant and potentially more incriminating matters, including the cover-up activities beginning in October.

The report of Tower's review board gave Reagan a further boost, despite its numerous criticisms of the president's leadership. Reagan's admirers praised him simply for establishing the board, and for refusing (unlike Nixon) to invoke executive privilege in order to evade scrutiny. One of the president's most levelheaded supporters during the crisis, the U.S. ambassador to NATO, David Abshire, later commended Reagan for his honest desire to uncover the truth, and extolled the board members for producing "a credible and broadly accepted document that created the foundation for restoring the Reagan presidency." The board's explicit objective, however, was not to save Reagan's presidency but to examine the circumstances surrounding the Iran-contra matter and evaluate the role of the NSC staff. Even though its mandate expressly stated that the board would neither "assess individual culpability" nor stand as "the final arbiter of the facts," its final report assessed culpability as it saw fit—and set a powerful tone for all subsequent inquiry and debate.

As a creation of the executive branch it was investigating, the board lacked any standing as an independent body within the Constitution's system of checks and balances. It also lacked the legal authority to subpoena documents, compel testimony, or swear witnesses. Much new information did surface, but without broad investigative powers, the board could not clear up conflicting testimony or settle such basic questions as when Oliver North first became involved in supplying the contras. Even if it had been given broader powers, the tight, arbitrary deadline set for the completion of its work precluded anything approaching an exhaustive investigation. Yet by the time the board issued its final report in February, it had acquired the air of an unencumbered, authoritative commission, which had honored the president's often quoted insistence that he wanted "all the facts to come out."

The report of the Tower Commission did rebuke Reagan for placing "the principal responsibility for policy review and implementation on the shoulders of his advisers." But that criticism, apart from being fundamentally inaccurate, was actually more exculpatory than damning. At no point, except possibly with regard to the diversion of funds, did Reagan relinquish either his responsibility for or his active engagement in policy review over defying the Boland Amendment or selling arms to Iran. On other matters he may have been detached or uninformed—but on these matters, the record showed a president who was passionately engaged and constantly informed. He may not have known every fine detail about operations; few presidents do. But he was fully aware that he had approved and helped engage in secret fund-raising for the contras, and that he had approved the sale of missiles to Iraq in the futile hope that this would free all the hostages. And he knew that these approvals, undertaken covertly in order to avoid the attention and skirt the will of Congress, were quite possibly unlawful and even unconstitutional.

The review board more gently chided Reagan for his lax "management style"—but aside, perhaps, from the diversion, nothing that resulted from Reagan's reliance on McFarlane, Poindexter, and North in the Iran-contra affair departed in any significant way from his actual policies (which were not always the same as his publicly stated policies). The report lent credence to groundless claims that the dealings with Iran originally had little or nothing at all to do with the hostages, and only gradually and accidentally became an arms-for-hostages arrangement. By emphasizing matters of style instead of Reagan's deliberate and emphatic political decisions, it also turned a dubious caricature, popular among some of Reagan's liberal detractors—the president as a doddering old man at the mercy of his manipulative advisers—into a rationale for not judging him too harshly.

Above all, the report fed widespread public misconceptions of the scandal by focusing on the diversion to the contras and concluding that Reagan had had "no knowledge" of it until Meese informed him in late November 1986. No matter what its pretenses were about refusing to assess individual guilt, and no matter what its criticisms were of unsound procedures and "process," with that flat judgment the report essentially exonerated Reagan. Reagan himself recognized as much. A month after the report was released he joked genially at the White House with Abshire about how he had been found not guilty. "Plainly, there was no smoking gun in the president's hand," Abshire later wrote of the board's findings.

The report irritated Shultz and Weinberger, who at different points had stoutly opposed the initiative in Iran but whom the board criticized for not doing more before they "distanced themselves from the march of events." The report also found fault with Casey for giving too much power to North and for insufficiently informing the president—but by the time the report appeared, Casey was terminally ill and beyond accountability. The board had especially severe words for the chief of staff, Donald Regan, charging that he bore primary responsibility for the disorder inside the White House; and Regan hit the roof, knowing that he would now be forced to resign. (He agreed to do so, and the president confided in his diary, "My prayers have really been answered. . . . Thank you God.") Otherwise, those around the president breathed a sigh of relief. And the president, now fully recovered from his prostate surgery (and, it seemed, from the Iran-contra scandal), returned to the fray reinvigorated.

He began in earnest on March 4, with a prime-time speech to the nation in which he publicly accepted the conclusions of the Tower Commission. The well-crafted address earned raves, even from shrewd reporters and political commentators. One of them, R. W. Apple, the chief political reporter for the *New York Times*, praised Reagan for speaking "in a spirit of contrition that has not been heard from the White House in a quarter century." In his "contrition," though, Reagan sustained the illusion that he had approved the original arms sales solely "in order to develop relations" with Iranian moderates. "What began as a strategic opening to Iran," he shamelessly asserted "deteriorated, in its implementation, into trading arms for hostages"—as if he had not been interested chiefly in the hostages from the start, and that without this concern, the initiative would never have gone forward. The president made it sound as if all the illicit and shady activities related to Iran and Nicaragua for which he was now gallantly shouldering the burden, and not just the diversion to the contras, had been "undertaken without my knowledge." He admitted he had been too slack and too trusting, but nothing worse than that. He stated that his heart and best intentions—the things Americans most admired about him—still told him he had *never* traded arms for hostages. Even if he had, his intentions were still pure. And the quiet self-pardoning contained in these erroneous statements and incongruities eluded serious rebuttal.*

The Iran-contra affair dragged on, with occasional bursts of excitement, for several months more, playing itself out in the congressional hearings that took up the late spring and early summer of 1987. The hearings began with renewed expectations of high political drama. Unlike the Tower Commission, the intelligence committees in the House and Senate had the full power to subpoena documents and force unwilling witnesses to testify under oath. With the Democrats now holding the majority in both houses, there was a chance that new and damaging evidence would come to light, or so the critics of the administration hoped. But the board's vindication of Reagan had dampened public concern. Thanks to some high-minded decisions and political lapses by senior Democrats in Congress, and to unbridled efforts by the Republicans to undermine the investigations, the administration's good fortune held. The theatrical climax of the hearings came not in a shattering exposé of the administration's misdeeds, but in the televised glorification of Oliver North.

Some of the defects in the congressional hearings arose, ironically, from the determination of the chairman of the Senate Intelligence Committee,

---

* Reagan himself came closest to rebutting—or at any rate correcting—his own continuing self-defense when he told a group of southern journalists in mid-May that he was "very definitely involved in decisions about support for the freedom fighters. It was my idea to begin with." For months, the White House had been claiming that it knew no details about the effort to supply the contras; Reagan himself had told reporters in October 1986 that "we did not know the exact particulars" about the program. The later statement was in line with the new, more aggressive line advanced by the White House and Republicans on Capitol Hill during the congressional hearings on the affair (these hearings had then just gotten under way) that the efforts to aid the contras did not in any way violate the Boland Amendments. Reagan, "Informal Exchange with Reporters on the Budget, October 8, 1986," transcript at http://www.presidency.ucsb.edu/ws/index.php?pid=36565&st=&st1=. Steven V. Roberts, "Aide Cites Reagan Foreign Policy Power," *New York Times*, May 15, 1987, p. A13; "Private Aid Idea for Rebels Is His, President Asserts," *New York Times*, May 16, 1987, p. 1; Stuart Taylor Jr., "A New Stand over Contras," *New York Times*, May 25, 1987, p. 1.

Daniel K. Inouye of Hawaii, that they be conducted with bipartisan fairness, restraint, and decorum. A much-decorated hero of the World War II who lost an arm at the end of the Italian campaign, Inouye had served on the Senate Watergate Committee that paved the way for the impeachment proceedings against President Nixon, and earned praise for his calm and judicious manner. A strong Democrat but a patriot first, Inouye wanted to promote a sense of national unity as well as probity in this new time of trouble. Yet Inouye's aversion to conflict led him and his colleagues to commit tactical errors that helped stack the deck in favor of the White House and its unwavering loyalists.

Fearing that simultaneous investigations by House and Senate committees would create a media circus, Inouye helped persuade his colleagues to hold a single set of hearings before select committees from the House and Senate, working jointly. Fair and efficient in theory, the plan overlooked the very different styles of debate and partisanship in the two houses: the gentlemanliness of the Senate, to which Inouye was accustomed, was very different from the more rough-and-tumble, polarized atmosphere in the House. Consequently, the combined committees found themselves struggling with intense partisan divisions. Conservative Republicans in the House acidulously challenged the legitimacy of the very investigation they were supposed to be helping to conduct, attacking all probes of the administration's actions as efforts by liberals to subvert a popular president. The Democrats, intent on exposing what they perceived as gross abuse of executive power by the president, were caught by surprise and left virtually speechless and defenseless. Instead of comity, the plan brought rancor.

Some of the committee's other decisions limited the scope and power of the investigation. Not wanting to embarrass the president or vice president at a critical moment in the cold war, Inouye successfully opposed any effort to subpoena Reagan or Bush—giving a pass to two of the most important potential witnesses. Inouye also favored acceding to demands by Oliver North's abrasive lawyer, Brendan V. Sullivan, that his client be granted immunity from criminal prosecution based on his testimony before Congress, and that the time allowed for the committee to question him be strictly limited. Inouye and others worried that if the committee did not give in, Sullivan would raise objections and make court appeals that would drag the hearings well past the committee's self-imposed deadline in October.

Other well-intentioned decisions came back to haunt the hearings when the televised proceedings began. As the lead counsel for the Senate, a group of three senators, headed by the committee's vice chairman, Warren

Rudman of New Hampshire, selected the brilliant and distinguished New York attorney Arthur Liman. On the House side, the chair of the House Intelligence Committee, Lee Hamilton, picked as chief Democratic counsel a younger lawyer, John Nields, who had impressed Hamilton with his work in an earlier congressional ethics investigation. (The Republican minority from the House, under the ranking member, Dick Cheney of Wyoming, also had its own minority counsel as well as its own committee staff.)

Solely on the merits, Liman and Nields were excellent choices. But as televised events, the hearings inevitably became political theater as well as legal proceedings. None of the Democrats gave any thought to the obvious implications for public relations. Liman, for his part, came across on television like a provincial stereotype of a New York Jew, strands of hair covering his balding forehead, as he glowered at witnesses he found unpersuasive.[*] Nields's youthfulness and shoulder-length hair made him look like a student rebel of the 1960s trying to disguise himself in a suit and tie. The confrontation pitting them against the star witness, the superpatriot Oliver North, in his Marine uniform, would appear to many viewers as two incarnations of eastern, elitist liberalism persecuting Ronald Reagan's purebred, wholesome all-American.

The hearings had become fractious well before North appeared in mid-July. Richard Secord, the first witness, presented himself in four days of testimony as an unfairly accused, proud, selfless American who had served his country long and well. When Liman bore in with damaging questions about Secord's profit making, Secord responded with disdain that bordered on ridicule. Yet the immediate and surprising public response strongly favored Secord as an embattled soldier. And while Liman began receiving hate mail, some of it menacing and viciously anti-Semitic, Republican conservatives on the committee praised Secord and cast aspersions on Liman, Nields, and the Democrats. One of the most outspoken Republicans, Representative Henry J. Hyde of Illinois, openly sided with Secord and gibed sarcastically that the witness had been "charged with the high crime of ambiguity of intention." So it continued, as one witness after another—some

---

[*] David Abshire has perhaps come closest to expressing, in all its ugliness, how many Americans in the heartland perceived the encounter, in a startling passage contrasting the "handsome" Richard Secord with his "fine military bearing," which Abshire admired, and "his inquisitor" Liman with "[h]is spaghetti hair, New York accent and culture, and abrasive, aggressive manner." David Abshire, *Saving the Reagan Presidency: Trust Is the Coin of the Realm* (College Station, TX, 2005), 170–171.

arrogant, others grave—withstood Liman's and Nields's questions while the Republicans intensified the attacks on their Democratic colleagues.

Oliver North strode into this simmering atmosphere to deliver a boiling hot piece of right-wing performance art. His Marine uniform's left breast bedecked with medals (these were permitted, to their later regret, by the Democrats), North played the incorruptible action hero facing down the mean-spirited lawyers and politicians. Like his commander in chief, Ronald Reagan, North was a man of very simple, unashamed black-and-white views; like Reagan, he presented himself as friendly and accessible, quick with a smile. But unlike Reagan, he was a genuine military man, a decorated veteran of Vietnam who had never stopped fighting the good fight. And whereas Reagan, the supposed archconservative, had raised eyebrows by selling American arms to the archenemy Iran, North, the uniformed patriot, would turn the conservatives' contempt for government into a dark defense of everything that had happened in connection with the Iran-contra affair.

In his way, North became the man who would try, finally, to redeem the shame, hurt, and frustration suffered by the dutiful, heroic veterans of Khe San and Hamburger Hill. According to right-wing myth (propounded by Reagan) the U.S. government, abetted by the stab-in-the-back liberal media, had failed these heroes by refusing to go all-out to win the Vietnam War. North updated that mythology to save his neck, turning the hearings into a forum where an invented authentic America would wreak its vengeance at last. Some critics likened North to another military authoritarian, General Douglas MacArthur, who in the early 1950s had wrapped himself bathetically in the American flag and caused a sensation after being dismissed by President Truman for disobeying orders. North certainly waved the flag, but he also did something else, portraying Nicaragua as the latest Vietnam, the front line of America's war against the forces of brutal, tyrannical communism, where, once again, meddlesome, weak-kneed politicians were doing the devil's work. In the continuing disquiet after Vietnam, North put himself forward as a true braveheart who would stop at nothing to ensure that freedom's cause prevailed.

North endlessly repeated that he was simply a good Marine who had followed orders and undertaken initiatives of his own only with the full approval of his superiors. Granted congressional immunity in exchange for his testimony, he freely admitted that he had shredded documents; lied to Congress and to the CIA; and falsified financial records to cover up, among other things, the purchase of a personal home security system bought with proceeds from the Enterprise. (North deflected that last charge by claim-ing—absurdly and without evidence—that he built the fence as protection against the terrorist Abu Nidal, and by referring the committee to a grisly photograph of one of Nidal's victims, an eleven-year-old American girl—a girl "not perhaps a whole lot different" from his own eleven-year-old daugh-ter, North said, suddenly husky-voiced.) All of North's deeds could be justi-fied as the leatherneck means to a glorious end—unseemly, certainly, and maybe even illegal, but imperative given the astronomical stakes. Every-thing that the committee members deemed a possible crime, including sub-version of the Constitution, North calmly but firmly threw back in their faces as the indispensable deeds of a valiant, realistic American. The real villain, he charged, was Congress, which had failed to provide consistent support to the contras.

Neither Liman nor Nields nor the committee members had expected North to be such a powerful witness, but they found out quickly enough when he opened his defense. "I think it is very important for the American people to understand that this is a dangerous world," he said grimly in re-sponse to a straightforward question from Nields:

> That we live at risk and that this nation is at risk in a dangerous world. And that they ought not to be led to believe, as a consequence of these hearings, that this nation cannot or should not conduct covert operations. By their very nature, covert operations or special activities are a lie. There is great deceit, deception in the conduct of covert operations. They are in essence a lie.

At one level, this was a brazenly obvious and illogical evasion. Nields had never suggested that the world was a safe place; nor had he or anyone else on the committee said that the country should cease conducting covert operations. That some lies must be told in covert operations hardly justi-fied North's lies or his particular covert operations. At another level, it was a brilliant distillation of a zealous will to power, a kind of cynical Bolshe-vism turned inside out. Since the nation is perpetually, as North put it, "at risk," appeals to constitutional restrictions and to checks and balances play into the hands of the enemy, signifying weakness and hampering America's own resolute freedom fighters like Oliver North.

Most of the committee members were chilled and angered by North's politicized contempt for the truth and his convenient twisting of the Constitution (including his tendentious claims that, in foreign affairs, the executive branch's prerogatives reign supreme.)[*] One of the angriest, the Republican senator Warren Rudman, had actually supported aid to the contras, but he upbraided North for attacking Congress. Pointing out that public opinion polls had been strongly against aid to the contras, Rudman instructed North that, like it or not, "this Congress represents the people." Yet in the heat of the moment, North, not Rudman and his colleagues, seemed to have captured the public's affection. Mail supporting North and denouncing the committee poured into Washington; individual members were alarmed by how many letter writers expressed a desire to see them hanged along with "that Jew, Liman"; all around the country, a personality cult of "Ollie!" sprang up instantaneously.

Conservative Republican committee members from the House, meanwhile, cheered North from the start, at once feeding and feeding on the popular frenzy. The ranking Republican member, Dick Cheney, used North's testimony as a pretext for charging that news reporters and editors were systematically spreading falsehoods about North and the White House—prompting appreciative words from President Reagan about how Cheney had "blasted the press." When not jumping in to interrupt Liman's questioning, several others went so far as to endorse North's diversion to the contras as a stroke of genius, which fleeced Ayatollah Khomeini in order to supply the freedom fighters. Still others, led once more by Henry Hyde, defended North as a high-minded, patriotic practitioner of situational ethics, regardless of his truthfulness or adherence to the Constitution. "The end doesn't justify the means," Hyde said. "It's a useful ethical statement, I suppose, but I'll tell you, that phrase doesn't seem to me to establish the moral context for every tough decision someone in government has to make."

Other star witnesses followed North, including John Poindexter (who testified that he had insulated Reagan from knowing about the diversion to the contras) and George Shultz (who fended off charges from Republicans in the House that he lacked integrity and should have resigned after he failed to dissuade the president from selling arms to Iran). But after North

---

[*] At one point, North cited George Washington to support his contentions. The passage from President Washington, dating from 1796, relates why the need for caution and secrecy was an important reason "for vesting the power of making treaties in the president, with the advice and consent of the Senate." North's rendition conveniently excised the final clause. See Washington, "Message to the House of Representatives Regarding Documents Relative to the Jay Treaty, March 30, 1796," at http://www.presidency.ucsb.edu/ws/index.php?pid=65520&st=&stl=.

departed, the high drama ended; and once Poindexter seemed to clear the president of the only charge that many thought mattered, the rest was anticlimactic. The joint committees, divided from within, ended up submitting two starkly different reports. The majority report placed the blame for the affair entirely on Reagan, and charged that by allowing, even unwittingly, systematic lawbreaking by his subordinates, the president had failed in his duty, as stated in the Constitution, to "take care that the laws be faithfully executed." The report also charged that the solicitation of private and foreign funds, along with the diversion to the contras, clearly violated both the spirit and the letter of the Boland Amendment.

Under different circumstances, such accusations might well have become the basis for impeachment. But the committee, like the Tower Commission, found no "smoking gun"—no evidence that Reagan had even known about the supposedly all-important diversion; the Boland Amendment stipulated no criminal penalties for violations; and the Olliemania that developed during North's appearance banished any lingering thoughts of impeaching Reagan. Yet even if the report seemed to remove what one congressman called the "cloud hanging over the President," it was still unacceptable to all six Republican members from the House and two of the Republicans from the Senate. Their minority report called the entire investigation a witch hunt and claimed that, although mistakes were made, there was no constitutional crisis and no systematic lawbreaking. The minority report also attacked Secretary of State Shultz for "a record of disengagement," upheld the president's basic supremacy in foreign affairs, and lambasted Congress for encroaching on the president's authority.

The minority report read much like old attacks on the Watergate investigation as a brazen effort by Congress to undermine President Nixon's policies and usurp executive power. In the face of the evidence that officials in the Reagan White House had committed crimes in pursuit of their policies, the minority extolled some of those policies and dismissed any concerns about the Constitution and legal wrongdoing as cynical and politically motivated—the criminalization of policy differences, as some put it. On several points, the minority report actually converged with the views of what had been the pro-Casey and pro-North elements in the White House, including Casey's view that the Boland Amendment did not cover the NSC—the spark that set off the entire affair. The Republicans had shifted ground: instead of merely protesting the administration's innocence, they rationalized much of the lawlesness, commended decisions that had shocked the nation when exposed a year earlier, and spent considerable time attacking Con-

gress for usurping executive power. Not only did the report justify misconduct and lawbreaking by White House officials, it condemned Congress for
passing some of the laws in the first place.

The sale of arms to Iran, according to the minority report, was not a
reckless scheme but an inspired gesture to "establish a new US relationship
with Iran." Although it deplored the diversion of funds to the contras as extremely unwise, and acknowledged that Reagan's White House had made
mistakes, its worst mistake of all, according to the report, was Reagan's decision to sign the second Boland Amendment rather than veto it—even if
the veto might paralyze the government. A second mistake, stemming from
the first, was Reagan's continuing "less-than-robust defense of his office's
constitutional powers."

Two minority members took the lead in preparing and publicizing the
report. One, Henry Hyde, had been among the most scathing and sarcastic of the House Republicans during the televised hearings. The other, as
was his wont, spoke out bluntly when called on but generally took a much
quieter stance in public, preferring to wield his considerable power behind
the scenes. He was the ranking Republican member from the House, Dick
Cheney.

President Reagan, who had publicly embraced the report of the Tower
Commission (albeit on his own terms), scorned the findings of the congressional majority. (The official White House response dismissed the report as
"the subjective opinions of not even the unanimous judgment of the committee.") Reagan too had shifted his ground since February, now claiming
publicly that he could not find any serious fault in his former aides. Even
after Robert McFarlane, on March 11, 1988, pleaded guilty to four minor
counts of withholding information from Congress, and was followed, five
days later, by the return of indictments with twenty-three serious counts
against Oliver North, John Poindexter, Richard Secord, and Albert Hakim,
Reagan stood firm, insisting that they were innocent of any crime. When
a reporter pointed out the inconvenient fact of McFarlane's guilty plea, the
president, predictably, responded with mirth: "He just pleaded guilty to not
telling Congress everything it wanted to know." Then he chuckled: "I've
done that myself."

The president could afford to laugh—for he and his administration had
survived what could easily have become a political cataclysm. Contrary to
the committee's minority report, the Iran-contra affair was a major con-

stitutional battle over the respective powers of the executive and Congress. Although the issue had been debated as early as George Washington's time, never had it led to this sort of direct confrontation—or to the creation of what amounted to an unelected junta inside the White House to prosecute the president's policies outside the Constitution. Critics pointed out that the Constitution makes no distinction between foreign and domestic policy, and that, by approving and then executing the expenditure of funds not appropriated by Congress, administration officials had committed grave constitutional violations, quite apart from breaking specific laws. The committee's majority report quoted from Secretary of State Shultz's testimony: "You cannot spend funds that Congress doesn't either authorize you to obtain or appropriate. That is what the Constitution says, and we have to stick to it."

The other side held the view that, as the congressional minority put it, the Constitution gives the president "the primary role of conducting the foreign policy of the United States" and that any congressional efforts to "interfere with core presidential foreign policy functions . . . should be struck down." This view prevailed, in even starker terms, inside Reagan's White House, where Poindexter, North, and, occasionally, Reagan himself explicitly stated that the president has ultimate authority over foreign policy. With that view in mind, and with the president's full knowledge and participation, the White House purposefully and secretly evaded the expressed will of Congress, and flagrantly violated legal mandates about notification of Congress. The participants may have believed, some quite sincerely, that they were doing no more than previous administrations in evasively withholding sensitive information from a Congress that was maddeningly inconsistent on aid to the contras, and that they otherwise adhered to the law. But they also believed that, because they knew they were doing good, they could not possibly do wrong; that because their hearts were pure, their hands must be clean. So they wound up creating a foreign policy that not only was covert and directly contradicted stated administration positions, but was executed by an immense private network of shady foreign arms dealers, soldiers of fortune, cocaine-smuggling pilots, terrorizing brutes, and rip-off artists—all completely unaccountable to the American people.

The policies themselves also proved either stupid or ineffective. No Iranian moderates emerged after Ayatollah Khomeini's death in 1989; the arms deals turned out to be a sting operation by the Iranians more than anything else. (Three American hostages were freed during the fourteen months of the dealings, as Oliver North never tired of reminding the world—but over the same period, three more Americans were seized and one of the original hostages was executed.) Although the Sandinistas were indeed ousted from power in 1990, their ouster came not at the hands of the contras but as a result of diplomacy led by Costa Rica's president Oscar Arias (which the White House deplored) and of peaceful political organizing by democratic forces inside Nicaragua, which brought about the Sandinistas' defeat at the polls. But quite apart from the specific policies pursued, the White House and its supporters had followed an expansive view of executive power that forced a showdown.

The outcome of that showdown was mixed. Although Reagan, by denying that he knew anything, escaped scot-free, fourteen leading participants in the events were indicted, of whom eleven (including North and Poindexter) were convicted, in some cases of major felonies (North was convicted of destroying evidence, obstructing Congress, and accepting illegal gifts), in proceedings initiated by the special prosecutor Lawrence Walsh. When, early in 1988, Congress again voted to deny aid to the contras, and there was talk among conservatives about raising money from private sources, the White House swiftly renounced the efforts and laid the matter to rest. Yet many of those convicted over the Iran-contra affair would resurface in later years, including two, John Poindexter and Elliott Abrams, who would again serve in important posts in the executive branch.* (North's convictions were overturned on appeal in 1990, on the grounds that immunized testimony before Congress had been used in his trial. Poindexter's guilty verdicts were set aside for similar reasons. Later, President George H. W. Bush pardoned six people convicted in the scandal, including Abrams and Weinberger.) And the constitutional struggle that underlay Iran-contra would continue.

The more immediate political implications involved the makeup of the Reagan White House. Donald Regan's autocratic, centralized regime as

---

* Apart from Poindexter and Abrams, significant figures in and around the scandal and investigation who were later either elected or appointed to major positions in the executive branch include David S. Addington (assistant counsel at the CIA during William Casey's tenure and a member of the House committee minority's staff), John Bolton (a senior official at the Justice Department who advised Attorney General Meese when the scandal broke in November 1986), George H. W. Bush, Dick Cheney, Robert Gates (then deputy director of the CIA), John Negroponte (then U.S. ambassador to Honduras), and Otto Reich (then head of the Office of Public Diplomacy, charged with disseminating "white" propaganda). As we will see, several of these figures including Addington, Bolton, Cheney, Gates, and Negroponte, as well as Abrams and Poindexter, would occupy key positions in formulating the foreign policy of the George W. Bush administration.

chief of staff had been raising hackles for a long time, and his feud with Nancy Reagan had become fierce. The devastating discussion of his work contained in the report of the Tower Commission was, finally, the impetus behind the first lady's effort to force his resignation in March 1987. But Poindexter was also gone, as was Casey and, after November, Caspar Weinberger, who resigned, citing his wife's declining health. In their places (and with considerable input from Mrs. Reagan), the president chose strikingly more moderate men, most of whom had long been fixtures in Washington: former senator Howard Baker as chief of staff; Frank Carlucci (a longtime protégé of his roommate at Princeton, Donald Rumsfeld, and Poindexter's replacement as national security adviser) to be Secretary of Defense; Jimmy Carter's former director of the FBI, William Webster, to head the CIA; and Lieutenant General Colin Powell of the Army, formerly Weinberger's military assistant, as national security adviser. A year later, when the scandal-plagued Ed Meese finally resigned from the Justice Department, the president chose the moderate Republican Richard Thornburgh of Pennsylvania as his new attorney general. To revive his damaged presidency, Reagan fundamentally changed his inner circle, replacing sharpedged ideologues with temperate pragmatists.

The new team faced a difficult battle. Although the president had recovered some of the ground lost after the initial disclosure of Iran-contra, he would never recover the enthusiasm that vanished when the scandal broke. After half a century as a public figure, two decades as a political leader, and six years as a formidable president, Reagan seemed to have lost his magic touch. Even as the congressional committee wrapped up its investigation of Iran-contra, more bad news, political and personal, hit the administration. On October 5, the White House announced that Nancy Reagan had been diagnosed with breast cancer. Two weeks later she underwent a successful partial mastectomy. On October 19, the stock market crashed. On October 23, the Senate rejected the nomination of the troublesome Robert Bork to the Supreme Court, and soon after that the White House had to withdraw the nomination of Douglas Ginsburg. In mid-November, the president, under pressure from Congress, agreed to limit the testing of his cherished Strategic Defense Initiative.

But there was one very bright spot. On December 8, Reagan met in Washington with the premier of the Soviet Union, Mikhail Gorbachev, in their third summit since Gorbachev ascended to power in 1985. The two leaders signed a major treaty eliminating all intermediate- and short-range missiles from the U.S. and Soviet arsenals. The reunion was extremely

9

"ANOTHER TIME, ANOTHER ERA"

A T T H E E N D O F the summit in Washington, as his motorcade headed down Connecticut Avenue, Mikhail Gorbachev suddenly told his driver to halt, opened the door of his black Zil limousine, waded into a lunchtime crowd, and starting shaking hands like any American politician on the stump. Security guards cringed, but passersby were thrilled. "This is the most exciting thing that has ever happened to me," an office employee of the National Rifle Association said to a reporter. "I'm still shaking," said an account executive for Wang Laboratories. "It was like the coming of the second Messiah or something." Gorbachev elicited enthusiasm wherever he went: within just six months, Gorbymania had replaced Olliemania. Asked whether he minded being upstaged in his own capital city, Ronald Reagan, true to form, replied in good Hollywood humor. "I don't resent his popularity or anything else," the president quipped. "Good Lord, I once co-starred with Errol Flynn."

Reagan's contributions to changing U.S.-Soviet relations and hastening the end of the cold war are among the most misunderstood aspects of his presidency. When, in her eulogy at Reagan's funeral, the former British prime minister Margaret Thatcher said that he won the cold war "without firing a shot," she graciously exaggerated—but Thatcher, who knew better, did not claim that Reagan acted unilaterally, as many of his admirers have said. The contention that Reagan purposefully bankrupted the Soviets with his arms buildup, or that he thought of his far-fetched Strategic Defense Initiative as a means to frighten or outspend the Kremlin into submission, or that the Reagan Doctrine proved a smashing triumph, or even that Reagan's policies toward the Soviet Union were consistently hostile during the eight years of his administration, are as groundless as they are commonplace. Reagan's own ambassador to Moscow, Jack F. Matlock Jr., has ridiculed the assertion that Reagan set out "to bring the Soviet Union down" as false "rationalizations after the fact." Apart from mythologizing Reagan, these fictions imply that every action by the Soviet Union was merely a reaction to something America had done. Led by Gorbachev—whom Thatcher, in her eulogy of Reagan, called the Kremlin's "man of goodwill"—the Soviets had enormous reasons of their own to reverse the trends of militarization, economic disaster, and a futile war in Afghanistan, and, ultimately, to end the cold war.

Reagan's role in the drama was truly important. More than a year before Gorbachev took power, Reagan had begun offering the Soviet Union public and private assurances of his benign intentions and his hopes to improve relations between the superpowers. As his reaction to the scare over Able Archer indicated, Reagan regarded nuclear weapons, and the possibility of nuclear warfare, with horror. In addition to reviving the American will to resist communist tyranny and aggression (which unsettled liberals), he wanted to transform the basic terms of U.S.-Soviet affairs by rejecting the balance of nuclear terror in favor of actually eliminating nuclear weapons—an approach that earned the president contemptuous criticism from his allies in the conservative political establishment. Once they arrived at this shared vision about arms reduction, Reagan and Gorbachev—testily at first, and facing opposition from militants and ideologues in their own countries—undertook an astonishing new departure that revolutionized international relations. The denouement took three years and contained numerous ironies and unanticipated events. But together, the two unlikely costars seized the opportunity to complete one of the most dramatic turnabouts in modern history.

Mikhail Sergeyevich Gorbachev, during his six years as general secretary of the Communist Party of the Soviet Union, tried to salvage and vindicate what he saw as the ideals of his country's October Revolution after decades of political and economic decay. His reforms ended up hastening the collapse of both Soviet communism and the Soviet Union.

After being chosen premier on March 11, 1985, Gorbachev made clear

Above: Caspar Weinberger, Secretary of Health, Education, and Welfare, in the Oval Office to discuss welfare reform with President Richard M. Nixon, May 14, 1974, as the Watergate scandal raged. Weinberger urged Nixon not to resign, and Nixon assured him there was "no chance" he would. Less than three months later, Nixon was gone.

Right: A Marine changes the official presidential portraits hung at the American embassy in Bonn, West Germany, after Nixon announced his resignation on August 8, 1974.

President Gerald R. Ford meets with Deputy Chief of Staff Dick Cheney and Chief of Staff Don Rumsfeld in the Oval Office, April 23, 1975.

The counterculture pays a call: former Beatle George Harrison (*center*) and rock and roll organist Billy Preston (*left*) visit President Ford at the White House, December 13, 1974.

President Ford addresses delegates during the plenary session of the Conference on Security and Cooperation in Europe in Finlandia Hall, Helsinki, August 1, 1975.

Above: A demonstration by women in South Boston, led by antibusing advocate Louise Day Hicks (*center, wearing dark glasses*), protest federal school busing orders, September 12, 1975, as helmeted riot police line the street.

Right: Phyllis Schlafly, national leader of the "Stop the Equal Rights Amendment" movement, speaks with reporters at a rally in the Illinois state capitol, Springfield, March 4, 1975.

President Jimmy Carter and Rosalynn Carter walking down Pennsylvania Avenue following his swearing in at the U.S. Capitol, January 20, 1977.

Pat Caddell, polling expert and guru of the new politics, and President Carter at the White House, November 7, 1977.

Speaker of the House of Representatives Thomas P. "Tip" O'Neill, November 26, 1978. O'Neill bore the burden of President Carter's difficult relations with the Democratic Congress.

President Carter and the shah of Iran toast each other at a state dinner in Carter's honor, Tehran, December 31, 1977. This occasion would come back to haunt Carter and help ruin his presidency.

Prime Minister Menachem Begin of Israel playing chess with National Security Adviser Zbigniew Brzezinski during a break in the Camp David summit, September 9, 1978.

President Carter with Senator Edward M. Kennedy in the Oval Office, June 26, 1978. Relations between the two men were strained nearly to the breaking point over their clashing proposals for national health care legislation. Shortly after this photograph was taken, Kennedy publicly indicted Carter for exhibiting a "lack of leadership." The following September, officials inside the administration were circulating reports that Kennedy had already begun plotting to challenge the president for the Democratic nomination in 1980.

Ronald Reagan's fourth-grade class photograph, Tampico, Illinois, May 12, 1920. Reagan is in the second row at the far left, with his hand on his chin.

Reagan, president of the Screen Actors Guild, testifying before the House Committee on Un-American Activities, November 25, 1947. Reagan's anticommunism had already begun to lead him to the political right, although he would always retain traces of his earlier liberal politics.

Ronald Reagan and Nancy Reagan celebrating his victory in the California gubernatorial election, Los Angeles, November 8, 1966.

President Ronald Reagan eating lunch at his desk in the Oval Office less than a week after his inauguration, January 26, 1981.

President Reagan passes a jar of his favorite candy, jelly beans, to Budget Director David Stockman before a meeting at the White House with cabinet secretaries and budget advisers about reducing federal spending, February 11, 1981.

One month after a nearly fatal attempt on his life, President Reagan delivers a nationally televised address to a joint session of the Congress on what he calls his program for economic recovery, April 28, 1981.

President Reagan working at his desk in the Oval Office, May 6, 1982.

Below: President and Nancy Reagan attend a memorial service for those killed in action in Lebanon and Grenada, Camp Lejeune, North Carolina, November 4, 1983.

Above: A Marine in full combat gear stands guard outside the U.S. Embassy in Beirut after a bomb destroyed part of the building, killing sixty-three and wounding more than 100, April 18, 1983. Six months later, a terrorist attack on the Marine barracks at the Beirut airport would kill 241 American servicemen— the deadliest single attack on Americans abroad since World War II. Soon thereafter, the United States began its withdrawal from Lebanon.

President Reagan with (*from left to right*) Secretary of Defense Caspar Weinberger, Secretary of State George Shultz, Attorney-General Ed Meese, and Chief of Staff Don Regan, discussing the president's remarks to the press on the Iran-contra affair in the Oval Office, November 25, 1986. Reagan's performance was the worst of his presidency and possibly of his entire career.

Below: President Reagan meeting with his nominee to the Supreme Court, Robert Bork, at the White House residence, November 9, 1987.

Above: Lieutenant Colonel Oliver North testifying before the joint congressional committee on Iran-contra, seated beside his lawyer, Brendan Sullivan, July 14, 1987.

Above: President Reagan meets with General Secretary Gorbachev of the Soviet Union at Hofdi House during the Reykjavik summit, November 11, 1986.

Left: President Reagan speaking at Moscow State University, May 31, 1988.

Above (from left to right): Nancy Reagan, President Reagan, Vice President George H. W. Bush, and Barbara Bush, after Reagan endorsed Bush's run for the presidency in Washington, D.C., May 11, 1988. By this time, Bush was assured of the Republican Party's nomination, having turned back a challenge in the primaries by Senate Majority Leader Robert Dole.

Left: President Bush holds up a bag of crack cocaine during an address to the nation on his drug control strategy from the Oval Office, September 5, 1989. The dubious origins of the cocaine that Bush displayed later caused the administration some embarrassment.

Right: President Bush receives salutes from General Norman Schwarzkopf and troops during the Operation Desert Storm homecoming parade, July 8, 1991.

(*From left to right*) Senate Majority Leader Bob Dole, President Bill Clinton, and House Minority Whip Newt Gingrich plus an unidentified man (obscured behind Dole) conferring in the White House in 1993.

Bodies of Tutsi peasants murdered at Nyanza Hill in Rwanda, April 21–23, 1994.

Hillary Clinton campaigning on behalf of the administration's health care proposal, University of Colorado at Boulder, March 14, 1994.

Yitzhak Rabin, President Clinton, and Yasir Arafat mark the signing of the Oslo accords on the South Lawn of the White House, September 13, 1993.

President Clinton at a conference on his administration's economic policies, held in Atlanta, March 29, 1995. This gathering was reminiscent of the conference on the economy held in Little Rock late in 1992 while Clinton was still president-elect, and was intended to help stabilize the administration and get its message to the public following the Republican triumph in the midterm elections of 1994.

Hillary and Bill Clinton, and families of the victims, at the Time for Healing Prayer Service following the right-wing terrorist attack on the Alfred P. Murrah Federal Building, Oklahoma City, April 23, 1995.

Monica Lewinsky surrounded by photographers as she gets into a car headed for an appointment with investigators from the F.B.I., Los Angeles, May 27, 1998.

Independent Counsel Kenneth Starr testifying before the House Judiciary Committee in favor of the impeachment of President Clinton, November 19, 1998. Starr's ten hours of testimony, the dramatic culmination of his pursuit of the Lewinsky matter, pleased Republicans but offended his own ethics adviser, Samuel Dash, who resigned from the independent counsel's office.

Above: Noisy and violent protestors shutting down the recounting of votes by hand at the Miami-Dade County election office, November 22, 1998. The participants in what a writer for the *Wall Street Journal* later called a "bourgeois riot" included numerous Republican staffers and officials flown down to Florida from Washington. Among them (*pictured here in center, with blond hair, to the left of the man wearing a tie*) was Matt Schlapp, a Republican campaign aide who went on to become political director in the White House under President George W. Bush.

Vice President Al Gore speaking with reporters outside the White House, December 5, 2000.

President George W. Bush, Vice President Dick Cheney, and outgoing Secretary of Defense Donald Rumsfeld arrive outside the Pentagon for an armed forces full honor review to mark the end of Rumsfeld's tenure, Arlington, Virginia, December 15, 2006.

(privately if not always publicly) that fundamental economic, political, and diplomatic changes were in the offing. The diplomatic changes would include a timely exit from the war in Afghanistan (which Gorbachev from the start had thought a "fatal error" and now called a "bleeding wound") and recommencing serious arms limitations talks with the Americans. After the prolonged stagnation under Brezhnev and a rapid succession of dying leaders, the Soviet economy and the population's basic standard of living, already decrepit by Western standards, were crumbling. Gorbachev and the reformers he brought to power with him (including Foreign Minister Eduard Shevardnadze, Aleksandr Yakovlev, and Anatoly Chernyaev) were convinced that Brezhnev's leadership had ruinously forestalled economic improvement by fixating on achieving military parity with the United States.

To be sure, the annual growth rate of new Soviet military procurements had actually declined during the first half of the 1980s, despite the war in Afghanistan.* Still, a disastrous proportion of the Soviet Union's annual gross domestic product, on the order of 20 percent and more, remained earmarked for military spending. Despite differences over the specifics of foreign policy, there was broad agreement among the new political leadership that advancing domestic economic reform—and salvaging Soviet communism—required drastic reductions in military spending. "How long will our military-industrial complex keep devouring our economy, our agriculture, and our consumer goods?" demanded Yegor Ligachev (second in command to Gorbachev, but an older and far more conservative figure). "How long are we going to take this ogre, how long are we going to throw into its mouth the food of our children?" Chernyaev later explained that for Gorbachev, domestic reform "was the main thing. To do this he needed to stop the arms race."

Gorbachev and his closest advisers represented a new generation of Soviet leaders who had come of age after World War II. He was born to peasant parents in Stavropol in the northern Caucasus in 1931, but he was no rough provincial. Both of his grandfathers had suffered unjust impris-

---

* Reliable estimates show that the Soviet Union's annual rate of increase in procurements fell from an average of 7.02 percent between 1977 and 1982 to 5.94 percent over the next two years. The change appears to have begun in 1980. The figures contradict some of Reagan's assertions at the time—and they contradict the arguments that Reagan's arms buildup won the cold war by damaging the Soviet economy. Fred Chernoff, "Ending the Cold War: The Soviet Retreat and the U.S. Military Buildup," *International Affairs*, 67 (1991): 111–126.

onment for alleged crimes against the Soviet regime. Despite these difficulties, Gorbachev won state honors as a young farmworker and was admitted to the nation's most prestigious institution of higher education, Moscow State University, where he studied law, hoping to make his way in politics. (He would be the first Soviet leader since Lenin who had a university education.)

Rising quickly within the communist apparat, Gorbachev was named national party secretary in charge of agriculture in 1978, and two years later he became the youngest full voting member of the Politburo. A friend and protégé of Soviet leader Yuri Andropov (formerly the head of the KGB, and also a native of Stavropol), Gorbachev assumed enlarged responsibilities when kidney disease left Andropov increasingly incapacitated late in 1983. Andropov, who recognized the deep crisis of the Soviet system, died in February 1984, and was succeeded by a pro-Brezhnev old guard apparatchik, Konstantin Chernenko, himself in poor health; Gorbachev stepped in and presided at Politburo meetings when Chernenko could not attend, as happened far more often than not. When Chernenko died of emphysema after just thirteen months in power, Gorbachev, Andropov's younger heir apparent, was the favorite of Politburo leaders of differing views—and soon enough, he tested their loyalty.

Gorbachev called his agenda "new thinking." Later, it became better known as glasnost (openness) and perestroika (restructuring). Applying the new thinking to foreign policy required banishing the assumption, almost unshakable among the older generation—the generation of World War II—that the primary consideration ought always to be securing the Soviet Union from military attack, no matter what the cost. Gorbachev was inexperienced in foreign affairs and initially wary about sounding too unsettling—especially in dealing with allies in the Warsaw Pact. His first order of business, in any event, was to strengthen his grip as far as possible throughout the state bureaucracy. But Gorbachev came to power intent on making sweeping changes, having already expressed, as one aide recalled, "the feeling that our foreign policy had become too cast iron, too inflexible, too concentrated upon a number of positions that seemed to be impossible to change."

By mid-spring of 1985, Gorbachev was speaking bluntly about the need for major economic reforms while taking the first small steps toward altering the Soviet Union's foreign policy. In April, he announced a halt in the deployment of SS-20 missiles aimed at Western Europe; and six months later, in Paris, he announced a cut in the number of SS-20s actually deployed. In July, at a special meeting in Minsk with the entire highest-ranking Soviet military command, Gorbachev reasserted the primacy of guaranteeing national security, but insisted that world tensions needed to be reduced and, according to the chief of staff of the armed forces, "called on the military to modify their methods." In August, he imposed a unilateral moratorium on testing nuclear weapons, which would extend in stages through February 1987.

The Reagan administration, for its part, had never completely abandoned the conciliatory dealings with the Soviet Union favored by Secretary of State Shultz and given public voice by the president in January 1984. The bellicosity and ideological zeal that contributed to the Iran-contra affair revealed one important side of Reagan's thinking. The memoirs of U.S. diplomats and journalists who covered Reagan's foreign policy reveal another side, in which protecting the American people and reducing the likelihood of thermonuclear disaster were paramount. Andropov's death, only three weeks after Reagan's speech of January 16, seemed a serious blow to the latter effort, as the most backward of the old-line Stalinists took charge once more. Yet Reagan and Chernenko (as well as their intermediaries) exchanged numerous letters and public announcements, raising hopes that the superpowers would revive arms control talks. Chernenko, convinced that Reagan would win reelection in November, dropped Andropov's insistence on the removal of the Euromissiles as a precondition for negotiations.

Reagan set back the process in mid-August when, unaware that the tape was rolling, he cracked an ad-lib joke during the voice-level check for his weekly Saturday radio broadcast: "My fellow Americans, I am pleased to tell you today that I've signed legislation that will outlaw Russia forever. The bombing begins in five minutes." Outraged Soviet leaders—and Reagan's American critics as well as his European critics—took the facetious gaffe as evidence of his true beliefs and intentions. But through the efforts of Shultz, Reagan and the longtime Soviet foreign minister Andrey Gromyko met in September at the White House. Their talks produced no specific agreements, but each side came away impressed with the other's sincere desire for peace.

After Reagan was reelected in November, plans were announced for a high-profile negotiating session involving Shultz and Gromyko, to be held in Geneva in early January. Reagan left no doubt that he hoped it would lead to reducing and not simply limiting the superpowers' nuclear stockpiles. "I just happen to believe," he told an interviewer, "that we cannot go into another generation with the world living under the threat of those weapons and knowing that some madman can push the button some place." The sessions in Geneva were chilly but produced a compromise joint statement committing both sides to arms control negotiations. Two days before the scheduled new meetings were to commence in March, however, Chernenko died. A day later, the Communist Party Central Committee selected Gorbachev as the new general secretary and premier. The high-level meetings were postponed, but arms talks resumed in Geneva—and a new departure began.

Gorbachev's early cautious but unmistakable calls for reform were followed by even more sweeping pronouncements, but they failed to impress the conservative and neoconservative establishments in the United States. The influential conservative columnist George Will, a good friend of the Reagans (especially Nancy), dismissed hopes about Gorbachev as ludicrous, based on the notion that "the new generation is, well, younger." Early in 1986, a report by the Heritage Foundation described Gorbachev as a deceptive, brutal Stalinist who had brought "no essential change in the Soviet political scene." *National Review* argued that Gorbachev's foreign policies were mere posturing and assailed as "vintage Stalin" his consolidation of power in order to make domestic economic reforms. Glasnost, a typical article in *Commentary* later warned, was an elaborate ruse to "harness the power of the west to promote the Soviet Union's own objectives," including access to Western trade and credit.

Reagan, however, was forming very different impressions of the Soviet Union's new leadership. In their exchanges of letters during the months after Gorbachev took power, both he and Gorbachev candidly expressed profound differences, above all over the Americans' Strategic Defense Initiative (which, Reagan wrote, Gorbachev misunderstood as having "an offensive purpose for an attack on the Soviet Union"). But the two men aired their common concern, in Gorbachev's words, "not to let things come to the outbreak of a nuclear war." Other factors reinforced Reagan's willingness to be open-minded. Gorbachev's obvious vitality and charm differentiated him from the previous run of Soviet leaders. Margaret Thatcher (whom Gorbachev had met on an official visit to London before becoming general secretary) vouched for him to Reagan as a man whom she liked and with whom the West could do business.

Reagan was also was under pressure from his wife, who was increasingly influential after the Iran-contra scandal. Nancy Reagan distrusted the harsh ideologues around the Oval Office and urged him to restrain his own cold war rhetoric. More than most outside observers understood at the time, she could be an unofficial diplomat as well as adviser, effective at getting her point across. At an official dinner during Gromyko's visit to the White House in 1984, the foreign minister had raised a glass in a toast to the first lady and said he hoped she would whisper the word "peace" every night in the president's ear. "Oh sure—but I'll be whispering it in yours, too," Mrs. Reagan, coyly smiling, replied.

In his very first letter to Gorbachev, President Reagan wrote of pursuing arms control agreements and invited him to Washington; Gorbachev promptly accepted, if only "to search for mutual understanding." When the summit finally took place in November—in Geneva, not Washington—both sides had fairly low expectations. The conversation between the two heads of state included a good deal of the jousting that had become familiar during the cold war. Reagan complained of Soviet subversion in the third world and of the continuing war in Afghanistan. Gorbachev contended that the American military-industrial complex and right-wing think tanks like the Heritage Foundation were dictating U.S. policy.

Gorbachev also reemphasized the Soviets' suspicions that the Strategic Defense Initiative (SDI) was in reality an offensive missile plan. (Those suspicions had been heightened by the U.S. decision a month earlier to reinterpret the Anti-Ballistic Missile Treaty of 1972 in order to permit actual testing of a missile-defense system and not merely laboratory research.) "Who can control it?" Gorbachev asked of SDI. "Who can monitor it? It opens up an arms race in space." In any event, Gorbachev told Reagan, the Soviet Union had already designed a response to SDI that would be far cheaper to produce and would be deployed much faster. The impasse prevented any specific agreements.

Still, Gorbachev signaled to Reagan that, though he believed in a reformed communism, world domination was no longer a preoccupation of the Soviet Union, at one point joking that he did not awake "every day" thinking about "which country he would like to arrange a revolution in." Unlike every other Soviet leader, Reagan later observed, Gorbachev never declared "that he was dedicated to the Marxian philosophy of a one-world Communist state." And Reagan, while expressing his desire for both sides to make major cuts in nuclear armaments, delivered an impressive reproach about the Soviet Union's continued intervention in Afghanistan (a war, Reagan rightly perceived, for which Gorbachev had "no enthusiasm") and made a sincere effort to persuade his counterpart that SDI was truly intended to hasten the abolition of nuclear weapons. The genuine personal rapport that arose between the two men prompted participants to think, as Anatoly Chernyaev noted at the time, that "a turning point is noticeable in international relations." At Geneva, both Reagan and Gorbachev truly began to believe that neither side would start a nuclear war or "continue provoking it either in the name of communism or capitalism."

This is hardly to say that Reagan had broken away from his cold war dogma, especially on issues other than arms control. His stubbornness nearly proved costly when he reacted to revolutionary developments in the Philippines, a former U.S. possession. For decades, the United States had supported the anticommunist dictatorship of Ferdinand Marcos, chiefly to secure what the military considered vital naval and air installations at Subic Bay and Clark Air Field. Rising noncommunist democratic opposition crested following the assassination of the popular opposition leader Benigno Aquino on his return from a three-year exile in the United States in August 1983. Departing from the established lines of administration policy, American policy makers, including Assistant Secretary of State Paul Wolfowitz, urged prodding Marcos toward reforms while making symbolic gestures of friendliness to opposition leaders.

The shift in policy for the Philippines pressed by some neoconservatives marked an evolution in the thinking of influential voices within the administration, including Secretary of State Shultz and his assistant, the neoconservative Wolfowitz, about democracy and support for anticommunist dictatorships. The emergence of Solidarity in Poland—a popular democratic force quite different from third-world regimes such as Marcos's—led some of Reagan's officials to reject the long-held view, as reformulated by Jeane Kirkpatrick, that "traditional" anticommunist authoritarianism was tolerable. "You can't use democracy, as you appropriately should, as a battle with the Soviet Union, and then turn around and be completely hypocritical about it when it's on your side of the line," Wolfowitz later observed. There was always a temptation for Americans to idealize the situation in the Philippines as part of a universal democratic upsurge, and to overestimate their own influence in a struggle that was almost wholly the Filipinos'. Yet if the neoconservative idealists had their blind spots, the president, despite his support for building what he called the "infrastructure of democracy" abroad, could not yet envisage the push for democracy extending to anticommunist governments.

In late November 1985, Marcos shocked his countrymen by calling for a presidential election the following February, which he was confident he could win by fair means or foul, even after Aquino's widow, Corazon Aquino, emerged as his challenger. When Marcos declared himself the winner amid charges of gross fraud, Aquino's supporters filled the streets of Manila in nonviolent demonstrations of what they called "people power"—and Aquino declared that she, in fact, had won. Reagan, sticking to the cold war formulas, resisted efforts to abandon the United States' old ally Marcos and recognize a new government headed by Aquino. (The president even insisted, with no evidence, that the Marcos and Aquino forces had both tried to rig the election.) Finally, Secretary of State Shultz argued Reagan down, saying that allowing Marcos to remain in power would heighten, not reduce, the likelihood of a victorious communist insurgency. The Philippines became a model—too easily, in some minds—for the transition from dictatorship to democracy. But Reagan, while gradually warming to the new Soviet leadership, still clung reflexively to ideas that were more a hindrance than a help in reformulating American policy.[*]

Dramatic though the events in the Philippines were, however, U.S.-Soviet relations remained the paramount concern in Washington. And among American conservatives, even the administration's tentative moves toward serious negotiations raised alarms—along with, improbably, sudden strong doubts about their hero, Ronald Reagan. The qualms were being felt even before the summit began at Geneva. "Reagan is walking into a trap," Tom Bethell warned in the right-wing *American Spectator*. "The only way he can get success in negotiation is by doing what the Soviets want." George Will wrote years later, in a generally warm appreciation of "Reagan's era of good feelings," that the president had been "wildly wrong" about events inside the Soviet Union, and that by taking a more positive view of U.S.-Soviet relations, he had "accelerated the moral disarmament of the West—actual disarmament will follow—by elevating wishful thinking to the level of political philosophy." Just as Gorbachev had to deal with his adversaries in the military, so Reagan had to confront some of his oldest political supporters.

The twelve months after Geneva were crucial for Gorbachev's reform of the foreign policy of the Soviet Union. In December, he withdrew its long-

---

[*] In this respect, Reagan's old-line cold war thinking actually converged with the power-politics realism of his erstwhile adversary Henry Kissinger. "Are there no other overriding American interests?" Kissinger complained when the United States withdrew its support from Marcos. "Whatever else may be said about the Marcos regime, it contributed substantially to American security and had been extolled by American presidents for nearly two decades." Kissinger, "What Next When the U.S. Intervenes?" *Los Angeles Times*, March 9, 1986, part V, p. 1.

standing opposition to inspection of nuclear test sites required to verify moratoriums on testing. In mid-January 1986, he proposed the total elimination of all intermediate-range (INF) missiles in Europe and a phased plan for the total bilateral elimination of nuclear weapons by the year 2000—thereby, in effect, accepting the "zero-zero" option that had seemed a way to ensure the Soviet Union's opposition when proposed by the United States in 1981. ("It seems he really decided to end the arms race *at all costs*," Anatoly Chernyaev wrote in his diary.) At the annual Communist Party conference in late February and March, Gorbachev announced several basic shifts in the Kremlin's policy, including an embrace of the idea of common security vis-à-vis the United States. Over the next several months, he offered a significant reduction of Soviet forces based in Europe and froze the number of Soviet missiles deployed in Asia.

In late April, the catastrophic explosion of a nuclear reactor at Chernobyl in the Ukraine—the world's worst nuclear accident—initially brought a disturbing, prolonged silence from Moscow, followed by even more disturbing efforts to minimize the severity of the accident. But its domestic effects (it displaced populations on a scale unseen since World War II), along with the danger that radioactivity might spread across Europe, intensified antinuclear sentiments and compelled the Kremlin to look anew at nuclear disarmament as not only a political imperative but also a moral imperative. Gorbachev's closest advisers also interpreted the meltdown of the reactor as a symptom of the Soviet system's meltdown. (Chernobyl, Eduard Shevardnadze later wrote, "tore the blindfold from our eyes" and "convinced us that morality and politics could not diverge.") In late May, still affected by the disaster, Gorbachev delivered a lengthy address to the entire foreign policy bureaucracy of the Soviet Union on the "overriding importance for the new thinking to prevail in diplomacy." Soon afterward, he apprised the heads of the Warsaw Pact nations of the severity of Chernobyl—"It was like war," he said—and asserted that the tragedy "is closely related to the issue of disarmament." He discussed how "a lot of laziness" had to be overcome in light of "the challenge of current dynamic developments."

The dynamics were very different in Washington. The ebullience that followed the Geneva summit quickly faded, and distrust, even cynicism, prevailed. The administration reacted guardedly to Gorbachev's latest concessions as if they were just propaganda. The Soviet Union's proposal for abolishing nuclear weapons struck Reagan and others as a scheme to divide the United States from its Western European allies. Gorbachev's other proposals, in American eyes, were merely responses to Reagan's massive military buildup—and a sign that the United States ought to intensify the pressure. Concerns which had existed before Geneva about wrongful activities (including espionage) by personnel attached to the Soviet Union's mission at the United Nations, but which had been laid aside during the preparations for the summit, now produced an order by the United States to reduce the mission's staff dramatically—an order delivered, portentously, the day after the momentous Communist Party conference ended. An incident in March involving two U.S. Navy warships sailing in Soviet waters, provocatively close to the coast of Crimea, brought a rhetorical salvo from Moscow warning that any repetition would lead to "serious consequences." In early April, the United States conducted a new nuclear weapons test. Reagan's bombing of Libya following the terrorist attack at the discotheque in Berlin was quickly and predictably condemned by Moscow.

In late May, Reagan took the additional step of abandoning the U.S. adherence to the limitations on strategic offensive weapons in the SALT II treaty (which had never been ratified). For months, Weinberger, the secretary of defense; Casey, the director of the CIA; and other hawks in the administration had been campaigning to end voluntary compliance by the United States, in view of what they claimed was long-standing cheating by the Soviet Union. Over the objections of the chairman of the Joint Chiefs of Staff, Admiral William J. Crowe, and Secretary of State Shultz, Reagan gave way, although with a proviso that left open a possibility for reconsideration if the Soviet Union took "constructive steps" toward limiting its nuclear arsenal. Reagan at this juncture, although intrigued by the new Soviet leadership, gave little indication of grasping the enormous shift that Gorbachev represented.

His decision disturbed the Soviets, but not nearly as much as the administration's refusal to give an inch over testing and deployment of SDI. Reagan's advisers were themselves divided over the matter: whereas Shultz and the veteran arms negotiator Paul Nitze were willing to make concessions over SDI in order to reach agreements with the Soviets on arms reduction, Weinberger and his assistant secretary of defense, Richard Perle, dubious about all arms agreements, saw stubbornness over SDI as the surest means to sabotage efforts at reaching any. Reagan alone was determined to negotiate arms reductions while also going full speed ahead with SDI—the pillars of his utopian antinuclear strategy. But Gorbachev would agree to no arms reductions unless the United States confined SDI to the laboratory, under the original understanding of the terms of the ABM treaty. The goodwill generated at Geneva could not dissipate these fundamental differences.

Ironically, a spy scandal provided the impetus for another direct meeting of the two leaders. In August, FBI agents apprehended a Soviet physicist, Gennady Zakharov, who had been spying on the United States while on assignment at the UN in New York. The Soviets retaliated by arresting a senior American reporter in Moscow, Nicholas Daniloff. Shultz and Shevardnadze negotiated an exchange, which reinforced their high regard for each other. The surrounding controversy also produced (amid noisy exchanges of propaganda) a suggestion from Gorbachev for presummit discussions so that the new stalemate between the superpowers might be broken. Reagan instantly accepted, and the two sides gathered at Reykjavik, the capital of Iceland, in early October.

Expecting little on their arrival in Iceland, the Americans quickly discovered that Gorbachev was willing to make arms reductions far deeper than ever before and that his actions were not merely propagandistic posturing. In exchange for a return to the long-standing shared understanding of the ABM treaty (which would block development of SDI for a decade), he offered once again to accept the zero-zero option on INF missiles in Europe, with a proposed additional 50 percent cut in long-range ballistic missiles and a ban on nuclear testing. The cuts would severely affect the Soviet Union; Nitze thought this was the best Soviet proposal he had ever seen. Reagan and the stunned Americans pulled together a counteroffer, to eliminate all land-based ballistic missiles within a decade, after which the United States could fully deploy its SDI technology. Gorbachev replied with yet another proposal that accepted the arms reductions but suggested going all the way, to a complete elimination not simply of nuclear missiles but of all nuclear weapons. "It would be fine with me," Reagan replied, thereby signaling, almost off the cuff—and to the consternation of his aides—the elimination of the bulwarks of deterrence that had characterized the cold war for more than three decades.

It was too good to be true. Gorbachev had purposely held back on SDI, which he announced was a deal-breaker: either the United States would agree to limit its work on the program to laboratory research, or everything else was off. This was precisely the sort of trade-off that Shultz and Nitze had been looking for, but Reagan would have none of it: he thought of SDI as neither a bargaining chip nor a means to intimidate the Soviet Union but as a genuine guarantor of world peace. Did Gorbachev not understand, at long last, the president asked, that the United States was in earnest in promising to share the SDI technology once it was completed? Gorbachev scoffed at the idea, and wondered aloud why a purely defensive system would even be necessary if all nuclear weapons were abolished. "This meeting is over," Reagan brusquely announced. "Let's go George . . . we're leaving." Diplomatic niceties disappeared on the American side: "I was mad—he tried to act jovial but I acted mad & it showed," Reagan recalled in his diary.

The collapse of the talks at Reykjavik raised important questions about the role of SDI in the Reagan administration's nuclear strategy and about its effects on the Kremlin. There can be little doubt that the program initially frightened the Soviets; that Gorbachev feared it would prompt a militarization of outer space, which would ruin his reforms; and that he remained concerned about how its development would undermine the ABM treaty and all previous arms control agreements. That is, Gorbachev's opposition was chiefly based on political, not military, grounds. By late 1986, the Soviet Academy of Sciences had told him that the entire idea of a comprehensive antinuclear shield in space was impractical, and that even if portions of the technology could be perfected, modest countermeasures would offset them. Some scientists even advised the Kremlin that SDI was a hoax, designed to lure the Soviet Union into making massive defense outlays it could not afford. In any event, the Soviets never bothered to mount their own SDI program—contradicting the contention of some analysts that the initiative helped drive the Soviet Union into bankruptcy. And such was neither the intent nor the effect of U.S. policy, and certainly not what Ronald Reagan had in mind.* Reagan wanted exactly what he said he wanted: to offer Americans—and then the world—a shield against nuclear attack. Yet by raising the specter of an arms race in space, by undermining earlier arms treaties, and by strengthening the hand of hard-line elements within the Soviet military establishment, SDI hampered Gorbachev's reforms. In effect, Reagan's stubborn idealism and Gorbachev's own idealism, which converged on the general issue of nuclear disarmament, collided on the matter of SDI. And at Reykjavik, neither leader would back down.

---

* "I was present at many, if not most, of the discussions on [SDI]," Lieutenant General Edward L. Rowny recalled in 1998. "As the archives are opened, I would be greatly surprised if you find any serious talk about [outspending the Soviets] at all. I think it did come up once or twice in passing, but by and large, throughout the period, President Reagan's idea was 'Let's defend the people of the United States.'" The former national security adviser Robert McFarlane added that, in trying to correct a perceived strategic imbalance, the United States wanted to reduce its long-term costs by turning to its comparative advantage in technology rather than try and match the Soviet Union "tank for tank and ship for ship." Quotations in Beth A. Fischer, "Reagan and the Soviets," in W. Elliot Brownlee and Hugh Davis Graham, eds., *The Reagan Presidency: Pragmatic Conservatism and Its Legacy* (Lawrence, KA, 2003), 123.

* * *

The failure at Reykjavik, described on all sides immediately afterward as a disaster, instead made both sides more confident at home. Reagan boasted to the nation that by staying resolute on SDI, he had refused to compromise the national security of the United States. Yet he also emphasized the constructive aspects of the meetings, remarking, "The significance is that we got as close as we did." Gorbachev, meanwhile, was now fully convinced that Reagan had no intention of launching a nuclear first strike against the Soviet Union, a point he emphasized to the Politburo. With those reassurances about external security—and additional reassurances he would later receive from both Reagan and Shultz—he could accelerate the sharp defense cuts that were the precondition for his urgent domestic reforms. In November, the Politburo authorized the withdrawal of Soviet troops from Afghanistan, and Gorbachev told the governments of the Warsaw Pact nations that they could no longer rely on aid from the Soviet Union to sustain themselves. In January, reflecting the impact of Reykjavik and Chernobyl, Gorbachev announced his programs of perestroika, including replacing strict central planning with a greater reliance on the free market; and glasnost, permitting greater freedom and openness of discussion inside the Soviet Union.

The glasnost reforms were closely linked to changes in human rights policies, which in turn had ramifications for the Soviet Union's foreign policy. Beginning in December, the Kremlin undertook the release from prison and exile of most political dissidents, ceased jamming broadcasts by the Voice of America into the Soviet Union, and announced that it would permit larger numbers of Jews to emigrate. (Restrictions on emigration had been a source of conflict with the Americans since the mid-1970s.) Among the freed prisoners was the renowned physicist Andrey Sakharov, who was allowed to return to Moscow after seven years of banishment in the closed city of Gorki. Sakharov, a pioneer of the Soviet Union's thermonuclear arms program in the 1950s, had very strong ideas about SDI, ridiculing it as a "Maginot Line in space" that could be easily and inexpensively overcome. Predicting that a sizable reduction in nuclear arms would cause a similar reduction in popular support for SDI in the United States, Sakharov called for renewed talks with the Americans without reference to the controversial program.

Gorbachev had been thinking along similar lines, and even wondered whether his sturdy opposition to SDI wasn't causing more Americans to support it than might otherwise do so. (In the aftermath of Reykjavik, 70 percent of Americans polled favored deployment of SDI; and even skeptics such as George Shultz were coming around to support the program.) In any event, the meetings at Reykjavik had convinced Gorbachev that even a modest compromise would be unattainable during Reagan's last two years in office. The impasse would continue with no guarantee that Reagan's successor would be any less obdurate. International tensions could mount, costing Gorbachev even more valuable time in undertaking perestroika. How much direct influence Sakharov had in reinforcing Gorbachev's thinking is unclear, but at the end of February, Gorbachev announced that he was uncoupling his unconditional demand at Reykjavik regarding SDI from future negotiations about the removal of Soviet and American intermediate-range missiles from Europe. Eliminating the IMF would represent a cut of merely 4 percent in overall nuclear armaments, but would also eliminate an entire class of nuclear weapons—a significant first step toward wider agreements.

Gorbachev's announcement immediately bolstered Reagan's own optimism, and the more optimistic people around Reagan. In January, with fallout from the Iran-contra scandal descending on the White House, and with Reagan's popularity collapsing, the administration had issued its annual national security strategy report with a gloomy assessment of the Soviet Union's future intentions. Weinberger fed the president upbeat reports on the progress of SDI, and in early February asked for authorization for the Pentagon to begin deployment of certain elements of the anti-missile system, which had previously been thought to be a decade or more away. Shultz, along with Admiral Crowe of the Joint Chiefs, strongly objected that any such move would be provocative, but information leaked to the right-wing *Washington Times* suggested that Reagan was all in favor of pressing ahead.

Anger in Congress and pressure from European allies, though, persuaded the president to kill Weinberger's request. Instead, Gorbachev's decoupling proposal prompted Reagan to appear at the White House press room—his first appearance there since the disastrous press conference announcing the Iran-contra diversion—to welcome the new initiative. While trying to save his own political skin (and, as he saw the situation, salvage his country's economy), Gorbachev had given Reagan a helping hand to lift him out of the riptide of the Iran-contra affair. Reagan sincerely believed in what he was doing, but Gorbachev was additionally his political deus ex machina: without him, Reagan would have been stuck with a foreign policy that was mired in scandal. On March 6—two days after Reagan gave his speech accepting the report of the Tower Commission—the White House announced that Shultz would travel to Moscow in April to "maintain the momentum" toward an accord on INF and possibly arrange another summit meeting between Gorbachev and Reagan.

While Shultz and Gorbachev wrangled over the terms of a treaty and various other issues (including the ABM treaty and Afghanistan), a stroke of luck gave Gorbachev the opportunity to lighten his internal political situation. On May 28, a nineteen-year-old amateur pilot from Hamburg, Mathias Rust, landed a small single-engine airplane in Red Square, having flown all morning from Helsinki at low altitude. Rust carried with him a twenty-page plan for a nuclear-free world that he wanted to hand to Gorbachev; instead, having caused the Soviet military enormous embarrassment, he was locked up in a KGB prison. But rather than rebuke the intruder (who was released fourteen months later), Gorbachev, his closest military advisers, and the Politburo seized on an occasion to overthrow the military establishment and wipe away the main internal obstacle to arms reduction. A new, more congenial and compliant general took over as defense minister; more than 100 Soviet officers were removed from their posts; and after the quiet, yearlong purge that followed, the entire top echelon of the Soviet military had been replaced. "Let everyone here and in the West know where the power is—it is in the political leadership, in the Politburo," Gorbachev later remarked.

As plans developed for a summit in Washington later in the year, which would include the signing of a treaty on INF, Reagan, too, began to regain his political footing. In June, while the congressional Iran-contra hearings were under way, the president visited West Berlin, where, echoing President Kennedy, he reemerged as the valiant leader of the free world by delivering some ingratiating lines in German, and adding some soaring lines of his own, in a speech at the Brandenburg Gate: "General Secretary Gorbachev, if you seek peace, if you seek prosperity for the Soviet Union and Eastern Europe, if you seek liberalization: Come here to this gate! Mr. Gorbachev, open this gate! Mr. Gorbachev, tear down this wall!" Reagan was quick to credit Western resolve for getting the Soviets back to the bargaining table. Yet his dare to Gorbachev, by even mentioning peace and liberalization, showed how much his rhetoric had changed since his denunciation of the Soviet Union four years earlier as "the focus of evil in the modern world" (words that Soviet officials later said they had taken as stock propaganda). Reagan also noted that a point had been reached where it had become possible to envisage "not merely . . . limiting the growth of arms, but . . . eliminating, for the first time, an entire class of nuclear weapons from the face of the earth." In repairing his damaged presidency, Reagan gave freer rein to his old utopian side, reminiscent of *The Day the Earth Stood Still*. "I occasionally think," he told a baffled group at the United Nations in September, "how quickly our differences worldwide would vanish if we were facing an alien threat from outside this world."

Reagan's popularity at home improved—except in the hard-line conservative precincts. A few months earlier, activists in the new right and conservative Republicans were defending the militant president and railing at the critics of Iran-contra as the plotters of a liberal coup d'état. Now Reagan was castigated as the problem. Howard Phillips denounced him as "a very weak man with a very strong wife and a strong staff" who had become "a useful idiot for Kremlin propaganda." William Buckley and his *National Review* began a campaign to kill any treaty regarding the missiles in Europe. The familiar hard-liners in Congress such as Senator Jesse Helms of North Carolina were joined by newer faces—including Senator Dan Quayle—complaining that control of the White House's foreign policy had been seized by dupes and liberal quislings. The *Washington Times* likened Reagan to Neville Chamberlain, the weak-kneed British prime minister who tried to appease Hitler at Munich in 1938. Neoconservative columnists, such as Charles Krauthammer, repeatedly denounced the wider phenomenon of going "dizzy over Gorbachev."

The conservatives' frustration was understandable. Since the exposure of the Iran-contra affair, the exit of foreign policy hard-liners from the administration, their replacement by moderates, and the enlarged influence of Secretary of State Shultz had, indeed, dramatically shifted the balance of power in the White House. But Reagan also knew very well what he thought he was doing, and tried to explain himself to old allies like Buckley, though with little success. At the summit in Washington in early December, Reagan not only signed the INF accord (in the East Room of the White House, at a table once used by Abraham Lincoln) but also indulged Gorbachev's media offensive and did nothing to hide the basic warmth that the two leaders had developed. "*Doveryai, no proveryai,*" the president said at the signing ceremony, using a Russian phrase he had learned that meant "Trust but verify." "You repeat that at every meeting," Gorbachev replied, to great laughter. "I like it," Reagan retorted, to even greater laughter. The superpowers' antagonism had turned into vaudeville repartee.

The treaty stipulated the destruction by June 1, 1991, of the two countries' intermediate- and short-range missiles, and spelled out procedures for on-site monitoring—Reagan's *proveryai*. But unlike his counterpart, Reagan had to gain the consent of the U.S. Senate, where conservative opposition at first looked formidable. Gorbachev encouraged the ratification process by announcing that Soviet troops would at last leave Afghanistan and that the withdrawal would be complete by February 1989. Undaunted right-wing Republicans, led by Helms and Quayle (who called Reagan's criticisms of their resistance "totally irresponsible"), tried to block the treaty. But Reagan fought hard and peeled off the Republicans (including Quayle, whom Shultz warned, "Dan, you have to shut down!"); and in May the treaty passed, ninety-three to five. The elated president returned to his time-tested, goofy cinematic allusion. "I've often wondered," he said, "what if all of us in the world discovered we were threatened by a power from outer space, from another planet. Wouldn't we all of a sudden find we didn't have any differences between us at all?" (His national security adviser, Colin Powell, privately rolled his eyes at this latest appearance of Reagan's "little green men.")

Two days after the Senate ratified the treaty, Reagan and his wife arrived in Moscow for his fourth summit with Gorbachev. The chance of any major breakthroughs on disarmament was thin, as the two sides remained at loggerheads over SDI. Additionally, the Soviet Union claimed that even after its troops left Afghanistan, it was bound by treaty to give financial assistance to the Kabul government. This assertion prompted the Americans to vow that they would continue supplying military goods, including lethal antiaircraft Stinger missiles, to the mujahideen.* Distressed at the KGB's rough handling of the enthusiastic crowds that swarmed around him and Nancy on the Arbat, Reagan was heard to mutter, "This is still a police state."

Yet the summit at Moscow put the stamp on U.S.-Soviet rapprochement. With Moscow bedecked in festive regalia, the Kremlin mounted a three-day extravaganza, which included a speech by Reagan to students at Gorbachev's alma mater, Moscow State University; an evening at the Bolshoi ballet (where Reagan nodded off until Gorbachev gently prodded him awake just in time for the final curtain); and a visit to Danilov Monastery, the seat of the Russian Orthodox faith. Gorbachev was determined to demonstrate, as a further means of advancing perestroika, that the Soviet Union had nothing to fear from the American president. Reagan happily recipro-

---

* Reagan and Gorbachev did end up signing seven less momentous agreements on matters that included student exchanges and fishery rights.

cated. Asked by a reporter whether he still considered the Soviet Union an "evil empire," he replied, "I was talking another time, another era."

The symbolic high point of Reagan's visit was his speech at Moscow University. The scene was surreal, as the longtime American right-wing anti-communist addressed the assembled students while standing beneath a large white bust of Lenin. Reagan extolled an American democracy that he said was based on family and faith, but also unequivocally endorsed his communist hosts and the breath of freedom and hope that was filling the air:

> We do not know what the conclusion will be of this journey, but we're hopeful that the promise of reform will be fulfilled. In this Moscow spring, this May 1988, we may be allowed that hope: that freedom, like the fresh green sapling planted over Tolstoy's grave, will blossom forth at last in the rich fertile soil of your people and culture. We may be allowed to hope that the marvelous sound of a new openness will keep rising through, ringing through, leading to a new world of reconciliation, friendship, and peace.

It was the capstone of Reagan's presidency, his greatest, if least predictable, achievement. Not incidentally, it also dissipated any political ignominy left over from Iran-contra, and it began a rise in public approval that peaked during his last days in office.

At home, though, American politicians had been long anticipating the post-Reagan era; and by the time the president left Moscow, the fight to determine who would be his successor was well under way. Among some of Reagan's earliest supporters, there was a growing sense that the Gipper would be leaving the White House not a moment too soon. Some had quietly turned Reagan's picture to the wall and hung up a new one of Oliver North. One bellwether of hard-line conservative opinion complained that the president "has convinced himself that the man who heads the evil empire has ended its treachery . . . and facts to the contrary will not sway him." The world was changing, but many Americans, not all of them on the right, either could not comprehend what was happening or simply refused to believe it.

Ronald Reagan's unique appeal could not be replicated by any other Republican, and without the glue of Reagan's popularity, the Republican Party broke into its constituent elements. Beginning in 1987, a few television evangelists suffered though spectacular sexual and financial scandals. But one right-wing televangelist untouched by the scandals, the Reverend Pat Robertson, who was the son of a former U.S. senator, took up the flag-and-cross of the conservative crusade and (on God's instruction, he claimed) entered the race for the Republican nomination.

Other factions of Reagan's coalition championed their own candidates. Unrepentant supply-siders favored Representative Jack Kemp of New York, although some economic conservatives were drawn to Senator Pierre S. ("Pete") Du Pont of Delaware, who called for the partial privatization of Social Security. The embittered former secretary of state, Alexander Haig, attracted support from hawkish hard-liners. Donald Rumsfeld, who had served the Reagan White House in several advisory positions, briefly joined the race, drawing special attention to his role in building cooperation with the Iraqi dictator Saddam Hussein. But the two strongest candidates came from the mainstream of the Republican Party establishment.

The Senate majority leader, Robert Dole, had served President Nixon as national chairman of the Republican National Committee until late November 1972, when Nixon, concerned about Dole's reputation for bluntness and even meanness, replaced him with George H. W. Bush, who was then the U.S. ambassador to the United Nations. A mutual loathing then developed between Dole and Bush that would intensify over the years. Like Nixon, Dole had risen in politics the hard way—he was raised during the Depression era in a small Kansas town (where his family had to move into the basement and rent out the house in order to make ends meet); served heroically in World War II (where wounds suffered in Italy cost him the use of his right arm); and after two terms in the Kansas legislature was elected to the House of Representatives in 1960, and then to the Senate in 1968. Dole was a classic postwar midwestern Republican who rejected the old isolationism and accepted the new consensus on foreign policy, and who bridled at the panaceas of the starry-eyed new right. He was a skilled congressional insider, a nuts-and-bolts politician who had learned the arts of compromise in Washington as well as the uses of calculated partisan malice on the campaign trail.

Bush, by contrast, was to the manner born, the son of the investment banker and senator Prescott Bush of Connecticut. He had been nicknamed "Poppy" as a boy, had graduated from Phillips Andover Academy, had served in the war as the Navy's youngest fighter pilot (he was shot down and rescued in 1944), had graduated from Yale (where he was elected to Phi Beta Kappa and, like his father, was tapped for the exclusive secret society Skull and Bones), and had then relocated to Texas with other eager privileged easterners, using family money to make his own fortune in the oil field boom of the 1950s. Bush turned to politics at age forty, running unsuccessfully for the U.S. Senate as a Goldwater Republican in 1964. Although he retained his patrician Yankee demeanor (and personal ties), he had adapted to the Republicans' thrust toward the South and the West; and he would always present himself politically as a Texas conservative, unlike his Wall Street Republican father, opposing the Civil Rights Act of 1964, for example. Despite or perhaps because of his social and political advantages, Bush was an inconsistent politician, winning a safely Republican House seat in Houston in 1966—and returning to more moderate stances on some domestic issues (by supporting, among other measures, the Civil Rights Bill of 1968 that outlawed racial discrimination in housing)—but losing a race for the Senate four years later. Bush had terrible difficulty projecting popular appeal. When Bush lost his race in 1970, Nixon named him ambassador to the UN. After then serving as chair of the Republican National Committee through the Watergate disaster, with a total loyalty that almost proved disastrous for his political future, Bush continued to make his way upward through appointments, first as Gerald Ford's envoy to China, then (following the "Halloween massacre") as director of the CIA. Bush had hoped to be named Ford's vice president but lost out to Nelson Rockefeller; two years later, he saw Ford pick someone else as his vice presidential candidate—Bob Dole.

In 1980, Bush memorably denounced Reagan's "voodoo economics" and gave Reagan a scare in the Iowa caucuses, but showed he had neither mastered electoral politics nor shaken off his Yankee elitist image or his propensity for maladroit preppiness. (There is a story, perhaps apocryphal, that after Reagan attacked him as a Brooks Brothers Republican, "Poppy" Bush opened his suit jacket, with a smile, before a press conference, to reveal a J. Press label, leaving the reporters to shake their heads.) After securing the nomination, Reagan would have preferred to run either with his close friend Senator Paul Laxalt from Nevada or his would-be protégé Jack Kemp, but Laxalt was deemed too much like Reagan himself to aid the ticket, and unfounded, scurrilous sexual rumors about Kemp (from the days when he served as a youthful aide to Governor Reagan) eliminated him from consideration. When he received the call, Bush leaped for joy. Thereafter, and during his eight years as vice president, there would be no more talk of voodoo economics, and not even the slightest public hint of any other disagreement with the president. Bush knew the rules in Washington. "I'm following Mr. Reagan—blindly," he told one reporter.

Everything about Bush—his upper-crust background, his less than brilliant record as a candidate, his career built on connections and appointments, his open willingness to suppress his beliefs in favor of his ambitions—repelled Bob Dole. The years of Reagan's presidency widened the breach. Dole, serving as Senate majority leader, successfully tempered what he considered the administration's irresponsibility, especially on fiscal matters. It was thus all the more satisfying for Dole when he not only defeated Bush in the Iowa caucuses (which Bush had won eight years earlier) but saw the vice president finish third, behind Pat Robertson. Then Bush's campaign got serious—and rough. In the New Hampshire primary, Bush ran stark, negative television ads claiming that Dole was a "straddler" and the man personally responsible for whatever had gone wrong under Reagan, including the tax hikes, which were anathema to New Hampshire's Republicans. To suffocate the Dole campaign, Bush would out-Reagan Reagan by vowing never to raise taxes.

Bush's victory in New Hampshire left Dole embittered and also a bit mystified. ("There's nothing there," he would say of the vice president, as if recognizing, in horror, that nothingness had become a political asset.) And after New Hampshire, Bush's political operation, aided by President Reagan's rebound in the polls, was unstoppable. When Bush swept the southern primaries in March, the rest of the field dropped out. Bush's nomination was ensured—even though, curiously, his popularity actually trailed off during the coming months, once he had no one left to attack.

The Democratic field, meanwhile, grew quickly—and just as quickly thinned itself out. Two potentially imposing liberal figures decided not to run at all. Edward Kennedy had settled into his role as a senator, winning praise in Washington for his actions to limit Reagan's cuts in social spending. Governor Mario Cuomo of New York was a thoughtful, undogmatic, ethnic Roman Catholic upholder of the New Deal tradition, who also had a strong grasp of world politics. ("We should seize this moment in history—and try to begin to negotiate the end of the Cold War," he said in September 1987, after returning from meetings in Moscow with Soviet leaders.) But Cuomo backed out at the last minute, saying he was unable to reconcile a run for the presidency with fulfilling his continuing responsibilities to the citizens of New York.

Other leading contenders rapidly self-destructed. The early front-runner, Gary Hart, was even better informed than Cuomo was about where the cold war was headed, and he had refined his politics since his insurgent neoliberal candidacy in 1984, when he had nearly toppled Walter

Mondale—but now his candidacy ended abruptly when the press exposed an extramarital affair with a part-time model. Joseph Biden, a young, centrist liberal senator from Delaware who had helped undo Bork's nomination, felt compelled to withdraw when reporters learned he had plagiarized autobiographical campaign speeches from the oratory of the leader of the British Labour Party, Neil Kinnock.

Intraparty ideological fights were also costly. The Reverend Jesse Jackson returned to the fray and carried several southern state primaries as well as 55 percent of the vote in Michigan, which briefly made him look like the man to beat. But Jackson's leftism, his remark in 1984 about "Hymietown," and his past connections with militant, sometimes bizarre, black nationalists, thwarted any serious chance of the nomination. An earnest, moderate new candidate, Senator Albert Gore Jr. of Tennessee—a Vietnam veteran and military expert on the Armed Services Committee—also ran well in the South. But Gore became so closely tied, during the New York primary, to New York City's acidulous, polarizing former mayor, Edward Koch, that he alienated many voters and submerged the identity of his candidacy.[*]

The Democrats' disarray reflected, in part, shifts in the unwritten rules of presidential politics. There was a time, earlier in the century, when politicians could conduct reckless sexual adventures (and steal lines from other politicians' speeches) and safely assume that their actions would go unreported in the press. What happened after hours, in particular, was nobody's business. And some political leaders still seemed to enjoy immunity. (Ronald Reagan and his speechwriters blatantly lifted payoff lines, without attribution, from Spencer Tracy and Jimmy Stewart as well as from Franklin D. Roosevelt and John F. Kennedy, not to mention John Winthrop, yet nobody seemed to care or even to notice.) The full coverage by journalists and partisan operatives after the notorious drowning at Chappaquiddick and during the ensuing scandal involving Senator Edward M. Kennedy in 1969 proved an early sign of changing times. The investigative mind-set that then arose after Watergate gave reporters, as they saw it, license—indeed, a righteous moral imperative—to track down and report on a politician's slightest transgression or hypocrisy as if it were a political crime. Indeed, the line between the personal and the political became blurred. The feminist slogan from the 1970s, that the personal *is* the political, was twisted into a pretext

---

[*] Other hopefuls—Representative Richard Gephardt of Missouri who was favored by organized labor; from Illinois, the bow-tied Adlai Stevenson of the 1980s; and Senator Paul Simon—made no dent outside their institutional and regional support bases.

for disguising scandal-sheet prurience as valiant, public-spirited journalism. Scandalmongering, especially about sex, was hardly new to American politics, but now its scale expanded and its claim to be a serious form of political reporting grew bolder. A confused assumption that private acts have a direct bearing on public acts became an iron law, in time justifying dragnets, stakeout espionage, and other excesses in the media.

Still, the Democratic Party's shambling could not be blamed on the press corps, which simply preyed on vulnerabilities. Dazed by two successive Republican presidential triumphs; plagued by divisions of race, ideology, and political temperament that dated back to the late 1960s; unable to unite around a coherent set of attitudes, let alone ideas about foreign policy and the military or domestic issues; beholden to a disparate collection of special constituencies and interest groups, each with its own agenda, the quarrelsome Democrats made the fractured Republican Party look like a juggernaut. Even so, the Republicans' nominee was weak enough that the candidate who survived the primaries to win the Democratic nomination, Governor Michael Dukakis of Massachusetts, held a nearly twenty-point lead in the polls in midsummer.

Dukakis was the candidate of cool reason, the last man standing when the more impassioned Democratic contenders had fallen away. The son of successful Greek immigrants, a graduate of Swarthmore and Harvard Law School, Dukakis had served in the Massachusetts state legislature before being elected governor in 1974 on a platform of fiscal responsibility and reform of the state bureaucracy. Compelled to break his campaign promise and raise the state sales tax, he lost the renomination in a state primary to a conservative Democrat in 1978, taught courses on local and state government at the John F. Kennedy School of Government at Harvard, and then was elected governor again in 1982. In 1986 he was selected as the nation's most effective governor by the National Governors' Association. Dukakis presided over a boom in high-tech industries in Massachusetts (later called by his supporters the "Massachusetts miracle"), while gaining a reputation as an unpretentious man who rode the subway every workday from his home in Brookline to the state capitol.

Having come of age, politically, in the early 1960s, Dukakis identified with John F. Kennedy (who had been born in Brookline), and with the belief, imputed to Kennedy, that rational approaches to public problems, free of political dogma, could best address the common good. Although he detested the label (as he detested all political labels), Dukakis was a consummate technocrat, who governed in the best sense of that term. But his fixation on expertise and technique led him to draw all the wrong political conclusions about the Reagan era. The Iran-contra scandal, for example, had resulted, according to the Tower Commission, from lax management; as president, Dukakis said, he would correct all that. In his run for the nomination, Dukakis had outlasted men who had far greater national reputations than his, but who wore their values and beliefs on their sleeves—and thereby reinforced his own technocratic impulses. The country, he thought, was tired of the demagoguery, pandering, and political tags that had propelled national politics since the late 1960s. He offered another variation of the "new politics": the immigrants' son as an unruffled, tech-boom, government expert. (The satirist Mort Sahl called Dukakis "the only colorless Greek in America.") In his speech accepting the nomination, Dukakis described his updated version of the New Frontier not as a set of political promises but as a (vaguely articulated) set of challenges to be solved by his superior know-how. "Because," he said, "this election is not about ideology. It is about competence." As his running mate, Dukakis chose Senator Lloyd Bentsen of Texas, a social moderate but fiscal conservative—thereby seeming to re-create the Massachusetts-Texas axis that elected John Kennedy and Lyndon Johnson in 1960.

Bush looked like a sitting duck, already dismissed by the national media as a "wimp" (a term notoriously featured in a nasty cover story in *Newsweek*) and a political chameleon. Some Democrats harped on the absurdity of the patrician "Poppy" trying to run as a Texan in Reagan's populist mode who ate pork rinds and tossed horseshoes. "Poor George," said Governor Ann Richards, a bred-in-the-bone Texas liberal, at the Democratic convention: "He was born with a silver foot in his mouth." Such explicit class-based attacks, Democratic strategists believed, would undermine Bush's credibility and exploit the fissures within the Republican coalition. But Dukakis spurned such rhetoric as too emotional and too ideological. Instead, he would criticize Bush on matters of ineptness and irresponsibility, beginning with the vice president's still murky role in the Iran-contra affair.

Bush might have been vulnerable in that regard, having attended numerous high-level meetings and intelligence briefings about financing the contras and selling arms to Iran. But Bush, like Reagan, benefited from the singular preoccupation with the diversion of funds to the contras and, even more, from Reagan's rapprochement with Gorbachev, which pushed Iran-contra into the political background. Simply by repeating, like a mantra, that, as vice president, he had been "out of the loop" and that "mistakes were made," Bush evaded responsibility for the affair—even as he played up his eight years of hands-on experience in Reagan's White House. The press had already given up on pursuing what reporters and editors decided was an old story.

While he tried to look serenely detached from the grubbiness of political strategizing, Bush drew on Reagan's skillful political workers and on veteran Republican operatives. For his speech accepting the nomination, the former White House speechwriter Peggy Noonan provided him with a script that at once placed him in the no-nonsense Reagan mold (paraphrasing the tough-guy movie actor Clint Eastwood in his role as Dirty Harry: "Read my lips: no new taxes!"); gave a positive, even sentimental spin to slashing government social spending by extolling private charity and volunteerism ("a thousand points of light"); and promised a "kinder, gentler" conservative America. Yet in the New Orleans Superdome, where the convention was being held, there was abundant evidence that the Bush campaign did not include Democrats in this kinder, gentler America—for the simple reason that Democrats were un-American.

Jeane Kirkpatrick declared from the podium that the Democrats stood for "collectivism" and "weakness in defense." The keynote speaker, Tom Kean, who was the governor of New Jersey and the soul of what remained of moderate, "modern Republicanism," was driven to scorn the Democrats for their "pastel patriotism" and to charge that they "want to weaken America. But they won't admit it." For his running mate, Bush surprised the Republican Party and the political press corps by choosing Senator Dan Quayle, who was widely viewed as a political lightweight, but who was supposed to shore up Bush's credentials with the party's right wing. President Reagan's appearance was perhaps the most important political event of the convention. He reassured the country that his work with "Mr. Gorbachev" must continue, and that, by supporting continuity and voting for Bush, Americans would endorse the change his own election had initiated eight years earlier. "We are the change," said Reagan, stealing the thunder from the Democrats. Without Gorbachev as his partner in ending the cold war, Reagan's political vitality would have been greatly diminished, perhaps destroyed. But now Reagan had begun the rescue of the lagging Bush.

The campaign, as plotted by a young but experienced southern consultant, Lee Atwater, fiercely attacked Dukakis; "going negative" was at the core of Bush's themes. This effort was, in many respects, a reprise of a classic cold war campaign, even though the cold war was coming to an end. Since the late 1940s, Republicans, in the style of the young Richard Nixon, had been casting their opponents as soft on communism, even disloyal. In the late 1960s, the

Republicans, in a style pioneered by the "new" Richard Nixon, added the code words of its post–civil rights southern strategy. Atwater—a South Carolinian described by Reagan's White House political director Ed Rollins as "Oliver North in civilian clothes"—was well schooled in the techniques of the Republicans' post-1960s campaigning during the cold war. And by the late summer, the Bush campaign's attacks on Dukakis had become virulent.

Bush's researchers combed through Dukakis's record. In 1977, on sound advice from his state attorney general, Dukakis had vetoed a manifestly unconstitutional bill that would have penalized schoolteachers who did not lead their students in daily recitals of the Pledge of Allegiance. After an oblique reference made by Al Gore in a Democratic primary debate, Bush's staff also learned of a program in Massachusetts, initiated by Dukakis's Republican predecessor, which allowed brief furloughs to state prison inmates, and which Dukakis did not discontinue until after the primaries of 1988 were under way. Digging deeper, the Bush campaign learned that one prisoner, Willie Horton, convicted of first-degree murder, had, while on furlough, raped a white woman in Maryland, assaulted her husband, and stolen their car. As soon as Atwater saw a photograph of Horton, a black man with a menacing look, his hopes brightened.

State party committees and independent private groups prepared attack ads and brochures featuring Horton's picture, and the national Bush-Quayle committee renounced them—not the last time in national politics this convenient division of labor would give a national campaign an air of plausible deniability. Bush's team did approve television spots showing swarthy criminals entering and then leaving prison through a turnstile, thanks to Governor Dukakis's "revolving door prison policies"—so there was actually little doubt about the complicity of the national campaign from the start.

Even more fervent were the patriotic pageants whipped up around the Pledge of Allegiance. These rituals started at the Republican convention: when Bush finished reading Noonan's speech, but before the traditional hoopla began, he asked everyone in the hall to repeat after him: "I pledge allegiance. . . ." The campaign then wrapped itself in the flag. Bush held a rally at a flag factory, impugned Dukakis's loyalty with phrases drawn from the McCarthy era, and ended his campaign speeches, dutifully, with the pledge. Dukakis, Bush said, wasn't merely a member of the mollycoddle American Civil Liberties Union (ACLU), he was "a *card carrying* member of the ACLU." Bush also substituted "liberal" for "communist," then shortened it to "the L-word" (an epithet possibly first used by Reagan), uttered as if the term "liberal" reeked of the outhouse.

Amazingly, in the same year that the cold war was receding and that the Republicans' hero, Ronald Reagan, spoke of peace in Moscow beneath the bust of Lenin, the Republicans effectively red-baited the mild-mannered technocrat Michael Dukakis. That the Republicans also questioned the Americanism of a short, dark-haired Greek-American, plainly not in the traditional Anglo-Saxon (or, since John Kennedy, Celtic) presidential mold, made the assaults all the uglier. (One campaign T-shirt, spotted at a yacht-ing resort in Maine not far from the Bush family compound in Kennebunk-port, read "Don't step in the Dukakis"—combining the outhouse conno-tations of the "L-word" with a play on the candidate's foreign-sounding surname.) Some of Dukakis's advisers urged him to counterattack; and at one point the candidate seemed ready to denounce the Republican conven-tion as an extremist hate fest, which showed that the Republican Party had "gone so far to the right, they're wrong." But Dukakis refused, not wanting to run an inflammatory campaign. He was the candidate of competence. Everyone could see that. Any other judgment would be irrational.

Dukakis's rating in the polls collapsed by the end of August, and he would never recover. One effort to make him look tough by dressing him in combat gear and placing him in a tank for a television spot produced one of the most risible moments in modern political history. Dukakis did make something of a comeback in his first debate with Bush, appearing crisp and knowledgeable about domestic issues while the vice president rambled on about the Pledge of Allegiance and his opponent's extreme liberalism. But in the second debate, a black journalist on the panel asked Dukakis whether he would favor the death penalty for someone who raped and murdered his wife, and Dukakis sank himself with a passion-less answer about why capital punishment is not an effective deterrent to violent crime. In the final week of the campaign, Dukakis at last started attacking Bush as the candidate of the rich and wellborn—"He's on their side. Lloyd Bentsen and I are on your side," he declared—and his numbers in the polls rose. But Dukakis's populism was not credible, and it was too little and far too late.

Bush won the popular vote by 54 percent to 46 percent, and crushed Dukakis in the electoral college with 426 votes to 112. Not since 1928 had the Republican Party won three successive presidential elections; and not since 1836 had a sitting vice president been elected to the White House. But the public as a whole had responded to the candidates and their campaigns with cold indifference: barely 50 percent of the eligible voters went to the polls, the lowest turnout since 1924, when Calvin Coolidge defeated John

Davis. Between them, Bush and Dukakis had made politics look small as well as irrelevant. And although Bush's victory seemed overwhelming, he ran far less strongly than Reagan four years earlier, losing ten states as well as the District of Columbia. He did pick up several important states, including Illinois and Pennsylvania, but only by very slim margins.

When asked about the malicious tone of his campaign, the president-elect shrugged it off, remarking, "That's history." The outstanding feature of the election, though, had been neither Bush's demagoguery nor Dukakis's failure to defend the good name of liberalism, nor even the public's disenchantment. It was, rather, the campaign's almost total dissociation from the epochal events occurring all around it, thanks to the diplomacy of Ronald Reagan and Mikhail Gorbachev. The Republican strategists and their desperate candidate looked back to the tried-and-true themes and tactics of the past; and the Democrats failed even to hint that the Republicans' cold war demonology had been rendered obsolete and that the greatest political hero of the Republican Party had helped make it possible. The only important figure to register the point, along the way, was President Reagan himself—and he, of course, lent his backing and his reflected, renewed popularity to Bush. In one of the more bizarre presidential campaigns in American history, this was the ultimate irony.

On December 7, 1988, the forty-seventh anniversary of Japan's attack on Pearl Harbor, President Reagan returned to New York Harbor, with president-elect Bush in tow. But at this event, unlike the celebrations at the Statue of Liberty in 1986, there were no great crowds and no spectacular displays. Across the gray water, a ferry carried Mikhail Gorbachev, who had just give an address at the United Nations in which he had delivered the stunning news that the Soviet Union's conventional military forces would be reduced by half. Gorbachev disembarked at the military installation on Governors Island, where Reagan and Bush greeted him for a symbolic luncheon—a final get-together for the two costars and a handing of the torch to the incoming American president. Amid photo ops and reminiscing, the mood could not have been mellower. There was a discordant note when a skeptical Bush pressed for assurances of the success of perestroika and glasnost, and Gorbachev snapped, "Even Jesus Christ couldn't answer that question!" But this was an occasion for celebrating past achievements and new opportunities more than belaboring remaining difficulties. "A better attitude than at any of our previous meetings," Reagan noted. "[Gorbachev] sounded as if he saw us as partners making a better world." At one point, Gorbachev, noting Reagan's love of horses, asked him which side the rider mounted on. Effusively, Reagan answered, "On the left! On the left!" Gorbachev, not expecting Reagan to say the word "left" with such passion, broke up laughing.

The world truly had changed. But how much had Reagan and his presidency changed it? Writing of Reagan's impact, one astute observer has claimed that, far from being revolutionary, "Reaganism will eventually be seen as having helped conserve a predominantly status quo, middle-class welfare state." Useful as such assessments are in deflating persistent myths, however, the added perspective of twenty years shows that, quite apart from the cold war, Reagan's presidency made lasting changes, some of which would be felt only in the long run.

On the domestic side, William A. Niskanen, a member of Reagan's Council of Economic Advisers and then chairman of the Cato Institute, states flatly that although the economy improved substantially and changed a great deal, "there was no 'Reagan revolution.'" Reagan utterly failed in pursuit of his greatest stated initial goal, reducing the size of the federal government, and in modifying the basic structures of the New Deal's social benefits. The number of government workers actually increased during Reagan's administration faster than it had during Jimmy Carter's. Overall federal spending as a percentage of gross domestic product rose in the mid-1980s, before falling back to roughly the same level in 1989 (22.1 percent) as in 1981 (22.9 percent). Spending on social programs aimed particularly at the poor was slashed, and an estimated $70 billion was, in effect, transferred from domestic programs to the military, compared with expenditures before Reagan took office—yet total expenditures on social welfare programs, including Social Security and Medicare, rose between 1981 and 1989.

On the social and cultural issues dear to the religious right—ending federal protection of abortion, restoring prayer to public schools, reversing the trend toward toleration of homosexuality—the Reagan administration delivered virtually nothing at all besides speeches. Although some of Reagan's officials did their best to obstruct or ignore the execution of civil rights laws, those laws stayed on the books; and by the time Reagan left office, he was powerless to sustain his veto of the Civil Rights Restoration Act of 1988.

The administration's most conspicuous success in reducing the purview of government, aside from tax reform, was in the area of deregulation, as well as a relaxation of governmental oversight in contractual connections with the private sector. But the main fruits of that success were bitter: the savings and loan scandal, the politicization and plunder of the Environmental Protection Agency, the junk-bond boom and associated scandals on Wall Street, the outrages involving procurement at the Pentagon. If Reagan himself was free of direct culpability in these matters, his hands-off attitude toward federal regulation encouraged a permissiveness that ran directly counter to his tough talk about law and order. The extent of the criminal wrongdoing had not yet been determined when Reagan left office; its costs may never be fully counted.

The greatest domestic improvement during the Reagan years was, without question, the revival of the sputtering economy. When Reagan took office, the annual inflation rate was averaging about 12 percent, interest rates had jumped to more than 20 percent, and the unemployment rate was 7.2 percent; eight years later, those figures, respectively, were 4.4 percent, 9.3 percent, and 5.5 percent. Marked, after 1982, by the longest continuous period of peacetime economic growth in the nation's history, the Reagan years saw the nation's gross domestic product (GDP) increase twofold. Nearly 18 million new jobs were created.

With some historical perspective, however, the boom, although creditable, was not the soaring success that these figures suggest. Nor was the improvement attributable to Reagan's stewardship, apart from his continued support of the chairman of the Federal Reserve, Paul Volcker (who had been appointed by Jimmy Carter). Overall, the economy grew at a slower rate than it had in the 1960s and 1970s (and would again in the 1990s). The average annual growth in real GDP was actually lower during Reagan's eight years in office than during Carter's four years. Above all, the new prosperity was heavily skewed to the top: while average hourly wages and middle-class real hourly incomes stagnated during the 1980s, and while the average family real income for the bottom fifth of Americans fell by 7 percent, the share of the nation's wealth held by the top 1 percent of the population grew from 22 percent in 1979 to 39 percent in 1989. Instead of what now looked like a golden age of middle-class prosperity of the 1950s, the so-called Reagan boom brought inequalities of living standards reminscent of the nineteenth-century robber barons' gilded age.

Despite the celebrated tax cut of 1981, any suggestion that Reagan significantly lightened the nation's overall tax load is bogus. In 1981, 19.4 percent of the national income was diverted to federal taxes; in 1989, the figure was 19.3 percent—and many states and localities, meanwhile, had to raise their taxes to offset cuts in federal assistance. Where Reagan's federal tax reforms did succeed was in slashing marginal rates for the wealthy, making the system much more regressive, and further redistributing wealth to the top. Annual job growth was less vigorous, on average, under Reagan that it had been under any other president since 1960. And a large proportion of the new job growth in the 1980s came from an influx into the workforce of married women with young children; these women took work in order to make up for their husbands' declining real wages. The unemployment rate did not fall to the level of 1979 (5.9 percent) until 1988.

Reagan's fiscal policies succeeded mainly in raising deficits to astronomical levels while further enriching the already affluent. The chief stimulus to the economy was not added productive investments accrued from lower taxes, as supply-siders claimed it would be. Had it been so, the economy could have been expected to grow at an impressive rate, exceeding that of the boom years of the 1950s and 1960s, when top marginal tax rates were 70 percent and higher. Instead, the rate of private investment actually fell in the 1980s, as did total revenues from individual and corporate income taxes, adjusted for inflation, during the years immediately following the tax cut of 1981. Also contrary to the assurances of supply-siders, the overall disposable personal savings rate declined by nearly half during Reagan's second term alone, from 8 percent in 1984 to 4.4 percent in 1988.

Much of the capital redistributed to the top as a consequence of Reagan's tax reforms was spent either on luxury consumer items—according to one wit, Reagan's rising tide floated all yachts—or on speculative paper investments. Actually, the key to the recovery in the 1980s was the harsh interest-rate policies initiated by Volcker during Carter's administration and continued during Reagan's administration through 1982. Coupled with a precipitous decline in the price of crude oil after 1985 (caused by weaknesses within the OPEC cartel), those policies reversed the spiraling inflation rate.[*]

Another of Reagan's signal domestic successes added to his regressive legacy—hastening the decline of organized labor. Along with sharply progressive taxation, the growth of the union movement after the Great De-

---

[*] Another way to interpret the "Reagan recovery" is to say that Reaganomics was not, in the final analysis, supply-side economics at all, but an inverted form of liberal Keynesianism, in which massive federal borrowing and spending—totaling nearly $2 trillion between 1981 and 1989, and well over $500 billion in the years 1984–1986 alone—buoyed the miserable economy of the late Carter years.

pression was a primary cause of the narrowing of economic inequality and the expansion of mass middle-class prosperity during the decades following World War II. Quite apart from wage agreements, the strength of American labor, comparable to that of labor in other major industrialized nations, brought unionized workers numerous social benefits from their employers, including pensions and health insurance, which the government did not provide. Starting with Barry Goldwater (who first gained national attention in the early 1950s as an antiunion crusader), the resurgent conservative movement, backed strongly by employers' associations and corporate interests, was bitterly opposed to organized labor, and Reagan was no exception.

As president, Reagan—ironically, the only former union leader ever to be elected to the White House—put his antiunionism into practice with a flourish when he broke the PATCO strike in 1981. Thereafter, administration officials at the National Labor Relations Board and elsewhere enforced a regime that was deeply hostile to unions. Although economists have linked the decline of organized labor to numerous factors, the weakening and nonenforcement of labor laws during Reagan's administration had a major impact, undermining union organizing and collective bargaining. Having already gradually declined during the 1960s and 1970s from its historic highs of more than 35 percent, the percentage of the private-sector nonagricultural workforce that was unionized fell from 20.4 percent in 1980 to 12.1 percent a decade later—the lowest figure since 1915.[*]

Many pundits and scholars have asserted that despite these trends—or because of them—Reagan left office, in one historian's words, "an extraordinarily popular figure," but the claim is misleading. To be sure, Reagan won popular support at the moments when, as for any politician, it counted most, being the first president since Dwight Eisenhower to be reelected and to complete two terms. His margins of victory testify to his brilliance as a campaigner, although they also indicate the weakness of his opponents and of the Democratic Party in general in presidential politics. At different points in his presidency—following his shooting in 1981; at the height of the economic recovery in the summer of 1986; during the weeks just before he left office—Reagan received enviable performance ratings as well as personal ratings.

---

[*] The decline in union membership cannot be ascribed solely to the loss of manufacturing jobs during the Reagan years, because the percentage of union workers within the manufacturing sector also declined.

But Reagan's popularity suffered through some severe lows during the recession of 1982 and, even more, in the aftermath of the Iran-contra scandal. Among modern presidents, his average performance rating during his two terms places him in the middle tier, on a par with Lyndon Johnson and Bill Clinton but well below the leaders, John F. Kennedy, Franklin D. Roosevelt, and Dwight D. Eisenhower, and not much better than Nixon, Carter, Truman, and Ford. Reagan was also a polarizing figure—a divider, not a uniter—beloved by Republicans but despised by Democrats. The fifty-point gap between how supporters of the respective parties viewed him dwarfs the thirty- to thirty-five-point gap of his successor, the supposedly preternatural polarizer Bill Clinton. At the close of his presidency, Americans gave Reagan high ratings for his "charisma" and communications skills, as well as for his administration's relations with the Soviet Union and its conduct of foreign affairs generally. But the public split evenly over his economic policy and disapproved of his performance on judicial nominations, civil rights, education, ethics, housing, crime, welfare, and the deficit.

Americans certainly felt better about the country's direction under Reagan's leadership than they did at the end of Jimmy Carter's failed administration. But Reagan's presidency overall was not regarded as markedly better than others in this regard either. Over Reagan's two terms, an average of just 44 percent of respondents in the polls believed that the country was headed in the right direction, roughly the same as the overall average for the entire period from 1979 to mid-2004. Regarding the economy, supposedly the bellwether of Reagan's standing at home, only once during the boom years from 1985 to 1989 did 50 percent or more of Americans register approval.

In foreign policy, the connection between the unexpected ending of the cold war and Reagan's various foreign policies is highly problematic. The Reagan Doctrine contributed to a bloodbath in Central America, where as many as 200,000 people died in Nicaragua, El Salvador, and Guatemala fighting left-wing regimes or propping up right-wing regimes, with no discernible impact on the outcome of the cold war. Reagan's particular object of fixation, the Nicaraguan contras, certainly hurt the Sandinistas but never formed a credible political or military force, despite the attention and covert funding lavished on them. A continuation of Reagan's pro-contra policy, according to one designer of the policy, who was an official in Reagan's State Department, "would probably have meant many years of inconclusive struggle in Nicaragua." In any event, by late 1987, despite continued rhetoric from the White House about the Sandinistas' imminent threat to

U.S. security, administration insiders recognized that, with Gorbachev in power, any such threat had passed.

After the Iran-contra scandal, the administration, pushed by Congress, backed away from supporting a military solution and finally acceded to the diplomatic efforts led by the president of Costa Rica, Oscar Arias, that eventually brought a negotiated peace to the region. The reversal intensely displeased the hard-liners who had conceived of the Reagan Doctrine in the first place, and who regarded Arias's plan—in the fully mistaken words of one writer for *Commentary*—as a step toward "making Central America safe for Communism." Ironically, the Sandinistas did finally fall from power in 1990—in free elections supported by the United States: anticommunist liberals and centrists led by the newspaper publisher Violeta Chamorro (who had resigned from the Sandinista junta in 1980) carried the day. Also ironically, one pro-contra ally of the United States in the region, the government of Panama under the strongman (and drug trafficker) Manuel Noriega, soon proved to be such an open embarrassment to American policy makers that President George H. W. Bush ordered an invasion by U.S. forces to topple him.

Like the larger reforms in the Soviet bloc after 1985, the experience in Central America proved the falsity of a central, original premise in Reagan's policy—that antidemocratic left-wing regimes were immutable whereas friendly authoritarian right-wing regimes were open to reform. Indeed, one of the administration's few clear-cut successes in foreign policy before 1987—abandoning Ferdinand Marcos in the Philippines and opening the way for the ascension of Corazon Aquino—involved an implicit rejection of that premise. It also required Secretary of State Shultz's determined advocacy in order to overcome President Reagan, who was subbornly pro-Marcos.* In Afghanistan, the U.S support for the mujahideen unquestionably placed enormous military pressure on the Soviet-backed regime. Yet the Soviet Union under Gorbachev, who had inherited responsibility for the

---

* Even after the experience in the Philippines, the Reagan administration never openly repudiated its original propositions about dictators and democracies, as formulated by Jeane J. Kirkpatrick. Paul Wolfowitz, who came to support a more consistent pro-democracy policy, was among those who refused to acknowledge that he and other neoconservatives had changed their minds. But it is impossible to align Wolfowitz's declaration during the Philippine crisis—that "[t]he best antidote to communism is democracy"—with Kirkpatrick's earlier formulation of neoconservative doctrine. For a fuller discussion, see James Mann, *The Rise of the Vulcans: The History of Bush's War Cabinet* (New York, 2004), 135–137, quotation on 136.

occupation of Afghanistan, lacked the will to sustain the draining effort, especially after the hard-liners in the Soviet military establishment were removed. And after the Soviet Union withdrew, the devastated country devolved into a prolonged civil war among rival warlords and fundamentalist sects, reinforced with arms or money obtained for arms provided earlier by the United States. The Taliban, an extreme fundamentalist group, finally seized power in 1996 and welcomed the presence of a terrorist group headed by one of the mujahideen, Osama bin Laden.

In the Middle East, American misadventures in Lebanon and in its dealings with Iran brought no progress toward regional peace and security. The outstanding new ally recruited in the region was not the highly touted phalanx of Iranian moderates (who never materialized) but the Iraqi dictator Saddam Hussein, who waged the Iran-Iraq war to a standoff with crucial American support but still held his countrymen in an iron grip.

With regard to the Soviet Union, there is little credible evidence that Reagan's massive military buildup of the early 1980s did anything to persuade the Kremlin to come to the bargaining table. Much of the initial justification for the buildup arose from manifestly exaggerated estimates of the Soviet Union's military superiority provided by analysts in and around hard-line groups such as the Committee on the Present Danger, which were later proved wrong. New expenditures by the Soviet Union in the face of Reagan's buildup were not especially heavy in the 1980s, either before or after 1985, and certainly were not enough to cause major damage to its already racked economy. Much of the huge new American outlay, though, was consumed by fraud, waste, and mismanagement, including the $15 billion expended on the MX missile system and the $26 billion spent in research funds for SDI—neither of which would be deployed.

Reagan's adamant anticommunism and defense of human freedom did give a much-needed boost to the morale and aspirations of dissident forces within the Eastern bloc. Even if the administration's substantive responses to the crackdowns on pro-democracy forces in Poland, Czechoslovakia, East Germany, and elsewhere were often measured, Reagan's unstinting rhetoric of the evil empire, culminating in his speech at the Brandenburg Gate in 1987, was thrilling. Having the official communist press regularly denounce Reagan, especially in his early years, as an imperialist warmonger, raised his reputation among the anticommunist rebels. Adam Michnik, the eloquent young Polish dissident who was jailed for antigovernment activities, praised the American envoy to Warsaw, John Davis Jr., for playing a shrewd and helpful role for the dissidents—but Reagan, Michnik has said, stood as nothing less than a "national hero."

The great breakthrough in U.S.-Soviet relations, though, came with the advent of Mikhail Gorbachev in 1985 and his negotiations with Reagan. Without Gorbachev, it is conceivable that the Soviet Union might have carried on for decades, its nuclear deterrent strong enough to ward off threats from the West, its conventional forces powerful enough to contain rising discontent within its own satellites in eastern and central Europe. With Gorbachev, though, Reagan was able to seize on his own utopian antinuclear thinking and push for actual arms reductions, beginning with the INF treaty in 1987 that initiated the end of the cold war.

To complete that triumph of diplomacy and goodwill, Reagan had to withstand the criticism of many who had informed and reinforced his views of the Soviets for decades but who lacked his own understanding that with Gorbachev and other reformers now in charge of the Kremlin, a great change was at hand. Call it a triumph of character or idealism or perceptiveness or "wishful thinking" (in George Will's term), or some combination of these. But Reagan's ability to dispense with dogma (including his own) and negotiate with Gorbachev helped bring an end to a nuclear arms race that had terrified the world for forty years.

Reagan deserves posterity's honor not for adhering stubbornly to the ideas and strategies of cold war conservatism and neoconservatism, but for knowing when to transcend and, finally, reject outdated and counterproductive ideas regarding nuclear warfare and the Soviet Union. His success in helping finally to end the cold war is one of the greatest achievements by any president of the United States—and arguably the greatest single presidential achievement since 1945. On other fronts, Reagan and his presidency, if far less than "revolutionary," had a deep impact on American government and politics. He was "a successful candidate and effective president above all else because he stood for a set of ideas," his adversary Senator Edward Kennedy remarked in 1989. For better and for worse, he left several legacies that defined the age of Reagan.

By cementing the alliance between social conservatives and economic libertarian conservatives, Reagan completed the ideological enlargement of what had been a cranky, backward-looking political movement, and brought it from the margins of political life to the White House. With

his sunny temperament and odd mixture of nostalgia and futuristic optimism—in short, with his Reaganism—he put a new, smiling face on American conservative politics. Reagan also consolidated the Republican political
coalition pioneered by Richard Nixon in 1968. By the time he left office,
the once solidly Democratic South was an equally solid Republican South.
By winning, during his presidential runs, about one-quarter of the nom-
inally Democratic vote—including large numbers of blue-collar whites,
Roman Catholics, and other former mainstays of Franklin Roosevelt's New
Deal coalition as well as suburbanites—he fulfilled the Republican strategist Kevin Phillips's vision of a new Republican majority. How large that
majority actually was, how much of it translated from presidential politics
to other races (especially in light of the Republicans' loss of the Senate in
1986), and how permanent it would be remained unclear. But Reagan and
his conservative appeal managed to salvage a Republican Party battered by
Watergate and (somewhat ironically) secure the electoral base that Nixon
and his advisers had originally envisaged.

One effect of these changes was to make the Republican Party far more
conservative than it ever had been. Despite his rhetoric, Reagan neither
identified closely with the religious right nor expended much immediate
political capital on its behalf. (One writer has even described Reagan—a
divorced former actor who seldom attended church and who, along with
his wife, counted homosexuals among his friends and business acquain-
tances—as a "closet tolerant.") Yet by formally endorsing the evangelical
conservative cause and cultivating its political support, Reagan brought into
the Republican Party, especially at the state and local level, large cadres of
indefatigable culture warriors who would battle hard for the party's soul
and the nation's. Likewise, whatever his personal views were about racial
justice, Reagan's rhetoric as well as the policies of his Department of Justice
greatly reassured the enemies of civil rights reform, their politics forged in
reaction to the advances of the 1960s, that he was on their side. The Republican Party was no longer the party of Lincoln.

Although Reagan himself, as a union president and governor, was practiced in political compromise, not all conservative Republicans, in or outside
Washington, shared his temperament. Some truly saw themselves as political revolutionaries. In 1987, Pat Buchanan, while still serving as the White
House communications director, declared that "the greatest vacuum in
American politics is to the right of Ronald Reagan." (Ironically, when that
vacuum was filled, it would be with partisans whom Reagan had helped
mobilize and bring inside the corridors of power.) And with the ascendance

of more radical elements inside the party, the future was dark for moderate and liberal Republicans—who, in 1989, included, in the Senate, the New Englanders James Jeffords, John H. Chaffee, and William S. Cohen; and, in the House, a large portion of the Republican caucus from the northeastern states.

Reagan's chief legacy to American government was his pursuit of policies that might enable future administrations to make changes he himself could not complete. His most striking triumph lay in his judicial appointments, where the defeat of the unsettling Robert Bork was a rare exception. In its eight years, the Reagan administration won nearly 400 crucial appointments to the federal bench, elevating nominees who had survived a new, highly ideological screening process dominated by the White House's conservative hard-liners. According to the leading student of the subject, Reagan's appointments were "predominantly young white upper-middle-class males, with . . . reputations for legal conservatism." How much conservatives, who had long decried "judicial activism," would now feel free to pursue their own political and social agendas assertively from the bench would become clearer over succeeding decades. But in the short term—and in the long term, too—Reagan had startlingly politicized the process of judicial selection.

More subtly, but perhaps more powerfully, Reagan's fiscal policies left an enduring legacy to future lawmakers who might wish to build any new social programs even remotely resembling those of the New Deal or the Great Society. Some of Reagan's supporters blamed the crippling deficits of the Reagan years on a spendthrift Congress—although a subsequent review by the House Appropriations Committee showed that had Congress passed Reagan's budgets exactly as proposed, the national debt would have been $29.4 billion worse. Other supporters called them the necessary price for freedom—a regrettable but necessary result of the president's winning his top two priorities, cutting taxes and building up the military. But Reagan's critics were not so sure, agreeing with Senator Daniel Patrick Moynihan's charge (based, in part, on David Stockman's incautious, candid words) that the deficits were a deliberate attempt to allow a Republican administration and a Republican Senate to "use the budget deficit to force massive reductions in social programs," including Social Security.

Whether deliberate or not, Reagan's deficits, combined with his tax policies, altered some basic facts of American government. In the name of fairness and simplified taxes, the administration mauled the principles of progressive taxation that had seen the nation through the boom years of the

1950s and 1960s and hastened the great expansion of the American middle class. Now, faced with the deficits, Democrats would no longer be able even to consider any significant new domestic spending programs without proposing to raise taxes. And this is exactly what the Republicans hoped they would do, thereby reinforcing the Republicans' depiction of Democratic liberalism as "tax-and-spend" robbery to aid themselves (and their poor— read, black—political supporters) at the expense of honest, hardworking Americans. Coupled with the contention of the Reagan White House that colossal increases in the military budget were essential to achieve arms reductions and secure world peace, the changes left Democrats little political room (let alone fiscal room) in which to maneuver, even if some unexpected national emergency were to arise.

Reagan's legacy in foreign policy, even with the great achievements of his second term, was divided and contradictory. In the first years of his presidency, Reagan paid close heed to hawks who believed in belligerent displays of U.S. military superiority as the key to national security during the cold war. Mistrustful of détente, disgusted by what they saw as a pusillanimous "Vietnam syndrome," these powerful elements within the administration (as well as the conservative pundits) spurned Mikhail Gorbachev as a wily seducer. Among the best positioned and most single-minded of the hawks were the figures who led the administration into the Iran-contra mess—as well as those who, after the scandal was exposed, excused the behavior of the administration and attacked the president's critics as either spineless or disloyal. After Iran-contra, however, Reagan rid his administration of its most hawkish voices and paid greater attention to more moderate figures, such as George Shultz, while building on his own convictions about the need to eliminate nuclear weapons and about the sincerity of Gorbachev and the reformers. Yet because Reagan always depicted the hawkish approach as a necessary prelude to the great reversals of 1987 and 1988, he never actually appeared to choose one approach over the other. He bequeathed both to his successors.

Finally, and most ominously, Reagan handed over a confused and troubling legacy about the presidency and respect for law and the U.S. Constitution. "If ever the constitutional democracy of the United States is overthrown, we now have a better idea of how this is likely to be done," wrote Theodore Draper, the widely respected political writer and scholar of the Iran-contra affair. Instead of plotting to overthrow a president, the cabal inside the government that pursued the administration's covert policies on Nicaragua and Iran tried to dispense with the constitutional rule of law with the help of a president. The exposure of these activities, and the subsequent investigations, cast some light on the nation's vulnerability to strategically placed officials who would usurp power in the name of a higher cause. This was not a matter of paranoid speculation about all-powerful conspiracies; descriptions of the plot came directly from the papers and sworn testimony of the plotters themselves. Yet because the main official investigations in 1987 ascribed the affair to lax management, or even to gross negligence, by the president, the full extent of the danger was either overlooked or belittled.

Reagan did clean house once evidence of the diversion to the contras came to light and the affair became a political disaster. Thereafter, surrounded by pragmatic conservatives instead of zealots, he conducted foreign policy in a very different way, and the immediate threat to the Constitution abated. But in salvaging his own political position, Reagan not only evaded personal responsibility, he silently (and sometimes not so silently) condoned most of the covert policies that had led to the constitutional confrontation. Although he fired Oliver North over the contra affair, he also went out of his way, later, to praise North as "a national hero." He regretted what the evidence (though not his heart) told him, that he had allowed the strategic sale of arms to Iran to turn into an exchange for American hostages—yet even though he assumed responsibility for all wrongdoing, he never accepted the blame. Nor did he ever express any sense of culpability, let alone regret, about the repeated efforts to deceive Congress, violate its manifest will, break various federal laws, and delude the American people—many of them undertaken with his direct knowledge, and all of them undertaken in pursuit of his explicit general instructions. What little Reagan did say, chiefly about the covert effort to aid the contras—including his statement to one group of journalists that "it was my idea in the first place"—conformed with the conclusions of the Republican minority report from the congressional investigating committee, that the true guilty party in the affair was Congress itself and that Reagan's actions "were constitutionally protected exercises of inherent Presidential powers."

The political and constitutional fallout—or lack thereof—was disturbing enough. In future years, both the spirit of the episode and some of the very individuals who had either plotted the affair or defended it would resurface at the highest levels of American government. But the Reagan administration left a larger legacy as well, about the subordination of law to politics. In its politicization of the judicial selection process, in its highly selective enforcement of civil rights laws, in its abandonment of the Environmental Protection Agency and the Department of Housing and Urban Development to incompetents and looters, the Reagan White House established a pattern of disregard for the law as anything other than an ideological or partisan tool. Laws that advanced the interests of the administration were passed and heeded; those that did not were ignored, undermined, or (if necessary) violated. The administration's sorry record of corruption, partisan favoritism, and influence peddling stemmed in part from the shabby venality that is inherent in human affairs. But it also stemmed from an arrogance born of the same ideological zealotry that propelled Iran-contra—the belief that, in a world eternally "at risk," the true believers must take matters into their own hands and execute. The rule of law, by those lights, would always be subordinated to, and as far as possible aligned with, the rule of politics.

Finally, though, dissolving the Reagan myth by pointing out his presidency's many failures, regressive policies, and dangerous legacies should not obscure his essential importance. As Edward Kennedy observed, Reagan was an effective president because he took ideas seriously—he was a leader who would never diminish what his vice president later called "the vision thing" as if it were, as one British writer commented, a topic "like any other on which a politician should have a position." Although passionate—at times too passionate—in fighting for what he believed in, Reagan was a leader who understood American politics, and who, with the egregious exception of Iran-contra, practiced the art of compromise shrewdly. If greatness in a president is measured in terms of affecting the temper of the times, whether you like it or not, Reagan stands second to none among the presidents of the second half of the twentieth century. American history is filled with presidents who tried to build and consolidate a conservative reaction to previous eras of reform, including Andrew Johnson, Rutherford B. Hayes, and Calvin Coolidge. None came close to matching Reagan in redefining the politics of his era and in reshaping the basic terms on which politics and government would be conducted long after he left office. Add in Reagan's remarkable turnabout in helping to end the cold war, as well as his success, albeit easily exaggerated, in uplifting the country after the disaster in Vietnam and the Carter years, and his achievement actually looks more substantial than the claims invented by the Reaganite mythmakers. On Inauguration Day, January 20, 1989, as he prepared to fly off to his retirement in California, Ronald Reagan made clear which of his numerous legacies loomed foremost in his mind: "The Cold War is over," he declared. But his impact on American politics and

American life far exceeded that signal accomplishment. Now the consummate loyalist George H. W. Bush was in charge, much to Reagan's satisfaction. "He was the one I would rather see there doing this than anyone else," Reagan told reporters during the long flight west. The age of Reagan continued.

10

REAGANISM AND REALISM

IF RONALD REAGAN'S LIFE involved repeated, dramatic self-transformations, George H. W. Bush's involved adaptation, political job-seeking, and dutiful service—making him a cipher in the minds of some political professionals and an effete pushover in the minds of others. There was a great deal of unfairness in this, as Bush, an authentic combat veteran, was more of an active, competitive outdoorsman than the aging actor-politician Reagan. But Bush's evolution from patrician Yankee to conservative Texan was never completed in the public eye. His flimsy image remained, especially to the Reaganites.

Bush had stayed tethered to the Northeast and his father's moderate Republicanism, symbolized by his family's seacoast estate in Kennebunkport, Maine. His political career after his failed run for the U.S. Senate in 1970 was centered in Washington, not Houston. His closest associations and attachments were in establishment political circles, especially in foreign policy, as reflected in his appointments as U.S. ambassador to the United Nations, director of the CIA, and U.S. envoy to China. During the Republican primaries of 1980, Reagan scored points by scorning Bush's membership in the Council on Foreign Relations and the Trilateral Commission—viewed by hard-right ideologues as two East Coast, internationalist bogeys. Bush, by now an expert hint-taker, swiftly resigned from both groups, for which he had always had the highest respect. Reagan gibed, "He just melts under pressure," before acquiescing in the political necessity of uniting the Republican Party and naming Bush to the ticket. According to Ed Rollins, Nancy Reagan, who like many of Reagan's advisers initially opposed selecting Bush, privately made fun of Bush's speaking style and called him "Whiny."

By the time Bush finally won the presidential nomination at the Republican convention eight years later, he had altered his public stance even more, attacking gun control and legalized abortion, and fervently supporting capital punishment. And yet, there he stood at the Superdome, rolling his New England vowels and promising a "kinder, gentler" nation as he accepted the prize he had sought for so long, Bush joined in his campaign's demagoguery, but left most of the dirty work—such as the ads featuring Willie Horton—to his political staff. Meanwhile, he kept his mind peaceful with daily jogs around his estate in Maine and at stopovers on the campaign trail, listening, on his Walkman, over and over, to a tape of a soothing AM-radio hit, Bobby McFerrin's "Don't Worry, Be Happy." If his assaults on the Democratic nominee Michael Dukakis revealed little about any larger political outlook or program, he was not about to fill in the blanks. Nor would he add much more in his inauguration address, a paean to generosity, family, tolerance, and bipartisanship.

Two years after his swearing in, Bush's approval ratings were nearly 90 percent—the highest figure recorded since presidential opinion polling began in the early 1940s, and far higher than any Ronald Reagan had attained. In repelling Iraq's invasion of Kuwait, Bush had overseen the most impressive U.S. military display since 1945—and, it seemed, wiped away any shame that remained from Reagan's mishaps in the Middle East. Enthusiasm for the conquering hero—no longer a "wimp," as *Newsweek* had labeled him in 1987—persuaded many highly touted Democratic contenders to pass up running against him in the election of 1992. "George Bush will not need to visit a flag factory during his re-election campaign," Maureen Dowd of the *New York Times* wrote. "In the heady aftermath of the Persian Gulf war, Republicans are wearing the flag like Caesar's purple mantle, and Democrats are desperately tugging at the hem." Republicans began thinking that they had a permanent lock on the presidency.

But it was not to be, for reasons that stemmed from widening divisions within the Republican Party, fundamental confusion within the Bush administration, and the public's perception that Bush was indifferent to the concerns of ordinary Americans. Bush's presidency succumbed to an alternating pattern of triumph abroad and political ruin at home, which Bush and his supporters detected too late and could not reverse. And as the Bush administration successively conquered and floundered, there were fresh stirrings among the dilapidated Democrats.

* * *

Bush's impressive résumé in diplomacy and intelligence work, and the continuing rush of world events, virtually guaranteed that his presidency would focus mainly on foreign policy. Accordingly, he took special care in appointing his close friends James Baker and Brent Scowcroft as, respectively, secretary of state and national security adviser. To head the Defense Department, he reached back for another veteran of Ford's White House, the former chief of staff Dick Cheney. Cheney was more conservative ideologically than the others, but he was then known chiefly as a cool and collected team player with an extraordinary command of bureaucratic detail and an aversion to the limelight.* The selection in August, at Cheney's insistence, of Reagan's national security adviser, Colin Powell (whom Bush had just promoted to four-star general), as chairman of the Joint Chiefs of Staff completed Bush's foreign policy team.

The group had a much more sober, realist cast, reminiscent of Henry Kissinger (Scowcroft was Kissinger's protégé), than Reagan's original cold war hawks—and it consisted of politically astute men, virtually untouched by any direct involvement in the Iran-contra affair. (Dick Cheney, as the senior Republican member of the select congressional committee, had been a principal defender of the Reagan administration's plotting in Iran-contra, but he had reached the conclusion that "No policy can be effective for long without the wholehearted support of the Congress and the American people.") At the same time, though, Bush's White House, with its Kissingerian realpolitik, was initially much more skeptical about the Soviet Union than the outgoing Reagan administration had become in 1987 and 1988— privately criticizing Reagan for utopianism in what Scowcroft called a hasty "willingness to declare the end to the cold war," just as Bush and the others had quietly bridled at Reagan's anti-Soviet hard line before 1985.

(The outstanding anti-Kissingerian, Dick Cheney, never warmed to the Soviets as Reagan had. His views thus converged with those of Baker,

---

* Cheney got the job only after the Senate refused to confirm Bush's first choice, the Texas conservative John Tower, the former senator who had headed the Tower Commission on Iran-contra. Tower, an unpopular figure with his former colleagues, faced a range of allegations including improper ties to defense contractors as well as compulsive drinking and womanizing. After Tower's defeat, Scowcroft strongly backed Cheney, whom he considered conservative but not dogmatic and who, as a well-liked congressman, would easily win confirmation by the Senate.

Scowcroft, and other realist moderates, but his perspective and, at times, his bluntness, also made him distinct. After his confirmation, while the administration was still finding its feet, Cheney told an interviewer that he believed Gorbachev would "ultimately fail"—a bit of rash public candor for which the ever-prudent White House reprimanded him.)

Bush and his team could not have foreseen the magnitude of what would happen during the administration's first year. In April, students and workers occupied Tiananmen Square in Beijing in an around-the-clock pro-democracy demonstration that the Chinese leadership swiftly denounced as counterrevolutionary. Gorbachev's arrival in the city for three days in mid-May, on a mission to heal old divisions between the two communist superpowers, caused the crowd in Tiananmen Square to swell into the hundreds of thousands. Astonishing scenes of the nonviolent uprising, broadcast live by satellite around the world, finally led the infuriated Chinese government to crack down. On June 4, it sent in armed troops and tanks with orders to clear the square. In the ensuing bloodbath, at least 3,000 protesters were killed and 10,000 were wounded.

Bush's response, in character, was carefully calibrated. Sickened by the massacre, he ordered a halt to Chinese-U.S. military relations and held up loans from the World Bank to the People's Republic of China. But he would do nothing to endanger Sino-American economic and political connections, which had been growing since Nixon's historic visit to China in 1972, and which he himself had advanced in the mid-1970s as Gerald Ford's plenipo-tentiary to Beijing. "While angry rhetoric might be temporarily satisfying to some," Bush later wrote, "I believed it would hurt our efforts in the long run." Going out of his way to explain his actions to the Chinese commu-nist leadership, the president dispatched Scowcroft and Assistant Secretary of State Lawrence Eagleburger on two trips to Beijing, while the White House resisted efforts by Congress to impose tougher sanctions.[*]

Working mainly through back channels, Bush finally prevailed on the Chinese government, in mid-1990, to relax its repression and begin releas-ing jailed dissidents. By his lights, slow and steady diplomacy had worked without threatening political stability. But to critics on both the left and the right, Bush's realist approach in this instance seemed callous. A little-known

---

[*] The second mission to Beijing, in December 1990, came back to sting the administration when the infant Cable News Network (CNN) broadcast a tape of Scowcroft delivering a dinner toast to Chinese leaders, recorded by the Chinese government, in which he alluded to "negative forces" in both countries that "seek to frustrate our cooperation."

Democratic member of Congress from California, Nancy Pelosi, helped lead the fight to impose sterner sanctions and to protect Chinese students in the United States, in order, she said, to send "a very clear message to the butchers of Beijing" in the name of "human rights and principles." The columnist A. M. Rosenthal of the *New York Times* complained, "At a moment of passion in the story of democracy," the president "has been pale and thin." Even those who took a more charitable view agreed that Bush's deliberate actions affirmed his basic aversion to sudden changes in world politics.

Extraordinary upheavals in Europe, hastened by the events at Tiananmen Square, tested the limits of Bush's realism more severely. In August, the president of Poland, Wojciech Jaruzelski, asked an activist in Solidarity, Tadeusz Mazowiecki, to form a new government—the country's first non-communist government in forty years. On November 9, 1989, after weeks of civil disturbances and political unrest, East Germans began pulling and hammering down the Berlin Wall. Joyous scenes unfolded amid the rubble of what had long been an emblem of Soviet tyranny. During the next two months, democratic revolutions tore across eastern and central Europe—and the Kremlin did nothing to stop them.

Bush's initial responses were positive but less than ecstatic, in part out of a concern about saying anything that might upset the situation by rubbing salt into the Kremlin's wounds. "I don't think any single event is the end of what you might call the Iron Curtain, but clearly this is a long way from the harshest Iron Curtain days—a long way from that," he told reporters as the Berlin Wall crumbled. Still, even diehard skeptics such as Cheney could no longer doubt that great changes were overtaking the Soviet Union. At a mini-summit aboard a ship near Malta in early December, Bush and Gorbachev sized each other up and held a joint press conference that in effect declared the end of the cold war. "Bush is formulating his positions slowly, thoughtfully," Gorbachev reported back to the leaders of the nearly moribund Warsaw Pact.

In retrospect, these meetings would look like a major event, in which Bush and Gorbachev began building a strong personal and diplomatic connection of their own. Meanwhile, American policy makers were engaged chiefly in cleaning up one of their own messes, stemming from old cold war issues in Central America.

General Manuel Antonio Noriega of Panama had been on the payroll of the CIA and the Defense Department for nearly two decades—including the period when George Bush was the director of the CIA. After President Omar Torrijos died in a plane crash in 1981 (the result, some people claimed, of a plot by Noriega), Noriega amassed political power as head of the military command, and by 1983 he was Panama's de facto ruler. Through the mid-1980s, Noriega gave logistical support to the pro-American forces fighting in El Salvador and Nicaragua. But he was also becoming an embarrassment, implicated directly in rigged elections, the brutal assassination of one of his political adversaries, and extensive drug trafficking and money laundering in connection with a notorious drug cartel in Medellín, Colombia. Because sovereignty over the Panama Canal would be transferred to Panama in 2000, Noriega's ouster was becoming imperative.

Shortly after the summit with Gorbachev in Washington late in 1987, the Reagan administration tried and failed to persuade Noriega to step down; federal grand juries in Florida then indicted Noriega on charges of smuggling drugs. Accustomed to having the Americans turn a blind eye to his thuggery, Noriega clamped down more on his political opponents, rigged another election, and harassed U.S. citizens and businesses in Panama. Mounting economic pressure from Reagan's White House made Noriega even more dependent on the drug trade. And when an attempted coup failed in October 1989, the new Bush administration came under a cross fire of criticism from Congress, with some members criticizing the White House for doing too little to help the coup and others expressing concern that it had done too much. The conservative columnist George Will, who was no friend of Bush's, accused him of conducting an "unserious presidency."

Finally, in December, assaults on American servicemen by Panamanian troops gave Bush the casus belli he needed for an invasion. In the largest U.S. military operation since the Vietnam War, nearly 28,000 American troops and 300 American aircraft (including some of the most advanced, high-tech fighter jets) overwhelmed the Panamanian defense forces. After a weeklong standoff at the Vatican embassy, Noriega surrendered and was extradited to the United States. Tried for and convicted of drug smuggling, he was sentenced in 1992 to a forty-year prison term. Even Will saluted the invasion as a prime example of the "good neighbor policy" in action, although he still found Bush's public justifications "dry" and "understated"—symptomatic of the conservatives' continuing refusal to embrace the president.

Dwarfing in scope the Reagan administration's attack on Grenada, the invasion of Panama removed any doubts about Bush's willingness to unleash U.S. military power. Secretary of State Baker later claimed that the operation contributed to changing "the mindset of the American people about the use of force in the post-Vietnam era." Yet the invasion, called Operation Just Cause, was important chiefly as the nation's first post–cold war military intervention. Reagan's attack on Grenada was still part of the long struggle against communism, justified as necessary in order to rescue American medical students amid internal strife between far leftist factions. Operation Just Cause, however, toppled someone who was a former covert asset of the CIA and an anticommunist ally but who had become repulsive, with the stated purpose of spreading democracy but no mention of communism whatsoever. By fully exploiting new high-technology weaponry, thereby minimizing American casualties, the invasion of Panama also offered lessons for a new post–cold war military strategy, favoring highly mobile, rapid-deployment forces over conventional forces intended for lengthy campaigns.*

Settling on a more comprehensive post–cold war geopolitical policy proved more complicated. After the bloody overthrow of Romania's communist leader Nicolae Ceausescu on December 22, 1989, all of the satellite communist governments in the Warsaw Pact had been toppled. Liberal Democrats in Congress began speaking of an imminent "peace dividend," with funds cut from defense spending to be shifted to domestic spending. Supply-side Republicans contemplated further tax cuts; centrists in both parties advocated applying the dividend to reduce the deficit. The Pentagon, after initially discouraging all such talk, commissioned a full reassessment of national military strategy (overseen by Cheney's deputy, Paul Wolfowitz, who had most recently been Reagan's ambassador to the Indonesian dictatorship of General Sukarno). The report, released in full by President Bush in August 1990, recognized that the changes in eastern and central Europe were permanent, and called for a reduction by 25 percent of America's active-duty military force.

Yet both Bush and Cheney warned against any slackening of the nation's military resolve. Bush reminded everyone that the Soviets remained militarily formidable—and in any event, he went on to say, America remained at risk from other enemies: "Terrorism, hostage-taking, renegade regimes and unpredictable rulers, new sources of instability—all require a strong

---

* A total of twenty-three American troops were killed during the invasion—60 percent of the number killed in the operations connected to the far smaller *Mayaguez* incident in 1975.

and an engaged America." Cheney initially warned that the Soviet Union might become even more of a threat if it used its new connections with the West to obtained advanced military technology. In early 1991, he shifted his rationale, now suggesting that, instead of being too strong, the Soviet Union might implode and leave its former clients free to pursue whatever designs they pleased. The chairman of the Joint Chiefs of Staff, Colin Powell, made the general observation that even without the threat represented by the Soviet Union, the United States had to sustain a basic unilateral force to offset any unforeseen threats. In candid moments, Powell conceded that the actual threats were few. ("I'm running out of demons. I'm running out of villains," he half-joked in an interview that appeared in the spring of 1991. "I'm down to Castro and Kim Il Sung.") But mainly because of pressure from the White House, the peace dividend did not materialize. In 1989 and 1990, relative levels of defense and domestic discretionary spending remained stable while federal deficits continued to burgeon.

The Soviet Union, meanwhile, was too absorbed with its own difficulties to criticize the United States publicly over Panama, defense spending, or anything else. Since 1989, the Soviet Baltic states of Lithuania, Estonia, and Latvia had been in continual rebellion, met by Soviet force; by August 1989, all three had declared their independence. Inside Russia, Gorbachev felt pressure from his left for more rapid reform, led by a member of the Soviet parliament, Boris Yeltsin. The fall of the Warsaw Pact nations, especially East Germany, caused Gorbachev additional headaches by arousing the ire of surviving hard-liners in the Kremlin. Germany's future posed particularly thorny problems. Although the Germans themselves strongly favored the reunification of the two Germanys under a single government, Britain, as well as the Soviet Union, was unhappy at the prospect of a united German economic and political powerhouse in the heart of Europe.

The Bush administration displayed little enthusiasm for the secessionist stirrings in the Baltic (which it deemed potentially destabilizing) and none at all for Yeltsin's challenge to Gorbachev. But the White House faced renewed pressure from Congress to take a more active role after Gorbachev imposed an economic embargo on Lithuania in April; and within the administration, there were disagreements about how to handle the momentous issue of German reunification. Scowcroft shared the concerns of the British prime minister, Margaret Thatcher, about a resurgent unified Germany, but Secretary of State James Baker persuaded Bush to follow a careful, multilateral course toward reunification. Baker's plan, the "Two Plus Four Negotiations," called for the two German states to negotiate along with the four nations that had been victors in World War II (France, Great Britain, the Soviet Union, and the United States), with a prior understanding that the eventual settlement would approve reunification. Making strong use of personal, one-on-one diplomacy (on and off the telephone), his strongest suit, Bush cajoled Thatcher and Gorbachev through the early spring of 1990.

Gaining the agreement of the Soviet Union with regard to Germany was, obviously, crucial—but, given Gorbachev's increasingly tenuous political situation, it was difficult to obtain. In May, Bush and Gorbachev met at a major summit in Washington for which the "little summit" in Malta had been a preliminary. Gorbachev was almost desperate to sign a comprehensive trade pact with the Americans, including the granting of most-favored-nation trading status, and he succeeded—but only in exchange for a secret agreement to lift the embargo against Lithuania. Gorbachev appeared to hold fast on Germany, saying that, after its immense sacrifices in World War II, the Soviet Union had a "moral right" to specific security guarantees in the face of any reunited Germany. But he returned to Moscow to announce that he had dropped all objections to reunification, and would allow all West German troops to remain in NATO without a corresponding role for East German troops in the Warsaw Pact. In late August, the "Two Plus Four" negotiators reached an agreement to recognize a reunified Germany on October 3, with German national elections to follow two months later.

In his cautious way, Bush had established rapport with Gorbachev—and with Germany's swift and relatively untroubled reunification, he secured what would prove to be the greatest diplomatic feat of his presidency. There were, to be sure, political costs on both sides. American conservatives, already angry at Bush over China, were enraged at what they called his dithering over the Baltic republics. Gorbachev, for his part, had to relax the pressure on Lithuania, infuriating his own generals. But Gorbachev gained his trade agreement, crucial to his domestic reforms—and Bush had moved forward on creating a post–cold war world without damaging his own good relations with Gorbachev. One benefit of Bush's developing modus vivendi with Gorbachev after Malta had been the refusal of the Soviet Union to join in a clamor of international condemnation that followed Bush's invasion of Panama. The renewed détente would pay larger dividends after August 2, 1990, when Iraq suddenly invaded its oil-rich neighbor, Kuwait.

* * *

Iraq had suffered severely from its eight-year war with Iran. Quite apart from losing upwards of 250,000 soldiers killed, the country had expended about $250 billion and incurred a foreign debt of about $80 billion, at a time when the price of oil, the source of virtually all Iraq's revenue, was falling. The rise of nationalist movements within the Soviet movement also irked Saddam Hussein, who used chemical weapons against his own most troublesome ethnic minority, the Kurds. Although Saddam gave private assurances that he would do nothing, his public anti-Israel rhetoric became more inflammatory. Above all, he looked southward to Kuwait, whose existence as an independent state the Iraqis only grudgingly accepted. Other Arab leaders were perturbed when Kuwait, in defiance of the other OPEC nations, refused to cut back production of oil in order to raise prices, but Saddam was particularly incensed, calling it nothing less than "a kind of war against Iraq." The Iraqis further accused Kuwait of using "slant" drilling techniques to siphon oil that actually lay inside Iraq's borders. There was thus disquiet in the West in late July 1990, when three heavily armed divisions of the elite Iraqi Republican Guard began massing along Iraq's border with Kuwait. Although few observers expected that the Iraqis would actually invade, there was a chance that Saddam's forces might make a lightning strike against Kuwait's oil fields and then withdraw.

Saddam not only disproved the doubters: he marched to the capital, Kuwait City, plundered it, and proclaimed that Kuwait was now "the 19th Province—an eternal part of Iraq." He also sent detachments of his invasion force farther south to secure Kuwait's border with Saudi Arabia against counterattack—a move that, for a time, convinced the CIA and many American policy makers that he aimed to seize Saudi assets as well. But even with command of Kuwait alone, Saddam now controlled 21 percent of the world's oil supply. As far as the West was concerned, this was a naked act of aggression by an unstable dictator—"totally unacceptable . . . a total violation of international law," Prime Minister Thatcher declared. After Bush briefly hesitated, and not for the last time—"This [is] no time to go wobbly," Thatcher admonished him at one point—he arranged for the United Kingdom, France, West Germany, Japan, and six other nations to join the United States in freezing Iraqi assets, and applied pressure on the UN to halt Iraqi oil shipments.

More startlingly, and of crucial importance, the Kremlin, Saddam's long-

time ally, joined in the disavowals, despite the objections of pro-Iraq hard-liners in the Soviet military. The day after the invasion, Secretary of State James
Baker and Foreign Minister Eduard Shevardnadze of the Soviet Union held
a joint press conference outside Moscow in which the Soviet Union officially
joined the United States in condemning "the brutal and illegal invasion of
Kuwait" and in calling for an international embargo of all arms supplies
to Iraq. And with the Soviets' support, the United Nations passed two resolutions, the first condemning the invasion, and the second—Resolution
661—calling for a complete embargo on trade with Iraq and authorizing
nonmilitary measures to enforce the sanctions. By the end of August, three
more UN resolutions stiffened the resistence, including approval of forceful
measures to stop Iraqi-flagged vessels from exporting oil.

With his political flank covered by the United Nations, Bush focused
on protecting Saudi Arabia. Even though the Saudis, who controlled 17
percent of the world's oil, had been America's strongest ally in the region
since the fall of the shah of Iran in 1979, King Fahd had at least two reasons to be skeptical of American will: Carter's failure to sustain the shah,
and Reagan's disaster in Lebanon. The Saudis also worried about repercussions in the Arab world if they allowed Western troops on sacred Islamic soil. But for reasons that remain not wholly clear, possibly including
Thatcher's spine-stiffening, Bush quickly upped the ante, declaring that he
intended not simply to defend the Saudis from the Iraqis' aggression but to
do so by evicting the Iraqis from Kuwait. After receiving immediate assent
from Fahd, Bush announced he was sending 230,000 troops, including the
Eighty-Second Airborne Division and two squadrons of F-15 fighters, directly to Saudi Arabia.

By the end of August, 80,000 combat troops from the coalition initiated by the United States had arrived in the country, in what was called
Operation Desert Shield.* Saddam responded by twice reinforcing his own
army, so that he had, reportedly, ground forces composed of as many as
350,000 men. In a bid for Arab support, Saddam also promised to leave

---

* The armed coalition eventually consisted of thirty-five countries: Afghanistan, Argentina,
Australia, Bahrain, Bangladesh, Canada, Czechoslovakia, Denmark, Egypt, France, Ger-
many, Greece, Hungary, Honduras, Italy, Kuwait, Morocco, the Netherlands, New Zealand,
Niger, Norway, Oman, Pakistan, Poland, Portugal, Qatar, Saudi Arabia, Senegal, South
Korea, Spain, Syria, Turkey, the United Arab Emirates, the United Kingdom, and the United
States. Of the coalition's armed force, which at its height included 700,000 troops, 76 percent
were Americans.

Kuwait if the Israelis withdrew from the occupied territories in Palestine. But Saddam had finally worn out the patience of Arab governments, and on August 10, Syria and Egypt joined the coalition against Iraq. President Hosni Mubarak of Egypt, in an undisguised repudiation of Saddam's attempt to turn the standoff into an anti-Zionist campaign, called him "the new Hitler, since he has become a danger to the region, to the Arabs, and to the world."

Some of the planners at the White House, including Colin Powell, have since expressed doubt that Bush ever seriously believed the UN sanctions alone would force Saddam's hand. Yet Bush and his advisers were in a bind. By October, the UN sanctions appeared to have isolated Iraq, as no one would buy its oil; and increased production by Saudi Arabia, Venezuela, the United Arab Emirates, and Nigeria had made up for the loss of supplies from Kuwait. On the other hand, some experts predicted that it would take two years or more for the sanctions to dislodge Iraq from Kuwait. The long-term economic effects, on both the United States and the Arab nations, could be damaging. And it would not have been to Bush's political advantage to enter the election season of 1992 with the situation in Iraq unresolved.

Bush's closest advisers were divided about what to do. Baker and Powell counseled giving the sanctions and diplomacy more time to work, but Scowcroft, Cheney, and the deputy national security adviser, Robert Gates, favored removing Saddam from Kuwait by force. Bush himself, who had come of age during World War II, tended to perceive events through the prism of the 1930s and 1940s, and he echoed Mubarak's rhetoric describing Saddam as a new Hitler—"the rapist of Kuwait," he told one interviewer. He increased the American force in Saudi Arabia to 500,000. But the combination of heated rhetoric and military rumblings stirred misgivings among the American public. Antiwar protests, in the United States and around the world, were set off by Baker's comments about the economic stakes in Kuwait, and the protesters denounced Desert Shield as a cover for protecting American oil profits. On the right, a resurgent isolationism, spearheaded by Patrick Buchanan (the former hard-right aide to Nixon and Reagan, now a columnist and television talk-show host), attacked the operation as a quagmire in the making, and said that although Saddam Hussein menaced his neighbors, "he is no threat to us." Combined with conservatives' reactions to Bush's decision earlier in the year to raise taxes, balkiness over the Middle East caused the president's popularity rating to fall from 75 percent in August to 50 percent in early November.

Saddam Hussein, however, continued playing into Bush's hands. By taking hostage thousands of Western civilians (including 3,000 Americans) in Kuwait, and calling them "human shields," he inflamed pro-war feeling. In late September, the regime in Baghdad called on Iraqis to prepare for the "mother of all battles." Two months later, the United Nations passed a new resolution supporting all necessary means to expel Saddam if he did not withdraw from Kuwait by January 15, 1991. But Baker, cognizant of growing antiwar opinion in the United States, persuaded Bush to send him on one last good-faith mission to meet directly with the Iraqis and at least to appear to be dealing in good faith. In what quickly degenerated into a testy confrontation with Iraq's foreign minister, Tariq Aziz, in Geneva on January 5, Baker warned the Iraqis that they faced a far more lethal force now than they had ever faced in their war with Iran. "We accept war," Aziz replied.

Baker's course proved highly effective in moving American public opinion—and, more immediately important, moving opinion on Capitol Hill. Cheney, the White House counsel C. Boyden Gray, and Bush himself all agreed that under international law, the administration was on strong ground in deploying troops without congressional approval. Cheney, in particular, did not want to bring a war resolution to Congress now, lest it go down to defeat. But Bush overruled him, insisting that he did not want to seem like an impulsive American; instead, he hoped to gain enough support from the Democrats to present a united front to the country and the world—and to cover his political flank in case the operation failed. The two-day debate in both the House and Senate was resolute but civil, and it highlighted the persisting divisions among Democrats, as well as between the parties, over the deployment of U.S. forces abroad. The majority in the House against an antiwar resolution was solid, 250 to 183; but in the Senate, only the defection of nine Democrats, including Albert Gore Jr. of Tennessee, enabled the president's side to prevail by fifty-two to forty-seven. When it was over, Bush made clear that his mind was already made up and that he would have ordered his forces into combat even without a resolution of support from Congress. Regarding the Constitution, the president conceded nothing to those in Congress who insisted that the crisis fell under the provisions of the War Powers Act—but political prudence had demanded that he watch Congress go through with a vote anyway.

Before daybreak in Iraq on January 17, the first sorties of American helicopters destroyed important Iraqi radar systems. These actions were followed quickly by a wave of attacks on sites in Baghdad by F117A Stealth bombers and F-15C fighters. After nearly six weeks of constant bombardment, the coalition opened its ground attack on February 24, ousting the Iraqis from Kuwait City with astonishing ease and then smashing the chief defensive positions of the retreating Republican Guard. Exactly 100 hours after it had begun, the ground war ended in a cease-fire. Three days later, the American commander, General Norman Schwarzkopf, met with the Iraqi military leadership at Safwan, just north of the Kuwaiti border, and dictated the terms of peace.

The military outcome was never seriously in doubt. The Iraqi forces—much less formidable than had at first been feared, burdened with a rigid and incompetent command, and reliant on obsolete Soviet-made weaponry—were no match for the American-led coalition with its state-of-the-art military technology. By keeping the Israelis out of the conflict—despite Iraq's firing of forty relatively crude Scud missiles into Israel in a futile attempt at provocation—Bush achieved another diplomatic victory. Despite repeated targeting errors by the Americans and other mishaps (some not disclosed until later), the hundreds of spectacular air assaults—with pictures once again quickly televised around the world—seemed to mark the birth of an entirely new type of computerized warfare of which the United States was the undoubted master. The American military carefully hid evidence of deaths of Iraqi civilians and blocked depictions of American casualties by tightly constricting press coverage. Yet if the Persian Gulf War was far from antiseptic, the cost in American losses—148 killed in action and 458 wounded, low figures even when measured against the invasion of Panama—contributed to the mystique of technological warfare.

The only questions raised in this triumphal atmosphere concerned the decision by Bush and the military leaders to break off the fighting when they did, earlier than originally planned, instead of completely destroying Saddam's forces—or, perhaps, following up by sending the coalition all the way to Baghdad to remove Saddam from power. Continued attacks, as Iraqi forces retreated toward Basra along what became known as the "highway of death," seemed to the American leadership cruel and unnecessary once the Iraqis had returned inside their own borders and offered little serious resistance. Although some White House officials thought the terms Schwarzkopf dictated in Safwan were too lenient—especially in permitting Saddam the right to continued use of military helicopters because of the heavy damage inflicted on Iraq's roads and bridges—few foresaw exactly the dangerous results that followed. And the removal of Saddam had

simply never been a stated goal for Bush or the United Nations. To locate
and capture Saddam (an operation that had proved trying in the much simpler case of Manuel Noriega) would have required prolonged street fighting
in Baghdad, with inevitable heavy casualties for the coalition. And although
it has been reported that Bush privately hoped the Iraqis themselves might
overthrow the dictator in "some kind of Ceaucescu scenario," he was certain
that a conquest led by the United States would leave the Persian Gulf region
less stable than before, and tempt Iran and Syria to exploit the situation.

Sensible on its own terms, American policy did, if inadvertently, lead
to future disasters. Sensing that Saddam had been irreparably weakened,
Iraq's Shiite Muslim minority mounted a revolt in March, and the Kurds
in the north also revolted. Bush played an unwitting role in fomenting the
Kurdish uprising when he said after the coalition's victory that "the Iraqi
military and the Iraqi people should take matters into their own hands, to
force Saddam Hussein, the dictator, to step aside, and to comply with the
United Nations resolutions and then rejoin the family of peace-loving nations." American policy makers, though, had no intention of aiding the uprisings with U.S. troops or matériel; indeed, General Powell delivered to his
colleagues a specific and tightly reasoned military case against intervention
on behalf of revolts he believed were doomed. The combination of mixed
signals from Washington and wishful thinking on the rebels' part led to
catastrophe, as Saddam (using the helicopters Schwarzkopf had permitted
him to retain) brutally suppressed both uprisings. Forced to flee to refugee
camps in Iran and Turkey, the Kurds suffered severe hardships, but their
pleas for aid from the West were ignored.

More fateful, in the long run, was the decision to keep several thousand American troops stationed in Saudi Arabia, to help implement the
various economic and military sanctions now to be imposed on Iraq. Questionable in some minds even during the buildup to the Gulf War, the continued American presence around such Muslim holy sites as Mecca and
Medina seemed a pointless provocation to extremist Muslim elements once
the fighting had stopped. Many years later, Paul Wolfowitz, after returning to the Pentagon in the second Bush administration as deputy secretary
of defense, would concede that resentment over the United States' military
presence in Saudi Arabia became a "principal recruiting device" for anti-
American Muslim terrorists. The terrorists included the young renegade
and former mujahideen leader in Afghanistan, Osama bin Laden, who in
1990 had offered the Saudis some 12,000 fighters from his own new organi-

zation, Al Qaeda, to thwart the Iraqi invasion, but who was rebuffed by an unfriendly Saudi government and then departed for the Sudan in 1991.

There were some misgivings among the public in the United States after the war, less about the Kurds and Shiites, and still less about the little-known terrorist groups, than about Saddam Hussein's remaining an active presence in Persian Gulf politics, with one-third of his army still intact. But the doubts were stilled by an outburst of ardent patriotism that welcomed the troops home in early June. General Schwarzkopf became an instant celebrity, the greatest American military hero since Dwight Eisenhower. There was talk that Colin Powell or Dick Cheney or both would one day be elected president. As for the incumbent, his popularity ratings were now in the stratosphere, and he had the satisfaction of vindicating both his own honor and the country's, along with a vision of creating what he described, a bit vaguely, as a "new world order" to supplant the cold war—one "where the United Nations, freed from cold war stalemate, is poised to fulfill the historic vision of its founders," and "in which freedom and respect for human rights find a home among all nations." Not incidentally, the victory in the Persian Gulf also gave Bush the opportunity to wipe away some of the controversies that had arisen on the domestic front before 1991—and to turn his attention to a long-predicted economic recession that had begun to stifle the American economy even as Saddam Hussein ordered his doomed invasion.

Months before Bush's inauguration, it was clear that fiscal matters, and the growing federal deficits, would dominate the administration's handling of domestic issues. With the Democrats still in charge of both the House and the Senate—the Republicans actually had a net loss of two House seats without gaining in the Senate in 1988, unusual for a party winning the White House—Bush would be too busy vetoing Democratic spending pro-posals to offer any ambitious proposals of his own. (Bush ended up vetoing forty-four bills, of which Congress overrode only one, thanks mainly to di-visions among Democrats on Capitol Hill and partisan solidity among the Republicans.) The president felt constrained by his campaign pledge not to raise taxes, even though the General Accounting Office, only three weeks after the election, stated publicly that any credible effort to lower the deficit would require new tax revenues. Early in 1989, Bush sounded like a born-again supply-sider, avoiding any public mention of increased taxes while calling for a 50 percent cut in the capital gains tax that would bring it down to 15 percent.

Bush did select two areas for special attention: education and curtailing the use of illegal drugs. Shortly after taking office, he proposed a new $500 million program to reward what he called "merit schools," the best-performing schools in the nation, as well as for awards to superior individual teachers and science students. He also endorsed the concept of magnet schools as a way to expand parents' choices. Yet relative to what Bush's own secretary of education, Lauro Cavazos, called a crisis in U.S. education—in which test scores were falling and one in three American students failed to complete high school—the proposal seemed a pittance. Bush's plan also displeased movement conservatives, who wanted to see more forceful action in support of school choice, so-called values education, and instilling discipline. Bush tried to sustain his pro-education efforts by convening a rare summit of the nation's governors at Charlottesville, Virginia, in September to discuss education policy. Bush came away believing that the meeting had been a great success, and was particularly impressed by the young governor of Arkansas, the Democrat Bill Clinton; but the summit offered no specific recommendations.

Politics and budgetary concerns hampered the White House's education initiatives over the next two years. Late in 1989, Cavazos was forced to resign, following the harsh public reaction to a ruling by the Department of Education that scholarships granted only to minorities were an illegal form of reverse discrimination. Bush replaced Cavazos with a former governor of Tennessee, Lamar Alexander, who had been an active educational reformer—but the White House stuck by the decision to eliminate minority scholarships. Thereafter, Alexander formulated the administration's "America 2000" program, which called for voluntary national testing to raise standards, widened school choice with incentive grants, and proposed the construction of more than 500 new schools that would "break the mold of existing school design." But under Alexander's plan, even with up to $780 million allocated for encouragement, the major burden for funding and implementing the program would fall on the participating localities. Lacking sufficient federal funds except to cover enticements and one-time start-up costs, the White House in effect turned Bush's pet education reform into one of his thousand points of light. Alexander argued, unconvincingly, that he was conducting a grassroots campaign to improve schooling from the bottom up. Critics regarded the entire program as little more than an underfunded public relations gimmick.

Bush's war on drugs instantly gained attention and credibility when the president appointed the high-profile neoconservative William Bennett, who had been Reagan's secretary of education, as director of Office of the National Drug Control Policy—the nation's "drug czar," as he was commonly called. An outspoken, impatient, ambitious man, Bennett fought hard to beef up funding for policing and jail construction, find alternative sentencing programs (which he called "boot camps") for nonviolent drug offenders, and crack down on the smuggling of drugs into the country. Bush agreed with Bennett's punitive emphasis on enforcement and interdiction over treatment programs for drug abusers, claiming that the federal government lacked the funds to do both. In January 1990, the president asked Congress for a 50 percent increase in funds available to the military to halt the influx of drugs.

Yet with drugs, as with education, the White House seemed to be fighting a losing battle—at times embarrassingly so. In his first televised public address on drugs, in September 1989, Bush held up a small plastic bag of crack cocaine that he emphasized had been purchased undercover in Lafayette Park—directly across the street, shockingly, from the White House. Yet while Bush told the literal truth, the news quickly surfaced that men from the Drug Enforcement Agency had had to lure a teenage drug dealer to the park from another part of Washington—making it seem as if in selling the drug program to the public, the White House was engaged in criminal entrapment as well as in hype.

Thereafter, Bennett, as the "drug czar," complained loudly that the administration was failing to commit sufficient resources to triumph over the drug traffickers. Suspicion grew inside the White House that the media-hungry Bennett was using his post as a means to challenge Bush from the right in 1992. Finally, Bennett left the administration late in 1990 and was replaced by a former governor of Florida, Bob Martinez. Soon thereafter, Bush announced a new national drug program that increased federal spending for health incentives. But the increase did not appear in the White House's final budget proposal—and the nation seemed no closer to solving its drug problem than it had when Bush took office.

Bush would be able to claim substantive victories in two other areas. The Civil Rights Act of 1964 had not explicitly covered mentally or physically disabled Americans—a population numbering more than 40 million who faced widespread discrimination. Beginning in the mid-1980s, advocates for the handicapped began agitating for an Americans with Disabilities Act, and by the time Bush became president, a comprehensive bill had been proposed in Congress and was enacted. Although Bush does not deserve the credit sometimes given to him for creating the law, he did support it strongly (even mentioning the disabled in his inauguration address). Despite opposition from businesses who would have to cover the costs of adding new facilities for the disabled, Bush instructed the Department of Health and Human Services to make the bill a top priority, and he signed it into law in July 1990.

Bush the outdoorsman also cared about the environment, and he set about reversing the sorry record of the Reagan administration on protecting it. His efforts were given added urgency in March 1989, when an oil tanker, the *Exxon Valdez*, ran aground in Prince William Sound in Alaska, spilling 10 million gallons of oil that spread over thousands of square miles of ocean and spoiled 800 miles of shoreline. Environmental groups criticized the administration for moving too slowly, but Bush's secretary of transportation, Samuel Skinner, swiftly took charge of the situation, helped secure criminal indictments against Exxon for its contributions to the disaster, and by mid-September announced that the cleanup effort was complete.

With the added impetus of the *Exxon Valdez* spill, Bush endeavored to break what had become a long congressional impasse over updating and expanding the Clean Air Act of 1970. In the House, the powerful Democratic chairman of the Commerce Committee, John Dingell of Michigan, fought any further restrictions on toxic gas emissions from automobiles as an undue burden on ailing American automakers; and in the Senate, the Democrat Robert Byrd of West Virginia did likewise on behalf of his state's producers of bituminous coal. With the crucial aid of Majority Leader George Mitchell of Maine in the Senate and the moderate Republican Sherwood Boehlert of New York in the House, the administration managed to fashion a compromise bill that Bush signed in October 1990. With provisions covering issues such as controlling acid rain, reducing tailpipe emissions, and empowering the Environmental Protection Agency to make the first small efforts to combat the depletion of the earth's ozone layer, the Clean Air Act of 1990 was a major piece of legislation, the most auspicious domestic policy victory by the Bush White House. But it would be a rare domestic triumph, chiefly because of the challenges posed by the enormous deficits and the deregulation disasters of the Reagan years.

In 1989, the federal debt was $2.8 trillion, triple the size of the debt at the end of 1980. Debt service alone cost the government $200 billion a year.

Bush's early proposals to cut increases to federal spending to the rate of inflation, with the expectation that the deficit would shrink when economic growth began outpacing inflation, impressed most observers as wishful thinking at best, cynical at worst—"déjà voodoo" in the words of one editorialist, reminding the public of Bush's gibe during the Republican primary campaign of 1980 about Reagan's "voodoo economics." Bush managed to get his director of the Office of Management and Budget (OMB), Richard Darman (James Baker's capable deputy through the Reagan administration), as well Representative Dan Rostenkowski of Illinois, chairman of the House Ways and Means Committee, to hold off on any proposed tax increase for the first year of his presidency. But political pressure for a change of course was mounting—especially after the extent of the damage from the savings and loan (S&L) disaster of the Reagan years became fully apparent.

Bush had special liabilities in the S&L scandal, beyond his being part of the administration that let it happen. One of his sons, Jeb, had defaulted on a $4.56 million loan from a Florida thrift, leaving the taxpayers to cover more than $4 million in costs. Another son, Neil, had become a salaried director of the Silverado Savings and Loan in Denver in 1985, and approved more than $150 million in questionable loans to a pair of business associates, one of whom used part of the proceeds to buy Bush's failing oil business, JNB Exploration. When Silverado failed in 1988, the collapse cost taxpayers more than $1 billion. The president tried to finesse the larger problem with proposals for small fees on S&L deposits, and then for a bailout bond issue, the costs to be shouldered chiefly by the banks. But after these plans got nowhere, the administration was forced to admit that the overall cost would be much higher than expected; by the end of the summer, private projections of the cost for a federal bailout of the S&L system approached $200 billion. In August 1989, faced with a mind-boggling catastrophe, Congress approved legislation that established a large layer of new regulatory agencies while paying off the S&L losses directly from the Treasury. The law increased the federal deficit by $50 billion over the ensuing three years.

As Bush ended his first year in the White House, an economic recession seemed inevitable, especially as the new chairman of the Federal Reserve, Alan Greenspan (appointed by Reagan in 1987), raised interest rates in response to gradually rising inflation. Worse, Bush now faced the harsh realities of the Gramm-Rudman-Hollings Act, signed by President Reagan in 1981. The law stipulated that if Congress and the White House could not agree on a budget that adhered to reduction targets intended to produce a balanced budget by 1993, an automatic sequestering of funds would occur on October 1, 1990, requiring a shutdown of various government services. Democrats, sensing that, at long last, Reaganomics might be hoist with its own petard, and envisaging political gains in the upcoming midterm elections, refused to meet with the White House over the budget for 1991 until Bush publicly offered a concrete proposal. Wall Street, in turn, reacted to the uncertain climate with predictable panic. On October 13, the Dow Jones industrial average fell 190 points, and although it quickly regained half its value on the next day of trading, it then fell another thirty points.

Bush submitted his budget at the end of January 1990, sticking to the Gramm-Rudman-Hollings requirement by lowering the annual deficit to $64 billion while also leaving Social Security untouched, lowering the capital gains tax, and reducing defense spending only marginally, by 2.6 percent. But the proposal also included one of the tools that Darman, as director of the OMB, favored: a $14 billion increase in "users' fees," which, although not technically a raise in taxes, clearly signaled Bush's willingness to give way on his "read my lips" pledge, his most prominent promise during the campaign of 1988. After several months of negotiations with congressional leaders, Bush made the point explicitly, announcing that "both the size of the deficit problem and the need for a package that can be enacted" required "tax revenue increases."

The political reaction was immediate and intense. Although the Democratic leaders stuck to the high road and refrained from gloating, the rank and file could take comfort in knowing that Bush had conceded the most vital point of all. Conservative Republicans, overlooking the tax increases of the 1980s, furiously condemned Bush for having abandoned Reagan's one true way. Some of those who sounded most outraged—including a brash, up-and-coming Georgian, Newt Gingrich, who had succeeded Dick Cheney as the House minority whip—were actually well aware that new taxes were unavoidable at some point. (Gingrich did essay a semantic defense of the president, but it was lame: "He very explicitly didn't say, 'Raise taxes.' He said, 'Seek new revenues.'") The political timing, though, was abysmal: the announcement came before Bush could point to a finished compromise budget and claim a partial victory. Bush's campaign promise not to raise taxes had also been a firm political pledge to adhere to the Reagan legacy. Now right-wing Republicans (including Pat Buchanan as well as, soon enough, Newt Gingrich) called Bush's pursuit of a bipartisan budget agreement a perfidy that revealed the president's true anti-Reagan colors.

The politics of the budget became horrific for the administration during the succeeding months. Staring at the deadline, October 1, with added pressure from Saddam's invasion of Kuwait beginning in August, the bargaining between the White House and Congress turned brutal. Late in September, Bush threatened to veto any budget that failed to provide a "real spending reduction," but to no avail. The next day, the two sides announced their agreement—a budget that called for large cuts in both entitlement programs and discretionary spending (including substantial cuts in defense spending) but that also included $134 billion in new taxes, mostly to be raised by gradually increasing gasoline taxes. Bush declared that he did not welcome any tax increase, but said that this one would at least have the virtue of helping to reduce America's dependence on foreign oil.

Republican conservative hard-liners in Congress, led by Gingrich, would have none of it, and they joined with Democrats in the House to defeat the package. "I'm not sure about the President, but the people around him weren't in touch with reality," said Representative Silvio O. Conte of Massachusetts, a senior Republican. The House then approved a continuing resolution to keep the government going, but Bush, enraged, vetoed it—and with the October 1 deadline now passed, the government shut down for three days (although with a specific exemption for the military buildup in the Persian Gulf). An infuriated public vented its anger almost entirely at Bush, who now was forced to sign a continuing resolution to allow Congress to operate for two weeks more. Congress then overhauled the budget plan, replacing most of the gasoline tax with an increase in the income tax for upper-income households. Conservative Republicans remained disgruntled—only one in four members of the Republican Party in both houses voted for the measure—but support from the Democrats was strong enough to carry the day.

Ed Rollins, who had been the political director in Reagan's White House and was now cochair of the Republican National Committee, pronounced the budget deal disastrous, and advised Republican candidates to run away from the president in what was left of the autumn congressional election campaign. The advice failed: although the setbacks were not disastrous, the Republicans had a net loss of eight seats in the House and one in the Senate. (Bush, incensed at Rollins, ordered him fired when the election was over.) Several races were closer than expected; in Georgia Newt Gingrich, his district reapportioned, nearly lost his seat. The budget debacle also severely hurt Bush's standing with the public; his popularity rating, which had spiked with the burst of patriotism that immediately followed

Saddam Hussein's invasion of Kuwait in August, had declined by nearly twenty points by November. Bush, of course, recovered smartly over the next seven months, during the preparations for the Gulf War and then the war itself. But the domestic travails of his first two years provided hints, then unheeded, about what would become of his administration once the focus shifted from war and foreign policy back to domestic concerns.

The onset of the long-anticipated recession can be dated to August 1990, when the nation's three major automakers began suffering losses that by the year's end would reach a combined total of $1 billion. During the first few months of 1991, the big three either temporarily closed or slowed work in twenty plants and fired 60,000 workers. Other large corporations were forced to cut back on middle-management salaried positions as well as wage earners' jobs. By mid-1991, the national unemployment rate had risen to 7.8 percent, the highest level since the recovery from the recession of 1981–1982 during Reagan's administration. Yet the Bush White House, preoccupied with events in the Persian Gulf, stifled any discussion of the souring economy, refusing until late in 1991 even to admit that a recession existed, and forecast that it would be fairly mild, lasting no more than ten months. In fact, these predictions turned out to be fairly accurate: between June and September 1992, the rate of economic growth increased to 3.8 percent, and it would increase again, to 5.7 percent, in the final quarter of the year. Yet Americans did not feel as if the economy was recovering; rather, they thought Bush was out of touch with the suffering and anxieties of middle- and working-class citizens. In September 1991, Bush vetoed, on grounds of financial prudence, an Unemployment Insurance Reform Bill that would have increased benefits beyond what the bipartisan budget agreement allowed. Understandable in terms of fiscal responsibility, the move reinforced perceptions, by middle- and lower-income Americans, of Bush as a remote and uncaring elitist.

Other controversies after the triumph in the Gulf ate away at Bush's seemingly invincible political standing. In December 1991, the chief of staff, John Sununu, a gruff, thin-skinned former governor of New Hampshire who was one of Bush's strongest links to the Republican right, resigned under protest, after the *Washington Post* revealed that he had flown on various personal trips at great expense to the taxpayers. After the budget battle, Bush could ill afford to lose touch with the Republicans' conservative base; to compound the difficulty, Sununu's replacement, the highly competent secretary of transportation, Samuel Skinner, had no aptitude for the bureaucratic infighting that the job entailed.

The resignation from the Supreme Court of the legendary Justice Thurgood Marshall, in late June 1991, gave Bush an opportunity to improve relations with right-wing Republicans. A year earlier, when Justice William Brennan stepped down, Bush had wanted to nominate the Reagan administration's leading black conservative, Clarence Thomas, who had stifled action on discrimination complaints at the Equal Employment Opportunity Commission (EEOC) until Congress forced his hand. Attorney General Richard Thornburgh and the White House counsel, C. Boyden Gray, although sympathetic, thought Thomas lacked judicial experience, and Bush instead named the taciturn David Souter of the U.S. Court of Appeals for the First Circuit and appointed Thomas to the District of Columbia Circuit Court. Souter's nomination avoided a repetition of the fiasco that had developed over Robert Bork, and he won easy confirmation, after refusing to be drawn into substantial statements about his judicial philosophy. Once on the court, however, he proved to be much less of a conservative ideologue than the Republican right had hoped. And although Thomas had only a few months of experience on the bench when Marshall retired, he seemed to be the perfect political choice—not simply as a reliable conservative but as an African-American who would be taking over the "black" seat on the Court. Bush duly nominated him.

There turned out to be more to Thomas (as well as, in some ways, less) than met the eye. Few people took Bush seriously when he praised the inexperienced nominee as, without question, the best-qualified jurist in America to succeed Thurgood Marshall. (Making sure to avoid the political divisions that hampered Bork's nomination, the White House, through Sununu, made immediate common cause with leaders of the new right such as Paul Weyrich, who heartily supported Thomas and wrote glowingly of the effort on behalf of his confirmation.) A willing suspension of disbelief, combined with Thomas's compelling personal story of rising from poverty in Pin Point, Georgia, and his refusal to go into specifics with the Senate Judicary Committee, allowed the committee to vote thirteen to one to send the nomination to the Senate floor. But during the committee hearings, a background check by the FBI had turned up a black law professor at the University of Oklahoma, Anita Hill, who had worked with Thomas at the EEOC, and who provided a detailed statement that charged Thomas with sexual harassment, discussed his obsessive interest in pornographic movies, and described his boasting to female coworkers of his sexual prowess. When Hill's charges surfaced on National Public Radio and *Newsday*, all bets about Thomas's confirmation were off.

The convergence of sex, race, and high politics caused an eruption in Washington—and a national media spectacle. With Bush's permission, the Judiciary Committee reopened its televised hearings. Thomas delivered a diatribe of racialist paranoia, blasting his accusers for conducting a "high-tech lynching for uppity blacks." The scene was surreal, as a right-wing African-American with ties to pro–states' rights southern white conservatives conjured up images of persecuted sharecroppers and civil rights martyrs; alleged that he was being "lynched, destroyed, caricatured" for his judicial views; and implied that the aggrieved woman, Anita Hill, and her supporters on the Judiciary Committee embodied the spirit of the Ku Klux Klan. The scene grew more bizarre as Republicans on the committee, led by Senator Alan Simpson of Wyoming and Senator Arlen Specter of Pennsylvania, accused Hill of cleverly concocting her story. At one point, Simpson read passages from the novel *The Excorcist*, which he claimed Hill had plagiarized in her testimony. ("You were superb! Many thanks," Bush later told Simpson in a handwritten note.) Ultraright organizations such as the Council for National Policy kept the White House informed of rumors about Hill's nefarious mind-set and motivations in testifying against her former superior. Thomas eventually prevailed in the full Senate by a vote of fifty-two to forty-eight, as eleven male Democrats, most of them from the South, voted in favor of his confirmation.

For Bush, it was another pyrrhic victory. In building bridges to hard-line conservatives, he had given them a candidate with a morally dubious past. Any chance that Bush would carry the female vote in 1992 ended when Thomas's supporters in Congress mocked Hill's claims about sexual harassment and began treating her as either a scorned woman or a harridan. Nor did Bush, who early on had won strong ratings from blacks and other minorities, gain much favor from African-Americans with his defense of Thomas over Hill. (A month later, Bush sealed his doom with black voters when he signed a piece of civil rights legislation that permitted employers to avoid charges of discrimination if their racial disparities in hiring could be justified as a business necessity.) Above all, Bush appeared to be stubbornly placing his own sense of loyalty to a nominee above any reasonable assessment of competence or any sense of political wisdom. Standing by his man Thomas, Bush put the nation through a televised, emotional trauma while allowing himself to look inept.

By late 1991, Bush was even having difficulties in his favored area of foreign policy, in ways that gave fresh political advantage to his adversaries. During the Gulf War, Gorbachev, assuming that the Americans were too distracted to notice, cracked down hard on the Baltic republics, seizing government buildings and declaring martial law in Lithuania, and provoking riots that left fifteen dead and scores wounded. Bush, needing to keep Gorbachev on his side with regard to Iraq and as uneasy as ever about undermining the existing order, offered only muffled objections, even when Foreign Minister Eduard Shevardnadze resigned in protest over the repression. Bush also rejected advice that he abandon Gorbachev and support the upstart Boris Yeltsin, who was then the mayor of Moscow (and was soon to be elected president of the new Russian Federation). In July, Bush met Gorbachev for a summit in Moscow and to sign the START arms control agreement initiated during Reagan's presidency. Persuaded to take a side trip to the Ukraine, Bush delivered a speech that was broadly supportive of nationalist strivings (with one eye on the disintegrating government of Yugoslavia), but which conservatives deemed insufficiently anticommunist and insufficiently anti-Gorbachev. In his column for the *New York Times*, William Safire twisted Bush's remarks and labeled them the president's "Chicken Kiev" speech. But some liberals, as well, criticized Bush for acquiescing in what Senator Bill Bradley of New Jersey called old-line "totalitarian methods."

In the Soviet Union, even Gorbachev's turn to the right was insufficient for the orthodox communists, who finally made their move. On August 18, 1991, Gorbachev was placed under house arrest at his summer dacha on the Black Sea. The attempted coup was amateurish, and Yeltsin created a stir by courageously, if flamboyantly, opposing the plotters and rallying pro-democracy protesters in Moscow. Bush laconically supported Yeltsin, though only after it became clear that the coup would fail. Three days after Gorbachev's release, the parliament abolished the Communist Party. In late December eleven former Soviet republics established the Commonwealth of Independent States, and two days after that, Gorbachev resigned. The Communist Party of the Soviet Union and the Soviet Union itself, stunningly, ceased to exist. Yet in the United States, Bush, having stuck by Gorbachev long after it was too late, shared in little of the glory. Conservatives, conveniently glossing over their own records and their criticism of Reagan in 1987 and 1988, now began celebrating Reagan as a cunning statesman who had purposefully caused the downfall of the Soviet Union with a coherent and unchanging strategy that he followed from the beginning.

Trade policy also caused Bush political problems. Both Baker and Bush wanted to expand the free-trade agreement Reagan had reached with Canada in 1987 to include Mexico. Reagan himself had hoped one day to see completion of a comprehensive North American Free Trade Agreement (NAFTA), which would eliminate most tariff barriers among the three countries within a decade. The White House, trying to finish the job in advance of the elections in 1992, requested from Congress the same so-called fast track provisions that governed the negotiations with Canada, limiting the combined process of negotiation and congressional approval to six months. But with the economy now in trouble, the congressional debate over the fast track became an argument over what kind of wide-open agreement was likely to result. And the debate and ensuing negotiations gave ammunition to Bush's critics on the isolationist and neo-nativist right as well as in organized labor, who charged that he was trying to relocate American industry and high-wage American jobs to south of the border, where wages were low. Although Bush finally helped fulfill Reagan's dream, it came at a considerable political cost.

With the outstanding exceptions of the invasion of Panama, the Gulf War, and the reunification of Germany, the Bush administration seemed to have become adept at snatching political defeat out of the jaws of victory. Yet because his presidency followed Reagan's, Bush faced challenges that would have sorely tested anyone. It had been left to Bush to address two enormous fiscal messes—the deficits and the S&Ls—remaining from the Reagan years, to oversee the end of the cold war and the dissolution of the Soviet Union, and to advance what Reagan had started on issues such as judicial appointments and trade policy. Ironically, Reagan's legacy battered the presidency of his anointed successor. It was almost as if Reagan had set a trap with his supply-side profligacy, presiding over what looked like good times with the bill falling due when he left office. Bush, to be sure, lacked his predecessor's charm, and on matters such as the weird choice of Clarence Thomas, he mainly had himself to blame. But in areas where Bush carried through on popular policies, Reagan and not he got the credit; where he carried through on policies that had become unpopular, like NAFTA, he, not Reagan, got the blame; and the one area in domestic policy where Bush made a genuine contribution, environmental protection, was an area that Reagan had ignored. At the beginning of January 1992, Bush's popularity rating had fallen to 47 percent—one point lower than his disapproval rating.

* * *

"Our whole political problem is in the recession," an aide working for Bush's campaign complained in March 1992. "We face a twenty month recession, a 78 percent wrong track number, and (likely) a southern conservative Democrat. The situation is about as bad as it could be." In fact, the situation was much worse than that.

Since leaving the Reagan White House in 1987, Patrick Buchanan had returned to writing his syndicated column and cohosting one of the new, acerbic debate shows that had begun proliferating on cable television, CNN's *Crossfire*. Rumors of his running for president dated back to 1986, when his sister and political collaborator, a former treasurer of the United States, Angela Bay Buchanan Jackson, started a "Buchanan for President" effort. Right-wing Republicans were excited by the prospect: "Buchanan may be the Churchill of our times," said Jesse Helms's inflammatory campaign guru, Tom Ellis. Buchanan was ambivalent, and in 1988 he threw his support to his friend Representative Jack Kemp. But in 1992, the ambivalence was gone. Having lambasted Bush in print and on television as "King George," over issues such as taxes and free trade, Buchanan decided to challenge the president in the Republican primaries.

With relatively meager financial resources, Buchanan's campaign (which he called his "Pitchfork Brigades") had no reasonable chance of denying an incumbent president renomination. But fueled by ideological fervor and profiting from the media skills of its celebrity candidate, Buchanan's camp had an enthusiasm that the president's lacked. The departure of John Sununu had deprived Bush of his chief political link to the Republican right, especially in New Hampshire, which held its primary early; and Buchanan became the standard-bearer. He startled the political world by winning 34 percent of the vote in the New Hampshire primary. The gusto generated by that result, along with Buchanan's defiance of Republicans who warned that he was splitting the party, kept his campaign going through the Republican primaries and caucuses all the way to the party's national convention. Although his delegate count was, by conventional standards, unimpressive, Buchanan wound up winning 22.5 percent of total vote cast in all the Republican primaries (including, in March, nearly 28 percent of the primary vote in the president's home state, Texas). Even before the general election campaign got under way, the Bush campaign had been forced to spend $27 million to fend off Buchanan. It was a certain sign that Reagan's electoral coalition was in political trouble.

The oddball, independent, third-party candidacy of the billionaire Ross Perot, of Texas, added to the political and ideological confusion. Perot had

made his initial fortune in the 1960s, thanks to lucrative government contracts secured by his data processing company, Electronic Data Services,
which was based in Dallas. At the end of the 1960s and in the early 1970s,
Perot was an ardent supporter of the American war effort in Vietnam, and
he offered the Nixon administration large amounts of time and money to
help enhance Nixon's reputation and undermine the antiwar movement.
He was especially active in starting and publicizing a lobbying campaign
to repatriate American prisoners of war and Americans missing in action
behind enemy lines. (Their numbers reached into the thousands, Perot
claimed, despite abundant evidence to the contrary.) During the war, critics
said that the POW-MIA campaign was a cruel ploy, manipulating bereft
family members in order to distract the public from the expanding debacle. After 1975, for many years, as the campaign was carried on, it helped
develop the "stab-in-the-back" sentiments that blamed the defeat in Vietnam on pusillanimous government officials. Cultural phenomena such as
the *Rambo* revenge fantasy movies of Sylvester Stallone and the personality
cult of Oliver North could be traced directly to the climate created in part
by H. Ross Perot.*

Some officials in the Nixon administration found Perot's efforts to insert
himself into government affairs exasperating, and Perot and Nixon had a
falling-out around 1973. Reagan's officials, hoping to silence criticisms by
Perot that the administration was doing too little on the POW-MIA issue,
granted him access to classified documents. When Perot remained unconvinced and stepped up his attacks, Vice President Bush was given the un-
pleasant task of informing his fellow Texan that his security clearance had
been revoked. With this, Perot's contempt for Bush flourished, and it carried over into the campaign of 1992. (An aide of Perot's later told a reporter,
"If [Perot] denied Bush the presidency, he'll be on top of the world. He hates
Bush.") But instead of attacking Bush over his administration's continued
rebuffs about the POW-MIA question, Perot exploited a much broader popular sentiment, regarding federal power that, under Bush, had supposedly
grown ever more irresponsible and corrupt. Congressional wrangling over
appointments, Bush's reversal over raising taxes, scandals involving alleged
abuses of the House Credit Union and Post Office (the latter two ginned

---

* One of the most effective political marketing efforts of the age of Reagan, the POW-MIA
movement also succeeded in passing laws that, to this day, require the flying of special black
POW-MIA flags over government buildings, including the White House and every U.S. post
office, several days each year.

up by conservative Republicans in the House, led by Newt Gingrich, after an earlier scandal that toppled the Democratic House speaker Jim Wright in 1988)—all contributed to a growing perception among the public that the federal government was dysfunctional and that politics as usual had to cease.

Perot skillfully capitalized on this populist fervor. Seizing on the new cable television medium (particularly in his appearances on CNN's high-rated interview show *Larry King Live*), he presented himself as an angry, supercompetent businessman who was willing to lead the country out of its morass, but only if he was drafted by the American people themselves. The supposedly spontaneous grassroots pro-Perot effort, called United We Stand, turned out to be no more spontaneous than Perot's earlier ventures—but Perot's folksy twang, his blunt phrases ("It's just that simple" was one of his favored lines), and his stance as an outsider gave a ring of authenticity and captivated millions of alienated Americans, who had come to think that nobody in Washington could be trusted. Assuming the familiar American role of the village explainer, the uncorrupted man of common sense, Perot hit Bush especially hard over NAFTA and, to a lesser extent, over his failure to balance the federal budget. In late May, Perot's supporters managed a coup even more stunning than Buchanan's showing in New Hampshire: Perot won 15 percent of the vote in Oregon's Republican primary—all of it coming on write-in ballots.

Adding to the general sense of unpredictability, significant shifts seemed to be occurring within the Democratic Party. Many nationally known Democrats generally considered as real contenders—including Representative Dick Gephardt, Senator Bill Bradley, the Reverend Jesse Jackson, and Senator Sam Nunn of Georgia—backed out when Bush was still riding high in the polls. Governor Mario Cuomo of New York once again toyed with the idea of running, but pulled out literally while an airplane was waiting on the tarmac to take him to New Hampshire to open his campaign. This left a field of relative unknowns and retreads—and one candidate who proved an exceptional campaigner, Governor Bill Clinton of Arkansas. At forty-five, Clinton had already come far in life and in politics, rising from a troubled home in Hot Springs, Arkansas, to a Rhodes scholarship, a degree from Yale Law School, and election to five terms as governor of Arkansas. Long before, he had set his sights on winning the presidency, and he began his drive in earnest in the mid-1980s when he became head of the National Governors' Association. His successes in Arkansas in improving education, roads, and health care, despite a largely hostile conservative legislature, looked like a beacon of neoliberal reform—embracing economic development and alliances between business and government instead of the more traditional liberal government activism. And he had earned a reputation as a charismatic and tireless stump speaker as well as a serious thinker about domestic issues.

As with Jimmy Carter before him, Clinton's southern background attracted some party professionals who wanted to break through the Democrats' image as the party of effete, northern, liberal do-gooders. But Clinton brought much more than that to the campaign. In 1985, he became a founding member of the Democratic Leadership Council (DLC), a group formed in the aftermath of Walter Mondale's crushing defeat to try to reclaim the political center without abandoning the party's historic commitments to the underprivileged. In 1990, Clinton became chairman of the DLC and, in pulling together what would become his own major political themes, he articulated the need for both change and continuity in reshaping the party's basic ideas about government—a message some old-line Democrats of the New Deal and the 1960s found either confusing or treacherous.

Addressing the DLC national convention in May 1991, Clinton attacked the glorification of "the pursuit of greed and self-interest" during the 1980s, while poverty rates rose for women "and their little children." Yet he also endorsed such ideas as welfare reform and reducing the size of the federal bureaucracy, and he issued an urgent admonition to his fellow Democrats: "Too many of the people who used to vote for us, the very burdened middle class we are talking about, have not trusted us in national elections to defend our national interests abroad, to put their values into our social policy at home, or to take their tax money and spend it with discipline. We have got to turn those perceptions around or we cannot continue as a national party." The various interest groups that constituted the party's liberal core rankled at such heresy—Jesse Jackson dismissed the DLC as "Democrats for the Leisure Class" who "comb their hair to the left like Kennedy and move their policies to the right like Reagan"—but less dogmatic party leaders took notice. Just as the reborn post-Reagan Republican Party was dividing between its hard-right ideologues and its establishment conservatives, the Democrats seemed to have developed a new moderate liberal wing with real political talent. As the election season began in 1992, Clinton was the odds-on favorite for the nomination among professional Democrats as well as the pundits.

Clinton's major problems were personal, not political. Especially worrisome was his reputation—well known in Arkansas but only gradually gaining notice among Democratic insiders around the country—for an unruly sexual appetite. When, on the eve of the New Hampshire primary, a weekly national tabloid ran allegations about a twelve-year affair between Clinton and a nightclub singer in Little Rock, and then produced tapes of the two talking familiarly on the telephone, it seemed as if Clinton's candidacy would implode, just as Gary Hart's had done in 1988. But Clinton understood the uses of the campaign media as well as any of George Bush's other challengers did. With the support of his wife, the formidable lawyer and fellow graduate of Yale Law School Hillary Rodham Clinton, Clinton appeared on the respected CBS Television news program 60 *Minutes* (in a broadcast immediately following professional football's Super Bowl), where he admitted that he had caused "pain in my marriage" but denied the tabloid's allegations. Then, just as the campaign was righting itself, another set of charges arose, accusing Clinton of being less than forthright about his deferral from the military draft twenty-three years earlier. Yet Clinton persevered to finish a strong second in New Hampshire, behind the earnest but dour Senator Paul Tsongas of Massachusetts, emerging as the self-styled "comeback kid." Newly energized, Clinton's campaign withstood challenges from Tsongas, Senator Bob Kerrey of Nebraska, and, on the left, the former governor of California Jerry Brown, and wrapped up the nomination with a solid triumph in the New York primary in April.

President Bush, for his part, had a difficult time firing up his campaign. Some of his supporters attributed the apparent listlessness of his effort to the death from brain cancer of his chief political strategist, Lee Atwater, in 1991; others attributed it to the president's own health problems (which included an unforeseen diagnosis of Graves' disease, a disorder of the thyroid). And quite apart from Pat Buchanan's challenge, Bush's string of unforced errors and mishaps also continued through 1992, with damaging political consequences. During a state visit to Japan early in the year, the president contracted a sudden case of stomach flu and vomited into the lap of Prime Minister Kiichi Miyazawa—a blameless act that nevertheless made Bush the butt of ridicule rather than sympathy at home, where the scene was constantly replayed on televised videotape. More grievously, in April, the acquittal of four white police officers in Los Angeles accused, in a highly charged case, of mercilessly beating a black robbery suspect, Rodney King, touched off the worst urban rioting in American history. Fifty-two people died, 2,500 were injured, and nearly $500 million in property was destroyed. Bush immediately sent representatives of the White House to the ravaged city, but he did not see fit to visit Los Angeles personally and view the devastation until five days later—leaving himself open to more charges that he was out of touch and uncaring.*

And yet, despite all his misfortunes, Bush was still leading in the polls in early June—and the comparatively unknown Clinton, after the contentious primaries, was running a dismal third, behind the billionaire populist Perot. Three developments changed the dynamics of the election. First, Perot, for reasons he could never adequately explain, suddenly left the campaign in July, just before the Democratic convention, only to rejoin it in September. Besides giving the impression that he was too whimsical for the White House, his absence gave the voters two months to compare Bush and Clinton directly, to Clinton's advantage.

Second, Clinton and the Democrats held a remarkably united convention in New York, where Clinton, eschewing the conventional wisdom, favored generational politics over geography and selected Senator Al Gore Jr. of Tennessee as his running mate. Gore—whose military service in Vietnam and family life were beyond reproach—had the Washington experience that Clinton lacked, but without being thought of as a Capitol Hill baron. Also, Gore projected more gravitas than his opponent, Vice President Quayle. And Gore's presence on the ticket made the Democratic Party look youthful, vigorous, bursting with new ideas—but definitely not beholden to northeastern liberals.

Third, Bush's forces ran a disastrous convention in August. Needing to appease the Republican right wing, they overcompensated by giving the first night's prime speaking slot to Pat Buchanan. Buchanan rose to the occasion by delivering an unbridled attack on Clinton as a militant on homosexual rights, married to a radical feminist—a misfit from the 1960s who, if elected, would try to destroy every shred of American decency. "There is a religious war going on in our country for the soul of America," Buchanan declared, as the television cameras panned the delegates to find the smiling face of the Reverend Jerry Falwell. "It is a cultural war, as critical to the kind of nation we will one day be as was the Cold War itself." The convention later heard from Marilyn Quayle, the wife of the vice president, who

---

* Vice President Dan Quayle did not help the White House's cause when, in a speech in San Francisco on May 19, he blamed the rioting on a "poverty of values," and chose as one of his chief targets a popular television character, Murphy Brown, who he said had mocked "the importance of fathers by bearing a child alone, and calling it just another 'lifestyle choice.'" Social conservatives rushed to praise Quayle; the White House, recognizing the absurdity of blaming urban rioting on a television comedy, quietly backed off from his remarks.

offered an attack on the 1960s and a defense of traditional womanhood. By the time Bush finally gave his acceptance speech, apologizing for his tax hike, the convention had virtually declared that GOP stood for God's Own Party.

Clinton's campaign strategists knew well enough that the culture wars simply were not foremost in voters' minds in 1992. "It's the economy, stupid!" a message taped to a wall at Clinton's national headquarters in Little Rock proclaimed—a reminder to campaign workers to keep their eye on the ball, not to be distracted by the Republicans' attacks, and (the first rule of the new media politics) to stay on message. Clinton helped himself in the televised debates by coming across as crisp and knowledgeable. In the first debate, Bush tried lamely to explain his reversal regarding taxes; then he further damaged his image in the second debate by absentmindedly looking at his wristwatch, coming across as preoccupied and bored by the entire affair.

In the closing weeks of the campaign, Bush finally moved into an all-out attack, having his researchers stir up charges that Clinton had, suspiciously, visited Moscow and demonstrated against the United States during his years as a Rhodes scholar at Oxford University, and even at one point attempted to renounce his citizenship in order to dodge the draft. Bush also derided his opponents as a pair of "bozos." ("This guy," he added about Gore, growing incoherent "is so far off on the environment extreme, we'll be up to our neck in owls and out of work for every American. This guy's crazy. He is way out, far out. Far out, man.") These tactics were the last flailing of a desperate campaign.

Perot's reentry into the race obscured the final result. By winning an impressive 19 percent of the total vote, more than any third-party candidate since Theodore Roosevelt in 1912, Perot indicated that, in the aftermath of Reagan's presidency, the public alienation from politics that had begun in the Vietnam and Watergate eras had deepened—and that a sizable portion of the electorate was willing to vote for anyone who seemed to be an anti-politician in the angry populist vein. Yet the assertion by many Republicans—and by analysts across the political spectrum—that Perot threw the election to Clinton does not stand up under close scrutiny. More than 105 million Americans voted in 1992, an increase of more than 14 percent over 1988—and the first time since 1972 that the proportion of eligible voters who actually voted reached as high as 55 percent. Plainly, Perot's totals were swelled by voters who, had he not run, would have voted neither for Bush nor for Clinton. Studies afterward showed that, overall, those who voted for

Perot would have split evenly between Bush and Clinton. More important, Perot ran most weakly in Bush's strongest base in the Deep South (which Bush won handily), and ran most strongly in the sparsely populated mountain states (where Bush also won handily). Clinton won convincingly elsewhere, including the major electoral states of California, New York, and Illinois. Had Perot not run, Bush would have been reelected only if he carried virtually all of the fourteen states that, in the event, either he or Clinton won by less than 5 percent—mathematically, a nearly impossible outcome.

Still, having captured a mere 43 percent of the popular vote—the lowest figure for any president since Woodrow Wilson in 1912, and a smaller percentage than Michael Dukakis had won in 1988—Clinton would have trouble claiming a mandate. His party did still control both houses of Congress. As the first Democrat in the White House in twelve years, and the first of the post-1945 generation, Clinton would bring a different vision to Washington. But a strain of self-styled Reagan conservatism more dogmatic and fierce than Reagan's would prove much more powerful than any single election—or several elections—could alter.

11

THE POLITICS OF CLINTONISM

R EAGANISM IS FOR CONSERVATIVE Republicans still a term of pride, celebrated as the faith that restored freedom and morality after the long, dark night of the New Deal, New Frontier, and Great Society, and that rescued their party from the disgrace of Watergate. Clintonism, however, was used by critics across the political spectrum as a vague epithet. To leftists and some orthodox liberals, Clinton was either a mountebank (a conservative masquerading as a progressive) or an appeaser (unwilling, when the chips were down, to fight the good fight on matters of conscience). To orthodox conservatives, he was a dangerous deceiver, "Slick Willie," a 1960s radical disguised as a moderate. To many professional pundits and editorialists, he was a master manipulator with no stable set of beliefs, a man who believed in everything and therefore believed in nothing.

Clintonism acquired an additional sociological and psychological dimension at a time when many commentators considered attributes such as character and even personality as the chief qualifications for public service in a democracy. There was no end to the fanciful hypothesizing about the origins of Clinton's politics. The stepson of an abusive alcoholic, Clinton had come of age as a chubby overachiever who wanted everyone to love him. He was cast as the emotionally needy, guilt-stricken, womanizing husband of a supposedly cold, ambitious feminist. He was a sex addict, a food addict, avid for the attention of Hollywood celebrities—projected, in all things, as an embodiment of the baby boomers' culture of narcissism and self-gratification. Apart from Richard Nixon, no president, while still in office, was subjected to more armchair analysis than Bill Clinton. To many critics, Clintonism came to stand not just for unprincipled political expediency but also for a political pathology, the pathology actually being politics itself—in Clinton's case, the politics of re-creating liberalism during a long conservative era.

Since the end of Lyndon Johnson's Great Society and Richard Nixon's election in 1968, liberals in general, and especially the left wing of the Democratic Party, had acquired a distaste for the normal politics of compromise and maneuvering—an important current in the more general popular alienation from politics that was attributed to the age of Reagan. Whereas the conservative movement of the 1950s and 1960s sought political power and embraced it, the new left of the 1960s and the movements it generated became stuck in protest politics and regarded power and party politics warily as corrupt and unprincipled. Many on the left, despite all the evidence to the contrary in elections and opinion polls, even denied the country's turn toward political conservatism after the late 1960s. They believed that the problem, in fact, was a lack of ideological and political purity among the Democrats. An older generation of Democratic liberals suffered a crisis of legitimacy because they had supported the Vietnam War. Jimmy Carter's presidency, which had promised to rise above politics and was untainted by Vietnam, collapsed under the weight of post-Nixon foreign policy and economic woes, compounded by Carter's inadequacies—and it became seen, on the left, as more conservative than liberal. In the aftermath of Ronald Reagan, George H. W. Bush's presidency foundered on the contradictions of conservatism—astronomical deficits, recession, the ambiguities of foreign policy after the bipolar cold war, and the increasing strength of the divisive religious right within the Republican Party. But many liberals mistook the difficulties of conservatism as a sudden flowering of 1960s-style liberalism, as if the country were crying out for a new Great Society—or something even farther to the left.

Bill Clinton's election bore the weight of the self-deluding Democrats' unrealistic assessments and expectations. Despite his victory, his party remained fractured and largely unreformed. Most conspicuously, even though the cold war had ended, the bitter divisions among the Democrats over foreign policy and defense—divisions that had opened up during the Vietnam War—remained through the Gulf War. There were deeper problems as well. During the quarter century of Republican ascendancy in the White House, broken only by Carter's single term, the Democrats had mostly been in charge of Congress, where particular party constituencies gained a foothold and followed their agendas. The Democratic Party had become a congressional party, a loose coalition of contentious liberal and left-wing interests that were not especially interested in taking direction from a Democratic president. By comparison, even though Bush's defeat exposed fissures in the Republican Party, the Republicans' underlying strengths, which had been growing since 1980, remained.

Clinton was widely hailed, even by some of his detractors, as the most gifted politician of his generation—but the political tasks presented to him required continual bobbing and weaving, compromising and negotiating, retreating so as to advance. The chaotic situation he faced, more than anything else, defined what others hypothesized as the "character issue" that supposedly defined Clintonism. Clinton's early inexperience, the Republicans' residual political reserves, the self-destructive dynamics of the congressional Democrats and an unreconstructed Democratic Party, as well as an unsympathetic press corps that thrived on scandals—all contributed to the Democrats' losing control of both houses of Congress in 1994. And that loss shaped the rest of Clinton's presidency, both its high and its low points. The so-called character issue deepened, as Clinton was forced to establish a position independent of both the hostile Republican majority and the impotent Democratic minority. The ensuring confrontations that led to a federal government shutdown, Clinton's recovery in the election in 1996, and the impeachment proceedings two years later all stemmed from the political realities surrounding the Clinton White House.

Clinton's earnestness as well as his magnetism left him vulnerable to his critics' reductionism, and to the political attacks it usually disguised. At a time when expansive, tactile politicians in Lyndon B. Johnson's mold had supposedly gone out of fashion as inauthentic, Clinton updated the style and melded it with his intellectual prowess—disgusting primer political temperaments, including many on the left. Indeed, that Clinton was as successful as he was, with all his manifestly human traits—including his calculating, maneuvering side—outraged his critics even more. How could such a poseur and outsider have come so fast and so far—all the way to Washington, which the titular dean of American political journalism, David S. Broder of the *Washington Post*, pronounced was "not his place"? What made Clinton think he could get away with it? (In his detractors' eyes, Clinton was always trying to get away with something.) Although polls consistently showed that he was a less polarizing figure than Ronald Reagan with the general public, Clinton elicited far more distrust than Reagan did among the permanent fixtures of Washington society, most of whom had found Reagan and his mystique inexplicable and thus all the more intimidating politically. Confused by Reagan, they tried to dismiss his enormous political skills as acting, with which they more or less played along. Clinton was a very different matter.

In fact, Clinton was not one thing or another, but many things at the same time, and somehow they all hung together. He was a product of rakish Hot Springs, Arkansas, who was also a Rhodes scholar and a student of history and public policy. He was a white southerner who grew up in the civil rights era, identified closely with blacks, yet also understood the resentments of many southern whites. He was a man temperamentally drawn to reasoned conciliation and compromise who could also be sentimental, impulsive, and stubborn. He came across as a bundle of contradictions, eternally tangled up in nuance. Clinton's critics, though, refused to allow that in the White House this might be at least as much of an as asset as a drawback, especially when Clinton addressed the contradictory policy demands that he faced on taking office.

Lacking the infrastructure of well-funded conservative think tanks and institutes that helped inform and justify the Reagan White House, Clinton and his advisers figured out a great deal on the run. Clintonism turned out to be neither a set of public positions nor a psychological dysfunction, but an evolving, sometimes improvised, pragmatic politics, informed by liberal values and worked out on the job. To be sure, Clinton's personal foibles and flaws, as well as his political errors, nearly destroyed him, and with him his presidency. But Clinton was also hunted and accused of wrongdoing as few previous presidents had been—by members of the Washington press corps who harbored suspicions about his political integrity and resented his rapid rise, as well as by Republican conservatives who hated him passionately for his political values and considered his presidency illegitimate from the start. Under siege, though, Clinton survived to become, by the end of his second term, a singularly admired if controversial leader.

After a little more than two weeks in office, Clinton signed the Family and Medical Leave Act. Twice vetoed by Bush, the act guaranteed many workers up to twelve weeks a year in unpaid leave in case of family medical emergencies. To the relief of pro-choice advocates and health care professionals, the president also swiftly revoked a gag order that had prohibited abortion counseling in federally funded clinics and issued an executive order permitting the use of fetal tissue in medical research. With quick strokes, the new administration showed that it intended to govern very differently from its predecessors, especially when it could work within the fiscal constraints it inherited from the Reagan and Bush administrations. But these early political victories were fairly easy for the Clinton White House, when set against the difficult task of formulating new fiscal policies that broke with the orthodoxies of the left as well as the right.

One of the consuming dilemmas of Clinton's presidency would be finding ways to expand American opportunity by revitalizing an active federal presence while also confronting the daunting realities of the budget deficits incurred during the Reagan and Bush administrations—shortfalls that ran to $290 billion annually by the time Clinton took office. During the campaign of 1992, Clinton's program, summarized in his manifesto *Putting People First*, endorsed deficit reduction, but not as heartily as it advanced other proposals: a tax cut for the middle class, a surge of spending on public works to stimulate the sluggish economy, and $60 billion in what Clinton called "investments" in education, subsidies for child care, and other programs that would reap great human as well as fiscal rewards, especially universal health care. At a preinauguration economic summit in Little Rock, Clinton as president-elect heard from labor leaders, corporate executives, and economists of all stripes about the relative importance of cutting the deficit, practicing Keynesian spending, or doing nothing and letting the economy simply right itself. But Clinton remained confident that he could undertake his beloved investments while also halting the Reaganites' cycle of borrow-and-spend economics.

The fiscal realities, which had contributed to the undoing of his predecessor, were more challenging than Clinton imagined. Two weeks before the inauguration, the departing Bush administration announced that the projected federal deficit for 1997—the year by which, as a candidate, Clinton had promised to cut the deficit in half—was $60 billion higher than it had previously announced, an increase of about one-third. The stunned president-elect immediately consulted with his chief economic advisers, most prominent among them the incoming secretary of the treasury, Lloyd Bentsen (the former U.S. senator from Texas); the accomplished Wall Street investment banker who was Clinton's new assistant for economic policy, Robert Rubin; and a former congressman who was the incoming federal budget director, Leon Panetta. They instructed him on the pressing need to get serious about reducing the budget by means of both tax increases and reductions in spending, in order to persuade the chairman of the Federal Reserve, Alan Greenspan, and the capital markets to cut interest rates to lenders. Clinton, who was instinctively more of a traditional liberal than a business Democrat, bridled at the imperatives thrust on him. (Later, he would liken his administration, with self-mocking irritation, to "Eisenhower Republicans" fending off Reagan Republicans.) But he came to understand that he had been left with few practical choices, and that economic recovery was the top priority. Right away, he postponed his campaign offer of a tax cut for the middle class.

In facing up to the deficit, Clinton, not unlike Bush, aroused the political furies. Clinton's own liberal political advisers and many congressional Democrats, who had seen Clinton as a new vehicle for the redress of middle- and working-class grievances, and who regarded reduction of the deficit as a Republican obsession, took umbrage as he began seeking to impress the Federal Reserve and the bond market. "[T]he *deficit* isn't the core problem," wrote Robert Reich, an old friend of Clinton's from Oxford days, newly appointed as secretary of labor, who saw himself as the internal opponent of Rubin. "The problem is that the earnings of half our workforce have been stagnant or declining for years." Despite Clinton's actions, congressional Republicans were not assuaged, even as Clinton symbolically gave Alan Greenspan the seat of honor in the House gallery beside Hillary Rodham Clinton, the first lady, when he delivered his State of the Union message in mid-February. Although the president proposed devoting twice as much in revenue to reducing the deficit as to "investments," he still called for $30 billion in spending and tax reductions to help stimulate the economy. Quickly, Republicans killed the request for $16 billion to fund job creation for the summer of 1993. They also railed against Clinton's call for modest tax increases for those in the highest-income households.

Although his liberal supporters and many in the press began to scorn him as weak-kneed, Clinton secured most of what he requested when the budget battle finally ended in August. Spending cuts, both in defense and in social programs, remained modest. A higher marginal income tax rate of 39.6 percent on incomes of $250,000 or more went into effect, as did a 1 percent increase in the highest corporate tax rate. Clinton also expanded the earned income tax credit to low-income households with children, an important antipoverty tool first instituted in 1975. Even with its liberal provisions, the package was expected to achieve the president's stated goal of reducing the deficit by almost $500 billion within five years. In a sign of things to come, though, not a single Republican voted for the proposal in the House, where it barely squeaked through by 218 votes to 216. The package then cleared the Senate, where again not a single Republican voted for it, only when Vice President Al Gore broke a fifty-to-fifty stalemate. And by the time Clinton won what would eventually prove a historic fiscal victory, his early administration had been almost swamped by controversies and political scheming over other domestic matters.

Although Bill Clinton had graduated from Georgetown University and spent time as a congressional intern, his youthful experience in Washington offered scant preparation for what hit him and his administration. After the summit at Little Rock, he said he would initially focus on the economy "like a laser beam," but the distractions piled up quickly. First, in response to a reporter's question about one of his less than highly featured campaign pledges, the president-elect allowed that he would like to oversee reforms to permit homosexuals to serve openly in the military. Since he had not yet cleared the matter with the military brass or the relevant members of Congress, this was a careless statement about a sensitive issue that went to the heart of the culture wars. The chairman of the Joint Chiefs of Staff, Colin Powell, as well as the chairman of the Senate Armed Services Committee, Sam Nunn of Georgia, mounted a revolt of the military. Clinton, whose deferments during the Vietnam War had been a heated issue during the campaign, was immediately thrown on the defensive.

The proximate issue was gays in the military, but there was also the underlying issue of the power of General Powell, a longtime Republican favorite close to the Bush family, as well as suspicion within the military about the protester against the Vietnam War who was now president, the first of his generation. In his first weeks in office, Clinton was forced to back off from a position that he had not yet formed into a policy, infuriating gay organizations and their sympathizers, who declared him a betrayer. The eventual settlement, a form of benign willful ignorance known as "don't ask, don't tell," ended the furor, but Clinton had been weakened almost before he started. Over the ensuing decade, the "don't ask, don't tell" policy resulted in the discharge of upwards of 10,000 servicemen and servicewomen who revealed their homosexual preferences or were exposed by others.

Prolonged follies over the appointment of an attorney general compounded Clinton's political difficulties. His initial choice of the corporation lawyer Zoë Baird, a moderate, seemed uncontroversial, until a public scandal (stoked by the left-wing consumer advocate Ralph Nader, as well as by right-wing talk-radio hosts) ignited over her admission that she had em-

ployed two illegal immigrants to help with her child care. Baird's became
the first Cabinet nomination in 120 years to be voluntarily withdrawn.
Clinton's next choice, the federal judge Kimba Wood, another qualified
woman, was also discovered to have employed undocumented immigrants,
and she too hastily stepped aside. Determined to name the first woman to
head the Justice Department, Clinton finally found a successful nominee
in Janet Reno, state attorney for Dade County (now Miami-Dade County),
Florida. But in April, Reno came under heavy criticism because of the
FBI's handling of a standoff with the leader of a violent religious cult,
David Koresh, in Waco, Texas, which resulted in the deaths of Koresh
and more than seventy of his followers, including twenty-one children. A
commission headed by the former Republican senator John Danforth exonerated the FBI and Reno of any wrongdoing and put the entire blame
on Koresh, but the commission's report appeared eight years after the fact,
in 2001.

The imbroglio regarding Lani Guinier damaged Clinton's close relations with influential black professionals and politicians—and gave early
evidence of how mean-spirited the conservative opposition was becoming.
Guinier, an African-American, who was a rising authority on civil rights
law and a professor at the University of Pennsylvania law school, had trained
at Harvard and Yale, and had impeccable academic credentials; and Clinton (having known her for years) appointed her head of the civil rights division at the Justice Department. Yet at the instigation of Abigail Thern-
strom, a liberal turned neoconservative in Cambridge, Massachusetts, Clint
Bolick, a former assistant to Clarence Thomas at the EEOC who had long
been hostile to affirmative action, published in the *Wall Street Journal* an
attack on Guinier's academic writings. The article inflamed ugly prejudices
by calling Guinier a "quota queen" who, ominously, wanted to rig American elections in order to guarantee that blacks gained public office, as a per-
verse form of affirmative action.

As hypothetical intellectual exercises, Guinier's opinions certainly could
be unsettling—though mainly for their sympathy to ideas of the concur-
rent majority first elaborated before the Civil War by the advocate of states',
rights and nullification John C. Calhoun, normally a hero to the right.
Guinier's writings that explicitly criticized quotas and affirmative action
were ignored, as was her support for ideas about reform of elections and
representation that had been implemented in various places in the United
States as well as Europe—including a so-called supermajority voting plan
in Mobile, Alabama, that had won approval from the Reagan administra-

tion. Instead, the racially tinged attacks stuck. Guinier's relations with the Clintons chilled when she refused to bow to political reality and step aside quietly as Baird and Wood had done in similarly politically untenable situations; and the president once again looked ridiculous when, on withdrawing the nomination, he claimed that he had not seriously read Guinier's work until after nominating her.

A more mundane matter of malfeasance inside the White House travel office led to a fresh round of scandalmongering and to partisan attacks and official investigations that foreshadowed later momentous efforts to undermine Clinton's presidency. Late in 1988, a letter from a whistle-blower connected to the executive travel office (which arranged airline and hotel accommodations for the White House press corps) had led to an investigation by the FBI, which uncovered evidence of embezzlement and illegal gifts and favors, chiefly involving the office director, Billy Dale. The Bush White House had brushed the matter aside, but in May 1993, the Clinton administration responded by summarily firing the staff and replacing the director with a new appointee who, though professionally qualified, was also connected to family friends of the Clintons.

Nobody doubted Clinton's right to dismiss the compromised staff of the travel office and hire replacements—although the White House found it difficult to assert this right without an air of wounded sanctimony. Soon after the larceny charges first surfaced in 1988, Dale himself had admitted wrongdoing and even offered a plea bargain to prosecutors. But the press corps shared in the goodies doled out by the office and had close ties to Dale and his colleagues; and coverage of the matter ran heavily against the Clintons. Pundits, led by the columnist William Safire of the *New York Times*, harped on the incident as "Travelgate." Safire focused his attacks on Hillary Rodham Clinton, who, he would later charge, lied about the matter in order "to avoid being identified as a vindictive power player who used the FBI to ruin the lives of people standing in the way of juicy patronage." Two protracted inquiries—one of which, by the House Government Affairs and Oversight Committee, was not concluded until 1998—finally discovered no evidence of any wrongdoing. But the exonerations came too late to clear away the lingering cloud of charges that the president and his wife had abused presidential power and, with their friends, obstructed justice. Four months after the inauguration, Clinton's job approval rating had fallen twenty points, to 37 percent.

* * *

The first lady also became a lightning rod in the signal failure of domestic policy during Clinton's first term: formulating and securing a comprehensive national health care plan. By choosing to pursue health care reform with a large, high-profile effort, headed by Mrs. Clinton and assisted by her longtime associate, the policy strategist Ira Magaziner (another former friend of the president's at Oxford), Clinton wanted to put his best foot forward as a reformer. Since Harry Truman's presidency, Democrats had tried and failed to design a national health insurance system, in order to cover millions of uninsured Americans and bring the United States up to the standard of public health care provision of the other major industrialized nations. Clinton vowed to succeed, and he rashly promised to deliver a health care bill to Congress within his first 100 days in office. On January 25, 1993, less than a week after his swearing in, he announced the formation of his health care task force, with Hillary Rodham Clinton as its chief.

In its design and execution, Clinton's initiative raised profound political problems and faced concerted opposition from the start. The very idea that any White House task force could formulate a bill on so complex an issue as health care in just over three months displayed a self-assurance that bordered on arrogance—and diminished the president when it did not happen. Some influential figures in Congress, including Senator Daniel Patrick Moynihan of New York, were disappointed that the president did not first pursue his earlier promise to "end welfare as we know it" before taking on the less politically charged, more complex, and, in their eyes, less pressing issue of health care. Most important, the decision to initiate health care reform inside the White House instead of in the Democratic Congress was politically naive and foolhardy. Making Congress and its committees the focus of activity would have ensured congressional allegiance to legislation as it evolved. By instead presenting Congress with a fait accompli, the White House risked losing support from Democrats and moderate Republicans alike who agreed that the time had come to reform health care, and who had initially pledged their personal backing.

By placing Hillary Clinton at the head of the health care task force, the president chose a proven, qualified, highly competent, informed overseer, who had done excellent work on education reform (and impressed President Bush with her command of the issues) in Arkansas. But the appointment to a highly sensitive advisory post of an unelected spouse who would not require vetting and confirmation by the Senate immediately raised eyebrows.[*] The concerns deepened when the task force, numbering in the hundreds, met in closed sessions—the normal, even necessary procedure for internal policy-making counsels by any administration, but one that partisan newspapers and then the mainstream press portrayed as sinister in its secrecy. Finally, in September, after largely sidestepping the Congress in favor of academics and other outside authorities, the White House released, a bulky, ludicrously ill-explained proposal that filled more than 1,300 pages.

Despite its impossible complications, the Clinton health plan augured a genuine attack on the inequalities of the existing system. More flexible than the plans in force in some other countries, it called for most employers to pay for 80 percent of their employees' health benefits. Regional associations of insurance buyers would promote what the plan's advocates called "managed competition"—that is, competition overseen by the federal government—which would lower premiums. The government would pick up the costs for citizens who still remained uninsured.

Although it seemed counterintuitive to some people, several large American corporations supported the plan, expecting that it would actually reduce their own payouts for employees' health benefits while also expanding coverage to include all Americans. But apart from the air of arrogance that surrounded its origins, the plan itself raised hackles in various quarters. Liberals were angry that Clinton did not demand a Canadian-style single-payer program in which the federal government or some subcontracting entity assumed the costs for insurance—a simpler and fairer plan, in their view, even though in the short run it would require a substantial tax increase, about which Clinton was understandably wary. Ordinary Americans, most of whom were covered by fee-for-service plans, were easily frightened into thinking they might lose ground under a new, complicated national system, forced into a rationing of services without any choice over

---

[*] In 1961, President Kennedy wittily shrugged off charges of nepotism when he appointed his brother Robert as attorney general, joking with reporters that it seemed a good idea to give Bobby a little legal experience before he set up in practice on his own. (Since then, federal law has banned such family cabinet appointments.) President Clinton, by contrast, spoke earnestly of how, with him and his wife in the White House, the country would be getting two for one. The statement backfired less because it challenged traditional marriage than because to some it seemed presumptuous and undemocratic. In any event, Robert Kennedy's appointment had required approval by the Senate, as Hillary Clinton's did not.

their medical care. Employers' and insurance industry associations, allied with conservative Republicans, launched a propaganda counteroffensive to intensify these fears. Particularly notable were the clever and expensive television commercials by the Health Insurance Association of America, in which a fictional middle-class couple called "Harry and Louise" fretted and then raised questions laced with innuendo about the plan's bureaucratic constraints and financial viability.

Republicans in Washington gleefully fed the outrage. The brash, up-and-coming House minority whip, Newt Gingrich, rallied the congressional faithful by tacitly likening the Clintons to outmoded Soviet commissars, standing against "the entire tide of Western history" by trying to impose "centralized, command bureaucracies." On December 2, a leading conservative strategist, William Kristol (the son of the neoconservative Irving Kristol and lately Vice President Dan Quayle's chief of staff), circulated an action plan among Republicans in Congress, calling on them to kill (not merely amend) any plan Clinton offered, to prevent the Democrats from gaining the middle-class vote for decades to come. The venerable Washington political weekly *The New Republic*, an important forum of neoliberalism in the 1980s, ran a damaging, inaccurate attack on the program by an ambitious Republican political comer, over the heated objections of some of the magazine's senior editors—an article that the Republicans circulated widely. Having largely bypassed potentially supportive Democrats and the few remaining persuadable moderate Republicans in the conception of the plan, the White House now had to build crucial backing for its proposal after the fact.

Claiming that the various components of the managed competition system were all of a piece, and that nothing (including government support for the uninsured) could be sacrificed without destroying the whole, the administration precluded the kind of basic compromise inherent in any congressional negotiation, and further reinforced its growing reputation for self-righteous inflexibility. Although Hillary Clinton muted some of the critics when she testified knowledgably before Congress, the president's firm endorsement of the plan in all-or-nothing terms in a speech before Congress made winning a program more difficult.

A political fight on an entirely different issue that was dogging the White House at precisely the same moment, compounded the administration's problems. Shortly before he left office, President Bush completed negotiations with Mexico and Canada over the North American Free Trade Agreement (NAFTA). Clinton's leaning toward free trade and his belief in embracing what was becoming known as economic globalization, aligned him, with regard to NAFTA, more closely with leading corporate figures and Washington Republicans than with many Democrats. Clinton's basic argument was that ending trade barriers would force American exporters to be more efficient and competitive, and that this would increase their market share and, in turn, eventually benefit American workers. But to organized labor and its Democratic friends on Capitol Hill (notably the House majority leader, Richard Gephardt), NAFTA was merely a pretext for allowing American capital to shift jobs to Mexico, where labor was cheap and environmental protection requirements and other regulations were slight compared with those in the United States.

In addition, NAFTA was a bone in the throat for conservative isolationists such as Pat Buchanan, as well as the pesky protectionist H. Ross Perot, who spoke of the "giant sucking sound" of jobs being moved to Mexico because of the agreement. In November 1993, with House approval of the required implementation legislation weighing in the balance, Vice President Al Gore chose to debate Perot over NAFTA on the program *Larry King Live*; and, with a mixture of statistics and unexpected satirical humor, he trounced the self-styled populist Perot. Gore's performance helped tip the vote in the House and bruised Perot's public image by making him look peevish and ignorant. But Gore's victory did nothing to placate organized labor, which after its disastrous experience during the Reagan-Bush years had come to see NAFTA as a make-or-break struggle. And although Clinton tried to patch up relations with the president of the AFL-CIO, Lane Kirkland, the unions had invested too much energy and money fighting NAFTA to be of much help when the crunch came on health care. (Indeed, losing the fight over NAFTA fed anger within the AFL-CIO that would eventually lead to Kirkland's downfall.)

The struggle over NAFTA had the additional effect of forcing a postponement of congressional action on health care until 1994, which gave critics additional time to pick away at the plan. By trying to hew to the reformist center, the administration had alienated both liberals (still holding out for a single-payer plan) and conservative Democrats (dubious about such provisions as the guaranteed universality of coverage). Support for Clinton's plan, which had once had the backing of two-thirds of the general public, began to dwindle. With his own party badly divided, Clinton finally had to abandon the health care project in September 1994, before it even came up for a congressional vote. For a supposed master politician, this was a crushing defeat—all the more so because his own wife had been so closely tied to the initiative, making it impossible to distance the Oval Office from the outcome.

As if the health care fiasco was not bad enough, by the autumn of 1994, the Clinton administration was reeling from other errors and mishaps it could scarcely have anticipated. In particular, setbacks in foreign policy, chiefly concerning matters inherited from the Bush administration, appeared not only nettlesome but intractable.

During the final month of his presidency, President Bush made two major decisions related to foreign policy that had lasting effects. On Christmas eve, 1992, he issued presidential pardons to the former secretary of defense Caspar Weinberger (who had been indicted on four counts of perjury in connection with his testimony about the Iran-contra affair) and to five others who had either been convicted of or pleaded guilty to criminal charges in connection with Iran-contra, including the former national security adviser Robert MacFarlane and the former assistant secretary of state Elliott Abrams. Two weeks earlier, the independent counsel, Lawrence Walsh, first learned of the existence of an extensive private diary, previously not provided to investigators, that Bush had begun in November 1986. Numerous diary entries seemed to confirm that, as vice president, Bush had not been "out of the loop" on Iran-contra, as he had claimed during the 1988 campaign.

The pardon of Weinberger, among other things, ensured that Bush would never be called as a witness in a trial where his diary entries could be admitted as evidence. Bush's message about the pardon talked mainly of the past national service and patriotic motives of all those involved, and of Weinberger's declining health, as well as the need finally to lay the affair to rest. It also criticized the "profoundly troubling" new trend toward what Bush, echoing earlier critics of the investigations of Iran-contra, called "the criminalization of policy differences." Walsh, however, remained deeply suspicious that Bush was still involved in a cover-up; and when Bush placed sharp conditions on being questioned about the diary material, the judge dropped the matter lest there arise a "misleading impression of cooperation where there was none." Clinton, as president-elect, issued a noncommittal statement but expressed concern about any action "that sends a signal that if you work for the Government, you're beyond the law, or that not telling the truth to Congress under oath is somehow less serious than not telling the truth to some other body under oath."

Also in December, Bush dispatched more than 25,000 U.S. troops to join a UN humanitarian mission in Somalia in the horn of East Africa, where political unrest among contending warlords and chieftains had led to catastrophic famine. By the fall of 1993—long after the American forces had been expected to depart—Somalia had virtually become a protectorate of the United Nations, which was now engaged in nation-building in a country that basically had no effective central government (although the level of violence had been lowered). Clinton had reduced the America military presence, but a force of some 4,000 troops still remained as part of the UN mission, augmented in late August by 440 elite troops from the Delta Strike Force and special operations U.S. Army Rangers. On October 3, Black Hawk helicopters carrying U.S. Rangers descended into a neighborhood of Mogadishu, the capital city, where the most brutal and elusive of the defiant warlords, Mohammed Farah Aidid, was supposed to have taken refuge in a hotel. Suddenly, rocket-propelled grenades fired by Aidid's forces downed and disabled two of the helicopters, which were quickly surrounded by Somali fighters. In a fierce battle that lasted seventeen hours, Aidid's men killed eighteen Americans and wounded eighty-four. The American forces eventually restored order to the capital, but not before joyous crowds had dragged the corpse of one American soldier through the city's streets and then burned it in front of television cameras.

Apalled and outraged, Clinton blamed his aides for keeping him insufficiently apprised of the details of the operation in Somalia; then he announced that American troops would eventually be withdrawn. They finally departed in March 1994, when rival Somali factions signed a tenuous peace agreement that soon broke down. By then, Clinton's secretary of defense, Les Aspin, who had declined to supply the American mission with armored reinforcements, had shouldered most of the blame for the disaster and been forced to resign. More broadly, the events in Mogadishu—which inspired a graphic, compelling film, *Black Hawk Down*, released in 2001—revived popular wariness of ill-defined American military missions, especially if they were connected to post–cold war efforts to rebuild so-called failed states.

A week after the firefight in Mogadishu, the USS *Harlan County* arrived in the harbor of Port-au-Prince, Haiti. In 1991, a military junta had ousted and exiled Haiti's democratically elected populist president, the former priest Jean-Bertrand Aristide. The *Harlan County* was supposed to deliver 200 American and Canadian engineers as the first wave of an effort by the UN to return Aristide to power. But an anti-Aristide faction raised a mob of about 100 heavily armed thugs to meet the vessel at the pier and

prevent any disembarkation, while shouting derisively about "another Somalia." Caught unprepared, Clinton's national security advisers ordered the
ship to return home. Once again, the world's most powerful nation stood
humiliated, stuck between a desire to promote peace and democracy abroad
and wariness about endangering American personnel.

The costs of paralysis became hideously clear in April 1994, once again
in Africa, when mobs from the majority Hutu ethnic group in Rwanda,
incited by a political faction, undertook an astonishingly rapid genocide of
the Tutsi minority that, within three months, killed 800,000 in a country of 8 million—proportionally, the equivalent of 27 million Americans.
Even minimal armed intervention by the West would almost certainly have
curtailed the butchery. The National Security Council, alarmed when the
Hutu tortured and killed ten Belgian UN troops stationed in the capital,
Kigali, urged the creation of a protected zone for refugees, but the UN rejected the proposal and offered instead to send peacekeeping forces that
would take months to be fully deployed. The atrocities against the Belgians
were meant to evoke Mogadishu, and had the desired effect of increasing
Westerners' wariness about intervening to the point of paralysis.

The swiftness of the massacre, meanwhile, outpaced the international
debate. ("The difficulty has been one side not recognizing the other's government," the UN commander, General Romeo Dallaire of Canada, said,
more than a week after the genocide began. "But if we see another three
weeks of being cooped up and seeing them pound each other, then I have
to seriously assess the effectiveness of keeping troops here.") Rwanda was a
country in backwater central Africa, of no clear economic or strategic importance—and, after Somalia, there was little interest in undertaking military deployments in far-flung places. Apart from some persistent reporters
at official press briefings, no Americans of importance—among lawmakers, or even from pro-African lobbying groups led by blacks, such as Trans-
Africa—applied any pressure to intervene. Several African nations (notably
Senegal) sent troops to join the small UN force that remained in Kigali, but
the only intervention by westerners came from France, in the highly controversial Operation Turquoise in July—an action that many in Rwanda
believed was meant to provide cover for the killers, whose leaders had close
ties to France, rather than to protect the victims.

Inaction by westerners also haunted one of the ugliest outcomes of the
end of the cold war, a continuing crusade of what had acquired the hor-
rifically antiseptic label "ethnic cleansing" in the former Yugoslavia. In
1989, a former official of the Communist Party, Slobodan Milosevic, seized

power in Belgrade and quickly transformed himself into a Serbian nationalist, reviving and inflaming ancient ethnic enmities in order to forge a new dictatorship. His power grab hastened the disintegration of Yugoslavia, a nation-state cobbled together in the aftermath of the collapse of the Austro-Hungarian empire and as part of the settlement of World War I. First, Slovenia successfully declared its independence, and then Croatia, which Milosevic tried and failed to subdue in a brutal war. Finally, in 1992, Bosnia tried to break away. Divided between a cosmopolitan population of European Muslims, centered in the capital city, Sarajevo, and a minority of native Serbs, Bosnia became a killing field as Milosevic outfitted and armed Bosnian Serb forces that laid siege to Sarajevo.

The fighting in Bosnia—and the discovery of brutal concentration camps and incidents of mass rape and slaughter—raised alarms from some westerners, most auspiciously the outgoing prime minister Margaret Thatcher, who pleaded for concerted military intervention. But the realist Bush administration refused—the United States does "not have a dog in that fight," Secretary of State James Baker said—and the U.S. military leadership, including Colin Powell, concurred. Clinton criticized Bush's passivity during the campaign of 1992, but once he took office he was told by General Powell, still chairman of the Joint Chiefs of Staff, that intervening would require a minimum deployment of 500,000 U.S. troops. Leaders of the NATO countries (including the president of France, François Mitterrand—who supported the Serbs—and the new British prime minister, John Major) refused to lift an existing embargo on arms sales to Yugoslavia, or take any other action that might aid the persecuted Bosnian Muslims. A United Nations Protection Force (UNPROFOR) managed to keep the Sarajevo airport open for airlifts of humanitarian supplies, but was powerless to halt the atrocities. In the White House, most of Clinton's highest-level advisers, including Secretary of State Warren Christopher, deferred to General Powell's judgment that reversing the tide in Bosnia would require a very large number of troops, with no guarantee that the situation would not turn into another Vietnam. Swayed by this application of the Powell Doctrine—that the U.S. military should intervene only with overwhelmingly sufficient force and with a clear exit strategy—the White House remained for the moment frozen in the face of the Bosnian catastrophe.*

---

* The Powell Doctrine is sometimes said to be the basic formula behind the U.S. victory in the Persian Gulf War in 1991. Yet General Powell had initially favored continuing the sanctions rather than physically removing the Iraqis and was overruled.

The Clinton administration achieved the first of its diplomatic advances in the Middle East. In September 1993, secret negotiations between the Israeli government of Yitzhak Rabin and Yasir Arafat's Palestine Liberation Organization (PLO), facilitated by Norway, led to an unprecedented agreement. The so-called Oslo Accords ended the Palestinian armed uprising (or intifada) begun in 1987, and laid out a Declaration of Principles whereby control of portions of the Gaza Strip and the West Bank would be handed over to a new Palestinian Authority in exchange for the PLO's renunciation of terrorism and its recognition of Israel as a legitimate state. Having encouraged the pact, Clinton arranged for Rabin and Arafat to meet and shake hands in a highly publicized ceremony on the South Lawn of the White House.

Clinton's administration also moved more decisively with respect to terrorism and various troublesome regimes. In February 1993, Muslim extremists set off a bomb inside the World Trade Center in New York City, killing six people, injuring 1,000, and forcing 5,000 office workers to evacuate the two towers. Six days after the blast, authorities announced the capture of one of the plotters, Mohammed Salameh. In 1994, he and three others were convicted and sentenced to life imprisonment; over the next two years, two others, including the mastermind of the conspiracy, Sheik Omar Abdel-Rahman, were likewise tried and convicted. After Clinton ascertained that militants connected to Saddam Hussein of Iraq had tried to assassinate former president Bush in Kuwait early in 1993, he ordered a cruise missile attack on Baghdad, which targeted and destroyed Saddam's intelligence headquarters. Clinton also backed continuation of the UN's weapons inspections, no-fly zones, and economic sanctions imposed on Iraq in 1991. Toughening the United States' position in Haiti after the fiasco involving the *Harlan County*, Clinton threatened to send in troops. This threat resulted in the toppling of the military junta there and the restoration of the elected leader, Aristide, to power in September 1994, aided by American advisers who would help raise and train a Haitian professional constabulary. A month later, Clinton reached what was called an "agreed framework" with the North Koreans, whereby they would shut down their nuclear weapons development program and submit to international inspection in exchange for much-needed American supplies of food, medical supplies, and fuel oil.

At best, Clinton was groping, along with other Western leaders, to fix the contours of post–cold war diplomacy. President Bush's "new world order," vaguely defined, had not cohered, especially after the breakup of the Soviet

Union. Basic differences over foreign policy that cut across conventional political party lines emerged ever stronger. Some conservatives and liberals took cautious realist positions, counseling restraint in all but the most vital national security areas lest there be a repeat of Vietnam. Others—neoconservatives but also idealistic liberals—sought a more activist foreign policy; their goals included securing American global hegemony and advancing human rights against mass murderers such as Slobodan Milosevic and despots such as Saddam Hussein.

Through the end of 1994, Clinton, who had come to office with his mind chiefly on domestic policy, was still finding his feet in foreign affairs. The scenes from Mogadishu, in particular, hung heavily over the White House. There was a sense that, even with the cold war over, American power was bound by powerful restraints.

If foreign concerns were not troublesome enough, political dynamics at home, quite apart from the policy fights over health care and NAFTA, began looking as if they might overwhelm the new president. A shocking event had occurred in July 1993, when the body of the White House deputy counsel Vincent Foster, a longtime friend and colleague of the Clintons in Little Rock, was found in a park in Virginia, dead from a self-inflicted gunshot wound to the head. Over the months that followed, Foster's tragedy would be rendered as part of a conspiracy in a trumped-up scandal known as Whitewater.

Foster was clinically depressed when he killed himself, after having been singled out by the abusive, ultraconservative editorial page of the *Wall Street Journal*, which accused him of cronyism and dubious legal practices, and of nefarious complicity in the Travelgate affair. On the advice of friends, including President Clinton, he had consulted psychiatrists, but instead of following up he isolated himself in his bedroom with the curtains drawn. After Foster's death, the *Wall Street Journal* and other conservative voices, including the Reverend Jerry Falwell, had a field day, spinning yarns about how Foster had been wrapped up in plots and cover-ups that would make Watergate look tame by comparison. Above all, the scandalmongers alleged, Foster possessed damaging knowledge and information about the Clintons' involvement, before Clinton became president, in a failed land development project in the Ozarks called Whitewater—a scheme to which all sorts of other serious crimes were supposedly connected.

Clinton was no stranger to the more gothic political smears that arose out of politics in Arkansas. In his rapid progress from serving as an intern to Senator J. William Fulbright to becoming the state's governor, he had attracted many enemies across the state, some because of his racial liberalism, others for pettier political and personal reasons. One of Clinton's wildest adversaries, a former segregationist politician active in right-wing circles, "Justice" Jim Johnson, had encouraged the publication in 1992 of a book, written by Floyd Brown (an ultraconservative Republican operative), with a title that caught on—*Slick Willie: Why America Cannot Trust Bill Clinton*. It was filled with invective and included the charge that Clinton was an anti-Christian blasphemer for having called for a "new covenant" among the American people. A year later, Johnson himself turned up in Washington at the annual conference of the Conservative Political Action Committee, claiming special knowledge of the new president as "a queer-mongering, whore-hopping adulterer; a baby-killing, draft-dodging, dope-tolerating, lying, two-faced, treasonist activist." Out of all this arose a host of claims that Clinton was everything from a drug-trafficker to a serial murderer. But one set of charges, connected to the Whitewater deal, found its way to the front page of the *New York Times* in 1992, and so was a cause for greater concern.

In 1978, while Clinton was the boy wonder of Arkansas as its attorney general, he and his wife borrowed money from a former aide of Fulbright's and the former state Democratic Party chairman—a flashy, ingratiating businessman, James McDougal—to invest in a new project of McDougal's called Whitewater, developing vacation homes along the White River. Clinton had known McDougal for a decade, and was taken in by his eccentric, upbeat charm. But the investment failed, costing the Clintons $60,000— and McDougal proved to be shadier and more erratic than Clinton had suspected. After the Whitewater project and during the S&L frenzy of the 1980s, McDougal took control of an institution he named Madison Guaranty Savings and Loan, and he proceeded to turn it into a source of ready cash and loans—including, according to later unfounded allegations, his old friend (now the governor of Arkansas) Bill Clinton. But Madison Guaranty soon collapsed, requiring a $50 million federal bailout; McDougal, who had become an alcoholic and drug addict, suffered a psychological breakdown and stood trial for fraud, winning an acquittal in 1990. (He was later convicted of bank fraud conspiracy in 1996 and died in prison.)

Early in the campaign of 1992, an investigative reporter for the *New York Times*, Jeff Gerth, got wind of the connection between Clinton and McDougal. On March 8, the *Times* printed a front-page story by Gerth stating that the Arkansas securities commissioner, Beverly Bassett Schaffer, had granted favors to McDougal and Madison Guaranty at the direct prodding of Clinton and his wife. (In fact, Schaffer had requested federal authorities to shut down McDougal's operation, and she provided proof to the *Times* before it published its story, but Gerth and his editors ignored it.) Gerth's principal source was Sheffield Nelson, a former political rival of Clinton's, who had run unsuccessfully against him for governor, and had been McDougal's partner in a scheme that bilked Madison Guaranty. None of this appeared in the *Times*'s story. After the exposé appeared in the *Times*, another of Gerth's main sources, the unsteady McDougal, retracted his charges against the Clintons, and a close forensic investigation by a professional accounting firm of the tangled records led to a report that exonerated the Clintons of any wrongdoing. Yet as Bill Clinton advanced closer to the presidency, Republicans, all the way up to the White House, applied pressure to revive the stories about Whitewater and Madison Guaranty.

In Tulsa, Oklahoma, L. Jean Lewis, a regional investigator for the Resolution Trust Corporation (RTC)—the temporary agency established to sort out the finances of the S&L mess—read the *Times*'s article and on her own prepared an elaborate criminal referral directly implicating the Clintons. Although higher-ups at the RTC dismissed the claims of the referral—the investigator was known to be an ardent Republican partisan—the Bush campaign in Washington learned of the document and, in conjunction with Attorney General William Barr, pressured the RTC and officials at the Justice Department for further information. The FBI office in Little Rock repeatedly denied that there was any evidence to suggest that the Clintons even knew about McDougal's improprieties, let alone were party to them. At one point, the U.S. attorney in Little Rock, a Republican appointee, sent a severe letter to his superior, Attorney General Barr, saying that the entire affair "appears to suggest an intentional or unintentional attempt to intervene into the political process of the upcoming presidential election." With that, the Whitewater affair disappeared, but only temporarily.

Vincent Foster's suicide rekindled the interest of the press in the story. Various Arkansans (particularly a Republican municipal court judge in Little Rock, David Hale, convicted for embezzling funds from the federal Small Business Administration) began peddling fabricated stories about McDougal and the Clintons. The RTC investigator, L. Jean Lewis, resubmitted her criminal referral. By the autumn, the entire press corps was in a feeding frenzy, searching for any scrap of information dealing with Whitewater—and a small band of right-wing activists who had helped Floyd

Brown produce *Slick Willie* at "Justice" Jim Johnson's instigation began providing a stream of falsehoods to the broadcast news networks and the major
newspapers. (The activists included David Bossie, a Republican operative
who served as Brown's chief research assistant and is currently the president of a right-wing activist group, Citizens United.) The *Wall Street Journal* once again led the way in assailing the Clintons, demanding to know
whether taxpayers' money was siphoned "to fuel Bill's political ambitions."
But the furor was not restricted to conservative organs. "This is a man who
rode into Washington on a pledge to end politics as usual and every time
the White House dodges inquiries about the old days in Arkansas, reasonable people begin to wonder about a cover-up and Mr. Clinton's sincerity,"
the *New York Times* said in an editorial.

At the end of 1993 and in early 1994, the pressure on the Clintons became
so great that they had to face two difficult decisions, both of which divided
their in-house advisers. In the past, the Clinton White House had tried
to accommodate the political and public outcry for full disclosure, as in
the episodes involving Zoë Baird and Kimba Wood. But now the Clintons
were being asked to release their own personal legal and financial records
voluntarily, for scrutiny by reporters, including some who seemed hell-bent
on finding some sort of embarrassing irregularity. The press's clamoring
had come to the Clinton's own doorstep—and there were no guarantees
that giving up some records would not create demands for more and more,
thereby paralyzing the administration.

Speaking in favor of disclosure was the youthful White House communications aide (a veteran of the 1992 campaign) George Stephanopoulos, as
well as David Gergen, an experienced Republican political consultant and
former adviser to Nixon, Ford, and Reagan, whom Clinton had brought
into the administration earlier in the year to help improve public relations.
Stephanopoulos and Gergen endorsed the conventional post-Watergate
wisdom that voluntary disclosure was the only sure way to ward off further
accusations—and, more important, to prevent official investigations that
could prove disastrous. The White House counsel Bernard Nussbaum—
a highly respected lawyer from New York who had been counsel to the
House Judiciary Committee in its inquiry regarding the impeachment of
Richard Nixon and had served as an assistant U.S. attorney—argued that
nothing should be given up without a fight, and that anything the Clintons
provided to a voracious and self-important press would only worsen the
situation. The Clintons' personal lawyer, David Kendall, agreed, as did the
family's representative (and lawyer) Bruce Lindsey. Lindsey, in particular,

believed that it was time to halt once and for all the cannibalization that was becoming all too common in the press corps.

The president reportedly said he was willing to be accommodating, but he deferred to the first lady, who stood squarely with the lawyers. Later investigations would affirm that the papers contained nothing implicating the Clintons in any criminal wrongdoing. In the meantime, pressure to ask for an appointment of a special prosecutor was building among some senior Democrats in the Senate, as well as in the press. The White House deputy chief of staff, Harold Ickes, along with Stephanopoulos, thought an investigation was now inevitable. But Mrs. Clinton, who had served on the staff of the House Watergate committee, thought that appointing a special prosecutor when there was no legal basis for suspecting wrongdoing directly violated the spirit and the letter of the original independent counsel law. Nussbaum was even more pointed, denouncing the special prosecutor as an "evil" institution that would provide prosecutors with subpoena power with which they would wander endlessly through the president's business until they found something, anything, to justify their investigations. The Clintons, Nussbaum advised, should do all that they could (including now voluntarily releasing papers, which he had originally opposed) to avoid appointing a special counsel.

Nussbaum's analysis and advice proved prescient, but President Clinton, who was torn, finally decided he should "lance the boil," as Secretary of the Treasury Lloyd Bentsen put it. (Clinton made up his mind while he was mourning his mother, who had just died of cancer—and he later said it was the worst decision of his presidency.) On January 20, at Clinton's behest, Attorney General Reno named the widely respected attorney and former federal prosecutor Robert Fiske Jr. of New York, a Republican, as Whitewater special counsel. Fiske, an impartial investigator, uncovered no evidence implicating the Clintons in any crime. Effectively, his probe reaffirmed, independently, what early professional investigators had concluded. But Fiske's tenure as special prosecutor would be brief.

In August, after Congress renewed the independent counsel statute, a panel of three federal judges charged by the law to appoint independent counsels stepped in. The panel, called the Special Division—selected by Chief Justice William Rehnquist, and chaired since 1992 by Judge David Sentelle, a hard-line conservative who was a close friend of Senator Jesse Helms of North Carolina—ruled that Fiske must step aside, as he had been named to the job by Reno, a presidential appointee. The judges could just as easily have reappointed Fiske on their own authority, conforming to the newly reauthorized law and confirming Fiske's reputation for fairness. Instead, the panel replaced Fiske with Kenneth Starr, a former solicitor general of the United States during the Bush administration and a U.S. district court judge—a conservative with no prosecutorial experience. Starr was not thought of, at the time, as especially partisan or ideological. In 1991, the Bush administration had passed him over for the Supreme Court nomination that went to Clarence Thomas because officials at the Justice Department had labeled him a "squish"—movement argot for someone deemed ideologically unreliable. He had famously ruled in favor of the *Washington Post* in a libel suit brought against it by the chief of Mobil Oil, issuing a decision upholding freedom of the press in terms that might have been framed by the most liberal jurist. The Clintons even gave him a guided tour of the White House.

But over the months before he took over as special prosecutor, Starr quietly served as an adviser to a legal team on another explosive case. In May 1994, a former employee of the state of Arkansas, Paula Corbin Jones, filed a sexual harassment suit demanding $700,000 in an Arkansas federal court, charging that three years earlier, while he was governor, Clinton had propositioned her and lewdly exposed himself in a hotel room in Little Rock. The suit had clear political connections: the National Conservative Political Action Committee, a year after it was host to Jim Johnson, sponsored Jones's announcement that she would sue the president, with financial backing from conservative sources. Critics, including five former presidents of the American Bar Association, later complained, to no avail, that under the circumstances Starr's selection as independent prosecutor was wildly inappropriate. Clinton's legal as well as political troubles had taken a turn for the worse, just as the midterm congressional election season was opening.

In addition to the budget of 1993, the Clinton administration could point to several significant domestic achievements during its first two years. In 1994, Clinton's nominee for the Supreme Court, Stephen Breyer, a distinguished professor at the Harvard Law School, won easy confirmation from the Senate, and joined Clinton's successful nominee from the year before, Justice Ruth Bader Ginsburg, one of the nation's most prominent advocates of women's rights. The continuing Democratic congressional majority eased the confirmation process, and Breyer and Ginsburg, both pragmatic moderate liberals, did not dramatically change the court's overall judicial outlook. But their selection seemed to guarantee that, for the time being, the court majority would resist the rightward turn that had begun with the selection of Justices Scalia and Thomas, and the elevation of William Rehnquist to Chief Justice.

In September 1994, Clinton signed a law that banned the sale of nineteen kinds of semiautomatic assault weapons. Congress also passed the so-called motor-voter law that enabled citizens to register to vote when they applied for a driver's license; approved and modestly funded the new AmeriCorps program, offering young people federal aid to pay for college tuition in exchange for their community service work (more than 400,000 would sign up); authorized a new education bill that would send $2 billion to the states to improve education standards; and passed a law making obstruction of health clinics (a favored tactic of antiabortion militants) a federal crime. At the same time, Clinton won passage of a $30 billion crime bill that toughened penalties for federal crimes and provided money to add 100,000 new officers to police forces in communities around the country.

All these initiatives, major and minor, testified to the president's abiding attachment to federal programs as solutions to national problems—but they could not reverse the president's steady decline in popular esteem. Clinton's successes galvanized his opposition—for example, the gun manufacturers' lobby and the National Rifle Association, which mobilized against the new gun law. The continued scandalmongering over Whitewater and the Paula Jones case tarnished the president's image. Bad feelings persisted within his own party over NAFTA, and the AFL-CIO labor federation pledged not to help Democrats who had voted for the agreement. Above all, the final collapse of the health care initiative in September 1994 reinforced the impression that the administration, despite its early self-assurance, was inept as well as inexperienced.

Republicans, led by the House minority whip, Newt Gingrich, organized in order to make Clinton pay dearly for these failures in the midterm elections. Gingrich (originally named Newt McPherson) had been a lonely child, the stepson of an authoritarian army officer who relocated the family from one military base to another. He escaped by marrying one of his high school teachers, who taught him to drive, which his stepfather had forbidden him to do. Gingrich soon abandoned a floundering career as a history professor at West Georgia College in favor of politics, winning a seat in Congress in 1978 after two failed attempts, and rising within the House Republican caucus. A conservative ideologue and firebrand, Gingrich was not interested in making deals or compromises in the legislature; he sought the complete destruction of a Democratic congressional leadership that he considered antiquated, corrupt, and oppressive. A skilled tactician and ruthless infighter, Gingrich had engineered the overthrow of Representative Jim Wright of Texas—who was Tip O'Neill's successor as Speaker of the House and a canny, prickly politician. He achieved this by blowing up a casual arrangement whereby the Teamsters Union bought 1,000 copies of a compilation of Wright's speeches—an arrangement that bordered on being unethical but was not illegal and did not enrich Wright. Instructing his fellow Republicans to be fiercer in their attacks, Gingrich demonized Democrats and liberals (including the Clintons) as "counter-cultural McGoverniks," and he fancied himself as the "Definer of civilization." Aided by a group of young, southern conservatives in the House, including Richard Armey and Tom DeLay of Texas, Gingrich saw partisan politics as unending ideological war, in which character assassination was a preferred strategy. "I am a transformational figure," he proclaimed. "I'm a much tougher partisan than they've seen . . . much more intense, much more persistent, much more willing to take risks to get it done."

The indictment, in May 1994, of Dan Rostenkowski of Illinois, chairman of the House Ways and Means Committee, over embezzlement of House funds, gave Gingrich and his supporters a great political advantage by removing a powerful figure who might have helped Clinton in the battle over health care. The indictment also added to the growing impression, fed by the reporting of Whitewater, that the entire Democratic Party was corrupt. In order to exploit that mood, as well as the Democrats' disunity and their lack of clear political direction, Gingrich decided to nationalize the Republicans' fall campaign. Instead of running in 435 separate district elections, Republicans would fight as a team, coming across not as naysayers but as positive, principled, and ready to lead the nation—armed with a bold, conservative ideology that (Gingrich and his supporters believed) had been lost during the milquetoast, compromising years of the Bush administration.

Gingrich's main instrument was a ten-point program he devised with Dick Armey and others (and with help from the Republican pollster Frank Luntz) called the "Contract with America." The "contract" carefully avoided any mention of the divisive social issues that the Republican right had long favored, such as abortion and school prayer, lest it alienate libertarian conservatives and independents. Instead, it invoked Abraham Lincoln, attacked congressional malfeasance, attacked "one-party control" and "government that is too big, too intrusive" and offered a laundry list of reforms.

These included a dramatic overhaul of the federal welfare system, approval of a constitutional "balanced budget/tax limitation" amendment, a ban on U.S. troops serving under UN command, severe curtailment of federal regulations, and prescribed limits on the terms of senators and congressmen. A close look at the actual legislation proposed showed that the contract was far more radical than it sounded at first, auguring a full-scale, pro-business attack on reform traditions dating back to the Progressive era—including the virtual repeal of decades' worth of legislation protecting consumers and the environment. How much the voters understood the document, let alone how many found it persuasive, is dubious: later surveys found that not even one out of three respondents had heard of the contract. But as Republican candidates for the House flocked to sign on—367 endorsed it at a mass gathering at the Capitol in September—the program gave the party coherence and confidence, which the Democrats lacked.

Quite apart from the innovations by Gingrich and the House Republicans in strategy and tactics, the Democrats sensed that the country's mood had turned against them. As early as May, Clinton's pollster Stanley Greenberg was discovering in focus groups that the voters believed the president was in over his head—immature, indecisive, and struggling simply to handle his job. Hillary Clinton was shocked by what she saw in her barnstorming appearances to build support for health care, saying of one group of protesters in Seattle, numbering in the hundreds, that she had not seen such visceral hatred since the battles over segregation in the 1960s.

The waves of discontent turned into an electoral rout of historic proportions. In the House, the Democrats lost fifty-four seats, giving the Republicans the majority for the first time in forty years, by a margin of 230 to 204. The new Congress included seventy-three freshman Republicans, many of them southerners who stood well to the right of the traditional House Republican leadership—and, in many cases, to the right of the new leadership. The Republicans also regained control of the Senate by fifty-two seats to forty-eight. No incumbent Republican senator, congressman, or governor lost, whereas some nationally known Democrats, including Governor Mario Cuomo of New York, were turned out. The morning after the election, Clinton addressed the White House press corps, looking shell-shocked: "I think [the voters] were saying two things to me—or maybe three . . . maybe three hundred." Only halfway through his elected term, the fresh face Clinton had tried to put on politics after twelve years of Reagan and Bush seemed to have withered. In his place as the leading figure in American politics and government was the newly elected speaker of the Republican-dominated House, determined, he said, to complete the job Ronald Reagan had started—civilization's self-styled definer, Newt Gingrich.

Clinton knew he would have to retool the politics of his presidency, and to do so he reached out to an expert consultant, Dick Morris, a former associate who had lately worked mainly for Republicans. It had been Morris who, on the eve of the election, predicted to Clinton the devastating results that the president could not quite believe until the returns were actually in. In preparing for his State of the Union message in January, Clinton had Morris secretly conduct an elaborate poll to understand better the hundreds of things that the voters had told them. The results affirmed Morris's basic political instinct—that Clinton should co-opt the most popular features of Gingrich's program about reducing the deficit, shrinking the government, and reforming welfare, leaving the Republicans with only unpopular causes like opposing abortion rights and opposing environmental protection. By co-optation, Morris did not mean capitulation. Clinton, he said, should insist on a "Democratic way of achieving" the Republicans' priorities, including prudent trimming of government agencies rather than outright elimination as well as firm opposition to cuts in popular social programs such as Medicare.

Morris's long career had gained him a reputation, especially among liberals, as a cynical, even tawdry operator. (Hillary Clinton, who made the first call to Morris, tried to defend him to Harold Ickes, a longtime foe of Morris's, as a hardheaded man who knew how to win elections and understood the underside of politics. "He *is* the underside," Ickes retorted.) Morris's presence unsettled many of Clinton's advisers as well as his more liberal supporters in Washington and around the country. In particular, his name was closely linked to his term "triangulation," which came to be interpreted merely in terms of personal power: Clinton, supposedly, would abandon principle in order to seek (through polls, primarily) the maximally advantageous position, perched neatly between Democratic liberals and Republican conservatives. More than anything else, Clinton's new reliance on Morris turned Clintonism, in many quarters, into a byword for unprincipled opportunism and expediency.

Yet for Clinton, who understood American politics as the art of the possible, triangulation was not a cynical ploy but an obvious necessity after the elections of 1994—and a means to revive and reinforce the refurbishing of

American liberalism about which he had been talking long before his election. His choices had narrowed. He could not turn his presidency over to the Democrats in Congress, who were now the minority. Putting himself in the place of those whom he had once called the "very burdened middle class" and who now despised him, Clinton recognized that the New Deal consensus in favor of active federal government was in retreat. He later reflected that he actually agreed with many of the particulars in the "Contract with America," including welfare reform, although he thought the document itself "simplistic and hypocritical," especially on fiscal issues. Yet Clinton was not convinced that alienated middle-class voters were truly drawn to what he considered the hard-right, "gilded age," devil-take-the-hindmost conservatism of Gingrich and his troops, which they disguised as the principles of their futuristic "conservative opportunity society." More than ever, Clinton's self-imposed task was to reimagine a government-supported social compact that would be agreeable to the masses of Americans now skeptical and even resentful of large government programs—and that would spare the country what he called the Republicans' resentful "law of the jungle." "You can have good policies without good politics," he would later reflect, "but you can't give the people good government without both."

While Clinton worked on elaborating, in his State of the Union address, what he called a "new covenant," complete with a "middle-class bill of rights" consisting chiefly of tax credits, the new Republican leadership took command. As Speaker of the House, Newt Gingrich said he would emulate the activist style of the great nineteenth-century congressional leader Henry Clay (famously known as the "Great Conciliator," a title nobody would associate with Gingrich). Ignoring seniority rules, Gingrich ensured the selection of committee chairmen who were directly loyal to him, then forced through further changes in party rules that concentrated power inside the Republican caucus in his cadre of hard-line conservatives. Gingrich had promised to act on all ten items in the "Contract with America" within 100 days of taking power, and by April 7, the House had voted on all ten and passed nine. Gingrich himself was now the toast of Washington and of the national news media, actually capable of persuading several television networks to grant him airtime at the 100-day mark—a privilege normally granted only to presidents on momentous occasions. Yet even as Gingrich rode high, the new conservative dispensation was raising concern.

In part, Americans began getting a closer look at just who was now in power—and the sight could be very disturbing. Although Gingrich and his Republican hotspurs followed their hero Reagan in casting their conservatism as a forward-looking, optimistic creed, the radicalism of their antigovernment politics ran deeper than Reagan's. And their hatred of everything that they thought even slightly liberal could come across as truculent and mean-spirited. Richard Armey of Texas, now the House majority leader, was particularly prone to express hard-right Republicanism openly. In the House, Armey taunted the Democrats, referring to Clinton as "your president." He called the veteran, openly gay congressman Barney Frank of Massachusetts "Barney Fag." Social Security, according to Armey (a former economics professor who had failed to obtain tenure at North Texas State University), was a "rotten trick."

Swirling around the triumphant new majority, meanwhile, were signs of virulent, apocalyptic strains of right-wing politics, and signs that at least some Republicans on the right condoned them. With the cold war over, all sorts of marginal groups began turning their anger against the federal government—and these groups no longer seemed so marginal. The Reverend Pat Robertson's Christian Coalition now claimed 1.2 million members, and was, after the elections of 1994, more closely coordinated than ever with the Republican Party. Only three years earlier, Robertson had published an alarming tract, *The New World Order*, in which he projected immense conspiracies of Illuminati and Freemasons who, through the work of communists and liberals, were trying to create a single world government that would destroy Christian America. Other right-wing groups included some 800 armed militias organized in twenty-three states. One Republican, Representative Helen Chenoweth of Idaho, invited the leader of the militia movement in her home district to testify in local hearings about mysterious black helicopters supposedly flown by secret agents of the United Nations, preparing the way for an invasion. According to Chenoweth, most of the United States had fallen under "the control of the New World Order." Violence by antiabortion extremists, directed against doctors and patients, and including several murders, had also risen precipitously since Clinton signed the clinic-entrance act; and some antiabortion activists excused the killings as "justifiable homicide."

On April 18, the political fortunes of the White House reached a low. President Clinton held a press conference in prime time, but, in sharp contrast to the media coverage being lavished on Gingrich, only one network agreed to broadcast it. Responding to a pointed question about whether he feared he was not even being heard anymore, Clinton was pathetic. "The Constitution gives me relevance," he replied. "The power of our ideas gives me relevance. The record we have built up over the last two years and the things we're trying to do to implement it give it relevance. The president is relevant here." It was as if by pleading that he still counted, Clinton could somehow make it so.

At 9:02 the next morning, a rented truck packed with ammonium nitrate and nitromethane exploded outside the Alfred P. Murrah Federal Building in Oklahoma City. The blast ripped through government offices (as well as an office workers' child-care facility), killing 168 people, including nineteen children, and wounding 600. This was the worst incident of domestic terrorism in American history—and, within a few days, it became very clear that it had been the work of right-wing extremists in the militia movement. The conspirators, who were soon apprehended by the authorities, included Timothy McVeigh, who actually touched off the bomb, and his accomplices, the brothers Terry and James Nichols. McVeigh was especially frightening—a severe, hatchet-faced young man who wore a neo-Confederate T-shirt with the words of Abraham Lincoln's assassin, John Wilkes Booth, "Sic Semper Tyrannis" ("Ever Thus to Tyrants"). Given to proclaiming slogans of the extreme right-wing Christian Identity movement, McVeigh was a close reader of the neo-Nazi writer William Pierce, whose book *The Turner Diaries* described the overthrow of a Jewish-controlled U.S. government. The attack had been timed to coincide with the second anniversary of the tragedy at Waco involving David Koresh, which had become a source of bitter resentment on the farther reaches of the antigovernment right.

Four days after the crime, on a Sunday, President Clinton addressed 18,000 mourners packed inside an auditorium in Oklahoma City for a prayer and memorial service. "Let us let our own children know that we will stand up against the forces of fear," Clinton said. "When there is talk of hatred, let us stand up and talk against it." At one level, Clinton performed, with eloquence and grace, an act incumbent on all presidents, to help the nation cope with sudden, horrible events. At another level, his sermon paid homage to the public servants who had died senselessly—no longer faceless federal bureaucrats but men and women doing their jobs for the commonweal. And Clinton also stared down the incendiary hate that had been stirred up on the right, including portions of the hard Republican right. In a speech at Michigan State University in May, he underscored his rejection of the rancid politics that had led to the atrocity in Oklahoma City. "There is nothing patriotic about hating your country, or pretending you can love your country but despise your government," he said, his voice touched with anger. "How dare you suggest that we, in the freest nation on earth, live in tyranny?"

Clinton had now put his relevance as president on display, and the public responded; 84 percent of those contacted in a poll conducted by the *Wall Street Journal* and NBC News expressed approval of his handling of the tragedy. Yet Clinton had acted as something more than the nation's comforter, by providing a context for the nation's outrage as well as its grief. In doing so, he reversed the prevailing conservative militancy, at least for a moment, taking his stand against those who vilified the federal government as the enemy of the true America.

The full political significance of Oklahoma City would not become clear for months and even years. But by piercing through the antigovernment animus that underlay the tragedy, Clinton helped shift the political mood. The shift would dramatically alter the dynamics of his presidency.

CLINTON'S COMEBACK

IN POLITICS, HAVING THE right enemies can sometimes be as important and beneficial as having the right friends. The struggling Bill Clinton was not only beset by but also blessed with Newt Gingrich as his
chief political adversary in 1995 and early 1996. By masterminding the
Republicans' monumental congressional victory in 1994, Gingrich proved
he was formidable. In the process Gingrich created what he boasted of as
"the most explicitly ideologically committed House Republican Party in
modern history." Persuaded of his manifest historic greatness and the inevitability of his "conservative opportunity society," Gingrich was certain that
his ideas dominated the nation and his party as thoroughly as he dominated
the House. Yet following a classic revolutionary pattern, he proved to be too
tame for his more zealous lieutenants and foot soldiers, while his ascendancy united hitherto divided Democrats against him. And in the crunch,
Gingrich's self-important dramatics proved no match for Bill Clinton's
political adroitness, as Gingrich himself came to admit.

Thousands of miles away, Clinton faced a spine-chilling enemy in the
Serbian Slobodan Milosevic, the ex-communist turned nationalist strongman. In May 1995, a temporary cease-fire in the fighting in Bosnia, brokered by the former president Jimmy Carter, came to an end. Milosevic
and the Serbs decided to destroy Bosnia once and for all as an effective independent entity. After invading safety zones supposedly guarded by the
UN peacekeeping troops—the UNPROFOR—Serbian forces expanded
their "ethnic cleasing" campaign against the Bosnian Muslim population.
In May, Clinton finally arranged for some air strikes against Serb positions,

but these attacks emboldened the Serbs to seize UNPROFOR troops as hostages. When the UN soldiers were finally released, the Allied command, under control of the Europeans, ceased its bombing raids and declared that the UNPROFOR would return to its traditional peacekeeping mission. The way was cleared for the Serbs to begin the most gruesome campaign of mass murder in Europe since the Nazis' destruction of the Jews. Clinton, while engaged in a fight for his political life at home, now faced moral obloquy in Bosnia—but he lacked public support at home for a major commitment of U.S. troops.

Clinton struggled to regain the initiative simultaneously in domestic and foreign affairs. The first struggle, revolving around fierce budget negotiations, culminated in late December 1995, when for the second time in a month the Republicans' intransigence over the budget forced a shutdown of the federal government. The second struggle, involving an unprecedented bombing campaign by NATO in Bosnia, followed with a negotiated settlement ending the horror, concluded, also in December, when the first NATO troops deployed to enforce the new agreement arrived in Sarajevo.

By the time Clinton delivered his State of the Union message in late January 1996, he was well on his way toward winning a convincing reelection in the fall—a outcome that had appeared virtually impossible only two years earlier. There would be fresh battles along the way, above all with liberal Democrats over his signing of a major welfare reform bill in August 1996. But after the campaign of 1996 and through the first year of its second term, the Clinton administration seemed to have hit its full stride. Some liberals, to be sure, remained at best lukewarm, alienated by the president's centrist maneuvers. But to the shock and revulsion of Republican conservatives, what some had called Gingrich's revolution suddenly seemed to be running out of steam. And on the fate of that revolution, many Republicans believed, hinged the continuation or the collapse of the age of Reagan.

Clinton's first political crisis of 1995, curiously, found him siding with Gingrich against an odd coalition of liberal Democrats and conservative Republicans in Congress. In mid-January, Robert Rubin (who had just succeeded Lloyd Bentsen as secretary of the treasury) and the highest-ranking international economist at the treasury, now the deputy secretary, Lawrence Summers, apprised the president of the imminent default by the Mexican government of its foreign financial obligations, unless the United States committed up to $25 billion in loans to prop up the collapsing peso.

The risks were enormous, but Clinton, grasping that a failure by Mexico would have grave consequences for American national interests as well as for the global economy, committed himself early to providing the aid. Anti-NAFTA labor-oriented Democrats and congressional liberals suspected that a dark Wall Street plot lay behind the rescue plan, as did isolationist conservatives who also saw no reason to bail out a wretched nation that, in their eyes, gave America nothing but illegal immigrants and illicit drugs. (Gingrich, though, like Clinton, saw the emergency in Mexico as "the first crisis of the twenty-first century," pledged his support, and helped prevent his ally, the fiery talk-radio host Rush Limbaugh, from stirring up right-wing populists over the issue.) Despite Gingrich's position, Congress blocked the president, and so the White House provided the aid unilaterally by tapping the Economic Stabilization Fund, established in 1934 to minimize currency fluctuations. Within a few months, the Mexican economy was back on its feet, and a catastrophe had been averted.

Domestic fiscal and economic issues produced different sorts of political fights, pitting Clinton against Gingrich but also dividing the administration's inner councils. Through mid-spring, as the new Republican majority in the House moved into action, the administration was deliberately passive, excoriating Republicans' proposals for cuts in popular social programs such as Medicare but without offering any concrete budget proposal of its own. The strategy, arranged in concert with congressional Democrats, was to let the Republicans destroy themselves as the public gradually caught on to the harsh realities of their policies. But holding back made Clinton grow restive. He was also coming to share the view, put forward most vociferously by his political adviser Dick Morris but also favored by Vice President Gore and Hillary Clinton, that he ought to propose his own version of a balanced budget plan. For Morris, this was a straightforward matter of smart, triangulating politics. For Clinton, whose economic advisers had long told him that the deficit was a drag on capital formation and economic growth, it was both smart politics and smart policy.

In a brief speech to the nation on June 13—the major television networks grudgingly granted him only five minutes of airtime—Clinton announced his budget plan, attached to a proposal to balance the annual federal budget by 2005. Although he was careful to spell out his differences from the Republicans—by holding the line on education and Medicare, aiming tax cuts for the middle class and not the wealthy—the president seized the mantle of fiscal responsibility. Congressional Democrats—more liberal as a group after the defeat of many conservative Democrats in 1994—instantly called the president a turncoat, a "me-too" Democrat, and worse. (Representative Pat Schroeder of Colorado said the Republicans were playing with Clinton "like a kitten with a string.") But the budget speech was just the opening salvo in a strategic offensive, whereby Clinton outflanked the Republicans by stealing their more popular issues and phrases and Democratizing them.

The day before the president gave his speech about the budget, the Supreme Court handed down an important ruling on affirmative action, in *Adarand Constructors Inc. v. Pena*. The court sustained the basic idea of race-based preferences but also demanded specific and compelling evidence of past discrimination in all arrangements favoring minorities for government contracts. As it happened, the administration was completing its own lengthy review of affirmative action, and in late July, in a speech at the National Archives, Clinton presented the conclusions, which were in line with the court's reasoning: "No quotas in theory or practice," Clinton announced, "no illegal discrimination of any kind, including reverse discrimination; no preference for people who are not qualified for any job or other opportunity; and as soon as a program has succeeded it must be retired." The president summed up his position in a slogan—"Mend it, but don't end it"—and stressed his belief that affirmative action had benefited the country. But in sketching out its limits, he also tried to ease white voters' anxiety, exploited in election after election by Republicans, that the entire program was nothing but reverse discrimination on behalf of blacks and Hispanics.

Clinton pressed his summer offensive into the autumn, and on many fronts. In July, he spoke out on the contentious issue of school prayer, taking a middling position that would allow administrators, teachers, and students some latitude in honoring religious observance so long as it was not mandatory. (Earlier that month, referring to his own schooldays in Arkansas, when daily prayer was "as common as apple pie," Clinton had said, "Now, you could say, 'Well, it certainly didn't do any harm. It might have done a little good.'") He also endorsed a stream of initiatives and regulations aimed at curbing a perceived breakdown in moral and cultural standards, especially among young people: a ban on tobacco sales to minors; the mandatory wearing of school uniforms as an antidote to crime, violence, and drug use among youngsters; the installation of a V-chip device in television sets that would permit parents to block broadcasts they thought too violent or sexually graphic. "We have to do what we can to strengthen our families and to help them through these changing times," Clinton remarked in early August, during one of his weekly nationwide radio addresses.

In conventional political terms, Clinton appeared to be trying to salvage his presidency by moving as far to the right as any Democrat dared. Some liberals were appalled. Gingrich and the conservative Republicans, meanwhile, became more confident than ever, certain that they had Clinton cornered, interpreting the president's tactics as a sign of weakness. The big test would be the final negotiations over the budget—and the logic of triangulation seemed to dictate that Clinton would try to save face while basically surrendering to the majority in Congress.

But Gingrich founded his confidence on a misreading. The president may have sounded more conservative than ever, thumping in favor of order, accountability, family values, and fiscal discipline. But Clinton was also redefining conservative code words in liberal ways, linking the sustenance of all-American virtues to his own ideas of social justice and active government—and turning the code against the Republicans. "The congressional majority seems to be determined to cut back on programs that advance our family values," he said in August, when the House was passing deep cuts in social spending:

> How can you talk about family values in one breath, and in the next, take Head Start away from 50,000 poor children or cut back college loans and grants for students who need and deserve them or cut back worker training for people who are unemployed? But all that happened in the House of Representatives this week. They call it change. I say it shortchanges America's families in the fight for the future. This vote is antifamily, and I won't let it stand.

Having recovered from the shock of the midterm defeat, Clinton knew exactly where he was headed—even if some of his closest advisers did not.

Told by his political consultant Paul Begala that many in the White House now assumed he would eventually give way and approve a draconian budget agreeable to the Republicans, Clinton expressed astonishment.

"They can't really believe that, can they, Paulie?" he replied. "They can't really believe I'll cave to their demands?"

Still, over the coming months, Clinton would have to prove himself anew—and not simply over the budget.

By July 1995, the killing and mayhem were almost constant in Bosnia, and there was worse to come. On the morning of July 6, Bosnian Serb troops, working with the Milosevic regime, invaded the town of Srebenica, one of the enclaves that had been declared safe zones under the UNPROFOR and now teeming with tens of thousands of refugees from the surrounding region. The UN commanders rejected a radioed request for an air strike, and the Serbs had a free hand to carry out plans long in the making. The UNPROFOR troops were shoved aside; some 23,000 women and children were transported by bus and train to Muslim territory; and more than 7,000 men and boys were systematically executed and their bodies dumped in mass graves. The full extent of the horror would not be known for several weeks, but its basic shape—as the greatest single act of mass murder recorded since World War II—was immediately apparent.

The atrocity at Srebenica finally galvanized sentiment within the administration, even though American public opinion still ran against any major commitment of U.S. troops. The ambassador to the United Nations, Madeleine Albright, laid it on the line in a memo to the president: "Fairly or unfairly," she wrote, "your entire first term is going to be judged by how you deal with Bosnia." The secretary of defense, William Perry, and the chairman of the Joint Chiefs of Staff, John Shalikashvili (who had succeeded Colin Powell in 1993), had both been wary of intervening in Bosnia, but Srebenica shook them as well. Perry, in particular, had concluded that a major show of airpower would crush the Bosnian Serbs and Milosevic— "not a bomb or two, not a pinprick, but a massive air campaign."

Clinton charged his national security adviser, Anthony Lake, with formulating a comprehensive strategy to end the nightmare. In August, with encouragement from the United States, the Croat army, allied with Muslim forces, invaded Serbian Krajina and drove Bosnian Serbs out of Croatia and northwest Bosnia. Lake, meanwhile, presented Clinton with a plan that would involve an Allied air campaign, lifting the embargo on transfers of arms to the Bosnians, and an initiative by the United States to lead negotiations aimed at achieving a settlement among Serbs, Muslims, and Croats. There were many iffy propositions in Lake's design, not least getting the reluctant European powers to go along without endangering the Western alliance. ("I'm risking my presidency," Clinton warned his adviser.) But by telling the Europeans that the United States was prepared to act unilaterally if necessary, Lake gained their grudging assent. At the end of August, when an attack by the Serbs in Sarajevo killed at least thirty-six civilians, Clinton authorized participation by the United States with NATO forces in Operation Deliberate Force. Eighteen days of saturation bombing—the largest military action in NATO's history—smashed the Serbian positions on the hills ringing Sarajevo.

With the combined Croatian and Muslim ground forces still advancing aggressively, Milosevic sued for peace. The Americans were now committed to initiating the negotiating process, and Clinton sent as his chief diplomat the tenacious assistant secretary of state for European affairs, Richard Holbrooke. Talks among American and European representatives, Milosevic, and Croat and Bosnian Muslim leaders were scheduled to begin at an air force base outside Dayton, Ohio, on November 1. Yet there were still reservations about Clinton's resolve. Officials at the State Department wondered whether, with an election year approaching, the president would be willing to commit the thousands of American troops that would be necessary to police any territorial agreement in the Balkans. Some insiders conjectured that Clinton secretly hoped the talks at Dayton would fall short of achieving a bold and firm solution—or any solution at all. If, as many observers suspected at the time, Clinton was bound to buckle under to the Republicans regarding the budget, would he not also give in to political pressure with regard to Bosnia?

While these doubts hung over the administration, a shocking tragedy intervened four days after the talks started at Dayton. On a quiet Saturday afternoon, Tony Lake called the White House residence with the news that Yitzhak Rabin had been shot in Jerusalem, after a rally in favor of the peace process, by a youthful right-wing Israeli extremist. Clinton had come to know and admire Rabin as a world leader of epic proportions, and he rushed to the Oval Office. Word soon arrived that Rabin was dead. After a long stunned silence, the president announced that he would leave for Israel immediately to attend the funeral. Bosnia, the budget, and all other urgent issues suddenly appeared to recede.

An impressive delegation accompanied the president on the melancholy journey to Israel, including the Senate majority leader, Robert Dole, and Speaker of the House Newt Gingrich. During the long flight home, Dole and Gingrich thought Clinton might set aside some time to talk over the budget. Having presented him with a plan that promised large tax cuts for the wealthy and reduced spending on various social programs, especially Medicare, Congress set a deadline of midnight on November 14. After that, unless some deal was arranged with the White House, federal offices would be cut off from their monies and be forced either to curtail their operations or shut down completely.

Clinton's aides, apprehensive about what he might concede in a private session on Air Force One, made sure that Dole and Gingrich stayed in the back of the plane for the entire flight, then instructed them to disembark from the back as well, along with the White House staff and the traveling press. Bargaining went down to the wire. The Republicans touted their budget as, in Gingrich's words, "a basic shift toward traditional America of more decentralized government and balanced budgets," the grandest domestic decision since the advent of the New Deal. That shift included an attack on Medicare, the most important federal social program since the enactment of Social Security in 1935. The Republicans' budget called for deep slashes in Medicare funding; moved the responsibility for Medicare payments from the federal government to the states, where they would be cut further; and provided enticements for healthy senior citizens to drop out of the program, thereby eroding Medicare's financial base and eliminating its universality.* Republican leaders hoped that they could reach a minimal compromise on Medicare and perhaps give Clinton some minor face-saving concessions in education or the environment. Their basic proposal, though, would remain intact—imposing deep cuts in social programs for the poor such as the earned income tax credit that were nowhere near as popular as Medicare, while putting Medicare on the road to extinction.

On the evening of November 13, Dole, Gingrich, and the House majority leader, Richard Armey, came to the White House to make one last try. Dole and Gingrich were conciliatory; Armey was more confrontational. To their surprise, Clinton was adamant, telling them that he didn't care if his approval ratings in the polls dropped to 5 percent; he would never sign the Republicans' regressive budget. Armey exchanged some harsh words with the president. With that, the meeting ended and the government shutdown began.

By doing what he said he would do all along, and doing it with righteous anger, Clinton caught even some on his own staff by surprise. The president was, in effect, betting on his basic sense that most Americans, no matter how much they griped about "big government," approved of the services government delivered to them personally, such as delivering the mail and forecasting the weather. He was also betting that, even though, technically, his refusal to agree to Congress's budget caused the shutdown,

---

* Aware of Medicare's popularity, Gingrich and the Republicans claimed they were not cutting Medicare, because their proposal still increased the actual amount spent per senior. The White House and Democrats on Capitol Hill, they asserted, were guilty of the worst sort of demagoguery. But in their outrage, they failed to disclose that the increases they proposed came nowhere near matching the annual increases in medical costs—thereby camouflaging their reductions.

the onus would fall on the Republicans in Congress, with their antigovernment talk. The polls quickly confirmed that he had won both bets. The Republicans, meanwhile, had made no plans about what to do in case of a shutdown. A peevish Gingrich worsened matters when he told reporters that the president's snubbing of him on Air Force One had contributed to his intransigence over the budget and hence to the shutdown. Thinking he was still master of the capital, Gingrich came across as infantile. The New York *Daily News* famously depicted him on its front page as a wailing baby in a diaper.

After six days of negotiations and acrid recriminations, the government shutdown ended. The very next day, Clinton had important news to report from the negotiations in Dayton regarding the Balkans: after a momentary fear that the talks would break down because of the Muslims' territorial demands, Holbrooke had brokered an agreement. As expected, the United States would be extensively involved in keeping the fragile peace, deploying 20,000 American troops as part of a NATO force that would replace UN-PROFOR. To sell the proposition to a dubious public, Clinton said that the deployment would last only one year—a highly unlikely prediction even at the time. But Clinton and Holbrooke could take pride and satisfaction in having halted the carnage.

As it happened, the struggle in Washington over the budget was also nearing its last phases. Undaunted by public sentiment, the congressional majority went ahead and approved its budget proposal, which Clinton duly vetoed on December 6, forcing another shutdown ten days later. This one would last for three weeks: federal workers across the country missed a paycheck; numerous popular government operations, including national parks, closed; even the Vermeer exhibit at the National Gallery on the Mall in Washington was shut; and public displeasure with the Republicans deepened. Polls found that a large majority now considered Gingrich and his coterie as not simply disruptive but unfeeling and mean-spirited, willing to disrupt the government's ability to function in order to attack a cornerstone of the American welfare state. Finally, in early January, the Republicans retreated by agreeing to fund departments and agencies lacking money for the current fiscal year, and then accepted the White House's version of deficit reduction, now intended to end federal deficits by 2002. Coming after Dayton, Clinton's victory in the issue of the budget was doubly remarkable. Immediately, his public ratings began to climb—including, for the very first time in his presidency, majority approval for his handling of foreign policy and his performance as commander in chief.

Looking back at his defeat over the budget, Newt Gingrich admitted that he was a victim of his own overconfidence—and of his underestimation of Bill Clinton. "People feeling confident of their own strength often fail to take proper measure of their opponents," he observed. "That was certainly the case with us and the president. Had we done our homework about this man, especially about his career in Arkansas, we never would have been quite so confident of our ability to push him into signing our legislation into law." The same could have been said of those who thought Clinton would not press the Dayton accords. Now, with a State of the Union address in the offing to begin the election year, the president who had lifted his administration out of its trough was presented with a chance for a new beginning. Clinton could start trying to make up for lost time. The "comeback kid" was back again.

Clinton's State of the Union message for 1996, on one level, was a list of accomplishments—including achieving the lowest combined rate of inflation and unemployment since the end of the 1960s—as well as of the kinds of "triangulated" proposals he had been making for months: requiring a V-chip in television sets, cracking down on young people's smoking, and so forth. The most famous line in the speech—"The era of big government is over"—became a weapon for liberals who viewed Clinton as digging the grave of Democratic liberalism. Political pundits seized on the phrase and came to the same conclusion. Few remembered the very next passage:

> But we can't go back to the era of fending for yourself. We have to go forward to the era of working together as a community, as a team, as one America, with all of us reaching across these lines that divide us—the division, the discrimination, the rancor—we have to reach across it to find common ground. We have got to work together if we want America to work.

The speech did not repudiate activist government but aimed at refurbishing it. It did repudiate antigovernment Republicanism and the fearful politics of division—echoing, with its evocation of "one America," Clinton's speeches in the aftermath of the bombing at Oklahoma City.

One of Clinton's proposals in this speech, though, upset liberals more than any other—and seemed, superficially, to substantiate their complaints. This was his call for "sweeping welfare reform" that would "really move people from welfare to work." Clinton's plea was serious, as was his assertion that he and Congress were already in "near agreement." Along with deficit reduction, welfare reform would define the president as a new kind of Democrat, clearing away the racialized slurs about "welfare queens" that had been central to national Republican politics since the late 1960s, and giving himself added political space to campaign for reelection. But there were more important policy issues at stake as well—and, as Clinton had already discovered, more treacherous political pitfalls than he had originally foreseen.

In retrospect, Clinton might have been wiser to take up welfare reform much earlier than he did. He had pledged during the campaign of 1992 to "end welfare as we know it," and there were some people on Capitol Hill, notably Senator Daniel Patrick Moynihan of New York, who scorned the president for choosing to push for health care reform first. Yet Clinton's decision to make health care his main concern had political merits in 1993. He had, after all, campaigned even harder on the health care initiative. Once he had decided that deficit reduction was a more pressing priority than a tax cut for the middle class or new federal spending programs, working for welfare reform at the same time would have severely curtailed support from liberal Democrats in the administration's early months, when Clinton could least afford it. Ironically, as it happened, with his original Democratic Congress Clinton might just have achieved a welfare bill to his liking and then been in better political shape to proceed on health care. Instead, even with Democratic majorities in the House and Senate, health care failed, paving the way for the Republican takeover in 1994. And although Clinton and the Republicans both favored welfare reform, he differed forcefully with the approach to the issue taken by the new Republican majority.

Clinton had been drawn to the idea of welfare reform since the 1980s. It was, to him, a matter of humaneness and principle as well as politics. Like other skeptics (such as Moynihan), he believed that the established welfare system—Aid to Families with Dependent Children (AFDC)—which had grown out of the New Deal–era program of cash assistance payments, had become, as a policy, a disaster and a political albatross. Instead of uplifting the poor to hope and prosperity, it had trapped many recipients in a cycle of abasement and dependency that virtually ensured continued failure and hardship. Clinton wanted to cut the welfare rolls dramatically—but also to provide the poor with the job training and child care they would require to break free of dependency.

The Republicans saw the problem in more moralistic terms. Welfare, they believed, was a system that robbed the upright and industrious, gave to the lazy and improvident, and encouraged vice. The poor did not need more government subsidies at the taxpayers' expense in the form of training or child-care assistance; they needed to be left to their own devices. Yet what the Republican majority deemed the only just solution—letting the poor sink or swim on their own merits and moral choices—Clinton considered a moral abdication, a failure to live up to the ideals of "one America." And whereas Clinton thought that overhauling the welfare system might save money in the long run, at the start it would require substantial federal funding for training and child care.

By 1996, the Republican congressional majority had Clinton over a barrel on welfare reform. Twice, he had vetoed Republican bills that he thought punitive rather than ameliorative. Now, especially with the elections approaching, he deeply desired a bill he could sign. But for the Republicans, it made political sense to force Clinton into a third veto in order to exploit welfare as a wedge issue in the fall. At the end of July, Congress passed a bill that terminated AFDC, replaced it with a program of block grants to the states, required able-bodied heads of household to find work within two years or lose federal aid, and sharply curbed welfare assistance to legal immigrants. Clinton faced an agonizing decision. If he signed the bill, he would make a move popular with the voters but also enact a law containing some features he liked and others he detested. He would also greatly please Dick Morris (who warned him that a veto could cost the election) as well as a portion of the neoliberal policy intelligentsia—but enrage most of his advisers and offend a considerable portion of the Democratic Party's base. If he vetoed it, he would pay an untold political price and possibly kill any chance of fulfilling his own hopes to reform the welfare system.

The president held several meetings with his cabinet and staff. Most of the participants (including the secretary of the treasury, Rubin) spoke in favor of a veto. Two crucial advisers, however, took a different tack. Hillary Clinton, after encouraging her husband over the earlier vetoes and speaking publicly against any welfare reform bill that lacked sufficient support for child care, now took a more subdued line, noting that the Republicans' latest proposal at least was in some respects an improvement over earlier versions, and finally favored approving the bill. Al Gore, after waffling in one of the larger group sessions, told the president decisively that if he did not sign this bill, welfare reform would fade as an issue and the opportunity for reform would be lost. Clinton remained ambivalent for as long as he could, in his own earthy way, plainly miffed at being placed in such a tight political spot. (At one point, he described the Republicans' proposal as "a decent welfare bill wrapped in a sack of shit.") But he finally decided to sign the bill, telling reporters that despite its "serious flaws" this was the time to seize the moment and begin "to make welfare what it was meant to be, a second chance and not a way of life."

The reaction from Democrats and liberals was passionate. Senator Moynihan called the law "the most brutal act of social policy since Reconstruction." Marian Wright Edelman, who was the head of the Children's Defense Fund and a longtime friend and ally of Hillary Clinton's, called the reform inhuman; her husband, Peter Edelman, along with two others, resigned from the Department of Health and Human Services. Over the years that followed, liberals continued to say that the law effectively pushed poor women off welfare into the street or, at best, into exploitative, dead-end, low-wage jobs, which would not raise them out of poverty. But in the long term there were also signs that the effects of the reform were different from what its critics predicted. Welfare rolls dropped by nearly 60 percent by 2001, to the lowest level in a generation, and they would continue to decline even when the economy slowed in 2002 and 2003. Increased employment accounted for nearly the entire difference. And figures compiled by the Census Bureau later showed that poverty declined by 25 percent and child poverty by 30 percent during Clinton's presidency. (About 7 million people moved from welfare into jobs over the same span of time.)

Clinton also kept his promise to repair what he considered the flaws of the reform bill. He eventually succeeded in removing the restrictions on immigrants. He also secured a doubling of federal funding for child care and for the Head Start preschool program begun under Lyndon Johnson; and he fought successfully for an increase in the minimum wage as well as for tax reductions for the working poor. His Welfare-to-Work Partnership gained the participation of tens of thousands of companies, which ended up hiring more than 1 million former welfare recipients. More tacitly, Clinton also changed the racialized politics of welfare by all but removing one of the most effective wedge issues from public debate. No longer would conservative politicians bash Democrats over their coddling of the poor—that is, undeserving blacks—at the expense of the middle class—that is, hardworking white taxpayers. The shift took effect immediately in Clinton's reelection campaign against the Republicans' nominee, Senator Bob Dole, as welfare never became an issue. It would be the first time in more than a generation that race in coded form never made an appearance in a presidential campaign.

By reputation an acid-tongued, partisan political brawler, Dole emerged as one of the most poignant political figures of the Nixon years and Reagan era. A classic midwestern conservative, he had always deplored President Reagan's supply-side tax cuts as irresponsible and viewed Newt Gingrich with contempt. (The feeling was mutual: Gingrich blasted Dole as "the tax collector for the welfare state" and "a man devoid of vision.") Yet Dole's obstructionist tactics as the Senate majority leader—especially his use of filibusters to block Clinton's legislation, in order to advance his own presidential ambitions—had helped prepare the way for the success of Gingrich and the hard right in 1994.

In 1996, after having been nominated once for vice president and having run for the presidential nomination three times, Dole was next in line to be nominated for the presidency by the Republicans. However, he still had to face a challenge in the primaries from Pat Buchanan and the revived Pitchfork Brigades, who dealt him an embarrassing defeat in the New Hampshire primary. Thereafter, Dole stumbled from primary to primary, until he fell victorious across the finish line; but an incident on the campaign trail signaled the changing times. When Dole traveled to Arizona to receive the endorsement of the grand old man of Republican conservatism, Barry Goldwater, Goldwater denounced the new Republican right as zealots and fanatics who had "nearly ruined our party." "We're the new liberals of the Republican Party," Goldwater added. Dole, a bit taken aback, agreed, also accepting the accursed L-word that was still demonized in the Republicans' usual parlance.

Dole, the "liberal," actually did his best to accommodate the party's fervent right wing, going to the mat with Clinton over the government shutdown and welfare reform even though he regarded the shutdown as an act of lunacy. Once he had secured sufficient convention delegates to win the nomination, he thought he would run his campaign from the Senate floor, where he would be seen doing the job he did best. But the Democrats turned his obstructionist tactics against him, and the gridlock forced Dole to quit the Senate and campaign around the nation, where, in unfamiliar surroundings, he was likely at any moment to launch into a meandering speech filled with self-referential non sequiturs. Flagging badly in the polls as the Republican National Convention opened in San Diego, the candidate tried to stir up interest and secure the party's pro-Gingrich base by naming as his running mate a supply-sider, the former professional football star, Representative Jack Kemp—whom Dole had ridiculed from time to time as having played football "without a helmet." Although Dole had long resisted Reaganomics and the supply-side visionaries, he announced in his acceptance speech he had become a supply-sider himself, and came out for a 15 percent flat tax cut.

Now seventy-three years old, and having waited a political lifetime for this opportunity, Dole also presented himself as a man of experience who remembered an older, better America, and who wanted to serve as a bridge to "a time of tranquility, faith, and confidence in action." But this handed the Clinton campaign its own, far more effective campaign theme—of leading the country forward, not backward, by building "a bridge to the twenty-first century." There was little Dole could do to gain traction against the younger, energetic president. With the economy now running at full throttle, the Republicans' plan to cut taxes by 15 percent drew no interest from the public. Jack Kemp, a Gingrichite in policy but not in his ingratiating upbeat temperament, incensed his fellow conservatives by refusing to take up the vice presidential nominee's assigned role as hatchet man.

Dole's effort did get a lift in its final weeks, when news surfaced about possible irregular contributions to the Democrats by Asian fund-raisers and benefactors. Dole himself had been found in breach of campaign finance laws in the past; and in October 1996, his vice chairman for campaign finance pleaded guilty to seventy-four separate violations. But the press saw the stories about Clinton as much more colorful—involving, among other characters, an enterprising hustler named Johnny Chung, and also including the whiff of allegations (later proved false) about improper contributions from the Chinese government. There was also a sex scandal reported in the tabloids just before the Democratic convention: Dick Morris was discovered to have procured the services of a prostitute while working in Washington as Clinton's adviser. Clinton (who in any event did not seem to need Morris's advice any longer) summarily had him resign, but the story reminded the public of Clinton's own checkered past, including the continuing sexual harassment suit by Paula Corbin Jones. This, in turn, brought back to mind the seemingly dormant but still active Whitewater investigation being labored over by the independent counsel Kenneth Starr.

"Where is the outrage?" became Dole's campaign mantra. Although it had no discernible effect in decreasing Clinton's support, the issue of financing did hurt some Democratic candidates for Congress. In the closing days of the campaign, Clinton changed his schedule in order to campaign furiously for Senate and House candidates. Those efforts fell short of fulfilling the Democrats' hopes of regaining its majority in the House—and they certainly contributed to preventing Clinton from gaining the absolute majority

in the popular vote he so badly wanted, in order to end the Republicans' innuendo that, as a "minority" president, he somehow lacked legitimacy.

The results were still impressive, not unlike 1980 in reverse. Clinton won
49.2 percent of the popular vote to Dole's 40.7 percent. (Ross Perot, running as
the candidate of the fledgling Reform Party, which soon disintegrated, won
9 percent, less than half of his total in 1992. But his support was probably increased by the last-minute allegations about campaign finances, which also
ensured that Clinton did not receive his absolute majority.) In the Electoral
College, the Democratic ticket won 379 votes, or 70 percent of the total, from
thirty-one states in every region of the country. Yet some conservatives still
seemed unwilling to recognize the validity of the outcome. In the *Wall Street
Journal*, Paul Gigot's postmortem a year later was headed "A Stolen Election."

In his victory speech in Little Rock, Clinton claimed that the outcome
had vindicated the "vital American center." He had borrowed this phrase
from the eminent historian and Democratic liberal Arthur Schlesinger Jr.,
whose book *The Vital Center* (1949) defended liberal democracy and what
Schlesinger called the "free left" against communism as well as fascism.
Schlesinger, a supportive critic of the president, now wondered whether
Clinton knew the difference between creative moderation and the convenient middle of the road—between what he called the "vital center" and
the "dead center." Clinton was certain that he did, but he still had many
Democrats to convince. And more than he comprehended, he had many
new assaults from the right to endure.

On Inauguration Day, 1997, after he administered the presidential oath of
office to Bill Clinton for the second time, Chief Justice William Rehnquist
wished the president "Good luck," unsmilingly and in a tone more ominous
than cordial. Was Rehnquist just being his usual adversarial, conservative
self? Or did he have something more specific in mind? Over the weeks and
months to come, Clinton and his closest supporters would ponder the questions—and, in their darker moments, conclude that Rehnquist knew very
well about at least some of the political misfortunes, then undisclosed, that
would befall the White House. Only Clinton's wife immediately put an
exact and plausible construction on Rehnquist's remark.

Clinton, for his part, was eager to pick up the pace of reform, but he
understood that with conservative Republicans dominating Congress, he
would have to advance in a piecemeal fashion. In 1997, he succeeded in getting Congress to lift restrictions on assistance to legal immigrants included

in the welfare reform bill, and to sustain the earned income tax credit program for the poor. He also achieved legislation to provide tax credits for tuition payments for higher education and to expand federal aid for health care among poor children. And Congress was happy to pass his proposed reduction of the capital gains tax rate from 25 to 20 percent—a revision that testified to growing public recognition of just how vigorous the economy had become since the enactment of Clinton's budget of 1993, bringing an unexpectedly rapid improvement in the government's fiscal outlook.

According to every important indicator, the recovery from the sluggish economic times of 1990–1992 was a roaring success, markedly surpassing the prosperity of the Reagan years. Gross domestic product (GDP) per capita was rising dramatically, and would increase at an average annual rate of 3 percent a year during Clinton's second term. The unemployment rate, which stood at 7.3 percent when Clinton took office, had dropped to 5.3 percent by his second inauguration, on its way to bottoming out at just under 4 percent at the end of 2000. The average annual inflation rate, having dipped below 3 percent, would continue to fall until it reached 1.6 percent in 1998. Poverty rates were also falling, even more dramatically among blacks than whites. Although, overall, inequality remained a growing problem, median incomes rose across the board, including among Hispanics, African-Americans, and Native Americans.

When linked to the deficit reduction plan put into place by Clinton's economics team in 1993, the boom ended what had once looked like a string of federal deficits stretching as far as the eye could see. After hitting its peak of $290 billion in 1992, the annual federal shortfall had shrunk each year, reaching $22 billion in 1997. In the first week of 1998, there would actually be a surplus, for the first time since 1960—what the *New York Times* called "the fiscal equivalent of the fall of the Berlin Wall." The initial surpluses would be modest, and so long as the Republicans controlled Congress, any major new federal initiatives were off the table. (Clinton would propose applying much of the surplus of 1998 to shoring up Social Security.) And quite apart from its prosperity, the country looked as if it might be overcoming the constraints imposed on government and on future economic growth by the deficits of the Reagan and Bush administrations. Although numerous factors accounted for the reversal, the political reporter John Harris of the *Washington Post* noted that "no one who recalled the sense of national drift in 1992 could fail to credit the Clinton administration for at a minimum serving as an essential catalyst."

The Republicans, to be sure, did not give Clinton any credit for the prosperity. (Some of them even claimed, and some actually believed, that the upturn was the long-term result of Reagan's supply-side tax cuts, from which all blessings supposedly flowed.) Neither were Republicans eager to remind anyone of their discredited dire predictions about the effects of Clinton's budget for 1993, which not one Republican senator or congressman had voted to approve. But after the government shutdown and Clinton's reelection, the Speaker of the House—Newt Gingrich—and Dole's successor as the Senate majority leader, Trent Lott of Mississippi, were in a far more accommodating mood about the negotiations for the budget of 1997.[*] Clinton stepped back and chose as his new chief of staff an orderly North Carolinian banker, Erskine Bowles, who would serve as the White House's lead negotiator; and after strenuous but cordial talks with the Republicans' designates, Representative John Kasich of Ohio and Senator Pete Domenici of New Mexico, the two sides reached an agreement in midsummer. Clinton, at the formal signing ceremony in early August, saluted the new spirit of comity; Gingrich praised Clinton extravagantly for reaching out to Republicans. Democrats in the House, however, simmered over Clinton's agreement to cut taxes and trim the growth of Medicare funding; two out of five of them voted against the bargain. More ominously, many conservative Republicans were furious at Gingrich for failing to win larger tax cuts. But an odd new center momentarily held.

For nearly a year, Clinton had been likening his presidency to those in the early twentieth century, telling audiences (as he did in a commencement address at Princeton, Woodrow Wilson's alma mater, in 1996) that the nation stood "on the threshold of a new Progressive era." He was particularly fond of citing Theodore Roosevelt as his model. This evocation, though obviously meant to ennoble his own administration, also marked his efforts off from the Reaganite "gilded age" before 1992; and it likened the rapidly globalizing world of the 1990s to the turn of the twentieth century, when the United States emerge as a leading economic and political power. In some respects, of course, any attempt to draw a parallel between Clinton and Theodore Roosevelt was absurd: the Republican Roosevelt, born to privilege, was a man who relished personal confrontation and who spoke

---

[*] Gingrich had also been wounded in January 1997 by the release of a report by the House Ethics Committee documenting flagrant abuses by the Speaker of laws governing nonprofit institutions and conducting partisan activities at the taxpayers' expense. Gingrich was officially reprimanded and fined $300,000, the most severe penalty ever assessed against a Speaker of the House. Gingrich tried to shrug off the episode by blaming it on vengeful leftists.

and governed accordingly. But in 1997, as never before, Clinton seized on Roosevelt's concept of the presidency as a "bully pulpit," in order to preach his ideas and values to the public.

The initial results were meager at best. Early in the year, Clinton's aides let it be known that he would be lobbying state legislatures to support participation in voluntary national standards tests in the schools. In April, he appeared at what was billed as a "summit" in Philadelphia with Vice President Gore and the now retired general Colin Powell to encourage community voluntarism. The grandest project, the president's so-called "initiative on race," would send Clinton around the country to participate in discussions that would lead to a comprehensive report on the need for and opportunities of racial diversity. But Clinton ended up speaking to only three legislatures about education; after some photo-op sessions in a run-down neighborhood in Philadelphia, the volunteerism effort came to nothing; and the ambitious race initiative got bogged down in sectarian squabbling and identity politics.

Clinton's foreign policy bore more fruit. In the aftermath of the cold war, his main goal in Europe had been to expand NATO to include the former Soviet bloc countries of eastern and central Europe, and give their new governments an enhanced sense of security and diplomatic solidity. Some critics—including the gray eminence of American diplomacy, George Kennan, now in his nineties—thought the idea of expanding an old cold war alliance senseless and potentially dangerous. But Clinton insisted, and following his reelection, he pushed to accelerate the pace of expanding NATO. The great obstacle was Boris Yeltsin, who as the Russian president had become leader of the Russian Federation when Gorbachev stepped aside.

Clinton, more than his advisers, genuinely liked the colorful, hard-drinking Yeltsin and, on the basis of his own experience, empathized with Yeltsin's domestic political constraints. Even when the Russians, to international condemnation, used violence to try to suppress a secessionist insurgency in the province of Chechnya, Clinton turned a blind eye and continued his efforts, begun in his first year as president, to cultivate Yeltsin. The bond paid off in various ways, not least Russian military participation in enforcing the Dayton accords in the Balkans. In March 1997, Clinton and Yeltsin held a summit in Helsinki, where, after some blustering, Yeltsin agreed to let the expansion continue, with the Russian Federation given a consultative role in NATO's policy making.

Two months later, Clinton flew to Paris to attend the signing of the charter regularizing Russian relations with NATO. He then stopped off in

London to meet Tony Blair, who had become Britain's new prime minister only four weeks earlier. It was a joining of kindred spirits. After a long era of Tory rule under Margaret Thatcher and John Major, Blair had come to power by marginalizing both the old-line trade union leadership and younger Marxist sectarians within the Labour Party. Under the banner of "new Labour," he had pledged to build an innovative form of British social democracy, much as Clinton was trying to reinvent American liberalism—and, like similar center-left figures in Germany, Italy, and the Netherlands, Blair took Clinton as a model. Although Clinton and Blair were temperamentally very different—Clinton was more of a warm, charismatic pol than the sober, earnest, even self-righteous Englishman—their political commonalities turned this first encounter into a colloquium on the theory and practice of modern progressive politics. Soon, other European progressives would enlist in the course, under the rubric of what became known as the "third way"—an updated vital center, now standing between conservatism in the style of Reagan and Thatcher and orthodox western European socialism.

Clinton also had a cordial relationship with his German counterpart, the conservative Christian Democrat Helmut Kohl—a friendship based in part on their shared enjoyment of food, and in part on Kohl's willingness to support and to teach international politics to the neophyte American, sixteen years his junior, during Clinton's tentative early years in the White House. Kohl proved an especially valuable ally with regard to expanding NATO, especially when several member nations, headed by France, objected to the United States' insistence that the first wave of new admissions be limited to Poland, Hungary, and the Czech Republic. In July, when the chiefs of state of NATO met in Madrid to formalize the new arrangements, Kohl helped scuttle the French president Jacques Chirac's efforts to include Slovenia and Romania as well.

More unsettling was the continuing threat of various rogue nations and terrorist organizations. Although Clinton had reached an agreement with the North Koreans, there was widespread suspicion that the dictatorship in Pyongyang, now headed by the eccentric Kim Jong Il, was violating its pledge to halt development of nuclear weapons. Even more pressing, according to intelligence sources, was a rising tide of Muslim extremism in the Middle East. Iraq under Saddam Hussein remained a primary suspect in aiding extremist violence, as did the Iranian Shiite theocracy and its offshoot Hezbollah. And of ever-increasing concern were the terrorist forces allied to Osama bin Laden.

After his expulsion from the Sudan in 1996, bin Laden had gone to Afghanistan, where he established working relations with the fanatically anti-Western Taliban government that had come to power out of the disarray that followed the defeat of the Soviet Union's invasion in 1989. Bin Laden shared with the Taliban clerics an intense hatred of Western secularism, materialism, and egalitarian individualism (and, of course, contempt for women's rights), and he hated the United States in particular for its continuing military presence in Saudi Arabia, which he believed was corrupting the holiest sites of Islam. With financial backing from wealthy patrons throughout the Persian Gulf, bin Laden organized the network of terrorist cells called Al Qaeda ("the Base"), which in the mid- to late 1990s enlarged its recruiting and training operations in Afghanistan for terrorist agents. In July 1996, an explosion ripped through the Khorbar Towers, home to U.S. forces at the Dharhan military base in Saudi Arabia, killing nineteen people. No organization claimed responsibility, Saudi officials blocked American investigators, and it was generally suspected that Al Qaeda's operatives had been involved.[*] By 1996, some important figures in the Clinton administration—above all the chair of the National Security Council's Counter-Terrorism Security Group, Richard Clarke—were virtually obsessed with tracking down and thwarting Al Qaeda's threats, inside the United States as well as abroad.

The Americans were at a disadvantage in confronting the situation. Turf battles as well as legal restrictions enacted in the mid-1970s prevented the CIA and FBI from pooling their intelligence about terrorist threats coming from abroad. Past disasters, from the Bay of Pigs through Iran-contra, had contributed to a steady diminution of reliance on covert action and intelligence in favor of high-tech satellite surveillance. Combined with a basic lack of training of intelligence officers and analysts in Middle Eastern languages, the emphasis on space-age spy techniques left large gaps in Americans' understanding of actual conditions in the Middle East. Clinton's deteriorating relations with the director of the FBI, Louis Freeh—who was giving aid and comfort to his Republican political adversaries in order to prevent congressional scrutiny of abuses by the FBI—worsened matters.

Although bin Laden was known to federal investigators (who had already begun looking into his possible links to the bombing of the World Trade Center in 1993), he received little attention from the American

---

[*] In 2006, a U.S. district court issued a memorandum stating that the Iranian government had executed the bombing.

public. This was true even in February 1998, when he issued a public call for "*Jihad* [or, Holy War] against Jews and Crusaders," in which every true Muslim had a duty to kill Americans everywhere in the world.

The investigations that did receive enormous attention from the press and the public (apart from the sensational and sensationalized murder trial of the ex–football star O. J. Simpson) involved allegations, old and new, against the Clintons and certain members of the administration. In March 1995, Attorney General Reno appointed an independent counsel to investigate charges that the secretary of housing and urban development, Henry Cisneros, had lied to the FBI's investigators during the background check prior to his appointment, regarding the exact amount of money he had paid to a former mistress. Still under a cloud of suspicion, Cisneros resigned in January 1997, and eventually pleaded guilty to a misdemeanor—misleading the FBI—for which he was fined $10,000. But the independent investigation would carry on for nearly a decade to come, producing no further formal charges but allegations of an unspecified cover-up, at a cost to the taxpayers in excess of $21 million. Another independent-counsel investigation had forced the secretary of agriculture, Mike Espy, to resign in 1994: there were charges that he had received illegal gifts such as sports tickets, and these charges led to a thirty-count indictment in August 1997. Unlike Cisneros, Espy declined to plea-bargain and was acquitted of all charges in December 1998—after the independent counsel Donald Smaltz called seventy witnesses and spent $20 million in preparing and trying the case.

The Whitewater probe, now headed by Kenneth Starr and with an additional special investigation launched by Senate Banking Committee Chairman Alfonse D'Amato of New York, also appeared to be headed nowhere. Starr's and D'Amato's confrontations with the Clintons had heated up in December 1995 and January 1996—at the height of the crises over the budget and government shutdowns—when legal records of the first lady's that the independent counsel had long sought turned up in a crowded storage closet in the White House residence, amid piles of knickknacks and unsorted books. The records, concerning hourly billing charges on legal work Mrs. Clinton had performed in Arkansas, contained no incriminating or even embarrassing information—no information of the slightest significance about anything, in fact, that was not already in the public record. Senator D'Amato seized on their discovery anyway, and speculated darkly about a "smoking gun," and Starr subpoenaed Mrs. Clinton to appear in person before a federal grand jury to tell her story about the records. Yet neither the prosecutor's leaked speculation, nor the congressional hearings, nor Starr's decision to humiliate the first lady ever succeed in doing the impossible, which was to find any evidence of wrongdoing in connection with Whitewater, Madison Guaranty, or any of the other scandals charged against the Clintons.

D'Amato's committee did produce one sensational moment when it called as a witness (for a second time) L. Jean Lewis, the Republican partisan at the Resolution Trust Corporation who had prepared a criminal referral against the Clintons in 1992. After her initial appearance, one Republican, the moderate Representative Jim Leach of Iowa (who, as head of the House Banking Committee, had become the House point man on Whitewater) spoke about how the scandal had uncovered an "uplifting, indeed heroic story" of Middle Americans. Soon afterward, Jeff Gerth of the *New York Times*, the reporter who broke the *Times*'s original story on Whitewater, conducted a front-page, highly sympathetic interview with Lewis that featured unsubstantiated charges about improper outside obstruction of her investigation. But when Lewis appeared before D'Amato's committee for the second time in November 1995, Senator Paul Sarbanes, a Democrat from Maryland, calmly read the letter from the U.S. attorney's office that explained his refusal to act on her referral because doing so would amount to prosecutorial misconduct—and then, just as calmly, Sarbanes asked questions which revealed that Lewis lacked the most basic comprehension of federal banking laws. She responded by weeping and then fainting dead away, and had to be led off the stand, never to return.*

In June 1996, with Clinton's prospects for reelection looking stronger by the day, D'Amato and his chief counsel and alter ego, a former prosecutor in New Jersey, Michael Chertoff, finally closed down what had begun to look like a fishing expedition. Eight months later, Starr unexpectedly announced that he would leave his post in August to take up the deanship at the law school of Pepperdine University. But after coming under

---

* Neither the *New York Times* nor the *Washington Post* reported Lewis's breakdown on the stand. Having promoted the Whitewater story for years, in their news columns and editorial pages, both papers seemed unwilling to let it go—a phenomenon that the veteran journalist Marvin Kalb, among others, has documented and linked both to unprofessional excesses in pursuit of scandal and to a continuing, post-Watergate "climate of skepticism and cynicism about the political process." Kalb, *One Scandalous Story: Clinton, Lewinsky, and Thirteen Days That Tarnished American Journalism* (New York, 2001), 262.

heavy fire from conservatives (including William Safire, who blasted him in the *New York Times* as a "wimp"), he reversed his decision four days later. In April, Starr persuaded the U.S. district court to extend his White-water grand jury until early November, claiming that he had "extensive evidence" of obstruction of justice; in June, the *Washington Post* reported that Starr's office had begun questioning Arkansas state troopers about Clinton's alleged sexual affairs while he was governor; soon after that, the American Civil Liberties Union filed a suit charging that Starr was holding Jim McDougal's former wife in jail in barbaric conditions so as to coerce her to testify against the Clintons. On July 15, Starr's office finally reached one firm conclusion—that Vincent Foster's death was, indeed, a suicide—a conclusion already reported by the first Whitewater prosecutor, Robert Fiske, who had been forced from the post for stating the facts in the case. Had there not been indecent partisan speculation to the contrary more than four years earlier, Starr's investigation into the private life of the president, having nothing to do with his mandate, would almost certainly have never begun.

The sexual harassment suit by Paula Corbin Jones—which Starr's office was monitoring closely—also took some interesting twists and turns in 1997. Clinton's personal lawyer, Robert Bennett, regarded the action as friv-olous but potentially harmful and fought it on the traditional grounds that, as a civil suit, the matter should be postponed until after Clinton's presi-dency lest it interfere with his official duties. The presiding federal district judge in Arkansas, Susan Webber Wright, so ruled at the close of 1994, but just over a year later, a panel of the Eighth Circuit Appeals Court in St. Louis overturned her in a two-to-one decision. The case ended up at the Supreme Court, where opening arguments were heard exactly one week before Clinton's second inauguration. It would later dawn on the president's supporters that Chief Justice Rehnquist's mind could well have been on *Clinton v. Jones* when he growled "Good luck" at the swearing in. But Hill-ary Clinton had gotten the message instantly. "They're going to screw you on the Paula Jones case," she told her husband.

Paula Jones's lawyers of record were two otherwise unremarkable Re-publican attorneys in Virginia, Joe Cammerata and Gil Davis, but they were receiving considerable clandestine help from a team of high-powered conservative lawyers who were partners in major firms, including George Conway III of Wachtell, Lipton, Rosen, and Katz in New York; and Jerome Marcus of Berger and Montague in Philadelphia. Working secretly (in vio-lation of their companies' rules), Conway and Marcus were the principal authors of Jones's brief before the Supreme Court. They also helped prepare Gil Davis, who had never argued before the Supreme Court, by arranging a mock trial, for which Davis received coaching from two other, far better known conservative jurists: Robert Bork, President Reagan's nominee for the Supreme Court who had been rejected in 1987, and Theodore Olson, who was a former assistant attorney general under Reagan, a good friend and former law partner of Starr's, and a leading activist (with Starr) in the Federalist Society, a group of attorneys dedicated, in part, to stocking firms, law schools, and the judiciary with reliable conservatives.*

During the opening arguments at the Supreme Court, Chief Justice Rehnquist and Justice Scalia expressed contempt for Bennett's position that answering a civil suit could badly hamper a president's ability to do his job. And when the court handed down a ruling at the end of May, not just the conservative justices but all nine concurred that the Jones suit should go forward. According to the majority opinion, written by Justice John Paul Stevens, compelling Clinton to answer Jones's suit created no serious risk of exposing the presidency to "politically motivated harassing and frivolous litigation." Thereafter, though, the case passed through some strange convolutions that deepened its politically motivated character. As soon as the court decided *Clinton v. Jones*, Clinton and Bennett offered to pay Jones $700,000, so long as the proceeds went to charity and provided that the president not issue any admission or apology regarding the allegations. (With Clinton preparing to depart for the summit in Madrid on expanding NATO, Bennett lamented that the case was making the country a "laughingstock.") Jones's lawyers immediately rejected the offer. In August, Judge Wright in Arkansas scheduled the trial to begin in May 1998, while also dismissing charges from Jones's side that the president had defamed its client. By now, though, it had become less clear who actually made up and represented Jones's side.

In July, Susan Carpenter-McMillan, an ultraconservative antiabortion activist from suburban Los Angeles and a familiar presence on local television and radio talk shows, issued a press release announcing herself as Paula Jones's official spokeswoman. Carpenter-McMillan had befriended Jones years earlier after hearing about the case—inspired, Carpenter-McMillan now freely admitted, by a fixation on President Clinton: "Okay, good. We're

---

* Olson also oversaw the so-called Arkansas Project, a multimillion-dollar project to dig up and publicize salacious rumors about Clinton in Arkansas, funded by the ultraconservative billionaire Richard Mellon Scaife and run through the magazine *American Spectator*.

gonna get that little slimeball." Jones's attorneys of record, Cammerata and Davis, were infuriated, but Carpenter-McMillan managed to gain control of Jones's legal defense fund—and rewarded Jones with a thorough cosmetic makeover and a new luxury sedan. All the while, Clinton's lawyer, Bennett, kept working for a possible settlement, to get what he regarded as a group of grifters and political misfits out of the president's life. In August, Bennett offered full payment plus a general statement from Clinton, acknowledging no sexual misconduct but regretting that Jones's character and reputation had been harmed. It was a reasonable proposal, and Davis and Cammerata (who thought it was superb) strongly advised Jones to accept it.

Several forces and factors endangered a settlement. Jones's husband, Steve (they would divorce in 1999), demanded that the monetary portion be raised to $1.2 million. Carpenter-McMillan denounced the proposed expression of regret, saying it was full of "vanilla language" and not strong enough. And working in secret, at least some of Jones's other unofficial lawyers hoped no agreement was forthcoming. "We were terrified that Jones would settle. It was contrary to our purpose of bringing down the president," said one of their number, a young right-wing lawyer, Ann Coulter, who called the unofficial legal team the "elves," and described them as "a small, intricately-knit right-wing conspiracy." Jones, by every account easily manipulated by one and all, refused to settle. Davis and Cammerata declared that the suit had changed from a defense of Jones into a political offensive against President Clinton, and quit. Thanks to Carpenter-McMillan, Jones found new lawyers from the Rutherford Institute, a foundation based in Rockford, Illinois, and run by ultra-right-wing followers of R. J. Rushdoony, a Holocaust denier who favored capital punishment for doctors who performed abortions and for all homosexuals, and who believed that biblical scripture should replace the Constitution.

News about the case became increasingly strange. In early October, as formal depositions were about to begin, Jones's lawyers confirmed that she had signed an affidavit specifying an unusual "distinguishing characteristic" about the president's genitals. (One of the "elves," George Conway, had slipped the story in advance to a right-wing Internet scandalmonger based in Los Angeles, Matt Drudge, who featured it on his Web site for days until the mainstream press picked it up.) Bennett called the claim "baseless and easily refutable" and "a cynical and outrageous effort to embarrass the president." ("My question would be: How in the world do you know?" said Susan Carpenter-McMillan following Bennett's denial.) With the case now focused on the president's penis, and with Jones's forces looking increasingly grotesque, Clinton's side expressed confidence in private that the case was virtually won. Bennett had obtained signed affidavits proving that Jones's claim of sexual harassment on the job, the sole legal basis for her lawsuit, was instantly dismissible.

Jones's new lawyers, for their part, were quietly trolling Arkansas for any gossip about Clinton's supposed past sexual indiscretions. The president had faced similar accusations before (sometimes involving the same women) and always managed to put them behind him, acknowledging, as he had done in 1992, that he had caused pain in his marriage, but never getting pinned down on any specific example from the past—and always with the implication that he had ceased misbehaving. He had good reason to believe that the Jones case would be dismissed before any particulars surfaced as a matter of record—and that even if it did go on, he would escape unharmed.

The president received his first warning that this time the results might be different on December 6, at a five p.m. meeting in the Oval Office with Bennett and Bruce Lindsey. The lawyers had come to review recent developments in the case, including the names of the women Jones's new attorneys had placed on their witness list. One of those names was Monica S. Lewinsky. How Lewinsky's identity had come to the attention of Jones's lawyers was mysterious—but the fact that it had spelled potential trouble for the president.

Within six weeks, the entire world would know Monica Lewinsky's name. Clinton, having helped knock himself back into the trough, faced a yearlong legal and political struggle that would culminate in his impeachment by the House and trial by the Senate—causing the country yet another constitutional confrontation, the third in three decades.

13

ANIMOSITIES AND INTEREST: THE IMPEACHMENT OF CLINTON

ONICA LEWINSKY, A SPIRITED twenty-one-year-old Califor-
nian, was a recent college graduate, from a broken home but a
politically connected family. She arrived at the White House as
an intern in the summer of 1995. Smitten by the charming President Clinton, she edged close to him at official White House functions. On November 15, the second day of the initial government shutdown, while the White
House was working with a skeleton staff, she got close enough during the
workday to make an arousing flirtatious remark and gesture, after which
Clinton invited her to his private study off the Oval Office. What began as
embracing ended in her performing oral sex.

Over the next sixteen months, even after the White House transferred
her to a job at the Pentagon, they had nine more trysts—what the White
House aide Rahm Emanuel later described as "less than sex but more than
kissy-face." (Neither Clinton nor Lewinsky believed they had had "sex" as
they understood it, that is, sexual intercourse.) Clinton and Lewinsky also
exchanged gifts and engaged in several extended, graphic telephone conversations. After trying and failing several times to break off the relationship,
the president finally ended the sexual encounters in late May 1997, although
Clinton and Lewinsky continued to see each other and talk while she used
his friends' connections to leave Washington and find work in New York.
By the time the Revlon Corporation offered her a job, the story of her clan-

destine relations with the president was about to become a searing political scandal that would lead to the president's impeachment.

Clinton's affair with Lewinsky, as exposed and exploited by his adversaries, came extremely close to ending his presidency—closer than popular accounts have indicated, and far closer than Ronald Reagan ever came to impeachment as a result of the Iran-contra affair. How it happened involved a convergence of arrogance, betrayal, farce, vindictiveness, self-pity, plotting, prurience, tenacity, tawdriness, and hypocrisy, worthy at times of opera buffa and at times of classical drama, though more Roman than Greek. And the drama did not end when Clinton was acquitted by the Senate of charges that he had committed high crimes and misdemeanors. Momentous as it was, Clinton's impeachment laid the groundwork for another spectacular political confrontation—briefer, but just as driven by human nature, especially the will to power, or its absence, that decided Clinton's successor.

"This beautiful capital, like every capital since the dawn of civilization, is often a place of intrigue and calculation," Clinton said at his first inauguration in 1993. "Powerful people maneuver for position and worry endlessly about who is in and who is out, who is up and who is down, forgetting those people whose toil and sweat sends us here and pays our way." Many Washington insiders at the time—including some who would become Clinton's accusers during the impeachment episode—bridled at what they considered a personal gibe. Neither they nor he understood how they all would act out what Clinton described, and how it would affect the nation.

When Hillary Clinton, still in the dark about what had happened, famously blamed the early allegations about her husband on a "vast right-wing conspiracy," she was ridiculed as at once naive and paranoid. Yet if by a "vast conspiracy" one understands a diverse congeries of extremist conservatives devoted, as the plotter Ann Coulter put it, to "bringing down the president," Mrs. Clinton was correct about the basic matter, including how her husband's enemies were "using the criminal justice system to try to achieve political ends in this country." The first lady quickly and accurately detected that some sort of secret collaboration between the independent counsel's office and Clinton's right-wing opponents had led to the present situation. But she did not know at the time—because her husband had lied to her— that some of the most personally hurtful allegations about him were true.

The two human beings who knew the most stood at the center of a vortex of speculation and manipulation. Why Monica Lewinsky and Bill Clinton acted as they did will never fully be understood, even perhaps by themselves. The evidence extracted by the independent counsel's report describes two very different people, one more than twice the other's age, each a mixture of neediness and craftiness. The timing of their encounters, especially early on—while Clinton faced enormous strains over the budget showdown and Bosnia, and Hillary Clinton endured her worst torments from the special investigation of Whitewater—may help account for the president's initial frame of mind; his sense of guilt, shame, and dutifulness may help account for the sporadic liaison thereafter. Less clear is why the president ran such a risk of embarrassment inside the White House—and why, when confronted with possible legal consequences, he allowed himself to drift for a crucial month between the first appearance of Lewinsky's name on the list of witnesses drawn up by the lawyers for Paula Jones and his own deposition in the Jones case in mid-January 1998. As in any marriage or love affair, the motives and actions of the lovers were never completely clear, despite the omniscient pronouncements—some pseudo-clinical, others simply sanctimonious—that resounded in the media echo chamber in 1998.

At one remove from Clinton and Lewinsky stood two women—Linda Tripp and Lucianne Goldberg—whose motives were less mysterious. Linda Tripp had been a secretary at the White House with Republican connections. She had been held over from the Bush administration, but relocated (at a considerable rise in pay) to a job at the Pentagon in the summer of 1994. Tripp, a conservative who admired the Bushes, had always detested the Clintons, whom she regarded as interlopers. After Monica Lewinsky received her notice of a transfer to the Pentagon, Tripp—who was in her late forties—pretended to befriend the young woman, swapped stories with her about their experiences at the White House, and, once she learned about Lewinsky's relationship with Clinton, play-acted the role of a protective older sister.

When Lewinsky began confiding in her, Tripp contacted Lucianne Goldberg, a gossipy Washingtonian literary agent and writer of steamy novels who was a former White House secretary and had been a political spy for the Nixon campaign in 1972. Goldberg had met Tripp through Tony Snow, a former speechwriter of Bush's who was now an anchorman on the Fox News Network. Their meeting had been in connection with a possible book project by Tripp about Vince Foster. (Tripp had been Foster's secretary before he committed suicide, and had given some misleading testimony about him to the independent counsel's office.) Goldberg now instructed Tripp to tape-record, surreptitiously, her conversations with Lewinsky. Then Goldberg eagerly shared the tapes with friends in Paula Jones's legal camp, including the "elf" George Conway, and helped arranged for Tripp's attorney (another "elf," James Moody) to meet with a reporter for *Newsweek*, Michael Isikoff, who was covering what had become the Clinton scandal beat. At Conway's suggestion, Goldberg also encouraged Tripp to bring the tapes to Kenneth Starr and the Office of the Independent Counsel.

The next ring of participants was composed of Paula Jones's new legal team, headed by Donovan Campbell Jr., an attorney based in Dallas who was a member of the board of directors of the far-right Rutherford Institute. Under Campbell, Jones's team had aggressively followed up rumors of Clinton's past sexual misconduct, including the story of a volunteer at the White House, Kathleen Willey (a story that, ironically, her colleague, Linda Tripp, would challenge in testimony before a grand jury), that Clinton had sexually assaulted her in the White House in 1993. With little to go on in these cases but gossip and unsubstantiated, contested allegations, Campbell—like George Conway and the other lawyer "elves" working secretly around the Jones case—received Goldberg's news about Lewinsky as a godsend. On December 19, Jones's team subpoenaed Lewinsky, who signed an affidavit on January 7 denying any sexual relationship with the president. On the evening of January 16, hours before Clinton was due to testify in the Jones case, one of Campbell's colleagues, Wes Holmes, met with Tripp, who briefed him about what she knew and gave him permission to use the information in questioning Clinton.

The independent counsel—Starr—and his prosecutorial investigators had been poring over allegations against both of the Clintons far longer than Jones's new lawyers had—and they, too, had come up with nothing until the revelations about Lewinsky landed on their desks. Starr, in fact, had been probing Clinton's personal life, chasing rumors about sex, and demanding information about sex from witnesses since February 1997, when his investigation into the Whitewater story ran dry. On January 8, Goldberg and several of the lawyers working on the Jones case dined in Philadelphia with a member of Starr's staff and told him about the president and the intern. On January 12, Tripp, at Goldberg's prompting, contacted Starr's office to talk about Lewinsky, and four days later, her new attorney, James Moody, played the tapes for two of the "elves"—George Conway and Ann Coulter—at Coulter's apartment. Moody then presented seventeen of the tapes to the independent counsel's staff. On the basis of Tripp's story and Lewinsky's affidavit (a copy of which he had received courtesy of Jones's lawyers), Starr was certain that he had grounds for charging Clinton with suborning perjury and obstructing justice. He had his staff ask Tripp to arrange another meeting with Lewinsky at Pentagon City, but this time he outfitted Tripp with a wire provided by the FBI. Two days after the wired meeting, Starr received formal permission from Attorney General Reno to expand his investigation into Clinton's possible obstruction of justice in *Jones v. Clinton.*

The day after that, January 16, Lewinsky showed up for yet another rendezvous with Tripp at Pentagon City and was nabbed by men from Starr's office who detained and interrogated her in a nearby hotel room for several hours, threatening her with prison in an effort to get her to switch loyalties. Although Starr would later deny it, Lewinsky's apprehenders told her to wear a wire and secretly record conversations with more than one person: Clinton's secretary at the White House, Betty Currie; the president's close friend Vernon Jordan, a Washington power broker and former civil rights leader (who the investigators thought had helped arrange a job for Lewinsky in exchange for her false affadavit); and perhaps Clinton himself. Lewinsky, after venting her rage at the treacherous Tripp, grew silent, then broke down and sobbed for ninety minutes. Finally the investigators allowed her to call her mother, Marcia Lewis, and the questioning ended while all awaited Lewis's arrival from New York.

One group that would eventually prove crucial to the denouement, Congress, and especially the Republican majority in the House, was not yet fully engaged in the plotting, although Republicans were delighted at the president's torment in the Paula Jones case. As the moment neared for Clinton to give his deposition to Jones's lawyers, Speaker Gingrich was in, of all places, the fleshpots of Hollywood, delivering a speech to several hundred conservatives including the actor Charlton Heston and the host of the television game show *Wheel of Fortune*, Pat Sajak. Gingrich's appearance was sponsored by an activist funded by right-wing foundations, David Horowitz (described by the *New York Times* as "an author and prominent leftist turned rightist").

The final set of participants, the Washington press corps, was for the moment personified, thanks to Goldberg, by Michael Isikoff, although numerous other reporters, in both the mainstream and the partisan press, had already played a role in whipping up the scandal and would continue to do so. Alerted to Lewinsky's story by Goldberg, the scoop-hungry Isikoff and his editors were up against the magazine's Saturday night deadline, debating whether the evidence about the president's alleged affair and about the new departure in Starr's investigation was solid enough to run as a story. Late on Friday, around midnight, two members of Starr's staff met Tripp's lawyer, Moody, and George Conway at a Howard Johnson's near the Watergate apartment complex, and handed back one of the tapes Moody had given the independent counsel's office. Moody then bolted for the *Newsweek* office, where he played the tape for Isikoff and three of his colleagues.

So the clandestine lines converged—and after nightfall on Friday, January 16, scheming was general all over Washington. At her home in suburban Maryland, Linda Tripp, having spent the day fingering Lewinsky for Starr's men, was briefing one of Paula Jones's lawyers. Kenneth Starr's investigators were holding Monica Lewinsky in a hotel room at Pentagon City. Two of them then held a hugger-mugger meeting near the Watergate with two of the "elves" involved in the Jones case, one of whom was also Tripp's attorney. By early Saturday morning, Michael Isikoff, at the *Newsweek* office downtown, was himself listening to one of Tripp's tapes. At the White House, Bill Clinton was thinking about his testimony and steeling himself for the next day's deposition at his lawyer's office, where both Judge Susan Webber Wright and his accuser, Paula Jones, would be present. The president knew he would have to be nimble but did not foresee the coming broadside.

On Monday, January 19, Robert Bennett assured the first lady and the president's aides that Clinton's deposition had gone splendidly. "They didn't lay a glove on him," Bennett said. "On a scale of one to ten, it was a fifteen." Shut out by his client from the whole truth, Bennett was perplexed only by Clinton's obvious glumness after the questioning was done. In fact, the proceedings were almost disastrous for the president. Most of the interrogation concerned women other than Paula Jones, and Jones's leading attorney—Donovan Campbell's partner, Jim Fisher—asked Clinton some very pointed questions about Monica Lewinsky concerning their meetings in the White House, specific gifts they had exchanged, the twisted path of Lewinsky's job search, and more. Fisher also bluntly asked whether Clinton and Lewinsky had ever been alone and had ever had sexual relations. Clinton, thinking fast, answered all the questions in ways he thought technically truthful, including flat denials about sex. (He would later say he believed that the tortuous definition of "sexual relations," established for the purposes of the deposition, did not include his receiving oral sex.) He knew that there was a world of difference between the sexual harassment alleged by Paula Jones and his consensual encounters with Monica Lewinsky, and that his relations with Lewinsky were therefore irrelevant to Jones's case. Yet he also sensed that he had been lured toward perjury, and knew that his testimony included responses that may not have been technically perjurious but were still evasive and misleading. He was also now aware that the other side had somehow discovered a great deal about his private life.

Over the weekend after the deposition, the stories on Linda Tripp's tapes began filtering out. On Saturday, *Newsweek* finally declined to publish Isikoff's story—so Lucianne Goldberg and the "elves" e-mailed their version of it, related to them first by Isikoff, to Matt Drudge, the Internet gossip hound to whom George Conway had been sending titillating tips from Paula Jones's camp. At the time, Drudge was relatively obscure, a computer-savvy would-be Walter Winchell in a snap-brim hat and Hawaiian shirt—acting hard-boiled but also campy and louche. Aside from nudging *Newsweek* into publishing an earlier article of Isikoff's on Kathleen Willey, he was best known for posting on his Web site, The Drudge Report, the false and slanderous charge (later retracted) that a senior adviser at the White House and assistant to the president, Sidney Blumenthal, had beaten his wife. Yet by running, late on Saturday, a shocking if erroneous story about the Lewinsky affair—followed, the next day, by another flash report divulging Lewinsky's name—Drudge set off an unprecedented explosion in the press.

On Tuesday night, the *Washington Post* and ABC News were ready to release the first mainstream reports on the scandal. Thereafter, the press coverage turned into a bewildering roar. By the end of the week, the former White House adviser George Stephanopoulos—now a political commentator for ABC News on television (and a figure whom some in the White House regarded as unreliable in a crisis)—became the first person in the media to begin mentioning the inevitability of impeachment proceedings. Lucianne Goldberg and the "elves," with the assistance of The Drudge Report, had succeeded in setting the agenda.

Hit by a riptide of conflicting emotions, Clinton clung to his belief that what was afoot, fundamentally, was nothing more—and nothing less— than an effort to destroy him personally and politically, once and for all. As soon as the first report appeared in the *Washington Post*, he told his wife that, although he knew the troubled Lewinsky, the story about an affair was utterly untrue. He then turned quietly to Dick Morris, with whom he had maintained contact since Morris's dismissal under fire in August

1996, and with whom he could be more or less candid.* Morris commiserated, then commissioned a snap poll, which showed that whereas the respondents might forgive the president his marital infidelity, most of them would not condone perjury or obstruction of justice—but that, in any case, the national mood was too raw, too ugly, for Clinton to come clean immediately.

Clinton's tough response, later to become famous—"Well, we just have to win then"—reflected his determination to see himself as the victim of a political vendetta—the partial, self-validating view of the scandal that would carry him through the coming months. But Clinton's tough side was not his only side—or always, in the first days of the storm, his dominant side. Deciding to lie to the world, and above all to his wife and daughter, in order to rescue his presidency—and to do so not with clever prevarications but firm denials—left him flat and demoralized. At the end of the week, the White House deputy chief of staff John Podesta met the president in the study off the Oval Office and saw a man so haggard and dispirited that for the first time he thought Clinton's presidency might actually be collapsing.

Clinton's initial strategy of stonewalling—lying about Lewinsky and getting back to his work as president, while allowing his administration to counterattack—would permanently scar his reputation, batter his marriage and family, and throw him into additional legal jeopardy. Yet it also probably saved his presidency. Amid the media frenzy during the week after January 18, a forthright public admission by the president would almost surely have caused a fatal uproar, as Morris claimed. Even short of impeachment and removal by Congress, Clinton might have faced the likelihood of receiving a delegation of leading Democrats from Capitol Hill (some of whom had disliked him long before now) demanding his resignation.

By instead forcefully denying the charges, jabbing his finger for emphasis, after a brief appearance at the White House related to child care, on

---

* Morris would later testify to Starr's grand jury that Clinton told him, "With this girl, I didn't do what they said, but I did . . . do something. . . . And I may have done enough so that I don't know if I can prove my innocence." Morris testified further that Clinton added, "You know, ever since the election, I've tried to shut myself down. I've tried to shut my body down, sexually, I mean. . . . But sometimes I slipped up and with this girl I just slipped up." Dick Morris, grand jury testimony, August 18, 1998, as quoted in *Referral to the United States House of Representatives Pursuant to Title 28, United States Code, §595 (c), Submitted by the Office of the Independent Counsel, September 9, 1998*, at http://icireport.loc.gov/icireport/6narrit.htm#N_1107.

January 26, Clinton temporarily quieted the storm. By standing defiantly against the press and the lawyers on Jones's team and in Starr's office—saying, in effect, prove me guilty or else shut up—the president signaled that he would not surrender without a fierce fight. Four days later, Clinton delivered a substantive State of the Union address to Congress that was interrupted by applause 104 times. Even a leading conservative Republican congressman, Robert Livingston of Louisiana, hailed his "strong performance" and observed, "He has every reason to be proud." Less than two weeks after the scandal broke, Clinton had rallied his supporters' spirits (and his own) and made the case that doing his elected job was more important than dealing with scandalmongers.

Over the next six months, as the public had the time to absorb the story, the White House benefited from good luck made possible by hard work. On the night that Starr's men detained her for questioning, Lewinsky reached by phone, through her father, the malpractice attorney William Ginsburg of Los Angeles, who flew east the next day to serve as her legal counsel. A garrulous man who adored the limelight, Ginsburg quickly became an object of scorn and ridicule in the press. Yet he secured for his client a proffer and immunity agreement with two of Starr's assistants. Starr eventually rejected these in early February because Lewinsky stated that Clinton and Jordan had not engaged in any obstruction of justice. (If Starr had accepted Lewinsky's proffer, his whole investigation would have collapsed then and there.) Still, Ginsburg, who came to detest the independent counsel, had served his client well—and, as is now apparent, he slowed Starr's momentum.

Starr and his men also miscalculated by calling Clinton's secretary Betty Currie, and Lewinsky's mother, Marcia Lewis, before the Whitewater grand jury, appearing to the public to be browbeating two women. Starr compounded the error at the end of February by subpoenaing the White House senior adviser and veteran journalist, Matt Drudge's early target, Sidney Blumenthal. To this point, the press had been largely sympathetic to the Office of the Independent Counsel (OIC). In some instances, reporters were writing slanted stories based on illegal and often misleading leaks from the OIC. Blumenthal was trying to get reporters to pay attention to stories then surfacing, which raised doubts about Starr's investigation, as well as the role of the "elves." After his first day before the grand jury, Blumenthal denounced Starr in a speech delivered on the courthouse steps; this speech earned him the enmity of journalists bound to Starr but added to the wider impression that the independent counsel was out of control. At the beginning of March, the public's approval of Starr, the OIC, and the investigation dipped sharply.

Ten days later, Judge Susan Webber Wright in Little Rock barred Paula Jones's attorneys from introducing evidence gathered in the investigation of the Lewinsky affair. Three weeks after that, Judge Wright dismissed the Jones case altogether. The suit, which had produced the "elves," who in turn had given Starr's failed Whitewater inquiry a rationale to investigate Clinton's sex life and Clinton's attempts to conceal it, was now itself dead. Clinton and his supporters saw their torment ending at last, as the main lines of Starr's revived inquiry concerned the president's testimony in a case that now no longer existed. But Starr immediately made it clear that he considered the outcome in the Jones case irrelevant to his own task, which was to track down evidence of unlawful conduct of any kind by the president—evidence that he still believed would take him well beyond the Lewinsky case. Republican leaders in the House remained just as certain that Clinton was concealing additional misbehavior, and they were determined to bring down the president, by forced resignation if not by impeachment.

The revived campaign momentarily rescued Newt Gingrich from a difficult situation. Still the embodiment, to Democrats, of a regressive new Republican radicalism, Gingrich had fallen into disfavor with the more ardent young Republicans (including many of those who entered Congress in 1994) by allowing Clinton to outfox him. Having survived a plot by some of the young Turks to overthrow him in 1997, Gingrich had yet to regain the confidence of the right wing in the Republican caucus. ("We're drifting," said Representative David M. McIntosh of Indiana, a member of the hard-line Conservative Action Team.) Attacking Clinton over the Lewinsky scandal was one way for Gingrich to shore up his right flank, while also hitting the Democrats hard over their perceived "sick" moral laxity.

In April, Gingrich excoriated the president and pledged to return to the Lewinsky scandal in every speech he gave until the fall congressional elections. Gingrich's more grandiose side may also have gotten the better of him: reports circulated that he was already looking ahead to the impeachment and removal not simply of Clinton but of Vice President Gore—which would make Gingrich, who as Speaker of the House stood third in the line of succession, the next president by default. Against these dreams of glory, though, Gingrich had to weigh some inconvenient facts: having divorced his first wife and remarried, he was now involved in his own illicit affair with a woman who was young enough to be his daughter and whom he had personally added to the congressional payroll. Although no one had reported on it, Gingrich's affair was common knowledge among Washington insiders, so Gingrich would have to be on his guard.

Representative Henry J. Hyde of Illinois, the chairman of the House Judiciary Committee, also had problems. Hyde was regarded as a reliable conservative, not only because of his caustic defense of Oliver North during the Iran-contra scandal in 1987 but also because he had sponsored, in 1976, the Hyde Amendment, which forbade federal funding for abortions (and hit poor women on Medicaid especially hard). A longtime fixture in Congress, with an impressive white mane and an ingratiating manner that sometimes cloaked his pompous and sarcastic impulses, Hyde was treated with respect and even deference by the press corps, as "a man of courtliness and character," in *Time* magazine's phrase—a principled lawmaker who could lay his partisanship aside and ally himself with Democrats over specific issues such as gun control.

Yet Hyde was long past his prime. In recent years, he had suffered the death of his wife and then debilitating prostate surgery. It was obvious to those around him that he now lacked the energy, the will, and even the desire to oversee, as chairman of the judiciary committee, a full and impartial impeachment inquiry. During the months after the Lewinsky scandal broke, he often said that any legitimate impeachment proceedings would have to be perceived by the public as bipartisan—yet he did nothing to reach out to the committee's ranking Democrat, Representative John Conyers of Michigan. Having stalwartly defended one president's lying during the Iran-contra scandal, Hyde would now attack lying by another president about extramarital sex as an offense grave enough to warrant that president's removal. And Hyde's own past was not unblemished. Beginning in 1965, when he was forty-one, he had carried on an affair for four years with a married woman that broke up her marriage and endangered his own. Even Hyde's children had not learned of the incident until after the storm over Lewinsky began, and the man whom Hyde had wronged arranged to have the story published in order to condemn his hypocrisy at last.

Kenneth Starr was now determined to deliver to Congress a referral officially recommending Clinton's impeachment. Starr, who was about the same age as the president, had grown up in East Texas, the son of a barber who was also a minister in the conservative evangelical Church of Christ. After attending Harding College in Arkansas, a church-affiliated institution influenced by the John Birch Society, Starr had struck out for the east; earned degrees at George Washington University, Brown, and Duke Law School; and clerked for Chief Justice Warren Burger. He rose rapidly within Republican legal circles in Washington, although he kept up his contacts with more moderate and liberal colleagues. He had been the U.S. Solicitor General and a judge on the D.C. Circuit Court of Appeals, and was long mentioned as a possible nominee for the Supreme Court. The soft-spoken, undemonstrative Starr had agreed to take over the Whitewater inquiry in 1994, despite his lack of any prosecutorial experience, in the hope of burnishing his credentials—but also with the conviction that Clinton was a sexual demon. Linda Tripp's tapes not only recharged Starr's faltering investigation but so incited the upstanding, churchgoing independent counsel that his inquiry began to resemble a crusade. Yet the same sense of self-righteousness that drove Starr forward would also prove his undoing.

All summer, Starr called and recalled witnesses to his grand jury chamber. At the end of July, his office finally approved an immunity deal with Lewinsky, negotiated by two well-known Washington attorneys—Plato Cacheris and Jacob Stein—who had taken charge of Lewinsky's representation. Her latest statement to the OIC about what had happened with Clinton did not differ in substance from the statement that had accompanied the initial immunity agreement worked out by William Ginsburg, which Starr had rejected in February. The next day, Lewinsky handed over a blue dress (mentioned in rumors and press reports at the outset of the scandal) that she was sure had been stained by the president's semen.

As Clinton suffered his latest indignity—having his blood drawn for DNA testing—he almost certainly knew that his lies, public and private, were finally about to be exposed. He had already agreed to give a deposition to Starr's men in the White House on August 17; now he would have to figure out the best way to confess to his family as well as to the country. But suddenly and gruesomely, the world outside the bizarre universe of "Monicagate" intruded. On August 7, Osama bin Laden's terror network Al Qaeda blew up the American embassies in Kenya and Tanzania, killing 223 and wounding more than 4,000—the worst attack ever on American civilians and employees abroad. Once again, Clinton's domestic political problems were unfolding along with a grave and bloody foreign crisis.

At his grand jury deposition, having already confessed to his wife, Clinton read a prepared confession about indulging in inappropriate behavior with Lewinsky. That evening, he addressed the country on television, at last admitted his deceptions, and asked for forgiveness—but he also claimed that his evasive sworn testimony had been technically correct, and he unleashed his anger at Starr and Starr's investigators. Three days later, the president ordered retaliatory missile strikes on suspected Al Qaeda sites in Afghanistan and the Sudan. But neither the confession nor the forceful response to Osama bin Laden were sufficient to placate or deflect Clinton's critics—some of whom accused him of cynically attacking Al Qaeda in order to distract attention from his own problems.

On September 9, Starr delivered to the House a 445-page impeachment referral, which included graphic descriptions of Clinton and Lewinsky's sexual play (packed with explicit details that Starr thought necessary in order to prove that Clinton had committed perjury in his deposition in the Jones case) along with evidence allegedly confirming that Clinton had suborned perjury and obstructed justice. Two days later, at Gingrich's insistence, and with Starr's foreknowledge, the House released the report to the public over the Internet. The metropolitan press, setting the tone, expressed disgust at the president. Starr's report was "devastating," the *New York Times* said in an editorial; Clinton would now be remembered chiefly for the "tawdriness of his tastes and conduct and for the disrespect for which he treated a dwelling that is a revered symbol of Presidential dignity." The release of the Starr Report, however, did not have the same effect on the public, to the surprise and chagrin of the the Republican Congress and the prosecutor. The report was not the final blow turning Americans against the president; instead, a majority of the public became revolted at its prurience and at Starr's prying, and sympathetic to the man whose private life was being microscopically inspected. But Starr, the congressional Republicans, and much of the press corps refused to heed the public's mood.

On Capitol Hill, meanwhile, the Democrats buckled but did not break. The House minority leader, Richard Gephardt, already under pressure from his colleagues to demand that Clinton stand down, asked the Democrats' chief counsel to the Judiciary Committee, Abbe Lowell, to examine the enormous stacks of evidence which Starr had compiled for the grand jury (and which Hyde had arranged to he held in a sealed suite at a congressional office building). Lowell's assignment was to ascertain, over the coming weekend, whether the president had committed an impeachable offense. If he had, Gephardt said, the Democratic congressional leadership would go to the White House the following week "and it will be our sad duty to say that he has to resign."

Lowell reported back on Sunday: although the president had lied in his deposition in the Jones case, and possibly in his testimony to the grand jury, Lowell said, the rest of the charges did not stand up. Above all, Lowell explained, even the worst of Clinton's offenses was not impeachable. "It was all about sex," he explained. "It had no bearing on his public duties." Lowell was applying a standard, traditional interpretation of the Constitution's somewhat cryptic language: in stipulating that a president could be impeached for "high crimes and misdemeanors," the framers were thinking of crimes against the state committed in the exercise of executive power, in contrast to crimes against persons or property. As Alexander Hamilton had written in *Federalist* 65, impeachment was reserved for offenses "which may with peculiar propriety be denominated POLITICAL, as they relate chiefly to injuries done immediately to the society itself." Reassured, Gephardt canceled any thought of asking Clinton to resign.

Henry Hyde, his own past misbehavior now revealed on the Internet site *Salon*, was in no mood to compromise. On October 8, the House, in a partisan vote, approved Hyde's plan authorizing the judiciary committee to undertake an open-ended investigation into the president's misdeeds, without establishing constitutional standards for impeachment as had been done by the committee considering the impeachment of Nixon. The House also rejected an alternative that would have limited the hearings to allegations regarding Lewinsky. Whatever damning evidence Starr might have—about Whitewater, Travelgate, and who knew what else—would now be available to use in felling Clinton.

The Republicans then moved into full campaign mode. At the end of the month, Gingrich announced that he would spend $10 million in party election funds on ads attacking Clinton over the Lewinsky matter. Vice President Gore predicted that the Democrats would lose between forty and fifty seats in the House in the upcoming midterms. Yet, astonishingly, the Democrats actually picked up five seats in the House and held their own in the Senate. It had become virtually an iron rule of American politics that, in the sixth year of any president's term, his party lost House seats. The last time the opposite had occurred was in 1822—before the emergence of modern political parties and when James Monroe was president.

Across the political spectrum, experts and pundits in Washington, while busy listening to each other, had lost touch with the American public. Few of them noticed that, on the eve of the elections, Clinton's approval rating stood, enviably, above 65 percent, and had not fallen below 60 percent during the entire "Monicagate" frenzy. Starr, by contrast, received unfavorable ratings from two-thirds of the public as of the early autumn, and his standing deteriorated further in coming months. Plainly, the voters felt kindly toward Clinton's administration and its policies, even if they did not approve of his private behavior. Plainly, they had grown to dislike Starr and his allies, including the Republicans in the House. And as both the opinion polls and the returns confirmed, the public had concluded that Clinton's behavior, though indefensible, did not warrant his expulsion from office. In the days just before and immediately after the elections, hundreds of constitutional lawyers and historians signed statements endorsing publicly what Abbe Lowell had told Richard Gephardt privately: Clinton's alleged offenses, even if they proved to be true, did not rise to the level of impeachable high crimes and misdemeanors. The majority of the American people had already grasped that point instinctively.

The chief immediate victim of the elections was Gingrich, who, disgraced by the results and despised by his caucus, resigned his seat in Congress within days. In October, he had assured the House Republican caucus that their party would pick up twenty to thirty seats, at a minimum, in the upcoming congressional elections. Gingrich even called the president to warn him that Democrats in the House were on the verge of demanding his resignation. But less than a week after the elections, it was the disgraced Gingrich who resigned, not simply from the speaker's chair but from Congress altogether. His own adulterous affair, well known to Republicans, figured in the internal revolt that led to his resignation. And although the Republicans speedily named Robert Livingston of Louisiana as the new speaker-designate, effective power over the House fell to Gingrich's longtime rival, the ultraconservative House majority whip, Tom DeLay, a former insect exterminator from Sugarland, Texas.

DeLay considered Gingrich far too equivocal, especially in the budget showdown of 1995 and 1996. As party whip, DeLay also built a powerful machine of his own among the House Republicans, linking corporate interests, individual donors, and advocacy groups from around the country. By 1997, DeLay's operation was so formidable that when the coup against Gingrich, which he had masterminded, failed, Gingrich did not dare reprimand him. Unlike the egotistical Gingrich, DeLay preferred to wield power from the shadows and have his surrogates—including a group of his congressional minions informally called "the Committee"—do the dirty work, including whipping wayward colleagues back into line. Now, having put Livingston in Gingrich's place, DeLay set his sights on forcing out a president who, he later declared, lacked the correct "biblical world view" in politics.

Within hours of Gingrich's resignation, Henry Hyde announced to his Republican colleagues on the judiciary committee, through a telephone conference hookup, that he intended to move forward. "What can we do?" he said fatalistically. "Can we sweep it under the rug?" Having invited President Clinton to testify and been rebuffed, Hyde would compose a long list of questions to the president that would force Clinton to make some embarrassing replies. Hyde also planned to call Starr to testify, and to give the independent counsel one last opportunity to bring the entire terrible truth about Bill Clinton into public view—once again in the hope that it would suddenly turn the public against the president.

The televised hearings of the House Judiciary Committee lasted a month and produced far more heat than light. The committee majority produced friendly expert witnesses who claimed that the president's alleged perjury—indeed, any perjury—was a high crime, a systematic attack by the executive on a coordinate branch of the federal government. Other witnesses backfired on the Republicans. For example, the former coach of a women's basketball team described how she had lied under oath about hanging out in a lesbian bar called Puss 'n' Boots in Salt Lake City—a story utterly irrelevant to the impeachment of a president and to high crimes and misdemeanors, but puzzling and amusing in a way that made the impeachment seem ridiculous.

The high point in the hearings was Starr's marathon session. After a sometimes lofty, sometimes peevish performance (which the chairman, Hyde, praised as superb, even though it produced no dramatic new smoking gun), Starr received a standing ovation from the Republican side of the aisle and stony silence from the Democrats. He also made two important wrong moves. First, simply by appearing before the committee to advocate Clinton's impeachment, Starr stepped well beyond the precedent set by the independent counsel Leon Jaworski during the Watergate crisis and struck some as having exceeded his authority. The next day, Starr's ethics adviser, Sam Dash, who had served as co–chief counsel to the Senate Watergate Committee in 1973–1974, quit the OIC, charging publicly that Starr had "unlawfully intruded on the power of impeachment which the Constitution gives solely to the House." (Dash had earlier inspected all of Starr's evidence on Whitewater and the various other matters, concluded that there was nothing there, and urged Starr to act professionally by ending his investigation—advice that Starr dismissed.) Second, Starr let it drop, almost parenthetically, that his office had, some months earlier, cleared the Clintons of any wrongdoing in the Whitewater affair and all the other purported scandals he had investigated. Representative Barney Frank of Massachusetts picked up the point, noted that Starr's charge compelled him to release such information in a timely fashion, and pressed Starr with caustic wit about why he had waited until after the election to make public this important exoneration. Starr was left looking more than ever like a partisan witch hunter.

The hearings did not change a single mind on the committee. On December 11 and 12, the members approved, voting along strict party lines, four articles of impeachment: two alleging perjury, one alleging obstruction of justice, and one containing catchall charges stemming from Clinton's careful replies to the questionnaire sent to him by Hyde. Attention now focused on about two dozen Republican moderates, mainly from the Northeast, who had expressed reservations about impeachment and whose votes might still have tipped the balance. There are conflicting reports about how the majority whip, DeLay, handled these doubtfuls, and whether he delivered any direct threats. But Representative Peter King, a conservative Republican from Long Island, later gave a plausible account of what took place. "Coming out of the election, everyone thought impeachment was dead," King related:

> I didn't hear anyone discuss impeachment. It was over. Then DeLay assumed control. . . . In most districts in the country, a majority was against impeachment, maybe a majority of Republicans. But a majority who voted in the Republican primaries was for impeachment. When you put individual members under the gun, a lot of them could get killed in a primary. That was the way he did it. I heard of Christian radio stations going after the Republicans. Right-wing groups were stirring it up in parts of the country outside of the Northeast. Most of the pressure went through the Christian right network. It happened over a ten-day period.

Only five Republicans wound up crossing the aisle to vote against all four articles of impeachment, the same as the number of Democrats, from southern conservative districts, who defected to vote in favor.

One last piece of melodrama unfolded before the proceedings moved to the Senate. Earlier in the fall, the wheelchair-bound pornographer, Larry Flynt, publisher of *Hustler* magazine, offered cash rewards of up to $1 million for tips about the sexual indiscretions of House Republicans. He happened to pick up dirt on the speaker-designate, Representative Robert Livingston. Suddenly, in the middle of his speech from the floor on impeachment, Livingston announced sorrowfully that his marital infidelities had been "Larry Flynted," and he called on President Clinton to spare the country any more pain by doing the right thing and resign his post. "You resign! You resign!," Democratic members shouted; whereupon Livingston finished his remarks by doing just that and begging forgiveness from his family and his colleagues. Clinton, shaken by the latest downfall, reasonably suspected that DeLay had had a hand in crafting Livingston's resignation. Fearful that pressure might now increase for his own resignation, he immediately issued a statement asking Livingston to reconsider.

A few hours later, the House passed two of the four articles of impeachment, charging the president with perjury in his testimony to the grand jury and obstruction of justice in the investigations regarding Paula Jones and Lewinsky. There seemed to be little doubt that the Senate would fail to raise the two-thirds majority necessary to convict Clinton on either count and remove him from office. After the frightful scenes in the House, many if not most senators would have been just as happy if the entire matter went away. But Hyde and the other Republican members of the committee who had been selected to present the case to the Senate—officially, as the House managers—would not be easily cowed no matter how tired Chairman Hyde was. Having come this far, they intended to mount a full trial on the Senate floor, complete, they hoped, with live witnesses, in the strained hope that at long last some indisputably damning piece of evidence would emerge.

The Senate, however, under its majority leader, Trent Lott, voted to delay a decision about calling witnesses until after Hyde and the managers had presented their case. Eventually, the managers would present three witnesses—Monica Lewinsky, Vernon Jordan, and Sidney Blumenthal—but these three were questioned on videotape, not live. The videos contained nothing new. (Lewinsky was especially effective, as she ran rings around her inquisitor, Representative Ed Bryant of Tennessee, affirming once again that she had had sexual contact with Clinton but denying the charges about perjury and obstruction of justice.) Hoping that eloquence might do the trick, Hyde delivered a pair of impassioned speeches citing dozens of historical military battles, invoking the graves of the martyred dead, and wondering whether "if, after this culture war is over . . . an America will survive that will be worth fighting for to defend."

On the more mundane but relevant matters of evidence and analysis, the White House counsel Charles F. C. Ruff, who had been the last independent counsel in the Watergate scandal, nearly stole the show. In a neat refutation of the ballyhooed charges about Clinton's conspiring with Vernon Jordan to silence Lewinsky by offering her a job, Ruff dramatically showed that the House managers (as well as their lead counsel, David

Schippers, who was Hyde's crony and a former prosecutor from Chicago) had distorted basic facts. The former senator Dale Bumpers of Arkansas then wound up the defense with an earthy, eloquent speech that drew on humor by H. L. Mencken, alluded to the scholarship of the eminent southern historian C. Vann Woodward, and referred, above all, to the work of the framers. "We are here today," Bumpers told his former colleagues, "because the president suffered a terrible moral lapse of marital infidelity—not a breach of the public trust, not a crime against society." While conceding Clinton's wrongdoing, he drove home the "total lack of proportionality" in the attacks against the president.

On February 12, the Senate acquitted Clinton on the perjury article by a vote of forty-five ayes, fifty-five nays; and on the obstruction article by fifty to fifty. In the lingering mephitic atmosphere, perhaps few in Washington recalled that it was Abraham Lincoln's birthday.

Clinton's acquittal left the country momentarily exhausted and perplexed. The failure to remove the president or force his resignation felt anticlimactic, and muffled any sense that something important had actually occurred. Individuals, to be sure, had been affected deeply. Bill Clinton's sexual misdeeds in the White House and his efforts to conceal them under oath had been revealed, to his everlasting embarrassment.[*] Kenneth Starr had earned ignominy of a different kind as a vindictive zealot—a disgrace deepened by his subsequent efforts to prosecute others in connection with the Lewinsky affair, all of which ended in defeat. Newt Gingrich and Robert Livingston had lost their power and their dignity. The lives of Monica Lewinsky, Linda Tripp, and dozens of others were damaged. But the larger importance of this drama for the nation and its political institutions was not immediately evident, beyond the fanatical pursuit of a president's private flaw, egged on by a credulous and sensation-hungry press—a furious and sometimes idiotic tale that apparently signified nothing.

---

[*] Clinton would pay for his deceptions with a contempt citation from Judge Susan Webber Wright for giving false testimony, a $25,000 fine (to be paid to the Arkansas Bar Association), and a five-year suspension of his license to practice law, in addition to a mountain of legal fees. He would also pay Paula Jones and her lawyers $80,000, but with no apology, to get them to abandon any further legal proceedings against him. See Neil A. Lewis, "Transition in Washington: The President; Exiting Job, Clinton Accepts Immunity Deal," *New York Times*, January 20, 2001, p. A1.

Had Congress halted the drive for impeachment after the elections, the country would have been spared both the drama and the anticlimax. Congress would have offered a display of democratic responsiveness to the voters' will. But because it carried on into November and December, the impeachment exposed a fundamental breach over the Constitution and, more broadly, over authority and accountability in American politics. It also created ominous precedents and sent an important warning to future generations.

The breach became particularly evident in the actions and remarks of a single participant, Henry Hyde. In 1987, as noted above, Hyde had adamantly supported the lies, even under oath, of members of the Reagan administration. He went so far as to attend the verdict at Oliver North's trial—the only congressman to do so—and when North was convicted of making false statements and obstructing justice, Hyde rushed over to embrace him. Hyde acted very differently, though, in 1998 and 1999. In one of his speeches to the Senate during the impeachment proceedings, about the rule of law and the tombstones of fallen patriots, he attempted to explain that glaring difference. "Morally serious men and women can imagine the circumstances at the far edge of the morally permissible when, with the gravest matters of national interest at stake, a president could shade the truth in order to serve the common good," Hyde declared. "But under oath for private pleasure?" By this standard, the executive could be excused for lying about covert acts, no matter what their eventual consequences were, if, in the president's judgment, the lies served a severely imperiled national interest. This line of reasoning, which accorded completely with the earlier congressional minority report on the Iran-contra affair, granted the executive a great deal of power free from accountability to Congress or the public. It also viewed Clinton's misdeeds as all the more grievous because they lacked political grandeur, having been connected to private gratification and not public duties.

Hyde's critics came to exactly the opposite conclusion. They insisted that the framers had designed the Constitution primarily to correct political abuses by any branch of the government by making each accountable to the others. According to the critics, the framers would have frowned on any effort to evade that accountability, even by "morally serious" presidents who believed they were saving a nation at risk. By contrast, Clinton's lies, stemming from consensual if illicit sex, were trivial. Hyde and his supporters were appalled by such permissiveness, regarding it as the main source of what Hyde had invoked as "this culture war" and as a frontal attack on the rule of law—an attack that would lead the country to totalitarianism. In effect, they upheld a legal absolutism about allegations concerning private morality but a more forgiving approach to public morality—and interpreted the Constitution accordingly. Their critics were more flexible about private matters and alleged legal breaches connected to private matters, but much more stringent about alleged breaches concerning public power—and interpreted the Constitution accordingly.

Because the Senate acquitted Clinton, it is tempting to conclude that the latter view prevailed and to leave the lessons of the impeachment at that. But the success of the impeachment in the House suggests a very different conclusion. By impeaching Clinton in the manner and on the grounds that it did, the House altered the precedents established by the previous impeachment investigations of Andrew Johnson and Richard Nixon. With its approval of Hyde's plan authorizing impeachment over evidence of a crime that had not yet even been discovered, the House invented a truly novel constitutional theory. If allowed to stand, that theory could permit later government investigators to roam far and wide looking for crimes that presidents may have committed, harassing future administrations with an unending process of official search and accusation.

By impeaching Clinton for infractions that did not clearly rise to the level of high crimes and misdemeanors against the state, the House departed farther from precedent and lowered the bar for impeachment established by the framers. The members established a new standard whereby the House might impeach a president for any alleged crime at all, so long as a majority of members saw fit to label it a high crime. The House also openly treated impeachment as analogous to a grand jury proceeding, whereby the House members merely passed along a set of plausible charges to the Senate, which would act as the jury. Here again, though, the House diluted the framers' standard, which was that the House would impeach only if a majority was fully convinced that the president deserved removal.

Time would tell whether these new precedents would endure, or whether the example of 1998 would serve more as a warning than an invitation. But in one respect, this impeachment crisis—with its origins in deliberate efforts to topple President Clinton and with its bitter partisanship—clearly offered a dire warning. Writing in *Federalist* 65, Alexander Hamilton emphasized the constant danger that an impeachment battle would become connected to "the pre-existing factions" and would enlist "all their animosities, partialities, influence, and interest on one side or on the other." In such cases, Hamilton said, "there will always be the greatest danger that the decision will be regulated more by the comparative strength of parties, than by the real demonstrations of innocence or guilt." Two hundred ten years later, Hamilton's nightmare materialized in the impeachment of Bill Clinton.

Clinton drew the more immediate lesson that he ought to redouble the work he had undertaken in 1998, especially in foreign policy. Despite the obvious distractions of the Lewinsky scandal and the impeachment, the president had taken seriously his vow that the best thing he could do for the country and himself was to labor all the harder as president. In April, along with his skilled envoy, the former senator George Mitchell, he helped to negotiate the Good Friday Accords that halted more than two decades of sectarian violence between Protestants and Catholics in Northern Ireland. The process had begun in earnest when Tony Blair became prime minister of Britain in 1997. Blair saw Clinton (himself of distant Irish extraction) as a potential force for great good, and he agreed to name Mitchell as chief mediator in Northern Ireland. On Saint Patrick's Day in 1998, Clinton invited Northern Irish leaders from all sides to a party at the White House, where he spoke with them privately about the situation, preparing them for the negotiations that followed. The ensuing Good Friday agreement created a new elected assembly for Northern Ireland as well as new governmental bodies that brought together officials from the Irish Republic and Northern Ireland to deal with common problems. It also stipulated that all sides would henceforth renounce violence.

In September, Clinton helped negotiate the next steps in securing peace between the Israelis and Palestinians—a difficult task, given that the Israeli prime minister was now an obdurate conservative of the Likud Party, Benjamin Netanyahu; and that Yasir Arafat remained as intransigent and unreliable as ever. For eight days, the three leaders and their staffs holed up at Wye River Plantation in Maryland, along with, at Clinton's invitation, King Hussein of Jordan, who was dying of cancer. Hussein's calming, reasonable presence could not completely suppress the tension—on two occasions, Netanyahu threatened to walk out—but on September 23, Clinton returned to Washington with an agreement. The Israelis would cede to the control of the Palestinian Authority additional portions of the West Bank; the Palestinians would drop several harsh anti-Israel paragraphs from their national charter, while also agreeing to remand suspected terrorists to Israel, under the supervision of the CIA.

Renewed violence in the Balkans created a crisis that carried over into 1999, immediately after the impeachment trial. In the Serbian province of Kosovo, Albanian Muslims, representing the vast majority of the population, had undertaken their own drive for independence, led by the Kosovo Liberation Army (KLA). Slobodan Milosevic, however, considered Kosovo sacred Serbian soil, and in repressing the KLA, his troops turned again to a vicious campaign of ethnic cleansing in order to drive out the Muslims completely. By mid-1999, an estimated 863,000 Kosovars had been displaced and upwards of 10,000 killed. Clinton—backed by his secretary of defense, William Cohen, and by the Joint Chiefs of Staff—was wary of any new American intervention, in part because domestic public opinion opposed it and in part because many experts considered the KLA leaders a band of nationalist thugs little better than Milosevic. The United Nations would be of little use in stopping the violence, as Russia would certainly veto in the Security Council any military action against Serbia. The NATO nations, France above all, did not want to get involved. The new emergency began, eerily, to resemble the horror in Bosnia in 1995.

Like the earlier Balkans crisis, though, the fighting in Kosovo caused important officials within the administration to push Clinton toward decisive action. Madeleine Albright had succeeded Warren Christopher at the start of Clinton's second term, to become the nation's first woman secretary of state and the highest-ranking woman ever to serve in the federal government. Deeply concerned with the Balkans, Albright considered Milosevic a small-scale throwback to Adolf Hitler. Joined by the supreme allied commander of NATO's forces in Europe, the American general Wesley Clark, she called for intervention by NATO, including the dispatch of American troops. But Clinton refused, even when the failure of multilateral talks in Rambouillet, outside Paris, touched off renewed ethnic cleansing in March. Clinton did support light high-altitude bombing runs by NATO over Serbian positions, but these exercises in what one American general mocked as "tank plinking" actually encouraged Milosevic to intensify his ethnic attacks. Clinton accordingly agreed to a fierce escalation of the air war, which included high-tech bombing of Belgrade. Combined with some difficult diplomacy that brought about the Russians' withdrawal of support for the Serbians, the bombing forced Milosevic to sign an agreement in June.

The bombing campaign had killed an estimated 5,000 Serbian solders, 500 Kosovar rebels, and untold numbers of civilians. The peace agreement called for the disarming of the KLA without providing for an election that might lead to Kosovo's independence. Continuing murderous tension between Albanians and Serbs who remained in the province required the long-term stationing of 18,000 NATO troops (including 1,800 Americans) in addition to the American forces already stationed in Bosnia. The intervention was unpopular with the American public. Still, Clinton, after hesitating, had managed once again to win over recalcitrant members of NATO and stop a mass slaughter. Displaced Kosovars began returning to their villages. An International Criminal Tribunal for the former Yugoslavia, established by the United Nations in 1993, indicted Milosevic for war crimes in connection with the attacks on Kosovo, and in 2000 he was overthrown in a popular uprising; a year later he surrendered to security forces. (He would die of natural causes in 2006 in his jail cell in The Hague, his protracted trial still under way.) Clinton had found a way to overcome domestic resistance to military intervention—and to complete a multilateral operation without losing a single American life.

Clinton's military attack on Iraq at the height of the drive for impeachment stirred angrier controversy—a measure of how embittered politics in Washington had become. During 1997 and 1998, Saddam Hussein regularly halted and otherwise obstructed the UN's weapons inspections mandated after the Gulf War, causing one confrontation after another with the United States and Britain as well as United Nations officials. In February 1998, General Secretary of the United Nations Kofi Annan worked out an agreement with Saddam for the return of the inspectors in exchange for promises by the United Nations to consider lifting its economic sanctions against Iraq—but in August, Saddam reneged, claiming that he saw no progress on the UN's part. After several more diplomatic and military feints, the United Nations formally charged Iraq with systematic violations of the inspection accords. The United States and Great Britain launched Operation Desert Fox, a four-day campaign of massive bombing. The chief aim of the campaign, Clinton said, was to degrade Iraq's facilities devoted to research and development of unconventional mass weaponry, and to weaken Saddam's elite Republican Guard. (David Kay, director of the Iraq Survey Group, in his report on weapons of mass destruction, after the invasion of Iraq in 2003, stated his belief that Operation Desert Fox had destroyed the remaining weaponry facilities.)

Russia, China, and France objected and called for lifting the eight-year-old oil sanctions against Iraq. Other negative reactions came from inside the United States. Republicans in Congress, who had previously cast aspersions on Clinton's attacks against Al Qaeda, denounced Operation Desert Fox even more vociferously as a cynical effort to get impeachment off the front page of the newspapers. Senator Trent Lott, who had supported Clinton's earlier military action, now refused—an unprecedented move by any congressional leader while American forces remained in harm's way. (Interestingly, remnants of the campus-based leftists who had opposed the Vietnam War took a similar view and denounced Desert Fox as "Monica's war.") The former secretary of state Henry Kissinger, however, said that the bombing was not nearly as severe as it should have been and would not "make any significant difference." Other commentators considered the action necessary, proportionate, and useful, but warned that Saddam would have to be continually watched and contained in coming years.

If Saddam remained a constant cause of concern, Al Qaeda and the threat of terrorism by Muslim extremists became an obsession late in Clinton's presidency. On October 12, 2000, the USS *Cole* was at anchor at the Yemeni port of Aden for a routine fueling. Shortly before noon, two suicide bombers rammed the ship with a small inflatable craft laden with explosives, ripping a gash in the ship's hull, killing seventeen American sailors and wounding thirty-five. Although it would not be entirely clear for months to come that Al Qaeda had organized the attack, suspicion immediately centered on Osama bin Laden. And although, technically, an attack on a military target was not defined as an act of terrorism, bin Laden's growing brazenness caused great alarm among the White House's experts on terrorism—especially because other parts of the government, in particular the military, seemed unconcerned.

In 1997, the National Security Council, having identified Afghanistan and Yemen as strongholds for terrorists, sent a memo to the Pentagon about the heightened likelihood of terrorist attacks on American ships in foreign ports. But the Navy, which had been provided with a complete intelligence assessment specifically on Al Qaeda, disregarded the warning and then, in line with its emphasis on the personal responsibility of the commander, took no action about the security breach in Aden. "A more telling display of the persistent disbelief concerning the threat from al-Qaeda would be hard to imagine," said a later report by two of the White House's authorities on terrorism. Republicans, led by the former congressman Dick Cheney (now his party's nominee for vice president), saw the *Cole* incident as a political issue, and blamed it on what Cheney described as the Clinton administration's post–cold war indifference to the military. But on the change of administrations in January 2001, Clinton's counterterrorism coordinator Richard Clarke, who retained his position, swiftly and sternly warned the incoming foreign policy team that Al Qaeda was "not some narrow, little terrorist issue," and would demand continuing, primary attention from the White House.

On domestic issues, Clinton spent his last two years continuing to push for specifically targeted programs while protecting existing mandates such as Social Security and Medicare. The mounting annual federal surpluses—reaching $236 billion by 2000, the highest in U.S. history—vindicated Clinton's fiscal policies, but also stimulated renewed talk on the right about large regressive tax cuts, which fed on renewed talk on the left about new big-government programs. Clinton stuck to his center-left course, dedicating the surplus chiefly to Social Security while pushing for a wide range of specific reforms, including enlarged tax credits to ailing senior citizens and their families; expanding tax relief to cover college tuition; additional child-care provision to low-income families; and limited health care reform intended to lower the average cost of prescription medicines.

With the Republicans still in command on Capitol Hill, and House Republicans still smarting over the outcome of the impeachment, Congress had little interest in backing social spending of any kind. The congressional majority rejected Clinton's proposed "patient's bill of rights," legislation reducing the costs of prescription drugs to senior citizens, and a rise in the minimum wage. It also balked on passing new gun safety laws, even after a shocking massacre at a high school in Colorado by two disturbed teenage students. Yet Clinton and the Democrats could still look back and point to hard-won results over the previous seven years.

Despite some warning signals for the future—an unfavorable balance of trade, growing consumer debt, the collapsing values of many overpriced high-tech companies—the economic boom continued and the basic economy was strong. During the Clinton administration, the percentage of Americans who were poor or unemployed had decreased dramatically, as had rates of both violent crimes and property crimes. In his State of the Union address in 2000, the president could proclaim, "Never before has our nation enjoyed, at once, so much prosperity and social progress with so little internal crisis and so few external threats." Without erasing the shame of the Lewinsky scandal, Clinton had succeeded, yet again, in pulling his presidency out of the trough. Now, though, the "Comeback Kid" would be unable to ratify his latest recovery as he had done before—by running for office. If Clinton's success was to continue, it would depend on Vice President Al Gore.

14

IRREPARABLE HARM:
THE ELECTION OF 2000

A L GORE HAD BEEN Bill Clinton's heir apparent for all of Clinton's
presidency. Having greatly strengthened the Democratic ticket in
1992 and 1996, he had played an important role in administration
councils on numerous initiatives, including the budget for 1993, NAFTA,
welfare reform, and military intervention in the Balkans. As head of the
National Performance Review for streamlining government operations,
Gore had helped reduce the number of federal employees to its lowest level
since the early 1960s. Always a strong advocate for environmental protection policies, he also pushed hard for expanding access to the Internet in
the public schools. As the son of a respected liberal, Senator Albert Gore of
Tennessee, he had spent a lifetime in and around national politics, including four terms of his own in the House and eight years in the Senate; and
in 1988, at the age of forty, he had made a serious run for the Democratic presidential nomination. Not since John F. Kennedy in 1960 had the
Democrats presented a youthful figure groomed so thoroughly for the
White House.

By contrast, the Republican establishment looked almost tapped out following Bob Dole's defeat in 1996. The generation that had come of age
during the World War II was now past its prime in presidential politics. No
obvious younger figure who could unite and lead the party had emerged
from the ranks of the Reagan conservatives. The Republicans' dynastic tendency did, however, offer some rays of hope. Since 1952, with one exception,

the Republican national ticket had always included either a Nixon, a Dole, or a Bush.[*] Although Nixon's heirs lacked either the interest or the record to run for president, Dole's wife Elizabeth (thirteen years his junior) had been a cabinet member in both the Reagan administration and the Bush administration. After announcing a bid for the nomination, she dropped out in October 1999, before the first primary, because of inadequate fund-raising. The Bush family, though, had produced two possibilities: President Bush's son, Jeb, who after narrowly losing the gubernatorial race in Florida in 1994 won it four years later; and Jeb's older brother, George W., twice elected as governor of Texas. Although many observers considered Jeb the more talented of the two, George had the longer record in office and seniority—and, having prepared methodically for a run at the presidency since 1998, he was the clear favorite when the primary season began.

As it happened, Jeb Bush—as well as many of the Bush family's loyalists and retainers—would play a crucial role in the conflicts that decided the outcome of the 2000 election. Those conflicts tested American democracy's basic institutions.

Ordinarily, compiling a solid record of achievement in a two-term administration that had brought peace and prosperity would have made Gore the presumptive victor by a considerable margin. Yet the seeming inevitability of Gore's nomination, as well as his connections with Clinton, caused Gore vexing problems, including some that he himself compounded.

During and after the campaign of 1996, Republicans, looking to the future as well as the present, focused their continuing attacks on Gore in connection with alleged abuses of campaign financing. Although the accusations led nowhere, and Gore had done nothing illegal, they continued to dog his reputation for steadfast integrity. Then, in the immediate aftermath of Clinton's acquittal in the Senate, little stories began appearing in the press that challenged Gore's truthfulness and cast him as a compulsive fibber and an exaggerator about his own achievements. There was a confused story about how he had supposedly insisted, falsely, that he and his wife, Tipper, were the "models" for the lovers in Erich Segal's popular novel *Love Story* and the movie made from it in 1970. There were reports that he had claimed to be the inventor of the Internet (he was, in fact, the crucial

---

[*] The exception was the Barry Goldwater–William Miller ticket of 1964.

sponsor of the legislation that created the Internet); that he had lied about plowing fields as a boy on his family's farm in Carthage, Tennessee (he did, in fact, plow fields); and that he had mendaciously taken credit for breaking a national scandal in 1978 on the danger of toxic waste at Love Canal, New York (he did, in fact, as he claimed, help bring another toxic waste disaster to public attention at about the same time).

Each of these bogus stories, on its own, was trivial, but when the reports were trumpeted by the Washington press corps and hyped by the Republican National Committee, they attained the appearance of truth, even among some of Gore's former colleagues at the White House. George Stephanopoulos, who had become a political pundit on television, likened Gore to Pinocchio; the former secretary of labor Robert Reich, who opposed Gore's nomination from the left, added, "I don't know why he feels that he has to exaggerate and make some of this stuff up." The press, meanwhile, was determined to give credence to the stories, and reporters sometimes even invented tales themselves, chiefly by recycling their own misquotations. Although no evidence surfaced to show that mainstream journalists deliberately distorted facts in order to damage Gore's candidacy (except in conservative media such as Fox News), an anti-Gore bias clearly developed among leading political reporters and their editors. "Somewhere along the line," said Mark Halperin, the political director of ABC News, "the dominant political reporters for the most dominant news organizations decided that they didn't like [Gore], and they thought the story line on any given day was about his being a phony or a liar or a waffler."

The candidate, confused by the situation, responded weakly, either by trying to laugh off the accusations or by actually apologizing for misstating facts that he had not misstated. The decision by Gore's camp not to counterattack sharply and swiftly only deepened the reporters' suspicions, reinforced their bad habits, and encouraged fresh allegations. Eventually, the "Pinocchio" story line created a strong public impression of Gore as a devious, power-hungry, phony Washington insider—thereby tapping into the persisting public distrust of politics and politicians that had become a dominant theme of the age of Reagan and served the antigovernment line of conservative ideology.

Gore also had difficulty figuring out how to present himself vis-à-vis President Clinton after the Lewinsky scandal. Although Gore rallied to Clinton's side during the impeachment battle, he was genuinely offended at Clinton's behavior and said so in an interview in mid-1999. Gore also worried that his own campaign might suffer because of Clinton's infidelity and deceptions. Gore was especially alarmed by polls that showed the public's persistent personal disapproval of the president. When some of his advisers assured him that the voters would never confuse him with the rakish Clinton, and noted that the ratings of Clinton's job performance (the figures more predictive of electoral success) had actually peaked during the impeachment and remained high thereafter, Gore was unconvinced.

Presidential candidates from the incumbent's party must always find a way to escape from the shadow of the president and establish their independent bona fides. Gore, though, saw an additional need to distance himself from Clinton's improprieties—and did so by coming as close as possible to severing himself completely from Clinton, and from the record of achievement that he himself had helped build. He also sharply restricted Clinton's campaign appearances, even in Arkansas, thereby depriving the campaign of the president's proven appeal in places where Clinton might have been especially beneficial.

All the while, established Republican leaders prepared for the election on several fronts. Veterans of the Nixon, Ford, Reagan, and Bush administrations, along with the heads of some conservative think tanks and Republican members of Congress (and with the support of Newt Gingrich, who was then Speaker of the House) created a group called the Congressional Advisory Board, which began holding regular meetings on Capitol Hill in 1998. The board's major purpose was to develop lines of attack against the Clinton administration, lay the broad policy foundations for the Republicans' presidential campaign of 2000, and, not incidentally, provide a meeting ground and clearinghouse for people who hoped to occupy senior positions in a new Republican administration. Among the more conspicuous participants in the discussions of foreign policy were Donald Rumsfeld, the former secretary of defense; Dick Cheney, who had been Rumsfeld's associate since the Nixon administration and was also a former secretary of defense; and Paul Wolfowitz, who had served as Rumsfeld's foreign affairs deputy in the Dole for President campaign, in which Rumsfeld was campaign chairman. Condoleezza Rice, a young specialist on Soviet politics who was a protégée of both the former secretary of state George Shultz and the former national security adviser Brent Scowcroft, later joined the group. (Rice had become provost of Stanford University, which was also Shultz's base and the home of the influential conservative Hoover Institution.)

Early in 1998, Rumsfeld was selected as chairman of a congressional commission formed to examine and report on available intelligence concerning the threat to American security posed by ballistic missiles left over from the cold war. Wolfowitz was also named to the commission, which was modeled on the Team B that had provided alternative intelligence during the Ford years. The Rumsfeld Commission warned in July 1998 that the CIA and other U.S. intelligence agencies had badly underestimated the danger of these missiles. Although its final report, issued in July 1998, refrained from calling outright for a renewed American missile buildup, it specified that three countries had become the greatest menaces to the United States—Iran, Iraq, and North Korea.* (The neoconservative Wolfowitz had already taken the lead in raising special concerns about Iraq, and called flatly, late in 1997, for Saddam Hussein's overthrow—an appeal he repeated continually over the coming months in op-ed pieces, magazine articles, and testimony before Congress.)

While the Republicans' shadow foreign policy team took shape, the Republican establishment's presidential hopes focused on George W. Bush. Bush was only two years older than Gore, and had some other similarities to his Democratic rival, as the son of a political leader, as a product of prep school and the Ivy League, and as an experienced officeholder. Yet in every other way, the two men were utterly different. Unlike the steady, earnest, even bookish Gore, Bush was a reformed wastrel who had succeeded despite his repeated failures mainly because of his privileged family's connections in business and politics. An indifferent student, Bush nevertheless gained admission to Yale, which both his father and grandfather had attended, as a family legacy. By his own account, he wasted much of his early adulthood on parties and booze, until he underwent a religious conversion at the age of forty. In 1968, after he graduated from college, one of his father's friends placed a call to the speaker of the Texas house of representatives, and, jumping over several waiting lists, young Bush suddenly obtained a prized position in the Texas Air National Guard—known as the "champagne unit"—thereby avoiding military service during the Vietnam War. Gore, by contrast, enlisted and served in Vietnam. (For about a year, Bush, the party animal, was unaccountably absent from duty without official leave; his episode of going AWOL has never been explained.)

Rejected by the University of Texas Law School, Bush attended the Harvard Business School (having been accepted through the intervention

---

* In 2002, President George W. Bush would repeat these charges, calling Iraq, Iran, and North Korea the "axis of evil." George W. Bush, "Address Before a Joint Session of the Congress on the State of the Union, January 29, 2002," at http://www.presidency.ucsb.edu/ws/index. php?pid=29644&st=.

of his father). His subsequent efforts in business were mainly failures. One botched venture raised suspicions when a group of the elder Bush's friends at the Harken Energy Corporation bought young George's holdings and, in effect, gave him a large profit as a gift—just before his firm went belly-up. (Without explanation, the Securities and Exchange Commission, headed by one of his father's friends, dropped an investigation into his still murky dealings.) Bush also tried his hand at politics by running for Congress in 1978, but he lost to a candidate who stood far to his right. Bush's fortunes improved in 1989, when he and a syndicate of businessmen, including his father's campaign manager, purchased the Texas Rangers major-league baseball franchise—a sweetheart deal in which Bush, immediately named general managing partner at an annual salary of $200,000, saw his initial, borrowed stake of $500,000 increase in value to $14.9 million in nine years.

Whereas Gore took ideas as well as public policy seriously, no one would mistake Bush for an intellectual; nor did Bush have much patience with or use for intellectuals who did not directly serve his political ends. He was prone to malapropisms, more of a cutup than an orator. His strengths as a candidate were chiefly his beaming smile; his carefully cultivated, straight-shooter, even swaggering cowboy persona; and his instant name recognition. In fact, Bush's plain manner and generally mediocre record led many of his adversaries (as he put it in one of his more famous word manglings) to "misunderestimate" him. His unassuming exterior hid a sharp political intelligence, much as his Texas drawl hid his advantaged upbringing. Between losing business schemes, he had hung around his father's national campaigns, and had been apprenticed by his father to hardened southern Republican political operatives. In time he assumed the job of enforcing absolute loyalty to the candidate. In 1988, when the cutthroat campaign strategist Lee Atwater was given the assignment of minding him, Bush befriended Atwater, who deepened his political education. Atwater had first come to the Bush family's attention through his work on the controversial campaign of another up-and-coming strategist, a college dropout named Karl Rove, for national chairman of the College Republicans in 1973. Later that year, after clearing Rove of alleged misdeeds in that campaign, the elder Bush had hired him as an aide at the Republican National Committee; and in November, Rove first met the younger Bush and was reportedly "awe-struck" by his charisma. After resettling in Texas in 1977, Rove won a reputation of his own as a ruthless and effective strategist (in part from his work on George H. W. Bush's national campaigns from 1980 through

1992, which eventually got him into trouble with the candidate). Rove later masterminded George W. Bush's successful gubernatorial campaigns in 1994 and 1998.

Despite Gore's uncertainties and Bush's strengths, the presidential race of 2000 looked, early on, as if it would be Gore's to lose, at least according to most Washington pundits. Gore fairly easily overcame a challenge in the primaries from the former Rhodes scholar and professional basketball star Senator Bill Bradley of New Jersey (although Bradley, by harping on the vice president's supposed lack of trustworthiness, amplified the press's unfriendly reporting on Gore). Bush, however, faced a surprisingly stiff challenge from Senator John McCain of Arizona, who had been a hero and prisoner of war during the Vietnam War and had become known as a political maverick by taking independent stands on campaign-finance reform, regulation of the tobacco industry, and health care. McCain shocked Bush in the New Hampshire primary, where independents flooded the polls, trouncing him by 49 to 31 percent. The fight for the nomination came down to South Carolina, where Bush's faltering forces (in ways reminiscent of the efforts by the embattled Reagan campaign in North Carolina in 1976, but even more emphatically) tacked hard to the right, Dixie-style. Bush's strategists sidled up to neo-Confederates who favored keeping the rebel battle flag flying above the state capitol (a practice begun in the 1950s to endorse segregationist "massive resistance" to civil rights reform). The strategists had Bush speak at the controversial, fundamentalist Bob Jones University (which barred interracial dating among students). A well-financed dirty tricks campaign, funded by longtime supporters of Bush and directed by pro-Bush operatives, also helped spread scurrilous rumors to the effect that McCain had fathered an "illegitimate"; "black" child. (McCain and his wife had in fact adopted an East Asian girl.) McCain did not foresee how nasty the race would become—"They know no depths, do they?" he mused before reporters—and after he lost decisively in South Carolina, his campaign never recovered.

Having run so far to the right in order to win the nomination, Bush had to scramble in order to move back to the center for the general campaign—but with a combination of adroit rhetoric and cunning tactics, he succeeded. Superficially, he seemed to have learned some lessons from Bill Clinton's successful race in 1992. Just as Clinton ran as a new kind of Democrat, Bush presented himself as a new kind of Republican—a "reformer with results" who championed what he called "compassionate conservatism." On the conservative side, Bush favored deep, regressive tax cuts, both as a means to hand the new federal surpluses, as he put it, back to the people, and as supposed stimulant to further economic growth—a return, with a vengeance, to the supply-side ideal that his father had supposedly betrayed. Bush also openly displayed his evangelical faith, which made him even more popular with the religious right, and far more popular than his father had ever been. Bush's "compassion" appeared both as a political theme and in terms of policy in his calls to mobilize religious faith and charity on behalf of the less fortunate, in what he called "faith-based" initiatives—a religious version of his father's "thousand points of light." Like his father, Bush also proposed further raising national educational standards in order to combat "the soft bigotry of low expectations."

The Republicans' nominating convention, held in Philadelphia in July, symbolized the new "compassionate conservative" approach, and stood in stark contrast to the elder Bush's disastrous convention in Houston eight years earlier. Familiar right-wing firebrands such as the Reverend Jerry Falwell could be seen in and around the convention hall, but mostly they remained confined to the back rooms and hallways, out of sight of the television cameras. Onstage (and on television), the show consisted largely of minority singers, dancers, and speakers, in a political extravaganza calculated to soften the image of the Republican Party among independent, socially liberal suburban voters. Pride of place at the podium went to an African-American, the retired general Colin Powell, whose speech endorsing Bush also defended affirmative action, denounced poverty and racial discrimination, and attacked tax breaks for wealthy special interests. The only negative comments at the convention consisted of various speakers' promises to restore propriety and dignity to the White House—barely veiled allusions to the Lewinsky scandal and the unsubstantiated allegations about the Democrats' campaign finance abuses. Bush also promised to change the acrid partisan tone in post-impeachment Washington by governing as "a uniter, not a divider."

Bush said little about foreign affairs, about which he knew virtually nothing. (Although his father had been ambassador to the United Nations, plenipotentiary to China, and director of the CIA, young Bush had traveled hardly at all outside the United States.) But by the time Bush was nominated, the efforts by experienced Republicans to design a post-Clinton foreign policy had merged with his campaign. After delivering his quasi-official report on missile defense in 1998, Donald Rumsfeld continued to convene Republican leaders interested in the issue, including Condoleezza Rice and Paul Wolfowitz. In 1998, Rice also visited Kennebunkport for an extended stay, bonded with the younger Bush (in part because of their shared love of sports), and emerged as his chief adviser on foreign policy. That fall, Wolfowitz, who had served as an aide to both Shultz and Dick Cheney, joined the Bush campaign as a second foreign policy adviser.

The most important figure in the mix was Cheney. Since leaving the government in 1993, Cheney had served as chief executive officer of the Halliburton Corporation, a large military contractor. Selected by Bush early in 2000 to survey the field of possible nominees for the vice presidency, Cheney eventually decided that he wanted the position himself, and Bush instantly assented. Cheney had close ties to proponents of all shades of thought within the Republican Party about foreign affairs, from realism to neoconservatism. Apart from Rice, with her realist background, and his former aide when he had been secretary of defense, the neoconservative Wolfowitz, Cheney benefited from the loyal counsel of numerous veterans of the previous two Republican administrations, including the neoconservative Richard Perle, who had been an official in the Defense Department during the Reagan era, as well as Wolfowitz's former assistants at the Pentagon, Stephen Hadley and I. Lewis "Scooter" Libby. Cheney could also rely on his former mentor, Donald Rumsfeld, with whom the elder Bush had had uneasy relations ever since the days of the Ford administration.

The only major foreign policy figure not in Cheney's orbit was his antagonist from the Gulf War, Colin Powell. But weeks before Election Day, the younger Bush tapped Powell to head the State Department, even though Bush had developed virtually no personal connection with his father's chairman of the Joint Chiefs of Staff. In all, the Bush campaign presented what looked like a unified front of experienced Republican makers of foreign policy. Led by Cheney, they contributed campaign positions highly critical of the Clinton administration's "nation-building" interventions abroad, but they were also insistent about increasing rates of military spending, especially on missile defense.

During the general election, Gore tried to meet Bush head-on, especially over domestic issues. Instead of tax cuts, Gore promised that he would place surplus federal monies in a safe "lock box" dedicated to protecting Medicare. He denounced as risky and disruptive a proposal by Bush to allow younger workers to place their Social Security contributions in individual private equity accounts. On one issue after another, from environmental protection to education, Gore's command of the nuts and bolts of policy overmatched Bush's "compassionate conservative" rhetoric. But Gore's campaign was still plagued by its original dilemmas about how it should relate to the Clinton administration.

Gore made history by selecting as his running mate the first Jewish candidate to appear on a national ticket, Senator Joseph Lieberman of Connecticut. Widely considered a thoughtful lawmaker, Lieberman seemed to many to be a smart choice. Yet because Lieberman, at the height of the impeachment drama, had denounced Clinton's behavior as "immoral," his presence symbolized Gore's continuing, semi-paralyzing ambivalence about the administration he had helped lead for eight years. For Gore, Lieberman's moralistic stance on Clinton's private behavior was a major qualification. Searching for his own campaign themes, meanwhile, Gore settled on an older form of Democratic populism, standing as the candidate of the people against greedy corporate interests. But if these appeals pleased the party's pro-labor base, they confused voters who had come to think of Gore as a Clinton-style "new Democrat," and they seemed out of sync with the prosperity that the Clinton-Gore administration had managed.

Gore was also hampered by the protest candidacy of the celebrated gadfly and consumer advocate, Ralph Nader. After winning the nomination of the pro-environmentalist Green Party, Nader became a candidate for disaffected left-wing Democrats, especially those concentrated in college towns, who believed that Clinton and the new Democrats had moved the party too far to the right on issues related to economics and corporate power. According to Nader, there were no substantial differences between the Republican and Democratic parties, and there was no real choice between Bush and Gore—or, as Nader's supporters took to calling them, Gush and Bore.

Lacking any foreign policy beyond an anti-Israeli isolationism that was curiously reminiscent of Pat Buchanan's (and an anti-NAFTA protectionism also similar to Buchanan's), Nader had no chance of attaining the White House, or even of matching Ross Perot's totals in 1992. He instead wanted to make the Democrats pay for straying from his own pure conception of liberal politics. Asked whether he was running merely to spoil Gore's chances and help to elect Republicans by siphoning liberal votes, Nader expressed hostile indifference. At times, he even seemed eager to help defeat Gore, in order to give the Democratic Party the shock treatment he said it needed and to restore to power proponents of regressive policies that he claimed would spark genuine liberal resistance. The worse things were, Nader suggested, the better they would become for the left.

* * *

The campaign was volatile. Bush took a large lead in the polls after the Republican convention in July, only to lose it as soon the Democrats began counterattacking later in the summer. The three televised presidential debates seemed crucial—and, by every previous indication, Gore seemed to enjoy the advantage, having proved himself a master in the campaigns of 1992 and 1996. In the first encounter, on October 3 in Boston, the vice president outshone the challenger on the issues, and, according to polls conducted immediately afterward, won hands down among the general public. But Gore's microphone picked up his sighs and groans at some of Bush's vague answers—and these unguarded reactions became, in the pundits' theatrical commentary after the debate, its most telling moments, indicating Gore's elitism and arrogance.

Gore also misspoke in a minor way when he said he had accompanied Clinton's respected head of the Federal Emergency Management Agency, James Lee Witt, during a fire and flood in Texas. (Witt had accompanied Gore on many other trips responding to emergencies, but not, as it happened, this particular one; Gore had actually accompanied Witt's deputy to Texas.) The Republicans' researchers immediately caught Gore's slip and offered it as the latest example of his self-aggrandizing mendacity. The press predictably deepened the misimpression. Gore responded apologetically, as he had before, and he carried his defensive tone into the second debate, where his performance was disastrous. Browbeaten by his campaign consultants into believing he'd been too aggressive and had come across as personally unlikable in the first debate, Gore decided that he must be nice to Bush. At every point where he had an opportunity to articulate his differences with his opponent sharply, he instead responded, "I agree."

Only in the third and final debate, after he received terrible notices from the press corps, did the vice president begin to fight back—but in taking a different tack, he reinforced the Bush campaign's theme, harped on by the press, that he was really just a hack politician who would say anything to get votes. By then, Election Day was less than three weeks away, and the public's negative impressions of Gore were hardening. The vice presidential debate did nothing to improve the Democrats' hopes, as Lieberman handled Cheney, one of his old friends, with an agreeable politeness that bordered on obsequiousness.

On the eve of the election, with the candidates running neck and neck in the polls, Republican strategists worried that Bush might carry the popular vote but fail to win a majority in the Electoral College—in which case they were prepared to contest the outcome by railing against the Electoral College system as undemocratic, unjust, and antiquated. But when the tallies came in, that possibility evaporated: Gore seemed headed for a narrow but indisputable plurality of the popular vote. The trouble for the Democrats was that their total in the Electoral College remained at 266, four votes shy of victory. Early in the evening, exit polling data and early network projections showed that Gore had carried Florida, which would have put him over the top—but as the night wore on, the results in Florida turned out to be far tighter than either side expected. Finally, the conservative Fox News Network—where Bush's cousin John Ellis, with whom the candidate had been speaking by phone all day, was in charge of calling the projected winners—placed Florida in Bush's column, thereby giving Bush the electoral majority he needed. The major news networks quickly followed Fox's lead, prompting the stunned and incredulous Gore to place the customary phone call of congratulations to the new president-elect. But moments before Gore was about to deliver his public concession speech, he received word that the results in Florida were still uncertain, and he hastily called Bush to retract his concession. Voters in the eastern states who had gone to bed believing Bush was elected awoke to discover that the outcome was still in doubt and that everything would depend on the result in Florida—where Bush's brother, Jeb, happened to be the governor.

How the Lewinsky scandal and the impeachment directly affected the voting was not fully clear. Although anger at the zealous House Republicans riled Democrats and a significant portion of independents, the fallout from the events also shaped Gore's strategy, rendering it far less confident and forceful than it might have been, and providing the prideful candidate a reason to distance himself from the president. Without question, had Ralph Nader not run, Gore would have carried Florida and, thus, the election. (Nader won 97,488 votes in Florida, most of which would have gone to Gore had Nader abandoned his campaign, as some of his closest friends and colleagues begged him to do in the final weeks.) Even with Nader on the ballot, it is certain that a clear majority of Florida's voters had *intended* to vote for Gore, but thousands of their votes were disqualified. So the state and the nation tumbled into yet another constitutional calamity that revived the bitter partisan passions that had marked the Clinton years.

The calamity was partly the result of sheer human error, political miscalculation, and faulty technology. In Palm Beach County, home to many Jewish retirees, the election board approved the use of a bizarre ballot design, the so-called butterfly ballot, which easily confused people voting for Gore (though not those voting for Bush) into either mistakenly voting for the right-wing, anti-Israel candidate, Pat Buchanan, or spoiling their ballots by voting for both Gore and Buchanan. Even the die-hard Buchanan, now running as the candidate of what remained of Perot's old Reform Party, recognized that the totals in Palm Beach County were preposterous. The *Palm Beach Post*, after inspecting the ballots, concluded that nearly 10,000 votes meant for Gore either wound up going to Buchanan or were discarded as spoiled—a total which, if counted as the voters had intended, would have been more than sufficient to carry the state for the Democrats.

But the problems with the voting were even more widespread. In Duval County, a different poorly designed booklet ballot misled many voters, most of them African-Americans, into choosing two candidates for president. Out-of-date voting machines malfunctioned, creating ballot cards where the voter's choice could be determined only by individual manual inspection. That the faulty machines were particularly numerous in heavily minority and pro-Democratic districts heightened the suspicion that the state government—under the aegis of Governor Jeb Bush—had deliberately suppressed the Democratic vote. Before Election Day, on instructions from Florida's Republican secretary of state, Katherine Harris (who was also co-chairman of the state Bush-Cheney committee), county officials "scrubbed" thousands of African-Americans from the voter rolls, under the pretext (often erroneous) that those excluded were convicted felons who had served their sentences. There were also numerous confirmed reports that local police officers had blocked access to the polls in minority districts on Election Day, tactics that complemented and resembled other substantiated efforts of the Republican Party to minimize the Democratic vote by intimidating minority voters.

For Republicans, the controversy boiled down to a brazen attempt by the Democrats to steal the election. The original vote tally showed Bush with a lead of only 1,210 votes; and after the recounting of the statewide vote by machine (as stipulated by state law in all such tight races), Bush still had a 327-vote margin. The law had been followed to the letter; the vote, as Republican leaders never tired of repeating, had been counted and recounted. That all the major television networks had, at some point, declared Bush the winner reinforced the impression that everything was said and done. Mocking Democrats' complaints and their calls for more recounts, supporters of Bush and Cheney printed signs and buttons with the official Democratic campaign logo, but with the candidates' names altered to read: "Sore-Loserman 2000."

From the outset, the Republicans held an enormous political advantage. Having Jeb Bush operate the machinery at his command in Tallahassee was of crucial importance. The Republican-dominated state legislature stood by, ready to do whatever was necessary to ensure Bush's victory. As soon as the result fell into doubt. the Bush campaign dispatched the singularly able James Baker III to oversee an elaborate, fully staffed legal and political operation, which included public demonstrations of support for Bush. The operation was also heavily funded, with Halliburton and the Houston-based Enron Corporation providing private jets. And although it was not immediately evident to the press, scores of eager young congressional staffers, and even an out-of-state Republican congressman or two, flew down from Washington to help.

By contrast, the Gore campaign selected as its spokesman and point man in Florida the cautious, colorless, politically inexperienced former secretary of state Warren Christopher, as though what was needed in the political swamp warfare was an older career diplomat. From the start, the tone coming out of the Democrats' camp was subdued, almost defeatist, and certainly defensive. Not wanting to appear as if he was stirring up anything improper, Gore discouraged street protests and demonstrations (and personally told Jesse Jackson to cease and desist when Jackson mounted a protest on his own). Once again, Gore did not heed advice from President Clinton on the necessity of sharp political responses. The major force that might possibly favor the Democrats was the supreme court of Florida: all of the justices were Democratic appointees, and the constitution of Florida gave this court complete power to rule on disputes over state election laws. There were also some local judges and county officials, independents as well as Democrats, who believed that, in fairness—and especially under the unusual, momentous circumstances—all the ballots ought to be counted manually to ascertain the voters' intentions. There were so-called overvotes (in which more than one candidate had been chosen) and undervotes (in which the impressions left on the ballots by the voting machine were too indistinct to be registered by the recount machines).

The Republicans insisted, with dubious precedent, that under its "Safe Harbor" provisions, federal election law strictly barred challenges to previously certified state electors after December 12, six days before all the members of the Electoral College were scheduled to vote. The Republicans' clear aim, perfectly understandable from their viewpoint, was to make it as difficult as possible to conduct any manual recount, and to use the courts if necessary to tie up the process in litigation. Bush's legal team also began formulating the argument that any attempt by the state supreme court to intervene in the situation would violate Article II, section 1 of the U.S. Constitution, which stipulated that each state would appoint electors "in such manner as the State legislature thereof may direct." It was not a compelling argument, given its assumption that the framers' intention in this clause was to set aside the concept of state judicial review and to strip the people of any given state of the authority to use their state constitutions to restrict the actions of the state legislatures. There is no evidence from the framers' debate or writings to support such a reading, and some evidence to refute it; in any event, it ran counter to the principle of popular sovereignty that animated both the framing of the Constitution and the American Revolution itself. But despite their supposed veneration of the framers' "original intent," the Republicans saw in Article II an instrument to ward off what they took to be a politicized and mischievous state supreme court.

Two days after the election, once the machine recount had reduced Bush's lead, Gore's side asked for manual recounts in four counties where punch-card ballots had failed to register the clear intent of many voters. The Democrats contended that the law in Florida did not permit them at this point to demand a statewide manual count, so they chose four counties where the errors appeared to have been the most egregious. Gore also did not want to appear to be overreaching, and above all to appear reasonable. That these counties—Broward, Miami-Dade, Palm Beach, and Volusia—were also large Democratic strongholds was not surprising, as these were precisely the places where the outdated technology was still in place, and where irregularities could be expected to be most severe. But the Democrats' move allowed the Republicans to redouble their charges that the Democrats were perpetrating a fraud by cherry-picking friendly districts in order to inflate Gore's totals.

Secretary of State Harris quickly found her course being guided by a reliable Republican political operative, Jeb Bush's first campaign manager, Mac Stipanovich, whom Bush inserted into Harris's office. Repeatedly, Harris issued rulings that either hindered or blocked outright any manual recounts. The Palm Beach County canvassing board decided it would commence a recount on November 15; Harris then ruled that she would accept no results after November 14. A circuit court judge in Broward County told the county's board that it need not heed Harris's November 14 deadline; and Volusia County quickly completed a recount that gave Gore an additional ninety-eight votes. On November 15, however, Harris announced that she would certify the state's election results only three days later, leaving the remaining counties in question insufficient time to complete their recounts.

Florida's constitutional confrontation began that same day, when the Florida supreme court denied Harris's request to halt all the recounts, then followed up the next day by ruling that the manual recounts could proceed. Here, in the view of Bush's lawyers, was the interference they had long feared, by a runaway Democratic court that intended to steal the election. Gore's lawyers, however, immediately offered to halt all litigation if Bush would either agree to a statewide manual recount or accept the revised results in Broward, Miami-Dade, and Palm Beach counties, in addition to the results in the absentee ballots from overseas. By refusing the offer, the Bush camp tipped its hand. The charge that the Democrats were interested only in adding votes from select counties no longer applied (although it would be repeated constantly during the weeks to come). By refusing to assent to a statewide manual recount, the Republicans quietly affirmed that they feared a thorough accounting of all of Florida's votes would lead to their defeat. The last thing they wanted was a total recount—except for the admittedly flawed statewide machine recount, already completed, which had given them their tiny margin of victory.

All three branches of Florida's state government were now in a showdown. On November 18, Harris certified Bush's victory in Florida. Three days later, the Florida supreme court overruled her certification, calling it "arbitrary . . . contrary to law . . . contrary to the plain meaning of the statute." The court also declared that the uncompleted recounts in Broward, Miami-Dade, and Palm Beach counties were entirely legal and could continue for another five days. Governor Jeb Bush then stepped in, declaring he would sign a bill authorizing the legislature to select its own delegates to the Electoral College, pledged to the Bush-Cheney ticket, should the recounts wind up favoring Gore. Baker, accusing the Florida state supreme court of unfairly trying "to change the rules," filed suit with the U.S. Supreme Court seeking to overturn the Florida court's ruling.

Other pro-Bush stalwarts, impatient with the legal maneuvering, took the law into their own hands. The day after the state supreme court's ruling, a crowd of about fifty rushed the doors of the Clark Government Center, where the Miami-Dade canvassing board had just recommended its manual recounts. A few members of the mob were Cubans, alerted by a local right-wing Cuban radio station that had been contacted by Roger

Stone, a veteran Republican political operative recruited by Jim Baker. The rest were Republican congressional staffers from Washington—including staff members for Senator Trent Lott and the House majority whip, Tom DeLay—who had been given plane tickets and expense funds to join the struggle in Florida. At their head was Representative John Sweeney, a conservative Republican from New York, who started the chant, "Shut it down!" as the vigilantes assaulted members of the canvass board, punched the election supervisor David Leahy, and blocked the county Democratic Party chairman, Joe Geller, from reentering the canvassing room. Shaken and frightened, the canvass board workers abandoned the recount. "If it's possible to have a bourgeois riot," the *Wall Street Journal* editorial writer Paul Gigot, who was present, observed, "it happened here Wednesday. And it could end up saving the presidency for George W. Bush."

Despite the presence outside the county courthouse of hundreds of protesters organized by the Republicans, the Broward County canvassers did manage to complete their recount. They found 567 more votes for Gore. But in Palm Beach County, where the canvassers had an especially difficult time sorting out the ballots, the recount ceased when the Florida secretary of state, Harris, refused to extend the new deadline she had set following the state supreme court's ruling. When that deadline came, on November 26, George W. Bush appeared on national television and claimed victory—but Gore's forces had not yet surrendered. The next day, Gore's lawyers filed suit in Leon County to open recounts in three more counties; when a conservative county circuit court judge ruled against them, Gore's lawyers appealed to the state supreme court. Meanwhile, on December 4, the U.S. Supreme Court—which had surprised many legal observers by agreeing even to consider a matter that seemed outside its jurisdiction and was so obviously political—vacated the state court's decision of November 21 and sent the case back for the court to clarify the constitutional basis for its ruling.

Four days later, on December 8, the Florida supreme court dramatically voided the decision by the judge in Leon County, ordered that the approximately 45,000 "undervote" ballots statewide be recounted and included in the final tally, and added an additional 383 votes to Gore's total from the previously excluded Palm Beach County recount and the partial but interrupted recount in Miami-Dade. (As a result, Bush's margin in Florida was now only 154 votes out of more than 6 million cast.) It appeared, momentarily, that some approximation of a full accounting of the Florida vote would now be forthcoming—and that, if the previous recounts were any indication, Gore would eventually overtake Bush. But Baker appealed that ruling to the U.S. Supreme Court, which once again showed no compunction about intervening. On December 9, in a five-to-four decision, the Court ordered a stay of the Florida court's order to recount the undervotes. Arguments before the U.S. Supreme Court in the case of *Bush v. Gore* were scheduled for December 11—one day before, supposedly, no further challenges to the outcome in Florida could be made.

Justice Antonin Scalia's concurring opinion on the stay made it obvious to legal experts how the Court's majority would eventually rule. The further counting of votes "that are of questionable legality," Scalia contended, threatened "irreparable harm" both to Bush and to the nation by "casting a cloud upon what he claims to be the legitimacy of his election." It also endangered "the public acceptance democratic stability requires." To claim that the legality of the uncounted votes was at all "questionable"—even in the face of the Florida court's rulings to the contrary—revealed that Scalia and the rest of the majority were preparing to take over the situation in Florida entirely and dictate the outcome. The judgment that Bush would suffer "irreparable harm"—the high standard required for this sort of judicial stay—bordered on the frivolous, as Bush could always seek legal remedy if an improper recount went against him. Scalia's opinion also presumed that, if counted, these votes would produce a majority for Gore—an impermissible result, by Scalia's reasoning, because it would cast doubt on Bush's claim that he had been legitimately elected. "Democratic stability" required the Court to step in as the final arbiter—and ratify Bush's claims.

To argue its case, Bush's side chose Theodore Olson—the leader of the Federalist Society and a former official in the Justice Department during Reagan's administration, who had played an important part in the effort to oust Bill Clinton from office. Olson rehearsed in slightly altered form the basic arguments already offered by Bush's side, including the contention about the Florida court's violation of Article II. Almost in passing, Olson also presented the novel claim that tallying all of the still uncounted votes would violate the equal protection clause of the Fourteenth Amendment because the ballots would be counted by different standards in different counties. The relevance of the Fourteenth Amendment was questionable in a situation where, by law, different localities in Florida were permitted to construct different types of ballots. ("How can you have one standard when there are so many varieties of ballots?" one justice—probably Associate Justice Ruth Bader Ginsburg—reasonably asked.) It was also ironic, given the Rehnquist Court's often-expressed disdain for the equal protection clause.

Above all, acceptance of the equal protection argument would lead only to a court order sending the case back to Florida for a recount that adhered to proper standards. But Olson, perhaps without realizing it, had handed the court majority—and much more than the court majority—a piece of constitutional reasoning absent from Justice Scalia's opinion on the halting of the recounts.

Six, and possibly seven, members of the U.S. Supreme Court voted to overturn the Florida court's decision on the grounds of equal protection.* But astonishingly, five of them—all but David Souter and Stephen Breyer—also refused to allow the case to be returned to Florida, where the damage might be repaired and the recounting completed. At ten p.m. on December 12, the Supreme Court issued its five-to-four decision, reversing the Florida court's decision because it ignored equal protection guarantees. As, according to the Supreme Court, all votes had to be tabulated by December 12—in accord, the majority decision said, with the Florida election code and the state supreme court's dictates—any further action by the Florida court was impossible. The five most conservative justices—Rehnquist, O'Connor, Kennedy, Scalia, and Thomas, all Republican appointees (three appointed by Ronald Reagan and one by George H. W. Bush)—had aggressively moved in to conclude the entire matter. There would be no more recounting. George W. Bush had been made president.

Beneath numerous layers of questionable reasoning, the majority decision in *Bush v. Gore* contained, at its core, a falsehood. Having turned aside the contentions of Bush's lawyers about Article II, the decision had no basis for saying that the U.S. Supreme Court possessed any constitutional authority at all to rule on what the U.S. Constitution explicitly stated was a matter of state law. The decision thus turned on whether to remand the case back to Florida, in order to remedy the perceived deficiencies in the statewide recount on equal protection grounds. The majority in the Supreme Court decided, however, that this was impossible because it would stand "in violation of the Florida election code," as well as the Florida supreme court's supposedly explicit statement that the selection of state electors needed to be completed by December 12, as provided in federal law. In fact, the Florida court had said nothing of the kind. While recognizing the desirability

---

* Justice Breyer took seriously the equal protection argument but it was not fully clear that he wanted to overturn the Florida court's decision.

of completing the recounts by the technically preferred deadline, it always placed paramount importance on counting all the votes. The Florida election code, meanwhile, was silent about the federal deadline, but contained numerous provisions that emphasized the importance of counting every vote.

The most the majority could have accurately claimed about the Florida law was that it was unclear about what should occur if a full counting of the votes required working past December 12. But if they had done that, the Supreme Court would have been constitutionally required to send the case back to Florida. Instead, the majority's opinion fallaciously reported both Florida election law and the statements of the Florida supreme court, making it appear that by halting the recounts forever, the U.S. Supreme Court was merely adhering to Florida's statutes and to statements by the state supreme court. Either the majority was aware of its misrepresentations or the justices talked themselves and each other into believing that they were arguing and reasoning accurately.

That the Supreme Court was so bitterly divided, and that its ruling was contrary to the conservative majority's long-standing respect for states' rights and its hostility to the equal protection clause, immediately gave rise to charges that a group of Republican justices had made a deliberate partisan decision to elevate George W. Bush to the White House. In the days following December 12, bits and pieces of anecdotal reportage appeared to support those fears, including eyewitness claims that Justice O'Connor had been "very disappointed" at the first dispatches on election night that suggested Gore would win. And without question, partisanship could have operated, if only unconsciously, in the justices' thinking, though no doubt more so for some justices more than others.

Yet the fact that a case of such magnitude was decided so shoddily does not necessarily prove that the majority was engaged in a partisan judicial coup d'état. Another interpretation is that the Court may simply have wanted to bring the crisis to a speedy resolution—and the conservative majority saw itself, arrogantly, as better equipped to do so than any other governmental body, state or federal, legislative or judicial. The greatest irony of *Bush v. Gore* may be that conservative justices who had long railed against judicial activism had become the most activist justices in our history, or at least the most activist since the majority on the Taney Court handed down the notoriously slapdash decision in *Dred Scott v. Sandford* in 1857. The real loser in the case may turn out to have been not Gore and the Democrats, or even (as Justice John Paul Stevens wrote in his furious dissent) "the nation's confidence in the judge as an impartial guardian of the rule of law," but the basic American democratic principle that, messy as it might be, popular sovereignty is the bedrock of our political institutions.

Two things were clear, though, after *Bush v. Gore*. First, no matter how defective and unprecedented the Court's decision had been, the American people were willing to abide by it as authoritative. Gore helped calm the waters by delivering a speech to the nation right after the ruling was issued, taking strong issue with the outcome but accepting it graciously and conceding the election. (Ironically, this was one of his best appearances of the entire year.) On the damp, cold day of George W. Bush's inauguration, protesters filled the streets of Washington, carrying signs with slogans such as "Hail to the Thief!" Yet if a portion of the electorate would never accept Bush's legitimacy, the prevailing sentiment, even among Democratic leaders, was to wait and see what, exactly, Bush's "compassionate conservatism" amounted to—and whether the candidate who had run as "a uniter, not a divider" would deliver on his pledge.

Second, and most obviously, Clinton's presidency would not have what its members and supporters had hoped might, in effect, be a third term under Gore. Clinton had big dreams for his presidency, but many of them were dashed by his own early inexperience and indecisiveness, by the skill and ruthlessness of his political foes, and by his own curious cycles of political brilliance and achievement followed by personal and political crises. He had also accomplished a great deal, despite claims by his critics who confused political adroitness with capitulation: the greatest and most sustained period of prosperity in American history; the greatest reduction in the poverty rate and the greatest increase in family income and wages since the 1960s; a dramatic decrease in crime rates; the most extensive provision of loans, grants, and tax credits for higher education since Franklin Delano Roosevelt's GI Bill; and advances in foreign policy that left the international prestige of the United States as high as it had been since 1945. Clinton's policies had also turned the crippling federal deficits of the Reagan and Bush administrations into the largest surpluses ever, a reversal that would help guarantee the future solvency of Social Security and Medicare. The rise of the monster deficits, along with the massive redistribution of wealth through revisions in the tax code had, under Reagan and Bush, dramatically reduced the federal government's capacity to act on the nation's problems outside the military while deepening inequalities of wealth and power. Briefly, as Clinton recovered from the battering, self-inflicted and other, of the impeachment crisis, it seemed as if the age of Reagan might have concluded. But *Bush v. Gore* ended any speculation that a new center-left dispensation had begun. There would be no Gore presidency.

What would George W. Bush bring? The man himself remained a cipher, even after a national presidential campaign. He had gained the presidency in freakish circumstances, which suggested to some commentators that he would have to govern from the center, or as close to the center as he could get without losing touch with the Republicans' right-wing base. The circumstances of his ascension to the office also suggested that he would have to govern as his father's son. Bush had assembled around him respected older heads, not least his new vice president, Dick Cheney, who had served in his father's White House and lent the incoming administration a reassuring air of experience. Yet Bush and his team had fought ruthlessly to gain the presidency, from the South Carolina primary through the protracted chaos in Florida in November and December. His expertise on the issues facing the country, as displayed during the campaign, seemed, beyond the merest sloganeering, quite shallow. On Capitol Hill, Republicans would have the slenderest of majorities in the Senate and a somewhat stronger majority in the House, giving them control of the presidency and both chambers of Congress for the first time since 1955—with Trent Lott the majority leader of the Senate and Tom DeLay the effective power behind the scenes in the House. In the aftermath of *Bush v. Gore*, the Republican Party seemed in command of the federal judiciary as well, auguring one-party rule by Republicans of a sort unknown since the 1920s.

Would the second Bush presidency, given these unusual advantages, restore the age of Reagan, perhaps in his father's "kinder, gentler" form, after the Clinton interregnum? Or would it bring something entirely new—and if so, would it be more pragmatic than ideological, more centrist than hard right, or the other way around?

During his first nine months in the White House, George W. Bush did a great deal to answer these questions, in ways the public found disquieting. And then came an unprecedented horror.

OCTOBER 13, 2001

O N THE SIDE STREETS off lower Broadway, immigrant vendors sold little thin cloth Stars and Stripes fastened to sticks. Barely a month after the attacks, the shock had receded, just slightly; and on this Saturday, hushed throngs headed toward the Battery to get as close to the still smoldering mountain of death as the police would permit. The estimated count of the slain at the World Trade Center, as of now, stood at between 4,500 and 5,000—roughly double the number of Americans killed at Pearl Harbor on December 7, 1941. But these dead, unlike those at Pearl Harbor, were almost all civilians.* Federal officials had released details about the cockpit voice recorder tape retrieved from the wreckage of United Airlines Flight 93 in Pennsylvania, with its sounds of a wild and desperate struggle just before the plane went down. The White House had announced that it was giving about half of the $5.1 billion in emergency relief approved by Congress to the Defense Department for improving intelligence and repairing the damage that the third squad of terrorist hijackers

---

* It would take some time after the initial confusion to compile an accurate toll. The final accounting listed 2,973 fatalities, not including the nineteen hijackers: 2,602 at the World Trade Center towers and in the surrounding streets; 246 on the hijacked planes; and 125 at the Pentagon. They included 343 firefighters from the New York City Fire Department and sixty officers of the New York City and Port Authority police departments. Twenty-four persons still remain listed as missing. At Pearl Harbor, 2,335 military personnel and sixty-eight civilians were killed, and 1,143 military personnel and thirty-five civilians were wounded. Thus the attacks of September 11, 2001, were the deadliest foreign attacks ever on American soil.

had inflicted on the Pentagon building. But the devastation in lower Manhattan remained the focus of the shock, grief, and patriotism.

Almost exactly a quarter century earlier, during the bicentennial celebrations, revelers had swarmed through these same New York streets, joyously waving little American flags, craning their necks to see the tall ships in the harbor, enjoying what President Ford called "a super Fourth of July" beneath the immense twin towers that now were no more. Back then, in 1976, the feeling of national pride seemed manic, a little artificial, yet sincere—as if the celebrators were relieved and energized to discover that a common bond had survived the furious struggles over civil rights and Vietnam and the political trauma of Watergate. Now, the feeling was somber and frightened—a common bond *caused* by trauma, by fury, and also by fear, not just fear that terrorists might strike again at any moment but fear that the world had changed forever and nobody was prepared.

There was little foreboding when the terrorists struck, literally, out of a clear blue sky. At that moment, readers were absorbed by the sentimental story of a racehorse of the 1930s, Seabiscuit. Moviegoers were flocking to the dramatized biography of a brilliant but afflicted mathematician at Princeton, *A Beautiful Mind*. Only Bob Dylan, hitting the latest creative peak in his long career, somehow seemed to sense the fates in the song "High Water (for Charley Patton)," on his new album, *"Love and Theft,"* released, eerily, on September 11:

> *High water risin', six inches 'bove my head*
> *Coffins droppin' in the street*
> *Like balloons made out of lead*

The country turned to the president for leadership, reassurance, and explanations. George W. Bush, who was reading a book, *My Pet Goat*, to toddlers in a schoolroom in Florida when the first plane struck, seemed unsteady at first, freezing up when he received the news, then continuing to read. He flew thereafter to Omaha (a protective evasive action ordered by the Secret Service), and did not arrive back in Washington until night had fallen.

On September 14, Bush visited the disaster site in Manhattan, surrounded by a cordon of police officers, firefighters, and emergency rescue workers. The president stood on a pile of rubble, and some in the crowd shouted that they couldn't hear him. He replied through a bullhorn, "I can hear you. The rest of the world hears you. And the people who knocked these buildings down will hear all of us soon." (A hearty cheer of "USA! USA!" went up.) Six days later, Bush addressed a joint session of Congress, vowing that "whether we bring our enemies to justice or bring justice to our enemies, justice will be done." In this address the president also spoke, for the first time at length, of "[o]ur war on terror"—a war, not formally declared by Congress, which he would begin by attacking Osama bin Laden's Al Qaeda and bin Laden's Taliban hosts in Afghanistan and would not end "until every terrorist group of global reach has been found, stopped and defeated." (Later, former administration officials would reveal that during the early hours after the attack, Secretary of Defense Donald Rumsfeld and his deputy Paul Wolfowitz had scurried to find out if there was any way to link the atrocities to the Iraqi dictator Saddam Hussein—known to U.S. intelligence as an adversary, not a friend, of bin Laden.)

On October 5, American and British jets began bombing Afghanistan, targeting strongholds of Al Qaeda and the Taliban. On November 13, the Taliban fled Kabul and within a month Kandahar had fallen as well. Bin Laden and several hundred of Al Qaeda's fighters were cornered in a network of caves in the mountains of Tora Bora. The terrorists and their commanders were not eliminated—Mullah Mohammed Omar, the supreme head of the Taliban, made a nighttime escape on a motorcycle from Kandahar, and bin Laden slipped through the fingers of his attackers in Tora Bora. (The U.S. military assigned Afghan militia forces the task of capturing bin Laden and failed to order U.S. troops to close the lines around Tora Bora, and bin Laden escaped.) Yet the Taliban government had been toppled. Al Qaeda had been severely reduced and scattered from its Afghan training sites.

Bush had strong bipartisan support for the assault on Afghanistan, and his approval with the American public was the highest ever recorded in the history of opinion polling. He seemed decisive, focused, and strong; and the press hailed him as exactly the sort of leader Americans wanted and needed in an unnerving time. Yet in the eight months before the terrorist attacks, the peculiar character of George W. Bush's presidency had become evident—not as a new synthesis of "compassionate conservatism," but as a radicalized form of Reaganism. With the Republican Party controlling both houses of Congress, and with the courts leaning to the right, the president could freely pursue a dogmatic conservative agenda. Before September 11, the new administration was working hand in glove with a political machine, now known as the "K Street Project," directed by the House Republican majority leader, Tom DeLay. With the project's help, the White

House embarked on a partisan politicization of the federal government and an augmentation of executive power on an unprecedented scale, unimagined even during Richard Nixon's headiest days before Watergate. And after September 11, the Bush White House accelerated efforts to complete its version of the conservative revolution.

On September 10, 2001, George W. Bush had the lowest job approval ratings of any modern president to that point in a first term. (Only Gerald Ford, his popularity reeling after his pardon of Richard Nixon, had a comparably poor rating.) After the rancorous contest in Florida, the Washington press corps adopted as conventional wisdom that Bush, lacking a mandate, had to govern from the center. But instead of seeking moderation, Bush governed as if he had won in a landslide—and his politics and policies were far more conservative than his campaign rhetoric of 2000 had suggested. Most Americans, according to polls from this period, found all this disturbing.

During his first eight months in office, Bush spurned bipartisanship. He also undertook initiatives aimed at undoing fundamental structures of American government and diplomacy built up over the previous half century and more. In this sense, Bush was really no conservative at all, but a radical. Yet the Bush White House also represented a culmination of political trends that had marked the entire age of Reagan, even before Reagan himself was finally elected president, going back to Richard Nixon.

Two of the dominant figures in Bush's first term—Vice President Dick Cheney and Secretary of Defense Donald Rumsfeld—had started out in the executive branch under Nixon; Rumsfeld, in fact, had hired Cheney as his deputy. They had also been a team in Gerald Ford's White House—pushing Ford's administration to the right, especially in foreign policy, while they implacably resisted what they saw as the unconstitutional usurpation of executive power by Congress. Cheney, belying his phlegmatic manner, had remained a militant on these matters, as shown in the congressional minority report on the Iran-contra affair—a report influenced by the committee minority staff counsel David S. Addington, who entered the Bush administration as Cheney's legal counsel and, in 2006, became the vice president's chief of staff. Even before the attacks of September 11, Cheney and Addington were pressing to expand executive power at the expense of checks and balances. "[T]he idea of reducing Congress to a cipher was already in play," Bruce Fein, a former official in the Justice Department under Reagan, observed. "It was Cheney and Addington's political agenda."

The other dominant figure in the White House, Bush's political strategist, Karl Rove, got an early schooling in dirty tricks and the southern strategy as a protégé of Nixon's political advisers, and he refined his methods with Lee Atwater. Under the aegis of Cheney and Rumsfeld, meanwhile, Bush's foreign policy apparatus included numerous hard-line veteran neoconservatives and hawks from the Reagan years. Two of them had been convicted in the Iran-contra affair: the former national security adviser John M. Poindexter (named director of the Pentagon's Information Awareness Office in 2002), and the former assistant secretary of state Elliott Abrams (named special assistant to the president and senior director at the National Security Council in 2001).

A few moderate figures from the administrations of Reagan and the elder Bush were appointed to powerful positions, most conspicuously Secretary of State Colin Powell and National Security Adviser Condoleezza Rice. Yet Bush moved major aspects of American policy far to the right in the early months, repudiating not just his predecessor's policies but also some of those associated with his father—and he practically made it a point to humiliate Powell and the moderates. In March 2001, Bush withdrew from the continuing efforts to persuade the North Korean dictator Kim Jong Il to forswear the development and production of nuclear weapons. Powell, who had previously told the press that the United States remained committed to the negotiations with North Korea, had to contradict himself in public by officially announcing Bush's decision and immediately apologize for misspeaking—a deliberate humbling of Powell and a gesture of belittlement that would not be the last.

Bush also repudiated what had been for decades the traditional U.S. position as a mediator and negotiator among Israelis, Palestinians, and the Arab nations—a position his father had taken very seriously. He killed American support for the Kyoto Protocols to deal with global warming from greenhouse gases and substituted his own voluntary compliance plan, which won support from no other government and isolated the United States. As a candidate, Bush had promised to work for reductions in carbon dioxide emissions from power plants, but he quickly reversed himself once in office. He also struck down federal regulations that reduced the amounts of carcinogenic arsenic in drinking water.

The one piece of domestic legislation to which Bush committed himself heart and soul revived and extended Reaganite ideas—a large, regressive tax cut. Undertaken ostensibly to return the new federal surplus to the people who had earned it, the tax cut, approved by Congress, once again redistributed wealth upward to the wealthiest Americans, nullified the ideas of fiscal discipline advanced by both Bush's father and Clinton, drained the surplus, and contributed to staggering new federal deficits that required unprecedented borrowing from foreign lenders, especially China. Bush's secretary of the treasury, Paul O'Neill, the former CEO of Alcoa, warned the president of the consequences, but Bush ran roughshod over him.*

Bush actually went farther than Reagan in enshrining tax cuts as an instrument of social policy—in his case, virtually the only instrument of social policy, except for an educational program, "No Child Left Behind," that became an unfunded mandate; and proposals on pharmaceutical drugs for seniors and privatizing Social Security that won meager support. How deliberately the Reagan administration set out to crush activist government by accumulating huge deficits remains open to debate and conjecture. By 2001, however, it was perfectly understood from the experience of the Reagan years that supply-side economics were a delusion. The promise of increased investments and revenues accruing as a direct result of lowered taxes could never be a reality. The chief result of relentless, regressive tax cuts, apart from rewarding the wealthy, would be to preclude new social programs and exert pressure on existing ones. Under Bush, the chief domestic legacy of the age of Reagan became the purposeful core of domestic policy.

By cutting tax rates, and in numerous other ways, Bush seemed to many conservative Republicans—and not just Republicans—to be governing more like Ronald Reagan than his father had, before September 11 and for the rest of his first term. "On taxes, on education, it was the same. On Social Security, Bush's position was exactly what Reagan always

---

* Vice President Cheney also rebuked O'Neill, who resigned in December 2002. Early in 2004, in collaboration with the writer Ron Suskind, O'Neill published a memoir critical of the president. The administration immediately threatened to investigate and prosecute O'Neill for abusing classified information, an accusation that the White House dropped as soon as he ceased giving interviews about his book. Many people believed that Karl Rove was the chief instigator of the threats. More than six months before O'Neill resigned, Suskind, working on a magazine assignment, was waiting to interview Rove at the White House and overheard him complaining to an aide about a political operative who had displeased him. "It was," Suskind wrote, "like ignoring a tornado flinging parked cars. 'We will fuck him. Do you hear me? We will fuck him. We will ruin him. Like no one has ever fucked him!' As a reporter, you get around—curse words, anger, passionate intensity are not notable events—but the ferocity, the bellicosity, the violent imputations were, well, shocking. This went on without a break for a minute or two. Then the aide slipped out looking a bit ashen." Ron Suskind, "Why Are These Men Laughing?" *Esquire*, January 2003, p. 96.

wanted and talked about in the 1970s," Martin Anderson, a former aide of Reagan's, observed in 2003. "I just can't think of any major policy issue on which Bush was different." (Anderson might have added funding ballistic missile defense, partially privatizing welfare, determined deregulation of business, and hostility to organized labor, especially public service unions.) "I think he's the most Reagan-like politician we have seen, certainly in the White House," Michael Deaver said of Bush. "I mean, his father was supposed to be the third term of the Reagan presidency—but then he wasn't. This guy is." Bush's down-home style as well as his ability to exploit his adversaries' tendency to underestimate him, indicated, one writer for the *New York Times* remarked, that he was "the fruition of Reagan," and that he stood "a good chance of advancing a radical agenda that Reagan himself could carry only so far."

Although there are grounds for debate about how much the elder Bush turned away from Reagan's example, there can be no question that his son's presidency operated, from the start, squarely within the political terms of the age of Reagan. Yet in its willful partisanship and its radicalism, the George W. Bush administration also pushed well beyond Reagan during its very first months. Apart from taxes and Social Security, the administration's domestic policy—the heart of what still survived of "compassionate conservatism"—became subordinated to political and partisan imperatives: rewarding individual party loyalists, directing federal funds to constituency groups (notably efforts sponsored by evangelical conservatives), and, in time, replacing career professionals with ideologically approved appointees, to an extent even greater than during the 1980s. John DiIulio Jr., a professor of political science at the University of Pennsylvania, joined the administration early in 2001 as the first director of the White House Office of Faith-Based and Community Initiatives—but he quit in August, astonished and appalled. "There is no precedent in any modern White House for what is going on in this one: complete lack of a policy apparatus," DiIulio told a reporter for *Esquire* magazine. "What you've got is everything, and I mean everything, being run by the political arm. It's the reign of the Mayberry Machiavellis. . . . Besides the tax cut . . . the administration has not done much, either in absolute terms or in comparison to previous administrations on domestic policy. . . . They consistently talked and acted as if the height of political sophistication consisted in reducing every issue to its simplest black-and-white terms for public consumption, then steering legislative initiatives or policy proposals as far right as possible."

The Bush administration was also clear early on about its intention to concentrate power in the executive and shield the White House's policy making from public scrutiny and congressional oversight. For example, in the administration's first weeks, Vice President Cheney headed up an official task force on energy policy, meeting in private with numerous heads of corporations. Among those consulted was Kenneth Lay, the chief executive officer of the Enron corporation, who had been a partner in Bush's oil ventures and then became Bush's largest single financial backer in Texas. (Lay even provided company jets for the Bush campaign to use in the recount battle in Florida.) In the fall of 2001, the hollow shell that was Enron suddenly cracked, on its way to collapse, and Lay and others became embroiled in a huge scandal (which led to criminal convictions, including Lay's conviction in 2006 on ten counts of securities fraud and related charges, though he would die of a heart attack before he was sentenced). As soon as the scandal broke, Bush, who had nicknamed Lay "Kenny Boy," denied knowing him much at all, and distanced himself from the fiasco at Enron. But the scandal also intensified demands that the White House release a complete list of the names of those consulted along with Lay as part of Cheney's energy group—a demand the White House fought tooth and nail (and, finally, successfully) in the courts.

Bush's presidency was so extreme and single-minded at the outset that it actually cost the Republicans control of the Senate, which they had enjoyed by virtue of an equal partisan split in seats that gave Vice President Cheney the tie-breaking vote. In late May 2001, Senator Jim Jeffords of Vermont, a moderate Republican who had served in Congress since 1975, left his party and became an independent, announcing he would caucus with the Democrats. When a Democrat was in the White House, Jeffords observed, all shades of ideology in the Republican caucus had the freedom to argue their positions and influence party policy. "The election of President Bush changed that dramatically," Jeffords said. Radicalism in the White House fed radicalism in the Republican Party and in Congress—and vice versa—all but extinguishing what was left of moderate or even center-right Republicanism.

At the beginning of August 2001, Bush left the White House for his recently purchased ranch in Crawford, Texas, where he stayed the entire month. The most pressing issue he took up concerned possible restrictions on federal funding for stem cell research. On August 9, from the ranch, he delivered his decision in a nationwide speech that most analysts interpreted as a strong concession to restrictionists on the religious right. Three days earlier, Bush had received, as part of his daily briefing by the CIA, a document titled "Bin Laden Determined to Strike Inside U.S." The director of the CIA, George Tenet, would later testify that "the system was blinking red." But to this point, Bush's foreign policy had been aimed more at missile defense than at thwarting terrorism. Bush interpreted the CIA's briefing as essentially "historical" in nature, and thought it contained nothing new. He told his CIA briefer after the presentation of the memo of August 6 about bin Laden, "All right. You've covered your ass, now." There is no evidence that during the weeks between the briefing and the morning of September 11, the administration's highest officials held any discussions whatsoever about Al Qaeda or terrorism.

The atrocities of September 11 and Bush's response completely altered his presidency. Qualms about the legitimacy of his election evaporated. On the steps of the Capitol, Republicans and Democrats joined in a chorus of "God Bless America." Public support for the war in Afghanistan was virtually unanimous, according to opinion polls. More than at any time since the early 1960s—and perhaps since World War II—the American people seemed to think as one and regard the president as the living emblem of their patriotic unity. "[T]here is a resolve and a spirit that is just so fantastic to feel," Bush said at a town hall meeting in California, shortly after the fighting ended in the mountains of Tora Bora.

Yet there were also signals, substantive and rhetorical, that Bush and his advisers might bend the nation's resolute goodwill to their own purposes. In his address to Congress just after the attacks, the president had gone out of his way to sound reasonable and fair-minded as well as strong. He took special care to declare that, far from typical Muslims, the terrorists were "traitors to their own faith" who were "trying, in effect, to hijack Islam itself." But Bush also began speaking in more Manichean and even messianic terms, of leading what he called his "crusade" against the "evildoers." He declared, "Either you are with us, or you are with the terrorists"—suggesting that any disagreement with the administration's policy was anti-American and pro–Al Qaeda.

There were also alarming signs that the White House planned to use its "war on terror" for partisan advantage. In previous foreign wars, presidents had reached out to members of the opposing party in order to make America's fight truly national and above politics, especially by including members of the other party in the cabinet. Abraham Lincoln, during the Civil War, went to great lengths to make overtures to Democrats who were loyal to the Union effort. On the eve of World War II, sensing that the United States would inevitably be involved, Franklin D. Roosevelt made a Republican, Henry Stimson, secretary of war. At the height of the cold war, John F. Kennedy selected the Republican Robert McNamara as secretary of defense. And Bill Clinton, during the conflict in Kosovo, also had a Republican, William Cohen, as secretary of defense. But only two weeks after Bush had marveled at the new American spirit, Karl Rove addressed the Republican National Committee (RNC) and explained how the party had valid grounds for turning the public's anger and fear into a campaign theme: "We can go to the country on this issue because they trust the Republican Party to do a better job of protecting and strengthening America's military might and thereby protecting America." A spirit more akin to that of Joseph McCarthy and Richard Nixon than of Ronald Reagan—flatly equating partisan loyalty with patriotism—dominated the administration's rhetoric.

Inside the White House, the terrorist attacks contributed to the ascendancy of the neoconservatives on the president's foreign policy team and the marginalizing or outright purging of Republican realists, especially close associates of Bush's father. Vice President Cheney (working with his chief of staff, the longtime neoconservative I. Lewis "Scooter" Libby) was the main sponsor for the neoconservatives, although Secretary of Defense Rumsfeld was thoroughly cooperative. Under Cheney's and Rumsfeld's purview, policy makers such as Paul Wolfowitz (appointed deputy secretary of defense) and John Bolton (inserted by Cheney as undersecretary of state for arms control and later ambassador to the United Nations) advanced the neoconservative idea of maximizing U.S. force abroad while checking realists such as Secretary of State Colin Powell (who, although ever the dutiful soldier, found himself increasingly battered, until he decided to throw in the towel). The national security adviser, Condoleezza Rice, a realist by training, tailored her views to match the new fashion, thereby maintaining her viability within the White House and her loyalty to President Bush.

Cheney and Rumsfeld also pushed other political themes of the age of Reagan to their logical conclusion—and then took them farther. Under the cover of war, executive power was asserted and concentrated, and secrecy was justified. Applying a radical theory called the "unitary executive"—anticipated by Nixon and first broached during Reagan's presidency—the White House held that the president had absolute authority over independent federal agencies and that, in his presumed role as wartime commander in chief, he was not bound by congressional oversight or even by law. Whenever Congress passed legislation not to his liking, Bush would approve it but issue what were called "signing statements"—an old practice which he converted into fiats announcing that he would execute the law as he saw fit, an unabashed challenge to constitutional checks and balances.

In the continuing war on terror, Cheney remarked that it was sometimes necessary to go to the "dark side." The Bush White House did so, but in unprecedented ways. Bush authorized the detention of thousands of suspects in secret CIA prisons around the world, where they were denied legal due process. He ended the United States' adherence to the venerable international Geneva Conventions outlawing torture—provisions that the White House legal counsel (and later attorney general) Alberto Gonzales dismissed as "quaint." In 2006, Bush derided as "vague" Common Article Three of the Geneva Conventions, which spelled out the prohibition against torture.

The decision to take the war on terror into Iraq would be the most important—and, eventually, the most costly—of Bush's presidency. Cheney, Rumsfeld, and the neoconservatives were convinced that Saddam's brutal regime would always be a source of severe instability in a hostile world; that Iraq posed a direct and ever-present threat to American interests and allies in the region, including Israel; and that Saddam could be removed and replaced with a new, elective democratic regime quickly—in a "cakewalk," as a member of the Defense Policy Board, Kenneth Adelman, put it—and without a major long-term American military commitment. They then envisaged a secular democratic Iraq that would be a beacon of liberty in the region—and an example for freedom fighters in other countries.

Bush began preparing the way for war in early June 2002 by enunciating a profound and unsettling departure in the broad principles governing U.S. foreign policy, scrapping the principles of containment and deterrence that had guided American policy makers since the end of World War II. Under what became known at the Bush Doctrine, the United States would now assume the right to embark unilaterally on preventive war against any nation it deemed a potential threat, while also placing a special emphasis on extending democracy, free markets, and security to "every corner of the world." Realists, in and outside government, were appalled at the doctrine's recklessly aggressive implications, and expressed dismay as the groundswell for war grew during the summer of 2002. The critics included (publicly) a close friend of the elder Bush, the former national security adviser, Brent Scowcroft; and (privately) Secretary of State Powell. (Though he eventually went along with his president, Powell cautioned Bush that an American invasion of Iraq would saddle the United States with heavy responsibilities to oversee Iraq's reconstruction.) But Bush, under the sway of his own convictions as well as of his militant advisers, left no room for criticism, and seemed especially irritated by criticism from members of his father's administration. Asked by the reporter Bob Woodward if he ever sought advice from his father, the president replied, "There is a higher father that I appeal to."

The problem for the administration was to find a compelling casus belli that would persuade the American people to support an invasion. There was no hard evidence that Saddam had anything to do with supporting Al Qaeda or its operations, let alone the September 11 attacks—although Cheney, Rice, and other administration officials created the strong impression that such links did exist, even citing evidence that was later revealed as false. The argument that Saddam's regime was, in itself, cruel and menacing, and that his overthrow was justified along the lines of multilateral humanitarian interventions in the Balkans, was dismissed as a plea for "nation building," which the administration associated with Clinton. The administration instead seized on concerns Clinton himself had raised in 1998 about Saddam's intentions—even though many Republicans at the time disparaged and demeaned Clinton's separate attacks on Al Qaeda as well as Iraq. High-ranking officials at the White House flatly asserted that Saddam had built, and was hiding from the UN inspectors, unconventional "weapons of mass destruction" (WMD). The administration even hyped the possibility that Saddam (who, Bush and others claimed, was busy obtaining the necessary technology) would soon possess nuclear weapons. "We don't want the smoking gun to be a mushroom cloud," said Condoleezza Rice—a phrase echoed by other leading figures in the White House. This was the argument that finally turned congressional and public opinion decisively in favor of an invasion.

On March 20, 2003, using the latest "shock-and-awe" high-tech, rapid-deployment techniques favored by Rumsfeld, a "coalition of the willing" led by the United States—and including no other major Western power except the United Kingdom—began a massive bombardment centered on Baghdad. The invasion was on.

Saddam's regime quickly crumbled (although the dictator himself managed to elude capture until December). Within five weeks, the resistance from Saddam's troops either had been crushed or had melted away. On May 1, President Bush, wearing the uniform of an Air Force combat pilot, helped land a fighter jet on the deck of the aircraft carrier USS *Abraham*

Lincoln, a few miles west of San Diego, and then announced the conclusion of "major combat" in Iraq. A large banner aboard the carrier proclaimed, "Mission Accomplished." It was meant as the high point of Bush's presidency. Later it would look like an ironic embarrassment—and the beginning of the administration's gradual disintegration.

Bush managed to sustain his image as a warrior president long enough to win reelection in 2004—thereby outdoing his father once more. His campaign's basic message was that victory in Iraq was essential to the continuing war on terror, and that he was the only man who could prosecute that war successfully and keep the country safe from another terrorist attack. His opponent, Senator John Kerry of Massachusetts—a hero of the Vietnam War who then became a leader of the antiwar movement—did not learn the lessons of past presidential campaigns and failed to respond quickly and effectively to underhanded attacks on his record and his character. This failure certainly helped Bush. (Smear campaigns in the midterm campaigns of 2002 had signaled what was to come. Notably, the campaign against another hero of the Vietnam War, the triple amputee Senator Max Cleland of Georgia, had been crucial in helping the Republican Party win back the Senate majority that year.) Bush and his campaign team also polished his personal image, making his black-and-white rhetoric seem like the simple truth, his stubbornness seem like steeliness, his verbal miscues seem like the foibles of a normal guy. His religious piety was a constant reminder of his rectitude. One rank-and-file supporter spoke for many by describing Bush as "a Christian who actually acts on his deeply held beliefs." Although his narrow margins in the popular vote and in the Electoral College (the narrowest for reelection since 1916) hardly amounted to a mandate, this time Bush did win the election outright, becoming the first candidate to gain a majority of the popular vote since his father did in 1988.[*]

Yet even before the election, cracks were emerging in the seemingly impregnable political fortress represented by the White House. In 2003, critics of the administration included the Army chief of staff Eric Shinseki, who testified to Congress before the invasion that successful post-hostility operations would require 700,000 troops (a figure Rumsfeld and Wolfowitz ridiculed as too high). Another dissenter was the retired Marine Corps gen-

---

[*] Bush won 50.7 percent of the popular vote to Kerry's 48.2 percent. The contest in the Electoral College came down to the race in Ohio, which Bush also won narrowly.

eral and former head of Central Command Anthony Zinni, a Republican, who raised questions about the administration's basic judgment in going to war in Iraq. Shinseki and Zinni expressed sentiments that were widespread among senior military officers, who could not voice them on their own. In July 2003, a former U.S. ambassador, Joseph Wilson, published an op-ed article detailing how Bush had ignored evidence disproving claims that Saddam was seeking uranium for nuclear weapons from the African nation of Niger. Reports soon appeared in the press about the Pentagon's shadowy Office of Special Plans (OSP), the latest reprise of Team B, established by Donald Rumsfeld at the Pentagon and headed by a neoconservative veteran of the Reagan administration, Undersecretary of Defense for Policy Douglas Feith. (Under Feith, the OSP had gathered raw intelligence on Iraq, unvetted by professional intelligence analysts, and "stovepiped" it along to senior officials of the administration in order to bolster the case for war.) Early in 2004, at hearings held by the 9/11 Commission, Richard Clarke, held over as chief of counterterrorism on the National Security Council, testified that the administration had ignored terrorist threats before September 11.

Soon after the triumphant moment of Saddam's overthrow faded, it began to be apparent that the invasion force had found no trace of WMD in Iraq—the declared reason for the invasion. Rumsfeld, who like Cheney had stated categorically that Saddam possessed unconventional weapons, argued unpersuasively that Saddam might have destroyed them at the last minute in order to embarrass the Americans. In an interview, Wolfowitz explained, "For bureaucratic reasons, we settled on one issue, weapons of mass destruction, because it was the one reason everyone could agree on"— suggesting that the run-up to the war had been akin to a marketing campaign. Finally, the president attempted to laugh off the entire matter at the annual White House Correspondents Association banquet early in 2004, in a filmed skit in which he pretended to search for WMD all around the White House, even under his desk in the Oval Office, without success. The Washington press corps roared with appreciative laughter.

In April 2004, graphic accounts appeared, with shocking photographs, of systematic torture and abuse of Iraqi prisoners by American military personnel at Abu Ghraib prison in Baghdad. A few soldiers and the female general in charge of the prison were held responsible, but accountability stopped before it reached farther up the chain of command. The torture of prisoners at the detainee camp at Guantánamo Bay became so grotesque that the FBI issued orders that it would no longer participate. Undaunted

by criticism, Bush ordered the National Security Agency to conduct domestic spying without obtaining legally required warrants from special courts
established under the Foreign Intelligence Surveillance Act (FISA). Both
Bush and Cheney claimed that, had such actions been taken before September 11, the terrorist attacks might never have occurred—even though there
had never been any legal barriers under FISA that would have prevented
the White House from monitoring communications from the United States
to suspected members of Al Qaeda or any other terrorist group. When
pressed over the constitutionality of the warrantless eavesdropping, the administration produced memorandums from neoconservative lawyers at the
Justice Department reasserting that, in wartime, the commander in chief
had unchecked authority to protect national security regardless of the existing law.

Apart from the war, the subordination of policy to politics that had
marked Bush's early months as president came back to haunt him. In 2005,
Bush reinforced his ties to the Republicans' religious-right political base by
signing unprecedented legislation aimed at reversing decisions by federal
and Florida state courts permitting the husband of Terry Schiavo, a woman
who had been in a persistent vegetative state for fifteen years, to withdraw
her artificial life support. This case of family law turned into a dizzying
political affair when Senator Bill Frist of Tennessee, a medical doctor who
was the Senate majority leader, diagnosed the woman as sentient on the
basis of watching a videotape of her. The effort to thwart Schiavo's husband finally failed; the president's disregard for the legal process appeared
opportunistic; and in opinion polls the public registered revulsion at the
spectacle.

In September 2005, the administration's preparations for, and then its
catastrophically sluggish response to the devastation wrought by hurricane
Katrina, threw into sharp relief the president's isolation and apparent indifference, as well as the erosion of government. Bush, who had long ignored
scientists' warnings about the meteorological effects of global warming,
sloughed off warnings from the director of the National Hurricane Center
before Katrina hit. More important, for days and then weeks afterward, the
nation witnessed chilling scenes of suffering and death (some of the worst
of which unfolded among the suddenly displaced who were crammed into
the Louisiana Superdome arena), while the federal government offered one
empty reassurance after another.

Reorganized under the new Department of Homeland Security (now
headed by the former chief counsel to Senator Alfonse D'Amato's White-

water committee, Michael Chertoff), the once efficient Federal Emergency Management Agency (FEMA) had become, under Bush, a nest of crony-ism and incompetence. In place of the Clinton's expert appointee James Lee Witt, FEMA was now directed by a former head of the International Arabian Horse Association, Michael Brown—whom Bush praised, in the midst of the disaster, for doing a "heck of a job." Bush's hollowing out of the federal bureaucracy had badly compounded the human misery caused by the destruction of one of America's most vibrant and historically impor-tant cities. During the months immediately after the storm, Bush traveled to New Orleans eight times, promising massive aid for rebuilding from the federal government. Early in 2006, however, Bush's Gulf Coast coordina-tor admitted that it could take as long as twenty-five years for the city to recover.

From Katrina onward, the administration and the Republican Congress reeled from one disaster to another. A web of financial scandals involving a Republican superlobbyist, Jack Abramoff, soon ensnared and tainted, among other top Republicans, the House majority whip Tom DeLay. Thereafter, separate charges about illegal fund-raising in Texas led to DeLay's indict-ment, which in turn forced him to surrender his seat in Congress—and threw his political machine into disarray. In February 2006, Representative Heather Wilson of New Mexico became the first Republican on a congres-sional intelligence committee to call for an investigation of Bush's warrant-less wiretapping program.

A probe by the federal special prosecutor Patrick Fitzgerald into allega-tions surrounding efforts at the White House to discredit former ambas-sador Joseph Wilson after Wilson blew the whistle on the administration's misinformation about Iraq's nuclear weapons program led to the indict-ment on perjury charges of Vice President Cheney's chief of staff, "Scooter" Libby. (The last White House official of comparable standing to be in-dicted while still in office was President Ulysses S. Grant's personal secre-tary, in 1875.) A jury convicted Libby, and Fitzgerald declared that a cloud still hung over the vice president's office concerning the efforts to discredit Wilson and then to cover up those efforts. Bush's decision in early July 2007 to commute Libby's thirty-month jail sentence—a penalty that a federal judge appointed by Bush had imposed in full compliance with federal sen-tencing norms—stoked further allegations about the administration's disre-gard for the law.

Shortly afterward, Bush's surgeon general, Dr. Richard H. Carmona, having recently completed his four-year term, testified to Congress about

repeated efforts by administration officials to weaken or suppress important public health reports because of political considerations. On a range
of issues that included stem cell research, sex education, contraception, the
dangers of secondhand tobacco smoke, and the effects of global warming,
politics overruled science as in no previous White House; "I was told to stay
away from those [issues] because we've already decided which way we want
to go," Carmona related. No political consideration, according to Carmona's
testimony, was too petty to escape attention: administration officials, he
said, ordered him to mention President Bush three times on every page of
his speeches, and he was asked to support publicly Republican political candidates and attend political briefings. The White House even discouraged
Carmona from attending the Special Olympics for persons with disabilities
because "a prominent family"—known to be the Kennedys—had longtime
ties to the event. "Why would you want to help those people?" a senior aide
asked the surgeon general.

Above all, the unending military disaster in Iraq soured the public's
mood. During the run-up to the invasion, Bush's officials were full of
glowing predictions about how the Iraqi people would greet the Allied
forces as liberators. After several false starts under the Coalition Provisional Authority, or CPA (dissolved in 2004), an election was held early in
2005 to form a government that would draft a permanent constitution. By
then, though, the original optimistic assurances had come crashing down.
The coalition led by the United States appeared to the displaced Sunni
Muslims as heathen occupiers, and insurgent groups quickly took up
arms. With Saddam's cruel regime destroyed, the lid also came off vicious
sectarian hatreds between rival Iraqi Sunni Muslims (the minority, who
had been favored under Saddam) and Shia Muslims (the long subjected
majority, who had political as well as religious ties to neighboring Shiite
Iran). Ruinous blunders by the CPA, under the former ambassador and
foreign service officer L. Paul Bremer, notably the decision to disband the
existing Iraqi army, worsened popular alienation from the Americans. As
the insurgency intensified (despite assurances in 2006 from Cheney that it
was in its "last throes"), Iraq lurched toward civil war—while violent extremist groups (including Al Qaeda) used the American presence in Iraq
as the best recruiting device imaginable, replenishing their own numbers
after the defeats of late 2001. At the end of 2006, the number of American
military deaths climbed above 3,000—more (according to the revised figures) than the total number killed on September 11, 2001. Saddam Hussein, tried and convicted for crimes against humanity, was hanged in a

chaotic scene on December 30; but Osama bin Laden still remained at large.

In 2006, Bush and the Republicans paid a political price for their failures. In the first months of Bush's presidency, Karl Rove (to whom the president gave various nicknames, including "the Architect") fancied that he was on the brink of forming a permanent Republican realignment in American politics, a feat that, despite Nixon's landslide in 1972 and Reagan's landslide in 1984, had eluded the modern party. The uprising led by Gingrich in 1994 was supposed to have marked the beginning of the new dispensation, but President Clinton had outfoxed Gingrich in 1995 and 1996. Yet as Rove saw it, Clinton's presidency merely delayed what he would achieve—invincible one-party command of all three branches of the federal government, based on an enlarged electoral coalition of the solid Republican South, the plains and mountain states, and just enough of the battleground lower North (Pennsylvania, Ohio, and Indiana).

Republican political setbacks in 2006, though, atop the difficulties of 2005, upset Rove's best-laid plans. Late in the campaign season, a sex scandal was revealed involving a Republican congressman from Florida, Mark Foley, and several male congressional pages and interns. With the attendant charges of hypocrisy as well as of a cover-up, the scandal contributed to the final result. Against most predictions, the Democrats won a small majority in both the House and (by a single vote) the Senate. Although this would hardly be sufficient to redirect administration policy, let alone pass anything close to a legislative agenda, it gave the Democrats control of vital congressional committees that might, for the first time, exercise a measure of oversight over the administration. The day after the election, the White House announced Donald Rumsfeld's resignation as secretary of defense.

After nearly six years of one-party rule at both ends of Pennsylvania Avenue, the Democrats were understandably elated, but they had to learn quickly to curb their enthusiasm. The Democrats' earlier outbursts of euphoria had proved self-deluding—in the early 1970s, immediately following Watergate; in 1976, following Carter's election; and in the early 1990s, during Clinton's first term. If Karl Rove's visions of Republican dominance had proved, at best, premature, the Democrats had no reason to believe that the Bush administration's failures alone would bring the dawn of a new liberal political age. Unless, out of their own morass of competing interests and outlooks, they could unite behind a plausible public agenda and a set of governing ideas, the Democrats would fail as they had failed before.

And even if they succeeded, the effects of the Bush administration's first six years, along with the many changes in the basic structures of national government since 1980, posed enormous challenges to any liberal resurgence.

George W. Bush's Reaganite tax cuts—even during what he called wartime—drained Clinton's surpluses and helped create new monster deficits that added, according to projections through 2007, more than $2 trillion to the national debt. That reversal alone would severely hinder any return to active government to address basic social needs. Reagan and the elder Bush had also succeeded in overhauling the federal judiciary, from the Supreme Court down; and George W. Bush had resumed that overhaul, most strikingly by winning confirmation for two highly conservative Supreme Court nominees, John Roberts and Samuel Alito (with Roberts becoming William Rehnquist's successor as Chief Justice). By applying the same ideological rigor to permanent hiring in federal agencies and executive departments as to judicial appointments, the second Bush administration created an additional conservative firewall against future innovation. More than two decades earlier, Edwin Meese had emphasized the overriding imperative to "institutionalize the Reagan revolution so that it can't be put aside no matter what happens in future presidential elections." The struggle over how successfully Reagan and his Republican successors had fulfilled Meese's mandate was likely to continue long after George W. Bush's presidency ended.

As the elections of 2008 approached, there was, nevertheless, a sense that barring some catastrophic event like the terrorist attacks of 2001, or some new foreign policy crisis in the Persian Gulf region, the Reagan era was losing steam and may finally have run its course. The debacles in Iraq challenged conservatives' claim to superior wisdom in foreign and military affairs, which had been their major claim to competence. Other disasters, above all the government's handling of hurricane Katrina, showed the administration was not merely incompetent but dysfunctional—and it exposed the dark consequences of conservative small-government dogma. In some respects, the conservative movement was a victim of success: with the Soviet Union dissolved, inflation reduced to virtually negligible levels, and the top tax rate cut to nearly half of what it was in 1980, all of Ronald Reagan's major stated goals when he took office had been achieved, leaving perplexed and fractious conservatives to fight over where they might now lead the country. But there was also a growing awareness that Reaganism had exhausted itself politically as well as intellectually—and may well have been living, in a radicalized form, on borrowed time since the election of 2000.

A report in *Time* magazine early in 2007 said that the Republican Party had come to look "unsettlingly like the Democrats did in the 1980s . . . more a collection of interest groups than ideas, recognizable more by its campaign tactics than its philosophy." "It's gone," Ronald Reagan's former political director Ed Rollins said of the Reagan coalition. "The breakup of what was the Reagan coalition—social conservatives, defense conservatives, antitax conservatives—it doesn't mean a whole lot to people anymore." The conservative former senator Alan K. Simpson of Wyoming complained that continued unyielding dogmatism and political litmus tests for social issues such as abortion and gay rights were now "destroying the Republican Party." Although it was far too early to predict which party, let alone which candidate, would prevail in 2008, one of the earliest and most passionate advocates of the Reagan revolution, the former representative Mickey Edwards of Oklahoma, doubted that any Republican presidential nominee could "run hard enough or fast enough to escape the gravitational pull of the Bush administration."

The thinness of the Democratic majorities in the House and Senate, coupled with the virtually unanimous support for the White House from Republicans on Capitol Hill, did prevent the Democrats from gaining much political leverage in 2007. Efforts in Congress to constrain the White House's conduct of the war in Iraq failed to win sufficient support from Republicans to prevent filibusters in the Senate. Nor were there enough votes in the House of Representatives to override Bush's veto, in October, of a bipartisan bill renewing the Children's Health Insurance Program. (If enacted, the legislation would have enlarged health coverage for children in families with incomes too high to qualify for Medicaid but too low to pay for private insurance.) In announcing his intention to veto the bill, Bush echoed charges that conservatives and lobbyists for the medical industry had made for decades about the imminence of so-called socialized medicine—charges that had failed to halt the enactment of Medicare itself by President Lyndon Johnson in 1965. The proposed expansion, Bush said, would be a dangerous "incremental step toward the goal of government-run health care for every American." The president made it clear that, so long as he remained in office, he would not surrender an iota of his doctrinaire conservatism—and, evidently, he could not be forced to do so.

Left-wing Democrats, overlooking how the delicate partisan balance on Capitol Hill placed sharp political limits on the Democratic leadership, began harshly criticizing their own party for not doing more with its majorities in Congress. This was the sort of alienation that, in 2000, helped Ralph Nader drain away enough votes to ensure the defeat of Al Gore. Yet heading into 2008, it appeared that, despite the frustration on the left, the experience of the Bush years had concentrated Democrats' minds and dampened any enthusiasm for a schism that might end up keeping the presidency in Republican hands. Although matters of ideology, policy, and style separated the supporters of the front-runners for the Democratic nomination—including Hillary Rodham Clinton, now a twice-elected U.S. senator from New York; first-term senator Barack Obama of Illinois; and John Kerry's running mate from 2004, former senator John Edwards of North Carolina—the candidates' similarities greatly outweighed their differences, especially when compared with the Republicans. Nobody had ever gone broke overestimating the Democrats' ability to snatch defeat from the jaws of victory—but for once, the very early jostling seemed to augur eventual party unity.

Once the primaries began, though, the old divisions reappeared. Late in 2007 and early in 2008, party leftists and left liberals (notably in college and university towns, where the student vote was large) rallied behind Barack Obama, as did African-Americans proud to see one of their own running strong. Obama, an uplifting orator who had opposed the Iraq war while he was still a state legistlator in Illinois, turned his candidacy into a stampede by preaching the virtues of "hope" and "change." Although he was a political newcomer with a sketchy past, he deftly exploited Americans' dislike of the Bush administration, and promised to fulfill the public's recurring yearning for a new kind of leader that dated back to the Watergate scandal. Unreconstructed 1960s liberals, ex-Naderites, and others who had never forgiven Bill Clinton for his strategy of triangulation transferred their antipathy to his wife, whom they mocked as "Billary" and berated for supporting legislation in 2003 backing forceful inspections that the Bush administation had seized upon as congressional authorization to invade Iraq. Hillary Clinton, meanwhile, attracted solid support from traditionally Democratic low- and middle-income white voters, middle-aged and older women, Latinos, and a portion of the black vote, by arguing that her experience, pragmatism, and expertise—and her previous exposure to the worst Republican attacks—better suited her to beat the Republican nominee and then serve as a successful president. John Edwards conducted an old-fashioned populist campaign attacking corporate special interests, until he quit the race at the end of Januray.

By February, when the contests of Super Tuesday still left the final outcome in doubt, the early gentle jostling had become rough and, at times, ugly. After losing decisively to Obama in the Iowa caucuses, Clinton won a surprise victory in the New Hampshire primary, which led to charges in the media that covert racism on the part of New Hampshire's voters had turned the tide in her favor at the last minute. The wrangling between Clinton and Obama became truly nasty in South Carolina, where Obama won chiefly on the strength of a huge turnout by black voters. (Clinton had to contend with charges in the press that, in talking to an interviewer about Lyndon Johnson's role in enacting civil rights legislation, she had somehow injected race into the campaign, made a "distasteful" suggestion that blacks could change nothing without whites, and was "denigrating America's most revered black leader," the Reverend Dr. Martin Luther King Jr.) The Democrats would make history no matter whom they eventually nominated—but it remained an open question whether the renewed divisiveness of the primary season would ruin their chances in November.

The Republicans, meanwhile, had to contend with their own divisions, and with popular displeasure with the administration. George W. Bush's penultimate full year in office brought him and his party repeated political headaches. Contrary to the rosiest predictions, the introduction of more than 25,000 additional American troops into Iraq did not appreciably improve the political situation, although there were clear signs of military progress against the insurgents in parts of Baghdad and in Anbar province in the western portion of the country. By the end of 2007, the numbers of American casualties had fallen substantially from the grim figures of April, May, and June, when fatalities exceeded 100 each month. In September, U.S. Ambassador Ryan Crocker testified before Congress that the "cumulative trajectory" was upward. But in October, the retired lieutenant general Ricardo Sanchez, who had served as commander of the coalition ground forces in Iraq from June 2003 to June 2004, declared that, because of inept civilian leadership, the war had become "a nightmare with no end in sight."

Political controversy also roiled the home front in 2007. Karl Rove, besieged since the affair involving Joseph Wilson began, resigned from the White House staff in August. Additional allegations, investigated by Democrats in Congress, about the reported firings of various U.S. attorneys around the country for political reasons embroiled Attorney General Alberto Gonzales as well as Rove in controversy—and shortly before Rove's resignation took effect on August 31, Gonzales (like Rove a longtime personal friend and ally of the president's) announced that he too was stepping down. That same summer, two conservative Republican senators, James Vitter of Louisiana and Larry Craig of Idaho, were named in separate embarrassing sex scandals (the latter involving an arrest by an undercover officer who was policing homosexual activity in a men's rest room at the Minneapolis airport). Demoralization as well as sluggishness in making new administration appointments led to an alarming rate of vacancies in important posts throughout the federal bureaucracy. "In the long history of the country, I don't think the Justice Department has been in such disarray," said Senator Arlen Specter, a Pennsylvania Republican and ranking member of the Senate Judiciary Committee. Some Republicans, it seemed, could not get out of Washington fast enough.

The administration's travails colored the contest for the Republican presidential nomination in 2008. One very early favorite, George Allen of Virginia, fell by the wayside when a videotape camera caught him making what many observers perceived as a racist remark during his campaign for reelection to the Senate in 2006. The episode helped cost Allen his job as well as any chance of running for the presidency. Persistent talk that the president's brother Jeb, the governor of Florida through 2006, would try to succeed Bush ended when the president's popularity ratings began falling. Lacking any similar dynastic figure who might assemble an updated version of the Reagan coalition, the party appeared to be dissolving into its constituent elements. All the Republican candidates for president invoked the name of Ronald Reagan, each claiming over and over that he was Reagan's true political heir—rituals of conjuring which were among the strongest indications that the age of Reagan might be coming to an end.

The former mayor of New York, Rudolph Giuliani, an early favorite, won over pro-war voters by harping on the highly publicized (and, critics said, highly exaggerated) wisdom and courage he displayed in leading the city through the trauma caused by the attacks of September 11, 2001. Giuliani also appealed to what was left of the suburban white ethnic constituency, hostile to civil rights reform and to the cultural liberalism of the 1960s, that had turned out heavily for Ronald Reagan in the 1980s. Yet Giuliani's background—as a thrice-married Italian Catholic from New York City who had supported mild versions of abortion rights and gun control —dismayed a portion of the Republican base, especially the important sectors of the evangelical religious right. Poor strategy, negative news stories about his vindictive style, and a lack of focus on the campaign trail caused Giuliani's support to collapse, and at the end of January 2008, he dropped out of the race.

The other Republican contenders also had to deal with large minuses as well as pluses with the party's core supporters. Mitt Romney, the photogenic former governor of Massachusetts, pointed to his success as a businessman and a government official and seemed likely to attract political independents nationwide, much as he had in Massachusetts. But Romney, as a Mormon, was as unacceptable to a number of right-wing evangelical Protestants as the Catholic Giuliani was, and Romney's timely switch to more conservative positions on issues such as abortion made him seem unprincipled. After the Super Tuesday primaries in early February, he, too, dropped out.

Fred Thompson—a prominent lawyer, former senator from Tennessee, and sometime television actor—was supposed to evoke Ronald Reagan as well as stir the voters with his folksy twang and his hard-line stance about cracking down on illegal immigration. But Thompson's undemonstrative appearances early in the campaign gave some observers the impression that his heart was not in the race, and at the end of January, he gave up. The religious right rallied to Mike Huckabee, the former governor of Arkansas and a trained Baptist minister, who won an unexpected victory in the Iowa caucuses and later ran well in the South—but there was skepticism that, even with his populist economic proposals and personal charm, Huckabee could enlarge his appeal too far beyond the ranks of right-wing southern white evangelicals. Ron Paul, a Texas congressman, stood up for the libertarian wing of the Reagan coalition, and was the only Republican candidate to criticize the administration's war in Iraq—naturally estranging conservatives and other bitter-end supporters of Bush's foreign policy.

Senator John McCain of Arizona, the darling of leading political pundits and prognosticators, struck a political truce with President Bush, his adversary from 2000, but he did so at the exact moment when Bush's popularity began to decline precipitously. McCain's independent stance on issues such as health care, campaign finance reform, immigration, and (initially) Bush's tax cuts also made him suspect among various groups of Republicans. McCain's reputation for directness and his support for the Iraq war, though, rallied enough Republicans to stage an impressive comeback, win several important early primaries, and sew up the nomination in March. Still, even as the nominee, McCain would have to find a way to secure the solid confidence of leading right-wing spokesmen such as the evangelical leader James Dobson and the talk-radio host Rush Limbaugh, who had said that his candidacy would be disastrous for the Republican Party and the country. With his long political history in Washington as a pro-Reagan Republican and his generally conservative record, the westerner McCain, now nearly seventy-two years old, could make a more plausible claim than his rivals to Reagan's legacy—but important elements inside the party considered him a dangerous maverick and even a traitor to the Reaganite cause.

Even after McCain secured the Republican nomination, it seemed unclear that, if elected, he (let alone his Democratic opponent) would fully sustain the ideologically charged conservative politics that had begun under Reagan and then turned more radical under George W. Bush. Nor, despite their efforts to seize Reagan's mantle, did it seem that any of the contenders could match Reagan's combination of policies and personality. Nor, finally, was it clear that, in the more diverse America of the twenty-first century, the voters were even looking for a leader in Reagan's mold. The conservatism that had triumphed in 1980 had apparently reached a pass not unlike the one that New Deal and Great Society liberalism reached in the late 1960s. The death, in late February, of the intellectual founding father of the Reagan ascendancy, William F. Buckley Jr.—who had become sharply critical of Bush's Iraq war—appeared to symbolize that an era had passed.

One imponderable factor, which had the potential of changing the political landscape dramatically, was the Bush administration's heightened bellicosity about Iraq's neighbor, Iran. By choosing to overthrow Saddam Hussein, the administration had effectively strengthened the hand of Iran's Shiite rulers in the politics of the Persian Gulf region. In late 2007, both President Bush and Vice President Cheney delivered dire warnings about Tehran's nuclear ambitions. Halting the Iranians' efforts, Bush declared in October 2007, might be necessary "if you're interested in avoiding World War III"—and the president refused to rule out military action. How, exactly, efforts to expand the Bush Doctrine would affect public opinion in the United States—quite apart from how it would affect international politics—was by no means clear as the contest for the presidency geared up. But there could be little doubt that a new round of military action by the United States would profoundly affect the dynamics of the election of 2008. Nearly three decades after Ronald Reagan defeated Jimmy Carter, events in Iran once again were a factor in Americans' political calculations.

Deepening uncertainty in the nation's economic outlook also had powerful political implications—and worldwide repercussions. In 2006 and early 2007, a growing number of economists warned that the nation's prosperity had become far too dependent on an irrationally inflated real-estate market. Housing-market prices fell gradually in 2006 and then precipitously the following year, leading to a wave of foreclosures. The deflation culminated in August 2007, when markets in credit, hedge funds, and mortgages (especially so-called subprime mortgages, granted to home buyers with marginal credit ratings) all reached a crisis. On January 24, 2008, the National Association of Realtors announced that the previous twelve months had witnessed the largest drop in existing home sales in twenty-five years—quite possibly the first such decline, the association reported, "going back to the Great Depression."

A recession, possibly quite severe, seemed increasingly likely. The day after the realtors' report appeared, and following a week of heavy losses on Wall Street, President Bush announced an economic stimulus package consisting of tax incentives and rebates—and stock prices fell again. After an unsettled weekend, stock market average prices across Europe and Asia dropped sharply, a signal that foreign investors did not believe Bush's plan would stave off a recession in the United States. The chairman of the Federal Reserve Board, Ben Bernanke, had earlier vowed to act aggressively to head off a recession—and by the end of January, he announced two emergency cuts in the board's interest rate for loans to the banking system, bringing the benchmark figure down to 3 percent. Some analysts forecast that the Fed would eventually cut its interest rate below the rate of inflation (which had averaged out at 2.85 percent in 2007) in order to avert the first simultaneous decline in U.S. household wealth and household income since 1974—the year in which Richard Nixon fell from power.

The age of Reagan had by then lasted longer than most other such periods in our political history—longer than the ages of Jefferson and Jackson; longer than the "gilded age" or the Progressive era; and virtually as long as the combined era of the New Deal, Fair Deal, New Frontier, and Great Society. If it fell far short of eradicating Franklin Roosevelt's revolution in government or the reforms of the 1960s, it dramatically changed the sum and substance of American politics. It also hastened the downfall of the Soviet empire through Reagan's diplomatic engagement with Mikhail Gorbachev, without a single nuclear weapon being fired in anger. Yet the Republican ascendancy failed to check the popular political alienation born of the Vietnam War and Watergate; it compounded the constitutional crisis of 1973–1974 with new confrontations; and it left the country polarized. In the first decade of the new millennium, the vital center of American politics was badly in need of rescue and repair. The nation's future depended on who might best understand and lead that effort—and begin the world over again.

The Republicans' hopes that Richard Nixon's election had ushered in a new national Republican majority seemed to have run aground in the Watergate crisis in 1974. Few, if any, could sense after Watergate that the nation truly was at the beginning of an extended Republican political era, let alone a conservative Republican era whose outstanding leader would be Ronald Reagan. Gerald Ford's beleaguered presidency seemed to signal that the Republican Party was in mortal danger. Yet despite some interruptions over the next thirty-five years in the party's control of both Congress and the White House, and despite various ups and downs in individual political fortunes, the age of Reagan came to pass.

"The future remains indeterminate," the historian Arthur Schlesinger Jr. wrote in 1960, on the eve of John F. Kennedy's narrow victory. "Heroic leadership," Schlesinger said, could lead in any number of directions, "depending on what the leader does with his power, and what his people permit or encourage him to do." But just as the future grows out of the past, so any leader (and his or her party) would be fully equipped to meet the challenges ahead only after grappling with the history of the Reagan era and the questions it posed—about the character of America's political institutions; about American power in the world after Iraq; about the future of the global economy; about opportunity and equity in American life; about the rule of law and the fundamental meanings attached to the U.S. Constitution.

Not every leader or citizen has taken much interest in the historical dimension of our politics. When asked by a reporter what he thought about his place in history, President George W. Bush waved the matter aside: "History. We won't know. We'll all be dead." A much earlier Republican president, however, thought long and hard about the past and how his actions would touch the future. "Fellow-citizens, *we* cannot escape history," Abraham Lincoln said. "We of this Congress and this administration, will be remembered in spite of ourselves. No personal significance, or insignificance, can spare one or another of us. The fiery trial through which we pass, will light us down, in honor or dishonor, to the latest generation." So it was. And so it will be.

ACKNOWLEDGMENTS

I wrote most of this book while in residence at the Dorothy and Lewis B. Cullman Center for Scholars and Writers at the New York Public Library, where I was fortunate to hold a fellowship from the Mrs. Giles Whiting Foundation in 2006–2007. During the relatively brief period since its inception, the center has established itself as one of the most congenial and inspiring venues for thinking, research, and writing to be found anywhere. I am grateful to its director, Jean Strouse, for her imagination and intellectual instigation, and for many furlongs of kindness over the years. My fellow fellows quickly forged a smart and sympathetic community that I will always cherish. Pamela Leo and Adriana Nova were unfailingly helpful and encouraging. David Smith helped me obtain books and other materials with astonishing speed. To them all, as well as to the Cullmans and to the Whiting Foundation, my abiding thanks.

Apart from the public library, several other repositories were essential to my research. I especially wish to thank the directors, archivists, and their staffs at the Gerald R. Ford Presidential Library in Ann Arbor, the Jimmy Carter Library in Atlanta, the Ronald Reagan Presidential Library in Simi Valley, the George Bush Presidential Library in College Station, and the William Jefferson Clinton Presidential Library in Little Rock, for invaluable assistance both in situ and via e-mail. For nearly thirty years, Firestone Library at Princeton University has been my chief scholarly base, and it is a pleasure to record once again my indebtedness to everyone there.

Over the same three decades, I have had the privilege to teach in Princeton's department of History. To my colleagues and students, as well as the department's staff, my continuing admiration and thanks. Jeremy Adelman, the current department chair, was especially generous in helping me gain the funding and time I needed to get the job done.

My fellow Princeton historians Daniel T. Rodgers and Kevin Kruse took precious time away from their own important work on recent American politics to read an early version of the manuscript—no questions asked. Their scholarly expertise sharpened my thinking and spared me numerous blunders.

Dov Weinryb Grohsgal did a superb job as my research assistant in Princeton, and helped me with his own insight. Three indispensable friends, who know the Washington political scene—past and present—about as well as anybody can, read a late draft and offered invaluable observations from across the political spectrum. Without the help of former Congressman Mickey Edwards; my longtime editor at the *New Republic*, Leon Wieseltier; and former assistant to President Bill Clinton, Sidney Blumenthal, this book would have been far poorer—and so would the life of its author. To my other accomplices and interlocutors, too numerous to mention, a collective "thanks" until I can express my gratitude individually.

The idea for this book arose almost as an afterthought in a conversation with James Atlas, who gave my efforts vital encouragement early on. At HarperCollins, Jonathan Burnham has been a stalwart friend, not least in matching me up with an exceptional editor, Tim Duggan. Tim's contributions, in fine-tuning my prose and in pruning some overlong sections, have been enormous. Tim's assistant, Allison Lorentzen, has also been extremely helpful. Susan Gamer intelligently and meticulously copy-edited the manuscript. Without the acumen and support of my agent, Andrew Wylie, this book, most likely, would never have seen its way into print.

Although I purposefully conducted no interviews, Adam Michnik was happy to let the conversation turn to Reagan and Solidarnose (among other things) one April afternoon over drinks, and he kindly permitted me to quote from his remarks. I am, as ever, grateful to Jeff Rosen, his staff, and the founder of the feast for constant encouragement and generosity.

The continuing debts I owe to Christine Stansell, and to James Wilentz and Hannah Wilentz, have grown so deep and so wide that I dare not try to put them into writing here. Even words of devotion and love are just words.

Both of the dear friends whose names are on the dedication page adored this country—and would have disagreed with at least some of this book. That they are no longer around to argue about it makes me miss them all the more, but their amazing spirits abide.

SW
February 12, 2008

NOTES

INTRODUCTION

2 "further implementation": Executive Order 13233—Further Implementation of the President Records Act, at http://www.archives.gov/about/laws/appendix/13233. html. The act was signed by President Bush on November 1, 2001, following the terrorist attacks on September 11, supposedly as a national security measure. It covers all unreleased presidential material dating from 1980 to the present. Although researchers may seek declassification and release of specific documents, the process is numbingly time-consuming. Special requests for documents at the Ronald Reagan Presidential Library in Simi Valley, California, for example, have required as long as seven years simply to clear a classification review. On the procedures stipulated by Bush's order and their crippling effects, see Mary E. Stuckey, "Presidential Secrecy: Keeping Archives Open," *Rhetoric and Public Affairs*, 9 (2006): 138–144. The contemporary political consequences of the order have also been manifold. Its restrictions, for example, suppressed the release of important memos written for Reagan's Justice Department by John Roberts, now the Chief Justice of the United States, during Robert's confirmation hearings in the Senate. The recent publication, at the instigation of Nancy Reagan, of a professionally edited edition of Reagan's private diaries was a welcome step in the opposite direction. Some of the crucial entries in the diaries on the Iran-contra affair have already been reported by investigating bodies, biographers, and historians. The remainder, however, are often rich in fresh details, which I have found very useful, even when they do not appreciably alter the basic record of Reagan's presidency.

5 Nixon's knowledge: Douglas Brinkley, ed., *The Reagan Diaries* (New York, 2007), 424; entry, July 11, 1986.

6 "They say we offer": Reagan, "A Time for Choosing: An Address on Behalf of Senator Barry Goldwater, October 27, 1964," transcript at http://millercenter.virginia.edu/scripps/digitalarchive/speechDetail/32.

7 "one-*year* phenomenon"; "phaseout": David S. Broder, "The Phasing Out of Reaganism," *Washington Post*, January 12, 1983, p. A19.

9 "I have written": Theodore Draper, *Present History: On Nuclear War, Détente, and Other Controversies* (New York, 1984), xi.

PROLOGUE: JULY 4, 1976

14   "a super"; "I can still see":   Bernard J. Firestone and Alexj Ugrinsky, eds., *Gerald R. Ford and the Politics of Post-Watergate America* (Westport, CT, 1993), II, 671.

14   "for healing the land":   Ford quoted in Alan M. Webber, "Gerald Ford: The Statesman as CEO," *Harvard Business Review* (September–October 1987): 77. In the opening words of his inaugural address in 1977, Ford's successor, Jimmy Carter, also thanked Ford for "all he had done to heal our land"—praise that Ford never forgot. See Gerald Ford, *A Time to Heal: The Autobiography of Gerald R. Ford* (New York, 1979), 441.

15   "climate"; "even the will to learn":   John Russell, "Despite Serious Ills, City Keeps Chin Up," *New York Times*, July 5, 1976, p. 13.

16   "eaten away"; "and a lot of people":   Ibid.

16   "evil"; "serious assault"; "rightly resulted":   William Safire, "Ten Myths About the Reagan Debacle," *New York Times*, March 22, 1987, p. 21.

17   "the frenzied, almost maniacal"; "I have thrown down a gauntlet":   Kissinger and Nixon quoted in John Morton Blum, *Years of Discord: American Politics and Society, 1961–1974* (New York, 1991), 431, 433.

17   "White House horrors": Mitchell quoted in Stanley Kutler, *The Wars of Watergate: The Last Crisis of Richard Nixon* (New York, 1990), xiv.

18   "No longer was there the slightest doubt":   Ford, *Time to Heal*, 17.

18   "stupid":   Eisenhower to Edgar Newton Eisenhower, November 8, 1954, in Louis Galambos and Daun van Ee, eds., *The Papers of Dwight David Eisenhower* (Baltimore, MD, 1970–2001), XV, 1147. Also at: Doc. 1147. World Wide Web facsimile by Dwight D. Eisenhower Memorial Commission of the print edition; Baltimore, MD: Johns Hopkins University Press, 1996, http://www.eisenhowermemorial.org/presidential-papers/first-term/documents/1147.cfm. The entire relevant passage of this letter is worth reading to understand better how drastically the Republican Party would change in the 1960s and 1970s: "The political processes of our country are such that if a *rule of reason* is not applied in this effort, we will lose everything—even to a possible and drastic change in the Constitution. This is what I mean by my constant insistence upon 'moderation' in government. Should any political party attempt to abolish social security, unemployment insurance, and eliminate labor laws and farm programs, you would not hear of that party again in our political history. There is a tiny splinter group, of course, that believes you can do these things. Among them are H. L. Hunt (you possibly know his background), a few other Texas oil millionaires, and an occasional politician or business man from other areas. Their number is negligible and they are stupid." Hunt, ranked by *Fortune* magazine in 1957 as one of the ten richest Americans, was a prominent funder of and participant in various far-right groups, including the John Birch Society. Ten years later, Barry Goldwater would turn "moderation" into a word of opprobrium when, in his speech accepting the Republican presidential nomination, he famously declared: "I would remind you that extremism in the defense of liberty is no vice. And let me remind you also that moderation in the pursuit of justice is no virtue." Goldwater, "Speech Accepting the Presidential Nomination, Republican National Convention, San Francisco, July 16, 1964," at http://www.washingtonpost.com/wp-srv/politics/daily/may98/goldwaterspeech.htm.

19   "the Munich":   Goldwater, quoted in Robert Alan Goldberg, *Barry Goldwater* (New Haven, CT, 1995), 145.

20   "Goldwater Democrats":   Lippmann quoted in Rick Perlstein, *Before the Storm: Barry Goldwater and the Unmaking of the American Consensus* (New York, 2001), 213–214. Indeed, there is a strong argument to be made that, despite Goldwater's enormous defeat, 1964 marked a breakthrough for the conservative movement that never entirely abated. See J. William Middendorf II, *A Glorious Disaster: Barry Goldwater's Presidential Campaign and the Origins of the Conservative Movement* (New York, 2006).

20   "This country":   "Being Candid with Kandy," *Time*, September 28, 1970, p. 9.

20   "nattering nabobs":   James M. Naughton, "Agnew Aims Fire at G.O.P. Liberals," *New York Times*, September 12, 1970, p. 7.

21   "bitch mistress":   The phrase is commonly ascribed to Johnson; see, for example, the interview with David Gergen on CNN in 2003; transcript at http://transcripts.cnn.com/TRANSCRIPTS/0304/02/se.27.html. In *Lyndon Johnson and the American Dream*, Doris Kearns Goodwin writes that Johnson told her: "I knew from the start that I was bound to be crucified either way I moved. If I left the woman I really loved—the Great Society—in order to get involved with that bitch of a war on the other side of the world, then I would lose everything at home." Doris Kearns, *Lyndon Johnson and the American Dream* (New York, 1976), 251.

22   "It's silly":   Reagan quoted in *Fresno Bee*, October 10, 1965.

23   "fighting faith":   Arthur M. Schlesinger Jr., "Not Left, Not Right, but a Vital Center," *New York Times Magazine*, April 4, 1948, p. SM7. Schlesinger later expanded this into a book: *The Vital Center: The Politics of Freedom* (Boston, MA, 1949).

23   "long twilight struggle":   Kennedy, "Inaugural Address, January 20, 1961," at http://www.presidency.ucsb.edu/ws/index.php?pid=8032. As Kennedy saw it, the "twilight struggle" he spoke about also transcended the cold war and involved fighting against the "common enemies of man," including "poverty, disease and war itself."

25   "long national nightmare":   Ford, "Remarks on Taking the Oath of Office, August 9, 1974," at http://www.presidency.ucsb.edu/ws/index.php?pid=4409&st=&st1=.

CHAPTER 1: MEMORIES OF THE FORD ADMINISTRATION

26   "What had been unthinkable"; "For that matter":   John Updike, *Memories of the Ford Administration* (New York, 1992), 6, 76.

27   "*Idiot wind*":   Bob Dylan, "Idiot Wind," copyright © 1974 Ram's Horn Music.

27   "A computer on every desk and in every home":   Quoted in Janet Lowe, *Bill Gates Speaks: Insight from the World's Greatest Entrepreneur* (New York, 2001), 23.

28 "sputtering":   Gerald Ford, *A Time to Heal: The Autobiography of Gerald R. Ford* (New York, 1979), 142.

29 "and a noble thing to do":   Bernard J. Firestone and Alexj Ugrinsky, eds., *Gerald R. Ford and the Politics of Post-Watergate America* (Westport, CT, 1993), II, 671.

30 "*or* may have committed":   Ford, "Proclamation 4311: Granting Pardon to Richard Nixon, September 8, 1974," at http://www.presidency.ucsb.edu/ws/index.php?pid=4696&st=&st1=.

30 "The son of a bitch":   Bernstein quoted in David Greenberg, *Nixon's Shadow: The History of an Image* (New York, 2003), 125.

31 "presidents as well as plumbers":   Mansfield quoted in James T. Patterson, *Restless Giant: The United States from Watergate to Bush v. Gore* (New York, 2005), 5. Mansfield's statement was a pun, alluding to Nixon's shadowy "plumbers" unit—a group of operatives including E. Howard Hunt and G. Gordon Liddy who were dedicated to plugging suspected intelligence leaks, and whose clandestine illegal break-in at the Democratic National Committee headquarters had led directly to the Watergate scandal.

31 "an American tragedy":   Ford, "Remarks on Signing a Proclamation Granting Pardon to Richard Nixon, September 8, 1974," at http://www.presidency.ucsb.edu/ws/index.php?pid=4695&st=&st1=.

31 "if I am wrong":   Ibid.

32 "wrong in not acting":   Ibid.

33 "for all thirty months":   Hartmann quoted in John Robert Greene, *The Presidency of Gerald Ford* (Lawrence, KS, 1995), 27.

37 "public enemy number one":   Ford, "Address to a Joint Session of Congress on the Economy, October 8, 1974," at http://www.presidency.ucsb.edu/ws/index.php?pid=4434&st=&st1=.

37 "[A] lot of people":   Cannon quoted in Kenneth W. Thompson, ed., *The Ford Presidency: Twenty-Two Intimate Perspectives of Gerald R. Ford* (Lanham, MD, 1988), 352.

38 "We will swallow":   Ford quoted in Greene, *Presidency*, 77.

40 "far more serious":   Rockefeller in cabinet meeting minutes, September 17, 1975, Box 5 James E. Connor Files, Gerald R. Ford Presidential Library.

40 "Hell no!":   Rumsfeld quoted in Greene, *Presidency*, 93.

43 "I was one of the original":   "Interview with the President, October 30, 1975," Box 7, James M. Cannon Files, Ford Library.

43 "Since busing is the law of the land":   Parsons to Jim Cannon and Phil Buchen (memorandum), October 23, 1975, Box 1, "Busing," Richard B. Cheney Files, Ford Library.

44 "because the Governor":   Levi in cabinet meeting minutes, October 11, 1974, Box 5, James E. Connor Files, Ford Library.

44 "acted with great restraint":   Coleman in cabinet meeting minutes, September 17, 1975, Box 5, James E. Connor Files, Ford Library.

44 "Talk with me":   Ford to Rumsfeld, n.d. [October 1975], plus Robert Goldwin to Donald Rumsfeld, October 15, 1975; and Moynihan to Ford (memorandum), October 13, 1975, Box 10, "Presidential Commission on School Integration, 10/15/75," Richard B. Cheney Files, Ford Library. The poignant, even tragic concluding portions of Moynihan's memo presented numerous reasons why the president would be wise not to appoint a special commission on school integration—but also listed two reasons to go ahead with such a plan: the growing possibility that the politics of busing "could begin to turn the public at large against integration" and, "equally heart-breaking and even more calamitous," that if the country turned against busing, "American blacks could come to conclude that it had turned against *them*." Ford seems to have understood this dilemma, but did not come close to overcoming it.

45 "our common belief in civil rights": Ford, "Special Message to the Congress Transmitting Proposed School Busing Legislation, June 24, 1976," at http://www.presidency.ucsb.edu/ws/index.php?pid=6150&st=&st1=.

45 "There is no level": Coleman to Ford (memorandum), June 21, 1976, Box 7, "Busing—Presidential Meetings, June 18–22, 1976," James M. Cannon Files, Ford Library.

46 "absolutely, fantastically good": Rangel quoted in Ford, *Time to Heal*, 140.

47 "What has Ford done": In Ron Nessen, *It Sure Looks Different from the Inside* (Chicago, IL, 1978), 206.

CHAPTER 2: DÉTENTE AND ITS DISCONTENTS

49 "a specific authorization": "Public Law 93-148, 93rd Congress, H. J. Res. 542, November 7, 1973, Joint Resolution Concerning the War Powers of Congress and the President," at http://usinfo.state.gov/usa/infousa/laws/majorlaw/war-power.htm.

49 "clearly unconstitutional"; "to take away, by mere legislative act": Nixon, "Veto of the War Powers Resolution, October 24, 1973," at http://www.presidency.ucsb.edu/ws/index.php?pid=4021&st=&st1=.

49 "a serious legislative encroachment": Cheney in "CIA—The Colby Report, 12/19/74," draft memorandum, Box 5, "Intelligence—Colby Report," Richard B. Cheney Files, Gerald R. Ford Presidential Library. In a cover letter that accompanied Colby's initial report to the president, Secretary of State Kissinger agreed with Colby's assessment that Hersh's allegations had been exaggerated but conceded that the CIA had apparently committed some acts that were illegal and others that, although technically legal, raised "profound moral questions." Kissinger suggested that any presidential investigating committee initially limit itself to the matters contained in Colby's report. Kissinger to Ford (memorandum), December 25, 1974, ibid. The CIA's "family jewels" documents were finally declassified and released in June 2007. The documents confirm the CIA's involvement in various illegal activities including the surveillance of journalists and covert opening of mail. They also expose plots to kill foreign leaders. See www.gwu.edu/~nsarchiv/NSAEBB/NSAEBB/222/top02b.pdf.

49 "the CIA has engaged": *Report to the President by the Commission on CIA Activities within the United States* (Washington, DC, 1975), 10.

50 "rogue elephant":   Church Committee's report, quoted in John Robert Greene, *The Presidency of Gerald R. Ford* (Lawrence, KS, 1995), 112.

50 "strong team player":   Rumsfeld to Ford (memorandum), July 10, 1975, Box 5, "Intelligence—Appointment of CIA Director," Richard B. Cheney Files, Ford Library. Of the eight officials consulted, only three (including Cheney and Rumsfeld) named Bork. Other potential nominees, including Undersecretary of Commerce James Baker III, were named far more often. Rumsfeld put Bork's name at the top of the list anyway, using what he called "a simple aggregate of the number of times an individual favored one of the possible candidates to the number of times that person might have been recommended against." Bork had a reputation as an unconventional, highly conservative theorist on constitutional law but was best known for the Saturday-night massacre, when, as solicitor general, he was willing, at Nixon's direction, to fire Cox after Attorney General Elliot Richardson and Richardson's deputy William Ruckelshaus had resigned rather than comply. Having assumed the role of acting attorney general, Bork later resumed his duties as solicitor general, an office he held for the duration of Ford's presidency. Ford finally decided to move in a different direction in finding a new CIA chief, although he would select a Nixon loyalist. President Ronald Reagan would nominate Bork for the Supreme Court in 1987. See above, pp. 190–194.

54 "will be able to handle themselves":   Kissinger quoted in cabinet meeting notes, January 29, 1975, Box 4, James E. Connor Files, Ford Library. "We are asking for only enough to make it," Kissinger told the cabinet. "We must have enough! We are out of Vietnam, we brought 550,000 troops home with honor; but now the dissenters who wanted those troops out are asking for even more. The dissenters want to retroactively destroy everything that we have achieved. We maintain that this will hurt our credibility worldwide. . . . We will need this support for two, perhaps for three years before the Vietnamese will be able to handle themselves adequately."

54 "as far as America is concerned":   Ford, "Address at a Tulane University Convocation, April 23, 1975," at http://www.presidency.ucsb.edu/ws/index.php?pid=4859&st=&st1=.

55 "the sentiment in Congress":   Michel quoted in Charles Leppert Jr. to Jack Marsh (memorandum), April 2, 1975, Box 13, "Vietnam—General," Richard B. Cheney Files, Ford Library.

56 "FORD":   *Time*, May 26, 1975, cover.

56 "It's good":   Gerald Ford, *A Time to Heal: The Autobiography of Gerald R. Ford* (New York, 1979), 284.

57 "have been perfectly free":   Cheney to Rumsfeld (memorandum), July 8, 1975, Box 10, Folder: "Solzhenitsyn, Alexander," Richard B. Cheney Files, Ford Library.

57 "a goddamned horse's ass":   Ford quoted in Walter Isaacson, *Kissinger: A Biography* (New York, 1992), 658. Ford did do his best to contain with bland words the mounting pressure from inside the White House to force a meeting. After he received (most likely from Cheney) a copy of an article by the veteran right-wing journalist and campaigner Clare Boothe Luce praising Solzhenitsyn and condemning Kissinger, it arrived in Cheney's in-box with a single-word note from the president: "Interesting." Ford to Cheney, n.d. [June 1975] plus enclosure, Box 9, "Luce, Clare Boothe," Richard B. Cheney Files, Ford Library.

58 *"[T]he philosophy which permeates"*: Kissinger's briefing paper quoted in Greene, *Presidency*, 152–153.

58 "I am against it": Reagan quoted in Ford, *Time to Heal*, 300.

59 "All the new things": Kissinger in memorandum of conversation, cabinet meeting, August 8, 1975, Box 14, National Security Adviser, Memoranda of Conversations, 1973–1977, Ford Library.

60 "whenever his private ideology": Robert T. Hartmann, *Palace Politics: An Inside Account of the Ford Years* (New York, 1980), 283.

61 "relinquish my responsibilities": Rockefeller to Gerald R. Ford, December 16, 1975, in Box 3, "Domestic Council—Vice President's Role, 1/75–12/75, Richard B. Cheney Files, Ford Library. For somewhat cryptic documentation, see also Dick Cheney to Bob Hartmann, Phil Buchen, and Jack Marsh (memorandum), January 14, 1975, and enclosure; Cheney to Ford (memorandum), January 20, 1975; RBC to Kathie [secretary], February 3, 1976, plus enclosure; unsigned [Cheney] to Barb [secretary], February 13, 1976, plus enclosure.

61 "understood far better": Henry A. Kissinger, *Years of Renewal* (New York, 1999), 175.

61 "just a political ploy": Bruce Bradley quoted in T. D. Allman, "The Curse of Dick Cheney," *Rolling Stone*, August 25, 2004, at http://www.rollingstone.com/politics/story/6450422/the_curse_of_dick_cheney/.

61 "to go after Hersh papers": "5/28/75—Mtg., Buchen, A. G. Levi, Cheney," notes, Box 6, "Intelligence—New York Times Articles by Seymour Hersh 5/75–5/75," Richard B. Cheney Files, Ford Library. As Attorney General Levi strongly questioned the feasibility of any legal action, it appears that Cheney was among the more vociferous officials who supported taking legal reprisals. (Levi did, nevertheless, instruct the criminal division of the Justice Department and the FBI to prepare a proposal on investigating possible violations of the U.S. Criminal Code.) Cheney soon recommended that no investigation be launched; but his recommendation was based on a report from the Department of Defense, delivered by an officer at the National Security Counsel (NSC), that the submarine operations could continue despite the revelations, and that pursuing an investigation would only "generate publicity leading to a Soviet reaction." The NSC officer who reported to Cheney was, coincidentally, Robert "Bud" McFarlane. See also Cheney to Donald Rumsfeld (memorandum), May 29, 1975; Cheney to Rumsfeld (memorandum), May 30, 1975 (quotation). On Levi and the preliminary proposal, see Rumsfeld to Cheney (memorandum), May 31, 1975; Howard R. Tyler Jr. to W. E. Colby, June 2, 1975; Rex E. Lee and John C. Keeney to Edward Levi, June 2, 1975. I will discuss McFarlane in Chapter 8.

61 "sand in the gears": Cheney quoted in Stephen F. Hayes, *Cheney: The Untold Story of America's Most Powerful and Controversial Vice President* (New York,

2007), 111. In his interviews for Hayes's authorized, highly laudatory biography, Cheney briefly recounted with satisfaction his behind-the-scenes confrontations with Rockefeller and his efforts to humiliate the vice president. "You've got to watch vice presidents," he said at one point, with palpable irony (since he himself then held that office). "They're a sinister crowd" (112).

62 "the illusion that all of a sudden": Cheney to Rumsfeld (memorandum), July 8, 1975, Ford Library.

62 "Why don't you": Cheney to Goldwin (memorandum), February 14, 1975, Box 22, "Cheney, Richard," Robert Goldwin Papers, Ford Library. Kristol was in regular contact with Goldwin to suggest various policy ideas and initiatives, including the possible establishment of what Kristol called a "Council of Social Advisers." (See Goldwin to Cheney, November 20, 1974, and accompanying memorandum, Kristol to Goldwin, November 18, 1974, in Box 28, "Council of Social Advisers," Robert Goldwin Papers, Ford Library.) Other suggestions from Kristol included "doing something for a relatively small group of men who are, unbeknownst to it, being helpful to this Administration . . . the men who head small and sometimes obscure foundations which support useful research and activities of a kind the [liberal] Ford and Rockefeller Foundations take a dim view of." Among those Kristol mentioned were "the head of the Scaife Family Trust, the head of the Lilly Endowment, etc." He suggested an official show of appreciation such as an invitation to a state dinner at the White House. Kristol to Goldwin, January 30, 1975, Box 22, Robert Goldwin Papers, Ford Library. Rumsfeld also took an eager interest in Kristol, and urged Cheney to see if Goldwin could draw on some of Kristol's articles in order to "draft a basic speech for the President on the individual and too much government; re-privatization and de-regulation; and the general conservative philosophy." Rumsfeld to Cheney (memorandum), June 17, 1975. Cheney, Rumsfeld, and Goldwin also expressed interest in the work of Edward Banfield, Gertrude Himmelfarb, Michael Novak, and James Q. Wilson, among other luminaries in the emerging neoconservative camp. And Cheney spoke warmly of the ideas of a publicist for the *Wall Street Journal*, Jude Wanniski—"who's a friend," he told Goldwin—and of Wanniski's early formulations of what became known as supply-side economics. Cheney to Goldwin, June 11, 1975. In short, thanks largely to Cheney and Rumsfeld, conservative and neoconservative ideas and proposals that historians have linked most closely with the Reagan administration received a good deal of attention years earlier in Ford's White House. I will discuss the new conservative counterestablishment, Wanniski, and supply-side economics in Chapter 3.

63 "own team"; "the very best men": "Mtg of Senior Staff, Presdnt's remarks, 12:46 pm, 11/3/75," notes in Box 28, "Cabinet Reorganization 11/3/75," Robert Goldwin Papers, Ford Library.

64 "silent architect": Lou Cannon, "Rumsfeld: Silent Architect; Chief of Staff Seen as Force Behind Shake-Up," *Washington Post*, November 4, 1975, p. A1. See also "Rumsfeld Wins the Prize in Ford's Untidy Shuffle," *Economist* (London), November 8, 1975, pp. 69–73.

64 "We are going to forget":   Ford, "Remarks and a Question-and-Answer Session at Everett McKinley Dirksen Forum in Peoria, March 5, 1976," at http://www.presidency.ucsb.edu/ws/index.php?pid=5672&st=. At the beginning of March, Robert Goldwin sent Dick Cheney a full report on the etymology of "détente," which, Goldwin noted, "provide[s] a rationale for the President's decision to stop using the word." Goldwin had originally prepared the report at the request of Donald Rumsfeld in preparation for the hearings over Rumfeld's confirmation as secretary of defense. Robert Goldwin to Richard Cheney (memorandum), March 2, 1976, and accompanying report, Box 22, "Cheney, Richard," Robert Goldwin Papers, Ford Library.

64 "I am not appeased":   Reagan quoted in James Reston, "Mr. Ford's Machismo," *New York Times*, November 5, 1975, p. 43.

64 "I am going to make an announcement":   Reagan quoted in Ford, *Time to Heal*, 333.

67 "[W]e built it":   Reagan quoted in Greene, *Presidency*, 165.

67 "totally deceptive"; "telling the American people"; "if he knew more":   Robert D. Hershey Jr., "Goldwater Calls Reagan in Error," *New York Times*, May 3, 1976, p. 1.

67 "gross factual errors"; "a lack of understanding"; "a surprisingly dangerous":   "Honorable Barry Goldwater, Press Conference, Washington, D.C., May 4, 1976," in Box 16, Panama Canal, Michael Raoul-Duval Papers, Ford Library. The *Wall Street Journal* also ran an essay strongly criticizing Reagan, Thurmond, and the Veterans of Foreign Wars for their opposition to the canal negotiations. See Robert Keatley, "The Big Flap over the Canal," *Wall Street Journal*, April 29, 1976, p. 14.

67 "irresponsible":   Ford quoted in Greene, *Presidency*, 166. For Ford's own ideas about how to attack Reagan—on issues ranging from Reagan's "$90 billion" speech in Chicago to his possible acceptance of support from the John Birch Society and his stance on right-to-work laws—see Box 19, "Ronald Reagan," Richard B. Cheney Files, Ford Library.

68 "There's just no comparison":   Quotation in James M. Naughton, "Some Republicans Fearful Party Is on Last Legs," *New York Times*, May 31, 1976, p. 1. On early conservative rumblings about forming a third party, and divisions among hard-liners over the possibility, see Fred Slight to Jerry Jones (memorandum), June 6, 1975; and related materials in Box 16, "Conservative Third Party," Richard B. Cheney Files, Ford Library.

70 "high moral character":   Carter, "'Our Nation's Past and Future,' Address Accepting the Presidential Nomination at the Democratic National Convention in New York City, July 15, 1976," at http://www.presidency.ucsb.edu/ws/index.php?pid=25953&st=.

71 "There is no Soviet domination"; "And I would like to see Mr. Ford":   "Presidential Campaign Debate between Gerald R. Ford and Jimmy Carter, October 6, 1976," transcript at http://www.ford.utexas.edu/library/speeches/760854.htm. Not surprisingly, Ford's comments caused particular concern among leading Republican conservatives; see Jack Marsh to Dick Cheney (memorandum), October 7, 1976, Box 16, "Debates," Richard B. Cheney Files, Ford Library.

CHAPTER 3: JIMMY CARTER AND THE AGONIES OF ANTI-POLITICS

73 "Christ set some"; "committed adultery"; Christ says": Robert Scheer, "The Playboy Interview: Jimmy, We Hardly Knew Y'All," *Playboy*, November 1976, p. 136.

74 "the time for racial": Carter, "Inaugural Address as Governor of Georgia, January 12, 1971," at http://www.jimmycarterlibrary.org/documents/inaugural_address.pdf.

77 "malaise": Caddell quoted in Sidney Blumenthal, *The Permanent Campaign: Inside the World of Elite Political Operatives* (Boston, MA, 1980), 29.

77 "is a natural extension of the change in American politics": Caddell quoted ibid., 31.

79 "The road can be smooth": Byrd quoted in Peter G. Bourne, *Jimmy Carter: A Comprehensive Biography from Plains to Post-Presidency* (New York, 1997), 373.

80 "moral equivalent of war": Carter, "National Energy Plan—Address Delivered Before a Joint Session of Congress," April 20, 1977. Transcript available at http://www.presidency.ucsb.edu/ws/index.php?pid=7372&st=.

82 "the worst slum in America": Bob Schieffer quoted in Jill Jones, *South Bronx Rising: The Rise, Fall, and Resurrection of an American City* (New York, 2002), 316.

82 "[g]overnment cannot eliminate poverty": Carter, "The State of the Union Address Delivered Before a Joint Session of the Congress, January 19, 1978," at http://www.presidency.ucsb.edu/ws/index.php?pid=30856&st=&st1=.

83 "as antiquated and anachronistic": David S. Broder, *Changing of the Guard: Power and Leadership in America* (New York, 1980), 410.

84 "failure of leadership": Kennedy quoted in Victor Cohn, "Kennedy, Meany Assail Carter," *Washington Post*, July 29, 1978, p. A1.

86 "The entry of the United States": Norton to Jimmy Carter, memorandum, September 9, 1977, Box 2, "Bakke Case 5/77–7/78 [OA 5419]," Martha (Bunny) Mitchell Files, Jimmy Carter Presidential Library. As a follow-up, see Norton to Wade McCree, Memorandum, September 12, 1977.

87 "deterioration": Ibid.

87 "only one question": "Excerpts from U.S. Brief in Bakke Case," *New York Times*, September 20, 1977, p. 34.

87 "strongly committed"; "the recent decision": Carter, "Memorandum for the Heads of Executive Departments and Agencies, July 20, 1978," in Box 2, "Bakke Case 5/77–7/78 [OA 5419]," Martha (Bunny) Mitchell Files, Carter Library.

88 "last resort": Burton Kaufman, *The Presidency of James Earl Carter, Jr.* (Lawrence, KS, 1993), 110.

89 "fifty-year project":   Intercollegiate Studies Institute, "Our History," at http://www. isi.org/about/our_history/our_history.html.

90 "the stupid party":   See Bruce Chapman, "A 'Progressive's' Progress," *National Review*, April 17, 1981, p. 412. Chapman ascribes the use of the term to George Gilder in the 1960s.

91 "about twenty years for a research paper":   Wriston quoted in Sidney Blumenthal, *The Rise of the Counter-Establishment: From Conservative Ideology to Political Power* (New York, 1986), 54.

91 "stand athwart history, yelling Stop": William F. Buckley Jr., "Publisher's Statement," *National Review*, November 19, 1955, p. 5.

91 "sobering"; "the White community":   "Why the South Must Prevail," *National Review*, August 24, 1957, p. 148. The magazine, while preaching the necessity of rule by the minority (that is, southern whites) if the majority (that is, southern blacks) was debased, at times seemed also to condone segregationist violence, then being perpetrated chiefly by groups such as the Ku Klux Klan. In the same editorial that asserted white supremacy, the magazine observed: "Sometimes it becomes impossible to assert the will of the minority, in which case it must give way, and the society will regress; sometimes the numerical minority cannot prevail except by violence: then it must determine whether the prevalence of its will is worth the terrible price of violence."

93 "If you would like to know":   Falwell quoted in James T. Patterson, *Restless Giant: The United States from Watergate to Bush v. Gore* (New York, 2005), 139. The popular myth that abortion, school prayer, feminism, and related social issues galvanized Falwell to join with Weyrich remains sturdy. In the 1970s, the Catholic right was far more active in antiabortion politics than conservative Protestant evangelicals were. At the time, the white Southern Baptist Convention (which Falwell did not join until 1990) actually supported the decision in *Roe v. Wade*. And Weyrich's first entreaties to Falwell fell on deaf ears. Only later did Falwell become aroused over the future of his own Lynchburg (now Liberty) Christian Academy. "What changed their mind"—including Falwell's—"was Jimmy Carter's intervention against the Christian schools, trying to deny them tax-exempt status on the basis of so-called *de facto* segregation," Weyrich later recounted. In brief, the religious right, at its inception, was largely a continuation of the southern white "massive resistance" to desegregation in the 1960s. Weyrich quoted in Randall Balmer, *Thy Kingdom Come: How the Religious Right Distorts the Faith and Threatens America* (New York, 2006), 15.

94 "kingmakers":   Phyllis Schlafly, *A Choice Not an Echo* (Alton, IL, 1964), 6.

94 "paranoid style":   Richard Hofstadter, "The Paranoid Style in American Politics" in *The Paranoid Style in American Politics and Other Essays* (Cambridge, MA, 1996), originally published 1965.

94 "a conflagration on the Right":   Donald T. Critchlow, *Phyllis Schlafly and Grassroots Conservatism: A Woman's Crusade* (Princeton, NJ, 2005), 214.

97 "the true problems of our Nation"; "crisis of confidence"; "the meaning of our own

lives"; "very heart and soul and spirit":   Carter, "Energy and National Goals Address to the Nation, July 15, 1979," at http://www.presidency.ucsb.edu/ws/ index.php?pid=32596&st=&st1=.

CHAPTER 4: HUMAN RIGHTS AND DEMOCRATIC COLLAPSE

100   "the cause of human rights"; "the respect and the admiration and love"; "special relationship":   "Tehran, Iran Toasts of the President and the Shah at a State Dinner, December 31, 1977," at http://www.presidency.ucsb.edu/ws/index. php?pid=7080&st.

104   "internal settlement":   Burton Kaufman, *The Presidency of James Earl Carter, Jr.* (Lawrence, KS, 1993), 91.

106   "domestic flexibility":   Memorandum for the president from Jody Powell, February 21, 1977, Box 208, Stuart Eizenstat Papers, Jimmy Carter Presidential Library, quoted in Kaufman, *Presidency*, 39.

106   "an outspoken champion of human rights":   "U.S. Cautions Soviet on Sakharov Curbs," *New York Times*, January 28, 1977, p. A1.

108   "international marauders":   Brzezinski quoted in "Comrade Fidel Wants You," *Time*, July 10, 1978, p. 36.

108   "the polar bear to the north":   Brzezinski quoted in John A. Armitage, "China Ties and the U.S.-Soviet Balance," *Washington Post*, February 11, 1979, p. L7.

109   "the opportunity of giving":   Brzezinski quoted in *Le Nouvel Observateur*, January 15–21, 1998, p. 76.

113   "associated principles":   "Camp David Meeting on the Middle East Documents Agreed to at Camp David," September 17 1978," at http://www.presidency.ucsb. edu/ws/index.php?pid=29788&st=associated+principles&st1=.

115   "moderation":   Jimmy Carter, *Keeping Faith: Memoirs of a President* (Fayetteville, AR, 1995), 465, originally published 1982.

115   "There were objections in Iran":   Ibid.

116   "They are clearly *planning*":   Harris to Jordan, September 28, 1978, Box 78, "Kennedy, Edward," Chief of Staff Files, Carter Library.

116   "I'll whip his ass!":   Carter quoted in "Whip His What?" *Time*, June 25, 1979, pp. 20–21.

117   "our friend from Massachusetts":   Hamilton Jordan, *Crisis: The Last Year of the Carter Presidency* (New York, 1982), 19.

118   "America Held Hostage":   James T. Patterson, *Restless Giant: The United States from Watergate to Bush v. Gore* (New York, 2005), 125.

120   "Billygate":   William Safire, "None Dare Call It Billygate," *New York Times*, July 21, 1980, p. A17.

121   "voodoo economics":   Bush quoted in Hedrick Smith, "George Bush Running Hard, with Brand-New Track Suit," *New York Times*, April 27, 1980, p. E4.

121   "raucous": Francis X. Clines, "Grand Old Pandemonium; Voices in the Chaos," *New York Times*, February 25, 1980, p. A18. The incident at Nashua, which Reagan later claimed was the turning point of the primary campaign, appears to have resulted from a setup by the Reagan camp. In collaboration with the two leading contenders, Reagan and Bush, a newspaper in Nashua had scheduled a joint debate. One of the other candidates, Senator Robert Dole, complained to the Federal Elections Commission. After Bush's campaign refused to split the costs of the debate, Reagan's campaign agreed to cover them and then, without telling Bush, invited all the other candidates to participate. Bush arrived at a scene in the local high school for which he was completely unprepared, with several candidates onstage. Claiming that he had been ambushed, he refused to take part. Pandemonium broke out in the hall. Reagan seized the moment to explain what was going on, but the moderator, Jim Breen of the *Nashua Telegraph*, ruled him out of order. Reagan kept talking and Breen told the soundman to cut him off, but the technician (whom Reagan's men had made sure was one of their loyalists) would not. Reagan became furious and retorted (misstating the moderator's name), "I am paying for this microphone, Mr. Green." The tough talk and the thunderous ovation that followed played extremely well on television. As soon as the theatrics were over, all the candidates except Bush and Reagan departed; the debate proceeded as originally planned; and Bush, shaken, performed poorly. The trap had already worked even better than could have been foreseen. Reagan looked magnanimous and fearless next to the pinched, fussy Bush—and then took charge of the event manfully. Reagan's "microphone" line was quite similar to one delivered by Gary Cooper in Frank Capra's film *Meet John Doe* (1941), but this may have been a coincidence.

121 "the work goes on": "Democrats '80: Transcript of Kennedy's Speech on Economic Issues at Democratic Convention," *New York Times*, August 13, 1980, p. B2.

122 "states' rights": Reagan quoted in Douglas E. Kneeland, "Reagan Campaigns at Mississippi Fair," *New York Times*, August 4, 1980, p. A11.

122 "religious adviser": Peter Bourne, *Jimmy Carter: A Comprehensive Biography from Plains to Post-Presidency* (New York, 1997), 468.

122 "There is only one phrase": "Transcript of Reagan Speech Outlining Five-Year Economic Program for U.S.," *New York Times*, September 10, 1980, p. B4.

122 "You may not endorse me": Reagan quoted in Anthony Lewis, "Political Religion," *New York Times*, September 25, 1980, p. A27.

122 "A recession is when your neighbor loses his job": Reagan quoted in Lou Cannon, "Reagan: Denouncing Carter's Betrayal of Working People's Aspirations," *Washington Post*, September 2, 1980, p. A1.

122 "If Reagan keeps putting": Caddell quoted in Jordan, *Crisis*, 339.

123 "October surprise": Kaufman, *Presidency*, 205.

123 "Nuclear weaponry and the control": Carter quoted in "Carter-Reagan Presidential Debate, October 28, 1980, Cleveland, Ohio," at http://www.presidency.ucsb.edu/showdebate.php?debateid-10.

124 "There you go again": Although omitted from the official transcript of the

debate, Reagan's line appears in the Public Broadcasting System's transcript at http://www.pbs.org/newshout/debatingourdestiny/80debates/cart4.html.

124 "Are you better off":   Reagan quoted in "Carter-Reagan Presidential Debate, October 28, 1980, Cleveland, Ohio."

126 "You're kidding"; "No, sir":   Jordan, *Crisis*, 397.

CHAPTER 5: NEW MORNING

127 "Politics is just like show business":   Reagan quoted in Anthony R. Pratkanis and Elliot Aronson, *Age of Propaganda: The Everyday Use and Abuse of Persuasion* (New York, 2001), 140.

127 "When you've got to":   Goldwater quoted in Colman McCarthy, "A New Beginning with the Rich Right," *Washington Post*, February 1, 1981, p. G2.

127 "a bacchanalia of the haves":   Elisabeth Bumiller, "The Furs! The Food! The Crowds! The Clout!" *Washington Post*, January 19, 1981, p. B1.

128 "generation of self-seekers"; "The rulers of the exchange":   Roosevelt, "Inaugural Address, March 4, 1933," at http://www.presidency.ucsb.edu/ws/index.php?pid=14473.

128 "in the present crisis"; "terror"; "runaway living costs":   Reagan, "Inaugural Address, January 20, 1981," at http://www.presidency.ucsb.edu/ws/index.php?pid=43130. The image of government riding the people may have been borrowed from Thomas Jefferson: "[T]he mass of mankind has not been born with saddles on their backs, nor a favored few booted and spurred, ready to ride them legitimately, by the grace of God." Jefferson to Roger C. Weightman, June 24, 1826, Thomas Jefferson Papers, Library of Congress. By equating the modern welfare state with eighteenth-century monarchy and aristocracy, Reagan, throughout his political career, lifted rhetoric from early American liberals and radicals, including Jefferson and Thomas Paine. In his first inaugural address, Reagan also inserted a paraphrase of at least one line of movie dialogue, delivered by the actor Frank McHugh in the John Wayne film *Back to Bataan* (1944). And according to Lou Cannon, he included a patriotic, uplifting anecdote about a slain veteran that was conveniently embellished by inaccuracy. See Richard Reeves, *President Reagan: The Triumph of Imagination* (New York, 2005), 4; Lou Cannon, *President Reagan: The Role of a Lifetime* (New York, 2000), 76–77, originally published 1991.

128 "pay any price":   Kennedy, "Inaugural Address, January 20, 1961," at http://www.presidency.ucsb.edu/ws/index.php?pid=8032.

128 "our potential adversaries"; "The enemies"; "our own sovereignty":   Reagan, "Inaugural Address."

129 "an apparent airhead":   Edmund Morris, *Dutch: A Memoir of Ronald Reagan* (New York, 1999), 579.

130 "a sickness":   Nell Reagan quoted in Lou Cannon, *Reagan* (New York, 1982), 26.

130 "almost permanent anger and frustration":   Ronald Reagan and Richard Hubler,

Where's the Rest of Me? (New York, 1981), 54, originally published 1965.

130 "voracious reader": Ronald Reagan, *An American Life* (New York, 1990), 31.

130 "Huck Finn idyll": Reagan, *Where's the Rest*, 16.

130 "He had an inability": Margaret Cleaver quoted in Jules Tygiel, *Ronald Reagan and the Triumph of American Conservatism* (New York, 2006), 26, originally published 2004.

131 "hemophiliac liberal": Reagan, *Where's the Rest*, 139.

131 "a liberal who has": Kristol quoted in Douglas Murray, *Neoconservatism: Why We Need It* (New York, 2006), 34. This famous remark, ascribed to Kristol in the early 1970s, has been variously rendered as a liberal mugged by reality or simply a liberal who had been mugged; i.e., a victim of crime.

132 "We were told four years ago"; "You and I": Reagan, "A Time for Choosing: An Address on Behalf of Senator Barry Goldwater, October 27, 1964," transcript at http://www.reaganfoundation.org/reagan/speeches/rendezvous.asp.

133 "We recognized": Wick quoted in Sidney Blumenthal, *The Rise of the Counter-Establishment: From Conservative Ideology to Political Power* (New York, 1986), 63.

133 "I don't know": Reagan quoted in Lou Cannon, *Governor Reagan: His Rise to Power* (New York, 2003), 61.

134 "the role of a lifetime": Cannon, *President Reagan*. This phrase is the subtitle.

135 "The success story": Reagan, "Address to the Nation on the Fiscal Year 1983 Budget, April 29, 1982," transcript at http://www.presidency.ucsb.edu/wb/index.php?pid=42461&st=.

135 "What I want to see": Reagan, "The President's News Conference, July 28, 1983," at http://www.presidency.ucsb.edu/ws/index.php?pid=41535&st=.

135 "the extraordinary strength and character": Reagan, "Nomination Acceptance Speech, July 17, 1980," at http://www.presidency.ucsb.edu/ws/index.phpid=25970&st=.

136 "Did we forget": Reagan, "Remarks at the New York City Partnership Luncheon in New York, January 14, 1982," at http://www.presidency.ucsb.edu/ws/index.php?pid=42354&st=.

136 "in the spirit of sentimental appreciation": Richard Hofstadter, *The American Political Tradition and the Men Who Made It* (New York, 1948), v.

136 "the dream": "Transcript of Kennedy's Speech on Economics Issues at Democratic Convention," *New York Times*, August 13, 1980, p. B2.

137 "[T]here never was": Morris, *Dutch*, 394.

138 "noble": Reagan, "Remarks at Memorial Day Ceremonies Honoring an Unknown Serviceman of the Vietnam Conflict, May 28, 1984," at http://www.reagan.utexas.edu/archives/speeches/1984/52884a.htm.

138 "we would find out once and for all": Reagan, "Remarks to the Students and Faculty at Fallston High School in Fallston, Maryland, December 4, 1985," at http://www.presidency.ucsb.edu/ws/index.php?pid+38111&st=.

139 "fun and class": Hugh Sidey, "A Vodka Toast for Reagan," *Time*, November 24, 1980, p. 27.

140   "to occupy the land until He returns":   Watt quoted in Philip Shabecoff, "Watt Softening Attacks on Critics of His Policies," *New York Times*, October 10, 1981, p. A9.

142   "Honey, I forgot to duck":   Reagan quoted in Lynn Rossellini, "Honey, I Forgot to Duck, Injured Reagan Tells Wife," *New York Times*, March 31, 1981, p. A3.

142   "As of now, I am in control *here*":   Haig quoted in Martin Schram and Michael Getler, "Haig's Actions Again Raise Concerns over His Conduct," *Washington Post*, April 1, 1981, p. A1.

142   "The aura of heroism":   Wright quoted in John Farrell, *Tip O'Neill and the Democratic Century* (Boston, 2001), 553.

143   "It struck me as singular":   Rumsfeld quoted in Gil Troy, *Morning in America: How Ronald Reagan Invented the 1980s* (Princeton, NJ, 2005), 78.

144   "I'm getting the shit whaled out of me":   O'Neill quoted in Tony Kornheiser, "Tip O'Neill's Toughest Inning: The Sermon on the Mound," *Washington Post*, May 31, 1981, p. F1.

144   "Sometimes"; "So do I":   Deaver and Reagan quoted in Lou Cannon and Les Lescaze, "The Relaxed Approach," *Washington Post*, February 9, 1981, p. A1.

145   "a Trojan horse":   Stockman quoted in William Greider, "The Education of David Stockman," *Atlantic*, December 1981, p. 27.

146   "It's kind of hard": Ibid.

147   "Stockman was the original":   Kirkland quoted in Charles Alexander, "Reaganomics: Turbulent Takeoff," *Time*, December 28, 1981, p. 64.

147   "binge":   Reagan, "Remarks at the New York City Partnership Luncheon."

148   "tightening noose":   Stockman quoted in Greider, "The Education of David Stockman."

149   "breach of faith":   O'Neill, "Speaker's Statement, 20 May 1981," Press Statements, Box 9, Press Relations, Thomas P. O'Neill Papers, John J. Burns Library, Boston College, quoted in Troy, *Morning in America*, 104.

150   "The wolves in wolves' clothing":   Peter Rodino Letter, c. fall 1981, Democratic Congressional Campaign Committee Fund-Raising Letter, Box 5, Kirk O'Donnell Files, Staff Files, Thomas P. O'Neill Papers, Burns Library, Boston College, quoted in Troy, *Morning in America*, 109.

150   "stay the course":   Reagan quoted in James T. Patterson, *Restless Giant: The United States from Watergate to Bush v. Gore* (New York, 2005), 162.

150   "all signs we're now seeing":   Reagan, "Remarks and a Question-and-Answer Session with Editorial Page Writers on Domestic Issues, February 8, 1983," at http://www.presidency.ucsb.edu/ws/index.php?pid-40911&st=.

CHAPTER 6: CONFRONTING THE EVIL EMPIRE

151   "My idea of American policy":   Richard V. Allen, "The Man Who Won the Cold War," *Hoover Digest*, 1 (2000), at http://www.hoover.org/publications/digest/3476876.html.

152   "a one-way street":   Reagan, "The President's News Conference, January 29,

1981," at http://www.presidency.ucsb.edu/ws/index.php?pid=44101&st=&st1=.

152 "window of vulnerability": See, for example, Ronald Reagan, "Remarks on Board the USS *Constellation* off the Coast of California, August 20, 1981," at http://www.presidency.ucsb.edu/ws/index.php?pid=44172&st=.

153 "a kangaroo court": Ray Cline quoted in Paul C. Warnke, "Foreign Policy Fake, Arms Control Poseur," *New York Times*, October 14, 1988, p. A35.

153 "traditional autocracies": Jeane J. Kirkpatrick, "Dictatorships and Double Standards," *Commentary*, November 1979, pp. 38, 44.

154 "revolutionary autocracies": Ibid.

154 "They cannot vastly increase": Reagan, "Remarks and a Question-and-Answer Session at a Working Luncheon with Out-of-Town Editors, October 16, 1981," at http://www.presidency.ucsb.edu/ws/index.php?pid=43114&st=.

155 "a great revolutionary crisis": Reagan, "Address to the Members of the British Parliament, June 8, 1982," at http://www.presidency.ucsb.edu/ws/index.php?pid=42614&st=&st1=.

156 "political activists": Kirkpatrick quoted in Flora Lewis, "Keeping Us Honest," *New York Times*, March 27, 1981, p. A27.

156 "not credible": Abrams quoted in *Testimony in Hearing before the Committee on Foreign Relations, United States Senate, 97th Congress, 2nd Session, on the President's January 28, 1982 Certification Concerning Military Aid to El Salvador, February 8 and March 11, 1982* (Washington, DC, 1982), 22.

158 "strategic 'consensus' ": Haig quoted in Bernard Gwertzman, "Haig Says U.S. Seeks Consensus Strategy in the Middle East," *New York Times*, March 20, 1981, p. A1.

158 "Let friend and foe alike": Reagan, "Remarks on Board the USS *Constellation* off the Coast of California."

159 "any major reversal": United States Interests Section in Iraq Cable from William L. Eagleton Jr. to the United States Embassy in Jordan. "Talking Points for Amb. [Ambassador] Rumsfeld's Meeting with Tariq Aziz and Saddam Hussein," December 14, 1983, National Security Archive, at http://www.gwu.edu/~nsarchiv/NSAEBB/NSAEBB82/iraq29.pdf. Inconveniently for Rumsfeld and later U.S. policy makers, the Americans were already very well aware that the Iraqis were deploying banned chemical weapons, virtually on a daily basis, against the Iranians, and that they were possibly using American-made crop-dusting equipment. In 2002, as secretary of defense before the invasion of Iraq, Rumsfeld claimed that in his meetings with Saddam Hussein in 1983, he had warned Saddam not to use chemical weapons, but subsequently declassified documents show that the subject never arose. The record to date shows that Rumsfeld, working on behalf of the Reagan administration, turned a blind eye to Hussein's assaults with chemical weapons in 1983—even though he and other officials in the Bush administration cited those attacks in the catalog of reasons for invading Iraq in 2003. Instead of making the case that times had changed, Rumsfeld and others appear to have preferred to dissemble about what had happened under Reagan. See the useful analysis and compilation of documents by the National Security Archive staff on the tilt of the Reagan administration toward Iraq, National Security Archive, "Shaking Hands with Saddam: The U.S. Tilts Toward Iraq, 1980–1984," at http://www.gwu.edu/~nsarchiv/ NSAEBB/NSAEBB82/index.htm.

159 "restraint": Quotation ibid.

159 "Our long-term hope": David Newton quoted in Michael Dobbs, "U.S. Had Key Role in Iraq Buildup," *Washington Post*, December 30, 2002, p. A01.

160 "despicable": Reagan, "Remarks to Reporters on the Death of American and French Military Personnel in Beirut, Lebanon, October 23, 1983," at http:// www.presidency.ucsb.edu/ws/index/php?pid=40673&st=.

160 "not going to let": Bush quoted in R. W. Apple Jr., "Bush Says Act of Terrorism Won't Change U.S. Policies," *New York Times*, October 27, 1983, p. A8.

161 "Korean Air Lines massacre": Reagan, "Address to the Nation on the Soviet Attack on a Korean Civilian Airliner, September 5, 1983," at http://www.presi-dency.ucsb.edu/ws/index.php?pid=41788&st=&st1=.

161 "military psychosis": Richard S. Ovinnikov quoted in Bernard D. Nossiter, "'Murder' and 'Massacre' Charged as UN Council Starts Its Debate," *New York Times*, September 3, 1983, p. 1.

161 "deliberate": Ogarkov, "Transcript of Soviet Official's Statement and Excerpt from News Session," *New York Times*, September 10, 1983, p. 4.

162 "In the middle of a meeting": Douglas Brinkley, ed., *The Reagan Diaries*, (New York, 2007), 190, entry for October 24, 1983.

162 "We got there": Reagan, "Address to the Nation on Events in Lebanon and Gre-nada, October 27, 1983," at http://www.presidency.ucsb.edu/ws/index.php?pid= 40696&st=&st=1=.

162 "The precipitous way": Haig quoted in Richard Reeves, *President Reagan: The Triumph of Imagination* (New York, 2005), 117.

163 "to be a channel"; "this could be": Brinkley, ed., *Reagan Diaries*, 131, entry for February 15, 1983.

163 "the focus of evil"; "an evil empire": Reagan, "Remarks at the Annual Conven-tion of the National Association of Evangelicals in Orlando, Florida, March 8, 1983," at http://www.presidency.ucsb.edu/ws/index.php?pid=41023&st=&st1=.

164 "such as is already at hand": "Republican Party Platform of 1980, Adopted by the Republican National Convention, Detroit, Michigan, July 15, 1980," at http:// www.presidency.ucsb.edu/showplatforms.php?platindex=R1980.

165 "attempting to disarm": Andropov quoted in Dusko Doder, "Andropov Accuses Reagan of Lying About Soviet Arms," *Washington Post*, March 27, 1983, p. A1.

166 "freedom fighters": Reagan, "Radio Address to the Nation on United States Assistance for the Nicaraguan Democratic Resistance, June 8, 1985," at http:// www.presidency.ucsb.edu/ws/index.php?pid=38741&st=.

166 "and to bring": Reagan quoted in Anthony Lewis, "Obey Captain Disaster," *New York Times*, April 9, 1984, p. A19.

166 "If each of us determined": Reagan quoted in Don Oberdorfer, *From the Cold War to a New Era: The United States and the Soviet Union, 1983–1991* (Baltimore, MD, 1998), 47, originally published 1991.

166 "A nuclear war can never be won": Reagan, "Address Before the Japanese Diet in Tokyo, November 11, 1983," at http://www.presidency.ucsb.edu/ws/index. php?pid=40754&st=.

167 "get a top Soviet leader": Reagan, *Ronald Reagan: An American Life* (New York, 1990), 567.

167 "I am pissed off": Goldwater quoted in "Goldwater Writes CIA Director Scorching Letter," *Washington Post*, April 11, 1984, p. A17.

167 "a first step": Kennedy quoted in Martin Tolchin, "Senate, 84-12, Acts to Oppose Mining Nicaragua Ports; Rebuke to Reagan," *New York Times*, April 11, 1984, p. A1.

168 "a better working relationship": Reagan, "Address to the Nation and Other Countries on United States–Soviet Relations, January 16, 1984," at http://www. presidency.ucsb.edu/ws/index.php?pid=39806&st=&st1=. President Kennedy was apparently once again on Reagan's mind, and on his speechwriters' minds. The last line of this speech implicitly borrows from Kennedy's inaugural address; earlier, Reagan cited Kennedy explicitly on achieving cooperation between the United States and the Soviet Union.

168 "Together": Ibid.

168 "hackneyed ploys": Gromyko quoted in John Vinocur, "Gromyko, in Speech, Calls U.S. Main Threat to Peace," *New York Times*, January 19, 1984, p. A4.

168 "[T]he ice was cracked": Shultz quoted in Oberdorfer, *From the Cold War*, 74.

168 "Herbert Hoover with a smile": O'Neill quoted in Hugh Sidey, "The Art of Political Insult," *Time*, June 20, 1983, p. 24.

169 "every kind of mixture": Watt quoted in "Watt's Remark on Coal Panel Offends 4 Groups," *New York Times*, September 22, 1983, p. A15.

170 "This whole business": Brinkley, ed., *Reagan Diaries*, 136, entry for March 10, 1983.

170 "Stay the course": Reagan, "Message to the Congress Transmitting the Fiscal Year 1983 Budget, February 8, 1982," at http://www.presidency.ucsb.edu/ws/ index.php?pid=41977&st=.

172 "a future each generation must enlarge": Mondale, "Acceptance Speech, San Francisco, California, July 19, 1984," at http://www.presidency.ucsb.edu/ shownomination.php?convid=21.

172 "Hymies": Jackson quoted in "Post Reaffirms Report on Jackson Comment," *New York Times*, February 23, 1984, p. B13.

173 "Hymietown": Ibid.

173 "a candidate of the establishment past": Hart quoted in John Ehrman, *The Eighties: America in the Age of Reagan* (New Haven, CT, 2005), 83.

173 "Where's the beef?": Mondale quoted in "Excerpts from Transcript of 5 Candidates' Debate in Atlanta," *New York Times*, March 12, 1984, p. B8.

173 "blame America first": Kirkpatrick quoted in Dudley Clendinen, "Convention in Dallas: The Republicans; Viewing a TV Drama: As the Political World Turns," *New York Times*, August 22, 1984, p. A16.

173 "Paint Reagan": Quotation in Frances FitzGerald, *Way Out There in the Blue: Reagan, Star Wars, and the End of the Cold War* (New York, 2000), 233.

174 "It's morning again": Martin Schram, "Parties Resharpen Decades-Old Ideological Clash, GOP Seeks to Send a TV Message to Blue-Collar Democrats, Women," *Washington Post*, August 18, 1984, p. A1.

174   "I have to say":   Brinkley, ed., *Reagan Diaries*, 271, entry for October 6–7, 1984.

175   "There is a difference":   Kennedy quoted in Fay S. Joyce, "Kennedy Says Democratic Party Must Change to Regain Support," *New York Times*, March 31, 1985, p. A24.

CHAPTER 7: "CALL IT MYSTICISM IF YOU WILL"

176   "the greatest military buildup":   Reagan, "Inaugural Address, January 21, 1985," at http://www.presidency.ucsb.edu/ws/indexphp?pid=38688&st=.

176   "break faith":   Reagan, "Address before a Joint Session of the Congress on The State of the Union, February 6, 1985," at http://www.presidency.ucsb.edu/ws/index.php?pid=38069&st=.

176   "freedom fighters":   Ibid.

176   "the moral equivalent":   Reagan, "Remarks at the Annual Dinner of the Conservative Political Action Conference, March 1, 1985," at http://www.presidency.ucsb.edu/ws/index.php?pid=38274&st=&st1=.

179   "the Mice":   Quotation in Richard Reeves, *President Reagan: The Triumph of Imagination* (New York, 2005), 252.

180   "welfare queen":   Reagan quoted in " 'Welfare Queen' Becomes Issue in Reagan Campaign," *New York Times*, February 15, 1976, p. 51.

180   "strapping young buck":   Reagan quoted in Charlayne Hunter, "Blacks Organizing in Cities to Combat Crimes by Blacks," *New York Times*, February 22, 1976, p. 1.

180   "states' rights":   Reagan quoted in John Herbers, "Race Issue in Campaign: A Chain Reaction," *New York Times*, September 27, 1980, p. 8.

180   "humiliating to the South":   Reagan quoted in Lou Cannon, *President Reagan: The Role of a Lifetime* (New York, 2000), 458, originally published 1991.

181   "my man"; "a h—l of a good job":   Douglas Brinkley, ed., *The Reagan Diaries* (New York, 2007), 421, entry for June 23, 1986.

181   "one of the most conservative agencies":   Terry Eastland quoted in R. Jeffrey Smith, Amy Goldstein, and Jo Becker, "A Charter Member of Reagan Vanguard," *Washington Post*, August 1, 2005, p. A1.

182   "It is nothing short of criminal":   Hooks quoted in Glenn Fowler, "Private Schools Groups Assail Tax Rule Shift," *New York Times*, January 10, 1982, p. 19.

182   "whether it is the intention":   Quotation in Walter Isaacson, "Pirouetting on Civil Rights," *Time*, January 25, 1982, p. 24.

182   "the burden of racism":   Reagan, "Remarks at a Question-and-Answer Session with Employees at the Digital Equipment Corporation in Roxbury, Massachusetts, January 26, 1983," at http://www.presidency.ucsb.edu/ws/index.php?pid=41754&st=.

183 "We'll know in about thirty-five years": Reagan, "The President's News Conference, October 19, 1983," at http://www.presidency.ucsb.edu/ws/index.php?pid=40666&st=&st1=.

183 "I almost lost my dinner over that": Gergen quoted in Cannon, *President Reagan*, 462.

183 "come down in some of these cases": Metzenbaum quoted in Neil A. Lewis, "Hostile Questions Greet Nominee for Justice Department Post at Hearing," *New York Times*, June 5, 1985, p. B6.

183 "promise of liberty and justice for all": Reagan, "Address to High School Students on Martin Luther King Jr.'s Birthday, January 15, 1987," at http://www.presidency.ucsb.edu/ws/index.php?pid=33953&st=.

184 "vastly and unjustifiably expand": Reagan, "Message to the Senate Returning Without Approval the Civil Rights Restoration Act of 1987 and Transmitting Alternative Legislation, March 16, 1988," at http://www.presidency.ucsb.edu/ws/index.php?pid=35559&st=.

184 "closely identified with religious organizations": Ibid.

185 "The poor homosexuals": Buchanan quoted in Cannon, *President Reagan*, 733.

185 "gay plague": Quotation in James T. Patterson, *Restless Giant: The United States from Watergate to Bush v. Gore* (New York, 2005), 180.

185 "a sad thing": Reagan quoted in Cannon, *President Reagan*, 735.

185 "that in Hollywood he knew": Anderson quoted in Deroy Murdock, "Anti-Gay Gipper: A Lie About Reagan," *National Review Online*, December 3, 2003, at http://www.nationalreview.com/murdock/murdock200312030913.asp.

185 "public enemy number one": Reagan, "Remarks at a Luncheon for Members of the College of Physicians at Philadelphia, Pennsylvania, April 1, 1987," at http://www.presidency.ucsb.edu/ws/index.php?pid=34054&st=&st1=.

185 "He can be as stubborn": Brinkley, ed., *Reagan Diaries*, 517, entry for July 18, 1987. In the same entry, Reagan noted that William Bennett had volunteered to have a talk with the young man; "I hope it can be worked out," his father observed.

186 "a good friend": Ibid., 137, entry for March 15, 1983.

188 "institutionalize the Reagan revolution": Meese quoted in Lee Edwards, *The Conservative Revolution: The Movement That Remade America* (New York, 1999), 237.

188 "philosophical grounding": Markman quoted in W. Elliot Brownlee and Hugh Davis Graham, eds., *The Reagan Presidency: Pragmatic Conservatism and Its Legacies* (Lawrence, KS, 2003), 332.

190 "all medically acceptable": Quotation in "Answers to Some Accusations," *Time*, July 20, 1981, p. 11.

190 "conservative statism": Sidney Blumenthal, "Bill Rehnquist Is Big Government's Best Friend," *Washington Post*, September 21, 1986, p. C1.

191 "too extreme on race": Kennedy quoted in George Lardner and Al Kamen, "Kennedy Calls Rehnquist 'Too Extreme,'" *Washington Post*, July 30, 1986, p. A1.

191   "Rehnquisition":   Hatch quoted in Al Kamen, "Rehnquist Confirmed in 65–33 Senate Vote," *Washington Post*, September 18, 1986, p. A1.

192   "We'll get Bork confirmed":   Brinkley, ed., *Reagan Diaries*, 513, entry for July 6, 1986.

192   "in which women would be forced":   Kennedy quoted in Lou Cannon and Edward Walsh, "Reagan Nominates Appeals Judge Bork to Supreme Court," *Washington Post*, July 2, 1987, p. A1.

192   "Some of Judge Bork's":   Arthur B. Culvahouse Jr. to Howard H. Baker et al., Memorandum, September 8, 1987, Box 3, Series I: Subject File, "Judge Bork, Nomination of" (2), Howard H. Baker Jr. Files, Ronald W. Reagan Presidential Library. In this memo, Culvahouse went on to complain about a report in *Newsweek* that quoted a senior White House aide's description of Bork as a "right wing zealot." The remark, Culvahouse said, was *"very unhelpful,"* given the official White House line: "The mainstream jurist strategy *is* our strategy; there is no time for another strategy; and," he added almost as an afterthought, "it is true that Judge Bork is a mainstream jurist." Nothing seemed to be going quite right. Even in conservative Alabama, Culvahouse reported, Senators Richard Shelby and Howell Heflin were hearing "uncommon opposition to Bork" in their home districts, partly "from Christian groups concerned about a statement in *Time* some weeks ago that Bork was an agnostic." Culvahouse had served Baker as chief legislative assistant and counsel in the mid-1970s.

192   "confirmation conversion":   Leahy quoted in Edward Walsh and Al Kamen, "Senators Question Bork's Consistency; Nominee Sees No Constitutional Basis for D.C. Integration Ruling," *Washington Post*, September 17, 1987, p. A1.

193   "They never":   Brinkley, ed., *Reagan Diaries*, 532, entry for September 19–20, 1987. The day after the judiciary committee wrapped up its hearings, Chief of Staff Howard Baker reported that the Republican senator Arlen Specter of Pennsylvania seemed likely to vote no. "Would a meeting with Specter by me do any good?" President Reagan wrote at the bottom of Baker's memo. But Specter's mind was made up, much as Baker's report predicted. [Howard Baker] to Ken [Duberstein], Memorandum, October 1, 1987, Box 3, "Judge Bork, Nomination of" (1), Series I, Subject File, Howard H. Baker Files, Reagan Library.

195   "If you thought about deregulation in 1979":   Michael Fix quoted in Cannon, *President Reagan*, 740.

197   "reregulator":   Constance Horner quoted in ibid., 743.

198   "the weak, meek, and ignorant":   Keating quoted in Jules Tygiel, *Ronald Reagan and the Triumph of American Conservatism* (New York, 2006), 221.

199   "The administration was so ideologically blinded":   Edwin Gray quoted in Cannon, *President Reagan*, 744.

199   "Overall":   Ibid., 740.

200   "influence peddling, favoritism":   Quotation in Ronald J. Ostrow, "Panel Charges Pierce Steered Funds to Friends," *Los Angeles Times*, November 2, 1990.

200   "rampant bribery in Government":   Warner quoted in Ed Magnuson, "The Pentagon Up for Sale," *Time*, June 27, 1988.

200 "something in the big picture": Baker quoted in Cannon, *President Reagan*, 712.

201 "conduct which should not be tolerated": Quotation in "Meese Is Reportedly Denounced in Report by Justice Department," *New York Times*, January 17, 1989, p. A22.

201 "sleaze": George Lardner Jr., "Prosecutor Labels Meese 'A Sleaze'; U.S. Attorney Giuliani Said to Approve Language," *Washington Post*, July 23, 1988, p. A3. Months later, when Giuliani stepped down from his post, he had similarly harsh things to say about his former superior, although in less colorful language. See Howard Kurtz and R. Jeffrey Smith, "Meese Was in 'Wrong Job,'" *Washington Post*, February 17, 1989, p. A25.

202 "All in all": Reagan, "Remarks on Signing the Garn-St. Germain Depository Institutions Act of 1982, October 15, 1982," at http://www.presidency.ucsb.edu/ws/index.php?pid=41872&st=.

203 "I think greed is healthy": Boesky quoted in William Glaberson, "The Plunge: A Stunning Blow to a Gilded, Impudent Age," *New York Times*, December 13, 1987, p. A1.

203 "With the tax cuts of 1981": Ronald Reagan, *An American Life* (New York, 1990), 335.

204 "[I]t was seared into the consciousness": Charles P. Blahous III, cited in Martha Derthick and Steven N. Teles, "Riding the Third Rail, Social Security Reform," in W. Elliot Brownlee and Hugh Davis Graham, eds., *The Reagan Presidency: Pragmatic Conservatism and Its Legacies* (Lawrence, KS, 2003), 203.

205 "abominable": Quotation in Gareth Davies, "The Welfare State," Brownlee and Davis, eds., *The Reagan Presidency*, 223.

205 "so all taxpayers, big and small": Reagan, "Address Before a Joint Session of the Congress on the State of the Union, January 25, 1984," at http://www.presidency.ucsb.edu/ws/index.php?pid=40205&st=.

207 "Call it mysticism if you will": Reagan, "Remarks at the Opening Ceremonies of the Statue of Liberty Centennial Celebration in New York, New York, July 3, 1986," at http://www.presidency.ucsb.edu/ws/index.php?pid=37549&st=.

208 "[W]e are finally paying the piper": Frederick R. Zuckerman quoted in Alan Murray and Gerald F. Seib, "Reagan's Reversal: Stock Market Crash Makes Budget Accord, Tax Rise More Likely," *Wall Street Journal*, October 23, 1987, p. 1.

CHAPTER 8: "WE HAVE AN UNDERCOVER THING": THE IRAN-CONTRA AFFAIR

210 "were victims": Reagan, "Remarks and a Question-and-Answer Session with Regional Editors and Broadcasters, April 18, 1985," at http://www.presidency.ucsb.edu/ws/index.php?pid=38498&st=&st1=. Subsequent research discovered that most members of the Waffen SS buried at Bitburg were indeed young men between the ages of seventeen and twenty. But this did nothing to mitigate the intense emotions stirred up by the affair, compounded by the moral obtuseness

of Reagan's remarks. Nor did it overcome the fact that among the dead was a staff sergeant of the Waffen SS who had been awarded the German Cross for killing ten American soldiers.

210   "my 'Dreyfus' case":   Douglas Brinkley, ed., *The Reagan Diaries* (New York, 2007), 317, entry for April 19, 1985.

210   "Buchanan argued for a harder line":   Michael Deaver with Mickey Herskowitz, *Behind the Scenes: In Which the Author Talks About Ronald and Nancy Reagan . . . and Himself* (New York, 1987), 182.

210   "What is wrong with saying":   Brinkley, ed., *Reagan Diaries*, 315, entry for April 5–14, 1985. Vice President Bush also ardently supported Reagan's decision to go ahead with the visit to Bitburg and sent him a note after Reagan reassured Kohl that he would not back down: "Mr. President, I was very *proud* of your stand. If I can absorb some heat—send me into battle—It's not easy, but you are *right*!! George." Brinkley, ed., *Reagan Diaries*, 317, entry for April 19, 1985.

210   "I always felt":   Ibid., 323, entry for May 5, 1985.

210   "Reagan would never again fully recapture":   Lou Cannon, *President Reagan: The Role of a Lifetime* (New York, 2000), 519, originally published 1991.

212   "any nation, group, organization, movement, or individual":   Section 8066 of Public Law 98-473, the Continuing Appropriations Act for Fiscal Year 1985. In *Report of the Congressional Committees Investigating the Iran/Contra Affair, with Supplementary, Minority, and Additional Views* (Washington, DC, 1987), 398.

212   "crazies":   Cannon, *President Reagan*, 332.

212   "I want you to do whatever you have to do":   Reagan quoted in Richard Reeves, *President Reagan: The Triumph of Imagination* (New York, 2005), 221.

213   "the perfect No. 2 man":   Lou Cannon, "McFarlane's Hidden Hand Helps Shape Foreign Policy; Reagan Adviser Makes Mark as Conciliator," *Washington Post*, February 15, 1985, p. A1.

215   "crucial contribution":   United States Senate. Select Committee on Secret Military Assistance to Iran and the Nicaraguan Opposition, United States Congress. House Select Committee to Investigate Covert Arms Transactions with Iran. *Iran-Contra Investigation: Joint Hearings Before the Senate Select Committee on Secret Military Assistance to Iran and the Nicaraguan Opposition* (Washington, DC, 1988), 910.

216   "If such a story gets out":   Reagan quoted in National Security Planning Group Meeting, June 25, 1984, Minutes, National Security Archive transcript at http://www.gwu.edu/~nsarchiv/NSAEBB/NSAEBB210/index.htm. See also George Lardner Jr., "Reagan Urged Aid Secrecy; North Trial Hears Plan to Give Contras Third-Country Help," *Washington Post*, March 11, 1989, p. A1. At a crucial meeting of the National Security Planning Group on June 25, Ambassador Jeane Kirkpatrick as well as Bush spoke up in favor of seeking aid from other countries for the contras. Shultz, citing Baker, raised the specter of impeachment if such aid was sought; McFarlane urged that no solicitations occur until more information was available. The discussion and especially McFarlane's remarks were slightly absurd, as McFarlane had already obtained, in discreet language,

the first contribution agreement from Saudi Arabia, about which he promptly (and again discreetly) informed an approving President Reagan and Vice President Bush. See Theodore Draper, *A Very Thin Line: The Iran-Contra Affairs* (New York, 1991), 80–81. Although many of the relevant documents still remain classified, some material released between 1995 and 2000 affirms that the NSC's involvement with air shipments to the contras was well established during the summer of 1984. One memo from Oliver North's secretary, for instance, reveals North along with an official at NSC, Constantine Menges, working on "some covert activities" in connection with "Aircraft to Nicaragua." (Menges, like North, was a protégé of William Casey's, and was known by pragmatists in the White House and the State Department as "Constant Menace" for his unstinting support of covert aid to the contras.) See Fawn [Hall] to Ollie [Oliver North], August 13, 1984, Box 4, "Nicaragua—General" (2), Oliver L. North Files, Ronald W. Reagan Presidential Library.

216 "by all means available": Leslie H. Gelb, "'85 Reagan Ruling on Afghans Cited," *New York Times*, June 19, 1986, p. A7. The full text of the relevant document, National Security Decision Directive 166, "U.S. Policy, Programs, and Strategy in Afghanistan," signed on March 27, 1985, remains classified, but administration officials divulged its gist in mid-1986.

217 "supporting or cooperating": See materials on National Security Decision Directive 138, "Combating Terrorism," April 3, 1984, at http://www.fas.org/irp/offdocs/nsdd/nsdd-138.htm.

217 "gives terrorists no rewards": Reagan, "Remarks Announcing the Release of the Hostages from the Trans World Airlines Hijacking Incident, June 30, 1985," at http://www.presidency.ucsb.edu/ws/index.php?pid=38841&st=.

217 "outlaw states run by the strangest collection": Reagan, "Remarks at the Annual Convention of the American Bar Association, July 8, 1985," at http://www.presidency.ucsb.edu/ws/index.php?pid=38854&st=.

219 "Some strange soundings": Brinkley, ed., *Reagan Diaries*, 343, entry for July 17, 1985. When pressed, in a subsequent interview with investigators, about whether the president understood his proposal as chiefly "an attempt to get arms for hostages through the transfer from Israel to Iran," McFarlane replied, "Well, I think that was foremost in the President's mind." The interview continued:

> Q: So if he didn't state to you in so many words, Bud, go ahead and do it, he clearly led you to believe from the outset that here was a chance to bring some hostages out through a third country?
> A: It was unambiguously clear.

John G. Tower and Edmund S. Muskie, *The Tower Commission Report: The Full Text of the President's Special Review Board* (New York, 1987), 131.

219 "we were just falling into the arms-for-hostages business": Shultz quoted in *Report of the Congressional Committees Investigating the Iran/Contra Affair*, p. 167.

221   "a bit of a horror story":   North quoted in *Joint Hearings Before the Senate Select Committee on Secret Military Assistance*, 53.

221   "We have an undercover thing":   Brinkley, ed., *Reagan Diaries*, 371, entry for November 22, 1985.

221   "Hostage Rescue—Middle East"; "obtain the release":   Presidential Finding, signed December 4, 1985, MS draft (November 26, 1985) at National Security Archive, http://www.gwu.edu/~nsarchiv/NSAEBB/NSAEBB210/index. htm. Text in *Report of the Congressional Committees Investigating the Iran/Contra Affair*, 186.

221   "in a timely fashion":   *Report of the Congressional Committees Investigating the Iran/Contra Affair*, 9.

221   "our undercover effort"; "only a few of us"; "I won't even write":   Brinkley, ed., *Reagan Diaries*, 374, entry for December 5, 1985.

221   "President sd. he could answer":   Caspar Weinberger diary, December 7, 1985, MS, National Security Archives, at http://www.gwu.edu/~nsarchiv/NSAEBB/NSAEBB210/index.htm. Twelve days later, the State Department publicly released a report to Congress on Nicaragua prepared by the White House the previous month. (The White House was now required to prepare such a report every ninety days.) The report provided details on American humanitarian aid to the contras (under an executive order signed by Reagan in late August 1985), but no hint about the covert aid. The White House, Report on Nicaragua, November 6, 1985, Box 4, "Nicaragua—General" (1), Oliver L. North Files, Reagan Library.

221   "Reagan was not moved":   Michael Ledeen, *Perilous Statecraft: An Insider's View of the Iran-Contra Affair* (New York, 1988), 127.

222   "I gave a go ahead":   Brinkley, ed., *Reagan Diaries*, 384, entry for January 17, 1986.

223   "parallel efforts to provide":   McFarlane quoted in *Report of the Congressional Committees Investigating the Iran/Contra Affair*," 123.

223   "deliberate attempt to deceive":   Ibid., 133.

223   "a neat idea":   North quoted ibid., 271.

224   "This was a heartbreaking disappointment":   Brinkley, ed., *Reagan Diaries*, 415, entry for May 28, 1986.

224   "too disappointed":   McFarlane quoted in Draper, *Very Thin Line*, 330.

226   "no foundation":   Reagan, "Remarks on Signing the Immigration Reform and Control Act of 1986, November 6, 1986," transcript at http://www.presidency. ucsb.edu/ws/index.php?pid=36698&st=.

226   "off on a wild story":   Brinkley, ed., *Reagan Diaries*, 448, entry for November 7, 1986.

226   "effect the safe return of all hostages":   Reagan, "Address to the Nation on the Iran Arms and Contra Aid Controversy," November 13, 1986, at http://www. presidency.ucsb.edu/ws/index.php?pid=36728&st=. Reagan continued to write in his diary that the press was issuing "ridiculous falsehoods"; "based entirely on unsubstantiated rumors & out right inventions." Brinkley, ed., *Reagan Diaries*, 450, entry for November 13, 1986. Compounding the misinformation, Reagan also went on to insist repeatedly, at a press conference several days after the speech, that Israel had not been involved in the arms transactions. The White House press office was forced, quickly, to release a correction, stating that a third country, unnamed, had indeed been involved.

226 "speaking with one voice": *Report of the Congressional Committees Investigating the Iran/Contra Affair*, 305.

228 "our Col. North": Brinkley, ed., *Reagan Diaries*, 453, entry for November 24, 1986.

228 "in one aspect": Reagan, "Remarks Announcing the Review of the National Security Council's Role in the Iran Arms and Contra Aid Controversy, November 25, 1986," at http://www.presidency.ucsb.edu/ws/index.php?pid=36761&st=&st1=.

228 "the press would crucify him": Brinkley, ed., *Reagan Diaries*, 453–454, entry for November 25, 1986.

230 "a credible and broadly accepted document": David Abshire, *Saving the Reagan Presidency: Trust Is the Coin of the Realm* (College Station, TX, 2005), 138.

230 "assess individual culpability"; "the final arbiter": Tower and Muskie, *Tower Commission Report*, 2.

231 "all the facts to come out": "Remarks at a Meeting with the President's Special Review Board for the National Security Council," December 1, 1986, transcript at http://www.presidency.ucsb.edu/ws/index.php?pid=36766&st=.

231 "the principal responsibility for policy review": Tower and Muskie, *Tower Commission Report*, 79.

231 "management style": Ibid.

232 "no knowledge": Ibid., 55.

232 "process": Ibid., 62.

232 "Plainly, there was no smoking gun": Abshire, *Saving the Reagan Presidency*, 133.

232 "distanced themselves from the march of events": Tower and Muskie, *Tower Commission Report*, 82.

232 "My prayers": Brinkley, ed., *Reagan Diaries*, 478–479, entry for February 26, 1987.

232 "in a spirit of contrition": R. W. Apple, "The Reagan White House; In a Spirit of Contrition; Reagan's Concession on Iran Affair Evokes Memories of Kennedy's Bay of Pigs Speech," *New York Times*, March 5, 1987, p. A1.

232 "in order to develop relations": Reagan, "Address to the Nation on the Iran Arms and Contra Aid Controversy, March 4, 1987," at http://www.presidency. ucsb.edu/ws/index.php?pid=33938&st=. On the tortuous process of composing this speech, see Cannon, *President Reagan*, 653–658. Cannon quotes (657) the speechwriter Landon Parvin's conclusion "that what Reagan had really wanted to say was 'I didn't do it, and I'll never do it again.'"

235 "charged with the high crime": Hyde quoted in *Joint Hearings on the Iran-Contra Investigation—Testimony of Richard V. Secord* (Washington, DC, 1987), 321.

237 "not perhaps a whole lot different": North, quoted ibid., 131.

237 "I think it is very important": Ibid., 9.

238 "this Congress represents the people": Rudman, ibid., 127.

238 "that Jew, Liman": Theodore Draper, *A Present of Things Past* (New Brunswick, NJ, 2002), 222.

238 "blasted the press":   Brinkley, ed., *Reagan Diaries*, 515, entry for July 13, 1987. Three weeks later, Reagan consulted with Cheney about an upcoming speech, and the two agreed that "the public is fed up with the whole subject of Iran-Contra"; 524, entry for August 8, 1987.

238 "The end doesn't justify the means":   Hyde quoted in *Report of the Congressional Committees Investigating the Iran/Contra Affair*, 667.

239 "take care":   Ibid., 21.

239 "cloud hanging over the President":   McCollum quoted ibid., 675.

239 "a record of disengagement":   Ibid., 536.

240 "establish a new US relationship with Iran":   Ibid., 524.

240 "less-than-robust defense":   Ibid., 449. The report's chief author was Michael J. Malbin, a political scientist and former resident fellow at the American Enterprise Institute whom Cheney had appointed to the staff of the minority committee. As vice president, Cheney has cited the minority report as a good elaboration of "a robust view of the President's prerogatives with respect to the conduct of especially foreign policy and national security matters." Not every Republican at the time agreed. Senator Warren Rudman called the minority report "pathetic" and, quoting Adlai Stevenson, said that it had "separated the wheat from the chaff and left in the chaff." Cheney quoted in Richard W. Stevenson and Adam Liptak, "Cheney Defends Eavesdropping Without Warrants," *New York Times*, December 21, 2005, p. 36; Rudman quoted in Hays Gorey, "The Iconoclast of Capitol Hill," *Time*, September 3, 1990.

240 "the subjective opinions":   "Statement by Assistant to the President for Press Relations Fitzwater on the Report of the Congressional Committee Investigating the Iran Arms and Contra Aid Controversy, November 18, 1987," at http://www.presidency.ucsb.edu/ws/index.php?pid=33706&st=&st1=. Former President Nixon warmly congratulated Reagan after Reagan's speech to the nation at the conclusion of the congressional hearings. Nixon thought it was especially important that the president "sounded and looked *strong*. You gave the lie to the crap about your being over-the-hill, discouraged, etc." Nixon then added some words of presidential wisdom about handling scandals:

> If I could be permitted one word of advice: Don't *ever* comment on the Iran-Contra matter again. Have instructions issued to all White House staffers and Administration spokesmen that they must *never* answer any question on or off the record about that issue in the future. They should reply to all inquiries by stating firmly and categorically that the President has addressed the subject and that they have nothing to add.
>
> The committee labored for nine months and produced a stillborn midget. Let it rest in peace!

Nixon to Ronald Reagan, August 13, 1987, WHORM Subject File SP1169, case file 533859, Reagan Library. Reagan's reaction is unrecorded; he replied to the letter with a telephone call.

240   "He just pleaded guilty":   Reagan quoted in Reeves, *President Reagan*, 463.

241   "You cannot spend funds":   Shultz quoted in *Report of the Congressional Committees Investigating the Iran/Contra Affair*, 412.

241   "the primary role"; "interfere with core":   Ibid., 469.

CHAPTER 9: "ANOTHER TIME, ANOTHER ERA"

245   "This is the most exciting":   Quotation in Maureen Dowd, "The Summit; As 'Gorby' Works the Crowd, Backward Reels the KGB," *New York Times*, December 11, 1987, p A1.

245   "I'm still shaking":   Ibid.

245   "I don't resent his popularity":   Reagan, "Remarks and a Question-and-Answer Session with Area High School Seniors in Jacksonville, Florida, December 1, 1987," at http://www.presidency.ucsb.edu/ws/index.php?pid=33751&st=.

245   "without firing a shot":   "Margaret Thatcher," *Washington Post*, June 12, 2004, p. A25.

246   "man of goodwill":   Ibid.

247   "bleeding wound":   Gorbachev quoted in Don Oberdorfer, "A Diplomatic Solution to Stalemate; Gorbachev Never Wedded to the War," *Washington Post*, April 17, 1988, p. 1.

247   "How long will our military-industrial complex":   Ligachev quoted in Beth A. Fischer, "Reagan and the Soviets: Winning the Cold War?" in W. Elliot Brownlee and Hugh Davis Graham, eds., *The Reagan Presidency: Pragmatic Conservatism and Its Legacies* (Lawrence, KS, 2003), 125.

247   "was the main thing":   Chernyaev quoted ibid., 128.

248   "the feeling that our foreign policy":   Andrei Aleksandrov-Agentov quoted in Don Oberdorfer, *From the Cold War to a New Era: The United States and the Soviet Union 1983–1991* (Baltimore, MD, 1998), 112.

249   "called on the military":   Aleksandrov-Agentov, ibid., 114.

249   "My fellow Americans":   Reagan quoted in William R. Doemer, "Party Time in Dallas," *Time*, August 27, 1984, p. 8.

249   "I just happen to believe":   Reagan quoted in "An Interview with the President," *Time*, November 19, 1984, p. 52.

250   "the new generation is":   George Will, "The 'New Generation' Theory—Again," *Washington Post*, March 14, 1985, p. A19.

250   "no essential change":   Mikhail Tsypkin, "Gorbachev and the 27th Soviet Party Congress Say Nyet to Change," Heritage Foundation: *Issues*, April 16, 1986, at http://www.heritage.org/Research/RussiaandEurasia/bg504.cfm.

250   "vintage Stalin":   "The True Believer—Mikhail Gorbachev's Keynote Address at the Soviet Party Congress," *National Review*, March 28, 1986, p. 25.

250   "harness the power of the west":   Nick Eberstadt, "The Latest Myths About the Soviet Union," *Commentary*, May 1987, p. 27.

250   "an offensive purpose":   Reagan to Mikhail Gorbachev, April 30, 1985, Reagan

Library; also at http://www.gwu.edu/~nsarchiv/NSAEBB/NSAEBB172/Doc9.
pdf.

250   "not to let things come":   Gorbachev to Ronald Reagan, March 24, 1985, Reagan
Library; also at http://www.gwu.edu/~nsarchiv/NSAEBB/NSAEBB172/Doc6.
pdf.

251   "Oh sure":   Nancy Reagan quoted in Oberdorfer, *From the Cold War*, 92.

251   "to search for mutual understanding":   Gorbachev to Reagan, March 24,
1985.

251   "Who can control it?":   Gorbachev quoted in Evan Thomas, "Fencing at
the Fireside Summit," *Time*, December 2, 1985, p. 22. The Soviets had identified between twenty and thirty possible responses to SDI. It appears that
in Geneva, Gorbachev was referring to the *protivodeistvie* (counteraction)
program, undertaken in 1985, to develop the Topol-M missile, which the
Soviets believed could penetrate any space shield designed by the Americans in the foreseeable future. Work on the Topol-M continued even after
the collapse of the Soviet Union; the Russians finally deployed the missile
in 1998.

251   "which country he would like":   "Geneva Summit, Memorandum of Conversation, November 19, 1985, 10:20–11:20 a.m. First Private Meeting," at http://
www.gwu.edu/~nsarchiv/NSAEBB/NSAEBB172/Doc15.pdf.

251   "that he was dedicated":   Reagan quoted in Lou Cannon, *President Reagan: The
Role of a Lifetime* (New York, 2000), 677, originally published 1991.

252   "a turning point"; "continue provoking":   Anatoly Chernyaev, diary entry, November 24, 1985, at http://www.gwu.edu/~nsarchiv/NSAEBB/NSAEBB172/
Doc26.pdf.

252   "You can't use democracy":   Wolfowitz quoted in James Mann, *Rise of the Vulcans: The History of Bush's War Cabinet* (New York, 2004), 134.

252   "infrastructure of democracy":   Reagan, "Address to Members of the British Parliament, June 8, 1982," at http://www.presidency.ucsb.edu/ws/index.php?pid=
42614&st=&st1=. Reagan was referring in this speech to "the system of a
free press, unions, political parties, universities, which allows a people to
choose their own way to develop their own culture, to reconcile their own
differences through peaceful means." The impact of the Polish Solidarity movement was clear—and, in this respect, was as important in shap-
ing Reagan's thinking and, more profoundly and immediately, that of members of his administration, as the Reagan White House was in encouraging
Solidarity.

253   "Reagan is walking into a trap":   Bethell quoted in Dinesh D'Souza, "How
Reagan Won the Cold War," *National Review*, November 24, 1997, p. 36.

253   "Reagan's era"; "wildly wrong"; "accelerated the moral": George Will, "How
Reagan Changed America," *Newsweek*, January 9, 1989, p. 13.

254   "tore the blindfold from our eyes":   Shevardnadze quoted in Robert English,
"The Sociology of New Thinking: Elites, Identity Change, and the End of the
Cold War," *Journal of Cold War Studies*, 7 (2005): 61.

254 "overriding importance": Gorbachev quoted in Oberdorfer, *From the Cold War*, 163.

255 "serious consequences": Quotation ibid., 166.

255 "constructive steps": Reagan, "Statement on Soviet and United States Compliance with Arms Control Agreements, May 27, 1986," at http://www.presidency. ucsb.edu/ws/index.php?pid=37356&st=&st1=.

256 "It would be fine with me": Quoted in Oberdorfer, *From the Cold War*, 202.

257 "This meeting is over": Ronald Reagan, *An American Life* (New York, 1990), 679.

257 "I was mad": Douglas Brinkley, ed. *The Reagan Diaries* (New York, 2007), 444, entry for October 12, 1986.

258 "The significance is that": Reagan, "Remarks at a Meeting with Officials of the State Department and the U.S. Arms Control and Disarmament Agency on the Meetings in Iceland with Soviet General Secretary Gorbachev, October 14, 1986," at http://www.presidency.ucsb.edu/ws/index.php?pid= 36598&st=.

258 "Maginot Line in space": Andrei Sakharov, "Of Arms and Reforms," *Time*, March 16, 1987, p. 40.

260 "maintain the momentum": Quotation in Oberdorfer, *From the Cold War*, 217.

260 "Let everyone here and in the West know": Gorbachev quoted in Susanne Sternhal, *Gorbachev's Reforms: De-Stalinization through Demilitarization* (Westport, CT, 1997), 88.

260 "General Secretary Gorbachev, if you seek peace": Reagan, "Remarks on East-West Relations at the Brandenburg Gate in West Berlin," June 12, 1987, at http:// www.presidency.ucsb.edu/ws/index.php?pid=34390&st=. In preparing this carefully vetted speech, there was considerable jockeying among Reagan's speechwriters and advisers—including the national security adviser, Colin Powell; the staff of the NSC; and the State Department—over basic facts concerning American policy as well as about style and ideological shading. Some of its evolution can be traced in "Brandenburg Gate/Berlin, 6/12/87" 1-3, OA 18100, Speechwriting, WHO of: Research Office Rec., Reagan Library. In his book *How Ronald Reagan Changed My Life* (New York, 2003), the speechwriter Peter Robinson claims responsibility for certain crucial lines and passages in these remarks. For a broader, more complex view of the speech's origins and evolution, see John C. Kornblum, "Reagan's Brandenburg Concerto," American Interest Online, at http://www. the-american-interest.com/ai2/article.cfm?Id=286&MId=13. Kornblum, at the time, was U.S. minister and deputy commandant of the United States in Berlin, a post he had held since 1985. In an early draft prepared by Robinson that "incorporates NSC and other changes," Kornblum's name appears regularly in the marginalia marking suggestions as "Cornbloom," including one notation in the draft version about asking Gorbachev to come to the Berlin Wall. See Peter M. Robinson to Rhett Dawson (memorandum), May 29, 1987, "Brandenburg Gate/ Berlin, 6/12/87" 1, OA 18100, Speechwriting, WHO of: Research Office Rec., Reagan Library.

260   "not merely":   Reagan, "Remarks on East-West Relations at the Brandenburg
      Gate in West Berlin."

261   "I occasionally think":   Reagan, "Address to the 42d Session of the United Na-
      tions General Assembly in New York, NY, September 21, 1987," at http://www.
      reagan.utexas.edu/archives/speeches/1987/092187b.htm=.

261   "a very weak man":   Phillips quoted in Anthony Lewis, "Why the Summit,"
      New York Times, December 6, 1987, p. 31. See also E. J. Dionne Jr., "Arms Pact
      Has Major Effect on Presidential Race," *New York Times*, December 6, 1987,
      p. 1.

261   "dizzy over Gorbachev":   Krauthammer, "Dizzy over Gorbachev," *Washington
      Post*, December 3, 1987, p. A23.

261   *"Doveryai, no proveryai"*:   Reagan quoted in Thomas A. Sancton, "The Spirit of
      Washington," *Time*, December 21, 1987, p. 16.

261   "You repeat that at every meeting"; "I like it":   Gorbachev and Reagan quoted
      ibid.

262   "totally irresponsible":   Quayle quoted in Susan F. Rasky, "Treaty Critics Lash
      Back at Reagan," *New York Times*, December 5, 1987, p. 6.

262   "Dan, you have to shut down!":   George Shultz, *Turmoil and Triumph: My Years
      as Secretary of State* (New York, 1993), 1084.

262   "I've often wondered":   Reagan, "Remarks and a Question-and-Answer Session
      with Members of the National Strategy Forum in Chicago, Illinois, May 4, 1988,"
      transcript at http://www.presidency.ucsb.edu/ws/index.php?pid=35783&st=.

262   "little green men":   Powell quoted in Cannon, *President Reagan*, 42.

262   "This is still a police state":   Reagan quoted in George J. Church, "A Gentle
      Battle of Images," *Time*, June 13, 1988, p. 21.

263   "I was talking":   Reagan quoted in Lou Cannon, "Russians, Reagan: Sizing Up:
      'It's Better to See Once Than to Hear 100 Times,'" *Washington Post*, June 1, 1988,
      p. A1.

263   "We do not know what the conclusion":   Reagan, "Remarks and a Question-
      and-Answer Session with the Students and Faculty at Moscow State Univer-
      sity, May 1, 1988," transcript at http://www.presidency.ucsb.edu/ws/index.
      php?pid=35897&st=.

263   "has convinced himself":   *Manchester Union Leader* quoted in Jason Manning,
      Material Things: An Encyclopedia of the 1980s at http://eightiesclub.tripod.com/
      id337.htm.

265   "I'm following Mr. Reagan—blindly":   Bush quoted in Sidney Blumenthal,
      Pledging Allegiance: The Last Campaign of the Cold War (New York, 1990), 51.

266   "straddler":   Gerald M. Boyd, E. J. Dionne Jr., and Bernard Weinraub, "Bush vs.
      Dole: Behind the Turnaround," *New York Times*, March 17, 1988, p. A1.

266   "There's nothing there":   Dole quoted in Blumenthal, *Pledging Allegiance*, 91.

266   "We should seize":   Cuomo quoted ibid., 212.

268   "Massachusetts miracle":   David S. Broder, "Lessons of Defeat, Victory and
      Growth," *Washington Post*, June 29, 1987, p. A1.

269   "the only colorless Greek in America":   Sahl quoted in James Patterson, *Rest-*

less Giant: The United States from Watergate to Bush v. Gore (New York, 2005), 221.

269 "this election is not about ideology": "The Democrats in Atlanta; Transcript of the Speech by Dukakis Accepting the Democrats' Nomination," *New York Times*, July 22, 1988, p. A10.

269 "wimp": Margaret Garrard Warner, "Bush Battles the 'Wimp Factor,'" *Newsweek*, October 19, 1987, p. 28.

269 "Poor George": "Transcript of the Keynote Address by Ann Richards, the Texas Treasurer," *New York Times*, July 19, 1988, p. 18.

269 "out of the loop": Bush quoted in Joel Brinkley, "Bush's Role in Iran Affair: Questions and Answers," *New York Times*, January 29, 1988, p. A1.

269 "mistakes were made": Bush quoted in "The White House Crisis: 'We Gotta Take Our Lumps,' Excerpts from Speech by Bush in Capital: 'And If the Truth Hurts, So Be It,'" *New York Times*, December 4, 1986, p. A14. The connections would have been even clearer at the time had Bush complied with investigators' requests and handed over a damning personal diary covering the years 1985 and 1986. The diary would remain under lock and key until 1992.

270 "Read my lips: no new taxes!": Bush, "Address Accepting the Presidential Nomination at the Republican National Convention in New Orleans, August 18, 1988," at http://www.presidency.ucsb.edu/ws/index.php?pid=25955&st=.

270 "collectivism"; "weakness in defense": Quoted in R. W. Apple Jr., "The Republicans in New Orleans: Bush Chooses Senator Quayle of Indiana, A 41-Year-Old Conservative, for No. 2 Spot," *New York Times*, August 17, 1988, p. A1.

270 "pastel patriotism": "Kean Keynote Speech: 'Seasoned,' 'Steady' Bush," *New York Times*, August 17, 1988, p. A21.

270 "We are the change": Reagan, "Remarks at the Republican National Convention in New Orleans, Louisiana, August 15, 1988," at http://www.presidency. ucsb.edu/ws/index.php?pid=36273&st=.

271 "Oliver North in civilian clothes": Ed Rollins with Thomas M. Defrank, *Bare Knuckles and Back Rooms: My Life in American Politics* (New York, 1996), 125. "You start out in 1954 by saying, 'Nigger, nigger, nigger,'" Atwater told an interviewer in 1981. "By 1968 you can't say 'nigger'—that hurts you. Backfires. So you say stuff like forced busing, states' rights and all that stuff. You're getting so abstract now [that] you're talking about cutting taxes, and all these things you're talking about are totally economic things and a byproduct of them is [that] blacks get hurt worse than whites." Quoted in Bob Herbert, "Impossible, Ridiculous, Repugnant," *New York Times*, October 6, 2005, p. A37.

271 "revolving door prison policies": Bush quoted in David Hoffman, "Bush Made 'Good Decision' on Quayle," *Washington Post*, October 9, 1988, p. A19. The ads overlooked the fact that other states—including California during Ronald Reagan's tenure as governor—as well as the federal prison system had long since adopted similar furlough programs. Nor did the Dukakis campaign do much to clarify reality.

271 "a *card carrying* member of the ACLU":   Bush quoted in Anthony Lewis, "Freedom to Conform?" *New York Times*, August 18, 1988, p. 27.

271 "the L-word":   Reagan quoted in Steven V. Roberts "President Asserts Democrats Cloak Their True Colors," *New York Times*, July 24, 1988, p. 1.

272 "Don't step in":   Author's recollection.

272 "gone so far to the right":   Quotation in Blumenthal, *Pledging Allegiance*, 291.

272 "He's on their side":   Dukakis quoted in Robin Toner, "Dukakis Gets a Needed Boost for Campaign," *New York Times*, October 19, 1988, p. B7.

273 "That's history":   Bush quoted in David Hoffman, "Bush's Metamorphosis: From Loyal Subordinate to Self-Assured Leader," *Washington Post*, January 20, 1989, p. A1.

273 "Even Jesus Christ couldn't answer that question!":   Gorbachev quoted in Oberdorfer, *From the Cold War*, 321. In his memoir, Bush states that it was Reagan who, innocently, asked the question about perestroika, and that Gorbachev responded, "Have *you* completed all the reforms you need to complete?" Bush also writes that during the Washington summit in 1987 he had developed "a good feel for Gorbachev." George Bush and Brent Scoweroft, *A World Transformed* (New York, 1998), 5, 7.

273 "A better attitude":   Brinkley, ed., *Reagan Diaries*, 675, entry for December 7, 1988.

274 "On the left! On the left!":   Cannon, *President Reagan*, 710.

274 "Reaganism will eventually be seen":   Hugh Heclo quoted in William Schneider, "The Political Legacy of the Reagan Years," in Sidney Blumenthal and Thomas Byrne Edsall, eds., *The Reagan Legacy* (New York, 1988), 53.

274 "there was no 'Reagan revolution'":   William A. Niskanen, *Reaganomics: An Insider's Account of the Politics and the People* (New York, 1988), 363.

277 "an extraordinarily popular figure":   Jules Tygiel, *Ronald Reagan and the Triumph of American Conservatism* (New York, 1995), 235.

278 "would probably have meant":   Robert Kagan, *A Twilight Struggle: American Power and Nicaragua, 1977–1990* (New York, 1996), 723.

279 "making Central America":   Mark Falcoff, "Making Central America Safe for Communism," *Commentary*, June 1988, p. 17.

281 "national hero":   Michnik, conversation with the author, April 24, 2007.

281 "wishful thinking":   Will, "How Reagan Changed America," p. 13.

281 "a successful candidate":   Kennedy quoted in William C. Berman, *America's Right Turn: From Nixon to Bush* (Baltimore, MD, 1994), 143.

282 "closet tolerant":   Robert Kaiser, "This Puffed-Up Piety Is Perfectly Preposterous," *Washington Post*, March 18, 1984, p. C1.

282 "the greatest vacuum in American politics":   Buchanan quoted in Sidney Blumenthal, "Pat Buchanan and the Great Right Hope," *Washington Post*, January 8, 1987, p. C1.

283 "predominantly young white":   David M. O'Brien, "The Reagan Judges: His Most Enduring Legacy?" in Charles Jones, ed., *The Reagan Legacy: Promise and Performance* (Chatham, NJ, 1988), 75.

283 "use the budget deficit": Daniel Patrick Moynihan, "Reagan's Bankrupt Budget," *New Republic*, December 31, 1983, p. 18.

284 "If ever the constitutional democracy": Theodore Draper, "The Rise of the American Junta," *New York Review of Books*, October 8, 1987, p. 47.

285 "a national hero": Reagan quoted in Alessandra Stanley, "Faith in a True Believer," *Time*, February 16, 1987, p. 23.

285 "it was my idea in the first place": Reagan, "Informal Exchange with Reporters on the Budget, October 8, 1986," at http://www.presidency.ucsb.edu/ws/index.php?pid=36565&st=&st1=;.

285 "were constitutionally protected": *Report of the Congressional Committees Investigating the Iran/Contra Affair, with Supplementary, Minority, and Additional Views* (Washington, DC, 1987), 457.

286 "the vision thing"; "like any other": Frank Johnson, "Bush Beats About for Answer to the Wimp Factor," *Times* (London), February 16, 1988.

286 "The Cold War is over": Reagan quoted in Gil Troy, *Morning in America: How Ronald Reagan Invented the 1980s* (Princeton, NJ, 2005), 313.

287 "He was the one": Reagan quoted in Lou Cannon, "A Sentimental Journey," *Washington Post*, January 23, 1989, p. A2.

CHAPTER 10: REAGANISM AND REALISM

288 "He just melts under pressure": Reagan quoted in Lou Cannon, "Bush Wins the Boss' Respect," *Washington Post*, February 1, 1988, p. A2.

289 "Whiny": Ed Rollins with Tom DeFrank, *Bare Knuckles and Back Rooms: My Life in American Politics* (New York, 1996), 170.

289 "kinder, gentler": "The Republicans in New Orleans; Transcript of Bush Speech Accepting Nomination for President," *New York Times*, August 19, 1988, A14.

289 "wimp": "Fighting the 'Wimp Factor,'" *Newsweek*, October 19, 1987, cover.

289 "George Bush will not need": Maureen Dowd, "White House Memo: Unable to Out-Hero Bush, Democrats Just Join Him," *New York Times*, March 8, 1991.

290 "No policy can be effective for long": Cheney quoted in Karen Tumulty and Sara Fritz, "President, Panel Agree on Covert Action Rules," *Los Angeles Times*, August 8, 1987, p. 1.

290 "willingness to declare": George Bush and Brent Scowcroft, *A World Transformed* (New York, 1998), 12–13. Scowcroft, like many conservative ideologues as well as realists, suspected that Gorbachev was simply a front man for the old-line Stalinists in the Kremlin who wanted to use him to revitalize communism—thereby making the new Soviet leader, he wrote, "potentially more dangerous than his predecessors."

291 "ultimately fail": Cheney quoted in Bernard Weinraub, "Cheney Remarks on Soviet Future Ruffle the White House's Feathers," *New York Times*, May 2, 1989, p. A1.

291 "While angry rhetoric might be": Bush and Scowcroft, *World Transformed*, 89.

292 "a very clear message": Pelosi quoted in Marc Sandalow, "Human Rights Before

Trade; Pelosi's High-Stakes Stance on China," *San Francisco Chronicle*, May 9, 1994, p. A1.

292   "At a moment of passion":   Rosenthal quoted in John Robert Greene, *The Presidency of George Bush* (Lawrence, KS, 2000), 94.

292   "I don't think any single event":   Bush, "Remarks and a Question-and-Answer Session with Reporters on the Relaxation of East German Border Controls, November 9, 1989," at http://www.presidency.ucsb.edu/ws/index.php?pid=17783&st=&st1=. The president was equally measured and business-like out of public view. In a telephone conversation with the West German chancellor Helmut Kohl two days after the Berlin Wall began coming down, Bush expressed interest in the events, and Kohl offered a brief yet enthusiastic report—"It has the atmosphere of a festival," he said. Bush replied matter-of-factly, thanking West Germany for its handling of the outpouring, noting the increased importance of his forthcoming meeting with Gorbachev, saying that he would tell the press about Kohl's acknowledgment of the role played by the United States, and stressing how he wanted "to see our people continue to avoid especially hot rhetoric that might by mistake cause a problem." Memorandum of telephone conversation, November 10, 1989, White House Staff and Office Files, National Security Council, OA/ID CFO1731, George H. W. Bush Presidential Library. Bush, of course, was not alone, though he always tended to be more cautious than declamatory.

292   "Bush is formulating":   Gorbachev quoted in Don Oberdorfer, *From the Cold War to a New Era: The United States and the Soviet Union, 1983–1991* (Baltimore, MD, 1998), 384.

293   "unserious presidency":   Will quoted in R. W. Apple Jr., "Prudent Meets Timid: Bush's Critics Say He's Crossed the Line, but Public Still Sees Him as Presidential," *New York Times*, October 15, 1989, p. 1.

293   "good neighbor policy":   George F. Will, "Good Neighbor Policy," *Washington Post*, December 21, 1989, p. A29.

294   "the mindset of the American people":   Baker quoted in David Greenberg, "From Saigon to Baghdad," *New York Times Book Review*, March 14, 2004, p. 8.

294   "Terrorism, hostage-taking":   Bush, "Remarks at the Aspen Institute Symposium in Aspen, Colorado, August 2, 1990," at http://www.presidency.ucsb.edu/ws/index.php?pid=18731&st=.

295   "I'm running out of demons":   Powell quoted in Jim Wolff, "Powell: Running Out of Demons," *Army Times*, April 5, 1991.

296   "moral right":   Gorbachev, in "News Conference of President Bush and President Mikhail Gorbachev of the Soviet Union, June 3, 1990," at http://www.presidency.ucsb.edu/ws/index.php?pid=18549&st=.

297   "a kind of war":   Saddam Hussein quoted in Lawrence Freedman and Efriam Karsh, *The Gulf Conflict, 1990–1991: Diplomacy and War in the New World Order* (Princeton, NJ, 1993), 46.

297   "the 19th Province":   Saddam Hussein quoted in Susan Marquis, *Unconven-

tional Warfare: Rebuilding U.S. Special Operations Forces (Washington, DC, 1997), 227.

297   "totally unacceptable": Thatcher in "Remarks and a Question-and-Answer Session with Reporters in Aspen, Colorado, Following a Meeting with Prime Minister Margaret Thatcher of the United Kingdom, August 2, 1990," at http://www.presidency.ucsb.edu/ws/index.php?pid=18727&st=&st1=.

297   "This [is] no time": Margaret Thatcher, *The Downing Street Years* (New York, 1993), 824.

298   "the brutal and illegal": Bill Keller, "The Iraqi Invasion; Moscow Joins U.S. in Criticizing Iraq," *New York Times*, August 4, 1990, p. 6.

299   "the new Hitler": Mubarak quoted in Freedman and Karsh, *Gulf Conflict*, 98.

299   "the rapist of Kuwait": Bush quoted in Greene, *Presidency*, 122.

299   "he is no threat to us": Patrick Buchanan, "How the Gulf Crisis Is Rupturing the Right," syndicated column of August 25, 1990, in Micah L. Sifry and Christopher Cerf, eds., *The Gulf War Reader: History, Documents, Opinions* (New York, 1991), 213–215.

300   "mother of all battles": Alan Cowell, "Confrontation in the Gulf; Leaders Bluntly Prime Iraq for 'Mother of All Battles,'" *New York Times*, September 22, 1990, p. 4.

300   "We accept war": Aziz quoted in Bush and Scowcroft, *World Transformed*, 442.

302   "some kind of Ceaucescu scenario": Bush quoted in Greene, *Presidency*, 138.

302   "the Iraqi military and the Iraqi people": Bush, "Remarks to the American Association for the Advancement of Science, February 15, 1991," at http://www.presidency.ucsb.edu/ws/index.php?pid=19306&st=&st1=.

302   "principal recruiting device": Wolfowitz quoted in Karen DeYoung and Walter Pincus, "Despite Obstacles to War, White House Forges Ahead; Administration Unfazed by Iraq's Pledge to Destroy Missiles, Turkish Parliament's Rejection of Use of Bases," *Washington Post*, March 2, 2003, p. A18.

303   "new world order": Bush, "Address Before a Joint Session of the Congress on the Cessation of the Persian Gulf Conflict," March 6, 1991, at http://www.presidency.ucsb.edu/ws/index.php?pid=19364&st=&st1=.

304   "merit schools": Bush, "Address on Administration Goals Before a Joint Session of Congress, February 9, 1989," at http://www.presidency.ucsb.edu/ws/index.php?pid=16660&st=&st1=.

304   "break the mold": Alexander, "White House Fact Sheet on the President's Education Strategy, April 18, 1991," at http://www.presidency.ucsb.edu/ws/index.php?pid=19493&st=&st1=.

305   "boot camps": Quotation in Greene, *Presidency*, 72.

307   "déjà voodoo": Mortimer Zuckerman, "Déjà Voodoo All Over Again," *U.S. News and World Report*, October 9, 1989, p. 84.

308   "both the size"; "tax revenue increases": Bush, "Statement on the Federal Budget Negotiations, June 26, 1990," at http://www.presidency.ucsb.edu/ws/index.php?pid=18635&st=&st1=.

308   "He very explicitly": Gingrich quoted in Richard L. Berke, "Republicans Fear

a Kiss of Death as Bush Moves His Lips on Taxes," *New York Times*, June 27, 1990, p. A1.

309 "real spending reduction": Bush, "Remarks on the Federal Budget Negotiations, September 25th, 1990," at http://www.presidency.ucsb.edu/ws/index.php?pid=18859&st=&st1=.

309 "I'm not sure about the President": Conte quoted in David E. Rosenbaum, "The Budget Agreement; Bush Rejects Stopgap Bill After Budget Pact Defeat," *New York Times*, October 6, 1990, p. 1.

312 "high-tech lynching"; "lynched, destroyed, caricatured": Thomas quoted in "The Thomas Nomination; Excerpts from the Senate's Hearing on the Thomas Nomination," *New York Times,* October 12, 1991, p. 12.

312 "You were superb!": Bush to Simpson, October 15, 1991, OA/ID CF 00473, "Clarence Thomas Nomination (1)," Chief of Staff, John Sununu Files, George H. W. Bush Presidential Library.

313 "Chicken Kiev": Safire, "After the Fall," *New York Times*, August 29, 1991, p. A29.

313 "totalitarian methods": Bill Bradley, "Help the Russians, Not Gorbachev," *New York Times*, July 21, 1991, Section 4, p. 17.

315 "Our whole political problem": Fred Steeper to Bob Teeter, March 16, 1992, quoted in Greene, *Presidency*, 164.

315 "Buchanan may be": Ellis quoted in Sidney Blumenthal, "Pat Buchanan and the Great Right Hope," *Washington Post*, January 8, 1987, p. C1.

315 "King George": Buchanan quoted in Kevin Phillips, "Populists, Royalists, and the Trumpet of Revolt," *Washington Post*, February 23, 1992, p. C1.

316 "If [Perot] denied Bush the presidency": Quotation in Greene, *Presidency*, 167.

317 "It's just that simple": Perot quoted in "Getting Dizzy with Ross Perot," *New York Times*, October 27, 1992, p. A22. Perot did a good job of hiding evidence of how much of his personal fortune arose from cushy political deals, as well as strong-arm tactics and profiteering by Electronic Data Systems and its subsidiaries, objects of little-known investigations by the General Accounting Office in the early 1970s. He also managed to elude scrutiny of his past business calamities, including his management of the brokerage house DuPont Glore Forgan, which failed four years after Perot took command in the early 1970s.

318 "the pursuit of greed and self interest"; "their little children"; "Too many of the people": "Keynote Address of Governor Bill Clinton to the DLC's Cleveland Convention," May 6, 1991, at http://www.dlc.org/ndol_ci.cfm?kaid=86&subid=194&contentid=3166.

318 "Democrats for the Leisure Class"; "comb their hair": Jackson quoted in George J. Church, "Keeping the Faith," *Time*, August 18, 1986, p. 14.

320 "There is a religious war": Buchanan, "Speech to the Republican National Convention, Houston, Texas, August 17, 1992," at http://www.buchanan.org/pa-92-0817-rnc.html.

321 "bozos"; "This guy": Bush quoted in "The 1992 Campaign; In Their Own

Words," *New York Times*, October 30, 1992, p. A17. The charges about Clinton's student activities, first raised by the right-wing congressman Robert Dornan of California, drew the following comments from *Time* magazine: "In terms that recalled the red-baiting tactics of the McCarthy era, Bush told CNN talk-show host Larry King that Clinton should 'level with the American people on the draft, on whether he went to Moscow, how many demonstrations he led against his country from a foreign soil.' . . . Bush's comments marked the crescendo of a well-orchestrated campaign of rumors, leaks and innuendos. They ranged from wild suggestions of KGB links, to reports that Clinton had held multiple passports under different names while at Oxford, to dark hints that the young Arkansan may even have been planning to renounce his citizenship to avoid the draft. If Bush did have evidence for such charges that Clinton could not explain away, the results could be devastating. But so far no shadow of proof was forthcoming. . . . Few people were paying attention—except George Bush. In daily meetings with his top political advisers, the President pushed staffers to find ways to exploit Dornan's charges. Most of his advisers, deterred by Dornan's loose-cannon reputation and lack of proof, at first shied away from the allegations. But Bush just 'wouldn't let go,' says a top adviser, adding that the charges played on the President's aversion to anything he considers unpatriotic—'like the flag-burning thing.'" John Greenwald, "Anatomy of a Smear," *Time*, October 19, 1992, p. 28.

In fact, officials in the Bush campaign were pushing the effort beyond dropping "dark hints." It appears that in late September, James Baker, who was now directing campaign strategy, pressed the State Department to conduct an expedited search for Clinton's passport files, despite concerns about possible violations of privacy rights. On September 30, an official at the State Department, Elizabeth Tamposi, directed three subordinates to comb through the federal records in order to dig up dirt on Clinton. The search turned up only Clinton's passport application, with staple holes and a slight tear in one corner—evidence of nothing, but sufficient for Tamposi to work up a fanciful criminal referral to the Justice Department. News of the referral was leaked to *Newsweek*, which published the ominous story in early October, creating a pseudo scandal. Only rapid work by a Democratic congressional staffer, who tracked down the passport application and showed the ludicrous nature of the charge, prevented the report from turning into a major, and perhaps decisive, campaign issue. After the election, Baker felt so ashamed that he offered to resign.

The situation involved possibly serious criminal wrongdoing, and an investigation by an independent counsel was ordered. Fortunately for Bush, Baker, Tamposi, and the others involved, the three-judge selection panel, now headed by a hard-line conservative, Judge David Sentelle, chose another conservative hard-liner, a former U.S. attorney under Reagan, Joseph diGenova, who angrily dismissed any charges of criminal misconduct. DiGenova and his wife (and law partner) Victoria Toensing would later emerge as talking heads on television, as well as attorneys, on behalf of various conservative crusades—including, in 1998, the impeachment of President Bill Clinton. See Richard Pear, "Bush Aide Accused of Lying in Inquiry on Clinton Search," *New York Times*, December 22, 1992, p. A1; Walter Pincus, "White House Tied to Passport Search;Aim Was Clinton Letter, Tamposi Says," *Washington Post*, November 17, 1992, p. A1; Bob Woodward, *Shadow: Five Presidents and the Legacy of Watergate* (New York, 1997), 207–208.

CHAPTER 11: THE POLITICS OF CLINTONISM

323   "Slick Willie":   This slur seems to have been attached to Bill Clinton by Paul Greenberg, currently editor of the editorial page of the *Arkansas Democrat-Gazette*. See interview with Paul Greenberg, transcript available at http://www.pbs.org/wgbh/pages/frontline/shows/choice/bill/greenberg.html. Greenberg's account is affirmed in Kevin Merida, "It's Come to This: A Nickname That's Proven Hard to Slip," *Washington Post*, December 20, 1998, p. F1.

325   "not his place":   Broder quoted in Sally Quinn, "Not in Their Back Yard: In Washington, That Letdown Feeling," *Washington Post*, November 2, 1998, p. E1.

327   "investments":   Governor Bill Clinton and Senator Al Gore, *Putting People First* (New York, 1992), 4.

328   "[T]he *deficit* isn't the core problem":   Robert Reich, *Locked in the Cabinet* (New York, 1997), 29.

329   "like a laser beam":   Clinton quoted in R. W. Apple Jr., "The 1992 Elections: President Elect—The Overview: Clinton, Savoring Victory, Starts Sizing Up Job Ahead," *New York Times*, November 5, 1992, p. A1.

329   "don't ask, don't tell":   Sam Nunn quoted in Eric Schmitt, "Compromise on Military Gay Ban Gaining Support Among Senators," *New York Times*, May 12, 1993, p. A1.

330   "quota queen":   Clint Bolick, "Clinton's Quota Queen," *Wall Street Journal*, April 30, 1993, p. A1.

330   "supermajority":   See Michael Kramer, "Another Blown Opportunity," *Time*, June 14, 1993, p. 27.

331   "Travelgate":   See, for example, William Safire, "Scalpgate's Poetic Justice," *New York Times*, May 24, 1993, p. A15.

331   "to avoid being identified":   William Safire, "Blizzard of Lies," *New York Times*, January 8, 1996, p. 27.

332   "end welfare as we know it":   Clinton, "Acceptance Speech to the Democratic National Convention, July 16, 1992," at http://www.presidency.ucsb.edu/ws/index.php?pid=25958&st=.

334   "the entire tide of Western history":   Gingrich quoted in Gary Wills, "The Clinton Principle," *New York Times Magazine*, January 17, 1997, p. 28.

335   "giant sucking sound":   "The 1992 Campaign; Transcript of Second TV

Debate between Bush, Clinton and Perot," *New York Times*, October 16, 1992, p. A11.

336 "out of the loop": Bush quoted in Joel Brinkley, "Bush's Role in Iran Affair: Questions and Answers," *New York Times*, January 29, 1988, p. A1.

336 "profoundly troubling": Bush, "Proclamation 6518-Grant of Executive Clemency, December 24, 1992," at http://www.presidency.ucsb.edu/ws/index. php?pid=20265&st=.

336 "misleading impression": *Final Report of the Independent Council for Iran-Contra Matters* (Washington, DC, 1993), I, 474; also at http://www.fas.org/irp/off-docs/walsh/chap_28.htm. After the pardons, Bush refused to be interviewed by Walsh's investigators about the diary material, except over why the diary was not produced earlier. Deciding that such an interview "would not serve any basic investigative purpose," Walsh declined to accept Bush's conditions. Walsh also decided that, given the unlikelihood of now gaining an indictment against Bush, he would not proceed with any further criminal investigation of the president.

336 "that sends a signal": Clinton quoted in David Johnston, "The Pardons; Bush Pardons 6 in Iran Affair, Aborting a Weinberger Trial," *New York Times*, December 25, 1992, p. A1. These words might well have come back to haunt Clinton in later years, but seem to have been overlooked.

338 "another Somalia": Howard W. French, "Haitians Block Landing of U.S. Forces," *New York Times*, October 12, 1993, p. A1.

338 "The difficulty has been one side": Mark Huband, *The Skull Beneath the Skin: Africa After the Cold War* (Boulder, CO, 2001), 192.

339 "not have a dog in that fight": Baker quoted in Jane Perlez, "Showdown in Yugoslavia: The Diplomacy: Down the Years, A Slippery Foe Frustrated the U.S.," *New York Times*, October 8, 2000, p. 17.

340 "agreed framework": Alan Riding, "U.S. and North Korea Sign Pact to End Nuclear Dispute," *New York Times*, October 22, 1994, p. 5.

342 "new covenant": Floyd G. Brown, *"Slick Willie": Why America Cannot Trust Bill Clinton* (Annapolis, MD, and Washington, DC, 1993), 82–83. Brown, whose political involvements date back to Ronald Reagan's campaign in 1976, was chairman of the board of the right-wing group, Citizens United, and was one of the men who had been behind the notorious Willie Horton advertisement during the election of 1988. He also helped lead efforts to secure the nomination of Clarence Thomas to the Supreme Court. Brown, who is still active in the Republican Party, was a delegate to the party's national conventions in 1996 and 2000.

342 "a queer-mongering, whore-hopping": Jim Johnson quoted in James B. Stewart, *Blood Sport: The President and His Adversaries* (New York, 1997), 314.

343 "appears to suggest": Quotation in Joe Conason and Gene Lyons, *The Hunting of the President: The Ten-Year Campaign to Destroy Bill and Hillary Clinton* (New York, 2000), 44.

344 "to fuel Bill's political ambitions": "On Ethics: Arkansas Anxieties," *Wall Street Journal*, December 15, 1993, p. A1.

344   "This is a man":   "Open Up on Madison Guaranty," *New York Times*, December 20, 1993, p. A18.

345   "lance the boil":   Roger Altman quoting Lloyd Bentsen in Stewart, *Blood Sport*, 371.

346   "squish":   Quotation in Jeffrey Toobin, *A Vast Conspiracy: The Real Story of a Sex Scandal That Nearly Brought Down a President* (New York, 1999), 76.

348   "counter-cultural McGoverniks":   Gingrich quoted in John F. Harris, *The Survivor: Bill Clinton in the White House* (New York, 2005), 157.

348   "Definer of civilization":   Gingrich quoted in Andrew Ferguson, "Goodbye, Brave Newtworld," *Time*, November 16, 1998, p. 134. In 1994, Gingrich's political action committee, GOPAC, published a pamphlet, "Language: A Key Mechanism of Control," in which Gingrich offered a long list of words he thought useful for labeling Democrats, including "betray," "cheat," "collapse," "decay," "pathetic," "permissive," "sick," and "traitors."

348   "I am a transformational figure":   Gingrich quoted in Harris, *The Survivor*, 157.

348   "one-party control":   *The Republican Contract with America*, at http://www. house.gov/house/Contract/CONTRACT.html.

349   "I think [the voters]":   Clinton, "The President's News Conference, November 9, 1994," transcript at http://www.presidency.ucsb.edu/ws/index. php?pid=49468&st=.

350   "Democratic way of achieving":   Dick Morris, *Behind the Oval Office: Getting Reelected Against All Odds* (New York, 1998), 37–38.

350   "He *is* the underside":   Ickes quoted in Harris, *The Survivor*, 161.

351   "very burdened middle class":   Clinton quoted in Robin Toner, "Democrat Session Previews '92 Race," *New York Times*, May 8, 1991, p. A18.

351   "simplistic and hypocritical":   Bill Clinton, *My Life* (New York, 2004), 622.

351   "conservative opportunity society":   Adam Clymer, "House Revolutionary," *New York Times Magazine*, August 23, 1992, p. SM41.

351   "law of the jungle":   Clinton quoted in Harris, *The Survivor*, 160.

351   "You can have good policies":   Clinton, *My Life*, 632.

351   "new covenant"; "middle-class bill of rights":   Clinton, "Address Accepting the Presidential Nomination at the Democratic National Convention in New York, July 16, 1992," at http://www.presidency.ucsb.edu/ws/index. php?pid=25958&st=.

352   "your president":   Armey quoted in Katharine Q. Seelye, "Man in the News; Ascendance of an Improbable Leader—Richard Keith Armey," *New York Times*, December 6, 1994, p. B9.

352   "Barney Fag":   Armey quoted in Jerry Gray, "No. 2 House Leader Refers to Colleague with Anti-Gay Slur," *New York Times*, January 28, 1995, p. 1.

352   "rotten trick":   Armey quoted in David Maraniss, "Armey Arsenal: Plain Talk and Dramatic Tales," *Washington Post*, February 21, 1995, p. A1.

352   "the control of the New World Order":   Chenoweth quoted in Timothy Egan, "Terror in Oklahoma: In Congress; Trying to Explain Contract with Paramilitary Groups," *New York Times*, May 2, 1995, p. A19.

352 "justifiable homicide": Quotation in David C. Trosch, "Justifiable Homicide," letter addressed to the U.S. Congress, July 16, 1994. Feminist Majority Foundation, "1994 Clinic Violence Survey Report," at http://www.feminist.org/research/cvsurveys/cv_main.html.

352 "The Constitution gives me relevance": Clinton, "The President's News Conference, April 18, 1995," at http://www.presidency.ucsb.edu/ws/index.php?pid=51237&st=.

353 "Let us let our own children": Clinton, "Remarks at a Memorial Service for the Bombing Victims in Oklahoma City, Oklahoma," April 23, 1995, at http://www.presidency.ucsb.edu/ws/index.php?pid=51265&st=.

353 "There is nothing patriotic": Clinton, "Remarks at the Michigan State University Commencement Ceremony in East Lansing, Michigan, May 5, 1995," at http://www.presidency.ucsb.edu/ws/index.php?pid=51317&st=.

CHAPTER 12: CLINTON'S COMEBACK

355 "the most explicitly ideologically committed": Gingrich quoted in E. J. Dionne Jr., *They Only Look Dead: Why Progressives Will Dominate the Next Political Era* (New York, 1996), 222.

355 "conservative opportunity society": Adam Clymer, "House Revolutionary," *New York Times Magazine*, August 23, 1992, p. SM40.

357 "the first crisis of the twenty-first century": Gingrich quoted in Robert Rubin with Jacob Weisberg, *In an Uncertain World: Tough Choices from Wall Street to Washington* (New York, 2003), 16.

358 "like a kitten with a string": Patricia Schroeder quoted in Adam Clymer, "Whether Friend or Foe, Most Think Clinton Is Playing Politics on the Budget," *New York Times*, June 16, 1995, p. A24.

358 "No quotas in theory or practice": Clinton, "Remarks at the National Archives and Records Administration, July 19, 1995," at http://www.presidency.ucsb.edu/ws/index.php?pid=51631&st=.

358 "as common as apple pie": Clinton, "Remarks at the James Madison High School in Vienna, Virginia, July 12, 1995," at http://www.presidency.ucsb.edu/ws/index.php?pid=51608&st=.

358 "We have to do": Clinton, "The President's Radio Address, August 5, 1995," at http://www.presidency.ucsb.edu/ws/index.php?pid=51714&st=.

359 "The congressional majority"; "How can you talk": Ibid.

359 "They can't really believe that": Clinton quoted in John F. Harris, *The Survivor: Bill Clinton in the White House* (New York, 2005), 190.

360 "Fairly or unfairly": Albright quoted in Sidney Blumenthal, *The Clinton Wars* (New York, 2003), 153.

360 "not a bomb or two": Perry quoted in Derek Chollet, *The Road to the Dayton Accords: A Study of American Statecraft* (New York, 2005), 26.

360 "I'm risking my presidency": Clinton quoted in Bob Woodward, *The Choice* (New York, 1996), 265.

362 "a basic shift toward traditional America": Gingrich quoted in John E. Yang and Eric Pianin, "House Approves Bill to Balance Budget," *Washington Post*, October 27, 1995, p. A1.

364 "People feeling confident": Newt Gingrich, *Lessons Learned the Hard Way* (New York, 1998), 55.

364 "The era of big government is over"; "But we can't go back"; "one America": Clinton, "Address Before a Joint Session of the Congress on the State of the Union, January 23, 1996," at http://www.presidency.ucsb.edu/ws/index.php?pid=53091&st=.

364 "sweeping welfare reform"; "really move"; "near agreement": Ibid.

365 "end welfare as we know it": Clinton, "Address Accepting the Presidential Nomination at the Democratic National Convention in New York, July 16, 1992," at http://www.presidency.ucsb.edu/ws/index.php?pid=25958&st=.

367 "a decent welfare bill": Clinton quoted in Harris, *Survivor*, 238.

367 "serious flaws"; "to make welfare": Clinton, "Remarks on Welfare Reform Legislation and an Exchange with Reporters, July 31, 1996," at http://www.presidency.ucsb.edu/ws/index.php?pid=53140&st=.

367 "the most brutal act of social policy": Moynihan, congressional press release, March 4, 1996, quoted in Harris, *Survivor*, 234.

368 "the tax collector for the welfare state": Gingrich quoted in Helen Dewar, "Republicans Wage Verbal Civil War; Gingrich Leads Rebels," *Washington Post*, November 19, 1984, p. A1.

368 "a man devoid of vision": Blumenthal, *Clinton Wars*, 160.

368 "nearly ruined our party": Goldwater quoted in Anthony Lewis, "Merchants of Hate," *New York Times*, July 15, 1994, p. A27.

368 "We're the new liberals": Barry Goldwater quoted in Katherine Q. Seelye, "In Visit to Arizona, Senator Emphasizes Goldwater Roots," *New York Times*, February 26, 1996, p. B7.

368 "without a helmet": Dole quoted in Blumenthal, *Clinton Wars*, 162.

369 "a time of tranquility": Dole quoted in Richard L. Berke, "The Republicans: The Overview; Dole, 'The Most Optimistic Man in America,' Vows Return to Nation's Enduring Values," *New York Times*, August 16, 1996, p. A1.

369 "a bridge to the twenty-first century": Clinton, "Remarks Accepting the Presidential Nomination at the Democratic National Convention in Chicago, August 29, 1996," at http://www.presidency.ucsb.edu/ws/index.php?pid=53253&st=.

369 "Where is the outrage?": Dole quoted in Katharine Q. Seelye, "Dole Is Imploring Voters to 'Rise Up' Against the Press," *New York Times*, October 26, 1996, p. 1.

370 "A Stolen Election,": Paul Gigot, "A Stolen Election," *Wall Street Journal*, October 17, 1997, p. 1.

370 "vital American center": Clinton, "Remarks at a Victory Celebration in Little Rock, Arkansas, November 5, 1996," at http://www.presidency.ucsb.edu/ws/index.php?pid=52218&st=.

370 "free left": Arthur M. Schlesinger Jr., *The Vital Center: The Politics of Freedom* (Boston, MA, 1949), 130.

370 "vital center"; "dead center":   Arthur M. Schlesinger Jr., *A Life in the Twentieth Century: Innocent Beginnings, 1917–1950* (Boston, MA, 2000).

370 "Good luck":   Hillary Rodham Clinton, *Living History* (New York, 2003), 396. The first lady added: "Something about his tone made me think we would need it." Other reports state that Rehnquist actually added, "You'll need it."

371 "the fiscal equivalent":   James Bennet, "The Balanced Budget: The Overview; Clinton Will Seek Balanced Budget in '99 Instead of '02," *New York Times*, January 6, 1998, p. A1.

371 "no one who recalled":   Harris, *The Survivor*, 432.

372 "on the threshold":   Clinton, "Remarks at the Princeton University Commencement Ceremony in Princeton, New Jersey," June 4, 1996, at http://www.presidency.ucsb.edu/ws/index.php?pid=52906&st=.

373 "bully pulpit":   Clinton, "The President's News Conference, November 10, 1993," transcript at http://www.presidency.ucsb.edu/ws/index.php?pid=46092&st=.

373 "initiative on race" :   Clinton, "Remarks at a Democratic National Committee Dinner, June 16, 1997," at http://www.presidency.ucsb.edu/ws/index.php?pid=54273&st=.

376 "*Jihad* [or, Holy War]":   Bin Laden, available at http: www.washingtonpost.com/ac2/wp-dyn?pagename=article&node=&contentId=A4993-2001Sep21.

376 "smoking gun":   D'Amato quoted in Stephen Labaton, "Clinton Aide Removed Files About Legal Work on S&L," *New York Times*, December 12, 1995, p. A1.

377 "uplifting, indeed heroic story":   Leach quoted in *The Failure of Madison Guaranty Savings and Loan Association and Related Matters—Part 3, Hearing Before the Committee on Banking and Financial Services, House of Representatives, One Hundred Fourth Congress, First Session, August 8*, 1995 (Washington, DC, 1996), 1.

378 "wimp":   William Safire, "The Big Flinch," *New York Times*, January 20, 1997, p. A23.

378 "extensive evidence":   Starr quoted in Neil A. Lewis, "Whitewater Counsel Says He Has Evidence of Obstructing Justice," *New York Times*, April 23, 1997, p. A1.

378 "They're going to screw you":   Clinton quoted in Blumenthal, *Clinton Wars*, 192.

379 "politically motivated":   "Excerpts from Supreme Court Ruling on a Lawsuit Against the President," *New York Times*, May 28, 1997, p. A16.

379 "laughingstock":   Bennett quoted in Peter Baker, "Clinton Lawyer Suggests Way to Settle Jones Case; Payment to Charity, but No Apology, Proposed," *Washington Post*, June 2, 1997, p. A1.

379 "Okay, good":   Carpenter-McMillan quoted in Lloyd Grove, "Cause Celebre; An Antiabortion Activist Makes Herself the Unofficial Mouthpiece for Paula Jones," *Washington Post*, July 23, 1997, p. C1.

380 "vanilla language":   Carpenter-McMillan quoted in Peter Baker, "Paula Jones Lawyers Ask to Quit Case," *Washington Post*, September 9, 1997, p. A1.

380 "We were terrified":   Coulter quoted in Michael Isikoff, *Uncovering Clinton: A Reporter's Story* (New York, 1999), p. 183.

380 "a small, intricately-knit": Coulter quoted in Joe Conason and Gene Lyons, *The Hunting of the President: The Ten-Year Campaign to Destroy Bill and Hillary Clinton* (New York, 2000), 302.

380 "distinguishing characteristic": "Clinton Makes Firm Denial in Sexual Harassment Case," *New York Times*, July 4, 1997, p. A12.

380 "baseless and easily refutable": Bennett quoted in "Clinton's Attorney Denies Jones' Claim of 'Distinguishing Characteristics,'" *Washington Post*, October 8, 1997, p. A14.

380 "My question would be": Carpenter-McMillan quoted ibid.

CHAPTER 13: ANIMOSITIES AND INTEREST: THE IMPEACHMENT OF CLINTON

382 "less than sex but more than kissy-face": Emanuel quoted in John F. Harris, *The Survivor: Bill Clinton in the White House* (New York, 2006), 315.

383 "This beautiful capital": Clinton, "Inaugural Address, January 20, 1993," at http://www.presidency.ucsb.edu/ws/index.php?pid=46366&st=.

383 "vast right-wing conspiracy": Clinton, interview with Matt Lauer, *Today*, NBC, January 27, 1998, quoted in David Maraniss, "First Lady Launches Counterattack; Prosecutor called 'Politically Motivated' Ally of 'Right-Wing' Conspiracy," *Washington Post*, January 28, 1998, p. A1.

383 "bringing down the president": Coulter quoted in Michael Isikoff, *Uncovering Clinton: A Reporter's Story* (New York, 1999), 183.

383 "using the criminal justice system": Clinton, interview with Matt Lauer, in Maraniss, "First Lady Launches Counterattack."

386 "an author and prominent": Alison Mitchell, "Gingrich Draws Well in a Democratic Stronghold, Hollywood," *New York Times*, January 16, 1998, p. A13.

387 "They didn't lay a glove on him": Bennett quoted in Sidney Blumenthal, *Clinton Wars* (New York, 2003), 319.

387 "sexual relations": Clinton was lucky that the lawyer's questions were not even more pointed. Fisher could have asked him any number of direct embarrassing queries about the physical specifics of the sexual encounters, which would have forced Clinton to lie beyond cavil. Instead, Fisher stuck to a convoluted definition of "sexual relations," based on an even more confusing definition that Jones's lawyers offered at the start of the deposition so that they could avoid using more graphic language. Clinton was also lucky that Judge Susan Webber Wright, at his lawyer Bennett's request, agreed to attend the deposition. At the outset, Judge Wright simplified the definition of "sexual relations" proposed by Jones's team—a ruling which inadvertently allowed Clinton to claim that he had not had sexual contact with Lewinsky because (he asserted) he received oral sex from her without touching her genitals or breasts. The claim defied adult common sense, and it contradicted Lewinsky's own subsequent testimony—but it was Clinton's story, he stuck to it, and nobody, even Lewinsky, could prove it a lie.

389 "Well, we just have to win then": Clinton quoted in Dick Morris, grand jury
testimony, August 18, 1998, in *The Starr Report: The Findings of the Independent Counsel Kenneth W. Starr on President Clinton and the Lewinsky Affair* (New
York, 1998), 149.

390 "strong performance": Livingston quoted in John Harris, "Clinton Pledges Activist Agenda," *Washington Post*, January 28, 1998, p. A1.

391 "We're drifting": McIntosh quoted in Katherine Q. Seelye, "Gingrich Continues to Reach Out to GOP Conservatives," *New York Times*, April 11, 1997, p.
A22.

392 "a man of courtliness and character": John F. Dickerson, "A Nice Guy in a
Nasty Fight," *Time*, October 12, 1998, p. 34.

394 "devastating"; "tawdriness": "Shame at the White House," *New York Times*,
September 12, 1998, p. A18.

394 "and it will be our sad duty": Gephardt in Jeffrey Toobin, *A Vast Conspiracy:
The Real Story of the Sex Scandal That Nearly Brought Down a President* (New
York, 1999), 332.

395 "It was all about sex": Lowell quoted ibid., 335.

395 "which may with peculiar propriety": Hamilton in Clinton Rossiter, ed., *The
Federalist Papers* (New York, 1961), 396.

396 "biblical world view": DeLay quoted in Alan Cooperman, "DeLay Criticized
for 'Only Christianity' Remarks," *Washington Post*, April 20, 2002, p. A5.

397 "What can we do?": Hyde quoted in Toobin, *Vast Conspiracy*, 346.

397 "unlawfully intruded": Sam Dash, "Letter of Resignation from Ethics Adviser
and Starr's Letter in Response," *New York Times*, November 21, 1998, p. A10.

398 "Coming out of the election": King quoted in Blumenthal, *Clinton Wars*, 539.

398 "Larry Flynted": Livingston quoted in Richard Lacayo, "Washington Burning," *Time*, December 28, 1998, p. 60.

399 "You resign! You resign!": Ibid.

399 "if, after this culture war is over": Hyde in "Trial of William Jefferson Clinton,
President of the United States," *Congressional Record—Senate*, February 8, 1999.
106th Congress, 1st Session, 145 Cong Rec S 1337, Vol. 145, No. 22, S. Res. 30,
S1365.

400 "We are here today": Bumpers in "Trial of William Jefferson Clinton, President
of the United States," *Congressional Record—Senate*, January 21, 1999. 106th
Congress, 1st Session, 145 Cong Rec S 832, Vol. 145, No. 9, S. Res. 16, S845.

400 "total lack of proportionality": Ibid., S846.

401 "Morally serious men and women": Hyde in "Trial of William Jefferson Clinton, President of the United States," *Congressional Record—Senate*, January 16,
1999, 106th Congress, 1st Session, 145 Cong Rec S 281, Vol. 145, No. 7, S. Res.
16, S299.

402 "the pre-existing factions"; "all their animosities"; "there will always be": Hamilton in Rossiter, ed., *Federalist Papers*, 396.

404 "tank plinking": Interview with General Michael C. Short, transcript at http://
www.pbs.org/wgbh/pages/frontline/shows/kosovo/interviews/short.

406 "make any significant difference":   Kissinger quoted in an interview with Margaret Warner, "Mission Accomplished?" *PBS NewsHour*, December 21, 1998, transcript at http://www.pbs.org/newshour/bb/middle_east/july-dec98/iraq; sf12-21.html.

406 "A more telling display":   Daniel Benjamin and Steven Simon, *Age of Sacred Terror: Radical Islam's War Against America* (New York, 2002), 323–324.

406 "not some narrow":   Richard Clarke to Condoleezza Rice (memorandum), January 25, 2001, quoted in National Commission on Terroist Attacks upon the United States, *The 9/11 Commission Report* (New York, 2004), 201.

407 "Never before has our nation enjoyed":   Clinton, "Address Before a Joint Session of the Congress on the State of the Union," January 27, 2000, at http://www. presidency.ucsb.edu/ws/index.php?pid=58708&st=&st1=.

CHAPTER 14: IRREPARABLE HARM: THE ELECTION OF 2000

409 "models":   In 1997, the Nashville *Tennessean* inaccurately reported, on the basis of an interview with Segal, that the Gores were the models for his leading characters. Gore noticed the report and mentioned it to two journalists at the time—not knowing that Segal had been misquoted. *Time* magazine contacted Segal for verification, and Segal clarified the *Tennessean*'s garbled quotation: Gore was one of the models for one character but Tipper was not a model for any character. *Time* reported the story in December with the implication that Gore had fabricated everything. "Al attributed [the story] to a newspaper. *Time* thought it was more piquant to leave that out," Segal observed soon afterward. See Melinda Henneberger, "Author of 'Love Story' Disputes a Gore Story," *New York Times*, December 14, 1997, p. 40. In March 1999, researchers for the Republican National Committee (RNC) unearthed the story in *Time* and began sending out faxes to the media about Gore's impulsive boasting. Eventually, both the *Boston Globe* and the *New York Times* reported the matter, drawing on the inaccurate version in *Time* as hyped by the RNC.

On November 30, 1999, visiting a high school in New Hampshire, Gore urged the students to take an active interest in politics. Thanks to a letter from a student, he said, he had been alerted to the dangers of toxic waste in the student's hometown—Toone, Tennessee. He then found out about Love Canal and went to work on the toxic waste problem. "Had the first hearing on that issue, and Toone, Tennessee—that was the one you didn't hear of. But that was the one that started it all." While taking credit for holding hearings, he did not claim that he was the first official to discover Love Canal, which had already been evacuated; rather, he listed it as the most famous of the disasters discussed at the hearings prompted by the student's letter about Toone. But the next day, the *Washington Post* reported that "Gore boasted about his efforts in Congress 20 years ago to publicize the dangers of toxic waste." Without mentioning Toone or the student's letter, the *Post* continued: " 'I found a little place in upstate New York called Love Canal,' he said, referring to the Niagara homes evacuated in

August 1978 because of chemical contamination. 'I had the first hearing on this issue. . . . ' Gore said his efforts made a lasting impact. . . . 'I was the one that started it all.'" The *New York Times* also reported the false quotation, but edited the grammar: "I was the one who started it all." The eager Republicans spread the alarm by fax. "Al Gore is simply unbelievable—in the most literal sense of that term," James Nicholson, the chairman of the RNC, proclaimed. Numerous pundits—including Chris Matthews on CNBC, Ceci Connolly in the *Washington Post*, George Stephanopoulos, William Kristol, and Cokie Roberts on ABC—repeated the misrepresentation about Gore and Love Canal as if it were true, and ridiculed the candidate as self-deluded or a liar. For a review of these and Gore's other alleged exaggerations and lies, see Sean Wilentz, "Will Pseudo-Scandals Decide the Election?" *American Prospect*, September 25–October 9, 2000, pp. 45–50.

410 "I don't know why": Reich quoted in Robert Parry, "He's No Pinocchio," *Washington Monthly*, April 2000, p. 23.

410 "Somewhere along the line": Halperin quoted in Howard Kurtz, "By Stepping Aside, Gore Stands Out," *Washington Post*, December 23, 2002, p. C1.

412 "champagne unit": David Barstow, "In the Haze of Guard Records, a Bit of Clarity," *New York Times*, February 15, 2004, p. N24.

413 "misunderestimate": Bush, "The President's News Conference," March 29, 2001, at http://www.presidency.ucsb.edu/ws/index.php?pid=45705&st=.

413 "awe-struck": Tom Hamburger and Peter Wallsten, "Uproar Has Roots in Rove's Vast Reach," *Los Angeles Times*, July 13, 2005. Rove was fired from George H. W. Bush's reelection campaign of 1992 because, campaign officials said, he had leaked some damaging information about Bush's Texas campaign chairman and close friend Robert Mosbacher to a friendly reporter— namely, Robert Novak. The event would receive fleeting notice in 2005, when a leak to Novak sparked the affair concerning the former ambassador Joseph Wilson, which eventually led to the conviction of "Scooter" Libby for perjury.

414 "illegitimate"; "black": Glenn Frankel, "The McCain Makeover; Does the Veteran Republican Rebel Really Mean All Those Nice Things He's Saying About George W. Bush?" *Washington Post Magazine*, August 27, 2006, p. W12.

414 "They know no depths, do they?": McCain quoted in Mark Sherman and Ken Herman, "McCain Blasts Bush Ad Blitz," *Atlanta Journal and Constitution*, March 5, 2000, p. 3B.

414 "reformer with results": Howard Kurtz, "Team Bush's Very Defensive Strategy," *Washington Post*, March 6, 2000, p. C1.

415 "compassionate conservatism": Bush, "Texas Gov. George W. Bush's Acceptance Speech; They Have Not Led. We Will," *Washington Post*, August 4, 2000, p. A20.

415 "the soft bigotry of low expectations": Ibid.

415 "a uniter, not a divider": Bush quoted in Rich Lowry, "'I'm a Uniter, Not a Divider,' Bush Talks About Rising Above It All. But That's No Way to Govern," *Washington Post*, October 29, 2000, p. B1.

416 "nation-building": Bush quoted in "The 2000 Campaign: Second Presidential Debate Between Governor Bush and Vice President Gore," *New York Times*, October 12, 2000, p. A22.

416 "lock box": Gore quoted in "The 2000 Campaign; Transcript of Debate Between Vice President Gore and Governor Bush," *New York Times*, October 4, 2000, p. A30.

417 "immoral": Lieberman quoted in Elaine Sciolino, "For Lieberman, 'Loyalty' Is to the Public Interest," *New York Times*, September 4, 1998, p. A18.

418 "I agree": Gore quoted in "The 2000 Campaign: Second Presidential Debate Between Governor Bush and Vice President Gore," p. A22.

420 "scrubbed": See Sean Wilentz, "Jim Crow, Republican Style," in Andrew Cuomo, ed., *Crossroads: The Future of American Politics* (New York, 2003), 278–284, which carries forward to controversies about the suppression of voters in the elections of 2002.

421 "Sore Loserman 2000": David Barstow, "Counting the Vote: The Parties; Voting Battle Threatens Florida's Uneasy Truce Between Political Parties," *New York Times*, November 20, 2000, p. A15.

421 "Safe Harbor": David Greenberg, "What's the Rush?" *Salon*, December 13, 2000. As Greenberg points out, contests in 1960 over the allocation of Hawaii's electoral votes following an extremely close result in the popular vote continued long after the "Safe Harbor" date.

423 "arbitrary . . . contrary to law": Supreme Court of Florida, *Palm Beach Canvassing Board, Petitioner, v. Katherine Harris, etc., et al., Respondents*. November 21, 2000, at http://www.presidency.ucsb.edu/docs/florida2000/11-21_fla_opinion.pdf.

423 "to change the rules": Baker quoted in Frank Bruni, "Bush Camp, Outraged, Vows to Seek Recourse to Ruling," *New York Times*, November 22, 2000, p. A1.

424 "Shut it down!": Sweeney quoted in Jonathan Schell, "Vesuvius," *The Nation*, December 18, 2000, p. 4.

424 "If it's possible": Paul Gigot, "Burgher Rebellion: GOP Turns Up Miami Heat," *Wall Street Journal*, November 24, 2000, p. A16. The following evening, the Bush campaign treated the rioters to free food and drink at a hotel in Fort Lauderdale. Both Bush and Cheney congratulated the revelers by phone hookup, and the Las Vegas lounge singer Wayne Newton provided entertainment including a rendition of "Danke Schoen." A few of the rioters later had important positions in George W. Bush's administration. They included Matt Schlapp (special assistant to the president and later political director at the White House); Garry Malphrus (deputy director of the White House Domestic Policy Council, appointed a federal immigration judge in 2005); and Rory Cooper (White House Homeland Security Council).

425 "that are of questionable legality": Scalia in *George W. Bush and Richard Cheney v. Albert Gore, Jr., et al.,* No. 00-949 (00A504), Supreme Court of the United

States, 531 U.S. 1046; 121 S. Ct. 512; 148 L. Ed. 2d 553; 2000 U.S. LEXIS 8277; 69 U.S.L.W. 3396, December 9, 2000.

425 "How can you have one standard":   Ginsberg quoted in "Contesting the Vote; Excepts from Arguments Before Supreme Court on the Florida Recount," *New York Times*, December 12, 2000, p. A27; also at http://www.pbs.org/newshour/election2000/scotus/olson2_12-11.html. The sources disagree over which justice actually posed this question; the *Washington Post* reported that it was Justice O'Connor, and some sources have repeated the claim. See Edward Walsh, "On the Minds of the Court's Nine," *Washington Post*, December 12, 2000, p. A34; see also http://www.presidency.ucsb.edu/showflorida2000.php?fileid=12-11_us_supreme_transcript.

426 "in violation of the Florida election code":   *George W. Bush and Richard Cheney, Petitioners v. Albert Gore, Jr., et al.,* No. 00-949, Supreme Court of the United States, 531 U.S. 98; 121 S. Ct. 525; 148 L. Ed. 2d 388; 2000 U.S. LEXIS 8430; 69 U.S.L.W. 4029, December 12, 2000.

427 "very disappointed":   *Newsweek* magazine, for example, reported that, at a party on Election Night, Justice Sandra Day O'Connor was overheard to express horror at early returns that seemed to presage a victory by Gore. The article described her husband, John, explaining that the couple had wanted to retire to Arizona but that a Gore victory meant they would have to wait another four years. "She's very disappointed," he said, "because she was hoping to retire"—but with a Republican president in office to appoint her successor. Another report said that at a social gathering on the evening of December 4, after the Supreme Court had released its first opinion on the election, O'Connor railed against "the Gore people," and repeated unproved accusations about vote fraud by Democrats, which previously "had circulated only in the more eccentric right-wing outlets." See Evan Thomas and Michael Isikoff, "The Truth Behind the Pillars," *Newsweek*, December 25, 2000/January 1, 2001, p. 46; Richard K. Neumann Jr., "Conflicts of Interest in Bush v. Gore: Did Some Justices Vote Illegally?" *Georgetown Journal of Legal Ethics*, 16 (2003): 375–443.

427 "the nation's confidence in the judge":   Stevens, dissenting, in *George W. Bush and Richard Cheney, Petitioners v. Albert Gore, Jr., et al.* Had the Court heeded the previous examples of deadlocked presidential elections—in 1800, 1824, and 1876—it would have deferred to Congress to decide the matter. Given the Republican majorities in the outgoing House and Senate, a Republican victory might have been anticipated—although neither party controlled an absolute majority of the individual House delegations. In any event, though, the process would have been more democratic, if much messier, than the one the Court majority arrogated to itself. As is suggested by the history of the *Dred Scott* decision—where hard evidence of improper political tampering, which had been widely suspected, actually surfaced decades after the case was decided—it could be many years before the entire story of partisanship and *Bush v. Gore* is known.

428   "Hail to the Thief!":   Joel Achenbach, "In This Political Theater, a Supporting Cast of Thousands," *Washington Post*, January 21, 2005, p. A19.

EPILOGUE: OCTOBER 13, 2001

433   *"High water risin'"*:   Bob Dylan, "High Water (for Charley Patton)," copyright © 2001 Special Rider Music.

433   "I can hear you":   Bush, "Remarks to Police, Firemen, and Rescue Workers at the World Trade Center Site in New York City, September 14, 2001," at http://www.presidency.ucsb.edu/ws/index.php?pid=65078&st=.

434   "whether we bring":   Bush, "Address Before a Joint Session of the Congress on the United States Response to the Terrorist Attacks of September 11, September 20, 2001," at http://www.presidency.ucsb.edu/ws/index.php?pid=64731&st=.

435   "[T]he idea of reducing Congress":   Fein quoted in Jane Mayer, "Letter from Washington: The Hidden Power," *New Yorker*, July 3, 2006, p. 44.

437   "On taxes, ":   Bill Keller, "The Radical Presidency of George W. Bush; Reagan's Son," *New York Times Magazine*, January 26, 2003, p. 26.

438   "I just can't think": Ibid.

438   "the fruition of Reagan": Ibid.

438   "There is no precedent":   DiIulio quoted in Ron Suskind, "Why Are These Men Laughing?" *Esquire*, January 2003, p. 96.

439   "The election of President Bush":   Jeffords quoted in John Lancaster and Helen Dewar, "Jeffords Tips Senate Power; Democrats Prepare to Take Over as Vermont Senator Quits GOP," *Washington Post*, May 25, 2001, p. A1.

440   "Bin Laden Determined":   Tom Shales, "Cool, Calm Condoleezza Rice," *Washington Post*, April 9, 2004, p. C1.

440   "the system was blinking red":   Tenet quoted in National Commission on Terrorist Attacks upon the United States, *The 9/11 Commission Report* (New York, 2004), 259.

440   "historical":   Ibid., 260.

440   "All right":   Bush quoted in Ron Suskind, *The One Percent Doctrine: Deep Inside America's Pursuit of Its Enemies Since 9/11* (New York, 2006), 2.

440   "[T]here is a resolve and a spirit":   Bush, "Remarks at a Town Hall Meeting in Ontario, California, January 5, 2002," at http://www.presidency.ucsb.edu/ws/index.php?pid=62589&st=.

440   "traitors to their own faith":   Bush, "Address Before a Joint Session of the Congress . . . Response to the Terrorist Attacks of September 11."

440   "crusade":   Bush, "Remarks on Arrival at the White House and an Exchange with Reporters, September 16, 2001," at http://www.presidency.ucsb.edu/ws/index.php?pid=63346&st=.

440   "Either you are with us":   Bush, "Address Before a Joint Session of Congress . . . Response to the Terrorist Attacks of September 11."

441   "We can go to the country":   Rove quoted in Thomas B. Edsall, "GOP Touts War as Campaign Issue; Bush Advisor Infuriates Democrats with Strategy Outlined at RNC Meeting," *Washington Post*, January 19, 2002, p. A2.

442 "dark side": Cheney, interview on *Meet the Press*, NBC, September 16, 2001, transcript at http://www.whitehouse.gov/vicepresident/news-speeches/speeches/vp20010916.html.

442 "quaint": "Excerpts from Gonzales's Legal Writings," *New York Times*, November 11, 2004, p. A30.

442 "vague": Bush, "The President's News Conference, September 15, 2006," at http://www.presidency.ucsb.edu/ws/index.php?pid=861&st=.

442 "cakewalk": Ken Adelman, "Cakewalk in Iraq," *Washington Post*, February 13, 2002, p. A27.

442 "every corner of the world": Bush in *The National Security of the United States of America, September* 2002 (Washington, DC, 2002), v.

443 "There is a higher father": Bush quoted in Bob Woodward, *Plan of Attack* (New York, 2004), 421.

443 "weapons of mass destruction"; "We don't want the smoking gun": Rice quoted in Todd S. Purdum, "Threats and Responses: The Administration; Bush Officials Say the Time Has Come for Action on Iraq," *New York Times*, September 9, 2002, p. A1.

444 "major combat": Bush, "Address to the Nation on Iraq from the USS *Abraham Lincoln*, May 1, 2003," at http://www.presidency.ucsb.edu/ws/index.php?pid=68675&st=.

444 "a Christian who actually acts": Quotation in Richard Reeves, e-mail archive, at http://www.richardreeves.com/email_archive.html.

445 "For bureaucratic reasons": Wolfowitz quoted in Sam Tanenhaus, "Bush's Brain Trust," *Vanity Fair*, July 2003, p. 114.

447 "heck of a job": Bush, "Remarks on the Aftermath of Hurricane Katrina in Mobile, Alabama, September 2, 2005," at http://www.presidency.ucsb.edu/ws/index.php?pid=64973&st=.

448 "I was told"; "Why would you": Carmona quoted in Gardiner Harris, "Surgeon General Sees 4-Year Term as Compromised," *New York Times*, July 11, 2007, p. A1.

448 "last throes": Dick Cheney, interview with Larry King, *Larry King Live*, CNN, May 30, 2005, transcript at http://transcripts.cnn.com/TRANSCRIPTS/0505/30/lkl.01.html.

450 "institutionalize the Reagan revolution": Meese quoted in Lee Edwards, *The Conservative Revolution: The Movement That Remade America* (New York, 1999), 237.

451 "unsettlingly like the Democrats did": Karen Tumulty, "How the Right Went Wrong," *Time*, March 15, 2007, p. 26.

451 "It's gone": Rollins quoted in David D. Kirkpatrick, "Shake, Rattle, and Roil: The Grand Ol' Coalition," *New York Times*, December 30, 2007, section 4, p. 1.

451 "destroying the Republican Party": Simpson quoted in Adam Nagourney and John Broder, "Some in GOP Express Worry over '08 Hopes," *New York Times*, April 11, 2007, p. A1.

451 "run hard enough or fast enough": Edwards quoted ibid.

453   "distasteful"; "denigrating": "Unite, Not Divide, This Time," *New York Times,* January 9, 2008, p. A18; "Race and Politics," *New York Times*, January 17, 2007, p. A30.

453   "cumulative trajectory":   Crocker quoted in Daniel Henninger, "Iraq Hearings Prove Dems Should Move On," OpnionJournal.com from the *Wall Street Journal*, September 13, 2007, at http://www.realclearpolitics.com/articles/2007/09/ Iraq_hearings_prove_Dems_need.html.

453   "a nightmare":   David S. Cloud, "Ex-Commander Calls Iraq Effort 'A Nightmare,'" *New York Times*, October 13, 2007, p. A1.

454   "In the long history":   Philip Shenon, "Interim Leaders Increasingly Run Federal Agencies," *New York Times*, October, 15, 2007, p. A1.

456   "if you're interested":   Bush quoted in Gay Stolberg, "Nuclear-Armed Iran, Risks 'World War III,' Bush Says," *New York Times,* October 18, 2007, p. A1.

457   "going back to the Great Depression":   Michael M. Grynbaum, "Home Prices Sank in 2007, and Buyers Hid," *New York Times*, January 25, 2008, p. C5.

458   "The future":   Arthur M. Schlesinger Jr., *The Politics of Hope* (Boston, MA, 1963), 20.

458   "History":   Bush quoted in Woodward, *Plan of Attack,* 443.

458   "Fellow-citizens, *we* cannot escape":   Abraham Lincoln, "Annual Message to Congress, December 1, 1862," in Roy P. Basler, ed., *The Collected Works of Abraham Lincoln* (New Brunswick, NJ, 1953), V, 537.

SELECTED SOURCES
AND READINGS

Some of the topics covered in this book—the Nixon administration (especially the Watergate scandal); the rise of the conservative movement; the end of the cold war; the attacks of September 11 and the ensuing war on terror—are each the subject of a large and contentious literature. Other topics, particularly the ups and downs of the Reagan administration, are now receiving their due. Still others, especially events that occurred during the presidencies of George H. W. Bush and Bill Clinton, have only just begun to receive serious historical study.

The Age of Reagan has relied chiefly on the public record contained in official reports and transcripts, and on newspapers, newsmagazines, and journals of opinion, as well as on secondary sources. It has also drawn on memoirs and autobiographies. Whenever possible, I have checked the secondary sources against the official record to ensure accuracy in reporting and analysis. I have also supplemented these sources at important junctures with archival research, to fill in important gaps. The interpretations, however, are my own, and I take sole responsibility for their shortcomings.

The following sources and readings were among those I found the most useful.

PRIMARY SOURCES

Because this book largely concerns the view from Washington, the presidential libraries for the administrations covered have been essential resources, much as they have for many of the scholarly studies on which this book has drawn. Despite the daunting task of processing and cataloging mountains of material, compounded by restrictions on the public release of material, the archivists and staff of the National Archives and Records Administration do an excellent job at making available to researchers what sources they can. Because so much of the available material in the Ford and Carter libraries has already been combed through by historians, I have consulted the libraries' respective holdings on very specific topics, as indicated in my notes. The most severe of the latest restrictions, adopted in November 2001, apply to the period after 1980. Fortunately, some important documents were released through requests made in accordance with the Freedom of Information Act (FOIA) before those restrictions came into effect, and the libraries have opened these papers (as well as much smaller amounts of material requested under FOIA and released since then) to all researchers. I thus was able to consult worthwhile material in the holdings of the Reagan and George H. W. Bush libraries. Even then, however, I discovered that some documents, still considered highly classified, have been withdrawn from the files. These range from material on obviously sensitive topics such as Oliver North's activities relating to Nicaragua to seemingly innocuous matters such as the budget negotiations in 1990. The Clinton library had just begun processing interesting material when I began work; scholars will want to consult important collections there as they become open.

The National Security Archive at George Washington University has done a fine job of gaining the declassification of significant documents on American foreign and security policy, as well as previously unobtainable documents from the Soviet Union, and making some of the most important of them available online at: http://www.gwu.edu/~nsarchiv/.

Modern political historians have long relied on the imposing series *Public Papers of the Presidents* for the official transcripts of speeches, press conferences, and other formal and informal presidential texts. The American Presidency Project overseen by John Woolley and Gerhard Peters at the University of California at Santa Barbara has now made all those volumes, and a great deal more, easily accessible online at the project's Web site, http://www.presidency.ucsb.edu/. Bowing to the wonders of the Internet, I have abandoned a long-standing practice and in my notes directed readers to the relevant URLs either at the Santa Barbara site or at other sites where official material is easy to find.

I made extensive use of newspaper and magazine holdings from the 1970s onward, especially those of the *New York Times*, the *Washington Post, Newsweek*, and *Time*. Journals of conservative and neoconservative opinion were of enormous value, especially for the years from the late 1970s through the early 1990s, above all *National Review, Commentary*, and the *Public Interest* (later the *National Interest*), supplemented in more recent years by the *Weekly Standard*. Newsletters and articles by the main conservative and right-libertarian think tanks, including the Heritage Foundation, the American Enterprise Institute, and the Cato Institute, also helped me trace the political course of the right. Liberal and neoliberal opinion (along with a dose of neoconservatism, especially in the 1990s) appeared in the *New Republic*. Early neoliberal articles also appeared in *Washington Monthly*. Farther to the left, the most reliable weekly source is the *Nation*. From social democratic and left-liberal perspectives, there are revealing and perceptive articles in *Dissent*, supplemented since 1990 by the *American Prospect*.

GENERAL WORKS

As the book went to press, the historical study that best covered most of the events treated here was James Patterson's *Restless Giant: The United States from Watergate to Bush v. Gore* (New York, 2005). Thorough and judicious, Patterson's book describes all the major political events of the period and aligns them with larger cultural and social trends. It should, though, be supplemented with Godfrey Hodgson's more analytical and argumentative studies, *The World Turned Right Side Up: A History of the Conservative Ascendancy in America* (Boston, MA, 1996); and *More Equal Than Others: America from Nixon to the New Century* (Princeton, NJ, 2004). See also E. J. Dionne Jr., *Why Americans Hate Politics* (New York, 1991), which incisively examines both the failure of liberalism and what the author calls the emergence of a "conservative impasse" from the 1960s through the elections of 1988. There are also several other useful general studies on portions of the period, including William C. Berman, *America's Right Turn: From Nixon to Clinton* (1993; Baltimore, MD, 1998); John Ehrman, *The Eighties: America in the Age of Reagan* (New Haven, CT, 2006); Philip Jenkins, *Decade of Nightmares: The End of the Sixties and the Making of Eighties America* (New York, 2006); Michael Schaller, *Right Turn: American Life in the Reagan-Bush Era* (New York, 2007); Bruce J. Schulman, *The Seventies: The Great Shift in American Culture, Society, and Politics* (New York, 2001); and Gil Troy, *Morning in America: How Ronald Reagan Invented the 1980s* (Princeton, NJ, 2005).

PROLOGUE

On Richard Nixon and his long career, Stephen E. Ambrose's three-volume study, *Nixon—The Education of a Politician, 1912–1962* (New York, 1991); *The Triumph of a Politician, 1962–1972* (New York, 1991); and *Ruin and Recovery, 1972–1990* (New York, 1992)—is greatly informative if disputable on various interpretations. Garry Wills, *Nixon Agonistes: The Crisis of the Self-Made Man* (1970; New York, 2002), is remarkable for its ambition, range, and acute observation, and remains stimulating nearly forty years after it first appeared. I also found undimmed good sense and sharp analysis in another classic work, covering the quarter century before Nixon's election, Godfrey Hodgson, *America in Our Time: From World War II to Nixon, What Happened and Why* (New York, 1976). *The Age of Reagan: The Fall of the Old Liberal Order, 1964–1980* (New York, 2001), by Steven Hayward, is marred by its one-sided polemical tone but includes a great deal of astute analysis and valuable detail, especially on the 1970s. Fred Siegel's terser *Troubled Journey: From Pearl Harbor to Ronald Reagan* (New York, 1984) covers a longer period and is also full of shrewd appraisals.

There are now scores of books and articles on the Johnson years and the collapse of the liberalism of the 1960s. In addition to Hodgson's *America in Our Time*, listed above, readers should start with Allen Matusow, *The Unraveling of America: A History of Liberalism in the 1960s* (New York, 1984). A briefer and more recent assessment appears in H. W. Brands, *The Strange Death of American Liberalism* (New Haven, CT, 2001). On Lyndon Johnson, the contrasting, distinguished, multivolume biographies by Robert Caro (still in progress) and Robert Dallek have now been joined by Randall B. Woods's perceptive and sympathetic *LBJ: Architect of Ambition* (New York, 2006). On conservatives' reactions to the reformism of the 1960s and the rise of the southern strategy, it is most useful to read the closest thing to a primary source: Kevin Phillips, *The Emerging Republican Majority* (New Rochelle, NY, 1969). Regarding what is conventionally referred to as the liberal consensus of the 1960s, one important local study on a crucial northern constituency dates the first signs of the collapse of that consensus much earlier, in the 1950s and even the 1940s, chiefly because of civil rights issues and racial divisions: Thomas J. Sugrue, *The Origins of the Urban Crisis: Race and Inequality in Post-War Detroit* (1996; Princeton, NJ, 2005).

On the Watergate scandals and their fallout, there are books from several political persuasions (written with varying degrees of scholarly care), as well as several straightforward narratives. (This is not to mention memoirs, which include books by everyone from the chief "plumber," E. Howard Hunt, to Nixon himself.) I found that the closest attention to the available sources—some of which the author himself helped make available to researchers and the public—was paid in Stanley I. Kutler's *The Wars of Watergate: The Last Crisis of Richard Nixon* (New York, 1990) and *Abuse of Power: The New Nixon Tapes* (New York, 1997); as well as in Fred Emery, *Watergate: The Corruption of American Power and the Fall of Richard Nixon* (New York, 1994). Still indispensable, not only for their documentation but for their sense of watching history unfold, are the report of the special Senate investigating committee headed by Senator Sam Ervin and later published as *The Senate Watergate Report* (New York, 2004); and the House Judiciary Committee report: U.S. House. Committee on the Judiciary, *Impeachment of Richard M. Nixon, President of the United States: Report of the Committee on the Judiciary, House of Representatives, Peter W Rodino, Jr., Chairman*, 93rd Cong., 2d Sess. August 20, 1974 (Washington, DC, 1974). On changing memories and interpretations of Watergate, see Michael Schudson, *Watergate in American Memory: How We Remember, Forget, and Reconstruct the Past* (1992; New York, 2005), which corrects numerous stubborn myths and explains how they came to be.

The account here of the bicentennial celebrations of 1976 draws chiefly on reports in the *New York Times*, July 1–6, 1976.

FORD (CHAPTERS 1 AND 2)

John Robert Greene, *The Presidency of Gerald R. Ford* (Lawrence, KS, 1995), is the best place to begin any study of the Ford administration. Greene has also provided a useful bibliography, *Gerald Ford: A Bibliography* (Westport, CT, 1994). See also the interpretation in Yanek Mieczkowski, *Gerald Ford and the Challenges of the* 1970s (Lexington, KY, 2005). Bernard Firestone and Alexj Ugrinsky, *Gerald R. Ford and the Politics of Post-Watergate America* (Westport, CT, 1993), is an important two-volume collection of reflections by administration officials and historians on numerous topics, drawn from a conference held at Hofstra University in 1989. Also useful are the recollections in Kenneth W. Thompson, ed., *The Ford Presidency: Twenty-Two Intimate Perspectives of Gerald Ford* (Lanham, MD, 1988). Less helpful is another collection of conference papers, Herbert Storing, ed., *The Ford White House* (Lanham, MD, 1986). See also a stimulating scholarly work by a member of Ford's staff, A. James Reichley, *Conservatives in an Age of Change: The Nixon and Ford Administrations* (Washington, DC, 1981), which gives the Ford administration much higher marks in domestic affairs than in foreign policy.

Among biographies, Richard Reeves, *A Ford, Not a Lincoln* (New York, 1975), appeared while Ford was still in office and is especially hard on the president for his pardon of Nixon, a verdict Reeves has since rejected. A briefer and more sympathetic account, concentrating on the presidential years, appears in Douglas Brinkley, *Gerald R. Ford* (New York, 2007). On the prepresidential years, see also Edward L. Schapsmaeier and Frederick H. Schapsmaeier, *Gerald R. Ford's Date with Destiny: A Political Biogra-*

phy (New York, 1989). On the specifics of Ford's elevation as minority leader in 1965, in which Representative Donald Rumsfeld played a leading role, see Henry Z. Scheele, "An Examination of the Gerald R. Ford–Charles A. Halleck House Minority Leadership Contest," *Presidential Studies Quarterly*, 25 (1995): 767–785.

Several memoirs and autobiographies cast light on Ford's career, and especially his presidency, from very different angles. First and foremost, obviously, is *A Time to Heal: The Autobiography of Gerald R. Ford* (New York, 1979), ghostwritten by Trevor Ambrister. Of uncommon importance for its insights about the tensions with the Ford White House and other matters is Robert Hartmann, *Palace Politics: An Insider's Account of the Ford Years* (New York, 1980). Other works of varying value include John J. Casserly, *The Ford White House: The Diary of a Speechwriter* (Boulder, CO, 1977); James A. Cannon, *Time and Chance: Gerald Ford's Appointment with History* (New York, 1994); David Hume Kennerly, *Shooter* (New York, 1979); and Ron Nessen, *It Sure Looks Different from the Inside* (Chicago, IL, 1978). On foreign policy, Henry A. Kissinger, *Years of Renewal* (New York, 1999), is indispensable, if sometimes predictable. (Its title is misleading, as the Ford years saw a steady unraveling of Kissingerian foreign policy far more than any renewal.) Although surprisingly lacking in literary flair, Betty Ford with Chris Chase, *The Times of My Life* (New York, 1978), reveals another side of the president and his administration.

On the politics and complex negotiations surrounding the pardoning of Nixon and the early days of Ford's presidency, see Robert Sam Anson, *Exile: The Unquiet Oblivion of Richard M. Nixon* (New York, 1984), as well as the relevant portions of Stanley Kutler's *Wars of Watergate*, listed above. An investigative article by Seymour Hersh, "The Pardon: Nixon, Ford, Haig, and the Transfer of Power," *Atlantic*, August 1983, pp. 55–78, included the first details of Ford's pre-resignation talks with Alexander Haig about a possible pardon. On Ford's proposal of clemency, see Lawrence Baskir and William A. Strauss, *Chance and Circumstance: The Draft, the War, and the Vietnam Generation* (New York, 1978). Tragically, Cary Reich died before he could write a second volume to follow his excellent *The Life of Nelson A. Rockefeller: Worlds to Conquer, 1908–1958* (New York, 1996); but see Michael Turner, *The Vice President as Policy Maker: Rockefeller in the Ford White House* (Westport, CT, 1982).

The economic and energy policies of the Ford administration have yet to receive full scholarly treatment, but I found much useful information and analysis in Roger B. Porter, *Presidential Decision Making: The Economic Policy Board* (Cambridge, MA, 1980); and Herbert Stein, *Presidential Economics: The Making of Economic Policy from Roosevelt to Reagan and Beyond* (New York, 1984). Andrew D. Moran, "Gerald R. Ford and the 1975 Tax Cut," *Presidential Studies Quarterly*, 26 (1996): 738–754, treats the sudden reversal of course on fiscal policy. See also John W. Sloan's brief overview of the political and ideological direction of Ford's economic policy, in "The Ford Presidency: A Conservative Approach to Economic Management," *Presidential Studies Quarterly*, 14 (1984): 526–537. William E. Simon, *A Time for Truth* (New York, 1978), is disappointingly tendentious; see also Simon's *A Time for Reflection: An Autobiography* (Washington, DC, 2004), written with John M. Caher. Alan Greenspan's memoir, *The Age of Turbulence: Adventures in a New World* (New York, 2007), appeared too late for me to incorporate it thoroughly in my thinking, but has a great deal of important information. Martin J. Shefter, *Political Crisis/Fiscal Crisis: The Collapse and Revival of New York City* (New York, 1985), is the best study of a tangled subject; but see also Robert W. Bailey, *The Crisis Regime: The New York City Financial Crisis* (Albany, NY, 1984).

The approach of the Ford administration to school desegregation is concisely and astutely covered in Lawrence J. McAndrews, "Missing the Bus: Gerald Ford and School Desegregation," *Presidential Studies Quarterly*, 27 (1997): 791–804. The outstanding work on the busing crisis in Boston, as seen from multiple angles, is J. Anthony Lukas, *Common Ground: A Turbulent Decade in the Lives of Three American Families* (New York, 1985); but see also Ronald P. Formisano, *Boston Against Busing: Race, Class, and Ethnicity in the 1960s and 1970s* (1991; Chapel Hill, NC, 2004).

On the CIA and the investigations into its abuses, I found a good deal of forceful and sober assessment in William Colby, *Honorable Men: My Life in the CIA* (New York, 1978), although the author plainly wished to defend his record before and after he became the director of the CIA. On the inquiries in particular, see Frank J. Smist Jr., *Congress Oversees the United States Intelligence Community, 1947–1989* (Knoxville, TN, 1990). Kathrun Olmstead, "Reclaiming Executive Power: The Ford Administration's Response to the Intelligence Investigations," *Presidential Studies Quarterly*, 26 (1996): 725–737, helps place the inquiries and the efforts by the White House to contain them in the context of the broader battle over executive power that began with Vietnam and Watergate and has now continued into the war on terror.

Important studies of U.S. foreign policy in the immediate aftermath of the Vietnam War include Robert S. Litwak, *Détente and the Nixon Doctrine: American Foreign Policy and the Pursuit of Stability, 1969–1976* (Cambridge, MA, 1984); and William C. Ryland, *Mortal Rivals: Superpower Relations from Nixon to Reagan* (New York, 1987). For two views of Henry Kissinger, see Walter Isaacson, *Kissinger: A Biography* (New York, 1992); and Roger Morris, *Uncertain Greatness: Henry Kissinger and American Foreign Policy* (New York, 1977).

On the end of U.S. involvement in Southeast Asia, see Arnold R. Isaacs, *Without Honor: Defeat in Vietnam and Cambodia* (New York, 1981). Two articles are sharply critical of the administration's role in the denouement: T. Christopher Jesperson, "The Bitter End and the Lost Chance in Vietnam: Congress, the Ford Administration, and the Battle over Vietnam, 1975–1976," *Diplomatic History*, 24 (2000): 265–293; and Jesperson, "Kissinger, Ford, and Congress: The Very Bitter End in Vietnam," *Pacific Historical Review*, 71 (2002): 429–473.

On Middle East policy, William S. Quandt, *Decade of Decisions: American Policy Toward the Arab-Israeli Conflict, 1967–1976* (Berkeley, CA, 1977), offers an overview. On U.S.-Soviet relations, the place to start is Raymond Garthoff's massive *Détente and Confrontation: American-Soviet Relations from Nixon to Reagan* (Washington, DC, 1985). There is a strong chapter in Paula Stern, *Domestic Politics and the Making of American Foreign Policy* (Westport, CT, 1979), about the gradual shift away from détente. The SALT II negotiations are well covered in John Newhouse, *War and Peace in the Nuclear Age* (New York, 1989).

For contrasting views of the *Mayaguez* affair, consult Richard Head et al., *Crisis*

Resolution: Presidential Decision Making in the Mayaguez and Korean Confrontations (Boulder, CO, 1978); and Christopher Jon Lamb, *Belief Systems and Decision Making in the Mayaguez Crisis* (Gainesville, FL, 1988). The Solzhenitsyn affair awaits its historian. Vojtech Mastny, ed., *Helsinki, Human Rights, and European Security* (Durham, NC, 1986), is cogent and excellent. Barry Werth, *31 Days: The Crisis That Gave Us the Government We Have Today* (New York, 2006), is suggestive about Donald Rumsfeld, Dick Cheney, and their role in the Ford White House, but is of limited significance because it stops more than a year before the "Halloween massacre." On the events of October–November 1975, see the materials cited in my notes, especially the reporting of Lou Cannon.

On the campaign of 1976, useful works by journalists include Elizabeth Drew, *American Journal: The Events of 1976* (New York, 1976); and Jules Witcover, *The Pursuit of the Presidency, 1972–1976* (New York, 1977). Craig Shirley, *Reagan's Revolution: The Untold Story of the Campaign That Started It All* (Nashville, TN, 2005), is a strongly pro-Reagan account with a good deal of telling information about the Republican primaries. Farley Yang, "Turning a Runaway into a Race: The Role of Foreign Policy Issues in the 1976 Republican Primaries," *Michigan Journal of Political Science*, 7 (1986): 107–128, emphasizes the political effectiveness of Reagan's bellicose charges and rhetoric on the Panama Canal and foreign affairs in general. On Ford's campaign, see Malcolm Mac-Dougall, *We Almost Made It* (New York, 1977). On Carter's, see Martin Schram, *Running for President, 1976: The Carter Campaign* (New York, 1977); and Patrick Anderson, *Electing Jimmy Carter: The Campaign of 1976* (Baton Rouge, LA, 1994).

CARTER (CHAPTERS 3 AND 4)

Burton I. Kaufman's *The Presidency of James Earl Carter, Jr.* (1993; Lawrence, KS, 2006) is the fullest treatment of Carter's administration. It should be supplemented with the sympathetic accounts in Erwin C. Hargrove, *Jimmy Carter as President: Leadership and the Politics of the Public Good* (Baton Rouge, LA, 1988); and Charles O. Jones, *The Trusteeship Presidency: Jimmy Carter and the United States Congress* (Baton Rouge, LA, 1988). There is useful bibliographic information in George J. Lankevich, *James E. Carter, 1924–: Chronology, Documents, Bibliographical Aids* (Dobbs Ferry, NY, 1981). Two important collections of essays are M. Glenn Abernathy, Dilys Hill, and Phil Williams, eds., *The Carter Years: The President and Policymaking* (New York, 1984); and Gary M. Fink and Hugh Davis Graham, eds., *The Carter Presidency: Policy Choices in the Post–New Deal Era* (Lawrence, KS, 1988). There are also some suggestive essays in Frye Gaillard, *The Unfinished Presidency: Essays on Jimmy Carter* (Wingate, NC, 1986). An astute appraisal, sharply critical but fair, appears in Haynes Johnson, *In the Absence of Power: Governing America* (New York, 1980). See also the compendium of interviews in Kenneth W. Thompson, ed., *The Carter Presidency: Fourteen Intimate Perspectives of Jimmy Carter* (Lanham, MD, 1990.)

The fullest biography is Peter G. Bourne, *Jimmy Carter: A Comprehensive Biography from Plains to Post-Presidency* (New York, 1997). Readers may also wish to consult Betty Glad, *Jimmy Carter: In Search of the Great White House* (New York, 1980), for valuable details through the election of 1976; as well as William Lee Miller, *Yankee from Georgia: The Emergence of Jimmy Carter* (New York, 1978), which captures some of what I have described as Carter's "southern progressive" political outlook. Also highly suggestive is Leo P. Ribuffo, "Jimmy Carter and the Ironies of American Liberalism," *Gettysburg Review*, 1 (1988): 739–749. Related works, which examine Carter in relation to the New Deal tradition and come to very different conclusions (as much about the tradition as about Carter), are William Leuchtenberg, *In the Shadow of FDR: From Harry Truman to Ronald Reagan* (Ithaca, NY, 1983); and Alonzo Hamby, *Liberalism and Its Challengers: FDR to Reagan* (New York, 1985). For a different take, stressing the shortcomings of Carter's management and operational style, see Richard E. Neustadt, *Presidential Power: The Politics of Leadership from FDR to Carter* (New York, 1980). Carter's religious views have received nearly as much attention as his politics; I found particularly useful Niels C. Nielsen, *The Religion of President Carter* (Nashville, TN, 1977); and Wesley G. Pippert, *The Spiritual Journey of Jimmy Carter: In His Own Words* (New York, 1978). On Reinhold Niebuhr's influence, see Frank A. Ruechel, "Politics and Morality Revisited: Jimmy Carter and Reinhold Niebuhr," *Atlanta History*, 37 (1994): 19–31.

Carter's memoir, *Keeping Faith: Memoirs of a President* (New York, 1982), is helpful on the high points of his presidency, including the Camp David summit of 1978, but slim on other matters. There are numerous memoirs by members of the administration, including Griffin Bell with Ronald J. Ostrow, *Taking Care of the Law* (New York, 1982); Joseph A. Califano Jr., *Governing America: An Insider's Report from the White House and the Cabinet* (New York, 1981); Hedley Donovan, *Roosevelt to Reagan: A Reporter's Encounter with Nine Presidents* (New York, 1985); Hamilton Jordan, *Crisis: The Last Year of the Carter Presidency* (New York, 1982); Bert Lance with Bill Gilbert, *The Truth of the Matter: My Life In and Out of Politics* (New York, 1991); Jody Powell, *The Other Side of the Story* (New York, 1984); and Stansfield Turner, *Secrecy and Democracy: The CIA in Transition* (Boston, MA, 1985). The history of Carter's foreign policy is copiously covered in Zbigniew Brzezinski, *Power and Principle: Memoirs of the National Security Adviser, 1977–1981* (New York, 1983); and Cyrus Vance, *Hard Choices: Critical Years in America's Foreign Policy* (New York, 1983). Rosalynn Carter's memoir, *First Lady from Plains* (Boston, MA, 1984), also contains a good deal of information on policy and on political as well as personal matters.

On events at the other end of Pennsylvania Avenue, see the relevant chapters in Thomas P. O'Neill with William Novak, *Man of the House: The Life and Political Memoirs of Speaker Tip O'Neill* (New York, 1987). Carter's difficulties with Congress are covered from very different points of view in Mark Peterson, *Legislating Together: The White House and Capitol Hill from Eisenhower to Reagan* (Cambridge, MA, 1990); Nelson Polsby, *Consequences of Party Reform* (New York, 1983); and William E. Mullen, "Perceptions of Carter's Legislative Successes and Failures: Views from the Hill and the Liaison Staff," *Presidential Studies Quarterly*, 12 (1982): 522–544.

On what I have called anti-politics and on the role of Pat Caddell in Carter's rise to the presidency, Sidney Blumenthal, *The Permanent Campaign: Inside the World of Elite Political Operatives* (Boston, MA, 1980), is essential.

Foreign policy under Carter is in general better covered than domestic policy. On various specific domestic matters, see Laurence E. Lynn Jr. and D. F. Whitman, *The President as Policymaker: Jimmy Carter and Welfare Reform* (Philadelphia, PA, 1982); Harold L. Wolman and Astrid E. Merget, "The Presidency and Policy Formulation: President Carter and the Urban Policy," *Presidential Studies Quarterly*, 10 (1980): 402–415; W. Carl Biven, *Jimmy Carter's Economy: Policy in an Age of Limits* (Chapel Hill, NC, 2001); Anthony S. Campagna, *Economic Policy in the Carter Administration* (Westport, CT, 1995). In Abernathy, Hill, and Williams, eds., *The Carter Years*, see: Dilys Hill, "Domestic Policy," 13–34, Stephen Wollcock, "The Economy," 35–53; and M. Glenn Abernathy, "The Carter Administration and Domestic Civil Rights," 106–122. On the Bakke case, see Joel Dreyfuss and Charles Lawrence III, *The Bakke Case: The Politics of Inequality* (New York, 1979). On energy policy and the drift into the "malaise" speech, see J. William Holland, "The Great Gamble: Jimmy Carter and the 1979 Energy Crisis," *Prologue*, 22 (1990): 63–69; and Robert Strong, "Recapturing Leadership: The Carter Administration and the Crisis of Confidence," *Presidential Studies Quarterly*, 16 (1986): 636–660.

Readers interested in the rise of the "new right" should begin with Godfrey Hodgson's, *The World Turned Right Side Up*, mentioned above, as well as Sidney Blumenthal, *The Rise of the Counter-Establishment: From Conservative Ideology to Political Power* (New York, 1986); and George H. Nash, *The Conservative Intellectual Movement since 1945* (1976; Wilmington, DE, 1996). Much of the impetus for the new conservatism came from state and local developments, as has been shown in several fine recent studies, including Lisa McGirr, *Suburban Warriors: The Rise of the New American Right* (Princeton, NJ, 2001); and Kevin M. Kruse, *White Fight: Atlanta and the Rise of Modern American Conservatism* (Princeton, NJ, 2005). On the emergence of the neoconservative movement, see Peter Steinfels, *The Neo-Conservatives: The Men Who Are Changing America's Politics* (New York, 1979); and John Ehrman, *The Rise of Neo-Conservatism: Intellectuals and Foreign Policy, 1945–1994* (New Haven, CT, 1995). Apart from the files of *Commentary* and *Public Interest*, mentioned earlier, two memoirs cum political tracts are revealing: Irving Kristol, *Reflections of a Neo-Conservative: Looking Back, Looking Ahead* (New York, 1983); and Norman Podhoretz, *Breaking Ranks: A Political Memoir* (New York, 1979).

The Christian right, a complex phenomenon, has received a good deal of scholarly attention. An early and perceptive group of essays appeared in Robert C. Liebman and Robert C. Wuthnow, eds., *The New Christian Right: Mobilization and Legitimation* (Hawthorne, NY, 1983). Other stimulating works on the movement's rise, impact, and development include the relevant chapters in Frances FitzGerald, *Cities on a Hill: A Journey through Contemporary American Cultures* (New York, 1986); James Davison Hunter, *Culture Wars: The Struggle to Define America* (New York, 1991); Martin Durham, *The Christian Right: The Far Right and the Boundaries of American Conservatism* (Manchester, UK, 2000): and John C. Green, Mark J. Rozell, and Clyde Wilcox, *The Christian Right in American Politics: Marching to the Millennium* (Washington, DC, 2003). An early report from inside the movement is Jerry Falwell with Ed Dobson and Ed Hindson, eds., *The Fundamentalist Phenomenon: The Resurgence of Conservative Christianity* (New York, 1981). The best study of Falwell, and of how he and his allies transformed Protestant fundamentalism, is Susan Friend Harding, *The Book of Jerry Falwell: Fundamentalist Language and Politics* (Princeton, NJ, 2000), a study which better than most comprehends and interprets conservative evangelicalism on its own terms as well as the author's. For a warning about oversimplifying the Christian conservative impulse in the 1970s, see Robert Freedman, "The Religious Right and the Carter Administration," *Historical Journal*, 48 (2005): 231–260. On antecedents, see Leo P. Ribuffo's important book, *The Old Christian Right: The Protestant Far Right from the Great Depression to the Cold War* (Philadelphia, PA, 1983).

Donald T. Critchlow's biography, *Phyllis Schlafly and Grassroots Conservatism: A Woman's Crusade* (Princeton, NJ, 2005), offers a good deal of important information but avoids political analysis, and thereby oddly slights its larger subject, by interpreting Schlafly chiefly as a populist leader. Schlafly's career also suggests that there is a good deal more to be learned about the Roman Catholic as well as the evangelical Protestant influence in what is a diverse and not always cohesive Christian conservative movement.

Still the best survey of Carter's foreign policy is Gaddis Smith, *Morality, Reason, and Power: American Diplomacy in the Carter Years* (New York, 1986); but see also Robert A. Strong, *Working in the World: Jimmy Carter and the Making of American Foreign Policy* (Baton Rouge, LA, 2000); and David Skidmore, *Reversing Course: Carter's Foreign Policy, Domestic Policy, and the Failure of Reform* (Nashville, TN, 1996). A highly critical view of Carter's foreign policy appears in Raymond Moore, "The Carter Presidency and Foreign Policy," in Abernathy, Hill, and Williams, eds., *The Carter Presidency*, 54–83. Carter's policy of human rights is assessed in Sandy Vogelgesang, *American Dream, Global Nightmare: The Dilemma of U.S. Human Rights Policy* (New York, 1980); and subjected to a sharp critique in Joshua Muravchik, *The Uncertain Crusade: Jimmy Carter and the Dilemmas of Human Rights* (New York, 1986). On the larger history of détente and U.S.-Soviet relations, see Garthoff's *Détente and Confrontation*, cited above. Strobe Talbott offers a splendid account of the politics and diplomacy surrounding the SALT II treaty in *Endgame: The Inside Story of SALT II* (New York, 1979).

On the Panama Canal treaties, Robert Strong, "Jimmy Carter and the Panama Canal Treaties," *Presidential Studies Quarterly*, 21 (1991): 269–284, should be supplemented by Walter LaFeber, *The Panama Canal: The Crisis in Historical Perspective* (New York, 1978). As the present book went to press, Adam Clymer's study of the effect of the canal issue on domestic politics was about to appear, but readers should consult J. Michael Hogan, *The Panama Canal in American Politics* (Carbondale, IL, 1986); and George D. Moffett III, *The Limits of Victory: The Ratification of the Panama Canal Treaties* (Ithaca, NY, 1985).

Concerning Middle East politics, see Kenneth W. Stein, *Heroic Diplomacy: Sadat, Kissinger, Carter, Begin, and the Quest for Arab-Israeli Peace* (New York, 1999). See also Moshe Dayan's *Breakthrough: A Personal Account of the Egypt-Israel Peace Negotiations* (New York, 1981), which is part history, part memoir. There is a chapter on Carter's policies in Steven L. Spiegel, *The Other Arab-Israeli Conflict: Making America's Middle East Policy from Truman to Reagan* (Chicago, IL, 1985).

On the background and development of the crisis with Iran, see James A. Bill, *The*

Eagle and the Lion: The Tragedy of American-Iranian Relations (New Haven, CT, 1988); and Barry Rubin, *Paved with Good Intentions: The American Experience in Iran* (New York, 1980). On the events leading up to the hostage crisis and then the crisis itself, see Warren Christopher, ed., *American Hostages in Iran: The Conduct of a Crisis* (New Haven, CT, 1985); and, from another angle, Alexander Moens, "President Carter's Advisers and the Fall of the Shah," *Political Science Quarterly*, 106 (1991): 211–237, which is particularly critical of the national security adviser, Brzezinski.

The election of 1980 is recounted by two veteran journalists in Jack W. Germond and Jules Witcover, *Blue Smoke and Mirrors: How Reagan Won and Why Carter Lost the Election of 1980* (New York, 1981); but for a very different view, see Andrew E. Busch, *Reagan's Victory: The Presidential Election of 1980 and the Rise of the Right* (Lawrence, KS, 2005). On Edward Kennedy's challenge to Carter, see the relevant portions of Adam Clymer, *Edward M. Kennedy: A Biography* (New York, 1999). For left and left-liberal understandings and misunderstandings of Reagan's victory, see Thomas Ferguson and Joel Rogers, eds., *The Hidden Election: Politics and Economics in the 1980 Presidential Campaign* (New York, 1981).

REAGAN (CHAPTERS 5-9)

The literature on Reagan's presidency is as polarized as public opinion about Reagan was at the time. Admirers see him as an iconic leader who saved the economy, crushed the Soviet Union, and restored pride, patriotism, and morality; detractors see him as a reactionary if amiable dunce who did the nation much harm and who had nothing to do with the few things that went right. Both of these views are false, as a few outstanding works over the years have asserted. But a more nuanced and realistic body of scholarship about the Reagan White House has begun to emerge in recent years.

Useful surveys of Reagan's presidency include William E. Pemberton, *Exit with Honor: The Life and Presidency of Ronald Reagan* (Armonk, NY, 1998); and Jules Tygiel, *Ronald Reagan and the Triumph of American Conservatism* (2004; New York, 2006). Haynes Johnson, *Sleepwalking Through History: America in the Reagan Years* (New York, 1991), is a highly critical account by a seasoned journalist that is still worth reading. Garry Wills's *Innocents at Home: Reagan's America* (New York, 1987) was written during Reagan's second term and does not quite reach the level of the author's classic study of Nixon, but is very much worthwhile. See also Michael Schaller, *Reckoning with Reagan: America and Its President in the 1980s* (New York, 1992); and David Mervin, *Ronald Reagan and the American Presidency* (White Plains, NY, 1990). John Ehrman's book *The Eighties*, listed above, concentrates almost entirely on domestic affairs, about which it is very stimulating; Gil Troy's *Morning in America* is broader-gauged and attuned to cultural as well as political trends. Reagan's difficulties in his second term, especially with the Iran-contra affair, are well covered in Jane Mayer and Doyle McManus, *Landslide: The Unmaking of the President, 1984–1988* (Boston, MA, 1988).

Emerging understandings of Reagan's place in history can be traced through several collections of essays, including these: Charles O. Jones, ed., *The Reagan Legacy: Promise and Performance* (Chatham, NJ, 1988); Larry Berman, ed., *Looking Back at the Reagan Presidency* (Baltimore, MD, 1990); Dilys Hills, Raymond A. Moore, and Phil Williams, *The Reagan Presidency: An Incomplete Revolution?* (New York, 1990); Richard S. Conley, ed., *Reassessing the Reagan Presidency* (Lanham, MD, 2003). In a class by itself is W. Elliott Brownlee and Hugh Davis Graham, *The Reagan Presidency: Pragmatic Conservatism and Its Legacy* (Lawrence, KS, 2003). An interesting collection of documents and commentary appears in Paul S. Boyer, ed., *Reagan as President* (Chicago, IL, 1990).

On other works about Reagan's presidency published during the first ten years after it ended, see Alan Metz, "The Reagan Presidency and Ronald Reagan: Post-Presidential Assessments, 1989–1998: A Bibliography," *Bulletin of Bibliography*, 56 (1999): 145–180.

Every student of Ronald Reagan's life and political career owes an enormous debt to the journalist Lou Cannon, who covered Reagan both as governor and as president. For the purposes of this book, Cannon's *President Reagan: The Role of a Lifetime* (1991; New York, 2000) was indispensable. See also his *Ronnie and Jesse: A Political Odyssey* (Garden City, NY, 1969); and *Governor Reagan: His Rise to Power* (New York, 2003).

The authorized biography, Edmund Morris, *Dutch: A Memoir of Ronald Reagan* (New York, 1999), has the drawbacks discussed in my introduction but is engrossing and contains some valuable information. On Reagan's childhood and early career, see Anne Edwards's massive *Early Reagan: The Rise to Power* (New York, 1987), as well as Bill Boyarsky, *The Rise of Ronald Reagan* (New York, 1968). On Reagan's Hollywood years, see above all Stephen Vaughan, *Ronald Reagan in Hollywood: Movies and Politics* (Cambridge, MA, 1994), as well as the critical but stimulating essays in Michael P. Rogin, *Ronald Reagan, the Movie: And Other Episodes of Political Demonology* (Berkeley, CA, 1987). On the campaign of 1966, see Matthew Dallek, *The Right Moment: Ronald Reagan's First Victory and the Decisive Turning Point in American Politics* (New York, 2000). Any assessment of Reagan's years as governor must come to terms with an important article by Jackson K. Putnam, "Governor Reagan: A Reappraisal," *California History*, 83 (2006): 24–45, 65–70, which argues persuasively that Reagan was not an ideologue but a conservative compromiser who was often willing to meet his adversaries more than halfway.

There is no shortage of memoirs and autobiographies from figures important to the Reagan White House. Reagan's efforts are obviously essential. The first suffers from being cast too much as a pilgrim's progress up from liberalism, and the second offers no historical revelations, but both capture Reagan's inimitable voice and convey the temperament that help make him so popular: Ronald Reagan with Richard Hubler, *Where's the Rest of Me? Ronald Reagan Tells His Own Story* (New York, 1965); and Reagan, *An American Story* (New York, 1995). *The Reagan Diaries*, ed. Douglas Brinkley (New York, 2007), is mandatory. Kiron R. Skinner, Annelise Anderson, and Martin Anderson, eds., *Reagan in His Own Hand: The Writings of Ronald Reagan That Reveal His Revolutionary Vision for America* (New York, 2001), is mainly a collection of the scripts Reagan wrote for his political radio show in the late 1970s, and is more useful than its breathless subtitle might suggest. The same editors have compiled an admiring selection from Reagan's correspondence, *Reagan: A Life in Letters* (New York, 2003).

Basic references from various corners of the Reagan White House include these: Martin Anderson, *Revolution: The Reagan Legacy* (New York, 1988); George P. Shultz, *Turmoil and Triumph: My Years as Secretary of State* (New York, 1993); Caspar Weinberger, *Fighting for Peace: Seven Critical Years in the Pentagon* (New York, 1990); Charles Fried, *Order and the Law: Arguing the Reagan Revolution* (New York, 1991); Edwin Meese III, *With Reagan: The Inside Story* (Washington, DC, 1992); and Michael Deaver with Mickey Herskowitz, *Behind the Scenes: In Which the Author Talks About Ronald and Nancy Reagan . . . and Himself* (New York, 1987). David Stockman, *The Triumph of Politics: How the Reagan Revolution Failed* (New York, 1986), puts its author's ideological idiosyncrasies on display and is essential. Donald T. Regan, *For the Record: From Wall Street to Washington* (New York, 1988), does not manage to rise above bitterness.

What might be called the Casey-North faction inside the Reagan administration is best represented in Constantine C. Menges, *Inside the National Security Council: The True Story of the Making and Unmaking of Reagan's Foreign Policy* (New York, 1988). See also Michael Ledeen, *Perilous Statecraft: An Insider's Account of the Iran-Contra Affair* (New York, 1988); and Elliott Abrams, *Undue Process: A Story of How Political Differences Are Turned into Crimes* (New York, 1993), although the latter deals mainly with Abrams's complaints about the special prosecutor Judge Lawrence Walsh's investigation into Iran-contra. Accounts from other quarters appear in Peggy Noonan, *What I Saw at the Revolution: A Political Life in the Reagan Era* (New York, 1990); Larry Speakes, *Speaking Out: Inside the Reagan White House* (New York, 1988); and Terrel H. Bell, *The Thirteenth Man: A Reagan Cabinet Memoir* (New York, 1988). Two of the more revealing volumes in an enormous literature of awestruck hero worship are by former staffers: Dinesh D'Souza, *Ronald Reagan: How an Ordinary Man Became an Extraordinary Leader* (New York, 1997); and Peggy Noonan, *When Character Was King: A Story of Ronald Reagan* (New York, 2001). Any student of Reagan's presidency must consult Nancy Reagan with William Novak, *My Turn: The Memoirs of Nancy Reagan* (New York, 1989).

On Congress and the leading Democrats, see Thomas P. O'Neill's *Man of the House*; and Adam Clymer's *Edward M. Kennedy*, both cited above. Above all, see Daniel Patrick Moynihan, *Came the Revolution: Argument in the Reagan Era* (San Diego, CA, and New York, 1988), which presents galled, at time incredulous, but always shrewd interpretations of what the Reagan administration was trying to accomplish, as well as of what it did accomplish.

There is, as might be expected, a lengthy as well as argumentative literature on Reagan's supply-side economic policies. Readers might begin with the propaganda works by Jude Wanniski, *The Way the World Works* (1978; New York, 1998); and George Gilder, *Wealth and Poverty* (New York, 1981). Then read the sympathetic accounts in William Niskanen, *Reaganomics: An Insider's Account of the Policies and the People* (New York, 1988); and Paul Craig Roberts, "Reaganomics: Myth and Reality," *Perspectives on Political Science*, 19 (1990): 114–117. Then go on to the critical assessments in Robert Lekachman, *Greed Is Not Enough: Reaganomics* (New York, 1982); and Paul R. Krugman, *Peddling Prosperity: Economic Sense and Nonsense in the Age of Diminished Expectations* (New York, 1994). Alan Greenspan's memoir, *The Age of Tur-*

bulence, cited above, offers the best insider's account thus far of the economic preoccupations of the 1980s, with candid appraisals of Reagan's strengths and weaknesses as president. Kevin Phillips, having forecast the political turn to the right in the 1960s, is very critical of the ensuing effects on wealth distribution and economic justice: see *The Politics of Rich and Poor: Wealth and the American Electorate in the Reagan Aftermath* (New York, 1990); and *Wealth and Democracy: A Political History of the American Rich* (New York, 2002). On labor, see a powerful case study with larger implications, Paul L. Butterworth, James T. Schultz, and Marian C. Schultz, "More Than a Labor Dispute: The PATCO Strike of 1981," *Essays in Economic and Business History*, 23 (2005): 125–139.

A positive review of Reagan's regulatory policies appears in Roger E. Meiners and Bruce Yandle, eds., *Regulation and the Reagan Era: Politics, Bureaucracy, and the Public Interest* (New York, 1989), which conveys the administration's general hostility to government involvement in what it fancied as the free market. On the most spectacular failure of government regulation under Reagan, see, among several useful studies, Kathleen Day, *S&L Hell: The People and the Politics Behind the $1 Trillion Savings and Loan Scandal* (New York, 1993); Martin Mayer, *The Greatest-Ever Bank Robbery: The Collapse of the Savings and Loan Industry* (New York, 1990); and Stephen Pizzo, *Inside Job: The Looting of America's Savings and Loans* (New York, 1989).

On civil rights, Raymond Wolters's *Right Turn: William Bradford Reynolds, the Reagan Administration, and Black Civil Rights* (New Brunswick, NJ, 1996) is completely admiring of the Reagan administration's policies and establishes Reynolds's importance to the political turn it describes. For the other side of the story, see Robert R. Detlefsen, *Civil Rights Under Reagan* (San Francisco, CA, 1991); and Stephen A. Schull, *A Kinder, Gentler Racism? The Reagan-Bush Civil Rights Legacy* (Armonk, NY, 1993), which also discuss Clarence Thomas's important role in the administration. On related matters concerning the cases of Bob Jones University and Grove City College, see Hugh Davis Graham, "The Storm over Grove City College: Civil Rights, Regulation, Higher Education, and the Reagan Administration," *History of Education Quarterly*, 38 (1998): 407–429.

On the culture wars, there is no end of jeremiads and counterattacks, but James Davison Hunter's *Culture Wars*, cited above, is the best place to start. See also the works on the Christian right listed in the preceding section on the Carter years. On the limits of the Reagan White House's commitment to the most conservative of the culture warriors, see Matthew C. Moen, "Ronald Reagan and the Social Issues: Rhetorical Support for the Christian Right," *Social Science Journal*, 27 (1990): 199–207. Randy Shilts, *And the Band Played On: Politics, People, and the AIDS Epidemic* (New York, 1987), is a powerful indictment; for an effort to vindicate Reagan on AIDS and gay rights, see Deroy Murdock, "Anti-Gay Gipper: A Lie About Reagan," in National Review Online, December 3, 2003, at http://www.nationalreview.com/murdock/murdock200312030913.asp.

Judicial and legal policy as seen from the inside are best understood in the memoirs listed above by Charles Fried and Edwin Meese III. By contrast, Herman Schwartz, *Packing the Courts: The Conservative Campaign to Rewrite the Constitution* (New York,

1988), is a thorough critique, which should be followed up with Cass R. Sunstein, *Radicals in Robes: Why Extreme Right-Wing Courts Are Wrong for America* (New York, 2005). The best study so far of the Bork debacle is by Ethan Bronner, *Battle for Justice: How the Bork Nomination Shook America* (New York, 1989).

On the election of 1984, see Jack W. Germond and Jules Witcover, *Wake Us When It's Over: Presidential Politics of 1984* (New York, 1985); William A. Henry III, *Visions of America: How We Saw the 1984 Election* (Boston, MA, 1985); Gerald M. Pomper et al., *The Election of 1984: Reports and Interpretations* (Chatham, NJ, 1985); and Dennis J. Mahoney and Peter W. Schramm, eds., *The 1984 Election and the Future of American Politics* (Durham, NC, 1987).

Like Carter's, Reagan's foreign policy has by now attracted a large literature—and has also been the source of the wildest and most durable myths about Reagan's presidency. An impressive early effort at an overview, focused on the gap between rhetoric and action in Reagan's foreign policy, is Coral Bell, *The Reagan Paradox: American Foreign Policy in the 1980s* (New Brunswick, NJ, 1989). Raymond L. Garthoff's *Détente and Confrontation* concludes before the end of Reagan's first term and must be supplemented with Garthoff's *The Great Transition: American-Soviet Relations and the End of the Cold War* (Washington, DC, 1994). The memoirs of Caspar Weinberger and (especially) George Shultz cited above are mandatory reading. On defense and foreign policy, see Daniel Wirls, *Buildup: The Politics of Defense in the Reagan Era* (Ithaca, NY, 1992). For a recent appraisal of the so-called Reagan Doctrine, see Chester Pach, "The Reagan Doctrine: Principle, Pragmatism, and Policy," *Presidential Studies Quarterly*, 36 (2006): 75–88. David Locke Hall, *The Reagan Wars: A Constitutional Perspective on War Powers and the Presidency* (Boulder, CO, 1991), appraises the constitutional proprieties of Reagan's military interventions in Lebanon, Libya, Grenada, and the Persian Gulf, finding more grounds for assent than disapproval.

Reagan's policies in Central and South America have been the source of controversy since the 1980s. For contrasting views, see Leslie Cockburn, *Out of Control: The Story of the Reagan Administration's Secret War in Nicaragua, the Illegal Arms Pipeline, and the Contra Drug Connection* (New York, 1987); Thomas Carothers, *In the Name of Democracy: U.S. Policy Toward Latin America in the Reagan Years* (Berkeley, CA, 1991); Robert Kagan, *A Twilight Struggle: American Power and Nicaragua, 1977–1990* (New York, 1996).

On the Middle East, see William B. Quandt, ed., *The Middle East: Ten Years after Camp David* (Washington, DC, 1988); and the relevant chapters in Quandt, ed., *Peace Process: American Diplomacy and the Arab-Israeli Conflict Since 1967* (Berkeley, CA, 2001). See also the brief discussion of Reagan's early years in Steven L. Spiegel, *The Other Arab-Israeli Conflict*, cited earlier. On an aspect of Reagan's Middle East policy that would have resounding importance in later decades, see Bruce W. Jentleson, *With Friends Like These: Reagan, Bush, and Saddam, 1982–1990* (New York, 1994).

Close study of the Iran-contra affair and the controversy it provoked requires reading the reports of the Tower Commission, the special congressional investigating committee, and the independent counsel, Judge Lawrence Walsh, as cited in my notes. By far the most thorough and authoritative account is Theodore Draper, *A Very Thin Line:*

The Iran-Contra Affairs (New York, 1991). On the effort to reform and moderate the National Security Council (NSC) in the aftermath of the scandal, see Colin L. Powell, "The NSC in the Last Two Years of the Reagan Administration," *Center for the Study of the Presidency: Proceedings*, 6 (1989): 204–218.

The central and most insidious myths about Reagan and his presidency concern the ending of the cold war. Supposedly, Reagan, from the start, aimed to destroy the Soviet Union by forcing the Kremlin to undertake an arms race it could not afford, plunged the Soviets into bankruptcy and pushed them into reform with his Strategic Defense Initiative, and in general set the stage for the collapse of Soviet communism between 1989 and 1991.

Such accounts are almost completely false. At the time, no one doubted that Reagan wanted to change U.S. policy toward the Soviets fundamentally, in order to ensure that the United States would always negotiate from as strong a position as possible. No one doubted that he wished to support anticommunist movements worldwide. Yet if Reagan hoped to hasten the destruction of the Soviet system, it is fanciful to see him as the demiurge who completed that destruction with a well-plotted plan. Everyone at the time recognized that the ending of the cold war was a complicated process, which involved Reagan's following up a fundamental shift in his own thinking between 1985 and 1987. Conservative hard-liners lamented that shift; liberals tended to find it confusing; but nobody doubted that it had occurred and was of crucial importance.

In an article written for *Foreign Affairs* just before Reagan left office, the distinguished and widely respected Sovietologist Robert W. Tucker assessed Reagan's foreign policy, and the extraordinary changes in U.S.-Soviet relations between 1980 and 1988. Because Tucker's evaluation is so cogent, and runs counter to the myths, it is worth quoting at length:

> [By 1988], the great fear of 1980—that Moscow would continue to make substantial inroads on the American position in the world—had all but disappeared. In its place was the belief that the Soviet threat had markedly diminished, that Soviet-American relations had taken a decided turn for the better and that the future held out the prospect for still further improvement in these relations.
>
> Ronald Reagan was undoubtedly the most important representative of this changed view, not only because of his position but because of the seemingly unshakable conviction he had always entertained of Soviet governments and more generally of the Soviet system. According to this conviction, the Soviet Union could no more change its malevolent character in any essential respects than the tiger could change its stripes. The sources of Soviet conduct defined the essence of the system and its eternal and implacable hostility to the West. The outgoing president had long accepted this as an article of faith, and he expressed it as recently as the beginning of his second term. Yet by 1988 Mr. Reagan declared that he had altered his deeply held views about the Soviet system in light of the institutional and doctrinal changes introduced by Mikhail Gorbachev. The president drew no explicit connection between domestic change in the Soviet Union and Soviet foreign policy. Still, it was apparent that the optimism with which he viewed future prospects for Soviet-American relations was based largely on the belief that a

greater liberalization in domestic institutions would lead to a greater moderation in foreign policy.

See Robert W. Tucker, "Reagan's Foreign Policy," *Foreign Affairs*, 68 (1989): 1–27.

At the time Tucker wrote, many of Reagan's erstwhile admirers and former staff members thought he had betrayed them and thereby destroyed his own policy. See, among many examples, Frank J. Gaffney Jr., "A Policy Abandoned: How the Reagan Administration Formulated, Implemented, and Retreated from Its Arms Control Policy," *National Interest*, 11 (1988): 43–52. Of late, however, some of Reagan's admirers have presented a spurious revisionist account of the president's single-handed, long-planned, beautifully executed attack on the Soviet Union, which crushed communism short of a nuclear war. The most full-throated versions of these ex post facto historical fantasies appear in Peter Schweizer, *Victory: The Reagan Administration's Secret Strategy That Hastened the Collapse of the Soviet Union* (New York, 1994); and, updated and fleshed out, in Schweizer, *Reagan's War: The Epic Story of His Forty-Year Struggle and Final Triumph over Communism* (New York, 2002); but see also the less bombastic account in Andrew E. Busch, "Ronald Reagan and the Defeat of the Soviet Empire," *Presidential Studies Quarterly*, 27 (1997): 451–466.

The most powerful refutation of these myths appears in the study by Reagan's ambassador to Moscow (and very much an admirer of the president), Jack Matlock, *Reagan and Gorbachev: How the Cold War Ended* (New York, 2004). Other relevant studies include Don Oberdorfer, *From the Cold War to a New Era: The United States and the Soviet Union, 1983–1990* (1991; Baltimore, MD, 1998); Beth Fischer, *The Reagan Reversal: Foreign Policy and the End of the Cold War* (Columbia, MO, 1997); Frances FitzGerald, *Way Out There in the Blue: Reagan, Star Wars, and the End of the Cold War* (New York, 2000); and Walter C. Uhler, "Misreading the Soviet Threat," *Journal of Slavic Military Studies*, 14 (2001): 171–182. The relevant sections in Archie Brown, *Seven Years That Changed the World: Perestroika in Perspective* (New York, 2007), gives Reagan too little credit, but demolishes claims that Gorbachev and the reformers undertook their overhaul in response to threats and unsettling initiatives by the Americans. On the other hand, the best study of Reagan's utopian abolitionism about nuclear weapons tends to overstate the effects of Reagan's arms race and SDI in pushing Soviet leaders toward reform; see Paul Letton, *Ronald Reagan and His Quest to Abolish Nuclear Weapons* (New York, 2005).

Concerning an important international political link that, among things, helped prepare the way for the thawing of U.S.-Soviet relations, see Geoffrey Smith, *Reagan and Thatcher: The Inside Story of the Friendship and Political Partnership That Changed World Events from the Falklands War to Perestroika* (New York, 1991).

On the election of 1988, Donald Morrison, ed., *The Winning of the White House, 1988* (New York, 1988); Sidney Blumenthal, *Pledging Allegiance: The Last Campaign of the Cold War* (New York, 1990); and Jack W. Germond and Jules Witcover, *Whose Broad Stripes and Bright Stars? The Trivial Pursuit of the Presidency, 1988* (New York, 1989), should be supplemented with Gerald M. Pomper, ed., *The Election of 1988: Reports and Interpretations* (Chatham, NJ, 1989). Richard Ben Cramer's *What It Takes: The*

Way to the White House (New York, 1992) contains a great deal of detail (most of it from the primaries), but eventually sinks under the weight of its own ambition to chronicle every aspect of presidential campaigning and the demands such campaigning makes on human character.

GEORGE H. W. BUSH (CHAPTER 10)

John Robert Greene, having already written well about Gerald Ford, did the same in *The Presidency of George Bush* (Lawrence, KS, 2000). Other useful general studies include Richard Rose, *The Postmodern President: George Bush Meets the World* (Chatham, NJ, 1991); Michael Duffy and Dan Goodgame, *Marching in Place: The Status-Quo Presidency of George Bush* (New York, 1992); David Mervin, *George Bush and the Guardianship Presidency* (New York, 1996); and Ryan J. Barilleaux and Mark J. Rozell, *Power and Prudence: The Presidency of George H. W. Bush* (College Station, TX, 2004). Somewhat narrower in perspective but still useful are Colin Campbell and Bert Rockman, eds., *The Bush Presidency: First Appraisals* (Chatham, NJ, 1991); Ryan J. Barilleaux and Mary E. Stuckey, eds., *Leadership and the Bush Presidency: Prudence or Drift in an Era of Change* (New York, 1992); Dilys Hill and Phil Williams, eds., *The Bush Presidency: Triumphs and Adversities* (New York, 1994); Kenneth W. Thompson, ed., *The Bush Presidency: Ten Intimate Perspectives of George Bush* (Lanham, MD, 1997–1998); Leslie D. Feldman and Rosanna Perotti, eds., *Honor and Loyalty: Inside the Politics of the George H. W. Bush White House* (Westport, CT, 2002); and William Levantrosser and Rosanna Perrotti, eds., *A Noble Calling: Character and the George H. W. Bush Presidency* (Westport, CT, 2004). Charles Tiefer, *The Semi-Sovereign Presidency: The Bush Administration's Strategy for Governing Without Congress* (Boulder, CO, 1994), takes up themes that would grow in importance under different circumstances after 2000.

Herbert S. Parmet, *George Bush: The Life of a Lone Star Yankee* (New York, 1997), the first proper biography, may now be supplemented with Tom Wicker's concise *George Herbert Walker Bush* (New York, 2004) and Timothy Naftali, *George H. W. Bush* (New York, 2007). Kevin Phillips's study of the Bush family, *American Dynasty: Aristocracy, Fortune, and the Politics of Deceit in the House of Bush* (New York, 2004), is scathing and incisive.

Bush has yet to publish a full autobiography covering his years as president. His campaign memoir, *Looking Forward: An Autobiography* (New York, 1987), written with Vic Gold, is a quickie production of little depth. On another level entirely is George Bush and Brent Scowcroft, *A World Transformed* (New York, 1998), a joint memoir concerning foreign policy supplemented with official documents of the time, many of which remain classified to this day. Although the book says nothing about domestic policy, it is the most interesting innovation in presidential memoirs in modern times, and consequently is more revealing than most.

Other important memoirs and autobiographical materials include these: James A. Baker III, *The Politics of Diplomacy: Revolution, War, and Peace* (New York, 1995); Colin Powell, *My American Journey* (New York, 1995); Charles Kolb, *White House Daze: The*

Unmaking of Domestic Policy in the Bush Years (New York, 1993); James P. Pinkerton, *What Comes Next: The End of Big Government—and the New Paradigm Ahead* (New York, 1995); and Richard Darman, *Who's in Control? Polar Politics and the Sensible Center* (New York, 1996). John Podhoretz offers a breezy account of a troubled administration in *Hell of a Ride: Backstage at the White House Follies, 1989–1993* (New York, 1993). Marlin Fitzwater, who came back to the White House to serve as Bush's press secretary after doing that job for Ronald Reagan at the end of Reagan's presidency, offers a wealth of anecdotes in *Call the Briefing! Bush and Reagan, Sam and Helen: A Decade with Presidents and the Press* (New York, 1995). See also Barbara Bush's utterly supportive *A Memoir* (New York, 1994).

Apart from Darman's *Who's in Control*, cited above, there is surprisingly little yet written on Bush's economic and fiscal policies. L. William Seidman, *Full Faith and Credit: The Great S&L Debacle and Other Washington Sagas* (New York, 1993), tells the story of bailing out the S&Ls and mopping up afterward from a self-interested insider's point of view. Nor have the rest of Bush's domestic policies been well covered, although that situation may soon change. See Richard Himelfarb and Rosanna Perotti, eds., *Principle over Politics? The Domestic Policy of the George H. W. Bush Presidency* (Westport, CT, 2004). On civil rights, see Stephen Schull's book, cited above in the section on Reagan. On the amendments to the Clear Air Act, the best study to date gives more credit to Senator George Mitchell (a Democrat) than to Bush: Richard E. Cohen, *Washington at Work: Back Rooms and Clean Air* (New York, 1992).

The debacle over the nomination of Clarence Thomas produced an enormous outpouring at the time. My research affirms how desperately the hard right fought to avoid another defeat like the rejection of Bork, and how—unlike the ambivalent Reagan White House under Howard Baker—the Bush White House stood firmly behind its nominee. Although many readers continue to disagree with its central contention—that Anita Hill told the truth before the Senate Judiciary Committee, and Thomas lied—the best single book on the subject remains Jane Mayer and Jill Abramson, *Strange Justice: The Selling of Clarence Thomas* (Boston, MA, 1994). Students will also want to read the original transcripts, usefully gathered as Anita Miller, ed., *The Complete Transcripts of the Clarence Thomas/Anita Hill Hearings* (Chicago, IL, 1994). The most vociferous and well-known attack on Hill, David Brock's *The Real Anita Hill: The Untold Story* (New York, 1993), has since been repudiated by its author. Clarence Thomas's *My Grandfather's Son: A Memoir* (New York, 2007) appeared as the present book was going to press.

On foreign policy, start with Steven Hurst's survey, *The Foreign Policy of the Bush Administration: In Search of a New World Order* (London and New York, 1999). Raymond Garthoff's *Great Transition* is as useful on Soviet-American relations under Bush as on the Reagan years, as is Don Oberdorfer's *From the Cold War*, both cited above. Jack F. Matlock, *Autopsy of an Empire: The American Ambassador's Account of the Collapse of the Soviet Union* (New York, 1995), is excellent, at once complex and dramatic. Overall, though, the best survey of Soviet-American relations is Michael Beschloss and Strobe Talbott, *At the Highest Levels: The Inside Story of the End of the Cold War* (Boston, MA, 1993), which finds reasons to vindicate Bush's cautious, realist approach to Gorbachev and perestroika. On German reunification, see Elizabeth Pond, *Beyond the Wall: Germany's Road to Reunification* (Washington, DC, 1993). On how events looked from the Russian standpoint, see Archie Brown, *The Gorbachev Factor* (New York, 1997).

The United States' link with Noriega and the U.S. invasion of Panama have been the subject of several studies, including John Dinges, *Our Man in Panama: How General Noriega Used the U.S.—and Made Millions in Drugs and Arms* (New York, 1990); and Bob Woodward, *The Commanders* (New York, 1991). On military policy in general, see David Halberstam, *War in a Time of Peace: Bush, Clinton, and the Generals* (New York, 2001).

On the Persian Gulf War, in addition to Bush and Scowcroft's book *A World Transformed* and Woodward's *The Commanders*, readers should consult Lawrence Freedman and Efriam Karsh, *The Gulf Conflict, 1990–1991: Diplomacy and War in the New World Order* (Princeton, NJ, 1993). For contemporary opinion, see also Micah L. Sifrey and Christopher Cerf, eds., *The Gulf War Reader: History, Documents, and Opinions* (New York, 1991). For critical assessments, see Stephen R. Graubard, *Mr. Bush's War: Adventures in the Politics of Illusion* (New York, 1992); and Alex Roberto Hybel, *Power over Rationality: The Bush Administration and the Gulf Crisis* (Albany, NY, 1993).

The election of 1992 is covered in Stephen J. Wayne, *The Road to the White House, 1996: The Politics of Presidential Elections* (New York, 1996); and Jack W. Germond and Jules Witcover, *Mad as Hell: Revolt at the Ballot Box* (New York, 1993). On Ross Perot and his movement, see Gerald Posner, *Citizen Perot: His Life and Times* (New York, 1996).

CLINTON (CHAPTERS 11–14)

The cacophony about Bill Clinton and his presidency has only just begun to subside in favor of more sober assessments, both admiring and critical. Ironically, though, because Clinton was such a controversial figure—a centrist liberal president in a conservative age—there is more published factual evidence available about his administration than for some other recent administrations. This is due partly to the intense (at times comically intense) scrutiny exercised by the press, as well as Clinton's political adversaries. It is crucial, however, to be cautious in sifting the facts out of the apologetics and the (far more numerous) assaults of the time.

The closest thing so far to a general history of Clinton's presidency is John F. Harris, *The Survivor: Bill Clinton in the White House* (New York, 2005), which, despite my disagreements on points of interpretation, I found judicious and informative. For a brief account, critical of Clinton from a left-liberal perspective, see William C. Berman, *From the Center to the Edge: The Politics and Policies of the Clinton Presidency* (Lanham, MD, 2001). There are also different interpretations in Roger Morris, *Partners in Power: The Clintons and Their America* (New York, 1996); and Joe Klein, *The Natural: The Misunderstood Presidency of Bill Clinton* (New York, 2002). Other general works include Colin Campbell and Bert A. Rockman, *The Clinton Presidency: First Appraisals* (Chatham, NJ, 1995); Colin Campbell and Bert A. Rockman, eds., *The Clinton Legacy* (Catham, NJ, 2000); Steven E. Schier, ed., *The Postmodern Presidency: Bill Clinton's Legacy in U.S. Pol-*

itics (Pittsburgh, PA, 2000); and Todd G. Shields, Jeannie M. Whayne, and Donald R. Kelley, eds., *The Clinton Riddle: Perspectives on the Forty-Second President* (Fayetteville, AK, 2004). On the disappointing early stages of press operations in the Clinton White House see Robert E. Denton Jr. and Rachel L. Holloway, eds., *The Clinton Presidency: Images, Issues, and Communication Strategies* (Westport, CT, 1996).

Clinton still lacks a full and balanced biography on the order of Herbert Parmet's study of George H. W. Bush, let alone Lou Cannon's several volumes on Reagan. On his early years and rise to power, see Charles F. Allen and Jonathan Portis, *The Comeback Kid: The Life and Career of Bill Clinton* (New York, 1992); and David Maraniss, *First in His Class: A Biography of Bill Clinton* (New York, 1995). There is also a useful collection of personal reminiscences from different perspectives, gathered in 1992, in David Gallen, ed., *Bill Clinton as They Know Him: An Oral Biography* (New York, 1992). On Clinton's life through 1992, Allan Metz, *Bill Clinton's Pre-Presidential Career: An Annotated Bibliography* (Westport, CT, 1994), is a useful research aid. Nigel Hamilton's two volumes—*Bill Clinton, American Journey: Great Expectations* (New York, 2003), and *Bill Clinton: Mastering the Presidency* (New York, 2007)—exemplify the recent fixations on psychology and character and the almost total disregard of politics. Less sensational examples include Stanley A. Renshon, *High Hopes: The Clinton Presidency and the Politics of Ambition* (New York, 1996); as well as the essays in Stanley A. Renshon, ed., *Campaigning, Governing, and the Psychology of Leadership* (Boulder, CO, 1994). Similar priorities—but in an openly hostile, pseudo-muckraking form that became familiar during the Clinton years—dominate Meredith Oakley, *On the Make: The Rise of Bill Clinton* (Washington, DC, 1994); and John Brummett, *High Wire: From the Backwoods to the Beltway—The Education of Bill Clinton* (New York, 1994).

Memoirs and autobiographies concerning Clinton and his presidency start with Clinton's own massive *My Life* (New York, 2004), best for its limning of growing up in Arkansas and of the author's role in the travails of Democratic politics in the 1980s as well as the 1990s. Because of her unusual importance in her husband's administration as both adviser and lightning rod, Hillary Rodham Clinton, *Living History* (New York, 2003), is more important than other first ladies' memoirs.

The earliest memoirs from inside the administration reflect the authors' disappointment in the Clinton's first term and in their respective roles in decision making at the White House: George Stephanopoulos, *All Too Human: A Political Education* (New York, 1999); and Robert B. Reich, *Locked in the Cabinet* (New York, 1997). Madeleine K. Albright with Bill Woodward, *Madam Secretary* (New York, 2003), is vital to understanding Clinton's foreign policy; so, on economic policy, is Robert E. Rubin with Jacob Weisberg, *In an Uncertain World: Tough Choices from Wall Street to Washington* (New York, 2003). Richard Holbrooke, *To End a War* (1998; New York, 1999), is a gripping account of the events leading to the signing of the Dayton Accords. George J. Mitchell has written a similarly valuable book on the peace agreement in Northern Ireland in *Making Peace* (New York, 1999). Strobe Talbott's *The Russia Hand: A Memoir of Presidential Diplomacy* (New York, 2002) is masterful. See also the relevant chapters in Joseph Wilson, *The Politics of Truth: A Diplomat's Memoir* (New York, 2004).

Less a memoir than a political field report, Stanley B. Greenberg, *Middle Class*

Dreams: The Politics and Power of the New American Majority (New York, 1995), is essential to any understanding of the political ideas and aspirations that drove the Clinton administration. On the administration's more hard-edged political side, see Dick Morris, *Behind the Oval Office: Winning the Presidency in the Nineties* (New York, 1997). On Clinton's second term generally, including the politics behind much of the scandalmongering that led to the impeachment, see Sidney Blumenthal's admiring and perceptive *The Clinton Wars* (New York, 2003), which has gained greater authority with the passing of time. The perspective of one of Clinton's chief speechwriters is well presented in Michael Waldman, *POTUS Speaks: Finding the Words That Defined Clinton's Presidency* (New York, 2000).

On the Republicans and their resurgence in 1994 and after, see Mel Steely, *The Gentleman from Georgia: The Biography of Newt Gingrich* (Macon, GA, 2000); *"Tell Newt to Shut Up!": Prize-Winning Washington Post Journalists Reveal How Reality Gagged the Gingrich Revolution* (New York, 1996), as well as the Elizabeth Drew's *Showdown: The Struggle Between the Gingrich Congress and the Clinton White House* (New York, 1997). Essential primary sources include Newt Gingrich, *To Renew America* (New York, 1995); Newt Gingrich, *Lessons Learned the Hard Way: A Personal Report* (New York, 1998); and Ed Gillespie and Bob Schellhaft, *The Contract with America: The Bold Plan by Rep. Newt Gingrich, Rep. Dick Armey, and the House Republicans to Change the Nation* (New York, 1994). The Contract with America is also available online at http://www.house. gov/house/Contract/CONTRACT.html.

On the early years of Clinton's presidency, see Koichi Suzuki, L. Alexander Norsworthy, and Helen C. Gleason, *The Clinton Revolution: An Inside Look at the New Administration* (Lanham, MD, 1993); Richard E. Cohen, *Changing Course in Washington: Clinton and the New Congress* (New York, 1993); Elizabeth Drew, *On the Edge: The Clinton Presidency* (New York, 1994); Bob Woodward, *The Agenda; Inside the Clinton White House* (New York, 1994); and Bob Woodward, *The Choice* (New York, 1996). For an insider's astute assessment of the debacle over the health care plan, see Paul Starr, "What Happened to Health Care Reform?" *American Prospect* (Winter 1995): 20–31; for a broader political view, see Haynes Johnson and David S. Broder, *The System: The American Way of Politics at the Breaking Point* (Boston, MA, 1996). See also the analysis in Theda Skocpol, *Boomerang: Clinton's Health Security Effort and the Turn Against Government in U.S. Politics* (New York, 1996). The struggle over NAFTA has produced mainly an adversarial literature on both sides of the matter, but for a fascinating account of the treaty negotiations, see Maxwell A. Cameron and Brian W. Tomlin, *The Making of NAFTA: How the Deal Was Done* (Ithaca, NY, 2000). For further reading, consult Allan Metz, *A NAFTA Bibliography* (Westport, CT, 1996).

On confrontation between the White House and Congress in 1995 and the aftermath, see Elizabeth Drew's *Showdown*, cited above, as well as Elizabeth Drew, *Whatever It Takes: The Real Struggle for Political Power in America* (New York, 1997); Charles O. Jones, *Clinton and Congress, 1993–1996: Risk, Restoration, and Reelection* (Norman, OK, 1999); and Evan Thomas et al., *Back from the Dead: How Clinton Survived the Republican Revolution* (New York, 1997). On the election of 1996, see also Gerald M. Pomper, ed., *The Election of 1996: Reports and Interpretations* (Chatham, NJ, 1997).

The list of books containing right-wing attacks on Clinton and his wife is extremely long. The urtext is Floyd Brown, *"Slick Willie": Why America Cannot Trust Bill Clinton* (Annapolis, MD, 1993). Other works representative of the genre (though not necessarily the most abrasive) include Paul Greenberg, *No Surprises: Two Decades of Clinton-Watching* (Washington, DC, 1996); William J. Bennett, *The Death of Outrage: Bill Clinton and the Assault on American Ideals* (New York, 1998); and, looking back on everything, Rich Lowery, *Legacy: Paying the Price for the Clinton Years* (Washington, DC, 2003). For an example of the lengths some of Clinton's ultraconservative adversaries went to in their attacks, see the VHS tape distributed by the Reverend Jerry Falwell, *The Clinton Chronicles* (1994), and the various sequels.

Although the conservatives' attacks were the noisiest and most consequential, Clinton hardly escaped sharp criticism from the left. For various shades of liberal and left-wing opinion, see James MacGregor Burns and Georgia J. Sorenson, with Robin Gerber and Scott W. Webster, *Dead Center: Clinton-Gore Leadership and the Perils of Moderation* (New York, 1999); Theodore J. Lowi and Benjamin Ginsberg, *Embattled Democracy: Politics and Policy in the Clinton Era* (New York, 1995); Lani Guinier, *Lift Every Voice: Turning a Civil Rights Setback into a New Vision of Social Justice* (New York, 1998); and Richard Reeves, *Running in Place: How Bill Clinton Disappointed America* (Kansas City, MO, 1996). See also Christopher Hitchens's polemic, *No One Left to Lie To: The Values of the Worst Family* (1999; New York, 2000), which at times condemns the Clintons over the same allegations raised by some of the wilder right-wing polemicists.

For an early evaluation of the Clinton administration's foreign policy, see William G. Hyland's disappointed assessment in *Clinton's World: Remaking American Foreign Policy* (Wesport, CT, 1999). A more positive interpretation appears in Stephen M. Walt, "Two Cheers for Clinton's Foreign Policy," *Foreign Affairs*, 79 (2000): 63–79. See also David Halberstam's *War in a Time of Peace*, cited earlier. On the persistent constitutional issues, see Ryan C. Hendrickson, *The Clinton Wars: The Constitution, Congress, and War Powers* (Nashville, TN, 2002). Not enough has yet been written on what became known as the "third way" or on Clinton's sometimes close, sometimes uneasy connection with the British prime minister Tony Blair, but for a start, see Flavio Romano's highly critical *Clinton and Blair: The Political Economy of the Third* Way (New York, 2006). On Rwanda, see, among many studies, Gérard Prunier, *The Rwanda Crisis: History of a Genocide* (New York, 1995); and Philip Gourevitch, *We Wish to Inform You That Tomorrow We Will Be Killed with Our Families: Stories from Rwanda* (New York, 1998). On Somalia, see Mark Bowden, *Black Hawk Down: A Story of Modern War* (New York, 2000); and on Haiti, see Philippe R. Girard, *Clinton in Haiti: The 1994 U.S. Invasion of Haiti* (New York, 2004).

On the Balkans, see Tim Judah, *The Serbs: History, Myth, and the Destruction of Yugoslavia* (1997; New Haven, CT, 2000); Tim Judah, *Kosovo: War and Revenge* (New Haven, CT, 2000); Noel Malcolm, *Kosovo: A Short History* (New York, 1998); and Misha Glenny, *The Balkans: Nationalism, War, and the Great Powers, 1804–1999* (New York, 2000). Richard Holbrooke's *To End a War* should be supplemented with Derek Chollet, *The Road to the Dayton Accords: A Study of American Statecraft* (New York, 2005).

For an overview of Middle East policy, begin with the relevant chapters in William B. Quandt's *Peace Process*, cited earlier. On the Irish peace negotiations, in addition to George Mitchell's *Making Peace*, see Conor O'Clery, *Daring Diplomacy: Clinton's Secret Search for Peace in Ireland* (New York, 1997). On U.S.-Russian relations, start with Strobe Talbott's *The Russia Hand*, but see also James M. Goldgeier and Michael McFaul, *Power and Purpose: U.S. Policy Toward Russia After the Cold War* (Washington, DC, 2003).

The political accusations and controversies that led to Clinton's impeachment began well before the first encounter between President Clinton and Monica Lewinsky. On the early battles, and especially the allegations over Whitewater, see James B. Stewart, *Blood Sport: The President and His Adversaries* (New York, 1996); and, for some needed debunking, Gene Lyons and the editors of Harper's Magazine, *Fools for Scandal: How the Media Invented Whitewater* (New York, 1996). The fullest account to date of the impeachment is Jeffrey Toobin, *A Vast Conspiracy: The Real Story of a Sex Scandal That Nearly Brought Down a President* (New York, 1999). For the reflections of a reporter who became a participant, see Michael Isikoff, *Uncovering Clinton: A Reporter's Story* (New York, 1999). For the most exacting account of the far-flung ranks of Clinton haters and their convergence in the impeachment episode, see Joe Conason and Gene Lyons, *The Hunting of the President: The Ten-Year Campaign to Destroy Bill and Hillary Clinton* (New York, 2000). Richard Posner's *An Affair of State: The Investigation, Impeachment, and Trial of William Jefferson Clinton* (Cambridge, MA, 1999) is an interpretation by a prolific, conservative federal judge that, although highly critical of the House Republicans, reserves its greatest scorn for the president and those who opposed the impeachment. The press's early feeding frenzy over the story and the sorry implications about the state of American journalism and its future are examined in Marvin Kalb, *One Scandalous Story: Clinton, Lewinsky, and Thirteen Days That Tarnished American Journalism* (New York, 2001). Other interpretations of the events include the essays in Mark J. Rozell and Clyde Wilcox, eds., *The Clinton Scandal and the Future of American Government* (Washington, DC, 2000); Robert Busby, *Defending the American Presidency: Clinton and the Lewinsky Scandal* (Houndmills, UK, and New York, 2001); and Nicol Rae and Colton C. Campbell, *Impeaching Clinton: Partisan Strife on Capitol Hill* (Lawrence, KS, 2004).

The presidential election of 2000 and its aftermath receive their first full treatment in Jeffrey Toobin, *Too Close to Call: The Thirty-Six-Day Battle to Decide the 2000 Election* (New York, 2001). Two books by leading newspaper staffs give a detailed narrative of events: the *New York Times's 36 Days: The Complete Chronicle of the 2000 Presidential Election Crisis* (New York, 2001); and the *Washington Post's Deadlock: The Inside Story of America's Closest Election* (New York, 2001). Also useful are the documents collected in E. J. Dionne and William Kristol, eds., *Bush v. Gore: The Court Cases and the Commentary* (Washington, DC, 2001). Richard A. Posner, *Breaking the Deadlock: The 2000 Election, the Constitution, and the Courts* (Princeton, NJ, 2001), offers a dense and unpersuasive defense of the Supreme Court's ruling on what the author calls "pragmatic" grounds, and fully supports the Court's aggressive appropriation of power at the expense of Congress. Angry critiques of the Court's ruling appear in Vincent Bugliosi, *The Betrayal of America: How the Supreme Court Undermined the Constitution and Chose Our President* (New York, 2001); and Alan Dershowitz, *Supreme Injustice: How the Su-*

preme Court Hijacked Election 2000 (New York, 2001). Additional commentary appears in two collections of essays, Cass R. Sunstein and Richard Epstein, eds., *The Vote: Bush, Gore, and the Supreme Court* (Chicago, IL, 2001); and Jack N. Rakove, ed., *The Unfinished Election of 2000: Leading Scholars Examine America's Strangest Election* (New York, 2001).

GEORGE W. BUSH (EPILOGUE)

My account of the scene in lower Manhattan in October 2001 draws on personal recollections as well as reports in the *New York Times*.

Although the George W. Bush administration has never lacked sharp critics, evaluations have passed through two basic phases: the first, when the country rallied behind the president following the attacks of September 11, 2001, and when, despite falling popularity ratings, most Americans stuck by him through the invasion of Iraq; and the second, beginning during the summer of 2005, when the controversies over the Terry Schiavo case and the government's bungling in the aftermath of hurricane Katrina, along with the deteriorating situation in Iraq, destroyed what had once appeared to be Bush's invincible popularity. Having a penchant for extreme secrecy, the administration made it difficult for official investigators, let alone journalists and historians, to obtain information about the formulation and implementation of basic policies. It may take many years longer to establish a reasonably full record of the Bush administration than it has for any administration since Richard Nixon's. Remarkably, though, the very radicalism of Bush's presidency has, over time, led to the publication of some revealing accounts of how it has operated behind the scenes. And this radicalism is sufficiently stark that the historical origins and implications of Bush's governance are less difficult to assess than is the case for other, more divided and pragmatic presidencies.

Among the noteworthy early general evaluations of the Bush years are Fred I. Greenstein, ed., *The George W. Bush Presidency: An Early Assessment* (Baltimore, MD, 2003); Colin Campbell and Bert A. Rockman, *The George W. Bush Presidency: Appraisals and Prospects* (Washington, DC, 2004); Gary L. Gregg and Mark Rozell, eds., *Considering the Bush Presidency* (New York, 2004); Bryan Hilliard, Tom Lansford, and Robert P. Watson, eds., *George W. Bush: Evaluating the President at Midterm* (Albany, NY, 2004); Steven E. Schier, ed., *High Risk and Big Ambition: The Presidency of George W. Bush* (Pittsburgh, PA, 2004); Robert Maranto, Doug Brattebo, and Tom Lansford, eds., *The Second Term of George W. Bush: Prospects and Perils* (New York, 2006); and John C. Fortier and Norman J. Ornstein, eds., *Second-Term Blues: How George W. Bush Has Governed* (Washington, DC, 2007).

Two enthusiastic general studies, both by established conservative writers (the first of whom was a speechwriter for Bush), are David Frum, *The Right Man: The Surprise Presidency of George W. Bush* (New York, 2003); and John Podhoretz, *Bush Country: How Dubya Became a Great President While Driving Liberals Insane* (New York, 2004). Ronald Kessler, the author of a tabloid-style thrashing of the lax morality and odd personalities that have dominated earlier administrations, finds nothing but probity and correctness in Bush's; see his *A Matter of Character: Inside the Bush White House* (New

York, 2004). In a class of its own is a book by Bush's communications adviser Karen Hughes, *George W. Bush: Portrait of a Leader* (Wheaton, IL, 2005), which depicts Bush as a hero and is replete with more than 100 photographs; it was released by a Christian publishing house that specializes in literary works "consistent with biblical principles." Negative general assessments include Elizabeth Drew, *Fear and Loathing in George W. Bush's Washington* (New York, 2004); Sidney Blumenthal, *How Bush Rules: Chronicles of a Radical Regime* (Princeton, NJ, 2006); and two books by Kevin P. Phillips, *American Dynasty*, cited earlier, and *American Theology: The Peril and Politics of Radical Religion, Oil, and Borrowed Money in the 21st Century* (New York, 2006), although the latter focuses more on the changing Republican Party than on the Bush White House per se. I ventured a preliminary, historical evaluation in "The Worst President in History?" *Rolling Stone* (May 4, 2006): 32–37.

Biographies have run the gamut from laudatory to damning. They include Bill Minutaglio, *First Son: George W. Bush and the Bush Family Dynasty* (New York, 1999); Arthur Frederick Ide, *George W. Bush: Portrait of a Compassionate Conservative* (Las Colinas, TX, 2000); J. H. Hatfield, *Fortunate Son: George W. Bush and the Making of an American President* (New York, 2001); and Frank Bruni, *Ambling into History: The Unlikely Odyssey of George W. Bush* (New York, 2002). Of equal interest is a spate of studies concerning Bush's longtime political adviser Karl Rove and Vice President Dick Cheney, who is formally as well as practically the most powerful vice president in American history. On Rove, see James Moore and Wayne Slater, *Bush's Brain: How Karl Rove Made George W. Bush Presidential* (Hoboken, NJ, 2003); James Moore and Wayne Slater, *The Architect: Karl Rove and the Master Plan for Absolute Power* (New York, 2006); and Lou Dubose, Jan Reid, and Carl M. Cannon, *Boy Genius: Karl Rove, the Brains Behind the Remarkable Political Triumph of George W. Bush* (New York, 2003). The only full-length study of Cheney is an authorized, uncritical biography, Steven F. Hayes, *Cheney: The Untold Story of America's Most Powerful Vice President* (New York, 2007), which contains some useful information and affirms primary material I have read about Cheney's earlier political career in the 1970s and 1980s. There is also a good deal to be learned in the relevant portions of James Mann, *Rise of the Vulcans: The History of Bush's War Cabinet* (New York, 2003). Mann's book is also a good place to start to learn about the rise of some of Bush's other foreign policy advisers: Donald Rumsfeld, Colin Powell, Richard Armitage, Condoleezza Rice, and Paul Wolfowitz.

Memoirs from the Bush White House began arriving early. Bush's own campaign biography, *A Charge to Keep: My Journey to the White House* (1999; New York, 2001), written with Karen Hughes and Mickey Herskowitz, is long on family anecdotes and short on political prescriptions, and it gives only the faintest hints of the direction his "compassionate conservatism" would take after Bush took office. Secretary of the Treasury Paul O'Neill's memoir of the White House, published as Ron Suskind, *The Price of Loyalty: George W. Bush, the White House, and the Education of Paul O'Neill* (New York, 2004), caused an immediate stir with its dispiriting account of an executive branch utterly without debate or free discussion, where policy was prearranged. Bush's first director of his new White House Office for Faith-Based and Community Initiatives, John DiIulio, resigned after a few months and sent a devastating on-the-record memo to Suskind, some of which appeared in Suskind's article "Why Are These Men Laughing?" in *Esquire* (January 2003). DiIulio described Bush personally in glowing terms as a truly caring man who "inspires trust, loyalty, and confidence in those around him." But his account of the hard-core politicized White House, in which policy is subordinated to partisan and personal political calculations by those DiIulio called "Mayberry Machiavellis," is still unnerving. The complete memo can be accessed at http://www.esquire.com/features/dilulio.

Richard Clarke advised presidents from Reagan to the second Bush on national security, with special expertise on antiterrorism policy. His memoir, *Against All Enemies: Inside the War on Terror* (New York, 2004), criticized the second Bush administration harshly for its indifference to Al Qaeda and terrorism before the attacks of September 11, 2001. George Tenet's *At the Center of the Storm: My Years at the CIA* (New York, 2007), written by Tenet (the former director of the CIA) with Bill Harlow, attempts to distance the author from some of the more egregious intelligence lapses that preceded the invasion of Iraq, and to attribute responsibility to other officials, including the veteran neoconservative Richard Perle, who was back in the White House as the chair of Bush's Defense Policy Board. L. Paul Bremer with Malcolm McConnell, *My Year in Iraq: The Struggle to Build a Future of Hope* (New York, 2006), tells of Bremer's efforts as head of the hapless, doomed Coalition Provisional Authority established to oversee Iraq's reconstruction after Saddam Hussein was overthrown. On the administration's contempt for the law, *The Terror Presidency: Law and Judgment Inside the Bush Administration* (New York, 2007), by Jack Goldsmith, a former head of the office of legal counsel in Bush's Justice Department, is especially damning because its author is a committed conservative who shares the administration's basic political outlook.

Apart from its aggressive, top-heavy tax cuts, the educational program No Child Left Behind (actually initiated by Senator Edward Kennedy), a failed proposal to privatize some of the Social Security program, and an expensive program for pharmaceutical price reform that would enrich the largest drug manufacturers, the Bush administration has not offered much in the way of a coherent domestic agenda. There have, though, been signs that its domestic policy has largely followed the course that enraged John DiIulio in 2001. Unfortunately, tight secrecy and the invocation of executive privilege have blocked inquiry into matters such as Vice President Cheney's meetings on energy policy in mid-2001 and the questions surrounding the hiring and firing of federal district attorneys. But the occasional streaks of light have been telling. In 2007, for example, the outgoing surgeon general of the United States, Richard H. Carmona, testified before Congress that officials at the Bush White House repeatedly and systematically blocked the release of information that might prove deleterious to the administration's corporate backers and friends on the Christian right; Carmona was also expected to give speeches full of positive remarks about President Bush, and to attend Republican Party political functions. See Gardiner Harris, "Surgeon General Sees 4-Year Term as Compromised," *New York Times*, July 11, 2007, p. A1.

On the election of 2004, see Evan Thomas et al., *Election 2004: How Bush Won and What You Can Expect in the Future* (New York, 2005). See also the clashing interpretations in Larry Sabato, ed., *Divided States of America: The Slash and Burn Politics of the*

2004 Presidential Election (New York, 2005); Kenneth R. Libbey, *Snatching Defeat from the Jaws of Victory: How the Democrats Lost the 2004 Election* (Lake Oswego, OR, 2005); and James W. Ceaser and Andrew E. Busch, *Red over Blue: The 2004 Elections and American Politics* (Lanham, MD, 2005).

The Terry Schiavo case has so far mainly been the subject of highly argumentative books and articles. The full political story and its implications have yet to be told, although some interesting facts are presented in a book whose title sums up its argument: Jon B. Eisenberg, *Using Terri: The Religious Right's Conspiracy to Take Away Our Rights* (San Francisco, CA, 2005). On the vexing ethical issues surrounding the case and others like it, see Arthur L. Caplan, James J. McCartney, and Dominic A. Sisti, eds., *The Case of Terri Schiavo: Ethics at the End of Life* (Amherst, NY, 2006).

On hurricane Katrina, the government's response, and the prolonged suffering, especially in New Orleans, see Jed Horne, *Breach of Faith: Hurricane Katrina and the Near Death of a Great American City* (New York, 2006); Ivor van Heerden and Mike Bryan, *The Storm: What Went Wrong and Why During Hurricane Katrina* (New York, 2006); Christopher Cooper and Robert Block, *Disaster: Katrina and the Failure of Homeland Security* (New York, 2007); and Douglas Brinkley, *The Great Deluge: Hurricane Katrina, New Orleans, and the Mississippi Gulf Coast* (New York, 2006).

A fascinating book remains to be written on the Joseph Wilson episode and the trial of I. Lewis "Scooter" Libby—a true-life hugger-mugger no matter how fully the story eventually is revealed. For the moment, readers should consult Murray Waas with Jeff Lomonaco, eds., *The United States v. I. Lewis Libby* (New York, 2007). Only one side of the controversy has yet to produce a substantial work, but see Joseph Wilson's *The Politics of Truth*, cited earlier.

The Bush administration has, of course, focused mainly on foreign policy—and, within foreign policy, on its war on terror—after the attacks of 2001, the ensuing assault on Afghanistan, and the invasion of Iraq in 2003. On the background to the terrorist attacks, Lawrence Wright, *The Looming Tower: Al Qaeda and the Road to 9/11* (New York, 2006), is the most helpful single volume. See also Paul L. Berman's challenging *Terror and Liberalism* (New York, 2004), which combines intellectual history with political commentary. There are now thousands of books that have some bearing on the events identified in shorthand as 9/11, ranging from collections of poetry to elaborations of bizarre conspiracy theories. Although it is not above criticism, the place to start is *The 9/11 Commission Report: Final Report of the National Commission on Terrorist Attacks upon the United States* (New York, 2004).

The buildup to the invasion of Iraq, the swift toppling of Saddam Hussein's regime, and the prolonged American military intervention ever since have each provoked contentious accounts. Along with the memoirs by Clarke, Wilson, Tenet, and Bremer cited earlier, as well as James Mann's *Rise of the Vulcans*, I have found the following especially informative: Thomas E. Ricks, *Fiasco: The American Military Adventure in Iraq* (New York, 2006); Michael R. Gordon and Bernard E. Trainor, *Cobra II: The Inside Story of the Invasion and Occupation of Iraq* (New York, 2006); Ali A. Allawi, *The Occupation of Iraq: Winning the War, Losing the Peace* (New Haven, CT, 2007); Christian Alfonsi, *Circle in the Sand: Why We Went Back to Iraq* (New York, 2006); Ron Suskind, *The One Percent*

Doctrine: Deep Inside America's Pursuit of Its Enemies Since 9/11 (New York, 2006); and Michael Isikoff and David Corn, *Hubris: The Inside Story of the Spin, Scandal, and Selling of the Iraq War* (New York, 2006). On the implications of the Bush administration's record in general, but especially in Iraq, for Americans' basic ideas of truth and objectivity, see the comprehensive recital in Frank Rich, *The Greatest Story Ever Sold: The Decline and Fall of Truth from 9/11 to Katrina* (New York, 2006). To conclude by coming full circle: Bob Woodward, whose reporting with Carl Bernstein for the *Washington Post* in 1972 and 1973 in many ways unwittingly set in motion the events that would open the way for the age of Reagan, has been writing extensively about the White House and the war on terror. In a continuing series of books, Woodward has shifted from almost uncritical admiration of President Bush and his aides to harsh condemnation—running in sync with the trends in general public opinion. See his *Bush at War* (New York, 2002); *Plan of Attack* (New York, 2004); and *State of Denial* (New York, 2006).

INDEX

Able Archer exercise, 166–67, 246
abortion issue, 27, 68, 89, 122, 186–87, 190, 192–93, 326, 352
Abramoff, Jack, 447
Abrams, Elliott, 156, 214, 225, 242, 336, 436
Abshire, David, 230, 232, 235
Abu Ghraib torture scandal, 445–46
Abzug, Bella, 34, 88
accountability, 401–2
    acquired immune deficiency syndrome (AIDS), 185–86
Addington, David S., 242, 435
Adelman, Kenneth, 442
affirmative action, 21, 46, 85–88, 183–84, 358. See also racial issues
Afghanistan
    George W. Bush administration war in, 434–35, 440
    Carter administration and, 109–10
    Clinton administration and, 394, 406
    Reagan administration and, 216, 279–80
    Soviet war in, 247, 258, 262
Africa, 103–5, 107
Age Discrimination Claims Assistance Act, 182
AIDS epidemic, 185–86
Aid to Families with Dependent Children (AFDC), 365

air traffic controllers' strike, 143–44
Albania, 404–5
Alfred P. Murrah Federal Building bombing, 353–54
Albright, Madeleine, 360, 404
Alexander, Lamar, 304
Alito, Samuel, 450
Allen, George, 454
Allen, Richard, 151
Al Qaeda, 303, 375, 393–94, 405–6, 434–35
America. See United States
American Enterprise Institute (AEI), 89, 132
Americans with Disabilities Act, 305–6
amnesty issue, 29, 78
Anderson, John, 118, 120
Anderson, Martin, 140, 438
Andropov, Yuri, 163, 165, 248–49
Angola, 104–5, 107, 157
Annan, Kofi, 405
anticommunism. See communism
antigoverment attitudes, 127–28, 135–37, 177, 274
anti-politics, 82–83, 98
antiwar protests, Reagan and, 133
Apple, R. W. "Johnny," 16, 232
Aquino, Benigno and Corazon, 252–53, 279
Arafat, Yasir, 53, 110, 159, 340, 403
Argentina, 157

Arias, Oscar, 242, 279
Aristide, Jean-Bertrand, 337–38
Arkansas Project, 379
Armey, Richard, 348, 352, 362
arms control. *See* Strategic Arms Limitation Treaty (SALT II); Strategic Arms Reduction Talks (START)
arms-for-hostages affair, Reagan's, 216–24, 241–42. *See also* Iran-contra affair
Ash, Roy, 32
Askew, Ruben, 171
Aspin, Les, 337
assassination attempts, 50, 64–65, 142
Atwater, Lee, 5, 270–71, 319, 413, 436
Aziz, Tariq, 300

Baird, Zoë, 329–30
Baker, Howard, 179, 194, 243
Baker, James, III, 139–40, 142, 146, 148, 178–79, 212, 215, 290–91, 294–300, 339, 421–24
Bakke, Allan, 86–87
Baldrige, Malcolm, 140
Balkans, 339, 355–56, 359–61, 363, 404–5
Baltic states, 295, 313
Baroody, William, 132
Barr, William, 343
Bartley, Robert, 90
Bayh, Birch, 69
Bazargan, Mehdi, 114–16
Beame, Abraham, 40
Begala, Paul, 359
Begin, Menachem, 111–13, 159–60
Bell, Griffin, 76, 86–87, 98
Bennett, Robert, 378–81, 387
Bennett, William, 185, 194, 305
Bentsen, Lloyd, 269, 327, 345, 356
Bernanke, Ben, 457
Bernstein, Carl, 25, 30
Bethell, Tom, 253
bicentennial celebration, 14–16

Biden, Joseph, 191–92, 267
big government. *See* federal government
Billings, Robert, 122
bin Laden, Osama, 280, 302–3, 374–76, 393, 406, 434–35
Bishop, Maurice, 161
black Monday panic, 208
Blackmun, Harry, 21
Blair, Tony, 374, 403
Blumenthal, Michael, 80, 98
Blumenthal, Sidney, 388, 390–91, 399
Boehlert, Sherwood, 306
Boesky, Ivan, 203
Boland, Edward, 166
Boland Amendments, 166–67, 212, 222–24, 239
Bolick, Clint, 330
Bolton, John, 242, 441
Bork, Robert, 50, 62, 190–94, 243, 283, 379
Bosnia, 339, 355–56, 359–61, 363
Bossie, David, 344
Bowles, Erskine, 372
Bradley, Bill, 205, 313, 317, 414
Brady, James, 142
Bremer, L. Paul, 448
Brennan, William, 311
Breyer, Stephen, 346, 426
Brezhnev, Leonid, 52–53, 58, 105–10, 163
Brezhnev Doctrine, 105, 109
Brock, William, 183–84
Broder, David, 7, 325
Brooke, Edward, 66
Brown, Edmund G. "Pat," 133
Brown, Edmund "Jerry," 69, 319
Brown, Floyd, 343–44
Brown, Harold, 107
Brown, Michael, 447
Browning, Herbert, 189
Brunei, 214, 225
Bryant, Ed, 399
Brzezinski, Zbigniew, 75–76, 101, 104, 118

Buchanan, Patrick J., 5, 179, 185, 210, 282, 299, 308, 315, 320, 335, 368
Buckley, James, 41
Buckley, William, 216–17, 220, 226
Buckley, William F., Jr., 89, 91–92, 261, 456
Budget Impoundment and Control Act, 17
budgets
    George H. W. Bush administration, 307–10
    Clinton administration, 326–29, 356, 357–64, 372
    Reagan administration, 141–43, 283–84
Bumpers, Dale, 400
bureaucratic decrees, 140
Burger, Warren, 21, 190, 207
Bush, George H. W., 288–322
    cabinet of, 290–91, 310–11
    campaign of, against Clinton, 315–22
    campaign of, against Dukakis, 264–73, 289
    career of, 288–89
    Chinese-U.S. relations and, 291–92
    as CIA director, 62–63, 153
    controversies of administration of, 310–14
    Bob Dole and, 264
    federal deficit, economic issues, and, 303–10
    Ford and, 33
    German reunification and, 294–96
    Iran-contra affair and, 215, 230, 336
    Iraqi invasion of Kuwait, Persian Gulf War, and, 297–303
    NAFTA and, 314
    Nixon administration and, 4–5
    Panama invasion of, 292–94
    Reagan on, 287
    Soviet-U.S. relations and, 292, 313

    Clarence Thomas appointment by, 311–12
    Reagan and, 120–21, 160, 287
Bush, George W., 408–57
    cabinet of, and neoconservative policies of, 242, 435–40
    campaign of, against Gore, 408–18
    campaign of, against Kerry, 444
    declining popularity of, and setbacks of, 444–50
    executive power issues, 8–9
    on history, 458
    overview of administration of, 432–35
    political controversies, Reaganism, and, 450–56
    Supreme Court ruling on election of, 7–8, 418–29
    war on terror of, 440–44
Bush, Jeb, 307, 409, 419–21, 423, 454
Bush, Neil, 307
Bush, Prescott, 264
business regulations. See deregulation
busing, desegregation, 42–47
Byrd, Robert, 79, 306

cabinets
    George H. W. Bush administration, 290–91
    George W. Bush administration, 411–12, 435–36
    Carter administration, 75–78, 98
    Clinton administration, 327–31, 376–78
    Ford administration, 32–33, 59–64
    Nixon administration, 5, 32–33
    Reagan administration, 139, 177–80, 242–43
Caddell, Patrick, 77–78, 82, 97–98, 122–23
Califano, Joseph, Jr., 76, 80, 81, 86, 98
California governor, Reagan as, 133–34
Cambodia, 54–56
Cammerata, Joe, 378–80
Campbell, Donovan, Jr., 385

Cannon, Lou, 2, 37, 64, 210
Carlucci, Frank, 243
Carmona, Richard H., 447–48
Carpenter-McMillan, Susan, 379–80
Carswell, G. Harrold, 21
Carter, Billy, 119–20, 123
Carter, Jimmy, 73–126
    Africa and, 103–5
    cabinet of, 75–78, 98
    campaign of, against Ford, 69–72
    campaign of, against Reagan,
        120–26
    Christians and, 73–74
    culture war issues, 85–89
    economic policies of, 78–85, 139–40
    Egyptian-Israeli accords and,
        110–13
    human rights policies of, 99–100
    inauguration of, 74–75
    Iranian revolution, hostage crisis,
        and, 113–20
    Iranian revolution, oil crisis, and,
        95–98
    liberalism of, 6
    management style of, 75–78
    new right conservative attacks on,
        89–95
    Nicaragua and, 102–3
    overview of administration of,
        73–75, 99–100
    Panama Canal issue and, 101–2
    Reagan vs., 278
    Soviet-American relations and,
        105–10
Carter, Rosalynn, 88–89
Casey, William, 153, 167, 212–17, 219,
    221, 226, 229, 232
Castro, Fidel, 50, 161
Cato Institute, 274
Cavazos, Lauro, 304
Central America, Reagan and, 157, 166,
    278. See also Iran-contra affair
Central Intelligence Agency (CIA), 18,
    49–51, 153, 167, 212, 265, 375, 439–40, 442
Chaffee, John H., 283

Chamorro, Violeta, 279
Channell, Carl "Spitz," 215
Chappaquiddick accident, 116, 267
character issue, Clinton and, 325
Cheney, Richard B. "Dick," 4–5, 49, 57,
    60–65, 67–68, 85, 223, 238, 240, 242,
    290–91, 295, 299–300, 406, 411, 416,
    429, 434–39, 441–42
Chenoweth, Helen, 352
Chernenko, Konstantin, 248–50
Chernobyl nuclear accident, 254–55
Chernyaev, Anatoly, 247, 252
Chertoff, Michael, 377, 447
Chile, 15, 49, 51
China
    George H. W. Bush and, 291–92
    Carter and, 107–8
    Ford and, 51, 65
    Nixon and, 21
Chodorov, Frank, 89
Christian Coalition, 352
Christians. See also religious
    conservatives
    George W. Bush and, 444
    Carter and, 73–74
    Oklahoma City bombing and, 353
Christian Voice, 92–93
Christopher, Warren, 339, 421
Church, Frank, 50, 125
Cisneros, Henry, 376
civil rights. See also affirmative action;
    racial issues
    George H. W. Bush administration
        and, 305–6, 312
    Carter administration and, 85–88
    conservatives and, 91–93
    Democratic Party and, 23
    Ford administration and, 42–47
    Nixon administration and, 19–20
    post-Watergate era, 6
    Reagan administration and, 180–87
Civil Rights Restoration Bill, 184
Clark, Dick, 50
Clark, Wesley, 404
Clark, William P., 162–63

Clarke, Richard, 375, 406, 445
Clean Air Act, 306
Cleland, Max, 444
Clifford, Clark, 97
Clinton, Bill, 323–407
    administration of, as Reagan post-
        lude, 4, 7
    budget negotiations and govern-
        ment shutdown, 356–64
    cabinet controversies, 329–31, 376
    campaign of, against Dole, 367–70
    campaign of, against George H. W.
        Bush, 317–22
    Clintonism term, 323–24, 350–53
    domestic policies of, 326–36,
        356–61
    education and, 304
    federal deficits and economic
        recovery policies of, 326–31,
        356–61, 370–73
    foreign policies of, 336–41, 355–56,
        373–76, 403–7
    gays in the military issue, 329
    Newt Gingrich's assault on, 346–50
    legacy of, and Al Gore, 410–11
    Monica Lewinsky affair and im-
        peachment of, 381–403 (see also
        impeachment, Clinton's)
    Dick Morris and congressional
        relations of, 350–53
    NAFTA issue, 334–36
    national health care issue, 322–36,
        365
    Oklahoma City bombing and,
        353–54
    overview of administration of,
        323–26, 355–56
    welfare reform issue, 364–67
    Whitewater controversy and Vin-
        cent Foster suicide, 341–46
    Whitewater investigation and
        Paula Jones sexual harassment
        suit, 376–81
Clinton, Hillary Rodham, 319, 328, 331–34,
    345, 366, 376–77, 383–84, 452–53

Cochran, Thad, 84
Cohen, William S., 283, 404
Colby, William, 49–50, 59, 62
Cole, bombing of, 406
Cole, Kenneth, 32
Coleman, William, 44–45
Colson, Charles, 32
communism. See also Soviet Union
    Carter and, 106
    Nixon and, 18–19
    Reagan and, 131, 136, 138, 151–52,
        157, 280–81
compromise politics, Clinton's, 326
Congress
    Black Caucus, 44, 46, 86–88
    Clinton impeachment hearings,
        396–403
    Democratic control of, 7, 449
    Iran-contra hearings, 233–40
    midterm elections, 7, 34–35, 37,
        84–85, 150, 309–10, 325, 346–50,
        395–96, 449
    Republican control of, 347–53, 439
    Tower Commission, 228–33
Congressional Advisory Board, 411
conservatism. See also Republican Party
    Clinton and, 359
    Democratic Party, 84–85
    federal judiciary and, 7–8, 21
    Ford's, 29
    neoconservatives, 28, 52, 62, 90–91,
        131
    new right, 89–95
    Nixon's, 5
    Reagan's, 1–11, 16, 127–29, 131–32,
        281–83
    religious (see religious conserva-
        tives)
    Donald Rumsfeld's and Dick
        Cheney's, 60–62
constitutional issues, 8–9, 17, 284–85,
    401–3
containment policy, 19, 23. See also
    détente policy
Contract with America, 348–49, 351

contras, 156, 166, 278–79. *See also* Iran-
  contra affair
Conway, George, III, 378–80, 385–88
Coolidge, Calvin, 137, 143
Cooper, Charles, 227
corruption, Reagan administration,
  200–203, 286. *See also* scandals
Coulter, Ann, 380, 383, 385
Council of Economic Advisers, 36–37
Council on Wage and Price Stability
  (COWPS), 95–96
Cox, Archibald, 50, 191
Craig, Larry, 454
Cranston, Alan, 198
Croatia, 339, 360–61
Crocker, Ryan, 453
Crowe, William J., 255, 259
Cruz, Arturo, 213, 223
Cuba, 104, 161–62
cultural issues
  Carter administration, 85–95
  Clinton administration, 329–31,
    401–2
  culture wars, 85–95, 320–21
  post-Vietnam War, 23–24
  post-Watergate, 26–28
  Reagan administration, 180–87, 274
Culvahouse, Arthur B., Jr., 192
Cuomo, Mario, 266, 317, 349
Currie, Betty, 386, 390

Dale, Billy, 331
Dallaire, Romeo, 338
D'Amato, Alfonse, 125, 376–77
Danforth, John, 181, 330
Daniloff, Nicholas, 256
Darman, Richard, 148, 179, 307–8
Dart, Justin, 133
Dash, Sam, 397
Davis, Gil, 378–80
Davis, John, 280–81
Davis, Loyal, 131
Day the Earth Stood Still, The (film), 138, 261
Deaver, Michael, 139, 142, 144, 146, 166,
  178–80, 200, 209–10, 438

debates
  Ford vs. Carter, 70–72
  Gore vs. George W. Bush, 418
  Gore vs. Perot, 335
  Reagan vs. Carter, 123–25
  Reagan vs. Mondale, 174
DeConcini, Dennis, 198
Decter, Midge, 91
de facto vs. de jure segregation, 42
deficits, federal. *See also* surpluses,
  federal
  George H. W. Bush administra-
    tion, 295, 303, 306–7, 314
  George W. Bush administration,
    437, 450
  Carter administration, 78–79
  Clinton administration, 326–29,
    363
  Reagan administration, 137,
    140–41, 146–47, 177, 206, 283–84
DeLay, Tom, 348, 396, 398–99, 424, 429,
  434–35, 447
Democratic Leadership Council (DLC),
  318
Democratic Party. *See also* liberalism
  George H. W. Bush and, 266–73,
    317, 320, 451–52
  Carter and, 82–83, 124–25
  civil rights and, 46
  Clinton and, 317–26
  congressional majority of, 7, 34–35
  neoconservatives, 28, 52, 62, 131,
    153
  Reagan and, 144, 171–75
  south and, 20
  Vietnam War and, 21–25
Denton, Jeremiah, 125
Department of Housing and Urban
  Development (HUD), 169, 200
deregulation, 39, 139–40, 169, 177,
  194–200, 274–75
desegregation, 5, 20, 42–47
détente policy, 5, 19, 23, 51–59, 64, 108,
  151–52
DiIulio, John, Jr., 438

Dingell, John, 306
discrimination, reverse, 86–87, 181, 184, 304
Dobrynin, Anatoly, 108, 163
Dobson, James, 455
Dolan, John "Terry," 92–93
Dole, Elizabeth, 201, 409
Dole, Robert J. "Bob," 69–70, 148, 181, 264, 266, 361–62, 367–70
Domenici, Pete, 372
domestic policies. *See also* civil rights; economic policies
   George H. W. Bush administration, 303–10
   George W. Bush administration, 436–40
   Carter administration, 78–85, 95–98
   Clinton administration, 326–36, 346–47, 357–58, 361–64, 370–73, 407
   Ford administration, 42–47, 71
   Al Gore on, 416–17
   Johnson administration, 23
   Nixon administration, 17–18
   Reagan administration, 8, 139–50, 168–71, 176–208, 273–78, 281–84
domestic surveillance, 17–18, 43, 49–50, 446
Donovan, Raymond, 201
Draper, Theodore, 9–10, 284
Drudge, Matt, 380, 388
drugs, 216, 293–95, 305
Dukakis, Michael, 6, 266–73, 289
Dylan, Bob, 27, 433

Eagleburger, Lawrence, 291
earned income tax credit, 328
East Germany, 292
economic policies
   George H. W. Bush administration, 303–10, 314
   Carter administration, 78–85, 95–98, 123
   Clinton administration, 321, 326–31, 357–58, 361–64, 370–73

Ford adminstration, 15, 35–41
   Mikhail Gorbachev's, 248–49, 258
   Johnson administration, 23
   Reagan administration, 127–28, 139–50, 168–78, 203–8, 274–76, 283–84 (*see also* supply-side economics)
Economic Policy Board (EPB), 36–37
Economic Stabilization Fund, 357
Edelman, Marian Wright and Peter, 76, 367
education issues, 304, 437
Edwards, John, 452
Edwards, Mickey, 451
Egyptian-Israeli accords, 53, 56–57, 110–13
Eizenstat, Stuart, 76, 80, 86–87
Ellis, John, 419
Ellis, Thomas, 66, 315
El Salvador, 156, 166, 217
Emanuel, Rahm, 382
Empire Savings and Loan, 199
energy policies
   George W. Bush administration, 439
   Carter administration, 75, 78–83, 95–98
   Ford administration, 38–39
Energy Security Corporation, 97
Enron Corporation, 421, 439
environmental issues
   George H. W. Bush and, 306
   Carter on, 82
   Reagan on, 169–70
Environmental Protection Agency (EPA), 170
equal protection argument, 425–26
Equal Rights Amendment, 27, 88, 94–95
Espy, Mike, 376
Ethiopia, 107
evangelical conservatives. *See* religious conservatives
evangelists, television, 263–64
executive branch politicization, 17, 435

executive power
George W. Bush and, 434–39,
441–42
Carter and, 83
Clinton's impeachment and, 401
Nixon and, 4, 8, 16–17, 48–49
Reagan and, 8–9, 194, 284–85,
240–42, 284–85
Donald Rumsfeld, Dick Cheney,
and, 61–62
executive privilege, Nixon and, 18
Exxon Valdez oil spill, 306

Fair Deal, 16
fairness doctrine, 195–96
fairness issue, 149–50
Falwell, Jerry, 89, 93, 186, 189, 320, 341,
415
Family and Medical Leave Act, 326–27
Family Support Bill, 204–5
Farrakhan, Louis, 171
Federal Bureau of Investigation (FBI),
18, 330, 375, 376
Federal Communications Commission
(FCC), 195–96
federal debt, 306–7. See also deficits,
federal; surpluses, federal
Federal Emergency Management
Agency (FEMA), 418, 447
Federal Energy Administration, 39
federal government
Clinton on, 364
Reagan on, 127–28, 136, 177, 274
shutdowns, 309, 356
federal judiciary, 7–8, 187–94, 429. See
also judicial appointments; Supreme
Court
Federal Reserve, 96, 147–48, 171, 208,
275–76, 307, 327–28, 457
Federal Savings and Loan Insurance
Corporation (FSLIC), 197–98
Fein, Bruce, 435
Feith, Douglas, 445
feminism, 6, 27, 88–89. See also women's
issues

Ferraro, Geraldine, 173
Feulner, Edwin, 90
fiscal policies. See economic policies
Fisher, Jim, 387
Fiske, Robert, Jr., 345–46, 378
Fitzgerald, Patrick, 447
Florida election dispute, 419–29
Flynt, Larry, 398–99
Foley, Mark, 449
Ford, Betty, 64–65
Ford, Gerald, 26–47
assassination attempts on, 64–65
bicentennial and, 14–16
cabinet of, 59–64
campaign of, against Carter, 69–72
campaign of, against Reagan, 65–69
civil rights and race relations poli-
cies of, 42–47
domestic policies of, 35–41
détente and foreign policies of, 48–64
Egyptian-Israeli accord, 56–57
intelligence reform and, 48–51
Mayaguez affair and, 55–56
overview of administration of, 4–5,
14–16, 26–28, 48
pardon of Nixon by, 28–35
Solzhenitsyn affair and, 57–58
Vietnam War and, 48
Watergate affair and, 18, 26–28
foreign policies
George H. W. Bush administration, 290–303, 312–14
George W. Bush administration,
415–16, 434–35, 440–46
Carter administration, 99–126
Clinton administration, 336–41,
355–61, 373–76, 403–7
Mikhail Gorbachev's, 248–57 (see
also Gorbachev, Mikhail)
Ford administration, 71
Nixon administration, 5, 17, 18–19,
21, 49–50
Reagan administration, 5, 128–29,
138, 151–68, 176, 278–81, 284 (see
also Iran-contra affair)

Foster, Vincent, 341, 343, 378, 384–85
Fox News Network, 196, 419
Frank, Barney, 352, 397–98
Freeh, Louis, 375
Frist, Bill, 446
Fromme, Lynette "Squeaky," 64

Garrity, Arthur, 42, 45
Gates, Robert, 242, 299
gay rights, 92–93, 185–86, 329
Geller, Joe, 424
Geneva Conventions, 442
Gephardt, Richard, 205, 267, 317, 335, 394–95
Gergen, David, 179, 183, 344
Germany, 209–11, 292, 294–96, 374
Gerth, Jeff, 342–43, 377
Ghorbanifar, Manucher, 218–25
Gigot, Paul, 370, 424
Gingrich, Newt, 85, 308–10, 317, 334, 347–53, 356–57, 359–64, 368, 372, 391–92, 395–96, 400, 411
Ginsburg, Douglas, 194, 243
Ginsburg, Ruth Bader, 346, 425–26
Ginsburg, William, 390, 393
Giuliani, Rudolph, 201, 454
glasnost (openness), 248, 250, 258, 273
Glenn, John, 171, 198
globalization, 335, 372
Goldberg, Lucianne, 384–85, 388
Goldwater, Barry, 19–20, 34, 67, 70, 127, 132–33, 167, 189, 277, 368, 409
Goldwin, Robert, 62
Gonzales, Alberto, 442, 452
Good Friday Accords, 403
Gorbachev, Mikhail
    George H. W. Bush and, 292
    career of, 246–49
    German reunification and, 295–96
    reforms of, 253–54, 258
    summit meetings with Reagan and, 243–46, 249–63, 284
    Boris Yeltsin and, 313
Gore, Albert, Jr., 9, 267, 300, 320, 366–67, 408–10, 416–29

Gorsuch Burford, Anne, 170
government. See federal government
Gramm, Philip, 141
Gramm-Rudman-Hollings Act, 307–8
Grant, Robert, 92
Gray, C. Boyden, 300, 311
Gray, Edwin, 197–99
Great Society, 16, 20, 23
Greenberg, Stanley, 349
Green Party, 417
Greenspan, Alan, 36–41, 140, 169, 307, 327–28
Greider, William, 145–46, 148
Grenada invasion, 161–62
Gromyko, Andrey, 107, 168, 249–51
Guantánamo Bay torture scandal, 445–46
Guinier, Lani, 330
Gulf Wars. See Iraq

Hadley, Stephen, 416
Haig, Alexander, 18, 30–33, 139, 142, 153, 156, 162–63, 264
Haiti, 337–38, 340
Hakim, Albert, 215, 223, 225, 240
Haldeman, H. R. "Bob," 32
Hale, David, 343
Hall, Fawn, 214
Halliburton, 421
Halloween massacre, 62–64
Halperin, Mark, 410
Hamilton, Alexander, 402–3
Hamilton, Lee, 235
Harris, Fred, 69
Harris, Hubert, 116
Harris, John, 371
Harris, Katherine, 420, 422–24
Harris, Patricia Roberts, 77c
Hart, Gary, 146, 171–73, 266–67
Hartmann, Robert, 33, 60–61
Hasenfus, Eugene, 225
Haynesworth, Clement F., 21
health care reform, 84, 332–36, 365
Helms, Jesse, 57, 66, 85, 101, 104, 183, 261–62

Helsinki accords, 58–59
Heritage Foundation, 27, 90, 157, 250
Hersh, Seymour, 49, 61
Hertzberg, Hendrik, 97
Hill, Anita, 311–12
Hinckley, John, Jr., 142
historical scholarship on Reagan, 1–5, 9–11
Hofstadter, Richard, 2, 94, 136
Holbrooke, Richard, 361, 363
Hollings, Ernest "Fritz," 171
Holmes, Wes, 385
home, Reagan on, 134–37
homosexual rights, 92–93, 185–86, 329
Hooks, Benjamin, 182
Hoover Institution, 89
Horton, Willie, 271, 289
hostage crisis, Carter and Iranian, 115–19, 123–24
hostage-for-arms affair, Reagan's, 216–24, 241–42. See also Iran-contra affair
House of Representatives. See Congress
Housing and Urban Development Department (HUD), 169, 200
Huckabee, Mike, 455
human rights
    Carter's policies on, 99–100, 105–6
    Gorbachev's policies on, 258
    Helsinki accords and, 58–59
Humphrey, Gordon, 84
Humphrey, Hubert H., 20, 22, 70, 131
hurricane Katrina, 446–47, 450
Hussein, Saddam, 123, 159, 297–303, 340, 374, 404–5, 412, 434, 448–49. See also Iraq
Hyde, Henry J., 235, 238. 240, 392, 395–99, 401

Ickes, Harold, 345, 350
impeachment, Nixon's, 17–18
impeachment, Clinton's, 381–403
    legacy of precedent set by, 8, 400–403

Monica Lewinsky affair and, 381–87
    Starr Report, congressional hearings, and Clinton's acquittal, 393–400
    Whitewater investigation, Kenneth Starr, and, 387–93
inaugurations
    George W. Bush's, 428
    Carter's, 74–75
    Clinton's, 370, 383
    Reagan's, 127–29, 139, 152, 176
individualism, Reagan on, 135–36
inflation, 23, 35–37, 78, 88, 95–98, 146–48, 170
Inouye, Daniel K., 234
intelligence
    George W. Bush Office of Special Plans, 445
    Ford administration reform, 48–51
    Rumsfeld Commission report, 411–12
Internal Revenue Service (IRS), 18, 182
Internet, 408, 409–10
investigative mind-set, 267
Iran. See also Iran-contra affair
    George W. Bush and, 456
    Carter and, 95–98, 100, 113–20, 123–24
    Reagan and, 158–59, 280
    war of Iraq with, 123
Iran-contra affair, 209–44
    arms-for-hostages deals with Iran, 216–24
    congressional hearings on, 233–40
    contra funding and, 211–16
    exposure and investigation of, 224–33
    legacy of, 8, 240–41, 285–86, 401
Iraq
    George H. W. Bush administration war with, 289, 300–303
    George W. Bush administration war with, 442–46, 448–49, 452

Clinton administration and, 340, 374, 405–6
    invasion of Kuwait by, 297–300
    Reagan administration and, 158–59, 280
    war of Iran with, 123
Irvine, Reed, 195–96
Isikoff, Michael, 385, 386–88
Islamic terrorism. *See* terrorism
Israel
    arms-for-hostages affair and, 217–24
    Carter administration and, 110–13
    Clinton administration and, 403
    Ford administration and, 53, 56–57
    Gulf War and, 301
    Yitzhak Rabin assassination, 361
    Reagan administration and, 159–60

Jackson, Henry "Scoop," 51–53, 58, 69
Jackson, Jesse, 97, 171–73, 267, 317–18, 421
Jacobson, David, 226
Japan, 319
Javits, Jacob, 125
Jaworski, Leon, 30
Jeffords, James, 283, 439
Johnson, Haynes, 201–2
Johnson, Jim "Justice," 342, 344, 346
Johnson, Lyndon B., 19–23, 70
Jones, Paula, 346, 369, 378–81, 387, 391, 400
Jordan, Hamilton, 76, 116, 123
Jordan, Vernon, 76, 386, 390, 399
judicial appointments
    George H. W. Bush's, 311–12
    Clinton's, 346–47
    Republican Party and, 429
    Nixon and, 5, 21
    Reagan and, 7–8, 187–94, 283, 285–86

Kahn, Alfred, 96
Kasich, John, 372

Katrina hurricane, 446–47, 450
Kay, David, 405
Kean, Tom, 270
Keating, Charles, 198–99
Keating five scandal, 198–99
Kemp, Jack, 121, 140–41, 149, 264–65, 368–69
Kemp-Roth Bill, 140–41
Kendall, David, 344
Kennan, George, 373
Kennedy, Anthony, 194, 426
Kennedy, Edward M., 46, 83–84, 96, 110, 113, 116–21, 144, 167, 175, 190–92, 266–67, 281, 286
Kennedy, John F., 1–2, 7, 19, 25, 268, 333
Kennedy, Robert F., 22, 333
Kerry, John, 444
Keynesian economics, 18, 23, 35
Khashoggi, Adnan, 218, 225
Khomeini, Ayatollah, 95, 114–16, 158, 211
Kimche, David, 217–20
King, Martin Luther, Jr., 22, 171, 182–83
King, Peter, 398
King, Rodney, 319
Kirkland, Lane, 97, 147, 335
Kirkpatrick, Jeane J., 153–54, 156–57, 159, 173, 252, 270, 279
Kissinger, Henry A., 17, 21, 28, 32, 34, 48, 51–64, 66–68, 106, 113–15, 207, 253, 406
Koch, Edward, 267
Kohl, Helmut, 209–10, 374
Korean Air Lines jet incident, 161
Koresh, David, 330
Krauthammer, Charles, 157, 261
Kreps, Juanita, 77
Kristol, Irving, 62, 91, 131
Kristol, William, 334
Kurds, 297, 302–3
Kuwait, 289, 297–303

labor unions
    Clinton, NAFTA, and, 335
    Reagan and, 143–44, 276–77

Laffer, Arthur, 121, 141
Laird, Melvin, 52
Lake, Anthony, 360
Lance, Bert, 76, 80
Lasch, Christopher, 26–27, 97
Lavelle, Rita, 170
law, Reagan's legacy and, 285–86
Laxalt, Paul, 59, 189, 265
Lay, Kenneth, 439
Leach, Jim, 377
Leahy, David, 424
Leahy, Patrick, 192
Lebanon, 159–61, 280
Ledeen, Michael, 219, 221
left. *See* Democratic Party; liberalism;
    new left
Levi, Edward, 43–45
Lewinsky, Monica, 381–94, 399–400. *See
    also* impeachment, Clinton's
Lewis, L. Jean, 343, 377
Libby, I. Lewis "Scooter," 416, 441, 447
liberalism. *See also* Democratic Party
    Carter's, 82–83
    Bill Clinton's, 323–26
    as epithet, 271
    New York City, 40
    tradition of, 15–16
    Reagan's early, 131–32
    Reagan's conservatism vs., 6–7, 136
Libya, 158
Lieberman, Joseph, 417
Liman, Arthur, 235–38
Limbaugh, Rush, 455
Lincoln, Abraham, 440–41, 458
Lincoln Savings and Loan, 198–99
Lindsey, Bruce, 344–45, 381
Lipshutz, Robert, 86–87
Livingston, Robert, 390, 396–400
Lott, Trent, 372, 399, 405–6, 424, 429
Lowell, Abbe, 394–95

McCain, John, 198, 414, 455–56
McCarthy, Eugene, 22
McCarthy, Joseph R., 18–19, 90
McDougal, James, 342–43, 378

McFarlane, Robert "Bud," 211–24, 227,
    229, 240, 257, 336
McGovern, George, 24–25, 125, 134, 171
McVeigh, Timothy, 353
Madison Guaranty Savings and Loan, 342
magnet schools, 304
Marcos, Ferdinand, 252–53, 279
Marcus, Jerome, 378–79
Markman, Stephen, 188
Marshall, Thurgood, 311
Martinez, Bob, 305
Matlock, Jack F., Jr., 246
Matthews, Christopher, 97
Mayaguez affair, 55–56
Medicare, 362
Meese, Edwin, III, 139, 146, 177–78,
    180, 183, 188, 201, 222, 226–28, 243
Mellon, Andrew, 137
Memories of the Ford Administration, 26
Metzenbaum, Howard, 183
Mexico, 313–14, 356–57
Michel, Bob, 55
Middle East
    Carter administration and, 110–13
    Clinton administration and, 340,
        374, 403
    Ford administration and, 56–57
    Reagan administration and,
        158–61, 280 (*see also* Iran-contra
        affair)
military
    gays in, 329
    Reagan's spending on, 137–38,
        152–55, 206, 280
    Soviet spending on, 154, 247
Milosevic, Slobodan, 338–39, 355–56,
    359–61, 404
minorities. *See* racial issues
Mitchell, George, 306
Mitchell, John N., 17, 20, 32
Mondale, Walter, 6, 69, 87, 104, 118–19,
    171–75
Moody, James, 385–87
morality, Carter and, 70, 73–74, 89–95
Moral Majority, 89, 93, 122

Morris, Dick, 350, 357, 369, 388–89
Moynihan, Daniel Patrick, 44, 145, 204, 283, 332, 365, 367
Mubarak, Hosni, 299
Mugabe, Robert, 104
Murkowski, Frank, 125
Muslims, Iraqi, 448–49
mythology, Reagan's, 134–38

Nader, Ralph, 329–30, 417, 419
NAFTA (North American Free Trade Agreement), 313–14, 334–36
narcissism, 27, 323–24
National Association of Realtors, 457
National Conservative Political Action Committee, 342, 346
national health care, 84, 332–36, 365
nationalism, 7
National Performance Review, 408
National Security Council (NSC), 100–101, 212
national testing, 304, 373
NATO (North Atlantic Treaty Organization), 373–74
Negroponte, John, 242
neoconservatives, 28, 52, 62, 90–91, 131, 153, 441
nepotism, 333
Nessen, Ron, 67
Netanyahu, Benjamin, 403
New Deal, 1–2, 6, 16, 18, 22–23, 40, 127–298
New Frontier, 1–2, 16, 19
new left, 22–24
New Orleans disaster, 446–47, 450
new right, 85, 89–95, 102, 122, 368
New York City, 14–16, 40–41, 59, 430–35
Nicaragua, 102–3, 156, 166–67, 242, 278–79. See also Iran-contra affair
Nichols, Terry and James, 353
Nields, John, 235–37
Nigeria, 103
Niskanen, William A., 274
Nitze, Paul, 255–56

Nixon, Richard
    campaign of, against Hubert Humphrey, 70
    Iran and, 113–14
    judicial appointments of, 187
    overview of administration of, 4–5, 16–25
    pardon of, by Ford, 28–35
    Reagan and, 139
    Watergate affair, 4, 8, 16, 25, 455–56
Nofziger, Lyn, 200–201
Noonan, Peggy, 270
Noriega, Manuel, 166, 279, 292–94
North, Oliver, 211–17, 220–28, 231–32, 236–40, 242, 285, 401
North American Free Trade Agreement (NAFTA), 313–14, 334–36
North Atlantic Treaty Organization (NATO), 373–74
Northern Ireland, 403
North Korea, 340, 374, 436
Norton, Eleanor Holmes, 86
nostalgia, Reagan's, 136–37
nuclear weapons, Reagan and, 165, 168, 246, 281
Nunn, Sam, 317, 329
Nussbaum, Bernard, 344–45

Obama, Barack, 452
objectivism, 89
objectivity, author's, 10–11
O'Connor, Sandra Day, 189–90, 426, 427
Office of Special Plans (OSP), 445
Office of the National Drug Control Policy, 305
Office of Thrift Supervision, 199
oil crisis, 35–36, 38–39, 95–98
Oklahoma City bombing, 353–54
Olson, Theodore B., 201, 379, 425–26
Olympic Games, 110, 167
O'Neill, Paul, 437
O'Neill, Thomas "Tip," 80, 81, 125, 139, 141, 144, 149, 168, 204
Operation CHAOS, 49–50

Operation Deliberate Force, 360–61
Operation Desert Fox, 405
Operation Desert Shield, 298
Operation Eagle Claw, 118–19
Operation Just Cause, 294
Operation Staunch, 218
optimism, Reagan's, 150
Organization of American States (OAS), 103
Organization of Petroleum Exporting Countries (OPEC), 35–36, 96
Orlov, Yuri, 59, 106
Oslo Accords, 340

Pahlavi, Mohammad Reza, 95, 100, 115
Palestine Authority, 403
Palestine Liberation Organization (PLO), 110, 112, 158–59, 340
Panama, 166, 279, 292–94
Panama Canal, 66–67, 101–2, 128
Panetta, Leon, 327
pardons
    by George H. W. Bush for Iran-contra figures, 242, 336
    by George W. Bush for Scooter Libby, 447
    by Ford for Nixon, 28–35
partisanship
    author's view of, 10–11
    George W. Bush's war on terror and, 440–41
PATCO (Professional Air Traffic Controllers Organization), 143–44, 277
Paul, Ron, 455
Pelosi, Nancy, 292
Pentagon
    procurement scandal, 200
    terrorist attack on, 432
People's Republic of China. See China
perestroika (restructuring), 248, 258, 262, 273
Perle, Richard, 52, 155, 255, 416
Perot, H. Ross, 315–17, 320, 321–22, 335
Perry, William, 360
Persian Gulf, 109–10. See also Iraq

Phillipines, 252–53, 279
Phillips, Howard, 92, 261
Phillips, Kevin, 20, 282
Pierce, Samuel, 200
Pipes, Richard, 153
Podesta, John, 389
Podhoretz, Norman, 59, 90–91
Poindexter, John M., 222, 226–30, 238, 240, 242, 436
Polish Solidarity movement, 155, 280–81, 292
political history, 1–11
politicization of federal government, 17, 188–89, 285–86, 435
populism, conservative, 85
Powell, Colin, 222, 243, 262, 290, 295, 299, 302–3, 329, 339, 415–16, 436, 441–43
Powell, Jody, 76, 106
Powell, Lewis, 87, 191
POW-MIA movement, 316
prayer, school, 358
presidential power. See executive power
Presidential Records Act, 2, 9
Professional Air Traffic Controllers Organization (PATCO), 143–44, 277
protest politics, 324
Proxmire, William, 74

Qaddafi, Muammar, 120, 158, 224
Quayle, J. Danforth "Dan," 125, 261–62, 270, 320
Quayle, Marilyn, 320–21

Rabin, Yitzhak, 53, 110–11, 340, 361
racial issues. See also affirmative action; civil rights
    George H. W. Bush administration, 311–2
    Carter administration, 74–77, 85–88
    Clinton administration, 330–31, 358
    Ford administration, 42–47
    Nixon administration, 21
    post-Watergate, 27

Reagan administration, 122, 180–85
Republican Party and, 19–20
radicalism, George W. Bush's, 439
Rafshoon, Gerald, 76, 97, 124
Reagan, Nancy Davis, 131, 146, 166, 178–80, 210, 243, 250–51, 288–89
Reagan, Ronald
  AIDS and, 185–86
  biographer of, 3
  cabinet and economic policies of, 139–44
  campaign of, against Carter, 120–26
  campaign of, against Ford, 16, 37, 59, 64, 65–69
  campaign of, against Mondale, 168–75
  campaign of, against Nixon, 21
  career of, 129–34
  civil rights and, 180–84
  controversial German visit of, 209–11
  culture wars and, 186–87
  deregulation and, 194–203
  Ford administration as prelude to, 14–16 (see also Ford, Gerald)
  foreign policies of, 151–75
  Grenada invasion by, 161–62
  historical scholarship about, 1–5
  inaugurations of, 127–29, 176
  Iran-contra affair (see Iran-contra affair)
  judicial appointments of, 187–94
  legacy of, 5–9, 281–87, 314, 434–39, 450
  Middle East and, 158–59
  myths of Reaganism, 134–38
  new right and, 92
  Nixon administration as prelude to, 5, 16–25 (see also Nixon, Richard)
  overview of administration of, 168–74, 176–77, 245–46, 273–81
  Reagan Doctrine and Soviet rela-
    tions of, 57–58, 151–57, 162–68, 176, 210–11, 216, 246, 278–81
  summit meetings of Gorbachev with, 243–46, 249–63
  supply-side Reaganomics of, 144–50, 274–76
  tax reform and, 203–8
  Vietnam War and, 22
Reaganism, 4, 127–29, 134–38, 434, 450–56
Reaganomics, 145, 168, 276
realism, 288–92, 442–43
realpolitik policy, 21, 52, 106, 113–14
recessions, 38, 122, 147–48, 310, 315
Regan, Donald, 139, 141, 178–79, 197, 205, 220, 232, 242–43
regulations. See deregulation
Rehnquist, William H., 21, 187–88, 190–91, 345, 370, 378–79, 426
Reich, Otto, 242
Reich, Robert, 328, 410
religious conservatives, 64–65, 70, 74, 85, 89, 92–93, 122, 163, 186–87, 282, 352–53, 415, 444, 446, 455
Reno, Janet, 330, 345, 376
Republican Party. See also conservatism
  George H. W. Bush and, 320–21
  George W. Bush legacy in, 450–56
  campaign of, against Al Gore, 409–17
  civil rights and, 45–47
  congressional majority of, 325, 347–53
  Dole's campaign against Clinton and, 367–70
  Newt Gingrich's Contract with America, 347–53
  new right, 89–95, 368
  Nixon and, 5, 18–21
  Reagan's campaign against Carter and, 120–26
  Reagan's campaign against Ford and, 65–68
  Reagan's legacy, 263–64, 281–87

Republican Party *(cont.)*
    southern strategy of, 4–5, 20–21,
        46–47, 122, 175, 282
    on welfare, 366
reverse discrimination, 86–87, 181, 184,
    304
Reynolds, William Bradford, 180–84,
    190, 227
Rhodesia, 103–4
Rice, Condoleezza, 411, 416, 436, 441,
    443
Richards, Ann, 269
Richardson, Elliot, 62, 191
Richardson, John, 227
Riegle, Donald, 198
Right. *See* conservatism; new right;
    Republican Party
Riney, Hal, 173–74
riots, Los Angeles, 319–20
Roberts, John, 450
Roberts, Paul Craig, 141, 148
Robertson, Pat, 264, 266, 352
Rockefeller, Nelson A., 19, 33–34,
    40–41, 49–50, 52, 59, 61, 63, 67
Rockefeller Commission, 49–50
Rodino, Peter, 149–50
Roe v. Wade, 21, 27, 89, 187
Rollins, Ed, 179, 271, 288, 309–10, 451
Romania, 294
Romney, Mitt, 455
Roosevelt, Franklin D., 1–2, 7, 127–28,
    132
Roosevelt, Theodore, 3, 129, 372
Rosenthal, A. M., 292
Rostenkowski, Dan, 307, 348
Rove, Karl, 5, 413–14, 436–37, 441, 449,
    452
Rubin, Robert, 327, 356, 366
Rudman, Warren, 235, 238
Rumsfeld, Donald, 4–5, 32–33, 40,
    43–44, 50, 57, 60–64, 143, 159, 264,
    411–12, 415–16, 434–35, 441–42,
    449
Rumsfeld Commission, 411–12
Rushdoony, R. J., 380

Russian Federation, 373. *See also* Soviet
    Union
Rutherford Institute, 380, 385
Rwanda, 338

Sadat, Anwar, 110–13, 158
"Safe Harbor" argument, 421–22
Safire, William, 5, 16, 20–21, 80, 313,
    331, 378
Sakharov, Andrey, 106, 258–59
Sandinistas, 102–3, 156, 242, 278–79. *See
    also* Iran-contra affair
Sandino, Augusto César, 102–3
Sarbanes, Paul, 377
Saudi Arabia, 158, 214, 298, 302
Savas, Emmanuel S., 169, 200
Savimbi, Jonas, 105, 157
savings and loan industry scandal,
    196–200, 307, 314
Saxbe, William, 43
Scaife, Richard Mellon, 90, 379
Scalia, Antonin, 190–91, 379, 425–26
scandals. *See also* sexual issues
    George H. W. Bush administra-
        tion, 307, 310–11, 316–17
    George W. Bush administration,
        444–50, 452
    Clinton administration, 329–31,
        369, 376–81 (*see also* impeach-
        ment, Clinton's)
    Democratic Party, 266–68
    Newt Gingrich, 372
    Reagan administration, 169–70,
        178–79, 194–203, 285–86
    television evangelists, 263–64
Schlafly, Phyllis, 19, 27, 89, 93–95
Schaffer, Beverly Bassett, 343
Schiavo, Terry, 446
Schlesinger, Arthur M., Jr., 2, 22–23,
    370, 458
Schlesinger, James, 32, 52–53, 59, 62–63,
    76, 79–80, 98
school desegregation, 5, 20, 42–47
school nutrition standards, 149
school prayer, 358

school testing, 304, 373
Schroeder, Pat, 358
Schultze, Charles, 76, 80–81
Schwarzkopf, Norman, 301–3
Schweiker, Richard, 68, 149
science, George W. Bush on, 448
Scowcroft, Brent, 62–63, 290–91, 295, 299, 411, 442
screening, judicial, 188–89
Secord, Richard V., 215, 220–24, 227–29, 235, 240
Senate. *See* Congress
Sentelle, David, 345
September 11 terrorist attacks, 430–35
Serbia, 338–39, 355–56, 359–61, 404–5
sexual issues. *See also* scandals
    Clinton's, 311–12, 346, 378–81 (*see also* impeachment, Clinton's)
    George W. Bush administration scandals, 449, 452
    Newt Gingrich's and Henry Hyde's, 391–92, 396
    homosexual rights, 92–93, 185–86, 329
    Robert Livingston's, 398–99
    politics and, 267–68, 319, 400
Shalikashvili, John, 360
Sharon, Ariel, 159
Shevardnadze, Eduard, 247, 254, 298, 313
Shinseki, Eric, 444
Shultz, George, 162–68, 184, 212–14, 218–22, 228, 232, 238–39, 241, 249–62, 279–80, 284, 411
shutdowns, government, 309, 356
Sidey, Hugh, 139
signing statements, 442
Silverado Savings and Loan, 307
Simon, Paul, 267
Simon, William, 32, 36–41, 90
simplicity, 6–7
Simpson, Alan, 312, 451
Sirica, John J., 30
Skinner, Samuel, 306, 311
Slovenia, 339
Smaltz, Donald, 376

Smith, Ian, 103–4
Smith, William French, 139, 177
Snow, Tony, 384
socialism, 136. *See also* communism
social issues. *See* cultural issues
Social Security, 66, 122, 149–50, 169, 204, 352, 407, 437–38
Solzhenitsyn, Aleksandr, 57–58, 62
Somalia, 336–37
Somoza family, 102–3
Souter, David, 311, 426
South Africa, 104–5, 184–85
southern strategy, Republican, 4–5, 20–21, 46–47, 122, 175, 282
South Vietnam, 54–55
Soviet Union. *See also* Gorbachev, Mikhail; Russian Federation
    Baltic rebellion in, 295, 313
    bicentennial celebration and, 15
    George H. W. Bush administration and, 290–92, 312–13
    Carter administration and, 104–10
    détente policy toward, 5, 19, 23, 51–59
    dissolution of, 313
    Ford administration and, 51–59
    Nixon administration and, 21
    Reagan administration and, 128–29, 138, 151–57, 162–68, 176, 243–44, 284
Speakes, Larry, 209
Specter, Arlen, 312, 454
Spencer, Stuart, 65, 127
stagflation, 6, 35, 41, 75, 128
Starr, Kenneth, 346, 369, 376–78, 385–98, 400. *See also* impeachment, Clinton's; Whitewater affair
Star Wars. *See* Strategic Defense Initiative (SDI)
states' rights, 122, 180
Statue of Liberty centenary, 207–8
Stephanopoulos, George, 344–45, 388, 410
Stevens, John Paul, 379, 427–28
Stipanovich, Mac, 422

Stockman, David, 141, 145–46, 148, 170, 179, 197

Stone, Roger, 423–24

STOP ERA, 89, 94–95

Strategic Arms Limitation Treaty (SALT II), 52–53, 58–59, 106–10, 255

Strategic Arms Reduction Talks (START), 155, 167, 313

Strategic Defense Initiative (SDI), 163–66, 176, 245–46, 250–51, 255–59, 280

strike-breaking, Reagan's, 143–44

Sudan, 394

Sullivan, Brendan V., 234

Summers, Lawrence, 356

Sununu, John, 310–11, 315

supply-side economics, 5, 121, 139–50, 276, 415, 417

Supreme Court. *See also* judicial appointments
    affirmative action ruling, 358
    George H. W. Bush nominations to, 311–12
    George W. Bush nominations to, 450
    Bush v. Gore election ruling by, 7, 8, 424–29
    civil rights rulings, 182, 184
    Clinton nominations to, 346–47
    Nixon and, 18, 21
    Reagan nominations to, 189–94
    reverse discrimination ruling, 86–87
    Roe v. Wade ruling, 21, 27, 89, 187
    school busing ruling, 45

surpluses, federal, 371, 407, 416, 437, 450. *See also* deficits, federal

surveillance, domestic, 17–18, 43, 49–50, 446

Suskind, Ron, 437

Sweeney, John, 424

Symms, Steven D., 125

Taliban, 280, 375, 434–35

Tax Equity and Fiscal Responsibility Act (TEFRA), 148–49

taxes. *See also* economic policies
    George H. W. Bush administration, 303–4, 308
    George W. Bush administration, 436–37, 450
    Carter administration, 79–85
    Ford administration, 37–42
    Reagan administration, 8, 121, 133–34, 140–50, 169, 203–8, 275–76, 283–84

Team B intelligence group, 153

Teeter, Robert, 47, 65

television evangelists, 263–64

Teller, Edward, 164

Tenet, George, 440

terHorst, Jerald, 29, 31

terrorism
    antiabortion, 352
    arms-for-hostages affair, 216–24
    Beirut bombings, 160–61
    bombing of USS *Cole*, 406
    George H. W. Bush and, 294–95
    embassy bombings in Kenya and Tanzania, 393
    first World Trade Center bombing, 340
    Khobar Towers bombing, 375
    Oklahoma City bombing, 353–54
    Libyan bombing and, 223–24
    September 11 attacks, 430–35
    war on, 8–9, 434–35, 440–46

testing, national, 304, 373

Thatcher, Margaret, 157, 162, 245, 250, 295–96, 297, 339

Thomas, Clarence, 181–82, 311–12, 314, 426

Thompson, Fred, 455

Thornburgh, Richard, 243, 311

Three Mile Island nuclear accident, 113

Thurmond, Strom, 21, 57, 85, 101, 188

Torrijos, Omar, 101–2, 293

torture, 442, 445–46

Tower, John, 228–33, 290

Tower Commission, 228–33

trade policy. *See* North American Free Trade Agreement (NAFTA)

travel office scandal, 331
Treaty of Paris, 53–54
trickle-down theory, 145–46, 168
Trilateral Commission, 75, 288
Tripp, Linda, 384–88
Triumph of Politics, The, 145
Trujillo, Rafael, 50
Truman, Harry S., 18, 131, 151
Tsongas, Paul, 319
Tyrell, R. Emmett, 91

Udall, Morris "Mo," 69, 83
unemployment, 147, 276, 310
unions. *See* labor unions
unitary executive theory, 8, 441–42. *See also* executive power
United Nations, 44, 101, 154, 265, 298, 300, 339, 355–56, 359–61, 405
United States
    bicentennial of, 14–16
    culture of greed in, 202–3
    culture of narcissism in, 27, 323–24
    post-Vietnam War culture of, 23–24
    post-Watergate culture of, 26–28
    Reaganism and culture of, 5–9
universal health care, 332–36, 365
users' fees, 308

Vance, Cyrus, 76, 100, 103–4, 106–7, 110–11, 118–19
"Vietnam syndrome," 153, 284
Vietnam War, 6, 20–25, 29, 48, 53–55, 78, 324, 329
Viguerie, Richard A., 85, 92–93, 129, 189
Vital Center, The, 22–23, 370
Vitter, James, 454
Volcker, Paul, 96, 147–48, 171, 275–76
voluntarism, 373
"voodoo economics," 121, 265
Vorster, B. J., 104

Wallace, George, 20, 69, 70

Walsh, Lawrence, 228, 242, 336
Wanniski, Jude, 90, 121, 145
Ward, Chester, 94
Warner, John, 200
war on terror, 8–9, 434–35, 440–46
War Powers Resolution, 49, 56, 61, 300
Warren, Earl, 21
Watergate affair, 4, 8, 16–18, 25, 455–56
Watt, James, 140, 169–70
weapons of mass disaster (WMD), 443, 445
Webster, William, 243
Wedtech scandal, 200–201
Weinberger, Caspar, 153, 157, 160, 164, 219–22, 229, 232, 242–43, 255, 259, 336
Weir, Benjamin, 220
Weizman, Ezer, 112
welfare reform, 80, 134, 204–5, 318, 351, 356, 364–67, 370–71
Weyrich, Paul, 27, 90, 92–93, 311
White House Judicial Selection Committee, 189
Whitewater affair, 341–46, 369, 376–81, 397–98. *See also* impeachment, Clinton's
Wick, Charles Z., 132–33
Wiesel, Elie, 210-
Will, George, 250, 253, 293
Willey, Kathleen, 385
Williams, Edward Bennett, 62
Wilson, Joseph, 445, 447, 453
window of vulnerability idea, 152–53
Wirthin, Richard, 140
Witt, James Lee, 418, 447
Wolfowitz, Paul, 252, 279, 294, 302, 411–12, 416, 441, 445
Wood, Kimba, 330
Woodward, Bob, 25, 30
women's issues. *See also* feminism
    George H. W. Bush administration, 312, 320–21
    Carter administration, 88–89
    Reagan administration, 185, 189

World Trade Center terrorist attacks,
    340, 375, 430–35
Wright, Jim, 142, 317, 348
Wright, Susan Webber, 378–79, 387,
    391, 400
Wriston, Walter, 91
Wyman, Jane, 131

Yakovlev, Aleksandr, 247

Yeltsin, Boris, 295, 313,
    373
Yemen, 406
Young, Andrew, 76–77, 101, 104
Yugoslavia, 338–39. *See also* Balkans

Zaccaro, John, 173
Zakharov, Gennady, 256
Zinni, Anthony, 445